SECRET CHA

Mohamed Heikal is one o
distinguished journalists and commentators. From 1957 to 1974 he was editor-in-chief of the Cairo daily newspaper *Al-Ahram*. A close friend of President Nasser, he was also a confidant of President Sadat until the mid-1970s, when they disagreed over Sadat's policies after the 1973 Yom Kippur War. Heikal was among prominent Egyptians arrested and imprisoned by Sadat in September 1981, but he was released three months later, following Sadat's assassination. Since then he has contributed countless articles to newspapers in the Arab world, the United States, Britain and Japan, and has written many books on Middle Eastern affairs. This is the eighth of his books to be published in English.

BY THE SAME AUTHOR

The Road to Ramadan
The Sphinx and the Commissar
Nasser: The Cairo Documents
Return of the Ayatollah: Iranian Revolution from Mossadeq to Khomeini
Autumn of Fury: The Assassination of Sadat
Cutting the Lion's Tail: Suez through Egyptian Eyes
Illusions of Triumph: An Arab View of the Gulf War

SECRET CHANNELS

The Inside Story of
Arab–Israeli Peace Negotiations

MOHAMED HEIKAL

HarperCollins*Publishers*

HarperCollins*Publishers*
77–85 Fulham Palace Road
Hammersmith, London W6 8JB

This paperback edition 1996
1 3 5 7 9 8 6 4 2

First published in Great Britain by
HarperCollins*Publishers* 1996

ISBN 0 00 638337 8

Set in Linotron Bembo and Castellar

Printed and bound in Great Britain by
Caledonian Book Manufacturing Ltd, Glasgow

CONTENTS

PART II

CHRONOLOGY

1798–1801	Napoleon's troops occupy Egypt.
1869	Suez Canal opened.
1882	British occupation of Egypt, lasting seventy-four years.
1882–1903	First wave of immigration into Palestine by European Jews.
1897	World Zionist Organization (WZO) founded.
July 1915–January 1916	'Hussein–McMahon correspondence'.
May 1916	Sykes–Picot Agreement.
2 November 1917	Balfour Declaration.
9 December 1917	British forces capture Jerusalem.
1918–48	British administration of Palestine.
May 1939	British White Paper on Palestine.
May 1942	Biltmore Conference, New York.
July 1946	King David Hotel, Jerusalem blown up by Irgun.
29 November 1947	UN General Assembly adopts a partition plan for Palestine.
14 May 1948	Proclamation of the state of Israel.
May 1948–January 1949	First Arab–Israeli war.
17 September 1948	Assassination of Count Bernadotte, UN mediator, in Jerusalem.
February–July 1949	Israeli–Arab armistice agreements.
20 July 1951	Assassination of King Abdullah of Jordan.
July 1952	Egyptian revolution.
February 1955	Lavon affair.
26 July 1956	Nasser announces nationalization of Suez Canal Company.

29 October 1956	Start of Suez crisis.
5 June 1967	Outbreak of Six Day War.
22 November 1967	UN Resolution 242.
February 1969	Yasser Arafat elected chairman of PLO.
October 1969	Rogers Plan.
7 August 1970	Israeli–Egyptian ceasefire under Rogers Initiative.
September 1970	Jordan crushes Palestinian *fedayeen*.
28 September 1970	Death of President Nasser.
November 1971	Assassination of Wasfi Tal, Jordanian prime minister.
6–22 October 1973	Yom Kippur War.
18 January 1974	First Israeli–Egyptian disengagement agreement.
31 May 1974	Israeli–Syrian disengagement agreement.
4 September 1975	Second Israeli–Egyptian agreement.
19 November 1977	Sadat visits Jerusalem.
February 1978	Sadat–Carter talks at Camp David.
26 March 1979	Egyptian–Israeli peace treaty.
6 October 1981	Sadat assassinated.
6 June 1982	Israeli invasion of Lebanon.
August 1982	PLO leaves Lebanon for Tunisia.
14 September 1982	Assassination of Bashir Gemayel, Lebanese president-elect.
16–18 September 1982	Sabra and Shatila massacres.
1 October 1985	Israel bombs PLO headquarters in Tunis.
7 November 1985	Arafat's Cairo Declaration.
9 December 1987	Beginning of the intifada.
November 1988	Palestine National Congress announces conditional acceptance of UN Resolutions 181, 242 and 338.
14 December 1988	Arafat accepts US terms for talks with PLO. Washington lifts ban on meetings with PLO.
20 June 1990	Suspension of US–PLO dialogue.
30 October 1991	Middle East peace conference in Madrid, followed by Washington peace talks.
December 1992–August 1993	Secret Oslo channel.

13 September 1993	Signing of PLO–Israel declaration of principles.
25 February 1994	Massacre of Palestinians at Tomb of the Patriarchs in Hebron.
6 and 13 April 1994	Reprisals by Hamas; Israeli buses attacked.
4 May 1994	Agreement on application of the PLO–Israel declaration of principles.
13 May 1994	Israel hands over Jericho to PLO.
1 July 1994	Arafat returns to Gaza.
25 July 1994	State of war between Israel and Jordan ends.
14 October 1994	Arafat, Rabin and Peres chosen to share 1994 Nobel Peace Prize.
19 October 1994	Further Hamas attack; twenty-two Israeli bus passengers killed.
26 October 1994	Signing of Israeli–Jordanian peace treaty.
22 January 1995	Twenty-one Israelis killed in another Hamas attack.
2 February 1995	First summit between leaders of Egypt, Jordan, PLO and Israel.

INTRODUCTION

Albert Einstein once said that the struggle between Israel and the Palestinian people was a conflict between two rights. Like many before and after him, the great physicist longed to bring those two rights into harmony, and tried secretly to use his personal standing as a bridge. This book is the story of peacemaking efforts by men like Einstein, and by the presidents, kings, politicians and academics whose love of peace – or whose personal ambition – drew them to one of the most intractable disputes of modern times. That work was by its nature secret.

The search for peace has involved many of the great figures of the twentieth century in largely unseen roles. Nehru, Eisenhower, Tito, de Gaulle, Kennedy, Brandt, Kreisky and Mitterrand were but a few of the statesmen who worked behind the scenes to achieve understanding. Some now remembered more for their mistakes than their accomplishments, including Ceausescu and Nixon, made important contributions. Other intermediaries, such as Henry Kissinger, conducted their roles in the glare of publicity. Every American president since Franklin Roosevelt has been part of the problem or part of the solution, or both. No American secretary of state since John Foster Dulles has been able to stay out of the peace process. The lives of every Egyptian and Syrian president, every Saudi and Jordanian monarch, and every Israeli prime minister have been dominated by the conflict.

Nothing has been harder to understand, for those who live outside the Middle East, than the twenty-five-year refusal of the Arab world to negotiate with Israel. The state of mind which lay behind the policy of ostracization is one of the themes of this book. Even in 1995, after twenty-one years of direct Arab–Israeli talks, echoes of that policy could still be heard in the Arab world.

More easily understood, but just as hard to resolve, has been Israel's sense of insecurity. Every Israeli leader since Weizmann has known that the key to security lay in recognition by the country's Arab neighbours. If that key remains unturned, it is because Israeli leaders have yet to realize that real recognition cannot be attained through peace treaties negotiated under duress. The Israeli dream of being accepted among Middle East states will remain a dream until Israel behaves like a partner. How much still remains to be learned was demonstrated anew in September 1994 when Shimon Peres, the Israeli foreign minister, rejected a request by his Egyptian counterpart that Israel should sign the Nuclear Non-Proliferation Treaty.

Many supposed that peace was at hand when PLO chairman Yasser Arafat and Israeli prime minister Yitzhak Rabin shook hands on the White House lawn in September 1993. A few months later Federico Mayor, secretary general of UNESCO, arranged a seminar between Arab and Israeli intellectuals to discuss how to shift the Middle East from a culture of war to one of peace. As a symbol of hope the venue was Grenada, a city which had witnessed peaceful cooperation between Muslims and Jews. The seminar was to have been called 'Peace Tomorrow', but when Arafat and Peres decided to attend, Mr Mayor promptly changed the title to 'Peace Today'. With a stroke of his pen the UNESCO secretary general sought to nudge history forwards. That was an act of optimism. An act of realism would have been to take a hard look at the agreement signed in Washington. A hard look would have led to a harder question: What made the architects of the PLO–Israel agreement think that peace could be achieved by postponing the difficult issues?

After decades of despair, the Middle East peace process has of late suffered from premature hope. The return of the PLO chairman to Gaza and Jericho in 1994 was widely reported as the end of the forty-six-year Palestinian nightmare. Rare was the journalist who distinguished between the marketing and the reality of the agreement. Much of the commentary in the West showed a suspension of critical faculties, a failure to apply normal tests of objectivity. Anyone who dared ask difficult questions risked being described as an enemy of peace. The Middle East yearns for hope, but the Arab–Israel conflict cannot yet be reported in the past tense. That day will come when Israel heeds the necessities of peace rather than the realities of power. If this book helps to explain why the 1993 agreement was a bandage rather than a cure, it will have made some contribution.

The arrival of the Jews in Palestine after an absence of nineteen centuries took 110 years, from the first influx in the 1880s to the slowdown in Soviet Jewish emigration in 1991. Israel is still a young society in the grip of an expansionist mentality. A journey of the mind towards a more mature view of Israel's relationships with its neighbours will be needed if peace is to dawn in the Middle East.

PART I

I Come From There

I come from there and I have memories.
Born as mortals are, I have a mother
And a house with many windows,
I have brothers, friends,
And a prison cell with one cold window.
Mine is the wave snatched by sea-gulls,
I have my own view,
And an extra blade of grass.
Mine is the moon at the far edge of words,
And the bounty of birds,
And the immortal olive tree.
I walked this land before the swords
Turned its living body into a laden table.
I come from there. I render the sky unto her mother
When the sky weeps for her mother.
And I weep to make myself known
To a returning cloud.
I learnt all the words worthy of the court of blood
So that I could break the rule.
I learnt all the words and broke them up
To make a single word: Homeland . . .

MAHMOUD DARWISH

1

A Wall of the Mind

An Overview of a Century of Conflict

When President Anwar Sadat flew to Jerusalem in 1977, to the astonishment of Jews and the fury of Palestinians, President Carter compared the event to Neil Armstrong's 'one small step for mankind' upon the moon. Sixteen years later, when Yasser Arafat shook hands with Yitzhak Rabin on the south lawn of the White House in September 1993, President Clinton drew a parallel with the fall of the Berlin Wall. Neither comparison was quite right, yet both contained elements of truth. Sadat's expedition to what then seemed an alien world proved to be just the start of a journey whose end is not yet in sight. If anything collapsed when Arafat took Rabin's hand it was the hope of an independent Palestine, not the communal wall of Arab–Jewish enmity.

Carter and Clinton saw, or thought they saw, the beginnings of an Arab–Israeli rapprochement, but that vision was premature. What these events in fact meant was that Egypt and subsequently the PLO had discarded the lever which might at some future time have squeezed Israel out of Arab lands. The nature of that lever was clear to Arab leaders in 1949, after a million Palestinians had been expelled from their homes or so intimidated that they fled. The Arab world could not in the short term defeat Israel in a major battle, but it could make the moral force of the Arab position felt by refusing to acknowledge, recognize or negotiate with Israel, hoping that a combination of limited military pressure, perseverance and demography would alter the balance of strength.

It was a strategy which called for superhuman patience on the part of Arab leaders, and for full-hearted public support. The first was in shorter supply than the second: in time pressures of state induced Arab leaders to reach out to their Israeli counterparts. The Arab public proved more constant than kings and presidents. The strategy of ostracization had entered the psyche of the humiliated masses, becoming a solace for their shock and impotence.

It was this strength of popular feeling which made contacts with Israel difficult, dangerous and necessarily secret. The first questions which came to any Arab leader's mind when opportunities for contact arose were: 'What if it leaks out?' and 'How can I cover myself politically?' These worries led Arab leaders to ask for advance assurances of Israeli concessions before entering into contacts.

The difficulty of negotiating on that basis was illustrated in 1977, during the period before Sadat announced his willingness to go to Jerusalem in search of peace. Knowing that his offer would be seen as a huge concession to Israel, the Egyptian leader tried to make sure that Israel was ready to give something in return. An envoy was dispatched to the Moroccan capital Rabat for a secret meeting with Moshe Dayan, the Israeli foreign minister. Such was the sensitivity of this encounter that Dayan hid his internationally recognizable features behind a stage beard, moustache and wig, and his blind eye, normally patched, behind impenetrable sunglasses, before boarding a plane to Paris. The ruse ensured that his departure from Israel was not noticed. In Paris Dayan changed planes and flew to Morocco, still wearing the disguise. As it turned out, the furtiveness was for nought: far from clarifying the situation, the secret meeting led to confusion. When Sadat told the Egyptian parliament: 'I am ready to go to the ends of the earth for peace, even to the Knesset [the Israeli parliament] itself,' he was under the incorrect impression that Israel was ready to hand over the occupied territories in exchange for peace.

Sadat's audacity won him accolades as a prince of peace, but these came from outside the Arab world. The reaction of the masses ranged from startled acquiescence in Egypt to furious accusations of betrayal from the rest of the Arab world. The Egyptian leader had trespassed upon an area of the Arab mind where the conflict in Palestine is inseparable from religion, because of Jerusalem's central importance. Judgement came five years later, in the form of thirty-six bullets delivered by fundamentalists. To the wider world Sadat was a statesman and peacemaker; to some of his own people, a traitor.

The Egyptian leader was neither the first nor the last to pay with his life for breaking the unwritten Arab pact of steadfast resistance to Israel. The assassination of King Abdullah of Jordan in 1951 was a direct result of lengthy secret negotiations he had conducted with Israeli leaders both before and after 1948. The killer was a young Palestinian acting, it was suspected, on the orders of the Islamic Liberation Party. Both Abdullah and Sadat were cut down at spots selected for their symbolism: Abdullah at the door of the al-Aksa mosque in old Jerusalem, which was then controlled by his British-trained forces; Sadat in the bosom of his power-base, the Egyptian army, while watching a military parade.

In 1982, a year after Sadat, President-elect Bashir Gemayel of Lebanon was murdered for being unduly cosy with Israel. Between 1948 and 1971 three Arab prime ministers were slaughtered by Arabs who objected to any concession to Israel. Mahmoud Fahmi El-Nokrashi Pasha, prime minister of Egypt, lost his life because he agreed to a truce during the 1948 war, and because he attempted to smother the Muslim Brotherhood, an organization which then alarmed Arab governments as much as Hamas does now. Wasfi El-Tal, prime minister of Jordan, was assassinated in 1971 after his government had stopped the PLO using Jordan as a base for attacks against Israel. Riad El-Solh, prime minister of Lebanon in 1951, did no more than talk about talks, but the price was the same.

Others were killed without defying the proscription directly but because they were associated in the Arab mind with Israel or its friends. In 1958 seventeen members of the Iraqi royal family fell in a single burst of sub-machinegun fire at the Palace of the Roses in Baghdad. They were seen as puppets of Britain, whose imperial power had made mass Jewish immigration into the Holy Land possible. Prime Minister Nuri El-Said Pasha, who had dominated Iraqi politics since the 1930s, was killed for the same reason two days later.

The motives of those who risked contacts with Israel were rarely as simple as a straightforward desire for peace. King Abdullah, one of the most astute Arab manipulators of his day, did business with Jewish leaders to further his own territorial ambitions, and was able to annex the west bank of the Jordan with Israel's connivance. No doubt he thought this was a success, but to many Palestinians it was treachery. Bashir Gemayel, a Christian militia leader, was widely seen as 'Israel's candidate' when he was elected president of Lebanon during an Israeli siege of Beirut in 1982. If the unwritten deal was his presidency in return for peace it was a failure on both counts, for Gemayel was murdered before he could take office, and the subsequent peace deal collapsed. President Sadat's moves were imaginative but were blighted by impatience and a sense of showmanship. If he erred it was in placing his short-term needs ahead of Palestinian and wider Arab interests.

Like all who entered into contact with Israel, Yasser Arafat frequently courted death, but his reasons were different. The PLO chairman's commitment to the Palestinian cause was beyond question, even if the two components of his psyche – half freedom fighter, half politician – were sometimes in conflict. Ultimately it was the politician in him who bowed, after a long struggle, to political and economic realities. By then the proscription against contacts had been abandoned not only by Egypt but by many within the PLO. In 1988 Arafat persuaded the Palestine National Congress to accept major changes in the PLO's aims and attitudes, opening the door to talks with Washington and later with Israel. Before 1988 Arafat had been at risk of assassination by Mossad; after 1988 the threat came from Palestinian militias which rejected any abandonment of the armed struggle.

The world rejoiced too soon at the 1988 policy change and the resulting negotiations. Nothing so clear as a change of heart by Palestinians as a whole had occurred. If the PLO had agreed to talk, it was because non-Palestinian Arabs were growing weary of the Palestinians, and older Palestinians were growing weary of the struggle. Younger Palestinians, on the other hand, wanted to continue the struggle, and were transferring their allegiance from the PLO to Hamas, a process which continued and intensified up to 1995.

Picking up the banner the PLO had dropped, Hamas underwent a personality change, adopting the 1949 ideas and blending them with the Islamic concept of *jihad*, or holy war. By mid-1994 some estimates put support for Hamas in the occupied territories as high as 40 per cent of the population. A strategy of no talks and no surrender had been handed down through two generations despite a desertion of the cause by many leaders.

To understand how a set of ideas so inimical to comfort survived for so long, a brief overview of the struggle is necessary. The conflict may be said to have lasted for a century, and to have begun some years after an influx of Jews into Palestine in the 1880s. Between then and the 1890s the Jews were a tiny minority, numbering between 8000 and 25,000 according to different counts, and relations with Arabs were reasonably cordial. Later, Jews arrived in larger numbers, and fears arose in Arab minds that something akin to a new crusade was beginning.

Arab–Jewish tension grew steadily between the two world wars, but the presence of a third party, the British mandate government, had a dampening effect. It was not until Britain's withdrawal and Israel's declaration of independence in May 1948 that all hope of a peaceful solution collapsed. The expulsion of most of the Palestinian population in 1948–49, and the loss of their land and homes, created more bitterness than any of the six periods of struggle which followed (the 1956 Suez crisis, the Six Day War of 1967, the 1968–70 War of Attrition, the Yom Kippur War of 1973, the 1982–83 Israeli invasion of Lebanon, and the 1987–92 Intifada).

Human misery cannot adequately be conveyed in figures, and yet the statistics give some order of scale. The Palestinian death toll from 1948 to 1993 was 261,000, with 186,000 wounded and 161,140 disabled. The refugees displaced in 1948 and 1967, and their descendants, numbered 5.4 million by the early 1990s, according to UN estimates. The civil wars in Lebanon which resulted from complications of the Arab–Israel conflict claimed a further 90,000 lives, 115,000 wounded, 9627 disabled, and 875,000 refugees.

Egypt's losses in five wars, (1948, 1956, 1967, 1968–70 and 1973) came to 39,000 dead, 73,000 wounded, and 61,000 disabled, while 2.1 million people living in the Suez Canal area were displaced twice (in 1956 and 1967). The canal was closed for two long periods, and the loss of revenue coupled with war costs amounted, according to President Sadat, to $43 billion.

The Arab public as a whole was opposed to contact with Israel for about thirty years, from 1948 until the Camp David accords in 1978, but the intensity of that feeling varied considerably. At its height soon after the 1948–49 war, any top-level direct contacts with Israel by Egypt or Syria, secret or otherwise, would have been unthinkable.

Arab anger was well understood by Dr Ralph Bunche, the first black American to reach high office in the US State Department, who was detached to work for the UN Palestine Commission. In the course of negotiating the 1949 Israel–Arab armistice agreements Bunche found that representatives of Arab countries could not be accommodated at the same table as Israelis. It was he who invented the 'Rhodes formula' (named after the island on which the talks were held), which consisted of installing Arab and Israeli delegates on different floors of the same hotel, while he shuttled between them. Bunche won the 1950 Nobel Peace Prize, but at the time peace was not on the cards; an absence of war was the most the Arab world could contemplate, and even that was controversial.

When new Israeli prime ministers took office they would declare their willingness to go to any Arab capital to talk peace. The Arab world knew that this was propaganda, given Israel's refusal to accept United Nations resolutions and its unwillingness to define its borders. Arab diplomats found a way of reminding other countries of Israel's defiance of the UN: whenever an Israeli delegate rose to address UN bodies, the entire company of Arab ambassadors would walk out.

Every Israeli peace plan had the principal aim of securing Arab recognition of Israel's right to exist, a demand which found sympathy in Western opinion but did not lack absurdity. How could a nuclear power imagine that it needed the permission of non-nuclear countries to exist? How could a nation which had seized the land of others and defied United Nations resolutions feel embattled and threatened? That Israel wanted recognition so badly showed the effectiveness of ostracization.

It was the Eisenhower administration which first realized that something more complex than ordinary post-war hostility was going on in the Arab mind. At the time, however, US interests were concerned less with promoting Arab–Israeli peace than with restraining Arab nationalism, fearing it might lead the Arab world into the Soviet camp.

John F. Kennedy had the same concerns but more hope, and made the first American effort to bring the parties together. His assassination brought that attempt to an end, but six years later the Nixon administration began to wear down the opposition of Arab leaders.

The limited prospects of that period were reflected in a private discussion in 1971 between William Rogers, then secretary of state, and Mahmoud Riad, the Egyptian foreign minister. Perhaps exhausted by the complexities of a region which had seen 112 revolutions, coups or attempted coups in the twenty-three years since the creation of

Israel, Rogers mused aloud about the afterlife, speculating that in another world he and Riad would find themselves together again, still discussing the minutiae of withdrawal agreements.

In spurning talks with Israel, the Arabs gave themselves time to build up their military power. By 1973 Egypt and Syria had acquired the strength to challenge Israel's occupation of parts of the Arab lands seized in 1967. The Yom Kippur War of October 1973 achieved an Arab psychological breakthrough, and yet failed to secure victory. That failure was partly caused by entering into indirect diplomatic contact with Israel. After achieving a surprise crossing of the Suez Canal, Sadat told Henry Kissinger that he had no intention of chasing the Israelis all the way back to their frontier. Kissinger passed this on to Golda Meir, as Sadat undoubtedly knew he would. Had Sadat been more cautious in what he told Kissinger, and had he pressed his military advantage, Egypt and Syria might have gained a more balanced basis for subsequent negotiations.

The Arab oil embargo of 1973–74 revived ostracization in a new guise, but was weakened and ultimately dropped as a result of Kissinger's shuttle diplomacy. The disengagement agreements between Israel, Egypt and Syria which Kissinger negotiated proved to be the wedge which eased Egypt away from ostracization and into direct talks.

Sadat became a willing captive first of Henry Kissinger and later of Jimmy Carter, leading to the neutralization of Egypt as a threat to Israel. Yet even in March 1977, when Carter took Sadat to his private quarters in the White House and tried to fathom his inner thoughts, Sadat was unable to imagine real peace. 'Maybe normal relations will be possible in my grandchildren's time, but not in my lifetime,' he said. The following year he signed the Camp David accords, a monument to hope which dared to imagine the unimaginable, and which formed the basis of all subsequent peace efforts.

Camp David was anathema to the PLO for a decade. As late as the spring of 1988 Arafat told President Mubarak of Egypt that he would sooner cut off his right hand than accept United Nations Resolution 242 (which required, among other things, the recognition of Israel's right to exist). In November that year George Shultz, the US secretary of state, refused Arafat a visa to address the United Nations, on the grounds that American law defined the PLO as a terrorist organization.

By then the PLO chairman was hesitating on the bank of his personal Rubicon, as Shultz knew when he took the decision to exclude him. Shultz also realized that the United States and Israel now held all the cards.

A month later, at a special session of the UN in Geneva and at a press conference afterwards, Arafat took the irrevocable step of publicly accepting Resolution 242. Ostracization was officially over, even if assassinations of PLO members who talked to Israelis continued. Arafat was fêted by President Mitterrand; even Margaret Thatcher was said to have been willing to see him, on condition he shaved first.

In retrospect, the PLO's change of direction in 1988 was probably the end of the main phase of the conflict, although the '*Intifada*' (uprising) would continue for a further four years, and Hamas had yet to make itself felt.

After that there was no turning back for the PLO, and the effects of the 1991 Gulf War accelerated the process. Arafat's support for Saddam Hussein cost him the backing of his richest Arab backers, causing both a cash crisis and a drastic loss of political weight. By 1992 the PLO was isolated, facing bankruptcy and divided within itself. American-sponsored direct talks had been under way for more than a year since their opening in Madrid in October 1991, and were heading for stalemate when the secret Oslo channel opened at the end of 1992. The need for secrecy now had less to do with the risk that PLO leaders might be assassinated (though that remained real) than with enabling the PLO to retreat from what its negotiators had been saying in the official talks.

The nine months of secret talks which followed were conducted under intense financial pressure. At one point the PLO had funds sufficient to last only three months, while Gulf oil states ignored its pleas for help. It was in these circumstances that the PLO settled, in the Oslo 'principles' of August 1993, on a deal far worse than the Camp David accords it had denounced in 1978. The Oslo agreement astonished only those who had failed to notice how much the PLO's old determination had faded.

After the White House handshake of September 1993 it took Arafat some time to adjust to being transformed in the eyes of Western governments and Israel from reformed sinner to Arab statesman. Shimon Peres, the Israeli foreign minister, and to a lesser extent Yitzhak

Rabin, the prime minister, now courted him almost as an ally. The Israeli government, which had fostered Hamas as a counterweight to the PLO, needed a stronger PLO to hold Hamas in check.

Nothing demonstrated the changed situation more clearly than the way the American government turned to the PLO for help after the massacre at Ibrahimi Mosque at Hebron on 25 February 1994.* Warren Christopher, US secretary of state, phoned Arafat five times that day urging him to view the massacre more as an attack on the peace process than as an anti-Palestinian outrage. His argument was that any suspension of the talks would be a victory for extremist elements in Israel.

Christopher's entreaties were reinforced by President Clinton, who said that after the Hebron massacre Arafat's leadership was more important than ever. Hardly able to believe his ears, Arafat put a hand over the phone, turned to the advisers around him and told them: 'Clinton says I am the flag and the symbol of the Palestinian cause.'

For a few hours the Americans believed they had persuaded Arafat not to withdraw from talks with Israel on implementing the 1993 agreement, and Arafat indeed appeared to waver, only to recover his political balance when news arrived of riots in protest at the massacre. A period of mourning was needed, and a suspension of several weeks was the minimum Arafat could allow without losing his remaining battered authority.

Forty days passed; then came the reaction from Hamas. Scenes of Israeli civilians torn apart by suicide-bomb attacks tested the fabric of the Labour-led coalition. By now Arafat and Peres were talking again, but the message from the slums of Gaza spoke louder. Hamas and its ever-expanding constituency would not buy a PLO–Israeli deal which failed to deal with the causes of the conflict. More than any Palestinian organization before it, Hamas was rehoisting the banners of 1949, updated to meet the post-Oslo situation: 'No deal, no surrender, no end to the conflict.' The attacks cannot be explained away as the work of an extreme fringe: even those who disliked the choice of targets supported the principle Hamas was upholding. The rapturous welcome Arafat received in July 1994 on his arrival in Gaza and Jericho marked a pause for celebration, not a reconciliation.

Such obduracy at a time when peace of a sort was within grasp can

* See pages 494–5.

only be explained in terms of psychology rather than politics. Had the issue been solely political, the vast majority of Palestinians would have accepted the Oslo agreement for the sake of a quieter, safer life. That so many tacitly approved the Hamas attacks showed that something extraordinary had been handed down by the survivors of the 1948–49 war to their children and grandchildren. That something was rooted in the 1949 strategy of ostracization, an idea which encapsulated the anger of the dispossessed, the humiliation of the defeated and the rejection of the oppressor, overlaid with social and cultural elements and religious convictions. Only one noun in the English language comes close to expressing so inchoate a blend of fury and revulsion. That word is 'taboo'.

2

The Making of a Taboo

In any other context the word 'taboo' would seem excessive as a description of one people's refusal to accept another. To understand how Israel came to bulk so large in Arab demonology it is necessary to ask a related question: Why did a country the size of Massachusetts or Wales, with fewer people than Austria or Hong Kong, seem so great a threat to an Arab world larger in land area and population than the United States?

In 1993 Yitzhak Rabin put the same query from an Israeli perspective: If the Arabs had twenty-one independent countries, was it too much for the Jews to have one? Formulating the question in that way masks the importance of the Palestinian issue. It was Palestinians who lost their homes and land when Israelis carved a homeland out of their territory, and it was Palestine which disappeared from the map. The impact on the frontline states, although serious, was of a different order.

In 1994 there were 800,000 Palestinians in Gaza, 1 million on the west bank, 2 million in Jordan and 400,000 in refugee camps in Lebanon, making a total of 4.2 million Palestinians living in lands close to their former homes. The Jewish part of Israel's population was about the same, including settlers in east Jerusalem, Gaza, the west bank and the Golan Heights.* In numerical terms there was an even balance between Israelis and Palestinians, but all the power was on one side.

The attitude of Palestinians (and other Arabs who shared their anguish) was not conditioned solely by the events of 1948. The taboo

* The Jewish population numbers substantially over 4 million if the 120,000 settlers in the occupied territories are included.

in the Arab mind was awakened by the bitterness of expulsion, but the roots of enmity ran much deeper. Buried in the collective memory were antagonisms accumulated over 3000 years, beginning with what was supposedly a family dispute.

It is enough to recall that both Arabs and Jews are believed to be descended from Ibrahim (known to Jews and Christians as Abraham) through his relationships with two women, and that he is revered by all three faiths. Abraham is the father of the Hebrews, but at the same time Ibrahim is the father of the Arabs and the founder of monotheism, which Islam restored to its original meaning. His descendants founded two nations which today speak related languages (both members of the Semitic subdivision of the Hamito-Semitic family) and use alphabets whose origins can be traced to Egyptian hieroglyphic writing. The story of Sarah, the barren wife of Abraham, who gave her husband an Egyptian slave girl called Hagar as a concubine but subsequently became jealous, is part of the common tradition of Jews, Arabs and Christians. Late in life Sarah bore a son, Isaac, and Hagar was evicted, together with her son Ismail (Ishmael to Jews and Christians). According to the Old Testament, God promised that although Isaac was the patriarch's heir, Ismail and his twelve sons would become a great people.

Whether the story of Isaac and Ismail is allegorical or based on fact, there is no reason to doubt that a split occurred. The date is usually put at around the middle of the second millennium B.C. The invasion of Canaan (the ancient name of Palestine) by the Israelites under the leadership of Joshua, successor of Moses, could be taken as the start of the territorial dispute. The Jews defeated the inhabitants, who were then nominally subjects of Egypt, and remained a power in the land until the Romans destroyed Jerusalem in 70 A.D. After periods under Persian and then Byzantine rule the Jews welcomed the Arab conquest of 640 A.D. The dispersal of Jews to other countries had begun earlier, and now it accelerated. From the seventh century until 1948 Islam was the dominant religion in Palestine, and for most of that period very few Jews lived there.

The crusades by European Christians between the eleventh and the thirteenth centuries were religiously motivated only in part. Princes went to Palestine to capture new lands with the blessing of Pope Urban II, slaughtering thousands of Arab civilians in the process. Despite their ultimate failure, the crusades retained romantic associations in the European mind. In 1830 the French used a dispute over trading privileges as a pretext for invading Algiers. As the troops disembarked their commander, Marechal de Bourmont, told them: 'Now you are resuming the crusades.' The French stayed for 132 years. When General Edmund Allenby led British forces into Jerusalem in 1917 he announced that the crusades had reached their goal. When French forces seized Syria after the First World War, their leader General Henri Gouraud* went to Saladin's tomb in Damascus and said: 'Nous voici de retour, Saladin.'

After Saladin's reconquest of Jerusalem in 1187 and the failure of subsequent crusades the territorial question seemed settled, and might have remained so but for two sets of problems which were in no way caused by the Arab world. The first was the struggle for empire between Britain and France, both of which wanted control of trade routes to the East. The second was the rise of European anti-Semitism (something which had never been practised by Arabs).

At the end of the eighteenth century Palestine had been in the hands of the Ottoman empire for nearly 200 years, but the empire was weak and Russia and Austria were nibbling at its extremities. It suited Britain to keep the Ottoman empire intact as a means of restraining Russia, and as a way of protecting the best trade route to India. Goods were shipped to Alexandria, carried by camel caravans via Cairo to Suez, and then reshipped for the journey across the Red Sea. In the event of trouble in Egypt, Britain would have needed to switch to the Palestine coast, with a long land journey to the Persian Gulf. The British government kept this option open by maintaining good relations with the Ottoman sultan.

The first threat to the Egyptian route came in 1798, when Napoleon occupied Egypt with the intention of bringing the Red Sea under French control. Hoping to close the secondary routes through Palestine too, he sought to populate the Holy Land with people who would be permanently in his debt. It was for this reason that Napoleon called upon the Jews in the Diaspora (dispersal) to return to the Holy Land and rebuild the civilization they had abandoned. 'Oh Israelites, come

* General Henri Eugene Gouraud was commander of eastern forces from 1915 to 1919, and then high commissioner of Syria until 1923.

to your holy places,' his proclamation beckoned. Nothing came of this because the Ottoman sultan, with the help of the British navy, sent a formidable army to oust the French, who withdrew in 1801. However, Napoleon's proposal sowed an idea which was taken up by the British later in the nineteenth century. The aim was to solve two problems at once: to persuade the Jews to leave Europe, where they were unpopular, and establish them in Palestine where they could guard the contingency routes.

Others, especially British Protestants, had religious motives for helping the Jews fulfil what many considered a biblical prophecy. Lord Ashley, an English Protestant and social reformer who later became the 7th Earl of Shaftesbury, was an early advocate of Zionism. Over dinner with Viscount Palmerston, the foreign secretary, in 1838, Ashley reinforced the religious argument with an economic one. Palestine was short of both labour and capital, and Jews could provide both. In a letter he wrote to Palmerston two years later pressing the same thought Ashley said: 'They will return at their own expense, and with no hazard but to themselves: they will submit to the existing form of government, having no preconceived theories to gratify, and having been almost everywhere trained in implicit obedience to autocratic rule.' Palmerston had in fact already written to his ambassador in Turkey instructing him to urge the sultan to pass a law permitting the free return of Jews to Palestine.

By now the Ottoman empire was known as 'the Sick Man of Europe' because of its indebtedness to European creditors and its inadequate military modernization. It was buffeted not only by European powers but by one of its own military leaders. Mohamed Ali, an exceptionally resourceful Macedonian soldier, had been sent to Egypt to help remove the French and had risen to become ruler. In 1832 he occupied Palestine and Syria and defeated the sultan's forces, creating a sub-empire which stretched from the southern borders of Turkey as far south as Khartoum in Sudan. Palmerston used this situation as one of his arguments for persuading the sultan to allow the Jews to return. A Jewish homeland would, he suggested in August 1840, create a human barrier to restrain Mohamed Ali.

France was now in agreement with the policy of keeping the sick man alive (but not well enough to recover), and at a conference in London in 1839 Britain, France, Germany, Russia and Austria agreed to provide military assistance. After destroying Mohamed Ali's fleet and cutting his communications lines the European powers forced the withdrawal of Egyptian forces from Syria and Palestine.

One of the founders of Zionism, Nahum Zokolov, wrote subsequently that if the Zionist idea had crystallized at that time, the London conference could have brought about the isolation of Syria and Palestine from the Ottoman empire, making possible the establishment of Israel much earlier.

Palmerston sent another message to the sultan in February 1841, this time stressing economic arguments for allowing Jews to return. Their wealth was well known, he said, and they would bring capital with them. Palmerston foresaw that such a policy would lead to trouble with the Arab population, and therefore proposed that the sultan should move the Palestinians to northern Iraq. He also suggested that the Palestinians (referred to in the letter as 'the inhabitants') would welcome the move because the land in northern Iraq was more fertile.

(Such an idea was under discussion again as recently as 1994. Iraq had been negotiating for the lifting of United Nations sanctions imposed during the 1991 Gulf War. The Americans hinted that they might agree if Iraq would allow the 600,000 Palestinian refugees living in Lebanon to be moved to northern Iraq. The advantage to the US would be a reduction of pressure on Israel to allow Palestinians to return. The advantage for Iraq's President Saddam Hussein, the Americans thought, would be a dilution of the Kurdish minority with large numbers of Sunni Muslims. As in 1841, the wishes of the Palestinians, who wanted to live in their own land, were considered unimportant.)

Palmerston told the sultan that Britain was doing what it could to hold the Ottoman empire together, and implied that it would do still more if the Jews were allowed to enter Palestine. The Jews would demand protection, which only Britain could provide (a clear hint that Palmerston wanted a British military presence). The foreign secretary, like Napoleon forty years earlier, wanted indirect control over Palestine.

The sultan vacillated between periods of allowing small numbers of Jews to settle and intervals of refusal. Those who entered were usually financed by donations from wealthy Jews in Europe such as Sir Moses Montefiore, a prominent British Jew who visited Palestine several times and helped to create Jewish institutions. One of

Montefiore's schemes was to build 200 Jewish villages, not in Palestine but in the eastern tip of Egypt near El-Arish, 'so that they can be near Palestine'. He apparently hoped that Mohamed Ali would be more amenable than the sultan, but made no progress. However, the idea was revived much later.

Britain also used its influence with the sultan to hold up construction of the Suez Canal, which required his permission. London had realized in the 1830s that the transportation economies a canal could offer would be offset by military and political costs. If a canal were built, Britain would have to deploy forces to keep it open. British pressure was among the causes of a twenty-year delay in authorizing the project.

A French company using Egyptian labour completed the canal in 1869, during the reign of Khedive (Viceroy) Ismail, a descendant of Mohamed Ali. This project and others, including railways and ports, indebted Egypt so heavily to European banks that Britain and France sent 'advisers' to manage the Egyptian economy. Such were the financial problems that the khedive decided in 1875 to sell Egypt's 44 per cent stake in the canal company, which was promptly snapped up by Britain. The decision was taken by Benjamin Disraeli, Britain's first prime minister of Jewish descent, and gave London a controlling interest, to the fury of Paris.

Despite their imperial rivalry Britain and France cooperated in forcing Ismail into exile in 1879, and three years later they sent a joint naval squadron to Alexandria to put down rioting by Egyptian nationalists. When the nationalists persisted France withdrew, but Britain attacked and slaughtered 10,000 Egyptians. Thus began the British military occupation of Egypt, which was to last seventy-four years. Subsequently Britain and France reached an agreement* under which France would not interfere in Egypt, nor Britain in Morocco, which later became a French protectorate.

In 1884 the European powers, together with the United States and Turkey, held a conference in Berlin aimed at settling colonial problems in Africa. The British government proposed a Zionist solution to the Jewish question, but this was rejected by Otto von Bismarck, the German Chancellor.

By now thousands of Jews had begun pouring out of Tsarist Russia,

* Part of the Entente Cordiale of 1904.

fleeing the pogroms which had begun in 1881. Most headed for the United States or Western Europe, but some went to Palestine, an influx which Jews call the first *'aliya'*.* The Ottoman government continued to vacillate, and funds provided by the Paris-based Jewish banker Baron Edmond de Rothschild enabled the settlers to establish themselves. The way some of them treated the Palestinians shamed the Jewish writer Asher Ginzberg (also known by the pseudonym Aham Ha'am). After a visit in 1891 Ginzberg wrote:

> They were slaves in the Diaspora, and all of a sudden they find themselves free without limits, freedom which has no deterrents, and that sudden transformation has created in them a tendency towards tyranny . . . they treat the Arabs with a spirit of enmity and violence and they despise them in a way which is not acceptable nor permissible and insult them unnecessarily. Some of our people think that Arabs are beasts and primitives who live like animals.

Ginzberg wrote this before serious problems began. At the turn of the century there were about 6000 settlers in twenty villages, not including Jews who had been there earlier, and large-scale immigration was yet to begin.

If Palmerston had foreseen trouble between Jews and Arabs in 1840, and Ginzberg witnessed the makings of conflict in 1891, one might suppose that Theodor Herzl, the founder of modern Zionism, would have been aware of the risks. Herzl, a Hungarian journalist, had become convinced while covering the Dreyfus affair† in France in the 1890s that the only solution to European anti-Semitism was the establishment of a Jewish national state. Herzl persuaded himself, against compelling evidence to the contrary, that Palestine was a land without people, ideally suited to a people without land. The problem, he thought, was mainly one of transportation. His concept was, in the opinion of Zionist leader Nahum Goldmann, that of a man with no sense of history, only geography. Herzl argued that Jews had lived for eighteen centuries in other countries, yet had put down no roots.

* *'Aliya'* expresses the idea that 'in the end of days' the Jews would return to Zion, the Holy Land.

† The trial of Alfred Dreyfus, a French army captain, on treason charges, was the most controversial case of the day. It was eventually proved that Dreyfus had been a scapegoat, selected because he was Jewish.

Some European governments would be glad to be rid of their Jewish populations if a way could be found to persuade the Ottoman empire to take them.

In his book *The Jewish State*, published in New York in 1895, Herzl wrote that only wealthy Jews succeeded in being assimilated in European societies. Those who were not wealthy should therefore emigrate to a place where they would not be persecuted or treated as outsiders. Some had suggested Argentina, but Herzl held that Palestine was unique in its hold on the Jewish mind. In this he and other Zionist writers were probably influenced by Hegel, the German philosopher, who taught that national identity was not a matter of choice but a biological bond between the individual, the community and the land.

Herzl seemed to assume that wealthy Jews would remain in the countries where they had made their money, a concept tantamount to visualizing Palestine as a Jewish poorhouse. He also believed that he had a mandate to represent the Jewish people as a whole. 'I manage the affairs of the Jews without any delegation from them, and I will be responsible for their fate in everything I do,' he wrote, listing the three great tasks before him as promoting Jewish action, obtaining international backing and facing Arab resistance. This last must have puzzled those who had understood the land to be without people.

Herzl's diaries for 1896 record a meeting with the sultan's secretary in which they discussed a decree to authorize Jewish immigration. The secretary, Mahmoud Gawid, stressed the importance of Jerusalem to Muslims. The Turkish records of the meeting show that Herzl assured Gawid that Jerusalem would be beyond the borders of the Jewish state because the city belonged to the whole civilized world. To quote these words in the 1990s, after nearly three decades of Jewish occupation of old Jerusalem, makes Herzl sound more moderate than his successors. At the time his remark was a statement of the obvious: even if Jerusalem lay within the Ottoman empire, its international nature was beyond dispute.

Jerusalem had been the original city towards which Muslims had faced when praying during the first seven years of the Prophet Mohamed's teachings, until the Koran commanded them to turn towards Mecca. The Dome of the Rock Mosque in East Jerusalem is considered the second holiest shrine in Islam, enclosing the rock where, according to tradition, Mohamed and the archangel Gabriel rose to heaven. The same area is equally sacred to Jews as the traditional site of the Patriarch Jacob's vision of angels ascending and descending the ladder between heaven and earth. The Jewish temple built by King Solomon was repeatedly destroyed and rebuilt until Titus razed it in 70 A.D., and the Wailing Wall, part of the Second Temple compound, is the last visible remnant. For Christians Jerusalem is the setting of the last chapter of Christ's life and contains some of Christianity's holiest places, including the Church of the Holy Sepulchre.

Herzl's assurance to Gawid was given half a century before the United Nations passed a resolution that Jerusalem should remain under international control, with the rest of Palestine divided into separate Arab and Jewish states. Had Herzl's view and the UN resolution been respected, much of the suffering which followed could have been avoided. But Jewish ambitions were never static, shifting steadily over the decades towards greater expansion. The Jews accepted the UN partition plan in 1947, but added to the captured territory during the 1948 war. In 1956 after the Suez conflict they annexed Sinai and renamed the Gulf of Aqaba the Gulf of Solomon, until forced by Eisenhower to reverse these moves. After the 1967 war they annexed Jerusalem and the Golan Heights.

Mahmoud Gawid, who was the son of the grand vizier, or prime minister, but nonetheless accepted bribes from Herzl to intercede with his masters, asked what relations were envisaged between the Zionist state and the Turkish empire. Herzl told him that the Jews did not want to defy or embarrass the Ottomans, and would accept a link similar to that between the empire and Egypt. At the time Egypt continued to acknowledge the sultan's suzerainty, even if this had little practical application.

Herzl sought to turn the sultan's financial problems to his advantage by proposing a scheme to purchase Palestine from the Ottoman empire. His diary for 15 June 1896 records an intention to pay the sultan 20 billion Turkish liras, of which 2 billion would be used to buy Palestine and 18 billion would be a gift to reform the state of Turkey itself. Herzl was making such plans at a time when the vast majority of Jewish refugees did not in fact want to go to Palestine, their preferred destination being the United States.

In a letter to the chief rabbi of Paris reporting on his meetings in Constantinople, Herzl said he had achieved stunning results. The sultan had received the offer to buy Palestine, and although unwilling to sell, 'made me feel that he would be ready for a deal if we found the proper formula'. The sultan was minded to issue an invitation for Jews to return to their homeland, on condition that they paid for the privilege. This was never implemented because the sultan felt unable to follow a consistent policy. When the empire needed favours from Britain the sultan would issue authorizations for Jews to enter; when Islamic leaders objected he would stop immigration.

Although increasing, Arab–Jewish tensions were not so strong as to preclude a sense of common purpose between nation-builders on either side of the divide. It was possible for a Zionist like Herzl to feel empathy for Arab nationalists struggling under the British yoke. Herzl got on well with Mustafa Kamel, a young Egyptian lawyer with a French education who was canvassing support for Egypt's independence. The two men met more than once in France, and Herzl recorded favourable impressions in his diaries. When Kamel asked for his help, Herzl was happy to oblige, reasoning that Egyptian nationalism might work to the advantage of Zionism. If the British were forced to leave Egypt they would have to build another canal to maintain the trade route to India. Any second canal would necessarily pass through Palestine, and this would strengthen Britain's interest in persuading the sultan to allow the Jews to return.

Herzl thought there were two possible routes for a canal: linking the Mediterranean to the Gulf of Aqaba, or connecting it to the Persian Gulf by crossing both Palestine and what is now Iraq (this would have been an immensely ambitious engineering project). The first option returned to the minds of Arab–Israeli negotiators in 1993 and 1994 following the Oslo agreement. A joint project between Jordan and Israel would link the Gulf of Aqaba to the Dead Sea, and from there an all-Israeli canal would be dug to the Mediterranean coast.

Herzl also attempted to enlist the support of Germany in bringing pressure upon the Ottoman sultan. In 1896, while Emperor Wilhelm II was preparing for a visit to Turkey and Palestine, Herzl visited the Grand Duke of Baden, father-in-law of the emperor, and delivered a letter for the emperor. The letter implicitly sought to exploit rivalries between European powers by hinting that if Germany used its influence to further Zionist aims, the Jews might prove helpful to German strategic interests.

'The only civilized element which can occupy Palestine is the Jews, because this country is poorer than to be of attraction to any other people,' the letter argued. 'It is meaningless to anybody but the Jews to be settled there, and I do not think you will permit a rush from other nations to that very important strategic area.'

Promising a warm welcome for the emperor from Jews in Palestine, Herzl continued: 'Our people will be waiting for you . . . you will have the historic opportunity to put our great project under your kind protection.'

The grand duke told Herzl that European Jews were not so ill-used that they would wish to emigrate, and suggested that it was Zionist agitators who were pressing them to leave. Herzl responded with flattery, suggesting that Jews were uniquely well-treated in the Duchy of Baden.

The grand duke persuaded his son-in-law the emperor to see Herzl, who reported in his diaries that the emperor asked: 'If you want me to talk to the sultan about the Jewish project, what would Turkey gain from that?' Herzl replied that a Jewish state would be a barrier to protect Turkey from Egypt.

In an article in the German newspaper *Die Welt* on 4 June 1897, Herzl extended this argument to include Russia: 'Our enemies are the same as the sultan's, they are our enemies. Those who want to divide the Ottoman empire are those who are standing against us.'

Three months later Herzl convened the first World Zionist Congress, which brought together Jewish representatives from many countries. It was held in Basel, Switzerland on 23 August 1897 and is regarded by Jews as a landmark in the creation of the state of Israel. The World Zionist Organization was created with the aim of establishing 'a home for the Jewish people in Palestine secured under public law'.

After the Basel conference the rabbis of Vienna decided to see for themselves what Herzl was talking about, and sent two representatives to Palestine. A cable sent by the two rabbis during their visit became famous: 'The bride is beautiful, but she is married to another man.' It was a message Zionists did not wish to hear, and the inconvenient husband was never acknowledged.

Herzl visited Egypt in 1903 and tried to interest the khedive in a project to colonize the area around El-Arish in the Sinai. The idea was not unlike the one Montefiore had put forward sixty-four years earlier, but it had an important additional element: Herzl wanted to channel water across the Sinai desert from the Nile to the proposed colony. The khedive supported the plan but was overruled by Sir Evelyn Baring (later Lord Cromer), Britain's proconsul in Egypt. Although Egypt was supposedly a self-ruling country within the Ottoman empire, the presence of British troops made this spurious. In all but name Baring was governor of Egypt from 1883 until 1907, and while Egyptians have no cause to cherish his memory, the decision to refuse Herzl's colony was sound. British engineers had reported that not enough Nile water was available for such a project.

The Israelis revived the water proposal during economic talks in 1993, but the opposing arguments remained as valid as they had been ninety years earlier. Apart from the insufficiency of water there was also a diplomatic issue: during the British colonial era a treaty had been forged between the countries through which the Nile flowed, establishing how much water each could extract. The diversion of any Nile water to Israel would have made renegotiation necessary. At the time of the original treaty Britain controlled or influenced most of the Nile countries, but any post-colonial renegotiation was sure to be difficult.

In 1903 Joseph Chamberlain, the British colonial secretary, offered Herzl a national home in Uganda, which had become a British protectorate nine years earlier. Chamberlain hoped the pleasant weather and rich farmland of the East African highlands would appeal to the Jews. According to Herzl's diary entry of 23 April 1903, Chamberlain said: 'I have found a gift for you, Mr Herzl.' But the Zionist leader declined: nowhere but Palestine would suffice.

More pogroms in Russia in 1903 and 1906 prompted a second wave of immigration, which lasted from 1904 to 1913 and brought 40,000 people to Palestine. During this period the composition of Palestine's Jewish minority changed fundamentally. When the Jews began dispersing after the Roman conquest they were a Semitic people with features similar to Arabs. When they returned they were a different race, modified by eighteen centuries of intermarriage. The 'blue-eyed Jews' who came from the Diaspora had little in common with the indigenous 'brown-eyed Jews' who had remained. The former, known as the Ashkenazim, were unable to speak Hebrew, though they used its script in written Yiddish, the German-based language which at that time was the tongue of 9 to 10 million Jews. The Ashkenazim gained the upper hand in the early years and retain it to this day, even if they are now in a minority. The numbers of 'brown-eyed Jews' were greatly increased by later waves of immigration, especially the arrival of descendants of Jews who had left Spain during the Inquisition and settled in Muslim countries. These were known as the Sephardim, and the term came to be applied to all Jews of oriental origin.

One might suppose that the Sephardim would be better disposed to Arabs than the Ashkenazim, but the opposite has been the case, perhaps because the Sephardim are more aware of failing their fellow Semites, and express that guilt through greater violence. The cruelty of Sephardi soldiers during the struggle on the Egyptian front in the 1948–49 war did much to reinforce the Arab taboo. Captured Egyptian soldiers would pray to be interrogated by an Ashkenazi rather than a Sephardi officer. Much later, Sephardi voters brought about the 1977 defeat of the Labour Party and the victory of the Likud alliance, a right-wing grouping whose aim was to frustrate the limited concessions which previous governments had offered Palestinians.

Another change brought by the second '*aliya*' from 1904 onwards was the introduction of socialist political ideas, which were put into practice in the first kibbutz, established in 1909. The kibbutzim* were mainly important because of the impression they made on public opinion outside Israel. The admiration which some newly independent African states professed for Israel in the 1960s was based on the idea that the Jews had invented an ideal community unit. It was only when Arab leaders explained, during a conference in Casablanca in 1961, that the kibbutzim had been used as a form of creeping colonization, comparing the movement with the slow conquest of South Africa by Dutch and British farmers, and the apartheid policies which followed, that African leaders took a different view. Kwame Nkrumah, president of Ghana, was among several who revised their opinion at that conference.

In the years after 1904 the impact of Jewish immigration on Arab consciousness grew immensely. Numerically Jews were still outnumbered twenty to one by Arabs, but their purchasing power made them masters. Jewish farmers were now hiring Arabs as farm hands

* *Kibbutzim* is the plural of *kibbutz*, from the Hebrew word for 'group'.

and paying above market price for Arab land. Large-scale purchases were made possible by an influx of capital from European and American Jewry. The Jewish National Fund had been established by the Zionist Congress to finance such purchases.

Theodor Herzl died in 1904, having aroused the Jews at a juncture in history when the British colonial mind thought they could serve imperial purposes, when European governments were seeking the riddance of a source of internal division, and when British Protestants supported the Zionist idea. Herzl's greatest disservice to the world was the falsehood that the Palestinians were either a non-existent people or one without consequence. Their existence was denied as late as 1968 by Golda Meir in a speech to a congress of the Socialist International in Vienna. The price of Herzl's blindness has been a century of conflict.

Two main strands of Zionist opinion grew from Herzl's seeds: one dedicated to the conquest of all lands which ultra-orthodox sects regarded as 'Eretz Yisrael', the land God gave the Jews,* the other willing in principle to accommodate some Arabs within Eretz Yisrael. The best-known exponent of the former faction was Vladimir Zeev Jabotinsky, who sought Jewish control of both banks of the Jordan river. The latter strand was exemplified by David Ben-Gurion, who favoured an autonomous Arab region within a Jewish state, an idea which Yitzhak Rabin continued to support in 1994. The second strand did not, however, pay more than lip-service to peaceful coexistence with Arabs. These two groups shared a common taste for violent methods, making their differences irrelevant to Palestinians.

If Herzl was primarily a dreamer, the next important figure in Israeli history, Chaim Weizmann, was a translator of ideas into action. The son of a Russian timber merchant, Weizmann made a career as a scientist in Britain and found himself at the right place at the right time. A new opportunity for Zionism, with British military power as its vehicle, was about to arise from events triggered by the 'Young Turks' revolution of 1908. Austria-Hungary annexed the Ottoman province of Bosnia-Herzegovina, and came into conflict with Serbia, leading to the Great War. In October 1914 Turkey declared war on Britain,

* Islam teaches that God gave the Jews the promised land, as recorded in the Old Testament, but that the Jews forfeited their inheritance because they strayed from the true path of monotheism.

France and Russia. In making common cause with Austria-Hungary and Germany, Turkey released Britain from inhibitions which had lasted more than a century. Since the days of William Pitt the younger British prime ministers had consciously resisted the temptation to redesign the Levant by force.

The opportunity created by war was attended by a fresh set of dilemmas. On one hand the British needed Arab support, or at least neutrality, to ensure the defeat of the Turks. On the other, the attractions of creating a Jewish homeland in Palestine remained undiminished. Overlaying both these considerations was the need for compromise between British and French ambitions in the Levant. Instead of choosing one or two of these goals, Britain adopted all three, regardless of their inherent contradictions.

In negotiations with Arabs, Britain gave the impression that a substantial portion of the Arab world would achieve unity and independence when the war was over. This induced Arabs to side with Britain, which in turn prevented Constantinople, as nominal head of the Muslim faith, from declaring a *jihad*, or holy war. A *jihad* would have caused a division of loyalties among Britain's Muslim forces in India. The Arabs also conducted a limited revolt against Turkey, in which T.E. Lawrence and other British officers participated.

In talks with the French, Britain reached a secret agreement on the division of the Ottoman spoils. The Jews, meanwhile, were working to change British policy from within, and had more success than either the Arabs or the French. Chaim Weizmann, who had contributed to the British war effort by developing an improvement in the chemistry of manufacturing explosives, was now the leading Zionist in Britain, and his views received much attention.

Sir Herbert Samuel, another leading British Jew, was the cabinet secretary. In January 1915 Samuel submitted a paper to the cabinet arguing the case for British annexation of Palestine. He said that the world's 12 million Jews aspired to 'the fulfilment of the hope and desire, held with unshakeable tenacity for 1800 years, for the restoration of the Jews to the land to which they are attached by ties almost as ancient as history itself'.

Samuel thought the time was not ripe for a Jewish state because there were only 80,000 to 90,000 Jews, compared with 500,000 to 600,000 Arabs. 'To attempt to realize the aspirations of the Jews one century too soon might throw back its actual realization for many centuries more,' he said.

The paper now seems extraordinary in its blatant appeal to the British sense of superiority. Annexation, Samuel held, 'would enable Britain to fulfil in yet another sphere her historic part of civilizer of the backward countries. Under the Turk, Palestine has been blighted. For hundreds of years she has produced neither men nor things useful to the world. Her native population is sunk in squalor. Under British administration, all this will be quickly changed. The country will be redeemed. What has been done in Egypt will be repeated here.'

Samuel pointed out that his plan would not be a complete solution to the Jewish question in Europe. Palestine was too small and too short of water to provide a home for all Jews, but could probably accommodate 3 to 4 million, 'and some relief could be given to the pressure in Russia and elsewhere'.

Three months later Samuel produced a revised and less jingoistic version of his paper, proposing a British protectorate rather than annexation. Although it was presented as a set of options, his own opinion was clear: if Britain did not decide the future of the Holy Land, France would do so by annexing Palestine.

Samuel's ideas did not immediately find favour with the cabinet, but in 1916 Lloyd George replaced Asquith as prime minister and appointed Arthur James Balfour as foreign secretary. The new government included more cabinet members who were favourably disposed to the Zionist idea, and the fact that the Zion Mule Corps* had participated in the Gallipoli Campaign of 1915–16 may have given Weizmann additional leverage.

In the autumn of 1917 General Edmund Allenby, leading the British forces in Egypt, began an offensive against Turkish forces in Palestine. As Allenby's men swept forward Balfour wrote a letter which was to become infamous in the Arab world. It was addressed to Lord Rothschild, a prominent Zionist leader:

> His Majesty's Government view with favour the establishment in Palestine of a national home for the Jewish people, and will use their best endeavours to facilitate the achievement of this object, it

* A volunteer force of 500 men organized by Vladimir Jabotinsky, whose main purpose was to gain training and experience for use in Palestine later.

> being clearly understood that nothing shall be done which may prejudice the civil and religious rights of existing non-Jewish communities in Palestine, or the rights and political status enjoyed by Jews in any other country.

Balfour asked Rothschild to bring the letter to the attention of the Zionist Federation of America (there were then 2 million Jews in the United States).

The Balfour Declaration was dated 2 November 1917, just five weeks before Allenby captured Jerusalem, ending 401 years of Turkish rule. The timing was significant, because by this time Britain's alliance with the Arabs had served its purpose. Once the Turks were defeated, Britain could afford to renege on its implied promise that Arabs should rule their own lands. That deception, and the Balfour Declaration, acted as powerful catalysts upon the alchemy of collective Arab phobia. Ancient antagonisms, reawakened from the sleep of centuries by mass Jewish immigration, sharpened by British duplicity, began to mutate into the poison of anger and resentment. The making of the Arab taboo had begun.

3

Deception, Collusion, Betrayal

The agreement signed at the White House in September 1993 set the principles for limited Palestinian autonomy in parts of the occupied territories. The stated intention was that self-rule should begin in Gaza and Jericho and would later be extended to other parts of the territories. Eight months of further negotiations passed before a start was made on implementing this accord, and by that time the initial optimism of Palestinians had faded. A majority suspected that 'Gaza and Jericho first' meant 'Gaza and Jericho only', and that nothing more would be obtained without a further struggle. This continuing scepticism was puzzling to many outside the Arab world. Israel had promised that the accord was only a beginning, and that negotiations on a permanent arrangement would begin within two years. Was it not reasonable to give Israel time to honour that undertaking? What made the many opponents of the agreement feel sure that Israel would renege?

No understanding of these suspicions is possible without appreciating the psychological impact on Arabs of promises broken during World War I, and of subsequent betrayals.

The least important of these disappointments stemmed from the wording of the Balfour Declaration. The phrase 'it being clearly understood that nothing shall be done which may prejudice the civil and religious rights of existing non-Jewish communities' sounded like a promise, but proved meaningless.* Balfour himself subsequently admitted that the Palestinians had been deceived.†

* The wording invited the question: Understood by whom? The Zionists or the British?

† The admission was made in a memorandum which Balfour wrote to cabinet colleagues in 1919. He attributed the deception to the 'Big Four' powers (the United States, France, Britain and Italy) rather than to Britain alone: 'So far as Palestine is

It could be argued that Balfour's reference to Palestinian rights was unimportant, because Arabs always realized that the declaration was a promise to Jews, not to Palestinians. However, there was no such ambiguity about the undertaking Britain made during the First World War to support Arab self-determination in specified Arab regions of the Ottoman empire. That promise had been made before the Balfour Declaration, and was repeated after it. Furthermore, the promise formed part of a clear bargain: Britain would help Arabs after the war if Arabs assisted Britain first.

The circumstances of the Anglo–Arab deal lie in the early months of World War I, before it became clear whether Arabs would side with the Allies or with the Central Powers. The question was hotly debated, to the point that different sons of one Arab emir argued for different sides.* Although Palestine, Syria, Iraq and the Arabian peninsula were still within the Ottoman empire, and still bound to Constantinople by religious ties, there was growing unrest. Turkey had lost much of its former administrative and military strength, but remained the focus of a commonwealth of nations headed by a Turkish caliph. Within the Ottoman empire each country had a sense of local nationalism, unconnected with its ties to Turkey.

This order of loyalties had remained unchanged for centuries, but was now being questioned by Arab intellectuals. Some had begun to call for the creation of a state uniting Arab peoples, rather than Muslims of all races. That concept was the result of a long passage of thought started a century earlier by scholars such as Rifa'a El-Tahtawi. Although not an Arab nationalist himself, El-Tahtawi helped to create the intellectual climate which led to differentiation between Islam and Arab nationalism.† El-Tahtawi was a member of an Egyptian delegation which was sent to France in 1826 by Mohamed Ali, the

concerned, the powers have made no statement of fact that is not admittedly wrong, and no declaration of policy which, at least in the letter, they have not always intended to violate.'

* Faisal, third son of Sharif Hussein of Mecca, initially leaned towards the Central Powers, although he subsequently became Britain's favourite. Abdullah, the second son, always preferred the Allies.

† The Ottoman empire was an Islamic nation, but Islamic nationalism was impossible because the empire was not racially or linguistically homogeneous. The Arabs, by contrast, were and are a nation in a racial and linguistic sense, which made Arab nationalism possible.

viceroy. After an extended visit El-Tahtawi wrote about the rationalist, humanitarian, liberal and scientific ideas which writers such as Voltaire, Montesquieu and Rousseau had brought to eighteenth-century European thought, and about the part which the Enlightenment had played in the French Revolution. El-Tahtawi's works brought to the Arab world an understanding of this 'Age of Reason' and the earlier ideas of the Renaissance, and helped to stimulate important changes in Egypt during Mohamed Ali's reign.* While remaining nominally subject to Turkey, Egypt acquired trappings of a nation-state, with a high degree of autonomy, a powerful army and a vision of modernization, especially in administrative, industrial and educational spheres. This interlude of Egyptian freedom did not last long,† but it had two lasting effects. One was to encourage Arab intellectuals outside Egypt to think of a pan-Arab union inspired by the Egyptian model. The second, paradoxically, was to delay Egyptian interest in Arab unity. Such was the pride in what had been achieved before the British occupation that nationalist feelings in Egypt were strictly Egyptian in character. Outside Egypt Arab nationalism became the focus of Arab intellectual debate by the early years of the twentieth century; inside Egypt that cause had its supporters, but forty years would pass before their views prevailed.

The area which proved most fertile for Arab nationalism was the Sham,‡ the lands of the east Mediterranean which had the strongest cultural links with Egypt, and which had been closely tied to Egypt before the Ottoman empire. Three factors combined to encourage a differentiation between Islamic and Arab loyalties: a strong intellectual tradition, especially in Damascus and Beirut; proximity to Turkey and the heavy-handedness of Turkish administrators; and the presence of large numbers of Christian Arabs,§ who were more willing than

* El-Tahtawi's most celebrated book was *The Extraction of Gold in the Description of Paris.*

† Mohamed Ali's reforms were continued by his successors, but the British occupation from 1882 ended an era of relative freedom.

‡ The Arabic word for the Levant.

§ Christian Arabs were equally prominent in promoting Arab nationalism in subsequent decades. George Antonius (1892–1942), a Palestinian with a pan-Arab vision, Michel Aflak (1910–89), the main theorist of the Ba'ath Socialist Party, Dr George Habash (b. 1925), leader of the Popular Front for the Liberation of Palestine, and Nayef Hawatmeh, leader of the Popular Democratic Front for the Liberation of Palestine, were among the best-known.

Muslims to renounce the empire. After living for four centuries under the umbrella of the holy state and the caliph, Muslim loyalties were entrenched in the mind, and might have remained strong but for the empire's inability to defend its possessions. As Arabs watched Algeria fall into French hands in 1830, followed by Tunisia in 1878 and Morocco in 1912, the realization spread that only Arabs could defend Arab lands.

The paradox Arab nationalists faced was that escape from one empire could only be achieved by enlisting the help of another; and yet the idea of approaching Britain, the occupier of Egypt, for help against Turkey remained unappealing. The outcome of these dilemmas was a reluctant Arab nationalist movement in Syria, which sought a religious cover to protect its flanks. Arab nationalist societies in Syria turned to the only Islamic figurehead whose prestige could rival that of the caliph: Hussein Ibn Ali,* Sharif of Mecca, descendant of the Prophet and leader of the Hashemite clan. They sent an emissary to offer Hussein their support for a revolution under his leadership, hoping that Hussein's spiritual authority and Anglo–French military power would together bring their dream to reality. Hussein accepted the offer, but his plan was to ride both horses, Arab nationalism and European imperialism, to a destination of his own choice.

It was obvious, although not explicitly stated, that Hussein's responsibilities as leader of the revolution would include contacts with outside powers. The revolution could not succeed without British and French acquiescence, and many thought American approval desirable, because of the moral authority the USA was beginning to exert on European empires.†

Hussein reached agreement with Britain, but not with France or the United States. It was not difficult for Hussein to negotiate with the British, because he had established contact with Lord Kitchener six months before the outbreak of war.‡ Kitchener understood the religious importance of Hussein's office: if a wedge could be placed

* The great-grandfather of the present (1995) King Hussein of Jordan.

† The Americans were seeking greater justice in a new world order, including the principle of government with the consent of the governed. These ideas emerged in January 1918 in the form of President Wilson's famous 'Fourteen Points'.

‡ Horatio Herbert Kitchener was the British representative in Egypt 1911–14, and returned to London as secretary for war from August 1914.

between Hussein and the Turkish caliph, the risk of a *jihad* would lapse, since tradition required any holy war to be declared from Mecca.

One drawback of channelling nationalist hopes through Hussein was that those aspirations became tied to the fortunes of the Hashemites. Hussein might have religious prestige, but his rule was limited to Hejaz, the eastern province of Arabia, and his relations with Ibn Saud, ruler of Nejd, the eastern province, and with El-Idrissi, ruler of 'Assir' (now the border area between Saudi Arabia and Yemen), were far from cordial. The British were now financing both Hussein and Saud.

A still greater disadvantage was that the right of the Hashemite family to be the guardians of Islam's holy places was open to question. Any descendant of Mohamed is accorded special respect, but the Prophet was a messenger of God, a mission which cannot be inherited. The Hashemite claim could have been based on Mohamed's other role as head of a state whose capital was Mecca, but that would have entailed thinking of the Prophet as the founder of a dynasty, which was contrary to the spirit of Islam.

Hussein yearned to extend his emirate to include other Arab lands, but wanted the peoples concerned to seek his leadership. His status as Sharif of Mecca and the ambiguity of the Hashemite claim made him reluctant to behave like an ordinary tribal leader. No such inhibitions were felt by his rival Ibn Saud, whose ambitions were limited only by political and economic factors.

Thus it was that Hussein, a man of little pan-Arab vision, became the symbol of an idea which was larger than himself. The sharif undertook a limited diplomatic effort conducted entirely on his own authority without reference to his sponsors, the societies in Damascus. That effort consisted of a lengthy exchange of letters with Sir Henry McMahon, the British high commissioner in Cairo. Egypt had been declared a British protectorate at the outbreak of war, and McMahon's writ included representing Britain in the western part of the Arabian peninsula.

During a year of correspondence, McMahon gave assurances which were understood by the sharif to mean that after the war Britain would help the Arabs achieve self-rule in the whole of the Arab peninsula and the area immediately to the north, between the Mediterranean and the Persian Gulf. McMahon made certain exclusions in Syria, but his remarks were vaguely worded, and Hussein was not as persistent as he could have been in clearing up ambiguities. The precise words used by McMahon are irrelevant, because on two occasions after the war the British government made statements reiterating its support for Arab self-determination. What mattered to Hussein and the Arab nationalists was the general British intention, and the fact that the assurances were conveyed at a high level.

The same Arab approach to negotiations has been evident in most negotiations from that day to this, including the Oslo talks: Arabs based their decisions on one man's word to another; Israelis and Westerners were mainly concerned with the precise meaning of words. If a promise was worded to deceive, the Western mind might interpret that as statecraft, while Arabs still had a semi-religious belief in the written word.

Trusting in British good faith, Hussein initiated an anti-Turkish revolt which was eventually led by his son Faisal and assisted by British officers, including T.E. Lawrence. Arab harassment of Turkish forces contributed to the British war effort on a limited but useful scale.

Hussein had no way of knowing that Britain and France had reached a secret deal on control of the lands lying between the Mediterranean and the Persian Gulf. A month before the first shots in the revolt were fired, British and French negotiators had drawn up a post-war map of the region. Mark Sykes and Georges Picot, acting on behalf of their governments, delineated zones of permanent British and French influence. The populated and fertile northern areas which Hussein was hoping to include in his expanded post-war kingdom were to be split into five new states. France was to have parts of Turkey, Syria and Lebanon as a state under direct French control, with a long Mediterranean coastline. A smaller British-controlled state was to be set up covering the remainder of the Mediterranean coast as far south as the Egyptian border and including parts of what are now Israel and Jordan, and within this there was to be an international mini-state including Jerusalem. Another British-controlled state was to be created in parts of what are now Iraq, Kuwait and Saudi Arabia. Two landlocked states were to be created in parts of what are now Syria, Jordan, Israel, Iraq and Saudi Arabia. These last were described as 'independent', but one was to be under British and the other under French tutelage. The fate of the rest of the peninsula was left unspecified.

The existence of this secret agreement was leaked a month before General Allenby's forces reached Jerusalem in December 1917, and just before the announcement of the Balfour Declaration.* It was now too late for any Arab change of heart to affect the outcome, but Britain hastened to assure Hussein that the McMahon assurances would be respected. Whatever his doubts, Hussein could only hope his trust had been justified. His followers had declared him king of the Arab countries, but this had no practical application.†

Realizing the sensitivity of the situation, Allenby sent a cable to London asking what flags he should raise when he reached Jerusalem. The decision taken by the war cabinet was as follows: 'Because of the unique nature of the city and because of the political and diplomatic complications which would be entailed, General Allenby should be advised not to raise any flags at all.'

Britain's three undertakings, to the French, to the Arabs and to the Jews, were now public knowledge, and yet Britain continued to act as if there were no contradiction between them. A government declaration to leading Arabs in Cairo supported 'the principle of the consent of the governed', and this was reinforced in even clearer language by a subsequent Anglo–French statement in November 1918. Both governments wanted to keep Arab nationalist passions in check while they secretly negotiated a revised version of the Sykes–Picot agreement and prepared for the Versailles Peace Conference.

Although shocked by the promises Britain had made to France and the Jews, the nationalists in Syria still thought something could be salvaged. Their hopes were now focused on Faisal, Hussein's third son, who had been picked by T.E. Lawrence as the member of the Hashemite family best suited to implement Britain's plans. Lawrence, who detested the French, did his best to undermine the Sykes–Picot agreement. His hope, based on the fact that the region was now under British military rule, was that the lands the French wanted could be absorbed in a new Arab kingdom combining Syria and Palestine, with Faisal as its monarch. Lawrence's aim was not to help Arab nationalism

* The leak came from the Bolsheviks, who had learned of the Sykes–Picot agreement during their revolution.

† France rejected the proclamation that Hussein was king of the Arab countries but accepted a British compromise under which he was recognized as king of the Hejaz. This ensured international acceptance that Hussein was a monarch, not an emir.

but to avoid making a gift to France of lands Britain had conquered. Some way had to be found of reconciling the scheme with the Balfour Declaration. Lawrence arranged meetings between Faisal and Chaim Weizmann, the British Zionist leader whose lobbying had helped bring about the declaration. After talks in Palestine and London an understanding began to emerge early in 1919 that Zionists would not seek a Jewish state in return for Arabs accepting large-scale Jewish immigration, subject to safeguards.

Meanwhile the Arab Bureau in Cairo sent Commander D.G. Hogarth, who had been Lawrence's mentor, to reassure King Hussein in Mecca. Hogarth reaffirmed the Allies' intention that the Arab people should have a chance to regain their existence as a nation, but said that this could only be achieved by the Arabs themselves. At the time Hussein was still hoping to bring Palestine, Syria and what are now Lebanon and Jordan under his rule. Hogarth said Britain was determined that the people of Palestine should not be ruled by anyone but themselves, although 'special arrangements' (meaning British rule) would be needed to administer Jerusalem. However the Ummar Mosque, also known as the Dome of the Rock, would be solely under Arab control. As for the Balfour Declaration, Hogarth emphasized that Jewish immigration should not affect the freedom of Palestine's existing inhabitants, either politically or economically. The Jews could help to obtain international backing for the Arab cause, and Jewish leaders wanted to achieve their aims 'through friendship and cooperation with the Arabs'.

Hogarth's memoirs show that Hussein understood that these assurances were little more than a statement of goodwill. The king's dreams were beginning to fade, but he did not yet know that he was to be sidelined by his children. Faisal's leadership of the Arab revolt had made him the popular choice to represent the Arabs at the Paris Peace Conference, which had been convened to convert the 1918 armistice into peace. Hussein authorized his son to go, but the French objected. Britain intervened and France relented, on condition that Faisal would represent solely the kingdom of Hejaz.

Weizmann, leader of the Zionist delegation to the conference, had submitted a memorandum setting out Zionist aims. These included recognition of the right of Jews to return to Palestine, putting Palestine under a British mandate, recognition of the Balfour Declaration and a pledge to implement it, and the setting up of a representative assembly for Jews in Palestine. These demands were repudiated by the Palestinian people, who sent a delegation asking the peace conference not to take any decision without hearing the Palestinian case first.

In March 1919 Faisal and Weizmann held a meeting as heads of delegations, an arrangement which inflated the importance of Weizmann, putting him on an equal footing with Faisal. The document which emerged makes bizarre reading in the light of subsequent developments. The two men recognized bonds of race and history between Arabs and Jews, and believed that the best way to achieve their respective aspirations was to intensify cooperation. In putting his name to this statement Faisal implicitly recognized the Balfour Declaration's goal of a national home for the Jews in Palestine. He also undertook to encourage immigration of Jews to Palestine, and the two men agreed that the British government should arbitrate any dispute between them.

The understanding Lawrence needed to make his scheme work was thus in place, but in the meantime the situation had changed. Lloyd George and Georges Clemenceau, prime minister of France, had reached an agreement during the Paris conference to divide the area between the Mediterranean and the Persian Gulf into zones of British and French hegemony.* The agreement, a modified version of the Sykes–Picot plan, made Lawrence's idea unworkable, because it confirmed what Lawrence was trying to avert: French control of Syria.

The Lloyd George–Clemenceau accord left many details to be settled later, but essentially set the framework of borders which were completed by 1922 and lasted until 1948. Nearly all subsequent changes to the political geography of the Levant have resulted from the Arab–Israeli conflict.

The Anglo-French decisions were later endorsed by the League of Nations, which had been created by the Treaty of Versailles. The American people had by now refused to join the League,† with the

* Lloyd George and Clemenceau were half of the 'Big Four' who took most of the decisions at the Paris conference. The other two were President Woodrow Wilson of the United States and Prime Minister Vittorio Emanuele Orlando of Italy.

† Contrary to the wishes of Woodrow Wilson they refused to ratify the Treaty of Versailles, thus beginning the era of American isolationism.

result that the new organization was overwhelmingly influenced by Britain and France. When the League's Supreme Council met in San Remo in May 1920, the two powers had little difficulty in persuading other countries to award them mandates over the territories they had selected. After the San Remo announcement there could be no further illusions that Britain would honour its promise to Hussein. Nationalists in Syria, Palestine and Iraq arose in anger but were crushed by French and British forces.

What had been Syria became two countries, Syria and Lebanon, under French mandate, a change which rankles with Syrians to this day. An echo of those feelings emerged when Warren Christopher held talks with President Hafez El-Assad of Syria in April 1994, to explore ways of unblocking Syrian–Israeli peace talks. The Americans understood that one of Assad's aims was to secure US recognition of Syria's dominant military and political influence in Lebanon.

Faisal, nominal king of the new smaller Syria, was ousted after only three months by the French, who had never accepted Britain's wish to promote the Hashemite family. The commander of the French forces which crushed Syrian resistance, General Henri Eugene Gouraud, replaced Faisal as effective ruler, with the title of haut commissaire.

Embarrassed by the actions of its European ally, the British government decided that Faisal would have to be compensated. Winston Churchill, then aged forty-seven, had recently been appointed colonial secretary after serving as secretary for war in 1917–18, and lost little time in making amends. By the spring of 1921 Faisal had been installed as king of Iraq, a throne he kept until his death in 1933. With this problem solved, Churchill went to Jerusalem, personally drew the borders of Transjordan, and asked Faisal's elder brother Abdullah to visit him. Abdullah felt entitled to a share of the cake, and had already staked his claim by occupying Amman with a small army. Churchill asked him to be the emir of Transjordan.

After the dishonour Faisal had suffered, Abdullah had made repeated threats to invade Syria and attack French forces. The emir's military strength was never sufficient for such a contest, but had he attempted it the real motive would not have been to avenge Faisal but to annex Syria. Abdullah was both jealous and contemptuous of Faisal, regarding him as Lawrence's favourite, and Faisal reciprocated this dislike.

Both brothers were also at odds with their father, who felt they had usurped his share of the territorial spoils.*

The British now insisted that Hussein should accept the San Remo decisions if he wanted military protection against his rival Ibn Saud, whose forces were menacing the Hejaz. Hussein put honour before pragmatism, refused to sign the treaty Britain offered, and was abandoned to face Saud. Five years later Saud ousted the Hashemites and absorbed the Hejaz, which eventually became part of Saudi Arabia. Relations between the Hashemite and Saudi clans remain less than cordial to this day.

Disillusioned Arab nationalists were exasperated with the whole Hashemite family. In their eyes Hussein had mishandled the negotiations with the British, Faisal had failed to stand up to Weizmann in Paris and to the French in Syria, and Abdullah had used the debacle in Syria to procure himself an emirate. After rewarding Abdullah and Faisal with thrones Britain felt free to keep Palestine, the jewel in the Arab crown, for its own designs.

Arabs had assisted the Allies on the basis that they would emerge free and united, within specified geographical limits, after the war; instead the Arabs had shrugged off the Ottoman yoke only to be saddled with British and French mandates and Jewish settlers. Arabs had invested much hope in McMahon's letters, not realizing that after the war British promises would be subject to a priority order: France first, Zionists second, Arabs last. Lloyd George might have modified those priorities if the Egyptian masses had risen to demand that the McMahon promises be honoured. But Egypt remained a world apart from Damascus and Beirut, still absorbed with dreams of Egyptian nationalism.

The Arab part in the First World War was well known to the British public because of romanticized accounts of Lawrence's role in the revolt against Turkey. This might have contributed to a greater appreciation of Arabs but for the fact that Zionists in key positions were working to belittle Arab qualities. In 1920, when Lloyd George asked for General Allenby's views on the future of the Sinai, one

* The eldest of Hussein's four sons, Ali, had stayed behind. When Hussein abdicated in 1924, Ali succeeded him but was quickly defeated by Ibn Saud, who became King of the Hejaz.

such Zionist found an opportunity. Allenby asked Colonel Richard Meinertzhagen, who had been his chief intelligence officer during the Palestine campaign, to prepare a memorandum. At the time Meinertzhagen was chief political officer for Palestine, which had been under British military rule since Allenby's conquest in 1917. The reply sent to Lloyd George took the form of a memorandum signed by Meinertzhagen with a covering letter from Allenby.

The memorandum said that the Paris Peace Conference had borne two siblings, Jewish nationalism and Arab nationalism, but there was a huge difference between them. The first was energetic, the second languid, filled with the stillness of the desert. The Jews, despite being scattered, were known for their loyalty, their cultural feelings and their knowledge, and had given Britain one of its great prime ministers. Jewish military capabilities had been proven at the time of the Roman invasion, whereas the Arab was known for his crudeness in war and his fondness for theft, killing and destruction. During the next half-century Jewish nationalism would flourish and Jews would achieve sovereignty. Arab nationalism would grow and Arabs would seek unity from the Persian Gulf to the Atlantic. Jewish immigration would lead to territorial expansion, Arabs would resist, two national ideas would collide, and there would be much bloodshed. As it was impossible to remain friendly with both Arabs and Jews, Britain should side with the latter who, being indebted, would be a loyal treasure for the future.

From this basis the memorandum argued that Britain should annex the Sinai, which had been an Ottoman possession under Egyptian administration, in order to secure its position in the Middle East when the time came to give the Suez Canal back to Egypt. Cooperation between Britain and the Jews and the construction of suitable facilities would forestall any Egyptian military threat. Britain would also have the opportunity to build a canal of its own between the Red Sea and the Mediterranean.

Palestinians living under British military government were well aware of the pro-Zionist views of some officials. The flavour of popular sentiment is reflected in a petition sent by their leaders to Brigadier-General C.F. Watson, commander of the 180th Brigade, which had been appointed to maintain order in Jerusalem. 'We have convinced our people that the British government is the best government in the world and will . . . look after the building of our country. [However] we look at the privileges which the Jews have been given . . . and we cry that are deprived of those privileges.' The petition went on to suggest that Jews were spreading Bolshevism in Palestine, and complained about their manners and morals. 'They are very arrogant with us, and even with you . . . Their young men, boys and girls, are really obscene; they go out hand in hand together, wearing clothes which are not decent. What is emerging in the settlements is a permissive society.'

The petition reflected the aggrieved but submissive mood of Palestinians at that time. 'We are an obedient people and we love whoever rules us,' it said. Such attitudes had been instilled during four centuries of Ottoman rule and would take time to change. Palestinian obedience to Constantinople had been based on the belief that the caliph was the Prophet's representative on earth.* The first wave of defiance did not come until 1920, when the British had been in Jerusalem for nearly three years. After Arab demonstrations against Jewish settlements the British took action against both sides, quelling the Arabs by force and imposing restrictions on Jewish land purchases. The Jewish Legion† was disbanded, but the Jews immediately created Hagana, a semi-secret defence force.

Jewish aims during the immediate post-war period had been outlined by Weizmann in a speech to Jews in London on 21 September 1919, six months after reaching agreement with Faisal: 'The Jewish state will come, but it will not come through pledges or political statements, it will come through the tears and blood of the Jewish people . . . As for the Balfour Declaration, it is but a golden key to open a door.' Weizmann spoke of flooding Palestine with huge numbers of Jews 'to create a society in Palestine which will be Jewish as much as England is English and America is American'.

Weizmann, who had assured Faisal in 1918 that there was no intention of creating a Jewish state, now implicitly endorsed that aim. 'Many people ask me: will Palestine be a Jewish state in the future or not, and on whom that task depends, and I tell you that is our task, not

* The word 'caliph' comes from the Arabic *khalifa*, meaning deputy of the Prophet.

† The Jewish legion was a volunteer force formed during World War I by Vladimir Jabotinsky. It fought as part of the British forces, notably in the Gallipoli campaign of 1915–16.

anybody else's.' The blessing of big powers was important, but it was Jewish organization, resources and knowledge which would make possible a Jewish state.

Zionist aims had taken an important step forward with the San Remo declaration, which apart from approving the British and French mandates also adopted the Balfour Declaration and gave Britain the task of implementing it. Palestinians strongly opposed this decision from the start, arguing that it broke the spirit of the Covenant of the League of Nations. The British mandate had been established under Article 22 of the Covenant, which spoke about 'peoples not yet able to stand by themselves' and said that the 'well-being and development of such peoples form a sacred trust of civilization', while the administration of those peoples 'should be entrusted to advanced nations'. Arabs wondered how Britain could claim to be safeguarding Palestinian well-being by foisting Jewish immigrants upon them.

Sir Herbert Samuel, the Jewish former cabinet secretary who had proposed a Zionist plan in 1915, was now selected as Britain's high commissioner in Palestine. His arrival in 1921 brought the British military government to an end, replacing it with a civilian administration made up of ten British officials, three of whom were Jewish, three representatives of the Jewish community in Palestine, four Muslims, and three Christian Arabs. The Muslims, who made up more than three quarters of the population, were thus greatly underrepresented. Samuel and his successors made numerous attempts to develop institutions of self-government, but were rebuffed. As Palestinians did not accept the decision to impose the Jewish national home upon them, they could not accept institutions whose aim was to implement that decision.

Samuel tried to placate the Arabs by halting immigration, but this proved to be only a temporary measure, and during the years 1919–1923 an influx of Russians added a further 34,000 Jews to the population. Hebrew was introduced as one of the three official languages of Palestine, on a par with Arabic and English, and in 1925 the Hebrew University of Jerusalem was opened. In the same year Vladimir Jabotinsky created the Revisionist Party, which demanded a Jewish state on both sides of the river Jordan.

The leader of Arab protests in 1920, Hajj Amin El-Husseini, had been imprisoned by the British, but was soon pardoned and became the dominant spokesman of Palestinian anger for the next three decades. His position was strengthened by two important titles: Grand Mufti of Jerusalem and head of the Supreme Muslim Council (a British invention). Although the post of Grand Mufti made him a religious figure, El-Husseini was primarily a resistance leader whose refusal to compromise remained an inspiration to many Palestinians long after his death. His grandson Faisal Husseini subsequently came to be seen as a living reminder of the Grand Mufti's example. During the 1993–94 talks between the PLO and Israel, Arafat sought to harness that aura for his own needs. When Arafat had to sign documents containing concessions to Israel, he would insist on being photographed with Faisal Husseini, to give the impression that the Grand Mufti would have approved. Faisal Husseini, however, eventually found a way of reminding Arafat of his grandfather's firmness. On 4 May 1994, when Arafat was in Cairo for the signing of the Gaza–Jericho agreement in its final form, Faisal Husseini remained at Orient House, his headquarters in East Jerusalem. A fax from Faisal Husseini to Arafat read: 'Mr Chairman, please do not sign this agreement.' Faisal Husseini's opposition proved short-lived, for he agreed a few weeks later to become a member of the Palestinian authority responsible for implementing the agreement which he had previously begged Arafat not to sign.

Amin El-Husseini was for many years the leading advocate of direct action against the Zionist invasion. In 1929 he played an important part in widespread Arab demonstrations against Jewish settlements, which led to two British investigations into the causes of Arab discontent.

These inquiries, by the Shaw Commission and by Sir John Hope-Simpson, produced conclusions which were sympathetic to Palestinian fears of loss of political and economic status, and Hope-Simpson also said that Palestine could not absorb another wave of immigrants without further economic development. These conclusions were adopted in a British White Paper issued in 1930 which introduced additional restrictions on Jewish land purchases and immigration, but the document provoked a storm of pro-Jewish protest in Britain. Ramsay MacDonald, then prime minister, backed down and sent Weizmann a letter confirming the cancellation of the most important provisions.* This

* Ramsay MacDonald's missive is known to Palestinians as 'the Black Letter'.

British refusal to respond to Arab concern was compounded by a lack of action to limit the activities of Hagana, which reorganized itself on a much larger scale and began establishing its own arms industry.

The frustration caused by these events did much to fuel the Arab nationalist movement, which now included several new leaders and writers. Their message, notably articulated by Satie El-Husari, was that Arabs were united by language, history, law and geography, and that all who shared these bonds, whether Muslim or Christian, were members of a great cultural entity which might some day achieve political unity.

If El-Husari's ideas were slow to gain ground in Egypt, the cause was the continuing strength of Egyptian nationalism. The discovery in 1922 of the intact 3000-year-old tomb of Tutankhamen and the astonishing standard of its art works had reinforced awareness of past greatness, and many Egyptians thought of their country as being Mediterranean rather than Arab in character.

Throughout the interval between the two world wars Egyptian nationalists were preoccupied with loosening Britain's military presence and regaining Egyptian control of Sudan, which had been dominated by Britain since Kitchener's conquest of 1898.* A series of crises in the 1920s and thirties resulted in negotiations which put the Anglo–Egyptian relationship on a new basis from 1936.† Although Egyptian and Palestinian nationalists were equally anxious to rid their countries of the British, there was no serious attempt to make common cause.

Despite these differences of outlook, Arab nationalism made its first practical impact on the Palestinian issue from 1931 onwards. Representatives of twenty-two countries met to show support for Palestinians, and subsequently the Arab world organized an economic boycott against British and Jewish companies.

Arab frustration was still running high in 1933 when the next major wave of immigration from Europe began, this time linked to Hitler's rise to power in Germany the same year. Arab protests were sternly suppressed by the British authorities, and the flood of immigrants

* Although the administration of Sudan was supposedly an Anglo–Egyptian condominium from 1898 to 1956, Britain kept the Egyptian role to a minimum.

† Under the Anglo–Egyptian Treaty of 1936, Britain agreed to remove its forces from Cairo and the Nile delta, while retaining bases along the Suez Canal. This partial withdrawal was delayed by World War II.

continued unchecked. Arab anger was focused not solely on Zionists but also on those Palestinians who sold their land and property to Jews. During a Palestinian meeting in 1933 Amin El-Husseini recounted the experience of a delegate who had protested to the British high commissioner about land purchases.* The high commissioner seemed astonished by the complaint. 'Why protest to me? Why don't you take it up with the people who are selling land?' he asked. The delegate pointed out that Jews were paying extraordinary prices because of overseas support. If Arabs had comparable financial and political backing they could buy large areas of any European capital. The high commissioner replied: 'Those who are selling land are not poor farmers, they are wealthy people like you.'

Proposals for taking direct action against those who sold were considered but rejected in favour of a religious approach. Abdullatif Bey Salah, a delegate at the meeting, recommended that all Palestinians, both Arab and Christian, should go to their mosques and churches, declare their anger against Britain and pray 'that those tyrants [the British] be sent another tyrant stronger than themselves'.

Another effect of the 1929 Arab unrest was that David Ben-Gurion, who later became Israel's first prime minister, came to understand the true reasons for Arab anger. After meeting several Arab leaders, Ben-Gurion proposed to Musa Alami, a former attorney general in the mandatory government, that in return for Arab acceptance of continued large-scale immigration, Zionists would support the creation of an Arab federation which would include Palestine. This would ensure that Arabs would remain a majority within the federation, even if they eventually became a minority within Palestine. Ben-Gurion also discussed his idea with George Antonius, whose subsequent book *The Arab Awakening* came to be seen as a definitive statement of the Arab nationalist idea. Not surprisingly, Ben-Gurion found no enthusiasm for his proposal. As Jewish immigration was the main source of concern, lifting Arab objections to immigration was out of the question.

The rebuff made Ben-Gurion realize that the Zionist–Arab dispute was essentially political rather than economic, something which was

* The Grand Mufti did not mention the high commissioner's name, but was presumably referring to Sir Arthur Wauchope, who served from 1931 to 1938.

obvious to Arabs but unacceptable to Jewish opinion. Most Jews had preferred to accept the British argument that Arab discontent reflected low living standards, and that as the Jews had come from more developed countries they would strengthen the economy. According to the British theory, Arab objections to Jewish immigration would fade as Arab living standards rose. Ben-Gurion was among the first major Zionist politicians to see that the theory was unsound, and to appreciate the consequences. If the division was as deep as it now appeared, the Jews had two options: to stop trying to impose themselves, or to prepare for a greater conflict.

In 1934 a variation of the idea Ben-Gurion had discussed with Palestinian leaders was taken up by Abdullah, Emir of Transjordan. Abdullah had never abandoned hope of uniting Palestine or Syria or both to his impoverished territory, and had been in continual contact with both Zionist and Palestinian leaders. His proposal was a federation of Palestine and Transjordan under his rule, each country to have its own legislative council and government. The Arabs would recognize the British mandate, including its aim of creating a Jewish homeland in Palestine, and the issues of Jewish immigration and land purchases would be settled within a separate agreement between Arabs and Jews.

This proposal, which amounted to abandoning the main principles of Palestinian resistance, would have been of little benefit to anyone except Abdullah, but was none the less given serious consideration. Hajj Amin El-Husseini led a great campaign against the plan, denouncing Abdullah as a friend of the Jews, and eventually the scheme was dropped.

The episode marked the beginning of a long era in which Palestinian nationalists frequently felt betrayed by other Arabs, including other Palestinians. That era was not finished at the time of the Gaza–Jericho accord. The assassinations of three PLO ambassadors during the decade and a half before the accord stemmed from suspicions of willingness to accept Israeli terms for peace. Sa'id Hammami, PLO representative in London, was murdered in 1978 after talking to British Jews; the same year the PLO's representative in Paris, Dr Ezzedin Kalak, met a similar fate. In 1983 a subsequent PLO representative in Paris, Dr Essam El-Sartawie, was killed while in Portugal trying to arrange a meeting with Shimon Peres. All three assassinations were attempts to prevent the PLO from breaking its own cardinal rule: no contact with the enemy. Even at that late stage, the price of defying the taboo was death.

At the time of Abdullah's proposal Jews were pouring into Israel from Germany and other countries in large numbers. Between 1933 and 1936 (a period known to Zionists as the fifth *aliya*) 166,000 Jewish immigrants were admitted to Palestine, and many more entered without permission, bringing the total Jewish population to 400,000 by 1936. The Jews were now a third of the population, and the risk that they might become the majority was no longer remote.

Arab anger eventually exploded in 1936 in Jaffa after a shipment of 537 cases of arms bound for Hagana was uncovered by British officials. Arab–Jewish skirmishes broke out in Jaffa and tensions throughout Palestine ran out of control. With every month that passed a peaceful solution looked less possible. Ben-Gurion now came round to the view of Jewish fundamentalists that war was inevitable. Some, like Jabotinsky, had long considered war not merely inevitable but desirable. Violence, in the mind of the most extreme elements, was not so much a necessary evil as an essential and valuable instrument of policy.

The psychology of that attitude was examined by a group of Palestinian intellectuals in a study entitled *Before the Arab Diaspora*, published in Beirut in 1987. The intellectuals tried to analyse why the Zionists used force not merely as a way of imposing their presence but also to oblige Palestinians to leave. They concluded that some Zionists were inwardly tormented by the contradiction of using irreligious methods to achieve a religious goal, and reacted by trying to erase Palestinians from their minds, from Palestine, and later from existence itself. Similar psychological tensions may have been at work again in 1994 when Baruch Goldstein massacred Muslims at prayer in Ibrahimi Mosque, Hebron. It is hard to imagine that Goldstein saw human beings when he looked through the sights of his assault rifle: what he perceived was an obstacle to the revival of Eretz Yisrael in its biblical form.

By the end of 1936 most of the causes of the post-1948 taboo were already in place. In chronological order these were the reawakening of ancient collective memories (1882 onwards), the untruth of Balfour's commitment to Palestinian rights (1914), the McMahon–Hussein affair (1915–21), reminders of the Crusades, caused by growing Zionist militarism and mass immigration (1930s onwards), and finally collusion between Zionists and Transjordan. In half a century the

Palestinian imagination had been assailed by biblical spectres, British deceit, broken promises, Zionist invasion, and betrayal by an Arab leader. Only the humiliation of defeat and dispossession now remained to complete the taboo.

4

Whispering Neighbours

The era of secret contacts between Arabs and Zionists began in the aftermath of Amin El-Husseini's campaign against King Abdullah. Until 1934 discussions between Transjordan's ruler and Ben-Gurion's emissaries had been discreet but not secret, since neither party yet realized how Palestinians would react to their collaboration. It was only after the Grand Mufti had aired his suspicions that the need for secrecy was appreciated.

Between 1936 and 1939 Palestine lived through the Arab Revolt, a period of protests and attacks against the Jews and the British. One effect of the revolt was to increase the appetite of Zionists for contact with the desert emirate across the Jordan river. War would come sooner of later, Zionists reasoned, even if they could not yet foresee circumstances in which Britain's military umbrella would be folded. Hagana was growing in training and organization but was as yet equipped only for quelling riots, with machineguns and armoured cars rather than tanks and artillery. Abdullah, on the other hand, had the most professional and best-equipped fighting force in the region, the Arab Legion, funded and trained by Britain, which also provided most of its senior officers. The Zionists realized that in any future conflict between Jews and Palestinians, the neutrality or involvement of the Arab Legion could decide the outcome.

Abdullah was just as interested as Zionists in contacts, hoping that the Jews could help bring to fruition his dreams of reigning over an expanded kingdom. While visiting London for the coronation of King George VI in 1936, Abdullah met a Jewish businessman* who offered a deal under which the emir would be paid for allowing Jews to settle

* Pinhas Rutenberg, who helped to develop Palestine's electricity generating systems.

in Transjordan. Abdullah declined, knowing that the British would not allow such a scheme, but contacts continued.

Throughout the next decade messages were passed frequently between Abdullah and the Jewish Agency, and these contacts gave both sides hope of bypassing Palestinian objections to their respective schemes. Abdullah used his interior minister Mohamed El-Unsi to convey ideas to Eliahu Sasson, head of the Jewish Agency's Arab Department. Sasson, then in his thirties, had come to Palestine from his native Damascus and spoke excellent Arabic. Apart from Abdullah's messages, El-Unsi also gave the Jewish Agency information on his own account, and was paid for his services. These early secret contacts prepared a relationship from which both sides were to profit later.

Throughout the late 1930s British officials searched fruitlessly for a way of defusing Arab anger. Several Arab parties had come together in 1936 to form the Arab Higher Committee, choosing Hajj Amin El-Husseini as leader, and the committee called a general strike which lasted seven months. The strike was regarded by Zionists as a failure, as it caused more economic harm to Palestinians than to Jews, but it proved effective as a way of raising awareness of the Palestinian case. A commission headed by Lord Peel was sent from London to investigate the causes of Arab discontent.

In its report, published in July 1937, the Peel Commission said that the British mandate was unworkable and recommended that Palestine should be partitioned into two states. A separate mini-state including Jerusalem should remain under British control. The Arab Higher Committee adamantly rejected the plan, while Abdullah was bound to support it because Peel proposed that the Palestinian state be unified with Transjordan. Weizmann, Ben-Gurion and Moshe Sharett (later foreign minister and prime minister) endorsed the plan, even if the state allotted to the Jews was smaller than they would have liked. Many other Zionist leaders, including Jabotinsky, rejected the plan. This division among Zionists resulted in an impression that Peel's proposals would be accepted by Jews only if they were altered in their favour, which was out of the question. The Peel plan therefore lapsed, but on both sides there were critics who felt that an opportunity had been missed. Nahum Goldmann described the Jewish response as a 'sin', while the Arab Higher Committee was blamed by some Arabs for failing to seize statehood when it was on offer. This latter criticism was unrealistic, because Palestinian public opinion was fiercely opposed to ceding territory to the invader, a principle which all Palestinian leaders upheld until 1988, when Arafat accepted UN Resolution 242. Even as late as the mid-eighties Arafat would explain his rejection of Resolution 242 by saying: 'I cannot start negotiating with Israel accepting *a priori* the surrender of more than half of Palestine.'

In 1937 Palestinian feelings were running high. Soon after the Peel report appeared the Arab Higher Committee stepped up the revolt, and during the following six months they gained military control of some areas, before the British quelled the fighting. The revolt also changed in character, becoming increasingly anti-British as well as anti-Zionist, although most of those killed were Arabs and Jews.* The mandate government disbanded the Arab Higher Committee, but this had limited effect, as Amin El-Husseini escaped to Syria, which became a base for raids into Palestine. The British also began to treat Hagana as a military partner, carrying out joint night raids on villages suspected of harbouring Palestinian commandos.

The situation changed suddenly in the autumn of 1938 when the British realized that Neville Chamberlain's appeasement of Hitler had failed. With another European war looming, the Foreign Office scrambled to shore up Britain's diplomatic and military position in the Middle East. The causes of anti-British feeling in Palestine could not be removed without abandoning the Balfour promise, but any undisguised retraction would inevitably arouse protests in Britain. The government's solution was to create a situation in which a change of policy could be presented as the wisdom of experience. Yet another British report was produced, full of arguments contradicting Lord Peel's recommendations. The thrust of its message, which was hardly original, was that Arab and Jewish populations were so intertwined as to make partition impractical. This new report provided justification for summoning Palestinians, Zionists and representatives of neighbouring Arab countries to London for a round-table conference in March 1939. Delegates arrived in London to find an atmosphere of crisis, with air raid shelters being dug in parks and gas masks at hand in homes and offices. Britain's need for a quick-fix solution to the

* Casualties during the Arab Revolt have been estimated at 500 Jews and a larger but uncertain number of Arabs.

Palestine problem was now self-evident. The settlement Britain proposed was a federal state which would come into being after a transitional period of five years, on terms which ensured that the Palestinians would remain in a majority permanently. The vehement opposition of Jewish delegates to this plan was no surprise, but the British were now mainly interested in Palestinian and Arab views. Against the advice of some supporters, Amin El-Husseini rejected the offer and the conference ended in failure.

Britain decided to ignore the Grand Mufti's objections and impose the plan, with certain changes. The new version was published on 17 May 1939 and differed from the March offer in that the state was to be unitary instead of federal and the transition was to take a decade instead of five years. This became known as the 1939 White Paper, which gives the incorrect impression that it was only a policy document. In peacetime Britain would have had to refer the recommendations to the League of Nations, but the League collapsed early in World War II and Britain implemented the white paper as it stood.

The British high commissioner was given powers to block further sales of land to Jews, who now owned 250,000 acres, or one ninth of the area suitable for cultivation. Britain planned to limit immigration to 75,000 during the next five years, bringing the Jewish minority to one third of the population. After five years no further Jewish immigration was to be permitted without Palestinian approval, and Britain declared its intention to hand over Palestine after ten years as a fully independent state with a two-thirds Arab majority. The Jewish population grew faster than planned, however, reaching 475,000 by the end of 1939.

The white paper came during the final exodus of German Jews before war closed the exits. Most went to the United States or Britain, but Palestine remained the choice of substantial numbers. Although infuriated by the immigration controls, Zionist leaders had little option but to cooperate with Britain, since Germany was the common enemy. Ben-Gurion announced that the Jews would wage 'war against the Nazis as though there were no white paper, and a struggle against the white paper as though there were no war'. Small paramilitary gangs carried out anti-British attacks, but the majority of Jews agreed with Ben-Gurion.

The white paper aroused neither enthusiasm nor anger in the Arab world. Amin El-Husseini, who spent the war in Italy and later Germany, and broadcast to Arabs from Berlin, was firmer in his opposition to British policy than were Palestinians as a whole. Some Arabs hoped for an Axis victory as a means of hastening Britain's withdrawal from the Middle East, but few sympathized with Nazi or Fascist ideas. The extermination of the Jews was not and never has been an Arab aim. Commando groups of young Arabs, including Anwar Sadat, undertook attacks against British forces in Egypt and passed information to German agents, but these were limited activities. The majority in Palestine and Egypt remained quiet: Britain's new policy had released just enough pressure to avert an explosion of Arab discontent during the Second World War.

Abdullah's support for the white paper did not endear him to Zionists, and contacts went into a quiet phase at the beginning of the war. For the next three years Zionists and Transjordanians waited to see whether the Axis powers would become the new overlords of the Middle East.

That possibility seemed very real on 29 May 1941 when Sir Anthony Eden, foreign secretary in Churchill's war cabinet, addressed the House of Commons. Rommel's surprise victory in Cyrenaica a month earlier had demonstrated that British tanks were not only obsolete but in poor condition as a result of inadequate maintenance. Eden now made a broad statement of sympathy for Arab nationalism, similar in its general thrust, its vague phrasing and its transparent intentions to the commitments McMahon had given in 1915–16. Britain knew that the white paper had not gone far enough towards Arab aspirations. Eden's statement, which amounted to recycling the unkept promise Britain had made during the First World War, was a bid for Arab cooperation or neutrality during the struggle against Rommel.

The Arab nation Eden was contemplating had geographical limits similar to those of the McMahon undertakings: essentially the Arabian peninsula and the Levant. A second statement by the foreign secretary in February 1942 specifically mentioned Egypt and was interpreted by some as a commitment to general Arab unity. The 1942 statement needs to be understood in the context of hectic preparations for the battle of Alamein. Eden could hardly avoid saying what Arab nationalists wished to hear at a time when Egypt was the most important outpost in the struggle against Germany. The 1942 statement meant less than it implied; the British government did not then think that Egyptian nationalism was closely linked to Arab nationalism.

Eden's two declarations probably helped Britain during the tense months when Rommel's Afrika Corps was hammering at Egypt's borders, but also complicated the rivalry between the Iraqi and Transjordanian branches of the Hashemite clan. Abdullah took Eden's words as a green light to promote his ambitions for an expanded kingdom based on the pre-World War I concept of Greater Syria. Meanwhile his cousins in Baghdad were plotting for a Fertile Crescent kingdom uniting Syria with Iraq.

Abdullah's brother Faisal I had died in 1933, and the Iraqi throne was now nominally occupied by Faisal II, grandson of Faisal I, aged only six. Real power was shared between Prince Abdel-Ilah, the regent, and Nuri El-Said Pasha. The pro-British prime minister had just been restored to office by British forces, replacing a nationalist government which Britain suspected of pro-German sympathies. Abdullah had sent his forces to assist in this coup, and for a time traditional rivalries between the two Hashemite branches subsided. The truce did not last long, and soon Nuri El-Said began actively promoting the Fertile Crescent kingdom idea.

The separate ambitions of Amman and Baghdad were followed with concern by Abd al-Aziz Ibn Saud, enemy of all Hashemites, who in 1932 had proclaimed himself king of the country which still bears his name. Any scheme which increased Hashemite strength was a potential threat to Saudi Arabia. At the same time advisers to King Farouk of Egypt, then aged twenty-one, were worried about Hashemite schemes for different reasons. The Sham had been bound to Egypt from the time of the Pharaohs until the Ottoman empire, with the exception of a brief period.* If a general rearrangement of borders after World War II was in prospect, Egypt wanted to be consulted. The outcome was a series of meetings between Farouk and Ibn Saud and an agreement to oppose the way the Hashemites were interpreting Eden's statements. A more profound change was that Egyptians began to feel drawn to Arab nationalism. Absorbed for decades by memories of past glory, the most populous Arab country was at last looking outwards.

* The exception was the Umayyad dynasty from 661 to 750 A.D., when Damascus was the capital of the Islamic world.

Ibn Saud, on the other hand, had been interested in the Palestinian cause since the mid-1930s. During the Arab Revolt, when Egypt offered Palestinians little more than moral support, Ibn Saud actively mediated between different Palestinian factions.* At the same time Ibn Saud was also looking to more distant horizons and realizing that his relationship with Britain was not necessarily advantageous. Oil had been discovered in large quantities in Saudi Arabia in 1938 but could not be developed until the war ended. It was already clear that if British companies developed Saudi oil they would keep production to a minimum, because Britain had more oil in Persia and Iraq than it could use. American companies, which knew that Texan reserves would soon be inadequate, had shown more interest. The king had to weigh the future importance of oil against the immediate reality of his agreement with the British-controlled government of India, and the annual subsidy paid in gold with which Britain retained his loyalty. There was no reason to think, at the outset of World War II, that the United States would be willing to take over this role if Ibn Saud decided to switch loyalties from London to Washington. The United States had so far shown little political interest in the region.

Although it was not obvious at the time, the solution to Ibn Saud's dilemma was provided by the Japanese attack on Pearl Harbor in December 1941. The raid did more than blow away American isolationism and reluctance to be involved in European quarrels; it also brought a realization that Middle East oil would alter American priorities after the war. Churchill unintentionally accelerated that thought process by urging President Roosevelt to give military priority to the Middle East at the same time as Europe, leaving Asia until later. After Montgomery's victory at Alamein in October 1942 American troops and tanks began arriving in North Africa in large numbers. Under Eisenhower's leadership these forces played a major role in forcing the surrender of the Afrika Corps six months later. From that moment on the American involvement in the region acquired a hidden extra purpose: to replace Britain as the dominant power in the Middle East.

Roosevelt had made it clear from the outset that the United States

* As a result of the interest Saudi Arabia had shown, Amin El-Husseini switched his loyalties from King Abdullah to Ibn Saud in 1934, after the Transjordanian proposal which had angered the Grand Mufti so much.

had no interest in sustaining old empires, but Churchill at first missed the full import of these remarks. The British governing classes watched American overtures to Arabs with amusement, marvelling at their inexperience. A telegram which Sir Miles Lampson, Britain's autocratic ambassador in Cairo, sent to Eden in June 1943 mocked the American habit of distributing chewing gum to Arab men and mirrors to women, and smugly suggested that such 'very primitive' methods of ingratiating themselves would have no success. A further two years would pass before complacency gave way to alarm; the British remembered too late that allies in battle could remain effective competitors in the diplomatic souk.

By 1942–43 the first stirrings of what would later be known as the Jewish lobby were being felt in Washington. The Roosevelt administration had shown interest in Jewish refugees as early as 1938 but was not then under significant political pressure. Tens of thousands of German Jews had fled to the United States during the Weimar Republic and the early years of the Third Reich, but they made little impact on American national politics. Most confined their activities to giving or raising money to help other Jews escape and to continue the preparation of Palestine as a Jewish national home. Two factors came together to alter this picture. The first was the fall of France in 1940 and the deportation by the Vichy government of French Jews to Germany. There was now no safe haven for Jews in Western Europe, given that Britain's future remained in doubt even after the successes of the RAF during the 1940 Battle of Britain. The uncertainty led to New York taking over London's role as the hub of Jewish political activity.

The second factor was that the more recent Jewish immigrants in America received word of what was happening to their relatives in Europe and began trying to mobilize other Jews. This was not difficult, as American Jewry was heavily concentrated around large cities, apart from remnants of rural communities established in the nineteenth century, when some Russian immigrants found work as farm hands. Jews in New York were now better established than other minorities, and by the late 1930s were already influential in the media, the arts and banking. Such people were reaching the upper strata of the cities just as the United States abandoned its self-imposed isolation, a coincidence which accounts for the rapid increase in Jewish political impact after 1942.

American Jews were by now very different in collective personality to their distant European cousins. After generations in the New World they had absorbed the vitality and optimism of American society, and equally its materialism and scarce interest in philosophical matters. Those from Europe, whether discreet bankers or poor artisans, were imbued with nostalgia for a land few had seen, but whose milk-and-honey memories had been passed down through eighteen centuries. Nahum Goldmann used to compare European Jewry with a violin, mournful of voice and light of weight. American Jewry was more like a piano, strident, booming, confident and massively built.

The event which made them play the same note took place at the Biltmore Hotel in New York in May 1942. More than 600 delegates from seventy countries came together for three days and passed resolutions whose effect on American foreign policy few could have foreseen.

The conference was influenced by the presence of three of the four best-known figures of recent Zionist history. After the death in 1904 of Theodor Herzl, founder of modern Zionism, Chaim Weizmann led the Zionist movement during decades when London was its political focus, and was instrumental in securing Arthur Balfour's promise in 1917. At the time of the Biltmore conference Weizmann was a leading figure in the World Zionist Organization, and six years later he was elected as Israel's first president.

David Ben-Gurion, born in Russian Poland in 1886, had come to prominence in Palestine as secretary general of Histadrut, the General Federation of Labour, and in 1942 he was chairman of the Jewish Agency Executive. In 1948 Ben-Gurion read the proclamation of the state of Israel and became prime minister and defence minister of the interim government.

Nahum Goldmann, born in Russia in 1894, had been an active Zionist since his days as a Heidelberg law student. He travelled widely but lived in Germany, working as a writer and publisher of the *Encyclopaedia Judaica*, until 1933 when he left the country just in time to escape arrest. In the early thirties he and Nahum Sokolov, then president of the World Zionist Organization, became active in fund-raising in America. Goldmann subsequently attained wide influence in securing American economic support and political protection for Zionism.

After the establishment of the state of Israel Goldmann led the World Zionist Organization, and later became an Israeli citizen.

These three leaders – the agent of the promise, the builder of the state, and the persuader of foreign protectors – were already celebrated figures among Zionists in 1942. They used the conference to convince American Jews that raising funds was no longer an adequate contribution to the Zionist cause. An active political role was needed, targeted on the Roosevelt administration, with the specific aim of securing American leverage to reverse Britain's abandonment of the Balfour Declaration.

The conference passed a resolution urging that a Jewish commonwealth should be established in Palestine after the war. The word 'state' was not used, but the vaguer term 'commonwealth' was intended to include hopes of statehood. European Zionists had been striving for a state for more than a generation, but American Zionists had never before agreed on a common goal. Indeed, there had not been a meeting of all American Zionist parties since the First World War.

The warning which Ben-Gurion, Weizmann and Goldmann brought was that the Jewish dream of a national home was now jeopardized by British hesitation. Generations of settlers in Palestine had built the infrastructure of a state, but all could be lost without a political push which could only come from the United States. Another goal, though many failed at the time to appreciate its importance, was to secure Arab acceptance of Jewish aspirations. Arms or political power might bring about a *fait accompli*, but a Jewish state would never have peace without the acceptance of those affected, the Palestinians. Bringing that hope to reality has been an aim of all US administrations since 1948.

The need for Arab acceptance was understood more clearly by Goldmann than by Ben-Gurion or Weizmann. After the 1948–49 war this difference between them gained another dimension, in that Goldmann feared that the excessive use of violence would debase the Jewish soul. Goldmann raised these thoughts with Ben-Gurion in a conversation a decade after the war. Ben-Gurion replied that he did not think Israel could have peace with the Arabs: 'If I were an Arab leader I would never sign an agreement with Israel . . . We have taken their land. It is true that God promised us this land but what do they care about that promise? Our God is not their God . . . They will forget after a generation or two, but for the time being there is no sign of them forgetting. We have to be strong, we have to have devastating power. This is our policy, otherwise the Arabs will annihilate us.'* Goldmann remained a voice of relative moderation in subsequent years, but his views did not prevail.

At the urging of Ben-Gurion a programme of political goals was adopted. These included the reaffirmation of the Balfour Declaration and the British mandate for Palestine, and the rejection of the British White Paper of 1939. Point eight of the programme demanded that 'the gates of Palestine be opened; that the Jewish Agency be vested with control of immigration into Palestine, and with the necessary authority for building the country'.

By the end of 1943 the Russians had defeated the Germans at Stalingrad and Kursk, Italy had surrendered and preparations were beginning for the Normandy landings. Meanwhile Washington was planning a silent conquest of Britain's political assets in the Middle East. An anguished telegram sent by Churchill to Roosevelt on 20 February 1944 shows that the war cabinet was now aware of this undeclared struggle.† Churchill was alarmed by American plans to hold a conference on Middle East oil, and spoke of fears that the US wanted to deprive Britain of its oil resources. He urged Roosevelt to accept private US–British discussions rather than an open conference, and warned that a dispute over oil would make a poor start to plans the two countries had made for the post-war period. Four days later he followed up this message with another letter expressing the anxiety of the whole cabinet and asking for a technical study of international oil questions before holding any conference.

The American tactic appears to have been to let the British think they might take everything, in order to force Britain to give up Saudi Arabia, the most important oil country. An understanding was reached within days, and is reflected in a further telegram sent by Churchill on 4 March. The prime minister assured Roosevelt that Britain would not stand in the way of US oil development in Saudi Arabia, and thanked Roosevelt for a pledge not to interfere with British oil interests

* Quoted in *Das Judisch Paradox* by Leon Abrahamovitch, 1970.

† The communications between the US and British leaders were released by the British Public Record Office after thirty years.

in Iran and Iraq. The importance of the British concession is not apparent in the telegram, which mainly expresses Churchill's relief.

Iran and Iraq were vastly more important to Churchill than Saudi Arabia, but the British leader was none the less upset when Roosevelt usurped what remained of British influence with Ibn Saud. After the 1945 Yalta conference Roosevelt flew to Egypt and boarded the US destroyer *Quincy*, which was anchored in the Bitter Lakes in Sinai. Ibn Saud was flown to Egypt to join him, and the meeting laid the basis of long-term Saudi–US cooperation. Britain had been squeezed out, and a trend had begun. Before Pearl Harbor America had been reluctant to come to Britain's rescue, but having won the battle the US was unwilling to leave Western Europe and the Middle East. The rise of communism provided a reason for staying, but Washington wanted its soldiers to do more than provide a garrison. Unconsciously, perhaps, the Americans were looking for an empire of their own, but of a different kind: more a club of US-dependent countries than a global stamp collection on the British model.

After his return to the US Roosevelt was incautious enough to refer to Ibn Saud as a 'noble savage' during conversations with American Jewish leaders, a remark which revealed how much Americans had yet to learn. The president questioned the wish of Jews to establish a national home so close to 'those savages', but found, as Joseph Chamberlain had discovered from Herzl four decades earlier, that no other destination would meet Zionist aspirations.

The dilemma which would eventually draw Washington into the Arab–Israeli dispute was beginning to take shape. On one hand the desire for a national home was a goal with which any American could sympathize, having parallels in US pioneer history. If Americans had driven the Indians from grazing lands to make space for themselves, why should they object to Jews expelling Palestinians? Jews had the skills, education and resources to build a modern state, while the Palestinians, as seen from America, were poor in everything except history. On the other hand the Palestinians had friends, including Ibn Saud and the Egyptians, who were important to Washington's plans for the future. It was therefore a relief to Washington that Britain, not the United States, was stuck with the Palestine problem. So long as Britain held the mandate, Washington could act as a spokesman for Zionist demands without jeopardizing its standing in the Arab world.

The difficulties of Britain's role had been underlined by the assassination of Lord Moyne, minister of state resident in the Middle East, in November 1944. Moyne, a personal friend of Churchill, was based in Cairo but responsible for British policy in the whole region, including implementation of the 1939 White Paper, and had refused to relax immigration restrictions in Palestine. He was entering his home in Zamalek, the most fashionable quarter of Cairo, when two members of the Stern gang shot him dead. The gang, also known as Lehi,* advocated the forcible expulsion of Arabs from lands which in biblical times had been Eretz Yisrael. It was founded by Abraham Stern as a splinter group which broke away from Irgun,† another extremist organization which Stern had also helped to create. Stern's followers included Yitzhak Shamir, who later became prime minister. Stern himself was shot dead by British police in 1942 after a large reward had been offered for his capture.

Moyne's death hardened Churchill's attitude towards the Zionists, but this became irrelevant with the Labour Party's crushing victory in the July 1945 British general election. The Attlee government was expected to tilt towards Zionism, but Ernest Bevin, the new foreign secretary, tried to uphold the 1939 White Paper. The limit of 75,000 immigrants had been greatly exceeded, bringing the Jewish population to 580,000, but Zionists were demanding unlimited entry for survivors of German concentration camps. Bevin now came under pressure from many quarters to relax the controls. David Ben-Gurion authorized Hagana to begin attacks against British troops and British installations throughout Palestine, resulting in disruption and many casualties.

Harry Truman, who had succeeded Roosevelt on the president's death in April 1945, called on Britain to allow 100,000 Jews to enter Palestine immediately. Bevin resented this interference, but Jewish organizations took Truman's support as a green light to test Britain's will. Sixty ships carrying 70,000 Jewish immigrants attempted to reach Palestine over the next three years, and although most were intercepted, the tactic succeeded in propaganda terms. Britain's stand was seen by the media in many parts of the world as inhuman in view of

* 'Lehi' is an acronym of Lohame Herut Israel (Fighters for the Freedom of Israel).
† Irgun's full name is Irgun Tz'vai L'umi (National Military Organization). It was founded by Jabotinsky's revisionists in 1937. Menachem Begin, later prime minister, was its commander-in-chief in 1942.

Jewish suffering during the war. An Anglo–American Commission of Inquiry, set up by the two governments, supported Truman's demand for the admission of 100,000 refugees. Tension between Britain and the Zionists reached its height in June and July 1946, when Britain carried out widespread arrests of Hagana members and Jewish Agency executive officials, and Irgun retaliated by blowing up the King David Hotel, where the British administration had many of its offices. The Jewish Agency then called a halt to military operations, but Irgun and Lehi disobeyed the order.

Britain now seemed to hesitate, unsure what to do next. The pressures from Truman, the Zionists and the world media had to be balanced against Britain's long-term economic and strategic interests, which required stability in the Middle East. Bevin, a shrewd politician, understood that the empire was an anachronism which Britain's ruined economy could no longer sustain in a global form. The decision to give India its freedom was not far away, but even without India Britain would still need guaranteed access to the Suez Canal, because of its oil interests in Iraq and Persia. Britain's vast chain of military installations strung out along the entire length of the canal was no longer accepted by other nations as an unchangeable political fact. The ink had barely dried on the United Nations Charter in 1945 when Egypt, one of the fifty-one founder nations, began using the new forum to sue for freedom. Bevin knew that Egypt had many sympathizers, and if Britain were forced to leave Egypt, its position in Palestine would become more important than ever. But that position depended on a mandate granted by a body which no longer existed, the League of Nations. The Palestinians had been demanding independence since World War I, and their case could not simply be ignored.

At the same time British public opinion was exasperated with foreign problems. The voters who had given Labour its huge 180-seat Parliamentary majority wanted undivided attention to be focused on demobilization, reconversion of factories, reconstruction, and above all the creation of peacetime jobs. The capital this needed had been spent on winning the war, which meant that seed money for recovery could only come from the United States, to which Britain was already heavily indebted for Lend-Lease aid. Bevin would not easily be pushed to do Washington's bidding, but there was a limit to how much he could defy the paymaster.

All this might have been clear to Bevin, but Zionists were only concerned with one facet of a multi-dimensional problem. The Jews were again pressing for partition of Palestine, a concept which Britain had abandoned at the end of 1938. In 1946, when Nahum Goldmann urged Bevin to grant a Jewish state in the coastal plain, Bevin asked: 'Do you expect me to give the Jews the keys to the most important strategic area?' Goldmann replied: 'Ernest, I have read and reread the Old and the New Testament, and I found no phrase saying that the keys shall be kept by the British empire for ever.'

Bevin knew that Zionists assumed he would eventually yield, and that military and diplomatic preparations were being made for that moment. The Foreign Office was also aware of the Zionists' links with Abdullah, and probably guessed that both parties were waiting for an opportunity to outflank the Palestinians.

Serious Zionist–Transjordanian planning had resumed as soon as Montgomery had broken Rommel's advance and long before the capitulation of the Afrika Corps. As early as November 1942 Moshe Sharett and Eliahu Sasson held talks with Abdullah to consider the post-war future. Abdullah was still dreaming of a Greater Syria under his reign, and the Zionists did not disturb that dream unduly. It suited their strategy to let him think they might cooperate, given the right terms.

Abdullah felt his plans were moving in the right direction after receiving formal independence from Britain in March 1946. At the same time Transjordan became the Hashemite Kingdom of Jordan, and Abdullah upgraded himself from emir to king. The all-important Arab Legion remained theoretically under Abdullah's command, even if ultimate authority lay in London.

Sasson now began having regular contacts with the king, following the death of Mohamed El-Unsi, Abdullah's interior minister and deputy prime minister, who had been a regular source of information for the Jewish Agency for fifteen years. It quickly became clear that Abdullah's ambitions had taken yet another leap to match his more exalted status. Up to this point Abdullah had been looking for ways of overcoming Palestinian objections by persuasion or evasion, but now he went further. If the Zionists would help Abdullah financially and in other ways, he was prepared to impose partition on the Palestinians. Abdullah probably thought the Jewish Agency would jump at such an offer, and was disappointed to receive only polite interest and a token payment.

Unknown to the king, Ben-Gurion and his colleagues were simultaneously negotiating for a larger prize: Egyptian acceptance of a Jewish state.

5

Palestine Lost

The Jewish Agency's contacts with Egypt were based on a two-track approach, one comparatively open, the other clandestine and known only to a handful of people. Ben-Gurion wanted the legitimacy which official talks implied, while deeper insights could best be obtained through people who understood and lived among Egyptians. The Jewish community in Cairo and Alexandria was firmly established at all social levels, enjoying the comfortable life of a well-accepted minority, not outsiders but part of the ancient fabric of society. In a sense all Jews had been Egyptians in antiquity, during the Middle Kingdom, and although most departed with Moses, some returned during the era of the Ptolemies. A millennium later, when Islam's missionary armies arrived from Mecca in 640 A.D., the Egyptian population was mainly Coptic with a Jewish minority. Both Muslims and Copts referred to Jews as '*ahl-El-Kitab*' (the People of the Holy Books), in recognition of the reverence accorded by all three religions to the Old Testament. During subsequent centuries the Muslim world was almost continuously in conflict with or threatened by one major European Christian power or another. The Jews remained outside this tension, and as they never represented a threat their relations with Muslims were mostly cordial. During the Mamluk dynasty of 1250–1517 A.D.,* most rulers preferred to have Jewish counsellors, who were less likely to be in contact with rivals, and could be entrusted with confidential information.

During the final century of the Ottoman empire many Jews in

* Mamluk means 'owned' in Arabic. The Mamluks were originally military slaves, but came to power because of their success in preventing the Arab world from being overrun by the Mongols.

Egypt preferred to be classed as foreigners in order to benefit from the capitulations,* but this was their own choice. After the arrival of the British in 1882 some Jewish families reached the top echelons of society. In the 1920s the recognized mistress of King Fuad was a Jewess, a Mrs Suarez, whose role went far beyond personal matters. Between the two world wars three Jewish families, the Kattawis, the Mosserys and the Harraris, enjoyed extraordinary prominence and influence. Kattawi Pasha was minister of finance in several Egyptian cabinets, while his wife was the long-serving First Lady of Honour to Queen Nazli, wife of King Fuad. Mossery Pasha and Harrari Pasha were prominent figures in business and industry.

By now it was quite normal for middle- and upper-income Jewish families to live in the same apartment blocks as Muslim and Coptic families. Neighbours of different faiths would invite each other to their homes, send each other cakes on feast days, and attend the same sporting events. Intermarriage remained restricted for religious reasons, but discreet relationships between Jewish girls and Muslim boys were often tolerated.

Jews at other social levels were accepted in many roles. No one was surprised if a boy from a good Muslim family was brought into the world by a Jewish midwife, treated by a Jewish doctor and even employed by a Jewish firm. The three Egyptian communist parties were all headed by Jewish leaders: the National Movement for Liberation by Henri Curiel, Iskra ('The Spark') by Helel Schwarz, and The Vanguard of the Working Class by Raymond Dueweik. Curiel was the son of a millionaire and lived in a villa overlooking the Nile in Zamalek, then the most luxurious quarter of Cairo. Poor Jews, who were usually not communists, lived in Jewish quarters of Cairo or Alexandria, but these were not closed areas, and therefore not ghettos. Anti-Semitism remained a European phenomenon which had no place in Egypt, nor in other parts of the Arab world.

Jews of the middle strata were especially prominent in banking and the media. Oswald Feny, who came from South Africa, owned the *Egyptian Gazette*, the *Egyptian Mail* and *La Bourse Egyptienne*, and shared with other Jews a near-monopoly of the advertising industry.

* Laws according special privileges to foreign nationals living in Egypt and other Ottoman countries.

Much of the best property in Alexandria was owned by a Jew named Smouha, who also gave his name to the city's most elegant club. In the late 1940s more than a quarter of the chairmen of Egyptian companies were Jews (about 200 out of a total of 750). The Jewish community at this time numbered 65,000 out of a population of 17 million, or one third of one per cent. Their influence was out of all proportion to their numbers.

The heads of the three religions, the Sheikh of al-Azhar, the Coptic Patriarch and the Chief Rabbi of Cairo, generally coexisted in mutual respect. Haim Nahum Effendi, the Chief Rabbi, had previously been the Great Rabbi of Istanbul, and had moved to Cairo when Turkey sided with Germany in the First World War. He was a leading scholar and a member of the High College of the Arabic Language.* Like many of his flock, the Chief Rabbi tried to be part of the country in which he lived. As a non-believer in Zionism he supported the Arabs during the 1948–49 war and again in 1956 when Israel invaded Egypt.

Egypt accepted some of the European Jews displaced by both world wars and provided emergency accommodation. During the First World War a refugee camp was set up in Alexandria under the patronage of an Egyptian princess, and a quarter of a century later Madame Kattawi Pasha, Queen Nazli's First Lady of Honour, was in charge of similar facilities. Those who came before and during the Second World War were given assistance to migrate to Palestine. This service was a charitable effort by Jews in Egypt and did not imply support for Zionism.

Like American Jews at the time, those in Egypt were happy to raise funds for Jewish good causes, but uneasy about the poor relations between Jews and Arabs in Palestine. Few supported the creation of a Jewish state, though they unconsciously felt a certain bond with Zionism. This division of loyalties created an inner conflict which some sought to resolve by delaying Egypt's awareness of an Arab as opposed to a Mediterranean identity. Harrari Pasha backed a publishing house which advocated Egypt for the Egyptians within a Mediterranean community of interest, not as part of the Arab world. This concept happened to suit Zionist interests, but was in no sense a Jewish invention.

* The Arab world's equivalent of the Academie Française, the bastion of French linguistic purity.

Some of Egypt's prominent writers and journalists have supported it, including the essayist Hussein Fawzi and the novelists Naguib Mahfouz, winner of the 1988 Nobel Prize for Literature, and Tawfik El-Hakim, his mentor. Ta'ha Hussein Pasha, editor of Harrari Pasha's prestigious magazine *Egyptian Scribe*, was no mere front man for his employer's views, having written a celebrated book, *The Future of Culture in Egypt*, on the same theme.

In the 1930s and early 1940s some of the Jews in Egypt passed messages for the Jewish Agency, but their role was secondary. The Agency's direct contacts with Egyptian leaders were working smoothly and the need for a second channel was minimal. Weizmann was received as an official guest, Ben-Gurion was a frequent visitor, and Sharett and Sasson had regular contacts with Egyptian ministers. The Jewish Agency thought it had an agreement with Ismail Sidki Pasha, the prime minister, that Egypt would accept Palestine being partitioned.

In the early part of the war Egypt became accustomed to the presence of thousands of Jews from Palestine, who had come to serve with the British army. The Jewish Brigade,* commanded by a British officer who was himself an ardent Zionist, Major-General Orde Wingate,† was based in Borg El-Arab. Jewish women in Cairo and Alexandria held fund-raising events for the troops, little realizing that military skills acquired during the war would later be used against Arabs, eventually causing the collapse of the Jewish position in Egypt. Abba Eban, later foreign minister of Israel, was stationed in Egypt as a spokesman for the British army and translated many of the works of Tawfik El-Hakim into English during the war.

The situation began to change after the assassination of Lord Moyne by Jewish extremists in November 1944. Contacts between the Jewish Agency and the Egyptian government then became secret, and gained greater urgency as the proclamation of Israel approached. Eliahu

* At the beginning of World War II Britain was reluctant to accept Jewish volunteers in the armed forces, fearing that this would contradict its recent pro-Arab policy shift. It was only after pressure from Roosevelt that London agreed to form the Jewish Brigade, which was subsequently involved in the Allied invasion of Italy.

† During the Arab Revolt Wingate had commanded the 'Special Night Squads' in Palestine in which British soldiers and members of Hagana worked together to combat Palestinian commandos.

Sasson had meetings with Hassan Youssef Pasha, deputy head of the royal cabinet, and with senior ministers, trying to persuade them that Egypt should recognize Israel. In return, the Agency offered to mobilize the Jews' formidable influence in the USA and Britain to bring about a complete British withdrawal from Egypt after the war. This was not an easy offer for the Jewish Agency to make. Many Zionists thought that the British presence along the Suez Canal would serve as a protective barrier, shielding the embryonic state. Others argued that no shield would be needed if Egypt recognized Israel.

The Jewish Agency's offer was overtaken by rapid changes in the situation. The vast Allied armies dispersed, the British withdrew from Cairo and the Nile delta into their Suez Canal fortifications, Sidki fell from power, and the search for identity and a desire for commitment and participation in the future of the region led Egyptians to give the Palestinian question more attention. Support was growing for all groups advocating uncompromising resistance to Zionism. Contacts between the Egyptian government and the Zionists continued, but in a changed atmosphere. The Jewish Agency now made increasing use of its second channel to the royal palace, relying on Jews resident in Egypt.

In the meantime Arab nationalism had taken a step forward with the creation of the Arab League. The need for an all-Arab forum had become clear during discussions over the post-war shape of the Middle East. It is often incorrectly said that the League was a British invention. The facts are that Anthony Eden's statements on Arab unity in 1941 and 1942 removed restraints which had inhibited debate, and the British had the political savvy to encourage the idea during its formative phase. The initiative came from Egypt, and was motivated partly by King Farouk's search for a more active role for his country and himself within the Arab world, and partly by the need to keep Hashemite ambitions in check. After an Arab conference in Alexandria in October 1944, at which the Palestinians were represented as observers, the treaty creating the League was signed in January 1945. The League almost immediately found sources of unity in two big issues: ridding the Arab world of its colonial masters, and the Palestinian question.

King Farouk had good reason to detest the British, having been humiliated in 1942 by Sir Miles Lampson (later Lord Killearn), the

British ambassador.* As soon as the war was over Farouk set out to renegotiate the 1936 Anglo–Egyptian Treaty. At the same time Arabs realized the danger that Britain might permit mass Jewish emigration to Palestine. Farouk called an Arab League summit in May 1946, which led to a consensus that Palestinians should be given military assistance. That decision was overtaken by events, for Jewish refugees now began to pour into Israel in huge numbers, evading British controls. The British arrested thousands at sea and interned them in camps in Cyprus, but were unable to stop the influx.

Amid fears that a Jewish state might force itself into existence with or without British assent, a meeting of Arab prime ministers was held at Bludan, just outside Damascus, in June 1946. The leaders agreed that if the Palestinians did not succeed in defending themselves, Arab states would send regular armies into Palestine. This decision, taken in the peaceful setting of a hotel surrounded by peach and apricot orchards, was intended to be secret, but Brigadier I.N. Clayton of the British Middle East Office, an orientalist, adventurer and soldier, was sending reports which kept the Foreign Office fully informed.

Eliahu Sasson was still in direct touch with the Egyptian government, but as tension grew the Jewish Agency's second channel became a more fruitful means of communication. War was becoming probable, yet King Farouk showed no sign of shunning his Jewish friends, often spending evenings with them at parties and poker sessions. The most illustrious Jewish families, who had previously felt uneasy about helping Zionists, now cooperated fully in the hope of averting war. Over the next year and a half they became the Jewish Agency's eyes, ears and messengers.

No one was better placed for this role than Irene Guinle, a Jewish beauty who had come to Farouk's notice at the beginning of World War II. Miss Guinle was a member of a family of cotton brokers who had settled in Alexandria in the eighteenth century, and she had no shortage of admirers. At first she reacted coolly to suggestions that she should meet the king, but an introduction was eventually made by Helen Moussery, one of the most wealthy and respected Jewish women of the time. The meeting led to an affair which was intense

* In 1942 Lampson surrounded the royal palace with tanks and forced King Farouk to form a new government under Nahas Pasha, leader of the Wafd Party.

for two years and afterwards continued in a more occasional way. The affair was not thought surprising, given that Farouk's father Fuad had had a Jewish mistress. Miss Guinle was never the king's only mistress, but she was considered the most beautiful and one of the most intelligent, speaking six languages.

Sir Miles Lampson, who patronizingly referred to Farouk as 'the boy', monitored the affair with interest. Ben-Gurion's diaries for the period make references to 'our girl' in Cairo passing messages to and from the king. Many suppose that he was referring to Miss Guinle.

The plans foreseen in the 1939 White Paper that Palestine should become an independent unitary state within ten years had not yet been abandoned. Britain made a final effort in January 1947 to bring Palestinians and Zionists together by convening another conference in London, but neither side was prepared to compromise. Ernest Bevin reluctantly concluded that there was nothing more Britain could do. The mandate was becoming an intolerable responsibility because of constant attacks against British forces by Irgun and Lehi. Both Jews and Arabs were preparing for war, regardless of British efforts to keep order, and Jewish refugees, encouraged by American support, were flouting British immigration controls. Bevin felt exasperated by Zionist leaders and their refusal to heed warnings that Britain might abandon Palestine unless they cooperated. The Zionists, who wanted Britain to remain until they were strong enough to stand alone, thought this an empty threat because of Palestine's strategic importance. Bevin realized that better relations with Arab countries could achieve the same strategic goals, and increasingly saw the Palestine issue as a distraction from more urgent priorities. The Allies were now alarmed by Russia's intentions, and Greece and Turkey seemed at imminent risk of falling into communist hands. Two world wars had now demonstrated the importance of relations with the Arab world, and now a third great struggle looked likely. Knowing that whatever he did would anger either the Jews or the Arabs, Bevin simply refused to choose. On 18 February 1947 Britain announced its intention to hand over responsibility to the United Nations.

The effect of Britain's decision was to remove restraints which had been holding back both Zionist and Hashemite ambitions. Abdullah used a secret meeting of the Arab League in March 1947 to press his Greater Syria scheme, but again received little encouragement from other Arab countries. The majority view was that the Arab Higher Committee should be supported in its demands for the immediate and total independence of Palestine, under Arab rule. All Arab countries except Jordan considered that the future of Palestine was a matter for the Palestinians, not the UN, and therefore refused to cooperate with the United Nations Special Committee on Palestine (UNSCOP) which was set up after Britain's decision.

The UN committee was unable to reach unanimity. In August 1947 it submitted a majority report and a minority report. The former proposed that Palestine should be partitioned into a Jewish state, an Arab state and an international enclave including Jerusalem. The latter called for a federal state in which the Arabs would have a permanent majority but Jews would be given wide autonomy. A meeting in London between representatives of the Jewish Agency and the Arab League's secretary general showed that there was no room for compromise. Any attempt to implement either plan was certain to cause war.

With Egyptian opinion constantly hardening, the Jewish Agency sought to expand its long-running relationship with Abdullah. The king was equally keen to cooperate with the Zionists, though for different reasons. In 1946 he had offered to impose partition on the Palestinians in return for Jewish financial aid. In 1947 what he wanted in return for partition was Jewish help in persuading the American government to recognize Jordan. The change of name from Transjordan to Jordan, and of Abdullah's title from emir to king, had been accepted by London but not Washington. If the Jews could secure American approval, Abdullah would agree to an independent Jewish state in part of Palestine with the rest being absorbed into Jordan. The Jewish Agency was unsure whether to believe this, fearing it might be a ploy to throw them off guard against attack by Jordan. The Arab Legion remained the most powerful military force under Arab control, feared by Hagana's top commanders.

The talks came to a head in November 1947 at a meeting held in Naharayim between Abdullah and Golda Meir, who was then acting head of the Jewish Agency's political department. The king agreed to the establishment of a Jewish state in parts of Palestine already occupied by Jews, on the basis that Jordan would annex the rest. Less than two weeks later, on 29 November, the UN General Assembly adopted the partition plan recommended by a majority of UNSCOP's members.

While this meeting was taking place Abdullah's forces entered Palestine as a reminder that military power would lie in Jordan's hands when Britain withdrew. This message was directed at the Arab League, which had reaffirmed, against Jordan's wishes, its policy of intervening directly in Palestine with regular Arab armies. Meanwhile Zionist armed groups, especially Hagana, were moving to secure parts of Palestine allotted by the UN plan to the Jews, and sometimes exceeding those lines.

A further Arab League meeting in December highlighted a division over the means to be used to prevent Palestine being partitioned. Fortified Jewish settlements in the Negev and Galilee were becoming more militarized and more active in controlling strategic areas, dominating crossroads and storing arms. The Palestinians were following a strategy of attrition, trying to wear down Hagana's strength. Hajj Amin El-Husseini wished to continue and intensify the attacks, but did not want outside Arab armies to become involved. The Grand Mufti correctly foresaw that if Abdullah's forces were permitted to occupy Palestine they would never leave. A majority of those present, including the Jordanian representative, preferred the earlier decision to use regular armies.

The only strong support for Amin El-Husseini's view came from Mahmoud Fahmi El-Nokrashi Pasha, the Egyptian prime minister. At the time there was intense debate in Egypt about whether to take part in any war with the Zionists. One of the strongest voices against participation was Sidki Pasha, a former prime minister, who argued that Egypt had no interests at stake in such a conflict. Without belittling Egypt's emerging sense of Arab identity, Sidki Pasha felt that Mediterranean contacts were more important.

El-Nokrashi Pasha was also against Egyptian involvement, but for a different reason, as he told the Egyptian parliament at the end of April. Egypt would not go to war, he said, because its primary objective was to persuade the British to leave the Suez Canal zone and give Egypt complete independence. The British were arguing that their departure would leave a vacuum which the Soviet Union could exploit. If Egyptian forces went to Palestine and fared badly, the British would feel confirmed in their doubts about Egypt's ability to defend itself.

Sidki Pasha and El-Nokrashi Pasha were opposed by leaders who had a wide range of reasons for wanting to save Palestine. Some were

Farouk loyalists who hoped that victory would restore his waning popularity, making him a king of kings in the Arab world. Farouk received encouragement from advisers, Arab nationalists, and adventurers in his court. Others favoured war as a means of taking the wind from the sails of radical groups including the Muslim Brotherhood, whose support was increasing.

The debate came to an end three weeks later when El-Nokrashi Pasha suddenly announced that Egypt would play its part as a member of the Arab League. The cause of this about-turn did not become clear until decades later. The British government had refused a request by the king for arms. That was the official response; unofficially, British arms somehow found their way to the Egyptian front. At the same time correspondence flew between different British ministries about the 'theft' of military stores from the canal base. About 20,000 Egyptian civilians worked at the base, but they were tightly controlled. The quantities taken were so great that convoys of lorries would have been needed to move them. It seems likely that the 'thefts' were ordered by the British themselves, the better to tempt Egypt into battle with the Zionists. London stood to gain in two ways: Zionists would be punished for terrorist attacks against the British army, and Egyptians would become absorbed in a goal other than British withdrawal from the Suez base. The 'theft' tactic kept all Britain's options open.

An anguished Foreign Office memorandum to the Ministry of War described the quantity of stores which had disappeared as 'astonishing'. Another document from the Foreign Office Egyptian desk to the embassy in Cairo said that the thefts were 'very embarrassing', especially as Britain was under contract to supply Saudi Arabia with weapons and had not done so. The amounts 'stolen' would have more than satisfied the obligation to Ibn Saud. A list attached to this letter included sixty-eight bombs weighing 500 pounds each, 993 anti-aircraft shells, 432,456 rounds of 9-millimetre ammunition, 27,575 bullet tracers and twenty-two military trucks weighing three tons each.

The UN had assumed that Britain would help implement the General Assembly's decision to partition Palestine, but London refused to do so without Arab approval. Britain also declined for the same reason to cooperate with a body set up by the UN for that purpose, and decided to withdraw its forces and administrators. When Palestine began to slide into chaos, the Attlee government decided to accelerate the withdrawal.

Britain's attitude led to rumours among Jews of a secret understanding between Abdullah and the British to use the Arab Legion, which still had British officers and funding, to attack the Jewish state as soon as it came into being. As it happened, there was indeed a secret understanding, but of a different nature. Ernest Bevin and Tawfik Abul Huda Pasha, the Jordanian prime minister, had agreed in February that when British troops withdrew from Palestine the Arab Legion would take up their positions in those areas which the UN plan had allotted to the Palestinians, but not in the Jewish parts.

The Zionists passed on to Washington their suspicions about Britain's intentions, resulting in an angry confrontation in April between Lewis Douglas, the US ambassador in London, and the British prime minister and foreign secretary. The ambassador demanded that the British should restrain Abdullah, while Clement Attlee and Ernest Bevin accused the United States of trying to bring about a Zionist victory. This dispute probably reinforced an incorrect American and Zionist impression of Anglo–Jordanian plans.

Suspecting that Abdullah had either double-crossed them or backed out of the deal, the Zionists now made a final effort to dissuade the king from joining the expected Arab League attack. The collapse of law and order had prevented top-level contacts for weeks, although the king's doctor, Shawkat Aziz as-Sati, often carried messages between Amman and the Jewish part of Jerusalem. On 10 May 1948 Golda Meir set out by car from Naharayim, disguised in Arab costume, and met Abdullah in Amman. The king said that the situation had changed because of a massacre of Palestinian civilians at the village of Deir Yassin a few days earlier. More than 250 people had been shot by Zionist gunmen, causing outrage throughout the Arab world, and the king now felt obliged to go along with the rest of the Arab League. Mrs Meir returned to Israel with confirmation that the secret Jordanian–Zionist agreement had collapsed. Abdullah and Ben-Gurion, who as young men had been students together at the same school in Istanbul, now faced each other as adversaries.

Just before the battle Abdullah ordered a massed parade of the Arab Legion outside the dusty town of Jericho, whose setting between mountains creates a natural gateway from Jordan to Palestine.

Thousands of troops marched to the strains of military bands, assembling at a parade ground set with patriotic flags.* The king was surrounded by British officers speaking in Arabic, addressing him as 'Sayyedna' (Our Master) and assuring him that with the help of God the army would be in Jerusalem within a week.

Abdullah, who had been appointed commander-in-chief of all Arab armies, made a speech from a podium exhorting the troops to battle, and then called for a certain blind Palestinian sheikh to give a sermon. The preacher was led by the hand to the podium and stood for some time in front of the microphone, hesitating. The king, who had turned away to talk to the officers, suddenly heard the sheikh's words coming over the loudspeakers: 'Oh Army –' a long pause; 'Oh Army, I wish you were ours.' The sheikh, who could not see the troops, had perceived what everyone but the king had missed: the troops were totally under British control, and Britain had no interest in creating a Palestinian state independent of Jordan. 'Get him out,' the king shouted. 'He deserves his blindness.' The blind man who could see too much was hurried away.

On 14 May 1948 the Zionist provisional council, forerunner of the Knesset, met inside Tel Aviv Museum to hear Ben-Gurion read the proclamation of the state of Israel. The Arab League had agreed a few days earlier on a coordinated attack by Egypt, Jordan, Iraq, Syria and Lebanon, which went into effect early on 15 May. Apart from Abdullah, most Arab leaders assumed that the combined forces would easily overwhelm Hagana, and were shocked when it became clear that the Zionist forces had a numerical advantage. Seven new Hagana brigades had been formed in the spring of 1948, bringing the total Jewish fighting strength to 60,000, armed with Czechoslovakian weapons which had been smuggled in under the noses of the British. The combined Arab armies were substantially outnumbered on the battlefield. If this now seems difficult to believe it is because of the success of the Zionists in presenting a David and Goliath version of the first Arab–Israeli war.

There were simple reasons for the inability of 40 million Arabs to match the fighting strength of 600,000 Jews. All the Arab countries which participated had been under British or French tutelage since the

* The author was present, and had travelled to the parade in the king's cavalcade.

First World War, with degrees of autonomy insufficient to function as modern states. The Zionists were able to call on resources of leadership, experience and technological skills from millions of Jews in the United States and Britain, who also provided funds. Finally, Hagana had benefited immensely from the military experience gained by the Jewish Legion in the First World War and the Jewish Brigade during the Second.

The Arabs also suffered from divisions over tactics, suspicions about each other's ambitions, and hasty preparation. Egypt had the special disadvantage that El-Nokrashi Pasha, the prime minister, initially decided not to use existing military units. Instead a special army of volunteers was raised from January 1948 onwards and sent to Palestine. On 14 May, the day of the proclamation of Israel, the prime minister reversed his decision and sent the regular Egyptian army as well.

Egyptian troops could not reach the front without passing across a British-held bridge at the Mediterranean end of the Suez Canal. Gamal Abdel Nasser, staff officer of the 6th Battalion Infantry, later remarked in his memoirs that in order to reach one enemy Egyptian forces had to pass under the inspection of a greater foe. These forces fought bravely and took heavy casualties, but had no chance of success. The total Egyptian forces deployed in Palestine by the end of the war amounted to only twelve battalions, while Syria and Lebanon mustered a further 4000 men. Jordan delayed the passage of Iraqi troops across its territory, causing the failure of military missions which had been assigned to Baghdad.

Fighting took place in four phases, interspersed with ceasefires between May 1948 and January 1949. The struggle was intense at first, but dwindled as the hopelessness of the odds against them became clearer to the Arab forces. The combined Arab armies, outnumbered approximately two to one by Israel's better-trained and -equipped troops, were unable to prevent the rapid expansion of the Zionist state.*

The Arab Legion, with 4500 highly trained troops, modern equipment and British officers, could have given the Zionists serious trouble, but the blind sheikh's prescience proved all too accurate. Gen-

* Estimates of casualties during the war were: Jordan, 611; Iraq, 1812; Syria, 5010; Egypt, 6000; Israel, 4800.

eral John Glubb, then the foremost British officer in the Middle East, led his four regiments into areas which had been allocated to Palestinians under the UN plan. He subsequently wrote that he was strictly forbidden by the British government to enter Jerusalem or areas which the UN had allotted to the Jewish state. The Zionists felt no such restraints, and quickly occupied mixed-faith areas of Jerusalem, which exposed the old city and its Arab population to a direct threat. Abdullah came under strong pressure from the entire Arab world to defend old Jerusalem and the holy places, but Glubb was reluctant because of his orders from London. The Foreign Office accepted that Abdullah could not allow the holy places to be occupied but insisted, under American pressure, that the Legion should not go beyond the Arab quarters of the city. Within four days of the proclamation of the state of Israel the Legion had carried out these orders and Abdullah became the protector of Islam's third holiest shrine, greatly enhancing his prestige. The division of Jerusalem had thus been brought about through Washington's direct influence with Britain and indirect influence with Abdullah.

Over the next seven months Hagana, now renamed the Israel Defence Army, drove the Palestinian population from their homes and herded them into other Arab countries. According to a British census the population of Palestine in 1947 was 1,157,000 Arab Muslims, 146,000 Arab Christians and 580,000 Jews. Two years later only 200,000 Arabs remained in the parts of Palestine which had become Israel. Another study showed that Jews had owned 12 per cent of the land in what became Israel in 1946, but 77 per cent after the 1948–49 war. A conciliation commission set up by the United Nations estimated that 80 per cent of the land the Jews gained was taken by force. The Jewish state then legalized the expropriation through a law on absentee ownership and other instruments. In subsequent years Jews claimed that the Palestinians had fled of their own accord, and censorship was used to prevent the truth from being published in Israel. As late as 1979 the memoirs of Yitzhak Rabin were censored, removing a passage which disclosed a small part of the story. Rabin recounted his own experience as commander of the Harel Brigade, which rounded up 50,000 Arabs from the towns of Lod and Ramlah and drove them out of Israel. Some were forced to walk up to fifteen miles to an area not wanted by Israeli forces, while others were moved by bus. Among those who had to walk were the family of George Habash, who later became leader of the Popular Front for the Liberation of Palestine. Rabin himself described the operation as 'harsh and cruel', but argued that it was a military necessity. The passage was censored because it showed that many Palestinians did not flee, and that the supposed heroism of Zionist troops was exaggerated.

The truth was that Lod and Ramlah were taken easily because Abdullah evacuated his forces from those areas without consulting other Arab armies. After the Jordanian withdrawal the Egyptian army in Negev found its flank exposed. Ben-Gurion considered attacking the Arab Legion directly, but was dissuaded by colleagues who realized that Abdullah was keeping to the agreement he had reached with Mrs Meir, even if he had repudiated it just before the war. Instead the full strength of the Israeli army was turned against the Egyptian army.

The British and American roles in influencing Abdullah did not become known in detail until much later, but enough could be deduced from events. Furious with London, Arab governments refused to accept a ceasefire resolution which Britain had tabled in the UN Security Council. The UN then appointed Count Bernadotte, nephew of King Gustav V of Sweden and president of the Swedish Red Cross, as official mediator. Bernadotte negotiated a truce which began on 11 June but soon broke down, leading to further heavy fighting in July. In the first week of September Bernadotte submitted a thirteen-point plan to the UN secretary general Trygve Lie. The plan, which was not made public until later, began by calling on the Arab world to accept that the Jewish state had been established. Bernadotte had little choice on this point because the four big powers, the United States, the Soviet Union, Britain and France, were solidly in favour of the Jewish state's existence, even if Britain disliked the way it had come into being. So eager was the Soviet Union to show its support that Moscow had announced official recognition on 15 May, the same day as the United States.*

Bernadotte's first point pleased the Zionists, but the plan contained

* At the time of Moscow's recognition of Israel, Soviet Jews held high offices in the Kremlin, and the Soviet Union regarded the Jewish cause as a class struggle. This caused confusion in the Arab world. Many Arab leaders feared that Israel would become a communist toehold in the Middle East. The fact that the three Egyptian communist parties were led by Jews contributed to this idea. These parties argued that the Jewish proletariat was the ally of the Arab proletariat.

another element which they liked less. Bernadotte realized that it was essential to avoid a physical division of the Arab world, with half in Asia and the other half in Africa and no land contact between the two. That risk could be averted only by leaving the Negev desert in Arab hands. The desert would therefore be allotted to the proposed Palestinian state and the Zionists would be compensated by extending Israel northwards to include the whole of Galilee. The plan was not yet public, but word of it reached an extremist Zionist group, which decided to eliminate Bernadotte. He was shot dead by three members of the Stern gang on 17 September as he crossed from the Arab into the Jewish quarter of Jerusalem. Yitzhak Shamir, later prime minister of Israel, was reported to have been one of the three. His memoirs refer to the incident without denying the reports. The irony was that Bernadotte had saved thousands of Jews from extermination during the Second World War, and was sympathetic to Israel in his analysis of the Palestinian–Zionist conflict.

After Bernadotte's death Israel moved quickly to obtain control of the Negev. At the time part of the Egyptian army was located in the north of the desert, in an area extending between Falluga and Irak El-Mansheya. These forces were linked by supply and communications lines to the General Command of Egyptian forces in Palestine, stationed at El-Arish (on Egyptian territory). General Fuad Sadek, the Egyptian commander-in-chief, was based there with reserve forces of three battalions, equipped with artillery and tanks. A third Egyptian force of nine battalions was located on the coastal plain north of Gaza, with its command headquarters at Majdal.

In an offensive beginning on 15 October Israel occupied a central area of the desert around Auja, thus cutting the Egyptian supply lines. A further attack, beginning on 25 December, proved to be the final offensive of the war. An Israeli force of three brigades, under the command of General Yigal Allon, dashed from the Auja area to the coast at Rafah (halfway between El-Arish and Gaza), thus isolating the Egyptian advance force in Majdal from its headquarters and reserves at El-Arish.

The division of Egyptian forces into three disconnected elements put Israel in a dominant position and left the Egyptian government in disarray. In a state of panic the minister of war, Mohamed Haydar Pasha, asked King Farouk and Prime Minister Ibrahim Abdel-Hadi to take political action. The king called Pinckney Tuck, the US ambassador, to protest and sent a message to President Truman. Similar steps were taken by the prime minister. Washington intervened, and soon afterwards a ceasefire was arranged, with an Israeli withdrawal to the Auja area. By this time a majority in the UN General Assembly regarded the Israeli victory as irreversible, and henceforward treated the Palestinian question as a refugee problem.

The General Assembly had passed a resolution on 11 December 1948 that displaced Palestinians should have a choice between repatriation and compensation, and instructed the conciliation commission to implement this decision. Israeli and Arab delegations attended an initial meeting in Lausanne and discussed an outline agreement on refugees and frontiers. The commission remained in existence for many years afterwards, but the Israeli delegation did not return to it. Zionists did not want to have to define their frontiers, since some factions still hoped to conquer the entire area of biblical Eretz Yisrael. That wish lingered on even after the Gaza–Jericho agreements of 1993 and 1994.

Dr Ralph Bunche's armistice talks began in Rhodes at the beginning of 1949 and led to agreements which delineated frontiers without establishing agreed borders. Any talk of peace was out of the question from an Arab point of view. Israel at first practised stalling tactics to give its forces more time to expand their gains. On 5 March, after an armistice with Egypt had been signed, Ben-Gurion sent two brigades to occupy the southern part of the Negev desert, up to the Red Sea coast. As the brigades approached General Glubb ordered the Arab Legion to evacuate its positions, with the result that Israeli troops took over the strategically vital area with minimal fighting. Glubb was acting on orders from London, which had come under heavy pressure from the United States. The code name of the Israeli action could hardly have been more expressive: Operation Fait Accompli. On 10 March, the day his forces reached what is now Eilat, Ben-Gurion became Israel's first prime minister, and the following day his negotiators in Rhodes signed a ceasefire with Jordan.

After this conquest the Arab world was divided, and Israel became a state of 8000 square miles, one third larger than the UN resolution of 1947 had intended. Israel was not, however, the only winner of the 1948–49 war. The other was Abdullah, whose secret (if briefly repudiated) deal with Golda Meir brought most of the spoils he had wanted. Israel did nothing to prevent Abdullah seizing the remaining 2200 square miles of the west bank, achieving his dream of a kingdom on both banks of the Jordan.

By the winter of 1948 most Palestinian leaders remaining in the west bank were ready to accept Abdullah as the lesser of evils, and called a congress at Jericho on 1 December to accept the inevitable. The congress was headed by Hajj Mohamed El-Gaa'bari, mayor of Hebron, and filled with west bank dignitaries who were now desperate for protection against further expansion by Israel. Other Arab states were not represented.

In a document proclaiming Abdullah as their king, the dignitaries described the unity of Palestine and Jordan as 'a true expression of history', which was the opposite of what most Palestinians felt. They saluted the king 'and his glorious army which fought and is still fighting for Palestine' (the Arab Legion having done nothing of the sort). Abdullah accepted their proclamation as 'a great blessing from God', a remark which with historical hindsight seems rich in hypocrisy and yet reflected the king's state of mind at the time. Abdullah was quite unable to see that he was collecting the spoils of collusion.*

The Jordanian House of Dignitaries unanimously approved the decision, and the west bank, including old Jerusalem, was formally annexed. Britain and Pakistan recognized the annexation but other countries condemned or ignored it. The rest of the Arab world, already angry with Abdullah for his betrayal during the war, reacted with fury. The king had defied the Arab League and taken a step towards the Greater Syria scheme which had worried Egypt and Iraq so much. A meeting of the Arab League in March and April 1950 became a virtual trial of Jordan on charges of making a separate deal with Israel, something which was obvious from events but legally unprovable.

Jordan, which risked expulsion from the League, effectively promised not to make further deals in return for being allowed to remain within the fold. As this understanding was secret, many were startled when Jordan voted in favour of a resolution on 1 April forbidding any member of the League from negotiating peace, or any other

* In an interview with the author at the time Abdullah emphasized the wisdom of the Hebron decision, but resisted efforts to delve into the logic of that wisdom.

type of agreement, with Israel, on pain of expulsion. Abdullah, who had initialled a secret understanding with Israel a few weeks before the Arab League meeting, sent the Zionists a message that Jordan's favourable vote meant nothing.

A further resolution on 13 April from the same lengthy Arab League meeting amounted to a politely worded order to Jordan to give the Palestinians self-rule, but did not threaten expulsion for non-compliance. The penalty was that Jordan (which was not directly named) 'would be considered to have reneged on its pledges and obligations' under the Arab League Pact. Jordan was the only country to vote against this resolution, whose lack of teeth amounted to tacit Arab League acceptance of Abdullah's annexation of the west bank in return for the promise to stop negotiating (which Abdullah had no intention of keeping).

The annexation of east Jerusalem by Abdullah and west Jerusalem by Israel outraged all who thought the city belonged to the world as a whole. An unlikely grouping of Catholic, Islamic and communist states had already passed a UN General Assembly resolution calling for Jerusalem to become a separate entity under UN control. The resolution so angered Ben-Gurion that he moved the Israeli government's offices from Tel Aviv to Jerusalem, ignoring objections from many within his own party.

Chaim Weizmann said in a public statement that he was 'astonished' by the annexation. Jerusalem had 'a special place in the heart of every Jew . . . If the Jews were unable through thousands of years to forget Israel how can they forget it now?'

Weizmann's tone was aggrieved rather than outraged, and he did not attack Abdullah by name. The reason for this was that the Israelis hoped to persuade Abdullah to sign a peace treaty. The secret understanding which Abdullah had initialled with Israel just before the Arab League meeting was the proposed text of such a treaty, but Abdullah had been unable to persuade his government to endorse it.

The peace document had emerged from secret talks which began immediately after the Jericho conference. The letters which led to these talks subsequently came to light, and their extraordinary tone shows how anxious the Israelis were to keep Abdullah in their camp. Israel might have defeated the Egyptian, Iraqi, Syrian and Lebanese armies, but was still ready to bow and scrape to the king of Jordan:

> My Great Master, humbleness and respect in front of your presence. I hope you are well and with good health, may God the Almighty always give you good health. My Master . . . the way you were talking to those Arabs [the Hebron dignitaries] was amazing. How I pray for [the success of] all that you are doing to secure peace . . . in that beautiful land which is so dear to Your Majesty and to us. I beg that Your Majesty, if you will again consent to give me the blessing of your kindness, will send someone to meet me and discuss . . . arrangements necessary for the new situation . . . May God give you a long life and keep you always, Amen, sincerely yours Eliahu Sasson.

A letter of 13 December, written in the same fawning tone, urged Abdullah to implement the Jericho decisions immediately 'so that he can put his enemies [meaning other Arabs] in front of a *fait accompli*'. The letter begged Abdullah not to make any decisions on the future of Jerusalem pending direct talks, proposed that the Israeli–Jordanian truce should be converted into a peace treaty, and asked him to expel Egyptian forces still in the west bank. It concluded with an offer: 'If Our Master His Majesty accepts the above points we pledge to make all the necessary propaganda . . . to secure acceptance of the Jericho decisions all over the world.'*

Throughout the last chapter of his life Abdullah was in almost continuous negotiation with the Israelis, apart from a brief suspension during and immediately after the Arab League meeting of March–April 1950. Abdullah ignored the promise he had given at that meeting and negotiated with the clear intention of securing peace and Israeli economic aid. His talks defied not only the Arab League but his own government which, to the extent that it was consulted, frequently objected to and contradicted his schemes.

Abdullah's talks went on for months without reaching a solution, because of the difficulty of finding terms which he could persuade his people to accept. The king was due to attend one of many such sessions on Saturday 21 July 1951 in Jerusalem, but was assassinated the day

* The letters were handed over to the Egyptian and Saudi governments by Colonel Abdul El-Tal, a Jordanian official who had been sent by Abdullah to see Sasson, and who defected rather than go through with this mission. The author obtained the letters and published them in an Egyptian newspaper in 1951. Abdullah did not deny their authenticity.

before while entering the al-Aksa mosque in Jerusalem to attend Friday prayers. After this Ben-Gurion virtually abandoned hope of coming to an arrangement with Jordan and had to be persuaded by colleagues not to seize more territory. The Jordanian throne passed briefly to Abdullah's son Talal, followed within a year by Hussein, Abdullah's grandson, who had witnessed his assassination. Although only seventeen at the time of his accession King Hussein showed an independent spirit, and soon made his mark. He has been the strongest champion of his grandfather's memory, arguing that Abdullah's qualities have been under-appreciated. Clement Attlee also paid warm tributes to Abdullah.

Abdullah's assassination came at a time of turmoil, bitterness and recrimination throughout the Arab world following Israel's victory. His collusion, the dispossession of the Palestinians and the duplicity of the British had created conditions for a collective psychological meltdown. When the defeated Arab armies returned home to find a grave economic crisis and a shortage of paid jobs, everyone who had been in a position of authority was held responsible. The catastrophe demanded scapegoats, and many were chosen unjustly. Accusations that ministers had profited from the war as arms traders began flying; many were true but some were false. The Egyptian prime minister El-Nokrashi Pasha, who had done nothing disloyal, was assassinated even before the fighting in Palestine ended, followed during the next two years by the commander of the Cairo police force Zaki Pasha, the chief judge of the Egyptian High Court Ahmed El-Khazendar, and the prime minister of Lebanon Riad El-Solh.

Bombs exploded in cinemas, nightclubs and shops, and not only those owned by foreigners. Amidst the confusion there were other kinds of violence that had understandable political motives. Commando groups began attacking British forces stationed in Egypt, with encouragement from the Wafd government,* which also ordered Egyptian civilian staff working for the British army to withdraw all labour. British troops over-reacted and slaughtered fifty Egyptian policemen in a single attack on a police station. This incident provoked a huge riot in Cairo in January 1952 leading to a fire which destroyed hundreds of buildings.

* The Wafd was a nationalist party founded in 1919.

Radical groups and parties, which led the riot and had carried out many of the earlier attacks against the British and on Egyptian politicians, now enjoyed unprecedented popularity among the Egyptian people, usually noted for their moderation. That support expressed a feeling that someone had to pay for so much Arab blood spilt in Palestine to so little effect. Hardly a village in Egypt, Syria or Lebanon had emerged from the 1948–49 war without losing some of its young men.

The Muslim Brotherhood, many of whose members had died in the fighting, argued that the Arabs had lost not just because of betrayal and incompetent planning but also because of insufficient devotion to Islam, while the Jews won because they had rediscovered their faith. Whatever the merits of this argument, its effect was considerable. Defeat, humiliation, bereavement, betrayal and economic hardship swirled together in the Arab mind, and now the Muslim Brotherhood added a religious dimension. The psychological chemistry of the taboo was becoming ever more complex, a blend of faith and fury, pride and shame, truth and myth, nationalism and mysticism. From now onwards anyone who treated with the enemy would face the implacable anger of the masses.

6

Messengers from Israel

The death throes of the old order in Egypt lasted for six months following the great fire of Cairo in January 1952. Four prime ministers came and went. Two were men of vision, but not of the calibre to confront the seven plagues of Egypt. As if colonialism, corruption, disease,* feudalism, humiliation, poverty and unemployment were not enough, even the monarchy had become a burden. King Farouk's efforts to negotiate British withdrawal were blighted by his lightweight personal image. It was easy for London to ignore Farouk's political demands so long as the British press focused mainly on the follies of the royal court. Law and order continued to crumble under his shaky rule, and by 1952 most Egyptians realized that firm government could be established in only one way. The question was not whether there would be a military coup but from which quarter of the army it would come. Farouk's spies were efficient enough to realize that a particular group of middle-ranking officers might be a threat. The 'Free Officers', as they secretly called themselves, had not yet decided to seize power, but they had a contingency plan. On 22 July 1952 word reached them that they were under suspicion. Deciding to pre-empt arrest, the officers implemented their plan, surrounding Cairo's main army barracks with tanks and seizing the radio station. The government fell without resistance, and four days later Farouk departed on his royal yacht, never to return. The monarchy was abolished a year later.†

One of the aims of the revolution announced in its first radio broad-

* Egypt suffered a severe epidemic of cholera immediately after the 1948–49 war.

† After Farouk's abdication his son Fuad II was named king, but ruled in name only until the abolition of the monarchy in 1953. Farouk died in Rome in March 1965.

cast was to 'cleanse the nation of tyrants', a reference to the British, Farouk, and wealthy landowners. The broadcast did not emphasize the Palestine issue.

It now became a top priority of the Israeli government to establish links with the coup leaders. David Ben-Gurion announced on 24 July that Israel looked with sympathy at what had happened in Egypt and wished the revolution luck, hoping for a new page in relations. The Free Officers ignored this declaration, and Israeli agents were unable to find out what policy they planned to follow on Egyptian–Israeli relations.

The truth was that the Free Officers had no real programme, only general aims, because the revolution had happened before they were ready. Those aims focused mainly on Egypt's internal rather than external problems. Secondly, it was not clear whose views were paramount. The Free Officers initially chose a collective form of decision-making with a paternal figure as nominal leader. General Mohamed Neguib,* a well-known and respected veteran of the 1948–49 war, was never more than the public face of the revolution. Several months passed before one man's leadership superseded the collective method.

Gamal Abdel Nasser, son of a postal worker from upper Egypt, was then thirty-four, a serious-minded young man who had briefly studied law, but who chose a military career because the army was the only institution which might some day obtain Egypt's freedom. The humiliation of Farouk by Sir Miles Lampson in 1942† had reinforced Nasser's determination to work for change, and in 1946 he began discussing ideas with like-minded colleagues at the Military Academy in Cairo, where he was an instructor. They continued discussions between battles in the 1948–49 war, and in 1950 nine of them formed the Free Officers' Movement, with Nasser as chairman. These young men shared strong nationalist feelings but had no uniform ideology. Nasser had read Marx, Lenin and the ideas of radical Islamic groups, but supported neither communism nor militant fundamentalism. The men he most admired were not ideologues but great military strategists.

* General Neguib was named commander-in-chief and president of the Revolutionary Command Council, but was removed from office in October 1954.
† See footnote p. 71.

All the Free Officers agreed that the top priority was British withdrawal from Suez. Previous Egyptian governments had looked to the United States for help in persuading the British to go, and there seemed no reason to change that approach. The difficulty was that Washington and London remained partners in the containment of the Soviet Union, and the Egyptian defeat in 1948–49 had strengthened Britain's argument for keeping its canal base.

The Truman administration continued pressing its policy of encircling the Soviet Union with defence pacts, thinking that this would solve three problems at once – the defence of the Middle East, Egyptian objections to the presence of foreign troops, and Egyptian–Israeli tension. The Americans had noticed that after the creation of the North Atlantic Treaty Organization in 1948, fewer Europeans were opposed to American bases in Europe. Washington hoped that something similar might be achieved in the Middle East. If Egypt could be persuaded to join a Middle East Defence Organization (MEDO), Egyptians might come to view foreign troops stationed along the canal as their defenders.

Secondly, such an organization would necessarily include Israel, because of its strategic location. Linking Israel and the Arab world in a defence pact should, the Americans thought, reduce the risks of Arab–Israeli conflict. In 1951 a proposal to create MEDO was put to Arab countries by the United States, Britain, France and Turkey,* but was rejected by Egypt, Syria, Saudi Arabia and others. Egyptian leaders both before and after the revolution felt that rivalry between the West and the Soviet Union was not Egypt's problem, and could not be used to justify continued occupation.

This rejection led the Americans to look for different ways of bringing the Egyptians into the Western fold. The Central Intelligence Agency, which had been formed in 1947, cooperated closely with representatives of major US oil companies in the Middle East to build up a network which could pursue US objectives without the limitations of ordinary diplomacy. The first prominent figure in this network was Kermit Roosevelt, a nephew of former president Theodore

* The inclusion of Turkey inevitably recalled memories of Ottoman suzerainty over the Arab world. Turkey became a member of NATO in 1952 and permitted the establishment of US military bases.

Roosevelt, who first appeared in the area as a journalist, but was later found to be responsible for the CIA's Middle East station.* Roosevelt established his presence before the revolution, interviewed Farouk, and was on good terms with some of the king's advisers. Jefferson Cafferey, the US ambassador, did not altogether approve of Roosevelt's activities. After the fire of Cairo both sets of Americans, official and unofficial, sought to persuade the king to make major changes. Farouk's most positive decisions, the appointment of Ali Maher Pasha and subsequently Naguib El-Hilaly Pasha as prime minister, were taken during this period, but too late to save the old order.

After the revolution the Americans and British quickly decided not to intervene, having established that the Free Officers were not communists. Within three weeks Jefferson Cafferey had sounded out the leaders and discovered that they were even more anti-British than the previous government, and just as unenthusiastic about MEDO. Kermit Roosevelt met Nasser in September 1952 and suggested peace with Israel, but found no interest. Nasser wanted to concentrate on British withdrawal and British recognition of Egyptian sovereignty in the Sudan. The latter issue had been of concern to all Egyptian governments since the nineteenth century.

Within a few weeks the Israeli government began sending messages to the new leaders through intermediaries. Direct contacts were out of the question, and Arab governments had agreed not to admit visitors whose passports showed that they had visited Israel. A stream of emissaries now found ways of bypassing these hurdles. The first was Richard Crossman, a British MP with an extensive knowledge of Jewish problems and some experience of Middle East affairs.† Crossman had been one of Ernest Bevin's appointees on the Anglo-American Committee of Inquiry on Palestine, but later turned against Bevin's policies, which he considered anti-Zionist, and led a revolt by Labour MPs. The charge of anti-Zionism was unwarranted: the foreign secre-

* Kermit Roosevelt's credibility in the Arab world was enhanced by his book *Arabs, Oil and History*.

† Crossman had spent some time among German and Austrian Jews before World War II, in which he served as deputy director of psychological warfare at Allied headquarters in Algiers in 1943–44. Immediately after the war he visited Nazi concentration camps.

tary was not against either side, but tried unsuccessfully to find a middle path at a difficult time.*

Crossman was on good terms with Sir Ralph Stevenson, then British ambassador in Cairo, and with the Americans. A meeting was arranged with Nasser at the home of William Lakeland, an American diplomat.† The Egyptians discovered later that Lakeland was also a CIA man under diplomatic cover. Five months had passed since the revolution and Nasser was now firmly in control, even if Neguib's name was still better known outside Egypt. As yet Nasser was inexperienced in foreign affairs, and what little he knew of Americans was based on films of the 1930s, especially those of Gary Cooper.

The meeting at Lakeland's home had barely begun when Crossman came to the point: 'I bring you greetings from a man who is watching what you are doing: David Ben-Gurion.' Nasser, who had not been warned of Crossman's sympathies, was visibly astonished, but was unable to escape Crossman's interrogation. The Egyptian leader explained that the Israeli question was not his priority, and that he had more urgent problems. 'How can you think that, Colonel?' Crossman asked, and then developed a provocative argument. 'I know my people [i.e. the British] better than you, and we will not leave unless you force us to go. You will have to fight us.' The British, he said, had left Palestine because the Jews forced them out through sustained attacks. 'Can your people fight?' Crossman asked. 'Can they make sacrifices?'

Nasser said he was exploring what to do about the British, and in the meantime wanted to concentrate on the development of Egypt. Crossman replied: 'If you don't want to fight you will have to make arrangements with us and with the Israelis. We will want to be sure before we leave that there will be no hostilities which could create an opening for the Russians.'

After a long, intense session Crossman said he was going back to Israel to tell Ben-Gurion what he had learned. Nasser may have secretly admired Crossman's frankness, but he could not condone his methods.

* Sir Harold Beeley, a Foreign Office Arabist and scholar who advised Bevin on Palestine issues, said that the British experience in Palestine was like carrying out a pioneering medical operation, with no precedent for guidance.

† Nasser seemed intrigued by the coal fire burning brightly in the grate at Lakeland's home. Few Egyptian homes had fireplaces, and Nasser had never seen one before.

'I do not want emissaries, open or secret, between me and Ben-Gurion,' Nasser said.

Crossman ignored Nasser's objections, went to see Ben-Gurion, and later returned to Egypt with a passport which showed no evidence of his having visited Israel.* Nasser refused to see Crossman again but asked Dr Mahmoud Fawzi, the foreign minister, to talk to him. Ben-Gurion's message was that Israel respected Egypt's desire for independence and understood inhibitions preventing contacts. If peace between Israel and Egypt was not a priority, the two countries should avoid any action which might complicate talks in the future, and look for practical ways of easing tension. When Crossman told Ben-Gurion that Nasser's priority was the development of Egypt, the Israeli prime minister replied: 'This is the worst news I have ever received from Egypt!' Ben-Gurion correctly foresaw that by addressing Egypt's internal problems, Nasser would create a stronger society more able to stand up to Israel.

The next emissary to meet Nasser was Barbara Castle, a former correspondent of the London *Daily Mirror* who had been elected as a Labour MP in 1945.† Mrs Castle had a specific mission to negotiate an exchange of nearly thirty Israeli prisoners who had been arrested by Egyptian authorities in Gaza for illegally crossing the lines or entering territorial waters. She subsequently made a second visit bringing a list of prisoners, and an exchange was made. This did not require contacts between Egypt and Israel.

Delegations of both Conservative and Labour MPs followed, and a pattern emerged. Those who were sympathetic towards Egyptian independence also admired Israel's socialist reforms. Those who disliked Israel's internal policies also thought that Britain's military presence in Egypt was essential.

One of the most persuasive visitors was Aneurin Bevan, who had helped to create Britain's National Health Service.‡ Bevan was almost

* The British government had begun issuing duplicate passports to businessmen, MPs and journalists who needed to travel both to the Arab world and to Israel.

† Mrs Castle later held senior government posts, including employment secretary (1968).

‡ Bevan had been minister of health and housing in the Attlee government, but was out of power when he saw Nasser, following the Conservative election victory in 1951.

as provocative as Crossman, but more constructive. 'Colonel Nasser, you think you are making a revolution; this is not a revolution; this is a façade,' he said, pointing out that nothing had yet been done to ease social injustice in Egypt. Nasser emerged from this meeting saying: 'The man is right.'

Streams of senior American and British journalists followed, many of whom had been to Israel first, and brought messages. Nasser welcomed the interviews and ignored the messages.

Although most of these early attempts to initiate a dialogue were orchestrated by Ben-Gurion, one approach came from a Jew whose renown transcended politics: Albert Einstein. The great physicist's intervention involved some improbable collaboration between Abba Eban, Israel's permanent representative at the United Nations, and Dr Mahmoud Azmi, senior counsellor to the Egyptian delegation at the UN. The two men had become acquainted during the Second World War, when Eban was stationed in Egypt as a British army press officer. Now they found themselves attending the same UN meetings, which was embarrassing because Azmi could not publicly acknowledge Eban. However, Eban often called at the Barbazon Plaza Hotel overlooking Central Park, where Azmi was staying, and the two men were believed to be holding discreet meetings.

Dr Azmi, a Sorbonne-educated academic and writer with progressive ideas, was also a good friend of mine. I called to see him while in New York in December 1952 and mentioned that I was planning to visit G.H. Gallup, founder of the American Institute of Public Opinion, in Princeton, New Jersey. Dr Azmi shook his head. If my destination was Princeton, the person to visit was not Gallup but Einstein, at the Institute for Advanced Study, he suggested. Two days later I found myself at Einstein's home. Although delighted to meet the great man I was not knowledgeable about relativity, which I thought would be his sole interest. It quickly became clear that Azmi's suggestion was not as casual as it had seemed: Einstein wanted to meet someone who could put him in touch with the new Egyptian leadership.

Before visiting Einstein I had been interviewed by the *New York Post* and had commented that General Neguib did not make the revolution; the revolution made Neguib. The *Post* mentioned my close friendship with Nasser. Einstein had been briefed on the *Post*'s article, and knew that the main inspiration of the revolution was a young colonel, though he had not previously heard of Nasser by name.

'What does he intend to do with my people?' Einstein asked. Seeing that his question left me blank, Einstein explained that he had spent his early life in Germany, and later took part with Chaim Weizmann in a fund-raising effort in the United States to finance the Hebrew University in Palestine. In 1934 the Nazis confiscated Einstein's property and deprived him of German citizenship, and he settled in America. The subsequent ordeal of Jews who remained in Germany troubled him deeply, but at the same time Einstein felt sorry for Palestinians who had been dispossessed by Jews, just as he had been by Nazis.

Einstein described the Arab–Zionist conflict as a struggle between two rights, and one which had caused him a crisis of conscience. He was happy for the Jews in that they had secured a state, sad for the Palestinians, and critical of the great powers, which could have done more to avert the 1948–49 disaster.

It was not the first time that Einstein had felt pulled in two different directions on a great issue. Although a convinced pacifist, he had taken it upon himself during World War II to make President Roosevelt aware of the possibility of developing a nuclear weapon. The physicist's intense dislike of violence reasserted itself in 1948 when Menachem Begin, the former commander-in-chief of Irgun, asked to see him. Begin wished to learn from one of the world's great teachers, but Einstein replied that he had no lessons to offer a man of violence, because such people were incurable. Einstein also wrote to the *New York Times* saying that a known killer should not have been allowed to visit the United States.

'What does your leader intend to do with my people?' Einstein asked again. Then he added: 'I mean the Jews.' He said that while the Jews needed a home, nothing could justify the misery they had caused the Palestinians, and recalled that when he ventured this opinion in a conversation with Weizmann after the 1948–49 war, the Israeli president replied: 'God promised the Holy Land to the Jews.' Einstein urged Weizmann not to use religious arguments, because all the sons of Abraham thought they had received some kind of promise from Allah or God.

'I am afraid the Zionists might become victims of a narrow nationalism of their own making,' Einstein told me. For most of their history

Jews had been cosmopolitan in outlook and global in distribution, and yet there had also been periods when they closed themselves in ghettos for protection. 'The Balfour Declaration gave free rein to the ghetto instinct, turning more than half of Palestine into a refuge against European anti-Semitism,' he said.

I explained that Nasser was not against Jews because of religion or race but as a result of their aggression against Palestinians. Einstein assumed that I was talking about extremists like Begin, and was surprised to learn that Egyptians saw little difference between Begin and Ben-Gurion. 'Ben-Gurion is quite different. There are so many good people in Israel but you should be able to know them,' Einstein insisted.

He asked me to convey an oral message to the Egyptian leadership expressing his wish to serve as a catalyst for peace. Einstein was not interested in becoming a mediator, but sought only to sow ideas in the minds of others. 'Tell him that my interest is humanitarian, and I have the same humanitarian feelings towards Arabs as towards Israelis.'

The message was delivered as requested and discussed within Nasser's inner circle. Einstein's stature and the way he had framed his approach made a negative reply difficult, but the taboo was overwhelming in its power. The only solution was to make no reply, with all the discourtesy which silence implied.

Later it emerged that the timing of Einstein's approach was significant. Weizmann had died in November 1952, and the Israeli government then invited Einstein to accept the presidency. In a telegram conveying the offer, Abba Eban reminded Einstein that this would involve taking Israeli nationality. Eban gave an assurance, on behalf of Ben-Gurion, that the post would not hinder Einstein's scientific work, and expressed 'the deep respect of the Jewish people to one of its great sons'. Israel, said Eban, was a small country in size but not in what it represented.

In his reply Einstein said he felt 'sad to the degree of shame' that he could not accept. After a lifetime dealing with objective matters he was unsuited to the human and ceremonial aspects of such a post, and his age (then seventy-three) left him no reserves of strength for additional responsibilities. He declined the presidency a few weeks before the initiative he made through me. It seems likely that his attempt to contact Nasser was a way of compensating for his decision on the presidency, by trying to light a path towards Arab–Israeli understanding.

When Einstein received no reply from Cairo he made a second approach through Dr Azmi, this time in writing. This again brought no response, so he enlisted the help of Jawaharal Nehru, prime minister of India, whose views carried great weight in the Third World. Nasser continued to feel that it was best not to respond.*

The Egyptian leader's determination to avoid contacts reflected his experiences during and after the 1948–49 war, and his personal belief in the Palestinian cause. Nasser had demonstrated that commitment by making plans to join the Egyptian volunteer force which went to Palestine at the beginning of 1948. At the last minute he decided to stay in Cairo to help organize the force, but went to Palestine later, when the Egyptian army officially entered the war. As the staff officer of the Sixth Battalion Infantry Nasser personally led Egyptian forces in the Battle of Irak-El-Mansheya, in which eighty-two Israeli military personnel were killed. This battle and subsequent events added a psychological element to Nasser's political convictions, inhibiting any post-war attempt to see Israel in a different light. Like any soldier who has watched friends fall in battle, Nasser felt an immense bond with his comrades, and the fact that armies from several Arab countries were constantly in touch with each other reinforced a powerful sense of common cause.

Nasser's subsequent distrust of peace initiatives was rooted in memories of Israeli breaches of UN-brokered ceasefire agreements. During one of these truces Israel broke through a military line running between Gaza and Beersheba in the northern part of the Negev, and later overran the desert to the south. The line held a particular military significance for Nasser, who had written a paper on its importance to the defence of Egypt. The young Egyptian officer was something of an expert on the strategy followed by General Edmund Allenby in his 1917 campaign to capture Palestine from the Turks, in which the Gaza–Beersheba line had figured prominently. The occupation of the Negev by Israel contradicted what Nasser saw as requirements for national security.

After this episode Israeli forces also broke through Egyptian lines

* Einstein died in 1955, without having achieved his wish to be a catalyst for peace.

further south and surrounded the Egyptian army at El-Arish in the Sinai. Meanwhile Nasser's brigade became encircled by Israelis at Falluga and was held under siege for four months. During that period Nasser was the liaison officer on truce committees, and came into contact with an Israeli counterpart, Captain Yeruhan Cohen. On one occasion Cohen crossed the lines to Egyptian positions for discussions with Nasser, bearing a white flag, and sought to convince Nasser that there was no reason for Egyptians and Israelis to be at war. Nasser did not want to be drawn into such a discussion and changed the subject.

Nasser also attended a meeting between the commander of the besieged forces, Brigadier El-Sayed Taha, and General Yigal Allon, Israeli commander of the southern front.* In this encounter, arranged by UN observers, Allon offered Egyptian forces safe conduct out of the area, provided they left their heavy weapons behind. Nasser was unhappy with the meeting and resented what he saw as Israeli arrogance, but thought that Egyptian political and military mismanagement was largely to blame for the plight of the besieged forces. Somewhat later, after the Egyptian–Israeli armistice agreement of February 1949, there arose a need for an Egyptian officer to show where Israeli soldiers killed in the battle of Irak-El-Mansheya had been buried. That role fell to Nasser, and again his Israeli counterpart was Yeruhan Cohen. On his way to the battlefield Nasser passed through the Negev and talked to Palestinians living under Israeli occupation, and later returned to Egypt feeling bitter about what he had seen and heard.

Professional, political and personal considerations thus played a part in Nasser's opposition to contacts with Israel, and his example helped to reinforce the wider Arab rejection of the Zionist state.

A further element of the Arab taboo was the consistently one-sided attitude shown by Harry Truman since his accession to power in April 1945. Truman's decision not to stand in the 1952 presidential election aroused hopes that the new incumbent might bring a more even balance to US policy in the Middle East. When the plain-speaking farmer from Missouri departed from the White House in January 1953 he left

* Allon subsequently held senior government posts, including deputy prime minister and foreign minister.

a deficit in the bank of US–Arab understanding. Truman would be remembered by Arabs as the president who encouraged Jewish refugees to defy British immigration controls in Palestine after World War II, as the president whose pressure on the British during the 1948–49 war contributed to Israel's victory, and as a president who apparently felt no remorse in tailoring US foreign policy to catch Jewish American votes. While Nasser was well disposed to Americans in other ways, Truman's legacy did not bode well for US–Egyptian relations.

7

The Eisenhower Initiative

Few American presidents come to office with their respect and popularity assured in advance. Dwight Eisenhower's stature as a war hero gave him not only an easy election victory but also the confidence to choose his own path. The Korean War was ended by negotiation six months after the new administration took office, leaving the president and his secretary of state John Foster Dulles free to concentrate on reducing tension in other areas, while completing Truman's ring of defence pacts around the Soviet Union. The difference in the Middle East was a more active US effort to bring Israel and the Arabs together. The Eisenhower–Dulles team was the first of many US administrations to dream of peace in the Holy Land.

The main US agencies involved in this effort were the State Department, the CIA and the Defense Department, coordinated by the Alpha group, a shadowy organization whose members mostly had more than one activity. Alpha members included Kermit Roosevelt, and to some extent the group was a continuation of the unofficial role Roosevelt had played before the revolution.

Dulles began to prepare for a visit to the Middle East, and quickly came under conflicting pressures from the British on one hand and the Israelis on the other. The British and Egyptians had solved one of their main differences, the Sudan issue,* and were inching towards accord on the Suez question, amid much acrimony. Anthony Eden† had by now come to terms with the inevitability of British withdrawal, but

* In February 1953 Britain and Egypt agreed that Sudan should be given autonomy immediately and self-determination in three years. This agreement ended the Anglo–Egyptian condominium in Sudan, which had existed since 1889.

† Eden had returned to office as foreign secretary following the Conservative election victory in 1951.

wanted Egypt to join the proposed Middle East Defence Organization first. After discussing this with Eisenhower, Eden thought that the Americans were putting insufficient pressure on Nasser to sign a pact. Sir Roger Makins, British ambassador to Washington, urged Dulles to be firm with Nasser.

At the same time the Israeli government was alarmed by Britain's intentions. Ben-Gurion had been trying since 1951 to interest London in transferring the British base from the Suez Canal to Gaza. Such a move would have kept a barrier between Egypt and Israel while retaining Britain's strategic position, but London was slow to respond. By 1953 the likelihood of British withdrawal from Suez was so strong that the Israelis could wait no longer. Abba Eban was instructed to press Dulles to find out Nasser's conditions for peace with Israel. The secretary of state replied that his experts had advised against carrying messages to Egypt. Eban commented: 'Mr Secretary, this advice smells of oil.'

Eban was close to the truth. The secretary of state's main concerns were Middle East oil and the need for a strong US presence in the region. These aims could best be advanced by exploiting Egypt's dispute with Britain and by not emphasizing the US relationship with Israel.

Dulles visited Nasser in March 1953, bringing a letter from Eisenhower which strongly supported Egypt's stand against British occupation. 'This government and the American people understand and appreciate the natural aspirations of Egypt for full sovereignty over its own territory. Similar aspirations have deep roots in the tradition of America.' Eisenhower also dealt with the defence pact issue in a way which was significantly different to what Britain wanted. Eden had insisted on Egyptian acceptance of a pact *before* British withdrawal; Eisenhower suggested that Egypt should 'favourably consider' such a pact *after* reaching outline agreement with London.

'America's desire in this situation is to see disappear a long misunderstanding between two friends,' wrote Eisenhower. As regards joint defence against the Soviet Union, this was indeed what Eisenhower wanted; in other respects the Anglo–Egyptian 'misunderstanding' served the US aim of supplanting Britain in the Middle East. Churchill was furious when he received reports of the Dulles visit.

Nasser and Dulles talked at length about the British problem before turning to Israel. Here again the secretary of state sought to present the US as an impartial friend trying to help. Dulles raised the question of peace with Israel but did not push for an agreement prior to British withdrawal, as Ben-Gurion had wished.

'Isn't peace with Israel the natural thing?' Dulles asked, arguing that as Jews and Arabs were Semites they should work together. Nasser retorted that the Israelis had come from ninety different countries, and their Semitic ancestry was open to discussion. 'Even if they are Semites they came here as invaders and imposed on Palestinians what they had learned from Nazis.'

Nasser thought that the most important issue was the division of the Arab world into two parts as a result of the Israeli annexation of the Negev desert. The Egyptian leader was surprised to find that Dulles needed the help of a map to understand this point.

Dulles asked whether Nasser considered peace with Israel to be impossible. Nasser replied: 'I don't see that peace can be based on a *fait accompli*.'

One of the ideas the Alpha group had suggested was that secondary differences between Arabs and Israelis should be tackled first, leaving the main issues until later. Dulles proposed starting with an agreement on division of the water of the Jordan river. This suggestion later led to an American offer to build nuclear-powered desalination plants to increase the fresh-water supply and ease differences over the Jordan's water. The Johnson administration subsequently proposed a different scheme based on a water-sharing treaty. Nothing came of these projects because the Israelis found that they could simply take the water they wanted.

The Alpha group also produced a bizarre proposal to meet Nasser's objection to the division of the Arab world. Arabia would be linked to North Africa by a highway overpass on stilts above the narrowest part of Israeli territory near Eilat. Nasser ironically pointed out that an Arab soldier on the overpass would only have to urinate on an Israeli soldier below to start a war.

On returning to Washington Dulles reported to Eisenhower that the Egyptians felt the weight of the colonial experience to a degree which prevented them from looking to the future. He recommended that the US should take an active role in negotiating British withdrawal, as a means of strengthening Washington's links with Cairo.

A year after the revolution Egypt had changed in fundamental ways. Feudal landlords had been emasculated by a law limiting land ownership to 200 feddans (about 204 acres). The assets of the royal family had been confiscated and were being used for a mixture of social and industrial programmes. Two new schools were being completed every three days and combined social centres, each including a hospital, a welfare centre and a school, were under construction. A law restricting the dismissal of workers had been passed. These were reforms which affected the lives of ordinary people, and brought a new spirit to the country.

The changes reinforced Israel's fear that a socially united Egypt would be a more dangerous enemy. The Israeli ambassador in London made repeated approaches to British officials demanding that any treaty on British withdrawal should include a provision that Egypt would not use military facilities evacuated by the British as bases for attacks on Israel.* Another demand was that Egypt should allow ships bound for Israel to pass through the Suez Canal. The Foreign Office was opposed to allowing Israel to be so closely involved in the making of British policy, but the Israelis had a powerful ally in Downing Street. In the spring of 1953 Churchill gave general instructions to the Foreign Office to be more cooperative towards Israel, which he described as the most important fighting power in the Middle East.† Churchill foresaw a need to cooperate with Israel against Egypt and strongly criticized the policies followed by Ernest Bevin. It had been wrong, Churchill said, to allow Egypt to prevent oil for Israel passing through the canal. Churchill implied that some in the Foreign Office were still loyal to Bevin's policies. In a further memorandum he added that he did not care if Cairo thought he was biased towards Israel, and rejected what he considered to be a 'sacrifice of Israel's interests' in order to persuade Egypt to allow British forces to remain in the Suez base. Britain should face the Egyptians squarely and cooperate with the Americans, Churchill said.

* The British officials involved in these talks were Anthony Nutting, a minister of state at the Foreign Office, Selwyn Lloyd, who was a minister of state at the time but became foreign secretary in 1955, and Sir William Strang, permanent undersecretary at the Foreign Office.

† The instructions were in a memorandum dated 23 April 1953 from Churchill to Sir William Strang and in related correspondence with Strang and Selwyn Lloyd.

These memoranda marked an important change of direction, away from the middle course Labour had tried to steer and back to the pro-Zionist policies Britain had followed before 1939. Bevin, exasperated by increasing Zionist demands, had decided that Britain's strategic interests could be secured through defence agreements with Arab countries. The Conservative victory of 1951 brought a partial revival of the old colonial mentality which Bevin had begun to dismantle. Churchill and Eden were accustomed to compliant Egyptian leaders who might grumble but would ultimately take orders; Nasser did not fit that mould.

In 1953, however, both Egypt and Britain thought an arrangement might be possible. Negotiations on the canal were continuing, Nasser had not ruled out joining a defence pact, and even Eden recognized that the new Egyptian government was more efficient than previous administrations had been. This brief hopeful period was strengthened by the resignation of Ben-Gurion and his replacement, in January 1954, by Moshe Sharett, the former Israeli foreign minister.

Sharett began telling colleagues that he had at last established contact with Egypt through the Israeli embassy in Paris. Word of his remarks reached Nasser, who had not authorized any contacts, and an investigation was carried out. The trail led to an Egyptian intelligence officer who had been sent to Paris to monitor increasing Israeli activity in the French capital. The officer met a member of the Israeli embassy, and began probing for information. Sensing the Egyptian's hunger for material, the Israeli suggested further meetings. The Egyptian then told his superiors that he had recruited an Israeli official, and began passing on any information he picked up, but omitted any political ideas put forward by the Israeli. The investigation uncovered a flagrant increase in the Egyptian's expense account, accompanied by a flow of largely worthless information.

The mirage of an Israeli–Egyptian channel coincided with an effort by a group of missionary American Quakers who met the Egyptian ambassador to Washington and told him they were going to the Middle East to pray and work for peace. They visited Egypt and met Dr Fawzi, the foreign minister, but nothing came of their 'project for peace in the Holy Land'. Their press conferences made greater waves than any contacts and proposals they initiated. But these two elements, the supposed Israeli–Egyptian channel and the 'project for peace', contributed to an illusion of declining tension.

After the Paris embassy disappointment Sharett revived an idea Ben-Gurion had put forward in 1951 to move the British base from the Suez Canal to a new site in Gaza, but gave it a fresh twist. The first proposal had been impractical because Gaza was under Egyptian control, so Sharett offered part of the Negev desert instead. The British, however, were unwilling to repeat the immense investment which had been poured into the Suez base, and the idea came to nothing. In July 1954 Britain and Egypt reached agreement on a timetable for British withdrawal.

In the meantime the United States and Britain had continued their attempts to encircle the Soviet Union. The South East Asia Treaty Organization, linking the three main Western powers with five Pacific and Asian countries, was signed in 1954. The Western powers were anxious to complete their defensive arrangements by setting up a Middle East Defence Organization (MEDO), but this was frustrated by Nasser's insistence that Britain should withdraw before Egypt gave any commitment. An attempt was made by NATO to build a defence system in two stages, beginning with a 'northern tier' of countries closest to the Soviet Union. Turkey, as a NATO member, took the initiative in negotiating an agreement with Iraq, which was signed on 24 February 1955. Six weeks later, Britain became a party, followed later in the year by Pakistan and Iran, and the agreement became known as the 'Baghdad Pact'. The five countries set up a permanent council to coordinate mutual defence arrangements.*

Iraq's eagerness to join increased Arab suspicions that the pact would perpetuate foreign domination of the Middle East. Baghdad sought to justify its decision by saying that any arms it received as a member of the pact would be used to fight Israel. Other Arab countries were not fooled, as a letter from King Saud† to his ambassador in Cairo showed: 'The Iraqis are lying and we should expose their lies to Arab peoples. They will not be able to use those arms against Israel.'

Nasser told Anthony Eden in February 1955 that the pact was badly

* The pact never expanded into the larger Middle East Defence Organization which the US and Britain had intended.

† King Saud came to the Saudi throne in 1953 on the death of his father Ibn Saud.

timed and conceived, and had impaired prospects for collaboration between the Arab world and the West. After this meeting Eden began to develop an obsessive hatred of the Egyptian leader, blaming him for any setback the British suffered in the Middle East. When riots broke out in Amman in December 1955, London thought Nasser had lit a fire to prevent King Hussein from taking Jordan into the pact. When King Hussein dismissed General Glubb in March 1956, a move which delighted Jordanians, Eden supposed the decision had been made in Cairo. At the same time the French were accusing Nasser of fomenting the Algerian revolution which had begun the previous November. These matters were connected with the Egyptian leader only in the general sense that Nasser had become a role model for groups and leaders throughout the Arab world.

Meanwhile the quiet period in Egypt's relations with Israel had come to an abrupt end following a series of explosions in American libraries and other public places in Egypt. An attempt to place another bomb inside an Alexandria cinema failed when the device exploded prematurely, injuring the terrorist who was carrying it. The man and an accomplice were arrested and found to be Israeli agents.

Unknown to Sharett, the agents had been sent to Egypt under orders supposedly issued by Pinhas Lavon, the acting Israeli minister of defence. As a result the scandal became known as the Lavon affair, but in fact Lavon's signature on the document issuing the orders had been forged. Sharett resigned in February 1955, disgusted with what had happened, and Ben-Gurion returned as prime minister later in the year.

When the agents were sentenced to death the Israelis mobilized leaders from all over the world to appeal for clemency. The prime minister of Burma, U Nu, wrote to Nasser: 'I accept your point of view politically but I am asking you for a human favour.' President Eisenhower, Pope Pius XII, Bertrand Russell and Nehru sent similar requests.*

Nasser authorized commandos to carry out attacks in reprisal for the bombs placed by the agents. Israel responded with a massive raid

* The executions were carried out in 1956. Egypt returned the agents' remains to Israel for burial after an agreement in 1967, following the Six Day war. Israel then acknowledged that the two men had been intelligence officers.

on the Egyptian headquarters in Gaza, in which fifty soldiers and civilians were killed. This episode had a critical effect on the formation of Nasser's subsequent policies.

The Lavon affair and the Gaza raid came at a time when Egypt was pressing the United States to provide military aid, and complaining that Washington was ready to help Israel but not Egypt. Cairo's high investments in social programmes had forced a reduction in military spending, leaving Egypt extremely vulnerable. Nasser felt that the danger came not from Israel's strength but from Egypt's weakness. 'I have lost my voice asking you for arms,' he told the American ambassador on 10 March.

Increased tension with Israel, and the US refusal to supply arms, helped to clarify a new policy which was forming in the Egyptian leader's mind. Egypt's place, he now realized, was neither with the West nor with the Soviet camp, but with a new independent grouping of nations. At the time preparations were under way for a conference of Afro-Asian countries to be held in April 1955 in Bandung, Indonesia. The arrangements were being made by three Asian countries – Burma, India and Ceylon – known as the Colombo Group, which had decided on certain rules for selecting the countries to be invited. Egypt joined the Colombo Group and then objected to an invitation being extended to Israel. Ben-Gurion, however, wanted Israel to participate and felt that as an Asian country it was entitled to a place at the conference. Nasser wrote to two leading prime ministers of the Colombo Group, U Nu of Burma and Jawaharlal Nehru of India, but his objection to Israel's inclusion was not well received. The Burmese and Indian statesmen felt that Nasser was imposing Egypt's quarrels on other countries. The Egyptian leader then pointed out that Israel had refused to define its borders, and that this refusal constituted a threat to its Asian and African neighbours.

The Burmese prime minister talked to Ben-Gurion, who again declined to accept the definition of Israel's borders contained in the UN plan of 1947. As a result Israel's invitation was withdrawn, while Egypt became a co-sponsor of the conference.

On the way to Indonesia Nasser met the Chinese leader Chou En-lai, and afterwards they travelled from Rangoon to Bandung. Nasser was now looking for a way to request Soviet arms without becoming part of the Soviet camp, and used the opportunity to ask Chou En-lai to sound out Moscow. The Chinese leader agreed, and expressed admiration for the stand Nasser had taken against the British, an attitude which was strongly endorsed by other Asian and African participants. It was the attention given to Nasser at the Bandung conference which made Arabs realize that the Egyptian leader was becoming an example to others beyond the Arab and Islamic worlds. The conference led to the creation of the Afro–Asian Solidarity Movement.

The United States, which did not recognize China's communist government, was surprised by Nasser's meeting with Chou En-lai and unhappy with Egypt's emerging role in the Non-Aligned Movement.* Surprise turned to anger in September when Nasser announced an agreement to buy Czechoslovakian weapons through the Soviet Union, a deal which stemmed from his request for Chou En-lai's help.

Realizing that the refusal to supply Egypt with US weapons had backfired, Washington became more anxious than ever to draw the most populous and politically important Middle East country into the Western camp. An opportunity arose two months later, when an Egyptian minister visited Washington to ask for financial aid. Egyptian leaders had long dreamed of building a high dam at Aswan to tame the waters of the Nile, preventing the floods which had been a feature of life in the river valley since the beginning of recorded time, and assuring an adequate year-round water supply. A civil engineering project of such magnitude called for a multinational financing package, which would be difficult without active encouragement from the United States. When the Egyptian finance minister sought US financing, Washington agreed in principle but attached political strings. Eisenhower sent Robert Anderson,† a close aide, to say that Egypt could have the dam if Nasser accepted a peace treaty with Israel. The Egyptian leader was being asked to break ranks with other Arab countries by settling Israeli–Egyptian differences in a separate deal. This would have destroyed Arab unity and left the Palestinians, Jordan, Syria and Lebanon even more vulnerable to Israeli domination.

Secret negotiations were conducted in the Tahira palace, a former royal residence in Cairo, and Anderson travelled between Israel and

* The Non-Aligned Movement grew out of a meeting between Nehru, Tito and Nasser in Yugoslavia in July 1956.

† Anderson served as deputy defense secretary 1954–55 and treasury secretary 1957–61.

Egypt via Cyprus passing messages. This forerunner of 'shuttle diplomacy' was an American way of circumventing Egypt's refusal to engage in contacts with Israel, but it was not well handled. Anderson attempted to tell Nasser what to say to Eisenhower; not just in outline, but the exact words. A letter for Nasser to send to the US president had been pre-written in Washington even before the consultations began, as had Eisenhower's reply. Such an approach would have angered any leader.

Nasser was supposed to declare that Egypt had no hostile intentions towards any other state (meaning Israel), would never be a party to aggression, and would try to prevent incidents along the armistice line between the two countries. Egypt would accept UN resolutions on Palestine and refugees 'notwithstanding the sense of injustice that will linger among generations of us', and would indicate its desire for permanent peace.

In return for these concessions, Egypt would expect Israel to give up enough territory to 'permit the Arabs of Asia and Africa to be joined together by a continuous and substantial land area under Arab sovereignty and peopled by Arabs'. Although not stated directly, this meant part of the Negev desert. After the territorial question had been settled the two sides would deal with the refugee issue, giving Palestinians a choice between repatriation or compensation.

The letter went on to offer detailed proposals on all the main points except Jerusalem. Nasser was to say: 'It is my feeling that the kingdom of Jordan should have the right of decision [on Jerusalem's future].'

Anderson also brought a proposed letter to be sent by Nasser to Eugene Black, president of the World Bank, requesting a loan of $200 million. In return for this loan Egypt would promise to follow 'sound financial and economic policies' calculated to ensure that it could service its foreign debts.

The letter strongly reminded Nasser and his colleagues of the nineteenth-century period of 'dual control', when Britain and France forced Ismail, the khedive, to allow European 'advisers' to help manage Egypt's economy. Ismail had accepted large European loans to finance infrastructure projects such as ports and railways, and had run into difficulties in servicing the debts.

Nasser knew that the World Bank would grant the $200 million only if the United States and Britain provided further loans totalling $70 million. The proposed deal was ready by December 1955, but the final decision took a further eight months. The two sets of US-prepared letters, one dealing with the dam, the other with peace, were inextricably linked. Egypt was being offered the dam and a separate peace with Israel, but not the dam without a separate peace. Few thought Cairo would prefer to accept neither, but in the end its choice was exactly that.

The atmosphere darkened further in May 1956, when Nasser announced that Egypt recognized the Chinese government, and when Western intelligence agencies noted an increase in Soviet weapons deliveries to Egypt. At this point the US administration decided that a tougher stand against Nasser was needed. On 19 July, while the Egyptian leader was travelling to Cairo after a meeting with Nehru and Tito, Washington announced that it was withdrawing from the financing scheme. The use of a public statement, instead of a private message, to convey this decision was clearly calculated to damage Nasser's prestige.

Britain was not consulted on the decision, perhaps because of strong personal dislike between Eden and Dulles.* Nevertheless, Britain was bound to follow Washington's lead, because the British part of the loan was only $14 million, compared with $56 million from the United States. Without US and British support the World Bank's conditions could not be met, and the finance package collapsed.† The failure of the Anderson mission, which had been the most important Middle East initiative of Eisenhower's presidency, set in train a series of major events.

A week after Washington's announcement Nasser retaliated with a move which delighted the Arab world and infuriated London and Paris. In a speech on the fourth anniversary of Farouk being sent into exile, Nasser told cheering crowds in Alexandria that the Suez Canal Company would be nationalized and revenue from the canal used to build the dam. As Nasser was speaking Egyptian engineers began

* Eden had become prime minister in 1955 following Churchill's retirement.

† The high dam project was revived in 1958 when the Soviet Union agreed to help. The only Soviet conditions were that Russian equipment should be used and that Soviet engineers should participate. Work began in January 1960 and the official completion ceremony was held eleven years later.

taking over the canal from British civilian staff. London thought that shipping would come to a halt without experienced British pilots, but the new Suez Canal Authority achieved a smooth takeover. Dulles fumed and Eden made exaggerated statements about 'theft' and 'blackmail', but as Egypt quickly promised compensation for shareholders the nationalization was legal under international law.

Nasser understood the risks he was taking. Britain and France had never hesitated to use force to keep the isthmus under their hegemony, and Israel was girding for war,* while Egypt's forces were still inexperienced in the use of their new Soviet weapons. The Egyptian leader also realized that his people were ready to face those risks. Every stand he took against Western pressure brought a further rise in his prestige, at first in Egypt, later in the whole Arab world. Nasser's two great refusals, no pact with the West and no peace with Israel, had sent his popularity soaring, giving him a 99.9 per cent victory in presidential elections in June. Not since Mohamed Ali had an Arab leader shown such resoluteness; not in the history of the Middle East had one man's strength so inspired Arabs from the Persian Gulf to the Atlantic. The making of a legend had begun.

Three tense months passed between the Alexandria speech and the inevitable violent reaction. The British and French slowly assembled troops and ships in Cyprus and Malta but did not decide until October how to act. Their resolve to use force was motivated not solely by the nationalization of the canal but by three other unconnected factors. The French military, smarting over criticism of its poor showing in Algeria, blamed Nasser for inspiring the rebels. At the same time Ben-Gurion, angered by Palestinian attacks across the Gaza border, was looking for a pretext to destroy Egypt's new weapons before the Egyptian army became proficient in using them. The third element was Anthony Eden's belief that Nasser was a new Hitler who needed to be crushed before he became too powerful.†

* Ben-Gurion had ordered Moshe Dayan, the Israeli chief-of-staff, to prepare for battle.

† Eden's far-fetched comparison sprang from memories of 1938, when he had resigned as foreign secretary in protest against Neville Chamberlain's appeasement of Hitler. His fear that history was repeating itself became an obsession, and Eden's increasingly commanding personality silenced objections from some who should have stood up to him. However Anthony Nutting, minister of state at the Foreign Office, resigned in protest.

These three elements came together at meetings in Britain and France involving, at different times, Eden, Selwyn Lloyd, Ben-Gurion, Dayan, the French prime minister Guy Mollet, two other French ministers and the head of the French air force. The conclusive session at Sèvres in France on 24 October resulted in a conspiracy extraordinary not only for its content but because it was committed to paper, and documentary evidence later came to light. It was agreed that Israel would send forces into the Sinai desert on 29 October, to provide a pretext for Britain and France to claim that the canal was endangered. The two European powers would then issue an ultimatum to Israel and Egypt to pull their forces back ten miles from either side of the canal. Britain and France then planned to seize the canal, using force if they met Egyptian resistance.

Nasser received intelligence reports about the Anglo-French build-up but did not believe the British would be foolish enough to conspire with the Israelis, because of the permanent damage this would cause to their standing in the Middle East. The Arab League declared that an attack against Egypt would be regarded as an attack against all, but the other countries were in no military position to help.

The plan was badly thought-out and clumsily executed. Britain and France underestimated both the strength of national and international reaction and the size of the force which would be needed to secure the canal. Field Marshal Montgomery, victor of the battle of Alamein, said later that a successful operation would have needed more than 100,000 troops occupying not just the canal zone but the whole Nile delta.

The Israeli 'invasion' force proved to be even smaller than the British and French had expected. Only a battalion was sent into Sinai initially, and only as far as the Mitla pass. This force was nowhere near the canal when the British and French issued their ultimatum. Israel's first priority was to ensure that Britain and France destroyed the Egyptian air force, and its second was to occupy Sharm El-Sheikh, the strategic point dominating the Strait of Tiran.

An Anglo-French invasion force landed near Port Said on 5 November, reduced much of the city to rubble and killed 2700 people, bombed Cairo and seized the head of the canal. The two European powers faced obstinate Egyptian resistance and massive international pressure to withdraw. The Soviet Union threatened nuclear attacks on London and Paris, the United Nations condemned the invasion,* Nehru warned that India might withdraw from the Commonwealth, and there was a run on sterling. The United States, annoyed because it had not been consulted and because the attack was timed to coincide with the presidential election, temporarily disowned its allies.

Faced with united international opposition, Britain and France backed down and withdrew when a United Nations Emergency Force arrived to take over on 21 November. By Christmas the forces of the two European powers had left, but the canal remained blocked by the hulks of fifty ships which had been sunk to prevent the invaders from using it.†

Britain paid dearly for the adventure, losing its last link with Suez. Although British troops had left Egypt the previous March, the base had remained under the control of British-paid maintenance staff. A seven-year agreement gave Britain the right to redeploy forces there in the event of a Soviet attack. After the Suez affair the base and its stores were taken over by Egyptian forces. Britain forfeited not only its strategic position, but esteem in the eyes of other Arab allies. British assets in Egypt were confiscated and hundreds of British residents expelled.

Eden's miscalculation also helped the Americans achieve their aim of replacing Britain as the dominant influence in the Middle East. Eden resigned in 1957 on grounds of ill health and never recovered the standing he had once had. France had less to lose.

Israel proved harder to dislodge than Britain and France. Having annexed the whole of the Sinai in November and renamed the Gulf of Aqaba the Gulf of Solomon, Ben-Gurion clearly intended to retain the conquered territory permanently. He gave way only under intense pressure from Eisenhower, who threatened economic sanctions. As Israeli forces departed they destroyed Egypt's military and civilian infrastructure in the Sinai.

* Dag Hammarskjöld, secretary general of the United Nations, submitted his resignation at the height of the crisis in protest against the involvement of two permanent members of the Security Council in aggression against a Third World country. He was persuaded to withdraw it. Hammarskjöld later considered trying to promote Arab–Israeli peace but realized after a visit to the Middle East that the idea was premature.

† The canal was restored to use by April 1957, and Britain subsequently paid dues for using it.

Two months later Washington rewarded Israel for withdrawing by giving a secret assurance that the Strait of Tiran would be kept open as an international waterway.* Until 1956 the strait had been controlled by the Egyptian navy, preventing Israeli access from Eilat to the Red Sea. The Israelis were thus the sole conspirators to emerge with anything to show for the campaign, yet they lost more than they gained, as their goal of obtaining Arab recognition moved still further out of reach, and the Arab taboo became stronger than ever.†

Despite casualties and much damage, the Egyptian people felt they had lived through their finest hour, resisting not just one but three aggressors. More than any other Arab–Israeli conflict, the Suez affair demonstrated that Israel was a bridgehead to serve foreign political interests. It was no coincidence that the greatest flowering of Arab unity occurred in the years immediately afterwards, and that peace prospects went into cold storage.

* The assurance was verbal but Dulles also gave Israel an aide-memoire confirming it, dated 11 February 1957. This was interpreted by Israel as a promise that the US would use force if necessary to keep the passage open.

† A further consequence of the Suez affair was that the position of the Jewish community in Egypt became untenable. Had the invasion not occurred, Egyptian Jews might eventually have resumed their pre-1948 role as a point of contact. By the end of 1957 nearly all had left Egypt.

8

Three Presidents; Three Perspectives

After 1956 Nasser was no longer just captain of Egypt but captor of the Arab masses, the leading Middle East statesman and a lion of the Third World. Millions looked to him as a symbol of resistance against Western military power. In another sense, the Egyptian president was just as much captive as captor of a popular mood he had helped to create. No Arab leader in such circumstances could have stepped beyond his people's psychological defences to attempt dialogue with the enemy. The all-powerful taboo was dominant.

If contact with Israel was out of the question, the need for a working relationship with Washington was greater than ever. The pre-Suez rows over the Egyptian–Soviet arms deal and the financing of the high dam remained fresh in Arab memories, but the Eisenhower administration had regained much credibility by refusing to support Britain and forcing Israel's withdrawal from Sinai. The collapse of British influence left the US as the only major power in a position to help. Suez was thus the historical turning point which made Washington's role as Middle East bridge-builder indispensable, though four more years were to pass before need coincided with opportunity. A period of adjustment intervened before the next serious US effort, and Eisenhower's Middle East activities during his second term consisted of coming to terms with the Nasser phenomenon, trying to contain it, and continuing the US effort to encircle the Soviet Union.

The US National Security Council devoted parts of six meetings to the rise of Arab nationalism, trying to decide whether it was the wave of the future or only a passing trend. In the late 1950s and early sixties that question was tantalizingly difficult to answer. If the Arabs succeeded in building a unified state, cordial US relations with the new entity would be vital to America's greater goal of containing communism. If not, the US could rely on defence pacts with a few Middle East states nearest to the Soviet Union.

In 1958 Arab nationalism seemed destined to change the map of the Middle East. Israel, Washington and London watched with mounting concern as Egypt and Syria merged in February to form the United Arab Republic, a new state under Nasser's presidency. Five months later a military coup in Iraq brought a nationalist government to power.* The US sent marines to Lebanon to protect the pro-Western government of President Camille Chamoun, while King Hussein of Jordan requested and received a British contingent. In the same year Yemen entered into a loose federation with the United Arab Republic.

Ben-Gurion saw the Egyptian–Syrian union as a nutcracker closing on Israel from above and below. In a letter to Eisenhower ten days after the Iraqi revolution he sought to draw the Americans into a deeper Middle East commitment by suggesting that Arab nationalism was a front for Soviet expansionism. Ben-Gurion said that Nasser's ambition was to dominate the whole Islamic world and Africa, and expressed doubts that the West-leaning governments of Lebanon and Jordan could be saved by US and British intervention. The majority of Muslims in Lebanon supported Nasser, he said, while the Christians were divided among themselves. Israel was trying to create a ring of friendly countries beyond its hostile neighbours and had entered into close links with Turkey, Iran, Ethiopia, and Sudan: 'Mr President, we are working seriously to contain that danger and to see what we can do. We started with countries of the northern tier, the outer tier around

* The coup on 14 July 1958 overthrew the former pro-British regime. The king, most of his family, and prime minister Nuri El-Said Pasha were killed. The new government, led by Brigadier General Abdul Karim Kassem, was divided in its attitude to Nasser and did not join the United Arab Republic.

us and around Nasser* . . . Our aim is to build a real high dam in front of the Nasserite–Soviet flood.'†

Ben-Gurion was in effect seeking American political cover and economic support to transform this loose grouping of countries into a steel barrier. 'With your help we can stand up to Nasser and to Soviet expansionism, which is being achieved through Nasser.' He implied that Israel was better placed than the United States to organize the containment of Nasser, because direct US involvement would arouse suspicions of neo-colonialism. 'I know that many are sensitive about giving such responsibilities to great powers . . . but because of the size of Israel nobody would think that we were really dominating them. I am not exaggerating our capacities . . . but let me tell you that we can build those forces.'

Ben-Gurion's proposal did not immediately change US policy, but the more general idea that US responsibilities in the Middle East could be delegated to Israel seeped into the thoughts of the Senate majority leader, Lyndon Johnson. A decade later that concept was to form an important part of Johnson's policies for the region.

Eisenhower made no major Middle East peace efforts during his second term (1957–61), but US relations with Egypt slowly improved. The Middle East now accounted for 25 per cent of total world oil production, and Washington knew that Cairo held the political keys to the Arab world. In 1958, when Nasser became involved in a dispute with Moscow after criticizing the Iraqi communist party, Washington saw an opportunity for stronger links. This led to a US decision to begin supplying Egypt with food aid. At the end of the Eisenhower era the two presidents met for the first and last time during a UN

* Israel and its 'outer tier' countries were not alone in wanting to keep Arab nationalism in check. King Saud of Saudi Arabia secretly opposed the creation of the United Arab Republic, although he pretended otherwise. In 1958, after the union had been proposed but before Nasser became president of the united country, one of Saud's fathers-in-law was given $2 million and told to transfer the money to Abdel-Hamid El-Sarraj, a colonel in the Syrian intelligence agency. The colonel was asked to bring about a military coup before Nasser arrived in Damascus on 22 February 1958, but he took the cheque to Nasser, resulting in a scandal which led to Saud's fall. The Saudi royal council, made up of family members, religious figures and senior advisers, ordered Saud to hand over his main powers to his brother Prince Faisal. Saud remained the titular monarch until 1964 and then abdicated.

† Ben-Gurion had no sooner sent this letter than his dam began to crumble, with the fall of Abdullah Khalil, prime minister of Sudan, swept away by a military coup.

function in New York, in September 1960. Eisenhower spoke of Egypt's progress with warmth and even admiration. Whatever their political differences, the old five-star general and the young colonel found an unexpected rapport.

When John F. Kennedy succeeded Eisenhower in January 1961 the Arab–Israel dispute was in a relatively quiet phase. The new president, attentive both to his substantial Jewish vote and to the growing importance of the Arab world, sought to bring a new approach to an old problem. Like many of his successors, Kennedy began his presidency with hopes of healing the breach between America's friends in the Middle East.

Ben-Gurion became agitated in February when Egypt carried out military exercises in the Sinai, showing off its Russian weapons. Meanwhile Israeli agents were attempting to assassinate German scientists involved in Egyptian research,* but such matters hardly warranted the attention of a US president. Indeed, the first letters between Kennedy and Nasser dealt with events in the Caribbean. After the Bay of Pigs operation in April,† Nasser sent a public message of support to Cuba's president Fidel Castro. Kennedy took this as an opportunity to write to Nasser, explaining the US viewpoint on Cuba, and Nasser sent a polite reply.

The ice now broken, Kennedy wrote again on 11 May dealing solely with the Arab–Israel dispute. The letter opened with a clear hint that Egypt could expect major US aid if it loosened ties with Moscow and recognized Israel. 'The United States . . . lends every appropriate

* After the 1948 war Egypt built three ordnance factories, and received technological training from a team of German officers led by General Eric Fahrenbachor. Production of arms in Egypt began after the 1952 revolution. Following the Suez crisis a fighter-aircraft programme started. The first prototype, the Cairo 100, was produced in 1959, followed by the Cairo 200 and 300 models. During the same period Egypt had a missile development programme, headed by Dr Wolfgang Pils, and the first rocket test was carried out in July 1962. The Israelis made twenty-six attempts to intimidate German scientists, or their assistants or secretaries, involved in the programme. One scientist was assassinated in Munich and other German staff were injured, including Dr Pils's secretary, Hilda Fromm, who lost an arm while opening a booby-trapped parcel.

† Just before leaving office Eisenhower broke off diplomatic relations with Cuba. In April 1961, three months after Kennedy had taken office, 1500 Cuban exiles trained and armed by the CIA landed at the Bahia de Cochinos intending to overthrow Fidel Castro. Most were killed or captured.

assistance to all Middle Eastern states that are determined to control their own destiny . . . and to allow their neighbours to pursue the same fundamental aims.' The letter went on to imply that Egypt could have some types of aid without these preconditions, and offered political help in solving differences with Israel, especially mentioning 'the tragic Palestinian refugee problem' and a dispute over the growing amount of water which Israel was diverting from the Jordan river.

While Kennedy's seven-page letter broke no new political ground, the energy and optimism of the young president was self-evident. At the same time the letter raised a question. Why should a US president involve himself in an apparently intractable issue at a time when no urgent US interest was at stake? Wanting to feel sure that Kennedy was not acting out of some hidden motive which might be harmful to Egypt, Nasser asked his top advisers and ministers to submit written opinions. Some realized that the letter reflected a genuine wish to reduce tension in the Middle East. Others were inclined to see obscure plots, and wrote long reports. Mahmoud Fawzi, the foreign minister, described the Kennedy approach as 'a letter of temptation' and suggested that the US president was trying to put Egypt in a difficult position. The arguments over different interpretations continued for two months before Nasser sent a long-overdue reply.

Nasser's letter recognized that Kennedy was seeking to 'open doors of understanding', and analyzed the issues from Egypt's viewpoint, beginning with a comment on the British Balfour Declaration: 'One who did not possess gave a promise to another who did not deserve, and these two managed by power and deceit to deprive those who both owned and deserved.' The letter included a stinging rebuke for America's role in the creation of Israel, saying that President Truman had 'put all his weight . . . against the principles of liberty and democracy'. Kennedy was also reminded of a rhetorical question once asked by Truman: 'How many votes do the Arabs have in US elections?'

Israel, the letter continued, had been used by imperialism to divide and threaten the Arab world. Continued immigration had created pressures within Israel for expansion, leading to further aggression against Arabs. The Middle East faced a future 'full of reasons for turbulence'.

After further criticisms of missed opportunities in the past the letter expressed a wish for better relations with Washington. 'We will go on stretching out our hand to the American nation even if we receive no reply to our satisfaction.' Nasser concluded by reaffirming that Egypt was still ready to accept the UN partition plan of 1947.

After this reply Kennedy and Nasser and their aides began an intense correspondence which ran to ninety-two letters during the twenty-two months of the Kennedy administration. Although Kennedy did not live long enough to achieve his aims, the tone of US–Egyptian relations improved greatly. The Kennedy administration also sought to reduce Israeli–Egyptian tension by assuring President Nasser in writing that Israel was not developing nuclear weapons. Kennedy may have believed this himself, but he was misinformed. Egyptian intelligence had obtained confirmation of Israel's programme.

A military pact between Egypt, Syria and Iraq in April 1963 provided Ben-Gurion with a pretext for a further attempt to engage the US administration more directly. In a letter to the US president on 26 April the Israeli prime minister claimed that the three countries had made a secret agreement to recapture Palestine.* Israel believed it could defeat all three armies, but was not eager for such a contest. Ben-Gurion asked for a joint US–Soviet guarantee of regional security and a declaration that civil and military assistance would be denied to any Middle East country which refused to acknowledge any other neighbour in the region.

This was a way of asking Kennedy to be less generous with US food aid to Egypt – Washington had been supplying wheat since Nasser's quarrel with Moscow in 1958. Ben-Gurion's aim was to extract a political price for continuing the deliveries, but so long as Kennedy lived the policy remained unchanged.

The assassination of Kennedy on 22 November 1963 ended an interlude of fairly relaxed US–Egyptian relations. Egyptians realized as soon as Kennedy's death was announced and the vice president Lyndon Baines Johnson took the oath of office that US policy would change in Israel's favour. Johnson's attitude in 1956, when as Senate majority leader he opposed Eisenhower's decision to force Israel to leave Sinai, had never been forgotten.

Soon after his inauguration Johnson asked Egypt to allow US inspectors to see its nuclear facilities, rockets and military aircraft. Nasser refused. Johnson then requested Egypt to stop broadcasting

* For further details of this pact see pp. 143–4.

propaganda hostile to the United States. This was out of the question, as the demand for US inspections had already created turbulence in relations. Johnson next asked Egypt to mediate with Hanoi over the Vietnamese War, but as Cairo was now a prominent leader among Third World countries* Nasser naturally sympathized with the North Vietnamese. A further element in Johnson's policy was that Britain had announced that its forces east of Suez would be withdrawn by 1967, including those in the Persian Gulf. Britain's departure left the United States to hold the ring against Soviet expansion. Washington became more anxious than ever to see an anti-communist government in Cairo.

By Christmas 1963, when Johnson had been in office for only five weeks, the main drift of his policy was already unmistakable. Realizing that Israel now had much stronger US support, Nasser called an Arab summit to consider how to face the new challenge.

The immediate issue when the heads of state met in Cairo in January 1964 was Israel's intention to divert part of the waters of the river Jordan to irrigate the Negev desert, which would inevitably reduce water supplies to Jordan and Syria. Arab governments had repeatedly expressed their intentions to forestall the Israeli project by building their own diversion schemes further upstream. But lack of Arab unity had prevented these plans from being implemented, and in the meantime the Israelis had carried out all the civil engineering their scheme needed.

One of the reasons for Arab inaction was the near certainty that any project which pre-empted the Israeli scheme would be attacked by Israeli forces. A report by Arab chiefs-of-staff to the summit said that their armies would be unable to prevent such attacks.

Nasser called for a unified Arab river water authority to build and manage the diversion schemes, and for a unified Arab military command to coordinate defence against Israel. The heads of state accepted these ideas and appointed an Egyptian general to lead the unified command. The same meeting set up the Palestine Liberation Organization and named its first leader, Ahmed Shukairy.†

* In 1964 Egypt hosted an Arab summit, a Non-Aligned summit and an African summit.

† See pp. 298–9, 301, 303.

The immediate effect of these steps was to buy time. Syria had been considering unilateral attacks against Israel's river diversion scheme, which might have drawn the Arab world into a general war with Israel. After the Cairo summit Damascus stayed its hand, but Arab leaders knew that action could not be long delayed. Over the next year the unified command was put into effect, the PLO began organizing itself, and PLO military units were created under the overall Egyptian umbrella.

Meanwhile Egypt patched up its relations with Moscow, which had been cool since 1958. In May 1964 Nikita Khrushchev attended the inauguration of the first stage of the Aswan high dam, which was being built with Soviet loans. At the same time President Johnson implemented Israel's long-standing request to attach strings to US food sales. Contracts for US wheat deliveries to Egypt had been renewed regularly for six years, but in November 1964, when Cairo asked about supplies for 1965, there was no reply. Leaks from the US administration to the media made it clear that there would be no further renewal unless Egypt changed direction.

In November 1964 Nasser received an extraordinary assessment of Johnson's policies from Mohamed El-Kouny, Egypt's permanent representative at the UN. El-Kouny had been invited to a function in New York by Adlai Stevenson,* and had fallen into conversation with a group of other envoys, including Lord Harlech, the British ambassador. In the presence of Stevenson and four ambassadors, Harlech severely criticized the new president's belligerent style and policies. El-Kouny reported that far from defending Johnson, Stevenson seemed to approve of Harlech's remarks. The British ambassador began by talking about the Gulf of Tonkin incident, in which Vietnamese gunboats allegedly attacked US warships. After the incident Congress had given Johnson a mandate for military action against Vietnam. Harlech said he believed the Americans had faked the attack to provide a pretext for escalating US involvement in the war.†

Harlech then turned to El-Kouny and warned that Johnson's obses-

* Stevenson, grandson of a former US vice president, was the unsuccessful Democratic candidate in the 1952 and 1956 presidential elections, and was a leading spokesman for liberal reform.

† Harlech's opinion was proved correct, although the facts were not established until 1974.

sion with Vietnam would have consequences in the Middle East. The president wanted to concentrate totally on defeating Hanoi, without other regional distractions. Although irritated by recent events in the Middle East, he was unwilling to give these matters his personal attention. Harlech believed that Johnson saw Israel as the natural ally of the United States, and would entrust the management of the Middle East to the Jewish state while the US focused on south-east Asia.

When El-Kouny expressed scepticism, Harlech replied that Johnson had been bitterly critical of Kennedy's 'weak' handling of the Middle East, accusing his predecessor of being over-influenced by British-educated Middle East experts. Johnson thought that Egypt's influence in world affairs was becoming excessive in relation to its power. Harlech further predicted that even in the event of a major incident in the Middle East, Johnson would leave matters to Israel as far as possible. He foresaw the possibility of an Israeli attack against its neighbours, and said that Egypt could no longer expect the near-unanimous international support it had enjoyed during the Suez affair. Friends of Israel now occupied key posts in the Pentagon, the National Security Council and the CIA. The Israelis were openly boasting that they could have defeated Egypt single-handed in 1956 and were telling Johnson: 'Give us the tools and we'll finish the job.'

El-Kouny's report cautioned that Harlech had been exceptionally close to the Kennedy administration and was perhaps over-critical of Johnson. Nevertheless, Harlech was in a position to know, and clearly felt strongly about what he had said. Nasser carefully read and annotated the report on 6 November 1964, but found it hard to accept Harlech's analysis. Three years later the British ambassador was proved right.

One of the strangest Arab–Israeli episodes of the mid-1960s arose from the civil war which had broken out in Yemen three years earlier. The war was prompted by a power struggle following the death in September 1962 of Imam Ahmad, autocratic leader of the ancient Zaidi imamate, where the style of administration had changed little in centuries. The imam's son Badr inherited the leadership but was challenged by army officers who seized the main towns and declared a republic. A five-year conflict ensued between Badr's supporters, who were mainly tribal, conservative and opposed to change, and the revolutionaries, who wanted a more modern society. Egypt backed the revolution from the start, while Badr received support from the main conservative elements in the region, including the Saudi and Hashemite monarchies, oil companies, arms traders, intelligence organizations and the British colonial administration in Aden.

The Egyptian involvement was seen by Israel as an important opportunity. The more deeply Egypt became drawn into the fighting, the fewer Egyptian troops would be left facing Israeli forces across the international border in Sinai. Israel therefore offered to supply Badr's forces with arms, communication equipment and intelligence information. Soundings to establish whether conservative Arabs would accept this kind of cooperation from Israel were conducted by British MPs who had formerly belonged to the 'Suez group' in the House of Commons. The best-known member of the group was Julian Amery, who formed a committee to oppose what he called 'Nasser's expansion' in Yemen. Amery saw Egypt's involvement as a threat to the West's oil lifeline, and feared that if revolution took hold in Yemen it might spread to the oil-producing states. There was also the risk, the British group supposed, that an Egyptian–Yemeni alliance would give revolutionary regimes a stranglehold on the Red Sea, because of Yemen's position controlling the strait of Bab el-Mandeb at the southern end, and Egypt's control of the north.

Amery, who was secretary of state for air, and then minister for aviation, between 1960 and 1964, made contact with King Hussein of Jordan. The king discussed the Israeli offer with the Saudi royal family and added that the Shah of Iran was also interested in helping Badr's supporters. The Saudis saw the importance of the offer, and soon Israel found itself working in tacit cooperation with some of its Arab enemies against the revolutionaries.

Israel's contacts with French intelligence, which had been important during the build-up to the Suez crisis, were reactivated. Djibouti, on the African side of the Bab el-Mandeb strait, was then still a French colony, and Israel was able to arrange airbase facilities on the shores facing Yemen. The Israeli air force supplied food and ammunition to tribal forces supporting Badr, especially in the Gawl area, the costs of the operation being paid by oil states and companies. Israel achieved its aim of embroiling Egypt in a hopeless and exhausting struggle. At one point Egypt's commitment rose to 50,000 troops supported by air power, causing a depletion of strength in Sinai.

This link between Israel and Arab conservatives was the first breach in the taboo after the rise of Arab nationalism in the 1950s. The earlier cooperation between Israel and the Hashemites had been dormant for several years because of heightened Arab opposition to any form of contact (a side effect of the greater Arab self-awareness promoted by Nasser).

A new element entered the Arab–Israeli equation on 1 January 1965 when the Palestinian organization al-Fatah carried out a sabotage attack against Israel's civil engineering works on the Jordan. Fatah, meaning 'Victory' in Arabic, had been formed by Yasser Arafat and others immediately after the Suez affair.* There was no connection then between Fatah and the PLO, which was still under Egyptian guidance. The attack was of little military significance, but it marked a psychological beginning and was followed by events which slowly pushed Egypt towards the war which Nasser wanted to avoid. Fatah felt that Egypt and Syria had the potential to do battle with Israel but were absorbed in their own less urgent problems. The organization's aim was to draw the two countries into a confrontation with the Zionist state so that justice for the Palestinians would become the common Arab cause. This strategy was known as '*tawreet*', literally 'pulling the legs', but in this context implying 'dragging them feet-first'.

In November 1966 Egypt and Syria reached an agreement to coordinate their defences more effectively, and at the same time a Palestinian land mine blew up an Israeli patrol car. Israel then carried out an air raid against Al-Samu, a Jordanian town on the west bank, with heavy loss of life. The attack caused uproar and rioting and King Hussein restored order only with difficulty. Amid bitter recriminations, directed against Arab leaders almost as much as Israelis, many Palestinians called for immediate war against Israel.

Events spiralled out of control after an Israeli–Syrian air battle on 7 April 1967 in which seven Syrian MiG-21s were shot down. On 13 May the Soviet authorities informed Anwar Sadat, the Egyptian vice president, that Israel had mobilized ten to thirteen brigades on the Syrian border. Nasser felt that immediate deterrent action was necessary, and declared a state of emergency. Egyptian troops were

* Arafat and other founders of al-Fatah were working in Kuwait when they first came together. At the time of the 1965 attack the organization was based in Syria.

deployed in Sinai while Syria reinforced its frontiers. Israel responded with further troop deployments, and Nasser raised the stakes by requesting the withdrawal of the United Nations Emergency Force from Sinai. The UNEF departed on 18 May, leaving a vacuum where there had been an international buffer. U Thant, the UN secretary general, was later criticized for complying too readily with the Egyptian request, but he had little choice at the time.

Egypt's moves were meant to be interpreted as a strong warning, not as a declaration of war. Nasser still held back from the more provocative step of closing the Strait of Tiran.

Levi Eshkol, who had succeeded Ben-Gurion as prime minister in June 1963, sought assurances from Johnson, but Lord Harlech's prediction that Johnson would be unwilling to give his full attention to the Middle East now started to come true. Eight crucial days were lost with no approach by Johnson to Nasser, and little sign that Washington was trying to avert war.

With Israeli forces at a high state of mobilization and the US apparently standing back, Nasser decided that he could wait no longer. In a meeting with air force officers at the Abu Suweir base on 22 May he announced that the Egyptian navy was closing the Strait of Tiran to Israeli shipping. At the same time Egypt and Syria mobilized their armies. War was now highly probable, but not inevitable given prompt US or UN mediation. Nasser assured U Thant a few days later that he would not take pre-emptive action against Israel, and repeated this in a public speech.

Johnson's first approach to Nasser since the start of the crisis was written just before Nasser's 22 May announcement and did not arrive until the following day. The letter proposed mediation by Hubert Humphrey, the vice president, but the closure of the straits had created a new situation, and nothing came of this offer.

The Israelis now reminded Robert McNamara, the US defense secretary, of the aide-memoire which Dulles had given Israel in 1957 confirming that the US regarded the Strait of Tiran as an international waterway. Israel wanted an assurance that the US would use force if necessary to keep the strait open, but Washington would not commit itself.

Britain proposed that a multinational force of warships should sail through the strait to demonstrate that closure would not be tolerated.

Washington failed to come to a decision on this idea because no one could answer the question: 'What happens if there is a clash with the Egyptian navy?' Any such incident was sure to be seen by Johnson's critics in Congress as a replay of the Gulf of Tonkin affair. The president might be accused of seeking a pretext for US military intervention in the Middle East.

The delay in US decision-making exasperated the Israelis, who claimed that an Egyptian attack was imminent. A crucial meeting was held at the White House on 26 May between Johnson and Abba Eban, the Israeli foreign minister.* Eban wanted a clear statement that the United States would use force if necessary to keep the strait open; Johnson said he could only act with Congressional support and on a multilateral basis. At the same time he warned Israel not to initiate hostilities, and implied that Israel could not expect to be rescued by the US if it ignored this advice.

The Israeli cabinet felt that Johnson was not absolutely forbidding an Israeli attack, even if he was withholding US blessing. During the last few days before the June war the Israelis made strenuous efforts to establish whether they had correctly interpreted Johnson's mind. The president's attention was now divided between the Middle East, Vietnam and Democratic fund-raising efforts. Most of the people Johnson saw during that period were either strongly or broadly pro-Israel in their views, including Mathilde Krim, a wealthy contributor to the party, Abe Fortas, a Supreme Court judge, Walt Rostow, the national security adviser, and Rostow's brother Eugene, under-secretary of state. Many of Johnson's closest advisers felt that the US should not allow itself to be diverted from the Vietnamese conflict, and that Israel could handle any problems in the Middle East, just as Harlech had predicted.

The administration's replies to Israeli requests for clarification did nothing to remove the impression that Johnson was not saying 'no', or at least not strongly. Observers have differed as to whether this amounted to giving Israel a green light or an amber light. What can be said for certain is that the US did not show a red light. Israel was free to attack, but on its own responsibility.

* Eban had left his diplomatic career in 1959 to enter politics. He served as deputy prime minister from 1963–66 and as foreign minister from 1966–74.

At this point Nasser was under the impression that there was still time to avoid hostilities. U Thant sent him a message asking for a breathing space of two weeks, and hinting that the Israelis would go along with this: 'I appeal to you, Mr President, as I am appealing to Prime Minister Eshkol . . . to exercise the utmost restraint at this critical juncture.' The UN secretary general had just returned from a visit to the Middle East when he wrote the message, and it reached Nasser on 29 May, eight days before the Six Day War. U Thant said that the aim of the request was 'to allow the [Security] Council to deal with the underlying causes of the present crisis, and to seek solutions'.

At the same time the Soviet Union continued to urge restraint upon Egypt. On 27 May Nasser was awoken at 3 a.m. by a visit from the Soviet ambassador pressing him not to attack. On 3 June a secret telegram from the State Department to American ambassadors in Arab capitals said: 'You should not assume that the United States can order Israel not to fight.'

The cunning of an aggressor in concealing his intentions lies at the heart of military tactics. The deception which made possible Israel's surprise attack on 5 June 1967 depended on three complicated relationships, between Israel and the United States, between the US and the Soviet Union, and between Moscow and Cairo. At the crucial moment when Israel was preparing to attack, Cairo believed that both superpowers were actively trying to prevent war.

Simultaneous Israel strikes against seventeen Egyptian airfields on 5 June crippled the Egyptian air force in a few hours. Most of the 300 planes destroyed were on the ground when hit by Israeli bombs. There were failures of foresight and coordination on the Egyptian side. Even if Egypt had reason not to expect immediate attack, the level of tension warranted greater precautions than those taken. Egyptian and Syrian troops put up fierce resistance against Israeli invasion forces, but once Israel had established command of the air the battle was lost.

Washington initially assumed that Israel mainly wanted to neutralize the two strongest Arab countries, not realizing that it also planned to capture the entire part of Jordan west of the river. Two days before the war Levi Eshkol had been unable to sleep, and his wife asked why he was so restless. 'We are going to take it all,' he replied. 'Take what?'

she asked. 'Jerusalem,' he explained.* The Israelis tried to hide their thrust into Jordan until key positions had been captured, and went so far as to bomb a US intelligence-gathering ship which was monitoring Israeli military signals from international waters thirty kilometres off the Sinai coast in the Mediterranean. Egyptian signals staff picked up the last words of the ship's radio operator: 'Sons of bitches, they're Israelis!'

Six days later the victory was complete, with the whole of Sinai up to the Suez Canal under Israeli control, as well as east Jerusalem, the west bank, the Golan Heights and the Syrian town of Quneitra. Jordan, Egypt and finally Syria accepted UN ceasefire resolutions, and fighting stopped at noon on 10 June 1967. The Soviet Union and all East European states except Romania broke off diplomatic relations with Israel. The major oil producers announced an immediate embargo against the US, which had colluded with Israel, and against European countries which had given moral support to the aggressor.

Israel now set about trying to convert victory into political gains. Eshkol† believed that captured Arab lands and domination of the Suez Canal could be used as hostages to bring Egypt, Syria and Jordan to the negotiating table. The concept of exchanging land for peace was born, but the Israelis had no intention of withdrawing completely.

After the 1948 and 1956 wars Israeli leaders had been criticized by hardliners for not seizing strategically or religiously important areas when the opportunity was available. Eshkol told the Knesset on 12 June that Israel would not return to the pre-1967 lines. Unlike Ben-Gurion, who had been forced by Eisenhower to withdraw from Sinai after the Suez affair, Eshkol knew he had a friend in the White House. Johnson confirmed in a speech at Glassboro, New Jersey on 19 June that the US would not demand Israeli withdrawal without peace. The same speech set out principles for a comprehensive peace agreement which were later included in UN Resolution 242, the United Nations framework for peace.

Documents subsequently released under the US Freedom of

* From an interview conducted by Professor Michael Brecher, quoted in *Decisions in Crisis*.

† Israel had formed a national unity government just before the attack. Eshkol, who was widely considered too weak for wartime leadership, kept his post as prime minister, but Moshe Dayan, the new defence minister, had more influence.

Information Act show an important shift in US policy during this period. Before the June war Israel had been a friend of the US, but a small and dependent one. After the war, having proved itself in the regional conflict which mattered most to Washington after Vietnam, Israel became a full partner in a symbiotic relationship. The change was not understood in the Arab world until some time later, but Israel began testing the limits of its enhanced freedom within weeks. By the end of June Israel had incorporated the Arab part of Jerusalem within new municipal boundaries, a step just short of annexation.

The Arab world emerged from the conflict with the same mixture of humiliation, anger and frustration which had been experienced in 1948, but no longer felt helpless against Israeli power. After the first Arab–Israel war returning soldiers had told extraordinary tales of Israel's fighting methods. Two world wars had taught the Israelis the use of greater than necessary violence as a means of daunting the enemy. By 1967 the gap between the fighting experience of the two sides was narrower. Arabs now felt that Israel had won the June war because of superior planes, tanks and artillery. Soviet weapons had been no match for those of the United States, and Soviet diplomacy had persuaded Egypt and Syria not to strike first. These criticisms of the Soviet Union were overstated to cover hurt pride, but nevertheless they contained a basis of truth. Intense bitterness towards the US, Britain and most European countries swept through the Arab world. (France was exempted because President de Gaulle had moved French foreign policy away from the pro-Israeli line it had followed since 1948. Israel could no longer count on supplies of French Mirage fighters.)

Nasser faced the daunting tasks of restoring national self-confidence, rebuilding the armed forces and finding some new way to face Israel. One of his first actions was to fly to Saudi Arabia to complete negotiations begun two years earlier, enabling Egypt to withdraw its forces from Yemen. Meanwhile the Israelis, convinced that Egypt would be anxious to reopen the Suez Canal, waited for a diplomatic olive branch from Nasser. But no approach came. 'What was taken by force cannot be retaken but by force,' the Egyptian leader declared, and his words became an oft-repeated slogan.

What Nasser meant by 'force' was not another full-scale confrontation, which Israel might win, but a long low-intensity campaign of attacks, relying on the Israeli press to remind Jews that every lost life weakened the Zionist state. The Egyptian strategy was to show Israel the emptiness of victory without peace, and to keep a candle lit in the gloom of Arab morale.

The war of attrition, as the period from mid-1967 to October 1973 became known, began within two weeks of the end of the Six Day War. The 10 June ceasefire broke down by the end of the month in a struggle over points in the Sinai which the Israelis had failed to occupy in their rush to the canal on 8 June. After a famous battle for a position called Ras El-Esh in the early days of July the fighting settled into a continuous rhythm. Later, after the sinking of the Israeli destroyer *Eilat*, Israel retaliated by bombing the towns of Suez, Ismailia and Port Said, which became virtually hostages to Israel because of their proximity to the front, and thousands of residents fled. Eventually it was decided to evacuate them completely, which gave the Egyptian army greater freedom to react to Israeli aggression.

Israel could not easily use the war of attrition to gain international sympathy, as the fighting was taking place on Israeli-occupied Arab territory. Israeli leaders sought to divert attention from this fact by overstating Arab aims. Golda Meir* claimed during a meeting of the Socialist International in Vienna that Arabs had declared an intention to destroy the Jewish state through a two-phase strategy. The first was to recover lands lost in 1967, and the second to liberate territory occupied in 1948. Mrs Meir must have known better.

The Arab world unintentionally lent credence to Israel's propaganda by issuing a hardline statement during a summit in Khartoum in August 1967. A resolution adopted by Arab heads of state declared that there should be no peace with Israel, no recognition of Israel, and no negotiations – the 'three no's'. Israel used these refusals to make the Arab world appear unreasonable to US and European public opinion. In reality, the resolution was a way of putting a brave face on defeat and papering over inter-Arab differences. The summit participants agreed to end the oil embargo, at the request of oil-producing states, in return for an annual subsidy of £125 million to Egypt, £40 million to Jordan and £25 million to the PLO, the cost to be split between Saudi Arabia, Libya and Kuwait.

* Mrs Meir had been foreign minister from 1956–65 and then became secretary general of MAPAI (Workers' Party for the Land of Israel). In 1968 MAPAI merged with two other parties to form the Labour Party, with Mrs Meir as secretary general.

Only Syria, among Israel's immediate neighbours, was in a position to respect the 'three no's'. Nasser had indicated willingness to accept the fact of Israel's existence as far back as the Bandung Conference, when he accepted the UN partition plan, while Jordan had been involved as a silent partner in Israel's creation. King Hussein's participation in the June war had been a surprising break with the past. Under intense pressure from Palestinians, who sensed a long-awaited opportunity to regain their lands, the king flew to Cairo on 30 May and signed a defence pact with Egypt. Hussein paid dearly for this departure from the policy his grandfather had followed during the 1948 war, losing all the territory King Abdullah had gained west of the Jordan river.

A sense of responsibility for Hussein's plight was uppermost in Nasser's mind when the two men met privately after the Khartoum summit. Nasser was not unduly worried about the Israeli occupation of Sinai, feeling that Egypt would eventually recover its territory, but realized that Israelis would try to establish roots in the west bank. 'I am afraid that with time the Israelis may find an opportunity to fill the west bank with settlements and change the character of Jerusalem,' he told Hussein. 'Although we have refused to negotiate, you are an exceptional case. Go to the Americans, kiss their hands if necessary, find a way to negotiate. The important thing is to regain those territories before the Israelis change their character, even if you have to make a separate agreement with Israel.' When Hussein pointed out the risks this could entail, Nasser offered to provide political cover if news of contacts leaked out. Both men were taking great risks, as the taboo had never been stronger. Nasser thus gave moral authority to Hussein to ignore the spirit of the 'three no's', even if he did not suggest direct talks with Israel.

Authority from Nasser still carried great weight, despite the June setback. Extraordinary scenes during the summit had demonstrated that his ability to move the masses was undiminished. The vanquished leader was mobbed by vast crowds of cheering supporters in the streets of Khartoum, to the amazement of the Western media. 'Hail the Conquered', said the cover of *Newsweek* magazine. Nasser's morale was much boosted.

The Egyptian leader felt that Jordan could make a separate agreement with Israel but Egypt could not. Nasser had already refused an

Israeli offer to return the whole of Sinai to Egypt immediately in return for an Egyptian–Israeli peace agreement.

King Hussein flew to New York and had a secret meeting at the Waldorf Astoria hotel with Abba Eban, the Israeli foreign minister, and separate contacts with US officials. Hussein felt encouraged by Eban's attitude. In another meeting with Eban a week later in London, at the home of Julian Amery* in Eaton Square, the king realized that the foreign minister was more open and reasonable than most other members of the Israeli cabinet. Eban's views were in line with those of Levi Eshkol, who had assured Washington that Israel had 'no colonial ambitions'. American diplomacy after the June war was based on a false assumption that the attitude of the Israel prime minister and foreign minister was shared by the cabinet as a whole.

Efforts were now under way at the United Nations to draft a resolution dealing with the war. Israel would not accept wording which demanded withdrawal from 'all the occupied territories', while Arabs would accept nothing less. Israel said it was willing to give up most of the captured territory, but wanted prior Arab concessions for doing so. Withdrawal should form part of a general peace agreement, Israel insisted, while Arabs wanted total withdrawal for peace.

During sporadic discussions over a period of five months the Israeli delegation gradually became more intransigent, reflecting pressure from hardliners like Menachem Begin who were campaigning for the whole of biblical 'Eretz Yisrael' to be incorporated within Israel's borders. Instead of showing firmness, as the Eisenhower administration had done when Israel made similar demands after the Suez crisis, the Johnson administration adjusted its views to suit Israel.

Abba Eban told a US official on 26 October that pressure by the UN to return to the borders Israel had had before the June war would play into the hands of hardliners. The Americans assumed that the Israeli cabinet was thinking of minor adjustments to former armistice lines, and told the Egyptians that the changes would not be detrimental to Arab interests. King Hussein received such an assurance from Dean Rusk, the secretary of state, and then from Johnson at the White House on 8 November.

The first draft resolution, put forward by India and other countries,

* A Conservative Member of Parliament and a former minister.

was rejected by Israel because it called for withdrawal from 'all the territories'. The United States now tried to skirt round Israel's objections by using phrases which could be interpreted in different ways by different delegations. The US draft called for withdrawal of armed force (rather than armed forces) from occupied territory (rather than the occupied territories). The Arabs rejected this.

On 16 November Lord Caradon, Britain's permanent representative at the UN, submitted a draft which called for 'withdrawal of Israeli armed forces from territories occupied in the recent conflict'. This retained the deliberate vagueness of the American draft, but struck a finer balance between claim and denial. Arabs could claim that the resolution meant full Israeli departure from lands captured in the June war; Israelis could (and did) say that they had not been told to withdraw all forces from all occupied territories. The ambiguity depended upon the precisely imprecise use of English, making exact translation into other official UN official languages difficult. The Russian, Chinese, French and Spanish texts did not achieve the same vacuity.

Six days passed between Caradon submitting his draft and the UN Security Council adopting it, the delay reflecting doubts on the part of several countries and intense efforts by US diplomats to secure support for the British compromise. The Russians submitted a rival draft calling on Israel to withdraw to lines held prior to 5 June, but dropped it for lack of support. The British draft was passed unanimously, which was a surprise, as any nine members of the fifteen-nation Council would have been sufficient.

United Nations Resolution 242 has become one of the most controversial Security Council pronouncements ever made, a triumph of form over substance, giving an impression of agreement where none existed, creating more problems than it solved. Among those who understood its faults was Henry Kissinger, then a Harvard professor.

Israel was the real winner, even if it did not announce its acceptance of the resolution until three years later. The victory was not over the Arabs, who had always felt that words were less important than intentions, but over the Americans. The revelation that Washington had forgotten how to say no was never forgotten by hardliners. Menachem Begin put the lesson to use when he came to power a decade later.

Egypt accepted Resolution 242 despite many misgivings. The resolution called for 'termination of all claims or states of belligerency and respect for and acknowledgement of the sovereignty, territorial integrity and political independence of every state in the area and their right to live in peace within secure and recognized borders free from threats or acts of force'. These words contradicted two of the three 'no's' of the Khartoum summit: no recognition of and no peace with Israel. Furthermore, the resolution did not mention the Palestinians by name, referring only to 'the necessity . . . for achieving a just settlement of the refugee problem'. The assumption was that Resolution 242 dealt with the aftermath of the 1967 war, while other UN resolutions from 1947 onwards had addressed the Palestinian problem as a whole, including the refugee aspect. Nevertheless, the emphasis was very different to the Khartoum declaration, which called for 'adherence to the rights of the Palestinian people in their country'.

Cairo's acceptance of Resolution 242 caused panic among Palestinians, who feared that their most powerful ally was forgetting what had happened in 1948–49. Syria and Iraq had rejected the resolution, but without Egypt their influence was limited.

The Palestinians now realized that freedom would depend on their own efforts, and they struck their first significant blow in March 1968 when Fatah commandos fought alongside Jordanian troops at the battle of Karamah in Jordan, killing many members of an Israeli raiding force. Later in the year PFLP commandos attacked an El Al plane at Athens airport, leading to a long series of hijackings and bombings of aircraft owned by Israel and its Western friends throughout the 1970s and eighties.

All through 1968 American and European attention remained focused on south-east Asia. Anti-war riots shook American universities, European students demonstrated against Johnson's policies, America's world standing declined, and the Viet Cong's Tet offensive gained moral support in many countries. At the height of the unrest Johnson announced his decision not to run for re-election in November, which had implications for the Arab–Israel conflict. Not wanting to leave office under the cloud of a foreign policy disaster, Johnson belatedly turned his attention to the Middle East, hoping for a success during his remaining months at the White House. Walt Rostow, the US national security adviser, sent a message to Cairo via Amintore Fanfani, president of the Italian senate, pointing out that the decision not to run freed Johnson from the pressure of Washington lobbies. 'He is still president and he can make daring moves which can surprise many. He feels the stamp of Vietnam on his administration and would like to end by being the peacemaker in the Middle East,' Fanfani reported.

Johnson's record over the previous five years inhibited enthusiasm for such an initiative. Nasser felt it best to wait, hoping that the next president would show a more balanced approach. Secondly, the taboo remained too strong for any initiative involving contacts or negotiations with Israel. The war of attrition was a daily reminder that Egypt wanted nothing less than Israeli withdrawal, and the level of fighting was constantly increasing, with major artillery duels across the Suez Canal. Egyptian commandos undertook raids across the canal to carry out sabotage and to capture Israeli soldiers for interrogation. The information gained in this way eased problems caused by Egypt's inability to send reconnaissance planes over Israeli lines. The Egyptian air force remained too depleted for such a role, after the destruction of most of its aircraft in 1967. Further insights into Israel's activities were gained through a highly successful code-breaking effort by Egyptian intelligence. From small beginnings, eavesdropping on the emergency communications network of the Israeli police, Egyptian intelligence succeeded by 1968 in breaking the codes used by the Israeli army in Sinai and the Israeli navy in the Red Sea.

Morale was beginning to recover, and Egypt was ready to step up the war of attrition. The Egyptian National Security Council recommended a policy of trying to draw the Soviet Union into the conflict militarily as well as politically, arguing that Egyptian interests would best be served by elevating the conflict from the regional to the global stage.

Nasser realized, however, that Moscow's priorities were to avoid confrontation with the US and to bring about a negotiated Arab–Israeli solution. At the time (mid-1968) that looked a forlorn hope. Gunnar Jarring, a Swedish diplomat appointed by the UN, had been conducting talks on implementing Resolution 242 for six months, but was making no headway.

The United States, the Soviet Union, France and Britain were attempting to play a four-power role, and had asked Egypt and Jordan, the parties which accepted Resolution 242, for their positions on various points. After months of fruitless discussions it became clear that Washington was not happy with the four-power format, and did not want the Europeans to play a role. Hoping to break the stalemate, Moscow thought that bilateral US–Soviet talks might be more effective. During a meeting in July 1968 at a hunting lodge outside Moscow Leonid Brezhnev and Alexei Kosygin* asked Nasser whether he would object to such a course. He encouraged them to go ahead. 'You have *carte blanche* to talk with the Americans,' he told Brezhnev. 'I have only two conditions: I do not want to negotiate a peace agreement under the weight of occupation. Secondly, should you arrive at an understanding with the Americans, I should under no circumstances be asked to give up Arab territories as a reward for aggression. Anything short of that I am ready to accept.' 'Comrade, fair enough,' Brezhnev replied.

Nasser's intention was to let Moscow discover for itself, through contacts with Washington, that Israel was not prepared to withdraw. This, he hoped, would lead the Russians to the conclusion he had reached early in the crisis: Israeli withdrawal could be achieved only by making the price of occupation unbearably high. Perhaps Moscow would then understand the futility of talking of peace without also considering how to break Israel's intransigence.

Nasser argued that any solution would depend on two elements: power and reason. Gunnar Jarring's efforts represented the use of reason without power, the moral authority of the UN being inadequate for such an approach. Israelis would not say what territories they were prepared to give up, and Arabs refused to define 'peace' without knowing how much territory would be returned.

Nasser sought a better balance between the two elements. To assist the course of reason, Egypt was prepared to recognize the pre-1967 lines and to accept Israeli shipping in the Gulf of Aqaba. To gain greater military power, Egypt needed more Soviet arms. Brezhnev asked if this demand reflected the Arab tradition of revenge. Nasser replied that no man responsible for the lives of his compatriots would recklessly lead them to war for the sake of revenge.

This conversation led to an intensification of US–Soviet talks and

* At the time power was shared between Brezhnev, general secretary of the Communist Party, and Kosygin, the prime minister.

an increase in Soviet military supplies to Egypt. As Nasser had expected, the Russians soon discovered the reality of Israel's attitude.

Meanwhile the White House and the State Department were looking for another way of ending the Johnson administration with a success linked to the Middle East. Washington proposed an agreement with the Soviet Union on limiting arms sales to the region, and talks between Dean Rusk and Gromyko were held in October. Moscow realized that the US proposal would leave the Arabs at a disadvantage, and insisted that any deal should come after, not before, a political settlement of the conflict.

Finding this path blocked, Washington made one last effort. In November, just before the Republican victory in the presidential election, Rusk told Cairo that the US would support complete Israeli withdrawal from Sinai as part of a peace deal. This proposal remained far short of Egypt's demand for withdrawal from all occupied territories before anything else. The US president's last action connected with the Middle East was to authorize the sale of fifty American F-4 Phantom jets to Israel.

Few in Egypt were sorry to see Lyndon Baines Johnson leave office. Of the three US presidents Nasser had dealt with during the sixteen years since the 1952 revolution, the Texan Democrat had been the least constructive.

9

1956–1968
Other Peacemakers

The role of a third-party mediator has parallels in mountaineering, requiring skill, stamina and a head for political heights. Between the 1950s and the 1970s four great struggles loomed high in the peacemaking range: the Cold War, the Korean War, the Vietnam War and the Arab–Israel conflict. The first was restricted to superpower summiteers; Eisenhower and Dulles conquered the second; the third lay in impossible territory; but the fourth, like Mount Everest before 1953, seemed just within the bounds of possibility. Climbers on the slopes of statesmanship felt that bringing Arab and Jew together would be a peak of achievement.

During the Nasser years many of Europe's leading politicians brought their skill, conviction, humanity and ambition to the Middle East. Some, like presidents Tito of Yugoslavia and Ceausescu of Romania, and Chancellor Bruno Kreisky of Austria, had excellent contacts with both Egypt and Israel. Others, like President Charles de Gaulle of France, Chancellor Willy Brandt of West Germany and French premier Pierre Mendès-France, had personal prestige but weaker contacts. Below this level another stratum of politicians, such as Giorgio La Pira, assistant secretary of the Italian Communist Party, were well motivated but inadequately placed for such a role. In a category of his own was Nahum Goldmann, president of the World Jewish Congress, who represented Jews living outside Israel. Goldmann proved exceptionally persistent.

One of the early non-American attempts to initiate an Egyptian–Israeli dialogue was prompted by the arms race which followed the 1948–49 war. The build-up had begun in a small way during the

British mandate, when Hagana was armed with guns produced in semi-secret Zionist workshops. Despite its vital political role in the creation of Israel, the Truman administration gave Israel little military help, and went so far as to impose an arms embargo before and during the war.* After 1949 Israel turned to France as its major supplier, and built up a close relationship with Paris. The fact that senior Israeli and French officers were in regular contact was a contributory factor in the tripartite plot of 1956. After the Suez invasion the French government agreed to supply Israel with a 24-megawatt nuclear reactor. That project was already in hand in 1958 when General de Gaulle was called out of retirement to become prime minister of France, and later president. De Gaulle subsequently tilted French policy in favour of the Arabs, but in 1958 his priority was to extract France from the Algerian War. Israel's nuclear programme had already started, and a reactor had been under construction at Dimona since 1957.

While this was under way Ben-Gurion approached Nahum Goldmann and asked him to raise $400 million, a huge sum at that time, from the Jews of the world. Ben-Gurion wanted the money in the form of a single-payment gift to Israel, to be used for 'national security'. The request disturbed Goldmann, who feared that Israel was selling its soul to buy an illusory form of security. In a meeting in November 1958 Goldmann and President Tito discussed the psychological factors behind Ben-Gurion's request. Goldmann quoted the Israeli prime minister as saying that since the Suez invasion the United States had reduced its public contacts with Israel, not wanting to anger the Arabs. Israel felt like a lonely illegitimate child, supported by its father in secret but rarely acknowledged in public.

Tito wrote to Nasser on 15 November passing on Goldmann's remarks, and suggested that Egypt should accept some form of contact. 'Goldmann tells me that he is afraid that maybe what Ben-Gurion means by this vague phrase about "national security" is that Israel is about to enter into a nuclear programme with high financial and moral costs.' According to Goldmann, the Jews of the world were anxious to see Israel at peace with its neighbours. If Arabs agreed to contacts

* During the war Washington threatened to lift the embargo on arms sales to Israel if Britain unleashed the Arab Legion against Israel. This was one of the reasons for the tight restraints which Britain imposed on King Abdullah.

with Israel, world Jewry would feel justified in refusing to finance Israel's nuclear weapons research. 'I thought, my friend, of telling you what I heard, leaving it to you to act as you wish,' Tito wrote. 'If you ask me as a friend, I would say: "Don't leave Goldmann's hand hanging in the air."'

In reply, Nasser pointed out that Israel's sense of isolation was self-inflicted. He had considerable admiration for Tito, but the taboo remained too strong for any such contacts.

Israel's nuclear programme went ahead, and the Dimona reactor was commissioned in 1963. It became the basis of a research programme whose participants included Edward Teller, 'father' of the first US hydrogen bomb. According to reports in the US media two decades later, James Angleton, counter-intelligence chief of the CIA, was in charge of the weapons project.

Egypt reacted to this development by setting up its own research facilities in the hope that it would eventually be in a position to match Israel's efforts. An atomic energy agency was established, and a programme of rocket development which had begun before the revolution was accelerated.*

Soon after Goldmann's unsuccessful approach, Tito and Jawaharlal Nehru, prime minister of India, held another meeting with Nasser. The Yugoslavian leader, looking for ways of reducing bitterness, took Nasser to task for saying that Arabs wanted to 'throw Israel into the sea'. 'I have never said that in my life,' Nasser protested. 'Are you sure?' Nehru asked, unconvinced. The remark had been frequently repeated by the Israeli media and was widely believed.

A committee consisting of senior officials from Yugoslavia, India and Egypt was set up to sift through all public remarks by Nasser and Egyptian ministers. After three months they found no trace of the alleged comment, but they did come across an interview which Abdul Rahman Azzam Pasha, secretary general of the Arab League, had given to the Voice of the Arabs radio station in 1948, before the proclamation of the state of Israel. Azzam Pasha was asked what would happen to the Jews if the Arabs refused to accept the creation of a Jewish state.

* In 1968 a ship carrying 200 tons of uranium to Italy was hijacked by Israeli agents, greatly increasing Dimona's supply of fissile material. During the Arab–Israeli war in October 1973 Golda Meir was reported to have ordered some Israeli bombers to be fitted with nuclear weapons on a standby basis.

He replied: 'They came by sea, and they can return by sea.' If this was the origin of the phrase, its transformation into a threat to throw Israel into the ocean was a remarkably successful piece of disinformation. As a result of constant repetition the phrase became widely associated with Nasser, contributing to an impression in the US and Britain that he held extreme views.

In the autumn of 1961, when President Kennedy was attempting to ease tension in the region, Goldmann decided to try again. His timing failed to take account of events in the Arab world. In September a military coup in Syria had brought opponents of Nasser to power in Damascus, resulting in a decision by the new government to leave the United Arab Republic. Nasser, who had devoted much of his energy to Arab nationalism, was deeply dispirited by this development but saw no point in trying to prevent the divorce. Realizing that Nasser's prestige had suffered a blow, Tito and Nehru decided to pay a morale-boosting visit to Egypt. This created an opening for Goldmann, who persuaded them to take another message to Nasser.

Goldmann's suggestion was that if Arabs felt unable to talk to the Israeli government, they could see representatives of world Jewry instead. In effect Goldmann was proposing himself as a middle man, in his capacity as leader of the World Jewish Congress. Nehru, a conciliator by nature, was in favour of Goldmann's proposal, but Nasser refused, commenting to friends that Arabs would think he was softening his stand at a moment of weakness. Once again, Goldmann's proffered hand was left hanging.

Eighteen months later the pendulum of Arab unity swung the other way. A coup in Iraq in the spring of 1963 brought a government led by the Ba'ath Party to power, and Colonel Abd el-Salam Aref, who had long proposed unity with Egypt, became president. Soon afterwards the Syrian government fell and was replaced by an alliance of the Syrian wing of the Ba'ath Party and supporters of Nasser. The two new governments approached Nasser proposing a three-nation federation, which was what the Egyptian leader had always wanted. The looser links with Yemen were to continue, and newly independent Algeria was seen as a kindred spirit.* The new entity would thus be

* The Algerian war ended with an agreement with France in March 1962. After a referendum on independence in July, Ahmed Ben Bella became prime minister in September and president in 1963.

the kernel of a vast area of Arab unity, and perhaps the first step towards a wider federation. Nasser was now torn between his desire for Arab unity and a wish to avoid repeating the hasty marriage with Syria of 1958 and its equally sudden divorce in 1961. His deliberations were overtaken by events, because the Ba'ath Party in Syria began suppressing pro-Nasser groups, and this brief opportunity for unity was lost, with the exception of a military alliance between Egypt, Syria and Iraq. The alliance alarmed Ben-Gurion and resulted in an Israeli approach to Kennedy in April 1963.*

Goldmann made another attempt to reduce Arab–Israeli tension in 1965 after a strange incident at an Arab summit. At the time the Johnson administration was shifting US policy away from the relatively balanced line Kennedy had followed and towards a clear pro-Israeli stance. With the risk of war growing the Arab League held several meetings to decide what to do. Pressure from the Arab masses to stand firm against Israel was strong, but Nasser did not want war unless or until Arab military strength was sufficient to ensure victory.

The gap between public expectations and military realities tempted some Arab leaders to indulge in tough but unrealistic talk. There was a tendency to make bellicose remarks during the supposedly secret proceedings of Arab summits, as it was known that leaks would ensure that everything was reported in the Arab press.

At a summit held in Alexandria in September 1964 the Syrian delegation seemed bent on outbidding all others in warlike statements. General Amin El-Hafiz, who later became head of state, said that Arab leaders should not be wasting time talking about issues like the division of water resources. The only subject worthy of their attention was the liberation of Palestine, and he was amazed that 'some leaders' (meaning Nasser) were hesitating.

Nasser replied: 'Very good, Hafiz. Now tell me how.' El-Hafiz started to outline an elaborate plan of attack, but Nasser, realizing how this would be reported, quickly stopped him by referring the matter to a committee.

A year later the Syrians requested another summit, which was held in Casablanca. Nasser arrived to find a worried-looking King Hassan of Morocco waiting for him at the airport. The king had discovered

* See p. 120.

that El-Hafiz was planning to call on General Ali Ali Amer, chief-of-staff of the United Arab Command, to present the Syrian proposal during the main session, when dozens of aides and advisers would be present. The details were bound to leak to the media and to Israel.

With Nasser's agreement, King Hassan called a closed session of heads of state, each accompanied by only one aide. General Amer distributed handwritten documents, to emphasize secrecy, and pointed out that the contents should be seen as an exercise in 'imaginative thinking'. The Syrian plan involved ten infantry brigades, one mechanized brigade, ten battalions of paratroopers, sixteen squadrons of fighter-bombers, a ring of airbases, and a detailed arrangement for sharing the costs. King Hassan immediately said that the paper was unacceptable even as a theoretical exercise, and urged the heads of state to turn to other subjects. Nothing more was heard of the matter until it leaked to the Israelis.

Nahum Goldmann initially thought, when he heard of the Syrian document, that so preposterous a plan could only be a fake. Hoping to avert an unnecessary scare in Israel, he asked Tito to obtain a statement from Nasser that no such plan had been contemplated. Nasser was considerably embarrassed at having to explain to Tito that the document was genuine but had never been taken seriously. Tito wondered how any document considered at summit level could be less than serious.

The document also reached Moscow, and Alexei Kosygin sent Nasser a letter of reproof. While understanding how Arab summits were conducted, Kosygin felt the document had been a political gift to the Israelis, helping them to mobilize American decision-makers against the Arabs.*

The American preoccupation with the Vietnam War increased the scope for European peace initiatives during the vital period between 1965 and June 1967. At the time no united Western European approach was feasible because of wide foreign policy differences between Britain and France. De Gaulle considered Britain to be an American captive,

* This incident led to a Soviet attempt at peacemaking a year later. Kosygin had recently brought India and Pakistan together using principles which became known as the 'Tashkent Formula', and wanted to try a similar approach to solve the Arab–Israeli conflict. Nasser felt that one superpower in the peacemaking business was more than enough, and persuaded Kosygin to desist.

and wanted any European approach to be led by France with support from other EEC members.* He disagreed with US policy on a wide range of issues, including the Arab–Israel conflict, and was shifting French policy towards a somewhat pro-Arab stance. Nasser felt that de Gaulle's interest was worth exploring and sent his war minister General Abdul-Hakim Amer on an official visit to France. 'We should have a bridge open to Western Europe and not appear to be with the USSR alone, even if such a bridge needs to be invented,' Nasser said.

A meeting between de Gaulle and General Amer at the Elysée Palace on 11 October 1965 carried these ideas forward. De Gaulle spent two hours asking Amer how Egypt thought the conflict might be brought to an end, and then set out his own views. He understood Arab fears of Israeli desires for expansion, and said he had warned many of Israel's leaders against turning Israel into a military garrison society. In de Gaulle's view, the Arab–Israeli conflict suited Washington well, allowing Johnson to use Israel to guard US interests in the Middle East. The Americans therefore had no interest in peace, and the British, who were trying to conceal their weakness through hypocrisy, would not step out of line with Washington.

De Gaulle felt that a French-led initiative by Continental Western Europe could solve the dispute. The French president knew the Middle East well as a result of his World War II experience, which included long stays in Syria and Lebanon and a period in Algiers, which became a base for rallying Free French forces in various French colonies.† He felt that this had given him an understanding of Arab sentiment, but also thought that Arabs should recognize that Jews had suffered greatly during the war, even if their plight was not of Arab making.

De Gaulle asked General Amer to tell Nasser that France was ready to help, but needed to know what kind of solution Egypt was prepared to accept. The Egyptian reply should be clear and precise, he insisted.

Nasser considered de Gaulle's suggestion but felt it lacked an essential element. Europe and France had no leverage with Israel, and Nasser

* The European Economic Community was established in 1958 as a six-nation trading group with federal aspirations. Britain did not join until 1973, and attempts to coordinate foreign policy were delayed until the late 1980s.

† After moving to London in 1940 following the fall of France and organizing Free French forces, de Gaulle became co-president of the French Committee of National Liberation, based in Algiers.

felt no need to confide precise negotiating positions to anyone, even someone as important as de Gaulle, who was not in a position to secure Israeli concessions.

After months without receiving a reply de Gaulle sent his friend André Malraux, a prominent intellectual and the minister for culture, to see Nasser. Their meeting began with a discussion of Middle East politics but drifted into the irresistible subject of ancient Egyptian civilization. Malraux remarked that the country which had invented eternity could wait for a solution.

De Gaulle made a second attempt immediately after the 1967 war, and on this occasion offered a different proposal. In a meeting on 22 June with Mahmoud Riad, Egypt's foreign minister, he said he was sure Israel had started the fighting. (Before the 5 June attack de Gaulle had appealed to both Arabs and Israelis to show restraint, adding that France would stand against any party which fired the first shot.) De Gaulle felt that Washington regarded the outcome of the war as an American triumph, because of its support for Israel, and thought that this attitude was a way of diverting attention away from the impending US defeat in Vietnam.* He urged that management of the Middle East crisis should not be left to the US, because any American solution would be on Israel's terms. France had already proposed a four-power summit consisting of the US, the Soviet Union, France and Britain to discuss the Middle East. Washington was against this idea, while Moscow seemed blind to the opportunity it offered. De Gaulle thought the Kremlin was full of stiff bureaucrats shorn of imagination. Part of the reason for US opposition and lack of Soviet interest was that Johnson and Kosygin had held a summit at Glassboro, New Jersey two days earlier, and immediately before this meeting Johnson had made a speech setting out the principles he considered essential for a Middle Eastern settlement. The way these principles were formulated showed a pro-Israeli bias and ignored the origins of the conflict.

De Gaulle decided to continue pressing for a four-power summit, thinking that the two superpowers could not monopolize the search for a solution indefinitely. If such a summit were held it should consider not just the outcome of the battle but the causes of the war. With

* At the time the US administration appeared confident of victory in Vietnam, but de Gaulle realized that this was false optimism.

that in mind, de Gaulle wanted to know what Nasser's attitude would be. He reminded Riad that Egypt had not replied to the French request two years earlier for a clear position statement. The difficulties Nasser and other Arab leaders faced in formulating a position were understandable, but the four-power idea offered a political advantage. De Gaulle thought that Arab leaders would find it less difficult to persuade their people to accept a solution which appeared to be imposed by the world's four main powers.

The French president's idea that Washington and Moscow were together monopolizing the search for a solution was not quite right. The two superpowers were mainly interested in managing the Middle East situation in such a way as to avoid conflict with each other. A secret briefing note prepared for Johnson's meeting in Glassboro said that the main point the US president should try to find out from Kosygin was whether Moscow was ready to reduce tension.* 'Do they [the Soviets] want to cool it off, or heat it up again?' the note asked, and went on to discuss tactics for the summit: 'He'll talk withdrawal; we want withdrawal to peace, not to June 4 [positions].' Emphasizing the need to coordinate with Moscow, the note continued: 'We will match our policy to theirs. We have absolutely no desire for another arms race, nor do we seek any "confrontation" with them. We don't think the Middle East is a promising place for either of us to play such games in – the players are too unpredictable. Moreover, we recognize that they can't make a 180-degree turn overnight, nor seem to abandon friends like Nasser – dangerous, unreliable and ineffective though Nasser has proved. But every move toward peaceful and constructive positions will get full understanding from us.'

These words, read more than a quarter of a century after they were written, give an impression that the two superpowers were on an equal footing in the Middle East. The true picture was one of immense US military, diplomatic and economic supremacy, a disparity which Arabs sensed at an early stage. Despite Soviet bravado about superpower parity, even Brezhnev was well aware of the gap, though he never acknowledged it directly. He preferred to talk about the defects of

* The note, dated 22 June 1967, was prepared by McGeorge Bundy, then president of the Ford Foundation, who had been Johnson's special adviser on the Middle East until 1966. It was declassified in 1993.

US presidents and the shallowness of US understanding. One of his favourite themes was that some presidents were adventurers, and some warmongers, but the US lacked understanding of the horrors of war, never having experienced a foreign invasion. The Soviet Union knew what it was to live under fire in devastated cities, or as refugees escaping from invading armies.

Anwar Sadat first noticed the chip on the superpower shoulder in 1968, while accompanying Nasser on a visit to Moscow. After the first session of talks Sadat sought out Nasser at 'Hospitality House Villa No 1', in Lenin Hills, and walked with him to the garden. Standing under a shady cherry tree Sadat whispered: 'Mr President, they feel inferior to the Americans.' Nasser replied: 'This is a late discovery. I realized it on my encounter with them in 1958.'

As much as Egypt valued Soviet support, the weakness of Moscow's position and its lack of influence with Israel were serious disadvantages. Brezhnev frequently reminded Arabs that the USSR would not expose itself to any confrontation which might lead to nuclear war with the United States. Moscow made no secret of the fact that any Arab–Israel solution would require US help, and openly encouraged Arab leaders to try to engage Washington in discussions. Kosygin argued that as US interests in the Middle East, including oil, pipelines, vital sea lanes and investments, were located in Arab countries rather than in Israel, the US would eventually have to come to terms with Arab governments. Israel, on the other hand, was an economic burden to the US.

The Soviet prime minister, like Khrushchev before him, thought that ties between Arabs and the US benefited from 1300 years of contacts between Arab and Western culture. Admittedly that shared history included the Crusades, centuries of rivalry and subsequently British, French and Italian colonialism, but even these negative periods tended to strengthen similarities between the two worlds. This Arab–Western cultural affinity naturally made Soviet leaders suspect that the Arab–Soviet relationship was a second-best arrangement from the Arab point of view, and a poor substitute for the friendship with the West which Arabs had never managed to achieve.

Nasser was once asked what he thought of the writings of Karl Marx, and replied that while he was not a Marxist, some of the ideas could in some cases be 'a fertilizer to the national experience'. Annoyed by the remark, Khrushchev said to Nasser: 'I hope you do not consider us a sort of manure!'

During the last year and a half of the Johnson era the Arab world came to terms with the dilemma left by the 1967 war. The United States had been the political and financial agent of Israel's victory, and was beginning, from 1968, to become its arms supplier.* The United States was also more powerful on every level than the Soviet Union. The Arabs accordingly believed that the US was the only country capable of persuading Israel to be reasonable in a negotiated settlement. This belief was shared by revolutionaries and traditionalists, rulers and masses alike, in all Arab capitals. No matter that Washington had demonstrated unswerving support for Israel, no matter the ambivalent or negative attitude towards Nasser shown by two of the last three US administrations; the Arabs were ready for Johnson's successor to take a leading role in solving the crisis. Thus while Richard Nixon inherited a Middle East filled with tensions which could have been avoided, he also found a readiness to listen to US initiatives.

* In the 1967 war the Israeli air force consisted mainly of Mirage fighter-bombers. France's subsequent refusal to continue supplying Mirages resulted in the Israeli air force being re-equipped with American Phantoms.

10

The Rogers Plan

The inauguration of Richard Nixon as president in January 1969 brought further changes in US foreign policy. Few American Jews had voted for Nixon, and the new president initially leaned towards the traditional State Department view that the US should be even-handed in the Middle East. William Rogers, the secretary of state, was given considerable freedom on Middle East policy at first, while Nixon concentrated on East–West affairs and the Vietnam War.

The intention, which soon broke down, was that Henry Kissinger, the national security adviser, should have little to do with the Arab–Israeli conflict. Nixon thought that Kissinger's Jewishness would be a disadvantage in any Middle East negotiations,* and Kissinger himself was inclined to agree.

Rogers strongly believed that peace in the Middle East was essential to American interests, and wanted to seek a comprehensive Arab–Israeli agreement. Another group of officials saw the conflict as an aspect of superpower relations, and wanted that perspective to dictate US policy. Henry Kissinger was the leading exponent of the second group. In his view, US interests lay with Israel so long as Egypt and Syria remained close to Moscow.

During the early months of the administration an attempt was made to coordinate Arab–Israeli policy with the Soviet Union, as a practical example of Nixon's policy of East–West détente. American officials held frequent meetings with their Soviet counterparts between spring and autumn 1969, with the aim of producing joint US–Soviet principles for a peace agreement. The sticking point was that the US and

* Nixon said this himself to Hafez Ismail, the Egyptian national security adviser, in a meeting at the Oval Office in February 1971.

Israel insisted on a peace treaty as a condition for withdrawal, while the Arabs did not want to negotiate peace under the weight of occupation.

The change of presidency was seen in Cairo as an opportunity to make good the damage US–Egyptian relations had suffered during the Johnson years. Nixon had been Eisenhower's vice president, and therefore a party to the pressure which the US put on Israel to leave Sinai in 1956. While out of office during the Kennedy and Johnson administrations Nixon had visited Egypt in 1963, and created a favourable impression by expressing regret for the Eisenhower–Dulles decision not to help Egypt build the high dam. It was 'agony', Nixon said after visiting Aswan, to see a monument to Egyptian–Soviet friendship at the dam.

An opportunity for Egypt to renew the relationship arose when Eisenhower died in March 1969, two months after Nixon had taken office. Nasser decided to send Dr Mahmoud Fawzi to the funeral, and afterwards Fawzi stayed to assess the administration's views on the Arab–Israel conflict. Nixon went beyond the usual courtesies in welcoming Fawzi and paying compliments to Nasser, but little of substance emerged either from the president or his national security adviser. Fawzi returned to Cairo feeling pessimistic, with little to report but generalities, and this contributed to a feeling in Cairo that nothing was moving.

Meanwhile the war of attrition was steadily escalating. The Egyptian artillery, which had a long tradition of high efficiency, shelled Israeli targets on the east bank of the Suez Canal on a daily basis. The Israelis replied, but did not get the better of the duels. Egyptian cities near the canal were now deserted, leaving Israel with few civilian targets within artillery range. Determined that Egyptian civilians should feel the effects of the war, Israel bombed targets deep inland, including a Nile river barrage at Naj Hammadi. Had Israel succeeded in destroying the barrage a quarter of a million acres would have been flooded. The strain of the unremitting crisis contributed to a heart attack Nasser suffered in September 1969.

Another Israeli 'deep penetration' attack later in the year was directed against Zafaran, a coastal village on the Gulf of Suez. In this raid Israelis landed with two helicopters, seized a radar station, and took parts of it away with them.

Unable to reach agreement with Moscow on a joint initiative, secretary of state Rogers decided in late autumn to put forward his own ideas. He suggested that Gunnar Jarring should conduct talks aimed at reaching two package agreements, one between Israel and Egypt, the other between Israel and Jordan. The principles he proposed for the Israel–Egypt agreement were Israeli withdrawal 'as part of a package settlement', cessation of the state of war, secure and recognized borders, demilitarized zones and special security arrangements in Gaza and Sharm El-Sheikh, freedom of navigation through the Strait of Tiran, Egypt to permit Israel to use the Suez Canal, 'a just settlement of the refugee problem' (meaning the Palestinians), and mutual respect for sovereignty. Finally, it was proposed that the agreement should be deposited with the UN, endorsed by the Security Council, and should be binding on both sides. Most aspects of the Palestinian problem were to form part of the parallel Israel–Jordan agreement. The media described this as the 'Rogers Plan',* but 'framework' would have been a more accurate description, as Rogers had suggested what should be done but not how agreement could be reached.

The framework was rejected in indignant tones by Golda Meir's government,† which accused Washington of seeking to appease the Arabs by imposing a solution upon Israel. The Soviet and Egyptian positions were discussed at talks in Moscow between Brezhnev and three Egyptian ministers.‡ After the Israeli rejection there seemed little point in pursuing the secretary of state's proposal. Moscow issued a formal rejection while Egypt made no further response.

In addition to the Israeli rejection, a further reason for the failure of the Rogers Plan was division within the US administration. President Nixon's attitude was conditioned by fears of negative public reaction, and he went so far as to tell American-Jewish leaders privately that the Rogers Plan did not have his full backing. Kissinger actively opposed the plan, arguing that Rogers was rewarding Egypt for its links with Moscow and punishing Israel for being loyal to Washington. He suggested a totally different policy: the US should delay any settle-

* The original name was the 'Joint US–USSR Working Paper, Fundamental Principles', but that was before the Soviet Union decided not to support the framework.

† Golda Meir had become prime minister of Israel in March 1969 following the death of Levi Eshkol.

‡ The Egyptian representatives were General Mohamed Fawzi, minister of war, Mahmoud Riad, foreign minister, and Anwar Sadat, vice president.

ment of the Arab–Israel conflict to make Arab countries realize that the Soviet Union alone was incapable of securing Israeli withdrawal.

These frictions showed that the original Nixon–Kissinger decision to give Rogers a free hand in Middle East affairs was beginning to break down. Kissinger was now too strongly opposed to the secretary of state's ideas to remain silent, and at the same time Nixon was more sensitive to American-Jewish attacks. The Jewish lobby had proved its ability to influence a wide spectrum of American opinion, not just the Democrats. The pressure to supply twenty-five Phantoms and 100 other planes which prime minister Golda Meir had requested was becoming uncontainable.*

Even without the extra aircraft, the Israeli air force was already causing immense damage, raising fears that supersonic fighter-bombers might succeed in penetrating air defences around the Aswan dam, destroying Egypt's most precious economic asset. During a visit to Moscow in January 1970 Nasser repeated earlier requests for better defences against low-flying tactics, and also asked Soviet forces to take responsibility for the air defence of the Egyptian interior. Moscow agreed, and Soviet missile systems were quickly deployed around the dam and other sites, followed soon afterwards by deliveries to Egypt of large quantities of military equipment. Moscow also sent military instructors and Soviet pilots to substitute for Egyptian air force personnel who were undergoing training. The pilots were to complete their training in six months and return to take over the defence of the Egyptian interior. On 18 April Israeli control command picked up and recorded communications between Soviet pilots aboard military aircraft scrambling from the base of Minya to engage an Israeli raiding formation. Meanwhile artillery duels across the canal reached a new intensity, with immense damage and casualties.

These developments lifted the tension from the regional to the superpower level. Fearing that Moscow was about to establish permanent bases in Egypt, changing the balance of power, Washington hurried to defuse the crisis. Joseph Sisco, assistant secretary of state under Rogers, was sent to Egypt in April 1970 to ask what sort of agreement Nasser might accept. Nasser welcomed Sisco and publicly invited the

* Golda Meir requested the aircraft during talks with Nixon in September 1969. Nixon did not commit himself at the time.

Americans to make another proposal. In a speech on 1 May Nasser made an open appeal to Nixon to follow one of two courses: either to make a sincere effort to find a political solution, or to stop arming Israel. If the US failed to make such a choice it would be considered an accomplice in the occupation of Arab territory.

Nasser's speech prompted Israel to make a further attempt to initiate talks with Cairo. Gideon Rafael, director general of the Israeli Foreign Ministry, sought the help of the Romanian government to convey a message to Nasser. The Romanian deputy foreign minister flew to see Nasser on 17 May and explained that Israel felt the peace process initiated by Resolution 242 was being taken over by the two superpowers. The Americans were beginning to interfere in Israel's internal affairs, and there was a growing fear that Washington and Moscow would do a deal over the heads of the parties to the conflict.

Rafael told the Romanians that Israel was prepared to discuss all issues with Egypt without preconditions, and would make a new offer once negotiations began. Israel had originally been opposed to repeating negotiations of the type held in Rhodes after the 1948–49 war, but was now prepared to accept that model.

The Romanian minister also conveyed a message from the Israeli government to President Nasser:

> The problem is a matter of misunderstanding. The Arabs believe that Israel wants territorial expansion by using power. At the same time the Israelis believe that the Arabs want to destroy it as a state. That historic misunderstanding cannot be left as it is and should be put to a test, and tested by the parties themselves, who should not wait for a solution from outside. The United States and Soviet Union control the situation in the region, but we are the ones who are paying with our blood.

Rafael made many additional points, of which three were important. Firstly, Israel would not take measures which might change the Jewish nature of the country. This meant that there was no plan to annex sizeable areas of Palestinian land, because that would dilute the Jewishness of Israel with large numbers of additional Arabs. Secondly, making the first point more explicit, Israel had no intention of annexing the occupied territories. This was so crucial that Rafael produced a note from his pocket and read it aloud in English to the Romanians.

Thirdly, Israel would offer solutions on all issues, but did not want to show its hand in advance of negotiations.

Nasser was also given a personal note from President Ceausescu of Romania saying that he thought the Israelis might be serious about this approach. After some reflection Nasser said he doubted Israel's sincerity because a majority in the Israeli cabinet was known to favour annexation of a large part of the occupied territories. The aim of the approach, he suspected, was to draw Egypt into contacts, which would then be leaked to the press, fanning the dispute between Egypt and the Arab world. Once Egypt had been isolated from other Arab countries, Israel would be able to dictate peace terms. Nasser expressed amazement that while Egypt declared its position openly, Israel refused to make an offer until talks started. 'They are keeping their options open and only dropping hints to lure us to the negotiating table,' he said.

Egypt's aim was total Israeli withdrawal from territories occupied in 1967, including east Jerusalem. No solution which left Jerusalem as a Jewish city would be acceptable. Egypt was ready to implement UN resolutions in full provided Israeli forces withdrew and the refugee problem was solved. However, time was against a peaceful solution because of the growing humiliation caused by Israeli occupation.

Nasser recalled that Nahum Goldmann had made numerous attempts to achieve talks with Egypt, using various intermediaries including President Tito. The Romanian minister then disclosed that Bucharest had checked Goldmann's credentials and discovered that he had no authority to speak for the Israeli government.

As the meeting ended Nasser said: 'We want a peaceful solution, but I don't think it is obtainable now. And I don't think we are ready for negotiations with Israel, either open or secret.' He also felt that Israel was trying to drive a wedge between Cairo and the Arab oil-producing countries which were paying an annual subsidy to the Egyptian economy. 'I know that there must be a solution, and I am able and ready to convince my people of it, but I don't believe that the way to go about it is to do anything secret.' Nasser implied that the situation might be different if the Arabs received clear assurances about Israeli intentions concerning withdrawal.

The heart of the problem was now apparent. Both sides had strong reasons to sue for peace, but the taboo made direct contacts perilous for any Arab leader. This explained the Arabs' insistence on knowing what the Israelis were prepared to offer before entering talks, something which Western countries never properly understood. The Israelis argued that there was little point in negotiations if they had to state their bottom line in advance. The same problem blighted many subsequent attempts at negotiation.

Golda Meir made another effort on 26 May to break the deadlock by announcing that Israel accepted Resolution 242. This decision was strongly attacked by Menachem Begin and the GAHAL bloc,* but meant little to Arabs, who were well aware that Israel's interpretation of the resolution was different to theirs.

Meanwhile the State Department had been working on new ideas since Nasser's invitation to the US to submit a fresh proposal. The main lesson learned from the failure of the Rogers Plan was that a simpler and less ambitious proposal was needed, involving a partial rather than a comprehensive settlement. On 19 June Rogers wrote to Mahmoud Riad, the Egyptian foreign minister, presenting an initiative which contained only three points: a ceasefire for three months, the reactivation of the Jarring peace talks during that period, with an active US role, and emphasis on withdrawal as the important phase of any agreement.

Ten days later Nasser visited Moscow and discussed the 'Rogers Initiative' with Brezhnev. 'Are you going to accept a plan with the stars and stripes on it?' Brezhnev asked. Nasser replied: 'I am going to accept it precisely for that reason. A plan with an American flag on it is more likely to be binding upon the Israelis.'

The war of attrition was wearing down Israel, as planned, but was taking its toll on Egypt too. Nasser was also exasperated by the half-hearted support of some of the wealthier Arab countries, which had virtually ignored an appeal for greater solidarity he had made at an Arab summit in Rabat in December 1969. At the same time he was becoming disillusioned with the Russians, suspecting that they were awed by the Americans.

By the end of the month Rogers knew that both Egypt and Jordan would cooperate, but another month passed while Washington haggled

* The GAHAL bloc consisted of the Herut and Liberal parties. In 1973 this grouping merged with two other elements to form Likud (Unity), with Begin as a joint chairman.

with Israel. Golda Meir at first thought the Rogers Initiative was a second attempt to impose the earlier Rogers Plan, and was persuaded only after Nixon had given Israel American electronic equipment to enable the Phantoms supplied earlier to evade Soviet anti-aircraft missiles. Her acceptance was not unconditional, but the State Department ignored her conditions.

The ceasefire went into effect on 7 August, and Egypt began making good the damage to its defensive systems. The Israelis interpreted this as a ceasefire violation and complained to Washington. Mrs Meir's anger was directed not just at Egypt but also at Rogers, for refusing to heed her ceasefire conditions, and at the US administration generally for arranging a ceasefire without a mechanism for dealing with violations. The State Department felt that the Israelis were making much of minor matters, but Nixon and Kissinger took Israel's side. The outcome was that the president and his national security adviser began conducting their own Middle East policy, often without informing Rogers. The secretary of state continued as before, and the administration found itself with two different views which only occasionally coincided. On 1 September a joint decision, involving both the White House and the State Department, was made to sell Israel eighteen of the twenty-five F-4 Phantoms Mrs Meir had requested.

The acceptance by Egypt and Jordan of the Rogers Initiative caused a dispute between Nasser and the Palestinians. Unrest among Palestinians had been at a high level since the previous December, when King Hussein was the only Arab leader to express approval of the Rogers Plan. Violent demonstrations in Jordan at that time had forced the king to take ever more repressive measures to maintain order. He saw the subsequent violence related to the Rogers Initiative as justification for expelling the PLO from Jordan,* thinking that in the circumstances Egypt would not object. This proved to be a miscalculation, for Nasser stood behind the Palestinians. During a meeting between the two leaders at Alexandria in August 1970, King Hussein was warned not to misunderstand Egypt's acceptance of the Rogers Initiative, and not to take it as a licence to liquidate the PLO. Nasser was convinced that the struggle would go on because there was no other way of making

* The PLO had broken away from Egyptian tutelage in the late 1960s to become a fully independent organization.

Israel withdraw. The Rogers Initiative had only a minimal hope of success, but was nevertheless worth accepting, if only to give Egyptian forces time to prepare for an attempt to recapture the east bank of the Suez Canal. Studies of such a campaign had been under way for some time, and in August Nasser signed the draft of a plan code named 'Granite One',* conceived by Abdel-Moneim Riad, the Egyptian chief-of-staff, and General Lashenko, chief Soviet adviser to the Egyptian army.

Despite Nasser's admonition to Hussein, the situation in Jordan was running out of control. Radical groups called for the overthrow of the Hashemite monarchy, and on 6 September the Popular Front for the Liberation of Palestine forced the conflict on to the front pages of newspapers around the world by hijacking three airliners, taking 500 hostages and then blowing up two of the planes at an airfield in Jordan.

Hussein formed a military government and turned the full weight of the Jordanian army against the Palestinian rebels. Syria then sent an armoured column into Jordan to show support for the Palestinians, a move which caused exaggerated alarm in Washington. The United States had already made contingency plans for direct US military intervention to help Hussein, but the Syrian development suggested that this might be too late to save the king. Both the US and Britain considered the survival of Jordan as a pro-Western state a matter of vital importance. The US made arrangements with Israel to send a column of Israeli tanks to intercept Syrian forces in Jordan, if King Hussein agreed. The crisis reached its height on 21 September, but by the following day Hussein's forces had regained control and no US or Israeli assistance was requested. This incident had an important impact on the wider Arab–Israel conflict by showing that Israel could sometimes become a party in Arab–Arab quarrels.

In the meantime Nasser had been working to stop the fratricidal fighting, and on 22 September he persuaded King Hussein and Yasser Arafat to come together under the auspices of an Arab summit. Nasser foresaw the risk of a permanent rift in the Arab world stemming from the bitter fighting, in which Hussein's troops had all but wiped out

* A reference to the solid rock upon which the Aswan dam was built. The plan was the basis for the one implemented on 6 October 1973, the first day of the Yom Kippur war.

Palestinian strongholds in Jordan. The events of what came to be known as 'Black September' rankle to this day with Palestinian survivors and their descendants. 'Black September' was later used as a name by Palestinian commandos claiming responsibility for attacks against Israeli targets, including the killing of eleven Israeli athletes at the Munich Olympics in 1972.

Hussein and Arafat met Nasser in Cairo on 27 September, and Nasser poured the last of his energy into securing an agreement to end the fighting. The following day, while seeing his guests off at Cairo airport, Nasser felt ill and went home. A few hours later he died of a heart attack, plunging the entire Arab world into mourning. Extraordinary scenes of mass grief at the funeral on 1 October confirmed that Gamal Abdel Nasser was that rarest of statesmen: a strong leader, genuinely loved by his people, who changed the course of their destiny.

11

From Hope to Disillusionment

Israel used Nasser's funeral to convey its hopes of improved relations with the new Egyptian administration. 'We understand your feelings at this moment and the sorrow that the loss of President Nasser has brought,' an Israeli message began. 'The Israeli government sends you assurances that it will not exploit any resulting confusion. We look eagerly to better times when we can establish contacts for dealing with our joint causes.'

The note was delivered by the Romanian delegation attending the funeral to Ali Sabri, secretary general of the Arab Socialist Union. It was similar to Israel's attempt to make a fresh start after Farouk's fall in 1954, and was equally unlucky in timing. Egypt was just as preoccupied with internal issues in October 1970 as in July 1952, although the nature of the problems was different. In 1970 the question on every lip was: 'Who will lead Egypt now?'

The loss of the visionary force which had dominated the Arab world for eighteen years had left Nasser's closest associates too shattered to face a leadership contest immediately. Agreement was quickly reached to follow the Egyptian constitution, which provided for a sixty-day consultation period under the vice president's temporary leadership.

Anwar Sadat, one of the original Free Officers, had been named vice president nine months earlier, but few saw him as a permanent successor. Sadat's role in the Nasser years had been steady rather than memorable. He served as secretary of the Islamic Congress and as speaker of the National Assembly, without emerging from the state president's shadow. His elevation to vice president was intended to fill a gap while Nasser went on a trip to other north African countries in December 1969.* The appointment was intended to be temporary, but Nasser never found time afterwards for a more considered choice. Lacking the qualities which had made Nasser an outstanding leader, Sadat was seen by many in Egypt and abroad as a transitional figure, to be followed by someone better able to take command of the post-Nasser power centres.† However, none of the expected contenders made an open bid for the presidency, and Sadat was appointed for lack of an opponent. Even then many expected him to serve as a ceremonial president, leaving the main decisions to powerful party or government members.

Nasser's death came at a time when Egypt had 850,000 troops massed on the west bank of the Suez Canal waiting for orders to cross. The ceasefire of 7 August was due to expire on 6 November, and Nasser had not planned to prolong the anxious waiting period unnecessarily. After his death it was realized that Alexei Kosygin and other statesmen attending the funeral would ask about Egypt's intentions. The Egyptian National Security Council therefore decided before the funeral to extend the ceasefire for three months.‡ As an untested leader, Sadat knew it was vital to gain the confidence of the army and the country before any decision to go ahead with the original plan. The ceasefire extension provided a vital breathing space.

The new president set out with the intention of continuing Nasser's main lines of policy while making reforms in certain areas. Gradually it became clear that some 'reforms' were in fact radical changes, and that Sadat, far from being a figurehead, intended to follow his own course. A struggle for power erupted, with important issues serving as ammunition in a fight for influence and authority. Sadat wanted to explore American intentions and attitudes, a path which his opponents considered dangerous.

Making contact with the US administration was complicated by the lack of diplomatic relations between Cairo and Washington. Sadat therefore approached a highly-placed Saudi who had close links with the administration. Kamal Adham, director of Saudi intelligence and brother of Queen Effat, the wife of King Faisal, had been in regular

* It was also a kind gesture on Nasser's part to enhance Sadat's pension rights. Sadat's pension on retirement would have been based on the highest position he reached.
† The Nixon administration initially shared this view.
‡ The decision was not made public until the previous ceasefire was about to expire.

touch with Richard Helms, former director of the CIA. During a meeting in November 1970 at Sadat's rest house at the Barrages outside Cairo, Adham explained that Washington would not bring pressure on Israel to leave Sinai so long as the Soviet Union retained a strong presence in Egypt. Sadat, who felt that Nasser had unnecessarily provoked the Americans, was personally willing to break with Moscow but knew it would be hard to gain the army's support.

Soon afterwards claims were published in the *Washington Post* that Sadat was being paid by Kamal Adham on behalf of the CIA. There is no proof that Adham gave the president money, but his gifts were sometimes generous.

Parts of Sadat's conversation with Kamal Adham were subsequently leaked to the US media, which reported that Sadat was prepared to expel Soviet advisers from Egypt. The article shocked Moscow and enraged powerful government and party figures. The Soviet Union began to watch the new president more closely.

The first ceasefire was now ending and the additional three months beginning. When Sadat announced the extension he said that the additional time should be used to resume the long-stalled UN peace talks under Gunnar Jarring. The US administration urged Israel to accept Sadat's proposal, but Golda Meir wanted Washington to give political guarantees and to promise further arms supplies before she took any decision.

Sensing that there was a new mood in Cairo, reflected in what Sadat had told Kamal Adham, Israeli defence minister Moshe Dayan proposed in November 1970 that Israel should pull its forces several kilometres back from the east bank of the canal, to allow Egypt to reopen the waterway. Dayan's idea was that an Israeli pull-back would be matched by a withdrawal of Egyptian forces from the west bank, leaving an arms-free strip on either side.

This idea was not supported by the Israeli cabinet as a whole, and Golda Meir was among the sceptics. Ever since the 1967 war Dayan had opposed Israel's domination of the canal, arguing that the Mitla and Giddi passes through the Sinai mountains would be easier to defend, and that Egypt would reconcile itself to a long-term Israeli presence in Sinai if the canal were reopened. His proposal of November 1970 was a variation of what he had been telling cabinet colleagues for three years. Dayan's strongest opponents were Yigal Allon, deputy prime minister, and Major General Haim Bar-Lev, principal architect of Israel's military fortifications along the east bank. The concept of the Bar-Lev line was that limited Israeli forces protected by attack barriers would be able to hold out against a surprise offensive until reinforcements arrived from Israel.

Most members of the Egyptian government dismissed Dayan's proposal as a trial balloon, but Sadat thought it worth exploring. He was dreading the prospect of having to order the army to cross the canal against fortified Israeli positions entrenched at the water's edge, because military experts, including the Soviets, estimated that the price of such a dangerous operation would be 25,000 casualties.

Soon afterwards Sadat was visited by Abd El-Moneim Amin, an Egyptian ambassador and former member of the Revolutionary Command Council. The ambassador was unusual in having close contacts with two widely different sectors of Egyptian life. As a military officer in 1952 he had played a role in persuading the Egyptian artillery to back the revolution. Unlike any other member of the Revolutionary Command Council Abd El-Moneim Amin was married to a wealthy society beauty who had a fine apartment. This made him a natural choice to arrange contacts with American diplomats in the weeks after the revolution, and later he took up a diplomatic career himself.* The ambassador, like Sadat, felt that Nasser had thrown away opportunities for better relations with the United States.

Abd El-Moneim Amin persuaded Sadat to let him approach the two principal US government officers in Cairo at the time, Donald Bergus, a professional diplomat, and Eugene Trone, the CIA representative. Although the US and Egypt did not have diplomatic relations, Bergus ran a US Interests Section under the aegis of the Spanish embassy.

With Sadat's blessing Abd El-Moneim Amin told the two Americans that if Washington could persuade Israel to agree to an interim arrangement, as a step towards full withdrawal, Egypt would be interested. This, however, was subject to an important condition: Israel would have to withdraw to the mountain passes, about forty kilometres east of the canal. Bergus and Trone passed on Sadat's interest in an interim solution to Washington, which in turn contacted Israel.

* He served as ambassador to Holland and later West Germany.

Sadat acted on his own, without consulting ministers opposed to compromise with Israel. Unknown to him, the Egyptian intelligence service had placed bugging devices in the homes of Bergus and Trone, and transcripts of the meeting were sent to two of Sadat's opponents, the minister of the interior and the minister of war, but not to Sadat. The recorders were kept rolling for months afterwards and picked up every word spoken in the two men's homes.

Some of the transcripts provided useful insights into American thinking. Report number 18,312 deals with a conversation between US Congressman Ernest Holling and Marshall Willie, first secretary at the US Interests Section in Cairo, at the home of Donald Bergus.

> HOLLING: What if the dam were hit?
> WILLIE: You're talking about bombing the high dam?
> HOLLING: I'm not saying we do it. I'm talking about the Israelis. They've got the fastest planes and if they don't have special bombs to do this they could manufacture one to destroy the dam. It would be purely an act of revenge. Do you get what I mean?

In December 1970 Sadat used the Bergus–Trone channel to inform the US administration that he was genuinely interested in peace with Israel, a statement which intrigued Washington and confirmed the suspicions of Sadat's opponents when they received the transcript.

At the end of the year Golda Meir lifted her objections to Jarring's peace mission after obtaining most of the concessions she wanted from Nixon. Jarring approached both sides, but his efforts were overtaken by an Egyptian initiative. In a speech to the Egyptian parliament on 4 February 1971, Sadat announced a further one-month extension of the ceasefire on condition that Israel used this period to begin a partial withdrawal of its forces from the east bank. If Israel complied, Egypt would clear the canal of debris and reopen it to international shipping. Sadat's critics in the government realized that this was a modified version of Dayan's idea, repackaged as an Egyptian proposal. The president had been warned by advisers to expect such a reaction, but thought that any deal which gave Egypt at least a token presence on the east bank was preferable to the slaughter of thousands of troops in an opposed crossing.

Sadat predicted that his initiative would transform Jarring's peace talks 'from ambiguous words into definite measures', but events took a different turn: the Jarring talks almost immediately ran into trouble. In his 4 February speech Sadat had made a vital concession in confirming that Egypt would enter into a formal peace agreement if Israel made a complete withdrawal. This brought Egypt closer to the Israeli and US position, but Israel's reply was a diplomatic slap in the face. Golda Meir reiterated Levi Eshkol's statement of 12 June 1967 that Israel would not make a complete withdrawal to the pre-1967 lines. There was now no basis for a comprehensive settlement, and the Swedish diplomat's role was finished. The Jarring talks had always had an air of unreality, dealing with comprehensive peace at a time when the taboo still made direct talks between Egypt and Israel impossible. A less ambitious accord involving a more prestigious intermediary seemed better suited to the mood of the time.

Just under a month after announcing his initiative Sadat visited the Soviet Union to ask for increased weapons supplies. During the visit a row broke out over an Egyptian request, originally made by Nasser, for Soviet bombers capable of inflicting on Israel the damage which Israeli air raids had caused in Egypt. Moscow considered this unduly provocative, despite a US decision in September 1970 to supply Israel with additional F-4 Phantoms.

Brezhnev said that bombers could be provided only if they remained in the USSR under Soviet control, with a Soviet military authority to operate them. Sadat refused to accept such an arrangement, and warned that Egypt might change sides. 'I cursed their fathers and their grandfathers,' Sadat told me on the phone when he returned from Moscow, describing his two long sessions with the Soviet leadership as 'nine hours of insults'. Our conversation was secretly recorded by Sadat's opponents in the intelligence service, and the transcript was later found in their files.

'I told them quite frankly: "You are destroying yourselves by keeping me two steps behind Israel. America is doing everything for Israel. And you are going to be the losers."'

Sadat pointed out that American willingness to put pressure on Israel was limited because of the Soviet advisers in Egypt: 'If you forfeited your presence on my territory you would lose a lot in the region and the world,' he warned.

Brezhnev agreed to provide most of the weapons Sadat wanted, apart from the bombers, allowing Sadat to return to Cairo with an apparent success. However, Moscow's hesitancy and unwillingness to risk confrontation with the US convinced Sadat that Egypt was in alliance with the wrong superpower. This made him more eager than ever to engage Washington's involvement in finding a diplomatic solution. The day after his return from Moscow Sadat wrote to Nixon asking for full US backing for his 4 February initiative.*

The US president replied to Sadat's letter in positive terms. It appears that Washington was unaware of Brezhnev's cautious attitude, and thought (incorrectly) that if Egyptian forces attempted a canal crossing, Moscow would be prepared to help. The Egyptian intelligence service recorded the following conversation between Eugene Trone and a visitor named Howe Baker Thomas.

> THOMAS: The Russians will undoubtedly help the Egyptians cross the canal with all this equipment and planes.
>
> TRONE: Did they say this? [It is unclear who is meant by 'they'.]
>
> THOMAS: Yes, which is why Sadat went to the USSR. [Speaks as if reading from something:] The Soviets signed an agreement saying they will assist in the canal crossing. On this basis and for the same reason they are sending troops and advisers. But I wonder if they are [insane] enough to send troops. Advisers maybe, but troops?

The conversation suggests that Washington had been given wrong information, as there was no such agreement.

The White House followed up Sadat's letter by asking Israel for an official response to the 4 February initiative. The Israeli cabinet was not entirely opposed to the Egyptian proposal but wanted a major modification to allow Israeli forces to remain in the Bar-Lev fortifications. Reopening the Suez Canal would make an Egyptian attack on Israeli forces less likely, because Cairo would not want to lose canal revenues. The Sinai would thus become a still more effective hostage

* The letter to Nixon was written as the one-month ceasefire extension was expiring. Sadat also explained that a further extension would not be given. However, non-renewal did not mean that military action was imminent.

to force Egypt to make peace with Israel at some future time. Secondly, reopening the canal would relieve strong international pressure, especially from the Soviet Union, which was complaining that its Indian Ocean fleet was separated from its Mediterranean fleet.

This huge modification was submitted to the US on 19 April 1971. It was not the limit of Israel's counter-demands. While Israeli forces stayed in their positions on the east bank, Israel wanted Egypt to evacuate its own fortifications on the west bank. Further, Israeli shipping should be allowed to use the canal when it was reopened. These terms were so unbalanced that the US held back from passing them on to Egypt.

Still unaware of Israel's reply, Sadat met Bergus and insisted that Egyptian forces should be allowed to cross the canal and take control of the Mitla and Giddi passes, as part of any interim agreement.

Meanwhile the growing differences between Sadat and his opponents were about to burst into the open. Egypt was moving towards a power struggle stemming from unresolved arguments on a wide range of issues. The president's opponents chose for tactical reasons to concentrate on a single point: Sadat's efforts to engage the US. The plan was to exploit the president's secret contacts by exposing evidence collected from the phone-tap transcripts. In addition to bugging the homes of Bergus and Trone, the Egyptian intelligence service was also monitoring the phone lines of everyone with whom the president was regularly in touch. Transcripts of conversations between Sadat and myself alone ran to 3600 pages.*

The plan was to disclose compromising extracts of the transcripts at a meeting of the Central Committee of the Arab Socialist Union (ASU), the highest organ of party power, with the aim of bringing about Sadat's dismissal and trial on charges of treason.

Before this could be implemented Sadat tried a diversionary move, giving his backing to a proposal that Egypt, Syria and Libya should be united in a federation. Both President Hafez El-Assad of Syria and Muammar Gadaffi of Libya favoured the scheme.† Egyptian public

* In these conversations my role was that of an informal adviser.

† Hafez El-Assad had become president of Syria in March 1971 after overturning another faction of the Ba'ath Party which had backed Syria's unsuccessful intervention in the Jordan crisis of 1970. Assad was a former head of the Syrian air force and had held government posts since 1966. Muammar Gadaffi had led Libya since the revolution of 1968, in which the pro-Western King Idris was overthrown.

opinion was unclear but probably supported federation, because Arab unity had always been Nasser's principal cause. Sadat's opponents realized that the scheme, by creating a new political structure, would affect their power base and strengthen the president at their expense. Hoping that Egyptians would rise up and overthrow the government, the opponents resigned *en bloc* from the Arab Socialist Union.

Ali Sabri, secretary general of the ASU and vice president of Egypt, was the most prominent of Sadat's opponents. Sabri had always been Sadat's deadliest rival and thought himself popular, but was a victim of self-delusion. At the beginning of May 1971 more than ninety of Sadat's opponents were arrested and Sabri lost his two posts. The conspirators, including Sabri, were subsequently tried and imprisoned. Sadat had sensed months earlier that confrontation with his opponents would come before long, and had ensured that the army chief-of-staff and the commander of the presidential guard were on his side. He kept the army's loyalty at a critical moment and strengthened his standing in the country as a whole.

Before announcing Sabri's dismissal Sadat had summoned Vladimir Vinogradov, the Soviet ambassador, to give notice of the decision. Vinogradov was surprised: 'Mr President, why are you telling me this? Your internal affairs are none of my business.' Sadat replied: 'I am telling you because I know that when I issue the order many people will rush to tell you that I have dismissed your best friend in Egypt.'

The dismissal of Sabri was designed to show the Egyptian government and army that Sadat could stand up to his opponents, and to give a signal to Washington that Moscow's friends had no hold over him. That message was fully understood by William Rogers, who visited Cairo two days later for talks with Sadat. The secretary of state complimented Sadat on his February initiative and gave the impression that Egypt had now made the concessions necessary to bring about a deal with Israel. These hopes were shattered a few days later when Rogers received a chilly welcome in Israel. Far from improving their 19 April offer, the Israelis, who knew that Rogers was only nominally in charge of US foreign policy, raised many new difficulties.

Rogers was well aware that his work was being undermined by the US national security adviser, Henry Kissinger, as he made clear during his visit to Cairo. He requested a visit to *al-Ahram*, and as the paper's editor I conducted him around the premises. We were followed by journalists and photographers until Rogers created a diversion by asking me to show him to the bathroom. As soon as we were alone he asked: 'Isn't there somewhere where we could talk for a few minutes?' We went to a private room and he said: 'I know many people are advising Sadat to deal with the White House rather than the State Department. You should know that Henry's first loyalty is to Henry, his second loyalty is to Henry, his third loyalty is to Henry, his fourth loyalty is to any boss he is serving, and his fifth loyalty is to his people [meaning the Jews].'

After the Rogers visit General Mohamed Fawzi,* the war minister, called a meeting of the Egyptian High Command and accused Sadat of conducting suspicious negotiations which amounted to an abandonment of national goals. This attempt to turn the army against the president failed because the chief-of-staff refused to allow the army to be drawn into a political dispute. General Fawzi then resigned.

With the army now firmly under his command, Sadat wanted to reassure Arabs that he was committed to the struggle to regain the occupied territories, and yet in reality he was still no closer to a decision on crossing the canal. To give himself more time he repeatedly referred to 1971 as 'the year of decision'.

A bugged conversation between Eugene Trone, Mrs Trone and an American guest shows that the CIA representative thought Sadat's position was secure:

> GUEST: How long can Sadat last? How much support does he have now?
> TRONE: I think he has a strong position in Cairo and other major cities. I think it is also strong in the military.
> GUEST: And with the intellectuals too?
> [No reply.]
> MRS TRONE: Do you think he enjoys the same degree of popularity as Nasser did, especially with the general public?
> TRONE: I think maybe more, for two reasons: First of all he is embarking upon projects for peaceful purposes, and secondly because he has never involved himself in a foreign venture as

* There were two Fawzis in the Egyptian government at the time: General Mohamed Fawzi and Dr Mahmoud Fawzi, the foreign minister, who became prime minister soon afterwards.

> Nasser had done. And from all that's said and done it is quite obvious that his government's policy is to retrieve what the country has lost before. He has offered a number of peace proposals that were quite acceptable and got support, and for the first time in twenty years Israel is in a defensive position before world opinion. All this indicates that he has succeeded where Nasser had failed, and once again he has agreed to the possibility of reopening the canal.

In the space of a few months Sadat had opened his lines to Washington, survived an attempt by opponents to oust him, established firm control of the army, and demonstrated his independence from Moscow. These changes were immediately noticed by both superpowers.

Sensing that the Egyptian president was manoeuvring towards a confrontation, Moscow made strenuous efforts to placate him. President Nikolae Podgorny visited Cairo on 25 May and persuaded Sadat to sign a fifteen-year Soviet–Egyptian friendship treaty. Sadat accepted because Egypt needed Soviet weapons, but he had no illusions about friendship. In another bugged phone conversation I pointed out to Sadat that the treaty was reminiscent of Egypt's former subservient relationship with Britain. Sadat replied that he had felt a need to appease Moscow, but that nothing had changed.*

The friendship treaty between Egypt and the Soviet Union puzzled Nixon, especially as William Rogers had just reported, after his visit to Cairo, that Egypt was beginning to emerge from Soviet tutelage. Podgorny's visit two weeks later gave the opposite impression. Nixon discussed the situation with King Faisal of Saudi Arabia, who was visiting the United States at the time. The king offered to talk to Sadat, and pass on some written questions from the US president. Faisal and Sadat dined together at a former royal palace in Alexandria on 19 June. During the meal Sadat wrote his replies directly on the US president's memorandum and handed it back to Faisal.

> NIXON: Will the treaty with the Soviet Union affect relations between Egypt and United States?
>
> SADAT: The treaty does not change anything in our position.

* In another measure to pacify Moscow, Sadat appointed several Egyptian communists to cabinet posts, replacing ministers who had been arrested in early May 1971.

NIXON: Does Egypt still have freedom of action to reach a peaceful settlement under the auspices of the United States?

SADAT: Our position is the same . . . and I am ready to sign a satisfactory agreement.

NIXON: Would Egypt restore its relations with the United States after the first phase of [Israeli] withdrawal?

SADAT: Yes.

NIXON: Would the Soviet forces leave Egypt right away after an agreement [between Egypt and Israel]?

SADAT: Yes, I am on my word.

Sadat had resolved to deal directly with the White House so far as possible, feeling that contact with Rogers was a waste of time. That feeling was fully shared by Nixon and Kissinger, who began trying to gain a better understanding of Egyptian thinking without using State Department connections. A close friend of the US president, Donald Kendall, chairman of PepsiCo, suggested that a meeting could be arranged between Kissinger and someone who knew Sadat's mind without being part of the Egyptian government. Kendall's first choice for that role was myself. He wrote to say that Kissinger had set aside two days in October to talk to me, and offered elaborate arrangements for the meeting, including the use of a private plane and of his own house in Connecticut. The offer was not unattractive, but there were too many uncertainties. It was unclear who was running US foreign policy, what Sadat was trying to obtain, and what he was willing to give in return.

The turning point in the White House–State Department tussle came in mid-July, when Kissinger's secret visit to China was made public.* The world now realized that any important foreign policy initiative would come from the White House and not the State Department. Egypt's ambassador to Washington, Ashraf Ghorbal, told Sadat that the national security adviser was the only member of the US administration capable of securing a deal. 'Kissinger is the man,' Ghorbal wrote in a letter to Sadat. The ambassador tried a personal

* Kissinger's visit to Peking on 9 July 1971 marked the beginning of one of Nixon's most important foreign policy achievements, opening relations between the US and China.

approach when Kissinger was ill, taking him flowers and a poem which amounted to an invitation to visit Cairo.

Sadat had not been told about the attempt in July to set up a meeting between Kissinger and myself, but in October Kendall tried again, using high-level contacts to ensure that the offer came to the president's personal attention.* Sadat urged me to go, but the situation had not changed. The Israeli inflexibility which had caused the collapse of the Rogers Initiative remained as rigid as ever, Kissinger seemed likely to ask for more Egyptian concessions as a way of tempting Israel into talks, and Egypt had already conceded too much. Sadat pointed out that in 1965 Nasser had asked me to make a secret trip to Yalta to request a loan of 200 million roubles from Khrushchev. The mission had proved successful. If I had acted as an emissary for the previous president, why not for the present one? I felt this was an over-simplification of a complicated situation.

In the autumn of 1971 the US administration began to adopt a new way of looking at the Arab–Israel conflict, reflecting Kissinger's views rather than those of Rogers. Kissinger wanted to increase US arms deliveries to Israel, arguing that Israel would come to a political settlement only if it felt militarily secure. He also wanted Egypt to feel that its friendship with Moscow had been a mistake. The United States should wait for Cairo to expel Soviet advisers before making any major mediation effort. The result of Kissinger's influence was that between November 1971 and October 1973 the United States did comparatively little to break the deadlock. Washington's relative inactivity was a contributory cause of the 1973 war.

The two years passed slowly in Cairo. It was a time of fatigue and sullen political introspection. Sadat was mocked when 1971 ended without a decision to use force. University students staged demonstrations, satirists suggested that 1971 had been extended, and the president fell into depression. The minister of war told him that the army needed yet more arms to conduct a successful attack, but the Russians were unwilling to go beyond earlier promises. Sadat felt that Moscow consistently supplied Egypt with second-rate weapons, while the US

* Mr Kendall approached Dr Mohamed Hassan El-Zayyat, Egypt's permanent representative at the UN, and repeated his offer. Dr Zayyat then contacted Dr Mahmoud Fawzi, the prime minister, with a strong recommendation that the offer should be accepted. Fawzi in turn approached Sadat, who asked me on 7 November 1971.

gave Israel the best available. He was now quarrelling both with his generals and with his main supplier, and simultaneously wondering how Egypt's dependence on the Soviet Union could be broken. An unhappy year ended on a sour note with a US announcement on 31 December that shipments of F-4 Phantoms to Israel would be resumed.

If 1971 had been frustrating, 1972 was worse. The US presidential election campaign gave the White House a further reason to suspend Middle East initiatives. Nixon's relations with Israel had improved so much that it looked as if significant numbers of American Jews might vote Republican in November, breaking with their traditional support for the Democrats. The only significant US diplomacy on the Middle East during the campaign was a set of principles for a future initiative, agreed between Kissinger and Andrei Gromyko, the Soviet foreign minister. This led to agreement between Nixon and Brezhnev at a summit in Moscow in May to conduct Middle East affairs in a way which would minimize risks of superpower confrontation.

The East–West accord came at a time when the Soviet Union was delaying deliveries of weapons promised to Egypt. Moscow was restraining Cairo to avoid jeopardizing East–West détente. Soon afterwards Sadat received further confirmation from Prince Sultan of Saudi Arabia, who had talked to Nixon, that the United States was now following Kissinger's policy of waiting for Egypt to break with its Soviet friends.

On 8 July 1972 Sadat went to see Dr Fawzi, who was now his principal foreign policy adviser, at his farm outside Cairo and said he had decided to expel all Soviet advisers, and would then start talking to the USSR on a new basis. Fawzi urged Sadat to negotiate first, but the president's mind was made up. Sadat called the minister of war and told him: 'I have a piece of news which will make you smile from ear to ear.' The minister's response was not a smile but a question: where would Egypt obtain arms in future? The president summoned me to see him, and like the prime minister Dr Aziz Sidki and the war minister I counselled caution. It was in any case too late. Sadat had already informed the Soviet ambassador that the 15,000 advisers should leave within ten days. Soviet officials were bewildered and hurt, but quickly provided a timetable for their departure.

As the advisers were packing to leave many in the Egyptian

government felt that Sadat's insult had been unnecessarily brutal. Aziz Sidki flew to Moscow on 13 July to try to smooth over the row, and was astonished when Soviet leaders offered more weapons and firm promises of a fixed delivery schedule. Sidki returned home with the biggest Soviet–Egyptian arms deal ever made.

Sadat was elated, but at the same time suspicious. Moscow had restrained Egypt when relations were close, and was now giving encouragement after the expulsion of Soviet advisers. Could it be, he wondered, that Moscow wanted to tempt him into battle with Israel, hoping that Egypt would lose and that a new and more pliable leader would emerge?

The expulsion of the Soviet advisers brought a warm message of admiration from Rogers, conveyed through Dr Mohamed El-Zayyat, who visited Washington in October.* However, Rogers also said that US leverage with Israel was limited; Washington would try to persuade the Israelis to cooperate, but could not force them. The secretary of state did not expect any progress on an interim settlement for at least six months. This was depressing news for Sadat, who realized that his sole reward for expelling Soviet advisers had been a pat on the head from a powerless secretary of state. In the same month Washington said that Kissinger was too busy with Vietnam to see Hafez Ismail, Sadat's national security adviser.

All these frustrations came at a time when Israel was carrying out raids in Syria and Lebanon in reprisal for the killing of eleven Israeli athletes at the Munich Olympics in September. Public pressure to hit back hard was growing, and the Arab League was talking of united action. Sadat was at this stage thinking of a limited battle, for which the weapons received from Moscow would be sufficient. General Mohamed Sadek, the Egyptian chief-of-staff, pointed out that no one could force Israel to keep a conflict within limits, and that Egyptian weapons stocks were insufficient for total war. After a long argument Sadat lost patience and dismissed Sadek on 26 October 1972, which almost led to a coup d'état. Wanting to secure his position, Sadat began to contemplate a battle in December, two months later. He sent his minister of war, Marshal Ahmed Ismail Ali, to Syria to discuss a joint

* El-Zayyat, formerly Egypt's permanent representative at the UN, had been appointed foreign minister.

Egyptian–Syrian attack. President Assad of Syria was astonished by this sudden rush.

Nixon had just begun his second term, and was anxious to resume Middle East diplomacy after the long delay caused by the election year.* Meanwhile Kissinger's status had taken another leap in January with the successful conclusion of talks with North Vietnamese negotiators in Paris.† Sadat felt that if Kissinger could stop the Vietnam War no political miracle was beyond his abilities. At the Egyptian president's request, Ahmed Ismail Ali called Eugene Trone, the CIA's representative in Egypt, and asked for a message to be passed to the US National Security Council, but not to the State Department. Kissinger's long-postponed meeting with the Egyptian national security adviser was scheduled for 25 and 26 February at Kendall's house in Connecticut. Hafez Ismail first had a brief meeting with Nixon, who said he realized that some Arabs distrusted Kissinger because of his Jewishness: 'Yes, he is a Jew. But he is loyal to me and he represents my point of view,' Nixon said.‡

The two national security advisers were oddly matched. Hafez Ismail, tall, dignified, pencil-slim, Sandhurst-trained and courteous to a fault, had been director of intelligence and subsequently ambassador to Paris; a man whose achievements were based on education, honesty and long service rather than mental dexterity. Sadat had chosen a ceremonial sword rather than a rapier to parry the thrusts of the fastest mind in the White House. Kissinger, then aged fifty, had been selected for office because of the powers of analysis demonstrated in his writings, his contributions to policy debate, and his academic career at Harvard. His works included essays and books on American foreign policy, nuclear weapons and the NATO alliance. As a participant in official and semi-official organizations dealing with defence, intelligence and foreign policy, he had become acquainted with the intrigues and power games of the US capital.

Sadat assumed that Kissinger would eventually propose a new for-

* Nixon won the November 1972 presidential election with nearly 61 per cent of the vote.

† Kissinger and Le Duc Tho of Vietnam reached an agreement in Paris on 13 January 1973, enabling US forces to withdraw from Vietnam and ending (for Washington but not for Saigon) a war which had lasted ten years.

‡ Extract from report by Hafez Ismail to Sadat.

mula based on the previous five years of diplomatic work. A solution which came from the White House would be easier to sell to the Egyptian government and army, and less likely to be refused by Israel. Kissinger, on the other hand, had little interest in the previous diplomatic work, partly because the starting point had been UN Resolution 242, which he despised, and partly because he disagreed with the Rogers approach. Secondly, he was in no hurry to submit a US proposal.

The two sides seemed to have a different understanding as to the nature of the negotiation. Hafez Ismail stated Egypt's maximum demands, and expected Kissinger to make a counter offer. Kissinger, whose Middle East experience was then limited, seems to have thought that the first Egyptian price was also the final price. His writings show that he considered Hafez Ismail's remarks unrealistic.

The report which Hafez Ismail wrote afterwards made discouraging reading for Sadat. Kissinger was not ready to offer ideas immediately, and any negotiating process would be long and slow. The US national security adviser had taken eighteen months to negotiate the opening to China, three and a half years to find a solution to the Vietnam conflict, and a year to reach accord with Moscow in the Strategic Arms Limitation Talks.

Kissinger's version was that the Egyptian 'was so courteous that he obscured Sadat's basic strategy, which was to elaborate the conditions for a showdown'.* This conclusion, which Kissinger reached long after the meeting, was wide of the mark. Far from seeking confrontation with Israel, Sadat was reaching out to Kissinger to help him avert war.

Hafez Ismail and Kissinger were in regular contact over the next three months and held a further secret meeting at a private house outside Paris on 20 May, but again nothing constructive emerged. The two versions of the Paris meeting were similar in substance, if not in detail. Hafez Ismail's report shows that he and Kissinger were still poles apart on basic matters, such as what role the United States should play.

> KISSINGER: Do you want us to be intermediaries?
> HAFEZ ISMAIL: You have expressed your desire so many times to be go-betweens.

* See *Years of Upheaval*, p. 212.

KISSINGER: Nonsense. You don't need us to convey messages to Israel. I am not a postman. You want us to convince Israel of your point of view. We are ready to back a solution, but a solution discussed by the parties.

Kissinger later came to the conclusion that Hafez Ismail had known at the time of the Paris meeting that Sadat was determined on war. Again, this was incorrect: had Kissinger shown a real US commitment to find a solution, Egypt would have waited. Sadat did not make his decision until he was sure that the secret channel had failed.

Much later there were signs that Kissinger regretted not having made a greater effort during this critical period. An Israeli writer quoted Kissinger as saying, in a conversation with Golda Meir after the 1973 war: 'I played with him [Hafez Ismail]. I toyed with him. My aim was to gain time and postpone the serious stage for another month, another year.' Hafez Ismail warned that there would be war if no solution were found, but Kissinger thought this was empty talk.* Kissinger was invited to Egypt, but did not make the time: 'We all thought he [Sadat] was a fool, a clown, a buffoon who goes on stage every other day to declare war.'

Sadat expressed his desperation to the Shah of Iran, who took the matter up during a visit to Washington. The Shah obtained a US position paper setting out Washington's views, and this was passed to Egypt. Sadat decided that the paper showed a clear US bias towards Israel and that further negotiations would be a waste of time. The US State Department later disclosed that a forecast at the end of May described the risk of war as 'better than even'.

In the first week of September Sadat informed his closest aides that the long-awaited decision had at last been taken. A plan had been worked out in Nasser's day for a crossing of the Suez Canal by five divisions, protected by missile batteries on the west bank, with the aim of establishing three bridgeheads. In January 1973 Egypt and Syria had worked out detailed arrangements for coordinating their attacks. These plans were now updated, and it was agreed that Damascus would give the Soviet Union four days' notice of the joint offensive.

* See Matti Golan, *Secret Conversations of Henry Kissinger*, Quadrangle, New York, 1976, p. 144. Publication of the book in Israel was delayed by censors for a year and became possible only after a legal battle.

The Palestinians presented a more sensitive problem. Sadat wanted their moral support, but dared not disclose too much. The solution, he thought, was to tell Yasser Arafat just enough to enable the PLO chairman to say afterwards that he had been informed in advance. In a meeting with Arafat and his colleague Abu Iyad,* Sadat said he wanted to 'light a spark' in the Middle East, but this was so vague that both PLO representatives missed his meaning. Paradoxically, Sadat told Arafat and Abu Iyad less than he had said in earlier public speeches, and less than he confided to the American banker David Rockefeller in a private meeting at Borg El-Arab in late September. Rockefeller was informed that the United States had left Egypt with no option other than war.

Some observers noted that Sadat, who had talked about war in almost every major statement since 1972, failed to mention the subject in a public speech on 28 September 1973 marking the anniversary of Nasser's death.

Washington was now absorbed with the drama of the dismissal of William Rogers as secretary of state and his replacement on 22 September by his arch-rival Kissinger. Six days later Palestinian commandos attacked a train carrying Jewish emigrants from the Soviet Union to a transit camp at Schönau in Austria. As the train crossed the Czechoslovakian border into Austria some of the Jews, whose ultimate destination was Israel, were taken hostage. Chancellor Kreisky of Austria agreed to close the Schönau camp in exchange for the hostages' release. The incident diverted international attention from the Middle East to Austria for a full week.

On 5 October, just twenty-four hours before war broke out, Kissinger held talks on a new peace initiative with Dr El-Zayyat, the Egyptian foreign minister, who was in New York to attend the UN General Assembly. On the same day, the Soviet Union evacuated its civilians from Cairo and Damascus. Golda Meir sent a message to Kissinger saying that she did not think Egypt or Syria was preparing to go to war. On 6 October the CIA interpreted the Soviet departure as evidence of a row between the two countries and Moscow. As the CIA report was being circulated, Egyptian forces were pouring across the Suez Canal, while the Syrian attack swept over the Golan Heights.

* Abu Iyad's real name was Salah Khalaf. He was assassinated in 1991.

A full month of hectic Egyptian and Syrian war preparations had been closely watched by the American and Israeli intelligence networks, yet both had come to the wrong conclusion. Neither country thought Sadat capable of leading his country to war, and neither rated Arab fighting abilities highly. Their prejudices and complacency were about to result in the greatest shock ever delivered to Israel's self-confidence.

Kissinger later came to the conclusion that Sadat must have decided to go to war much earlier, noting that Dr Aziz Sidki, the Egyptian prime minister, had announced a war budget on 11 February, before the first secret Egyptian–US meeting. In his memoirs Kissinger suggested that Sadat had followed an elaborate plan to throw the enemy off guard by threatening war so ostentatiously that he would not be believed.* That theory was an understandable but incorrect interpretation of several facts: in March Sadat spoke of preparations for 'total confrontation'; in April he publicly stated his intention to go to war; and in the same month Israel was sufficiently alarmed by Syrian troop movements and Egyptian canal-side deployments to mobilize its forces, only to demobilize them in May when nothing happened. Kissinger was further reinforced in his theory by Sadat himself, who felt flattered after the war by the notion that he had followed a masterly strategy of deception, and actively contributed to such speculation.

The truth was simpler: Sadat delayed war until his hope of a negotiated solution was exposed as an illusion. Kissinger was the last custodian of that hope, and must share responsibility with Israel for the transition from hope to disillusionment.

* See *Years of Upheaval*, p. 206.

12

Missiles and Missives

The Two Wars of Yom Kippur

The desperate struggle between Israel and the Arabs of October 1973 was extraordinary in that the battlefield outcome was partly determined by secret contacts. From the second day of the war, Sadat was in constant touch with Washington, and thus indirectly with Israel itself. While the fighting was a trial of valour, tactics, training and weapons, the encrypted signals flowing between Cairo and Washington tested Sadat's abilities as a strategist against those of Kissinger and Meir. Thousands were to die, but the value of their sacrifice depended on the hidden battle of wits.

The first twenty-four hours of the attack proved a success beyond the expectations of Cairo and Damascus. Egyptian forces punched through the Bar-Lev line with unexpected speed, taking only sixty-eight casualties in a crossing which might have cost thousands of lives. Bridgeheads were established at three points by forces landing from boats, floating bridges were set up, and tanks and artillery crossed to the west side. Israeli defenders were quickly driven back and parts of the Bar-Lev line captured. Meanwhile two Syrian divisions and 500 tanks swept into the Golan Heights, retaking some of the territory which Israel had captured in 1967. Within two hours of the crossing Brezhnev phoned Sadat to offer congratulations. 'You are fighting a wonderful battle and achieving your goals, *inshallah*,' he said through an interpreter, using the Arabic word for 'God willing'. Sadat laughed: 'Our friend Brezhnev is becoming a Moslem; he is saying *inshallah*.' The Egyptian president asked the interpreter to convey the gratitude of the Egyptian people for Soviet weapons and training. 'Tell him I will never forget the role of our sincere friends.' Brezhnev refrained from reminding him that those 'sincere friends' had been expelled from Egypt the previous year.

The scale of Egypt's success was mainly a reward for tight security,* sound preparation and military professionalism. Timing also played an important part, in that Yom Kippur, the Jewish day of atonement, created a holiday mood in Israel.† Israeli intelligence officials learned of Arab intentions at 4 a.m., and told the cabinet to expect an attack by sunset. This gave the impression that Israel had fourteen hours in which to prepare, whereas in fact the attack came within ten hours, at 2 p.m. The interval was partly wasted because of differing opinions as to what Israel should do, and mobilization proved unexpectedly slow, taking seventy-two hours to reach full strength. Israel lost 200 tanks and forty aircraft in twenty-four hours, prompting Moshe Dayan, the defence minister, to recommend a twelve-mile retreat from the Suez Canal.‡

In the first day of fighting three great myths were demolished: the supposed superiority of Israeli military organization and planning, the invincibility of the Bar-Lev line, and the quality of Israeli intelligence. Golda Meir later told Henry Kissinger: 'I have to admit that all the preparations and the timing of the attack were perfect.'§ Subsequent academic studies showed that the Israeli cabinet had been anything but cool and collected in this vital period. Confusion, disagreement and uncertainty reigned at the heart of the Israeli decision-making process.**

It was from this position of military advantage that Sadat sent a message of great importance to Kissinger in Washington. Without consulting his colleagues he ordered Hafez Ismail to transmit the note through Eugene Trone, the CIA representative in Cairo. The message began by referring to a peace formula which Kissinger had discussed with Dr Zayyat, the Egyptian foreign minister, during their meeting in New York on 5 October. This was an unfortunate opening, because

* Only Sadat, Assad and a handful of close advisers knew the exact time of the attack in advance.

† Yom Kippur is a day of fasting, prayer and repentance for past sins, and comes at the end of ten days of penitence.

‡ Dayan's proposal was seriously considered by the Israeli cabinet but ultimately rejected in favour of a counter-attack.

§ Matti Golan, *Secret Conversations with Henry Kissinger*.

** See Michael Brecher, *Decisions in Crisis: Israel 1967 and 1973*, University of California Press, 1980.

the letter should have emphasized that the outbreak of war had created a new situation. Hafez Ismail, writing on behalf of Sadat, said that the objective of the war was 'the achievement of peace in the Middle East and not . . . partial settlements'.

The importance of the message lay in item two, sub-paragraph six: 'We do not intend to deepen the engagement or widen the confrontation.' With this Sadat informed Washington, and hence Golda Meir, that Egypt had limited objectives and was not seeking to retake the whole of the Sinai desert by force, something which neither the US nor Israel could otherwise have guessed. Sadat had given the enemy an insight which he had not confided even to his military ally Hafez El-Assad, the Syrian president.

The message went on to state that if Israel withdrew from all occupied territories, Egypt would be prepared to participate in a peace conference under UN or other neutral auspices. Egypt would also agree to freedom of navigation in the Straits of Tiran and would accept an international presence in the straits as a guarantee for a limited period.

'This re-explanation of our position emanates from a real and genuine desire for . . . peace and not from readiness to start a series of concessions,' the message said. 'In fact we remember that Mr Rogers impaired peace chances when he mistakenly interpreted our peace initiative in 1970 in such a manner that it deviated from the true . . . objective.' The ending was surprisingly cordial in the circumstances: 'Please accept my best wishes, Hafez Ismail.'*

In using the secret CIA channel to communicate with Kissinger, Sadat set himself apart from Egypt's professional diplomatic service, which could have transmitted the message just as effectively. The sole purpose of this ruse was to keep the Egyptian government in the dark.

Kissinger was greatly, perhaps excessively, impressed by Sadat's approach. The man he had regarded as a buffoon now became, in his eyes, 'a statesman of the first order',† a man capable of devising a

* All messages between Cairo and Washington quoted in this chapter are based on the private archives of President Sadat. The statement in the 7 October message that Rogers 'impaired peace chances . . . in 1970' was a reference to Nasser's public invitation to the US in April 1970 to submit a new proposal, which led to the Rogers Initiative of 19 June 1970. See Chapter 10.

† *Years of Upheaval*, p. 482.

wholly new kind of strategy which no one had understood. Kissinger came to the conclusion that Sadat had conceived the war from the first as a struggle which Israel was bound to win in military terms, but which would demonstrate the strength and determination of the Arabs, heal their sense of humiliation, and open the way to a negotiated peace.

Kissinger's analysis was partly right, but lacked an essential element: an evolving thought-process. Sadat's ideas changed as the war progressed, reacting to developments rather than following a fully thought-out plan. The secretary of state was wrong to suppose that Sadat entered the war resigned to the probability of an Israeli military victory. The Egyptian leader understood the risks, but thought that the Arabs could regain at least some of their lost territory, as indeed they did.

The thought-process which led Sadat to tell Kissinger of his intentions can best be understood by following the Egyptian leader's moods, anxieties and moments of elation as the battle unfolded. In a conversation a few days before the attack, he told me: 'Nobody can blame me any more. The country wanted a war and we are having a war. Our losses may be great, but the country is big. Whatever happens we will have done what the people wanted.'* It was hardly the argument of a man expecting victory; if anything Sadat seemed to be preparing his lines of self-justification even before giving the order to attack.

Sadat's anxieties were forgotten on 6 October when the astounding success of the crossing became clear. Within ninety minutes of the first attack word reached the Egyptian high command that bridgeheads had been established. Unable to contain his elation, Sadat phoned Vladimir Vinogradov, the Soviet ambassador to Cairo: 'My boys have crossed, Vladimir. They are now approaching the fortified points in the Bar-Lev line and they have encircled some of them.'

In his excitement Sadat began to compare the Egyptian army's success with Israel's victory in the Six Day War of 1967. He made plans to address the nation on television that evening, and phoned me from high command to request notes for a speech. 'What do you want to

* Sadat, his wife and a few close friends spent hours talking almost every evening during this period. My notes of these conversations form part of this chapter.

say?' I asked. 'I'm going to tell the people that we won the Six Hour War,' he replied. 'Oh no,' I said, but he cut me short before I could point out that the struggle had barely started. Thousands of troops were at that moment crossing the Suez Canal on pontoon bridges which might be destroyed by Israeli air attacks.

Sadat's haste to claim victory was unnecessary, for the people were with him from the moment they realized that Egypt had seized the initiative from Israel. Apart from the first days of the 1948–49 war, Arabs had been on the defensive in every conflict. The dithering, insecure leader who had once been called a right winger without an ideology was forgotten: in his shoes stood a freedom fighter with 45 million followers, and a larger following beyond Egypt's borders. Sadat was suddenly the master of a powerful alliance, each of whose component groups had previously doubted him, but now found that their interests coincided with his. Two years of ill-tempered arguments with Moscow were quietly forgotten; the Soviet Union saw an opportunity to redress the disaster its image had suffered in the 1967 war, and perhaps strengthen its strategic position in the Middle East. The army, whose loyalty Sadat had never trusted, now willingly obeyed him. Other Arab leaders, who had previously laughed behind his back, were now bound to support him. The Third World, which had always felt that no one could replace Nasser, offered him its respect.

As a young man Sadat had been divided between desires for a comfortable life and dreams of a stage or film career. The actor in his personality came to the fore during the Yom Kippur War, making him want to look and behave like the commander-in-chief he was never cut out to be. Sadat had an office at high command stuffed with electronic gadgets, and separate high-tech command posts at his three principal homes, as if Egypt's victory depended upon his being in touch from minute to minute. He also asked the Mercedes company for a car equipped for use as a command post, at an estimated cost of $850,000. Ironically, when Brezhnev phoned from Moscow to congratulate him, Sadat was on his way from high command to his office at Tahira Palace, and was in another car.

By the time I had pushed my way through television crews to talk to the president at Tahira Palace on the evening of 6 October, there were confirmed reports that 35,000 Egyptian troops had crossed the canal safely. Fortified by this news and Brezhnev's call, which had at last reached him, Sadat pressed his idea for a speech on the 'Six Hour Victory'.

I pointed out that the situation could easily change for the worse, but Sadat was afraid that if he did not make the first claim the glory would be stolen by President Assad. Although the two men were on good terms, the Egyptian–Syrian alliance fell far short of being a confident partnership, and until early afternoon neither Sadat nor I had felt sure that Syrian forces would follow the agreed plan. 'I am not worried about what Assad does, I don't think you should start talking about a six hour war,' I said. Sadat accepted my advice with reluctance.

At the time Sadat seemed to be suggesting that crossing the canal was a sufficient achievement to be described as victory. In retrospect it seems clear that his real aim, consciously or otherwise, was to make his limited aims clear at this very early stage, hoping that Israel's response would be equally limited. When the idea of a speech was abandoned after strong objections, he passed the same information in his secret message to Kissinger. That communication remained secret until after Sadat's death eight years later.

Brezhnev followed up his phone call with a formal letter of congratulations which was delivered by Vladimir Vinogradov in person. While at Tahira Palace the Soviet ambassador asked: 'Mr President, what about the political side of the battle?' This was a reference to arrangements which had been made previously that the Soviet Union should use its political judgement to decide at what point to seek a UN resolution calling for a ceasefire. Sadat and Assad had agreed that if the fight went against their armies, Moscow should feel free to introduce a resolution immediately, without waiting for authorization from Cairo and Damascus, but if it went well there should be consultations before any resolution.

Sadat rose and stood before the ambassador. 'You see how I am dressed, Vladimir?' He was wearing a Pierre Cardin-designed version of a field marshal's uniform, a sartorial fantasy superb in its expensive understatement. 'Vladimir, you are talking to the commander-in-chief of the battle, and a military officer does not talk politics. If you need anything political, go and talk to Dr Fawzi.'

Vinogradov was too experienced to show his amusement, and too meticulous to believe his ears. 'Does this mean you are handing over political matters to your special assistant for foreign affairs, Mr President?' Sadat assured him that it meant exactly that. While the showman in Sadat's personality undoubtedly had the upper hand, his mental processes showed elements of cunning. By referring Vinogradov to Fawzi, Sadat diverted Moscow's attention from himself at a moment when he was playing a double game with Washington.

This stratagem was aimed solely at confusing Moscow; no Egyptian minister was given authority to bypass the president. Indeed Sadat seemed to want to decide every detail himself, apart from strictly military questions. Hafez Ismail wrote in his memoirs that this was a one-man battle in which no dissent from Sadat's views was acceptable.* I was among those who tried to argue with him, which was perhaps why our friendship later ended. One of our disagreements on 6 October concerned the strong religious tone which government propaganda was beginning to adopt. A leaflet distributed to the troops mentioned that a sheikh had had a dream in which the Prophet Mohamed was seen in the Sinai guiding Egyptian forces. I objected on the grounds that religion should not be confused with nationalism, and that a substantial proportion of the Egyptian soldiers were Coptic Christians. Sadat did not accept my point of view.

On 7 October the Egyptian advance continued, creating an unbroken line across the Sinai desert to a depth of five kilometres east of the canal. With Israel's east bank fortifications now fully in Egypt's hands, it no longer seemed implausible to talk of a victory of sorts. For the first time since coming to power Sadat had emerged from Nasser's shadow as a symbol of Egyptian nationalism. The troops became 'my sons in the army', the air force was composed of 'my aeroplanes' and the navy of 'my submarines'. Sadat refrained though from talking about 'my victory', although he knew that Egyptians considered it his.

The Egyptian leader's wish to focus attention on himself and to exclude others from the decision-making process had high costs. The knowledge of the Egyptian civil service and the experience of prominent leaders was left untapped while Sadat listened only to a handful of people, relying on hunch, intuition and a capacity for improvisation.

Egypt now had two diametrically opposed policies, both articulated

* See Hafez Ismail, *Egyptian National Security*, Al-Ahram, Egypt, 1987.

by Sadat to different audiences. Many an Arab and foreign ambassador was told that Egypt had no intention of stopping until its forces reached the border with Israel. The army, the government, indeed everyone in Egypt except Sadat and Hafez Ismail assumed that the military objective was the recapture of the Mitla and Giddi passes, the strategic keys to the whole of Sinai. Only the two countries with which Egypt had no diplomatic relations, the US and Israel, were privy to the president's secret policy. Kissinger was aware of both strands, and correctly guessed that the secret version was Sadat's real policy.* The secretary of state's plan was to delay any UN ceasefire resolution until Israel had recovered lost ground, which the CIA thought would take two or three days, and then to propose that both the Arabs and Israel should return to the lines they had occupied before the fighting. In other words, Egypt would give up any remaining positions on the east bank and Syria would forfeit any territory it managed to retain in the Golan Heights. Kissinger's policy was dictated by four priorities: the US alliance with Israel; the need to manage US–Soviet relations carefully; the fact that Nixon wanted him to orchestrate the post-war peace; and a feeling that Israel should be restrained from humiliating the Arabs, because that would make peace impossible. The last of these elements was not always given the importance it merited.

All through 7 October Israel kept the fighting on the Sinai front at a modest level while rushing reserve units to the Syrian front as they were mobilized. The Israeli air force ran four times as many sorties against Syrian positions as against the Egyptians. Although under intense pressure the Syrians by and large held their ground. The disagreement within the Israeli cabinet remained unresolved, defence minister Dayan continuing to advocate retreat in the south, while General David Elazar, the chief-of-staff, proposed a plan for a counter-attack the following morning. Elazar was given authority by the cabinet to visit the Sinai front and decide on the spot whether to attack. Meanwhile Israel requested and received permission for El Al airliners to collect supplies of US air-to-air missiles.

By the morning of 8 October the whole of Egypt was waiting for

* In *Years of Upheaval*, Kissinger recalls a National Security Council meeting on 7 October in which he predicted that Egyptian forces would remain in the positions they had captured without penetrating deeper into Sinai.

the second phase of the attack, in which the army was expected to capture the Giddi and Mitla mountain passes in central Sinai. The day passed with no attack in Sinai but with a massive Syrian effort on the Golan Heights, where Israeli defences collapsed in the southern sector during the morning. In the afternoon Syrian tanks penetrated Israeli defences in the central area, before being driven back with heavy losses. The Soviet Union was now pressing Sadat to give a clearer indication of his plans, because discussions were due to begin in the Security Council that evening and the Soviet delegate needed to know whether the Arabs wanted a ceasefire resolution.

Vinogradov was in a meeting with Sadat when I arrived at Tahira Palace in the evening, and as the ambassador emerged it was clear from his expression that there had been a disagreement. He asked to see me that night, and insisted on waiting up for me when I explained that I would be with the president until after midnight. 'It's very important,' he said.

I found Sadat pacing up and down the magnificently decorated salon of the former royal palace. 'What a black day, what a black day,' he was muttering. He had received word from Vinogradov of a heavy loss of Syrian tanks in fighting that day. This was a serious blow, but Sadat's mood suggested that something else was wrong. At that moment a waiter bringing orangeade and cola lost his balance, and the entire tray of glasses crashed to the floor. The president's self-control suddenly snapped. He began shouting and seemed about to pound the man with his fists. 'What is the matter?' I asked.

Sadat swung round and said: 'See what my Mussolini is doing to me.'

'Who is your Mussolini?'

'Assad. He is asking for a ceasefire.'

'Tell me what happened – and let us not use that metaphor, because if Assad is Mussolini, you must be Hitler.' My intention was to break the tension with a joke, but Sadat was not amused. It then emerged that he had understood Vinogradov to say that Damascus was asking the Soviet Union to arrange a ceasefire immediately.

I suggested that he should write to Assad to check whether this was indeed what he wanted, and Sadat agreed. The letter pointed out that stopping the war at that stage would leave Egypt in a worse position than before, because with international observers along the ceasefire lines it would be impossible to resume the war of attrition: 'The important thing now is not territory, the important thing is to fight to prove our will.'

Later that night I heard a very different version from Vinogradov. The ambassador said he had found Sadat in a highly nervous state, and had tried to reassure him. 'The situation is all right. Everything has gone well for Egypt so far, but you should start thinking about the next step,' Vinogradov had told Sadat. 'The situation is not good on the Syrian front. Do you want us to go ahead and ask for a ceasefire resolution?' According to Vinogradov, Sadat looked up sharply and asked: 'Did Assad ask for a ceasefire?' The ambassador replied that the Soviet ambassador in Damascus had not discussed the matter with Assad for several days, but would probably be doing so at about that time.

Assad replied to Sadat's letter the same night (8 October): 'I have not asked the Soviets for a ceasefire and I find it very strange that the Soviet ambassador has talked to you about this. What I told them [the Soviets] was that the ceasefire issue was connected with the liberation of land. And that was several days ago. There is nothing in the present situation that would induce me to ask for a ceasefire. The battle needs patience and is going on in a reasonable way. We are inflicting heavy losses on Israeli forces and our losses are within accepted norms . . . Be assured that an important subject like a ceasefire would not be decided without consultations with you.'

This showed that Vinogradov's account was correct and Sadat's interpretation entirely wrong. What lay behind this incident was that Sadat, whether he knew it or not, had begun to prepare himself psychologically for loosening his alliance with Syria, and was looking for a pretext. What he most wanted was the freedom to act alone, independently of Syria, if his contacts with Kissinger bore fruit. The fear that Syria might reject US proposals which Egypt would be prepared to accept was high in his mind.

During my meeting with Vinogradov the ambassador expressed his concern about the way Sadat was conducting the war. Soviet intelligence showed that the way was open for Egyptian forces to advance, and yet there was no movement. I had already asked the president the previous evening about the expected second phase. His reply had been that he wanted Egypt's positions on the east bank to be a rock against which the Israelis could batter their heads. That strategy had seemed to be working on the second day: the Israelis were only able to mobilize limited numbers of tanks from reserve stores, and these were driven to the front so fast that many broke down on the way. The dribbles of armour which reached Egypt's front were easily crushed.

Vinogradov shook his head when I recounted my conversation with Sadat. 'Your forces are too exposed in their present positions. They ought to move forward to the passes, where they will have more protection.' He took me to a map room in the embassy's military section and asked a military aide to point out to me the positions which Moscow thought Egypt should occupy. Information was streaming in continually from Moscow as we talked. 'There are practically no Israeli forces between your troops and the passes,' the ambassador said.

I tried to contact Sadat but found that he had taken his daughter to a mosque, leaving his bodyguards behind because he wanted to go 'incognito'. It was Ramadan and the mosques and streets were full of people talking excitedly about the war. Sadat was recognized, as he must have known he would be, and was hailed as a hero.

Later I spoke to the president and told him of Vinogradov's advice. Sadat hesitated for some time and then referred me to Ahmed Ismail, minister of war and commander-in-chief. On phoning Ismail's direct line I was told that he was asleep, but General Sa'ad El-Shazli, chief-of-staff and main planner of the 6 October canal crossing, was standing in. Shazli listened to me and then said: 'I suggest you wait until Ahmed Ismail awakes, and please don't let him know that you have told me about this.' This remark made me wonder whether Sadat had some non-military reason for holding back the Egyptian attack. That impression was strengthened a few hours later when I spoke to Ahmed Ismail. The commander-in-chief argued that it would be difficult to take the passes while also consolidating the bridgeheads, which was true but not a sufficient reason for inaction. In retrospect it seems likely that Ahmed Ismail was by this time aware of the secret dialogue with Kissinger.

A further reason for delay was that Sadat felt, and perhaps wanted to feel, that Vinogradov was still pressing for a ceasefire. Certainly Moscow behaved as if it were confident of securing Sadat's consent. The Soviet Union was in favour of a ceasefire in place, but not Kissinger's proposal for a ceasefire requiring a return to pre-war positions.

Kissinger had replied the same day (8 October) to Sadat's message of 7 October. He wanted to know whether Egypt was asking for total Israeli withdrawal before a peace conference, which had always been the Arab position, or whether Israeli agreement in principle would be sufficient. The message promised that the US would work to bring the fighting to an end, and finished with 'warm personal regards'.

Hafez Ismail replied on 9 October, reaffirming the standard Arab position that Israel would have to withdraw to the lines of 5 June 1967 prior to a peace conference. The only hint of flexibility lay in the way the demand was expressed, which was more conciliatory than previous formulations.

Kissinger learned the same day that Israel had lost forty-nine aircraft and 500 tanks, including 400 on the Egyptian front, in only two days of fighting. Now seriously worried, the Israeli cabinet pressed for replacements, and Washington quickly agreed. Kissinger's memoirs quote Nixon as saying: 'The Israelis must not be allowed to lose.' The US president's key decision was that all destroyed Israeli tanks and aircraft would be replaced by the United States. Although it was clearly impossible for the US to deliver the replacements before the war ended, the decision gave Israel greater flexibility to use military strategies which might otherwise have been too risky.

Moshe Dayan was still in a pessimistic mood on 9 October, telling Israeli newspaper editors that Israel would not be able to force Egyptian troops to retreat to the west bank of the Suez Canal. The main Israeli decision-making group was an inner cabinet consisting of Golda Meir, Yigal Allon and Yisrael Galili, replacing Mrs Meir's famous 'kitchen cabinet', which had been suspended for the duration of the war. Meanwhile Haim Bar-Lev had left his post as minister of industry to become commander-in-chief of the southern front.

The following day, 10 October, saw the start of a large-scale Soviet resupply operation to Syria, but not to Egypt, whose losses had so far been relatively light. Washington authorized the use of chartered planes to supplement the El Al airlift, which had begun collecting US supplies on the first day of the war. The Israelis were beginning to regain territory they had lost on the Syrian front but remained blocked by Egypt's solid defence line in Sinai. King Hussein of Jordan came under strong pressure to enter the war, and King Faisal of Saudi Arabia made plans to send a brigade to Damascus.

Meanwhile a misunderstanding was developing between the two superpowers. The United States was beginning to realize that its proposal for a return to the pre-war lines was unrealistic, but Israel had not yet come round to that view. At the same time Moscow was still trying to persuade Assad and Sadat to accept a ceasefire in place. According to Kissinger, Anatoly Dobrynin, the Soviet ambassador to Washington, told him on 10 October that Moscow would not block a resolution in the Security Council for a ceasefire in place.* At the time of the conversation no such resolution was yet before the Security Council. It appears that Kissinger thought Dobrynin was saying that Egypt and Syria would reluctantly go along with a ceasefire in place, and that Moscow was sounding Washington out before submitting a resolution. What Dobrynin meant was that Moscow had not yet secured Egyptian and Syrian approval, but would not veto such a resolution if Washington wanted to go ahead. This misunderstanding became the basis of an unfounded US accusation later in the war that Sadat had gone back on his word to accept a ceasefire resolution.

The first shift in Egypt's negotiating position was signalled the same day (10 October). In a message sent through the Hafez Ismail–Kissinger channel, Sadat modified the usual Arab demand for Israeli withdrawal prior to negotiations, proposing instead that Israel should withdraw under UN supervision within a specified period after a ceasefire.

Once Israeli troops had withdrawn the state of belligerency would come to an end, and within a specified further period a UN peace conference would be convened to discuss all issues. Kissinger realized that this showed a willingness to negotiate, but also felt that Sadat's demands were still too ambitious. American public interest in the war was deflected at this stage by the resignation on the same day of vice president Spiro Agnew amid a corruption scandal.†

The following day Hafez Ismail sent Kissinger a message marked 'Very Urgent' pointing out that Israeli air raids on civilian targets in

* See *Years of Upheaval*, p. 498.

† Agnew faced accusations over alleged payoffs during earlier public service as governor of Maryland. The scandal was not connected to Watergate.

the Nile delta on 10 and 11 October had left 500 dead and wounded. Ismail mentioned Sadat's name directly for the first time, in connection with an appeal to the US to restrain Israel. Attacks were also directed against Port Said, Damascus and a Syrian oil refinery, reflecting Israel's frustration at being unable to use its aircraft against Syrian and Egyptian forces because of the effectiveness of Soviet anti-aircraft missiles. In his reply the following day (12 October) Kissinger said that the US had made 'strong representations' to Israel not to attack civilian targets. He went on to deny reports that US forces were involved on Israel's side, but gave an implicit warning that Washington would reverse that policy if Soviet forces entered the war. This followed US intelligence reports that Moscow had placed airborne divisions on alert.

Haim Bar-Lev now began planning a campaign to break through the Egyptian lines guarding the east side of the canal. His strategy was to aim for a supposed weak point between the northern sector manned by the Egyptian second army and the southern sector controlled by the third army. The plan would not be feasible for several days until forces had been diverted from the Syrian front, and also needed new supplies of American arms and ammunition.

A major Israeli counter-attack against Syria began on 11 October and in three days pushed nearly seven miles into Syria beyond lines held before the war, bringing Israeli artillery within range of the outskirts of Damascus.

Washington, which had been putting off a reply to Dobrynin's message, began to bring pressure on Israel to complete its offensives on both fronts as soon as possible. This was unwelcome to Moshe Dayan, who felt that Israel needed more time, but the Israeli cabinet was watching Israel's dwindling ammunition stocks with anxiety. The US resupply effort had been slower than intended, and Golda Meir began to think that the delay was connected with Israel's reluctance to accept a ceasefire in place. At the same time the Arabs were continuing to show greater resistance on both fronts than Israel had anticipated, and intelligence reports said that a Saudi brigade had reached Syria. Iraq was sending reinforcements, and even Jordan, which had tried to stay out of the conflict, was prepared to assist Syria. Israeli accounts suggest that Mrs Meir felt under great stress during this period, realizing that if US supplies did not arrive quickly Israel might not be able to hold on to the territory captured in Syria. An exaggerated version of her concern was passed to the US administration, hinting that an Israeli defeat was in prospect. Mrs Meir announced that Israel was now prepared to accept a ceasefire in place and word was passed to Kissinger that the US could promote a UN resolution immediately. These hints that Israel was losing heart alarmed Kissinger and Nixon, who immediately investigated the cause of the delays.

Amid uproar in the US media, Washington denied that the delay had been a deliberate tactic to put pressure on Israel.* On 13 October Nixon ordered the use of American C-5A military transport aircraft to expedite deliveries. 'Send everything that flies,' Kissinger quoted the US president as saying.†

The timing of this more energetic US effort proved crucially important. Sadat had finally decided, after much delay and heart-searching, to go ahead with the second-phase attack which had been scheduled for 8 October. The decision was not taken until 12 October, for implementation two days later, which proved to be the worst possible moment. Once having given authority for the attack Sadat was obliged to reject the ceasefire-in-place proposal, and his refusal coincided with Israel's acceptance. Egyptian forces which on 8 or 9 October could have swept across the desert unopposed now faced strong Israeli positions. At 6 a.m. on 14 October, when the Egyptian advance began, the Israeli government already knew the period of vulnerability was over. American supplies were due to arrive later in the day, and there was no further need to conserve missiles and ammunition. Israel could throw everything it had into one of the biggest tank battles in history.

An Egyptian force of 1000 tanks and hundreds of heavy guns faced a comparable weight of Israeli armour and artillery, but the Israeli side had the important advantage of TOW anti-tank missiles, fired from helicopters operating from El-Arish airport. At the same time Israeli fighters were free to carry out close-support air strikes. Egyptian forces were now beyond the protective umbrella of the anti-aircraft missile batteries on the west bank of the canal, and had only portable missiles for cover, which proved inadequate. Faced with the full strength of the Israeli air force and armour, Egypt lost 390 tanks in a single day

* Kissinger claimed in *Years of Upheaval* that the delay was caused by the unwillingness of charter companies to allow their planes to be used in a war and by bureaucratic wrangles between two US government departments.

† In an interview with David Frost in May 1977.

and suffered a decisive defeat, for which Sadat must bear personal responsibility. Had Vinogradov's advice of 8 October been followed, Egypt would undoubtedly have seized and held the mountain passes. By the time Sadat made up his mind, the high command knew that the window of opportunity had passed. General Shazli, chief-of-staff, and General Saad Mahmoud of the first army, had placed their objections to the timing on record, but Sadat ignored their advice.

The 14 October battle ended at 3 p.m., and three hours later the first C-5A transport aircraft landed in Israel, beginning an operation which changed the balance of strength. From then on US supplies poured into Lod airport at a rate of 1000 tons a day and Israeli forces never again had to worry about shortages. The Soviet effort, which now included Egypt, was on a much smaller scale.*

The next day Kissinger sent Hafez Ismail a message seeking to justify the scale of the US effort. Unlike the cordial tone of previous correspondence, the 15 October note was written in the third person and was unsigned.

> As Dr Kissinger has pointed out to Mr Ismail the United States has reacted with great constraint to the recent events . . . the US has voiced no criticism of Arab actions either in the United Nations or in public statements . . . no resupply action to Israel was undertaken for a week despite insistent Israeli demands for supplies and equipment.† This restraint was observed by the United States even in the face of a massive Soviet airlift of military equipment to the Arab combatants.‡

Kissinger went on to say that the US had been 'forced to reconsider its position' on re-supplying Israel for two reasons. The first was that the Soviet Union had previously told Washington that Egypt was prepared to accept a ceasefire in place. Washington then obtained Israeli's agreement, only to find that Egypt was no longer willing to proceed (as already stated, this was the result of a misunderstanding

* Kissinger said in *Years of Upheaval* that on its first full day of operation the US airlift matched what the Soviet Union had sent to Egypt, Syria and Iraq in the previous four days.

† This statement overlooked the fact that El Al planes had been collecting US missiles since the first day of the war, as Kissinger acknowledged in his memoirs.

‡ The 'restraint' in US supplies after the Soviet airlift had begun was unintentional, according to the US administration's version (see footnote, p. 194).

between Kissinger and Dobrynin). The second was the 'massive Soviet airlift'. Kissinger said the US would stop re-supplying Israel as soon as a ceasefire was achieved.

The message ended on a more conciliatory note: 'The United States . . . recognizes the unacceptability to the Egyptian side of the conditions which existed prior to the outbreak of recent hostilities.' Kissinger then promised a major US diplomatic effort as soon as hostilities were terminated.

Sadat replied a few hours later with one of the most important messages of the war. Ignoring the terse phrasing of Kissinger's note, he wrote as if he were addressing a respected friend rather than his enemy's ally. The letter was sent in the name of Hafez Ismail but its main lines were undoubtedly dictated by the president, who wanted to show that Egypt was not beholden to the Soviet Union, and that US assistance to Israel did not diminish Cairo's hope that the US would bring about a solution. All this was implied rather than stated, but Kissinger could not, and did not, mistake Sadat's intention.

The letter began by reaffirming 'Egypt's wish to keep open this special channel of contact', and then pointed out that 'no other party [meaning the Soviet Union] speaks in Egypt's name'. This was a way of saying that what Kissinger had heard from the Soviet ambassador to Washington on 10 October about Egypt's willingness to accept a ceasefire was not necessarily accurate.

Sadat went on: 'Egypt wishes to make it clear that it does not seek to humiliate Israel, because Egypt has tasted what humiliation is.'

The Egyptian leader offered only the mildest rebuke imaginable for the massive US airlift, calling it 'unacceptable'. The letter did not depart from Egypt's demand for a complete Israeli withdrawal, but asked Kissinger to make a major effort to gain Israel's acceptance. In item eight Sadat said: 'Egypt will welcome Dr Kissinger in appreciation for his efforts.' In his memoirs Kissinger described this invitation as amazing. The message concluded: 'The Egyptian side will be prepared to discuss any subject, proposal or project, within the framework of the principles . . . that Egypt cannot make any concessions on land or sovereignty,' It was signed by Hafez Ismail 'with warmest regards'.

When the Egyptian national security adviser dispatched this message Israeli forces were making final preparations for the counter-attack which Haim Bar-Lev, commander-in-chief of the Israeli southern front, had been planning for several days. Bar-Lev concentrated his forces on a sector of the canal just north of Great Bitter Lake, in the supposed soft area between the Egyptian second army to the north and the third army to the south. The risk that Israel might try to drive a wedge between the two armies had been foreseen in military planning as early as 1969, and a scheme known as 'Plan 200' had been prepared to face that contingency. These precautions proved insufficient in the face of massed Israeli armour led by General Ariel Sharon. By 1.30 a.m. on 16 October an Israeli advance party had crossed the canal and begun establishing a bridgehead, and later in the day twenty-five Israel tanks succeeded in crossing on a pontoon bridge.

Sadat was making a major speech to the Egyptian parliament, announcing that Egypt would accept a ceasefire if Israel withdrew to its 1967 borders, when news agency tickers began carrying reports of a claim by Golda Meir to the Knesset that Israeli forces were fighting both east and west of the canal. As soon as Sadat left parliament I asked him about Mrs Meir's statement. He assumed that she was engaging in propaganda to deflect attention from his speech, but gradually it became clear that at least some Israelis had reached the west bank. Even then the extent of the operation was under-estimated. Ahmed Ismail, the minister of war, was under the impression for hours that the Israelis were carrying out a raid rather than creating a bridgehead. 'This is the first time I have seen guerrilla warfare by tanks,' he said.

Sadat continued to insist that the Israeli operation was a 'dance of the horses', an Arabic expression meaning a matter of little importance, until the presence of an Israeli general on the west bank was confirmed. By the time the Egyptian leadership took the threat seriously the Israeli bridgehead was established.

Alexei Kosygin, the Soviet prime minister, flew to Cairo the same day (16 October) and tried without success to persuade Sadat to accept a ceasefire in place. Soviet officials no longer hid their dismay at the conduct of the war and Cairo's lack of consultation with Moscow. Unknown to Kosygin, Sadat was now more likely to accept advice from Kissinger, who had just sent a long reply to Sadat's remarks of the previous day.

The secretary of state's aim was to make Sadat realize that time was now on Israel's side. The Arab armies had made their point, he felt, and the time had come for political realism. Nothing further would be achieved by continuing the fighting. 'Egyptian forces have already accomplished much,' he wrote. 'The humiliation which Egyptians and indeed the Arab world felt after 1967 has been erased. A new strategic situation has been established in which reliance by any country on permanent military supremacy has become illusory. Hence the necessity of a political settlement is becoming much clearer to all parties.'

Referring to Egypt's demand for a complete Israeli withdrawal immediately, the message said: 'In Dr Kissinger's judgement this is not achievable except by protracted war. No US influence can bring this goal about in present circumstances. What the US side can promise and will fulfil is to make every effort to assist in achieving a final, just settlement once a ceasefire is achieved.'

Further on Kissinger added: 'The Egyptian side therefore has an important decision to make. To insist on its maximum programme means continuation of the war and possible jeopardy of all that has been achieved. The outcome will then be decided by military measures. The US side will not speculate on this outcome but doubts whether it would be clear cut.' The message ended with thanks for the invitation to Egypt and warmest regards.

Sadat was now under pressure from both superpowers to accept a ceasefire in place and from Kissinger to set his political sights lower. Against this there were opposing arguments and developments which seemed to counsel against pessimism. On 17 October Arab oil producers announced after a meeting in Kuwait that production would be cut by 5 per cent immediately and by a further 5 per cent every month until Israel withdrew to its 5 June 1967 borders. This unleashing of the Arab oil weapon was to have an immense impact on Europe, and a less direct effect on Washington. Secondly, on the same day Nixon and Kissinger adopted an unexpectedly conciliatory attitude in a meeting with the foreign ministers of Saudi Arabia, Kuwait, Morocco and Algeria. Kissinger conceded that early US assumptions on the course of the war had been proved wrong. A report by El-Zayyat, the Egyptian foreign minister, said: 'When asked why [UN Resolution 242] had never been implemented, Kissinger replied quite frankly that being militarily superior Israel was not keen on its implementation. He said that one does not negotiate with the weak: the Arabs were weak but had now become strong and were fit to negotiate with.' In a press conference afterwards the Algerian minister pointed out that the US was now talking with the Arabs because of the success of the Arab military initiative.

A third reason for Sadat to delay any ceasefire resolution was that the Egyptian high command was not yet in agreement as to the scale of Israel's bridgehead on the west bank, nor on what to do about it. The next two days were lost in a dispute over tactics. Chief-of-staff General Shazli argued that two reserve divisions which had been used in the second phase attack on 14 October should be brought back to the west side to resist the Israeli bridgehead. A second school of thought held that Egyptian forces on the west side should try to close the gap which Israel had opened, with the aim of cutting off Sharon's supply lines from the east side. Minister of war Ahmed Ismail backed this second view against Shazli's recommendation, on the ground that withdrawing the two divisions could give an impression of a general retreat. He feared that this could have a disastrous effect on the morale of the second and third armies on the east bank. The debate was conducted in a reasonable manner until Sadat, siding with Ahmed Ismail, began to accuse Shazli of cowardice, which was unwarranted. The more Sadat insulted Shazli the greater the tension at high command became. Sadat later wrote that he dismissed Shazli because the general had lost his nerve.* While Sadat and his generals argued Sharon's tanks were knocking out the west bank missile shield post by post.

Kosygin, who had remained in Cairo after his unsuccessful meeting with Sadat, received Soviet satellite photographs on 18 October showing the scale of the Israeli bridgehead, which was now up to eight miles deep in places. With this evidence the Soviet prime minister approached Sadat again and managed to persuade him to accept a ceasefire. Sadat took this decision alone without consulting his cabinet, the Syrian president or any other Arab leader. When Gadaffi heard of it and phoned to ask for an explanation, Sadat felt no obligation to go into details. 'Muammar, I have calculated everything very carefully and I alone am responsible for my decisions,' he replied.

Within hours of obtaining Sadat's consent Moscow approached Washington to seek a UN resolution linked to Resolution 242. Kissinger

* Sadat gave this version in his memoirs, *In Search of Identity*, published in 1978.

knew that Israel, which had been anxious for a ceasefire six days earlier, now wanted more time to destroy Egypt's defences. By this time General Sharon's forces had 300 tanks on the west bank. The secretary of state did not reject the Soviet proposal but used delaying tactics.

Seeking a way of putting a time limit on US procrastination, Brezhnev asked Kissinger to fly to Moscow the following day (20 October) for talks. Kissinger accepted, partly because the travelling time and the need to adjust to jet-lag before conducting negotiations would gain a further two to three days for Israel to complete its military aims. Before leaving for Moscow Kissinger wrote to Hafez Ismail saying that his objective was 'to bring about an immediate ceasefire and to begin promptly a diplomatic process to move towards a fundamental settlement'. On the same afternoon (19 October) President Nixon approached Congress with a request for $2.2 billion in aid for Israel.

During the night of October 19–20 a strange incident in Cairo demonstrated growing unrest within the Egyptian army over the handling of the war. Sadat was sleeping at Tahira Palace when eleven officers from general command entered the building and asked to see him. Colonel Abdel-Ra'ouf Reda, a military liaison officer at the palace, tried to put them off, but the officers insisted. At first there were fears of a coup attempt, but eventually Reda decided to wake the president.

Sadat, who had always been nervous about the army's loyalty, was alarmed but emerged in dressing gown and pyjamas to talk to them. 'Yes, my sons?' he asked. The delegation had come to tell the president that senior officers at high command were constantly arguing and unable to make decisions. The situation was deteriorating and they appealed to him to take the situation in hand. 'All right, my sons, I'll see what I can do,' Sadat said calmly. As soon as the men had left he called Ahmed Ismail. The army chief wanted to identify and court-martial the officers, but Sadat vetoed any disciplinary action to avoid further aggravating the unrest.

Two days had passed since Sadat authorized the Soviet Union to proceed with a ceasefire resolution, and the delay was playing on the Egyptian leader's nerves, as the tone of a telegram he sent to Assad on 20 October showed:

> For the first four days Israel stood alone and we succeeded in exposing their positions . . . they admitted the loss of 800 tanks

> and more than 200 planes on both fronts. As for the last ten days, I have been fighting the US on the Egyptian front with its sophisticated military arsenal. I simply cannot fight the US or take on the historic responsibility of our armed forces being destroyed once again. I have therefore notified the USSR that I do accept a ceasefire in place on the following conditions:
>
> A Soviet–American guarantee of Israeli withdrawal, as the USSR has proposed.
>
> A UN peace conference to be held in order to reach an agreement, as the USSR has proposed.
>
> My heart bleeds as I tell you this but my sense of responsibility forces me to this decision.

News agency reports of heavy fighting worried King Faisal, who sent a telegram to Sadat: 'Please assure us about the situation.' Sadat replied: 'The situation is delicate because of the flow of American arms and volunteers operating tanks and planes, coming mainly from the US and also Europe. One pilot prisoner has admitted that US planes were being flown by American pilots. We have recorded this and will be broadcasting it. We are doing all that is humanly possible and more.'

Faisal had taken the lead in rallying Arab oil producers, proposing a 10 per cent reduction in output, instead of the 5 per cent cut which had been announced three days earlier, and a total embargo on oil sales to the United States and Holland.* This tightening of the screw was endorsed by other oil states and brought rapid political results. European countries dependent on Arab oil began to put pressure on the US administration to rein in Israel as quickly as possible.

While Kissinger was on his way to Moscow on 20 October the US administration was shaken by a further development in the Watergate scandal, forcing Nixon to concentrate totally on domestic politics.†

* King Faisal made this proposal on 17 October. Holland was included in the embargo because its statements during the war had favoured Israel.

† The scandal had begun in June 1972 when five men were caught inside the Democratic Party headquarters at the Watergate complex in Washington. The men were found to be linked to the Committee to Re-elect the President, which was promoting Nixon's campaign for a second term in the November 1972 presidential election, and to the CIA. The development which occurred while Kissinger was in Moscow was the 'Saturday night massacre', in which Nixon dismissed Archibald Cox, the special prosecutor appointed to investigate Watergate. Nixon's move prompted the attorney general Elliott Richardson and his deputy to resign in protest, and led to a determined effort by Nixon's opponents to bring about his impeachment.

From this point on Kissinger's role became more dominant than ever.

That night Hafez Ismail sent Kissinger a new three-point Egyptian proposal which reflected the secretary of state's earlier advice that Egypt should lower its expectations.* The important difference was that Cairo dropped its demand for an Israeli withdrawal within a specified time limit and instead called for a guarantee by the two superpowers that Israel would withdraw, without specifying when. Kissinger received this in Moscow before his meeting with Brezhnev and Gromyko.

On 21 October, while Kissinger was discussing the proposed ceasefire with Brezhnev and Gromyko, President Assad sent Sadat a telegram expressing optimism and suggesting that the battle should continue.

> I was touched by your message which I received yesterday . . . I have come to the conclusion that the situation does not call for pessimism and that it is possible for the conflict . . . to continue. The resumption of the battle can quite possibly lead to the destruction of enemy forces which have crossed the canal.
>
> Boosting the morale of our troops is imperative. The mere penetration of the front on their part does not necessarily mean that victory is theirs. They broke through the northern front a few days ago, but . . . we have succeeded in halting their advance in certain areas and I am certain we shall win back the areas we lost.

Brezhnev and Kosygin showed no sign of being aware of Assad's attitude during their talks with Kissinger. The two Soviet leaders seemed in such haste to negotiate a ceasefire that Kissinger was convinced he held all the negotiating cards. During four hours of talks on 21 October the three men settled the text of a UN resolution on terms that entirely suited the secretary of state. The text made no mention of Israeli withdrawal, merely calling for the immediate implementation of UN Resolution 242 of 1967, whose meaning had always been intentionally ambiguous. The Soviet leaders tried to include a reference to

* The three points of the Egyptian proposal were: a ceasefire on the present lines; convening a peace conference with the object of reaching a fundamental settlement; a guarantee by the United States and the Soviet Union of the ceasefire and the withdrawal of Israeli troops.

withdrawal, but dropped the demand when Kissinger insisted. Moscow had wanted a ceasefire since the early days of the war, and having secured Sadat's consent was determined to press ahead, with or without Assad's approval. The resolution also called for immediate negotiations between the parties 'under appropriate auspices', which meant the United States and the Soviet Union. The UN Security Council met a few hours later and passed Resolution 338 just after midnight (21–22 October) New York time.* The resolution was to go into effect twelve hours later, which would be the evening of 22 October in the Middle East. This gave Israel every incentive to press on until the last moment to improve its ceasefire positions. Fighting on the Syrian front, which had remained heavy since the Israeli advance of 11 October, intensified before the ceasefire and Israeli forces captured additional territory in the southern part of the Golan Heights.

A message which Kissinger sent Hafez Ismail on 22 October read: 'I can assure you that as the fighting ceases the United States will use its influence to secure a lasting peace in the Middle East on a basis just for all parties.' Israel was now pressing Kissinger to secure the release of prisoners taken by Egypt and Syria, an issue he had taken up with Brezhnev and Gromyko. 'The Soviet Union has assured us that they would use their maximum influence to bring about an immediate exchange of prisoners,' Kissinger wrote to Hafez Ismail. This was more a US hope than a reality: Moscow was unlikely to press Cairo and Damascus to give up a key factor in subsequent negotiations.

Subsequent messages informed Hafez Ismail that the ceasefire would go into effect at 6.52 p.m. Israeli time and that Kissinger was on his way from Moscow to the Middle East. Hafez Ismail sent Kissinger an invitation to call at Cairo, but he had already agreed to fly to Israel to tell Golda Meir about his talks in Moscow, and then to London to brief Sir Alec Douglas-Home, the British foreign secretary.

When Kissinger reached Tel Aviv a few hours before the ceasefire

* UN Security Council Resolution 338 stated: 'The Security Council 1) Calls upon all parties to the present fighting to cease all firing and terminate all military activity immediately, no later than twelve hours after the moment of adoption of this decision, in the positions they now occupy; 2) Calls upon the parties concerned to start immediately after the ceasefire the implementation of Security Council Resolution 242 (1967) in all its parts; 3) Decides that, immediately and concurrently with the ceasefire, negotiations start between the parties concerned under appropriate auspices aimed at establishing a just and durable peace in the Middle East.

he found the Israeli people exhausted, relieved that the fighting was about to stop, and rattled.* Israeli politicians later claimed that the Egyptian third army could have been destroyed if the ceasefire had been delayed for a further three days. This was unrealistic, because delaying the ceasefire and continuing American assistance at the level needed to destroy the third army would have caused a major US–Soviet crisis. The claims also overlooked the fact that the third army was not surrounded at the time of the ceasefire, and only became encircled later because Israel flouted the ceasefire while Washington turned a blind eye.

The mood in Cairo on 22 October was unlike that in Israel, but no calmer.

'It's going to end tonight,' Sadat told me at Tahira Palace, the strain showing in his voice.

'Have we informed the Syrians about the timing?' I asked.

'No, no, I am not going to inform them. The Soviets can do that.'†

'But why?' I asked. 'They agreed with you on going to war, not with Moscow.'

'No, don't bother me with these dilemmas,' he said.

'At least wait a few hours until United Nations observers are in place to monitor the ceasefire,' I suggested. 'You can't accept a law whose judge has not arrived.'

Sadat replied, 'No, I do not want my hands tied.'

The president's refusal to speak to Assad came from a wish to escape from Egypt's moral bond with Syria. Sadat knew that if his Kissinger-based policy were to work, he would have to distance himself from the Syrian leader. Washington was sure to regard Assad's close alliance with Moscow as an obstacle.

Sadat lost his temper when Hafez Ismail pressed the case for moving less quickly in accepting the ceasefire. 'What do you mean, Hafez?' the president snapped.

'Sir, we are rushing more than necessary.'

Sadat shouted at him furiously: 'What's got into you, Hafez? You're a military man, you ought to know better.' The national security adviser fell into silence, looking as if he were about to weep.

* See *Years of Upheaval*, p. 561.

† Syria accepted the ceasefire on 23 October.

These worries were quickly overtaken by events. Israel's forces on both banks of the canal paused for only a few hours after the ceasefire and then began an operation to encircle the third army in the southern sector. An angry message from Hafez Ismail to Kissinger on 23 October read: 'Israeli forces have broken the ceasefire and are attempting to exploit Egyptian compliance with Security Council Resolution 338 . . . by occupying new positions. If what is happening now is any indication, it certainly reflects the degree of worthiness to be attached to any future Israeli commitment. On its part Egypt is taking all necessary measures to ensure its security.'

A further Egyptian message a few hours later, marked 'Very Urgent', said that Israel was creating 'a new military situation' and asked for immediate US steps to make the Israelis return to the 22 October ceasefire lines. At almost the same time Kissinger received a report from the US ambassador in Israel that the Israeli army claimed it had been attacked by Egyptian forces, and that as a result Golda Meir had ordered her forces to continue fighting.* Neither Kenneth Keating, the US ambassador, nor Kissinger believed the Israeli version.

Kissinger wrote to Hafez Ismail: 'The US side is in urgent touch with the Israeli side regarding the maintenance of the ceasefire.' The same message discussed a further UN resolution and the possibility of deploying UN observer teams or troops in Sinai.

Frantic contacts involving the two superpowers, Israel and Kurt Waldheim, secretary general of the United Nations, continued during the next few hours, while Israeli forces swept ahead. Sadat sent a personal message to Nixon, using the Hafez Ismail–Kissinger link, asking for immediate US intervention even if that necessitated the use of force: 'The Egyptian government will consider the US government fully responsible for what is happening . . . in spite of your guarantees and of the Security Council resolution co-sponsored by the USA.' Sadat added: 'What is happening now in the light of your guarantee does not induce confidence in any other future guarantees.' Despite the terseness of this note it was signed 'with warm regards'.

Massive Israeli ceasefire violations had succeeded in cutting the supply line from Cairo to the Egyptian third army on the east side of the Suez Canal. Israeli forces on the west side now occupied a strip of

* See *Years of Upheaval*, p. 569.

territory running from just north of Great Bitter Lake to the Gulf of Suez, and were directly behind the third army on the east side of the canal. At the same time the third army remained hemmed in on its other flanks by Israeli units on the east side. Israel's tactic was to force the army of about 35,000 men to surrender for lack of water, medical supplies and food.

At the height of the crisis Hafez Ismail briefed the Egyptian cabinet on the true extent of Israel's presence on the west bank, which had been kept secret. The information so alarmed them that a minister suggested emergency preparations be made for a possible Israeli attempt to enter Cairo.* Hafez Ismail told the cabinet: 'I want to tell everybody that I am not responsible for what happened.' This was premature, because Egypt's military situation was not so serious as to warrant such talk. Nevertheless, the cabinet was beginning to realize the gravity of the situation.

Kissinger again played for time, pretending in messages to Hafez Ismail and to Moscow to be unsure which side had violated the ceasefire first. Brezhnev accused the Israelis of 'treachery' and the tone of superpower communications became heated. Later the same day the Security Council passed Resolution 339 urging both sides to return 'to the positions they occupied at the moment the ceasefire became effective'. This meant little in practice, because Israel argued that there was no way of determining what those positions had been.

Nixon replied to Sadat's message by denying that the US had guaranteed the ceasefire. 'All we guaranteed – no matter what you have been told from other sources – was to engage fully and constructively in promoting a political process.' The next day Kissinger informed Hafez Ismail that the US had made representations and that 'in response the Israeli government has told us that it will desist from any further offensive action', on condition that Egypt abstained from counter-attacks. A pattern was developing: Israel would pause for a few hours, claim that Egypt had broken the ceasefire, and resume fighting.

After further heavy fighting on 24 October and more Egyptian protests Nixon sent Sadat another message: 'The Israeli government

* Such an attempt was highly improbable, because Israeli military supply lines were already stretched out over a distance of 350 miles from the Red Sea to a front line twenty to twenty-five miles from Damascus.

has replied to the effect that the attacks are being initiated by the third Egyptian army; the Israeli forces are on the defensive and have been ordered only to shoot on attack. From here the true facts are impossible to determine. I want to assure you that the US is unalterably opposed to offensive military actions and is prepared to take effective steps to end them. In the meantime could you make sure that all military action is stopped also by your forces.' Nixon backed this up with another message later saying that Golda Meir had assured him that 'strict instructions' had been issued to Israeli forces to stay in defensive positions.

The US administration continued to claim that it was putting pressure on Israel, and Israeli forces continued to fight. A message from Kissinger to Hafez Ismail on 24 October said: 'The Israeli government was informed that further offensive operations would lead to a severe deterioration of relations between the Israeli and US governments . . . The president personally intervened with the prime minister of Israel to halt the fighting.'

Kissinger said that the Israelis claimed to have obtained a note issued to Egyptian forces by the Egyptian ministry of war at the height of the recent fighting. The note called on Egyptian forces to continue fighting, promised air support, and said that 250 tanks were being sent from Cairo to break through Israeli forces on the west bank.

Later the same day (24 October) Sadat informed Nixon that the Israelis had again resumed their attacks on the third army's positions both east and west of the canal: 'Let me reiterate that I am asking you to intervene, even on the ground, to force Israel to comply with the ceasefire. That much you have promised.'

The ceasefire violations continued and the tone of superpower contacts became steadily more tense, leading to a crisis on the night of 24–25 October. Brezhnev asked Nixon to participate in joint US–Soviet military measures to enforce the ceasefire, and indicated that Moscow would act alone if Washington declined to cooperate. Washington took this as a threat of direct Soviet involvement in the war, which would inevitably bring Soviet and US forces into conflict. Kissinger and the National Security Council then placed US forces around the world on a higher state of alert. Nixon, who was preoccupied with the Watergate scandal, had given him authority to act alone and was not consulted at the time.

Ironically, in the midst of what was technically a nuclear war alert, Kissinger and Hafez Ismail were calmly discussing dates for the secretary of state to visit Cairo, and agreed on 7 November.

Early on 25 October, while news of the US alert was breaking, Hafez Ismail sent Kissinger a message insisting on Egypt's position. The note began by referring to an earlier US decision to send a military attaché from the US embassy in Israel to monitor the ceasefire. 'It is our view that this is not sufficient,' Hafez Ismail said. 'We have asked for a joint US–Soviet presence to guarantee the ceasefire. Since the US refuses to take such a measure Egypt is asking the Security Council to provide an international force.'

Kissinger said in reply that he had learned that a resolution might be introduced at the Security Council that evening urging that outside military forces – including those of the US and the USSR – be sent to the Middle East to enforce the ceasefire resolution. He warned that if the resolution went ahead the US would use its veto power, and argued that bringing superpower forces into the conflict 'would introduce an extremely dangerous potential for direct great power rivalry in the area'. Sadat immediately sent a message to Nixon saying: 'I understand the considerations you have put forward [on] the use of a joint US–USSR force.'

A further Kissinger message said that 'the introduction of US–Soviet combat forces would have incalculable consequences'. However, Washington was ready to support an international force composed of troops from countries other than the five permanent members of the Security Council. Meanwhile in Washington the Defense Department was preparing contingency plans to send US forces to the Middle East. Washington was unsure whether Moscow was bluffing or not, and wanted to be prepared.

Hafez Ismail replied that Sadat would accept the US solution on condition that the proposed force had political backing from the permanent Security Council members, especially from the US and the Soviet Union.

Later Sadat complained that Israel was not only pursuing its ceasefire violations but was refusing to allow a United Nations helicopter carrying blood, plasma, medicine and provisions to reach wounded Egyptian soldiers on the east bank. 'I request your immediate and firm intervention,' he wrote.

Kissinger said in reply: 'The Israeli government has explained that it could not earlier allow helicopter flights since the helicopters would have Egyptian markings.'

Later Hafez Ismail reported that Israel was also preventing medical supplies from being sent by road: 'The medical supply column has been delayed along the route for several hours and when it reached the outskirts of Suez about sunset it was asked to go back again to Cairo and return on 26 October.'

The superpower crisis was finally resolved that night when the Security Council passed Resolution 340, which demanded an 'immediate and complete' ceasefire and a return to the 22 October positions. The resolution adopted the compromise proposal of a UN Emergency Force supplied by countries other than permanent members of the Security Council. The Soviet Union, the US and Egypt were happy with the resolution; Israel was not.* The Israeli military, the government and public opinion were still desperate to find any pretext to continue trying to destroy the third army.

In a message to Nixon on 26 October Sadat complained that the Israeli pressure on the third army was 'an attempt to isolate it and oblige it to surrender in humiliation. To this hour the Israelis are preventing UN observers reaching the area involved.' He added: 'I frankly do not see how we can provide for the appropriate atmosphere for constructive discussions with the secretary of state during his visit [to Cairo] if this situation continues to prevail.'

For a few hours afterwards the tone of messages on the Hafez Ismail–Kissinger link suggested a lull. The two men discussed Kissin-

* Security Council Resolution 340, adopted on 25 October, began with a preamble and then listed five points. 'The Security Council: 1) Demands that immediate and complete ceasefire be observed and that the parties return to the positions occupied by them at 16.50 hours GMT on 22 October 1973. 2) Requests the secretary general, as an immediate step, to increase the number of United Nations military observers on both sides. 3) Decides to set up immediately under its authority a United Nations Emergency Force to be composed of personnel drawn from states members of the United Nations except the permanent members of the Security Council, and requests the secretary general to report within twenty-four hours on the steps taken to this effect. 4) Requests the secretary general to report to the council on an urgent and continuing basis on the state of implementation of the present solution, as well as resolutions 338 (1973) and 339 (1973). 5) Requests all member states to extend their full cooperation to the United Nations in the implementation of the present resolution, as well as resolutions 338 (1973) and 339 (1973).

ger's plans to visit Cairo and arrangements to take medical supplies through Israeli lines to the third army, and Nixon sent Sadat a letter saying that he was 'very encouraged' by the preparations for Kissinger's visit. The reality in the desert was starker: the third army, already worryingly short of water, food and medical supplies, was trying to break out of Israel's vice, while Israeli forces were mounting another attack.

At 7.30 p.m. Cairo time Sadat sent an urgent message to Nixon: 'At the moment when I am receiving your encouraging message with respect to the future of peace, the Israelis are launching air and ground attacks against the third army under the false pretext that it has initiated the attack. I wish to advise you that the moment is critical and that the future of peace is in danger. Your guarantee of the Security Council resolutions is being defied under false pretences.'

Nixon replied that the Israeli government had given an account of the fighting which was the exact opposite of the Egyptian version. 'You must recognize that it is impossible for us to make proper judgements on who is keeping and who is violating the ceasefire,' he wrote.* He also said that Israel claimed it had permitted a medical supply convoy to enter Suez city, and that blood and plasma had been transferred directly to the third army. By this time UN personnel had set up observation posts along four key roads. Nixon suggested that the observers should be moved to places where attacks were taking place so that they could verify the claims. He said that if the observers confirmed the violations the United States would be prepared to oppose and publicly condemn 'those who have violated the ceasefire'. Nothing came of this offer because the observers arrived after the battle was over.

The third item of Resolution 338 had said that Arab–Israeli talks should start 'immediately and concurrently with the ceasefire' with the aim of 'establishing a just and durable peace'. When Kissinger, Brezhnev and Gromyko wrote these words they could hardly have realized the vast psychological hurdle such talks represented. The Arabs' taboo had made contact with Israel impossible in times of peace; now with the guns still hot the two sides were being asked to sit down together.

* Kissinger says in his memoirs that this message was in fact written by himself but sent in Nixon's name.

All the parties involved except Syria had the strongest reasons to bring item three to fruition: Washington because there could be no negotiated peace without talks; Moscow because talks offered hope of a Soviet role; Israel because its ultimate goal was Arab recognition of Israel; Sadat because his strategy depended on engaging Kissinger's full involvement. But no matter how much the parties' interests might seem to be converging, a major political effort at the highest level was still needed to make talks happen.

Kissinger and Hafez Ismail agreed in a message on 26 October that Egyptian and Israeli representatives would meet at 3 p.m. Cairo time the following day to discuss military aspects of resolutions 338 and 339. It was clear, however, that this depended on Israel allowing vital non-military supplies to reach the third army, which it had no intention of doing. On 27 October Kissinger passed on extracts from a letter which Washington had received from Golda Meir: 'We are prepared immediately to enter into discussions with Egyptians on how to solve this situation . . . We believe we have something to offer them – something which is neither surrender nor humiliation but an honourable way out of the situation.' This marked the full circle from Sadat's statement to Nixon on 15 October: 'Egypt wishes to make it clear that it does not seek to humiliate Israel, because Egypt has tasted what humiliation is.' Kissinger added that the US would use all its influence to produce an honourable solution.

Mrs Meir continued: 'All the Egyptians have to do is suggest the time, place and rank of their representative.' The reality was that Egypt's representative had been stopped at an Israeli roadblock and could not reach the rendezvous, while General Sharon's forces continued to obstruct an Egyptian convoy carrying non-military supplies to the third army. Kissinger called on both sides to engage in a 'calm and constructive dialogue'. Sadat sent Nixon a message saying: 'The Israeli side is still resorting to dilatory methods and reneging on its commitments in the hope of allowing itself time to achieve more territorial gains.'

Kissinger replied that an Israeli delegation had been waiting at the rendezvous, a point on the Cairo–Suez road, for three hours, 'and thus far no one from the Egyptian side has appeared'. According to him Israel was prepared to allow a convoy of non-military supplies to pass through its lines, but no convoy had appeared. It later emerged that the Israelis had 'forgotten' to give instructions to the roadblock guards to allow the Egyptian representatives to pass. By the end of the day neither problem had been resolved, although Kissinger told Hafez Ismail that he had talked 'personally and in the strongest terms' to Golda Meir, insisting on new arrangements for the following day and on a timetable for a convoy to pass.

Messages continued to fly at intervals of as little as five minutes. Nixon, Sadat and Meir were now personally handling details which in other circumstances could have been left to third secretaries, and yet in the Middle East made the difference between war and armistice. Brezhnev played a vital role in the crisis by dropping a hint of a further US–Soviet crisis, which had the effect of making Kissinger increase the pressure on Israel. In his memoirs Kissinger describes a showdown between himself and the Israeli ambassador to Washington. The secretary of state gave Israel an ultimatum to allow food, water and medicines to reach the Egyptian third army: 'I have to say again your course is suicidal. You will not be permitted to destroy this army. You are destroying the possibility for negotiations.'*

After a further show of defiance Israel reluctantly bowed to US pressure. A message from Nixon to Sadat later on the evening of 27 October said: 'I do want . . . to re-enforce secretary Kissinger's solemn assurances that my government will stand behind its commitments.' Finally, in the early hours of 28 October, the first direct talks between Israeli and Egyptian military delegations since the end of the 1948–49 war were held in the presence of UN observers, and the long-delayed convoy reached the third army the following morning.

As tension subsided it became clear that 26 October had been the last day of fighting and 28 October the end of the war. Most accounts of the final days assume that the superpower crisis showed the limits of détente in a situation where the US and the Soviet Union had conflicting interests. That analysis ignores an important point: the superpower crisis was not so much a consequence as a vital element in the struggle. Brezhnev's skill in using carefully modulated pressure on Washington, always stopping short of threatening the US directly, created the climate in which the US used its influence with Israel

* This encounter occurred during the night of 26 October Washington time (the morning of 27 October in Cairo). See *Years of Upheaval*, p. 609.

effectively. Kissinger was determined not to allow Sadat to gain the upper hand, but at the same time wanted to avoid any humiliation of the Arabs, because that would have complicated the post-war diplomacy. The secretary of state was looking for a balanced outcome, but failed to restrain Israel sufficiently until firm Soviet diplomacy left him with no option.

There has been much argument as to who won the war. The Arabs achieved a political and psychological victory partly offset by an unclear military result, in which Israel narrowly achieved the upper hand through massive US military aid. Israel lost most of the east bank of the Suez Canal, but also gained part of the west bank and increased the area of Syria under its control. Israel suffered fewer casualties than it inflicted in absolute terms, but about the same in proportional terms (taking account of differences in population). The lasting effects of the 1973 conflict, like many wars, lay more in intangibles than visible results. The failure of Israeli intelligence to predict the attack led to a political civil war in Israel which ultimately cost Golda Meir her job, while Sadat emerged vastly strengthened. A man who had been dismissed as a lightweight was now seen as an Arab statesman, freed from negative comparisons with his great predecessor. The fact that Sadat had robbed Egypt, or himself, of a considerable military victory did not become known until later.

Above all, the Yom Kippur War was the event which relieved Zionists of their self-confidence and Arabs of their humiliation. The haunted house of the Arab mind had lost one its ghosts, though many more remained to be exorcized. Having proved themselves in battle, and shown that Israel was dependent on having a more powerful backer, the Arabs could hold their heads high. The meeting between military representatives on the Cairo–Suez road on 28 October was similar in substance but different in psychological impact to the joint truce committees conducted under UN auspices after 1948. The first Arab–Israel war had been the single greatest event in causing the Arab taboo, while the Yom Kippur War created the first crack in that barrier. In a tense atmosphere amid confused feelings of anger and expectation, the Arab–Israel relationship had taken an important turn.

13

Kisses for Henry

In the Arab world, decisions made at the highest level are considered final, overruling the views of all lower strata of power and opinion. Sadat assumed that his meeting with Henry Kissinger on 7 November 1973, which had been arranged during the Yom Kippur War, would be conducted on the same basis of absolute individual authority.

Before the encounter Sadat sent Ismail Fahmy, the new Egyptian foreign minister, to Washington to seek a guarantee from the secretary of state that Israeli forces would not move against Egyptian positions while negotiations on implementing the latest UN resolutions were under way. Astonished by the request, Kissinger took a sheet of paper from his desk and wrote a 'guarantee' that the US would 'do its utmost' to prevent such offensive operations.* Sadat thought this meant using Washington's economic and political might, not realizing that the secretary of state was opposed to putting pressure on Israel, and that the armoury of US sanctions was locked by the multiple keys of presidential, congressional and US media power.

With Kissinger's 'guarantee' in hand Sadat felt in a strong position as he awaited the secretary of state's arrival. The actor in his soul relished the thought of dealing on a man-to-man basis with the superstar of US foreign policy. Sadat was clearly irritated when I suggested that it might be best to avoid one-to-one negotiations with Kissinger. 'If he talks to Brezhnev and Chou En-Lai alone, why not me?' I pointed

* The full text of the note read: 'In connection with any agreement between Egypt and Israel relating to implementation of paragraph 1 of the Security Council resolution 338 the United States guarantees that it will do its utmost to prevent offensive military operations by Israeli forces on the west bank against Egyptian forces while Israeli forces are on the west bank. Signed: H.A.K.' The note was undated, but Kissinger's meeting with Fahmy was on 29 October 1973 at the State Department.

out that he could hold a brief initial meeting with Kissinger and then withdraw, leaving the details to ministers, who would have to report back before reaching any agreement. This would give Sadat time for reflection and would prevent Kissinger from exploiting Sadat's absolute authority. My suggestion was not what the president wished to hear. An opportunity to focus the attention of the international media on himself was too good to pass up.

What occurred at Tahira Palace in Cairo on 7 November was the reverse of what I had proposed. The two delegations held a brief preliminary meeting and then Sadat and Kissinger withdrew for a tête-à-tête at which decisions of lasting importance for Egypt and the Arab–Israel conflict were taken.

Sadat opened the discussion by proposing that Israel should withdraw, as part of a disengagement agreement, from about half of Sinai, including the Mitla and Giddi passes. Kissinger gave an indirect reply, saying that it would be difficult to make Israel obey the UN resolutions demanding withdrawal to the 22 October lines. Egypt could mobilize international pressure on Israel, but that would embarrass the United States. Even if Israel fully obeyed the resolutions, Sharon's forces would still be on both sides of the Suez Canal. However, if Egypt abstained from insisting on the 22 October lines, the US would try to negotiate a full disengagement of forces, with the aim of persuading the Israelis to return to the east side of the canal.

Sadat could have replied that if Israel would not obey UN resolutions, hostilities would be resumed. A reorganization of forces had been carried out since the ceasefire, and the Egyptian army's morale was high. What he in fact said was: 'Henry, you disappoint me. I was expecting a discussion on the global level, and then you talk about minor points. I am a man of strategy and I know you are too.'* Sadat said he wanted to break with Nasser's legacy and alter Egypt's political course, treating the US as partner rather than indirect adversary. As if this were not music enough to Kissinger's ears, Sadat added that he would like to 'kick the Soviets out of Egypt, out of Africa and out of Asia'.

* This was Sadat's version, recounted in a conversation with the author. Kissinger's version was that Sadat thought in silence for some time and then accepted his suggestion without argument. See *Years of Upheaval*, p. 640.

This conversation was the beginning of a political affair which was to have extraordinary consequences for Egypt and Syria and the unity of the Arab world. Sadat very quickly came to offer Kissinger his unreserved trust and loyalty, while the secretary of state discovered respect and even affection for the man he had once called a buffoon. Both leaders subsequently heaped praise on each other in their memoirs. The chemistry of their symbiosis was clear even at the first meeting. Sadat needed Kissinger to help him accomplish grand designs for Egypt; Kissinger needed Sadat to achieve his goals of lasting security for Israel and permanent US dominance in the Middle East.

'You know, I did not lose to Israel, I lost to the United States,' Sadat told Kissinger.

'Yes, it is true that I made you lose the war, but, Mr President, be assured that I'll make you win the peace,' Kissinger replied.

Sadat accepted Kissinger's 'minor point' that the secretary of state should seek a full disengagement agreement rather than trying to secure Israel's withdrawal to the 22 October lines first. The Egyptian president must have realized that he was giving consent for 30,000 Egyptian troops to remain virtual hostages until Kissinger achieved success. The third army would remain imprisoned between Israeli forces on the east and west banks of the canal for weeks while disengagement negotiations took place.

Members of the two delegations, waiting outside in the sunny garden of Tahira Palace, assumed that the negotiations would begin when the stars recalled them after their tête-à-tête. Instead the officials, experts and ministers found that everything important had been settled over their heads. Sadat and Kissinger beckoned to Fahmy and Joseph Sisco, the assistant secretary of state, who were sitting just out of earshot. It then transpired that Kissinger, sensing Sadat's readiness to reach any agreement, had prepared a short cut. Sisco opened his briefcase and produced a ready-made six-point plan whose terms reflected demands which Golda Meir had made during a visit to Washington a week earlier. The main idea was to freeze the existing situation pending discussions on disengagement, without requiring Israel to obey UN resolutions. The sting, from Egypt's point of view, lay in the tail. Point six said: 'As soon as the UN checkpoints are established on the Cairo–Suez road, there will be an exchange of all prisoners of war, including wounded.'* In accepting this provision Sadat gave up one of Egypt's key negotiating assets, and received in return only an Israeli promise not to stop non-military supplies reaching the town of Suez and Egyptian forces on the east bank.

One of Sadat's few conditions in accepting the Israeli–American plan was that he should be able to present it to Egypt as his own. This method of selling concepts to the Egyptian public was used repeatedly in subsequent negotiations. Kissinger would listen to Golda Meir's ideas and propose them to Sadat as if they had come from the US; Sadat would present them to the Egyptian public as his own, and the Israelis would then be invited to accept their own demands. Mrs Meir was rarely satisfied with a single spin of this negotiating merry-go-round. Kissinger once told Israel's deputy premier Yigal Allon, who had been a student of his at Harvard, that it was a great achievement to persuade Israel to accept its own proposal.†

One of Sadat's tactics was never to allow negotiations to appear straightforward, however easy they might be in practice, so that journalists would give greater value to any concessions Egypt might obtain. The Americans went along with these tactics, with the result that media briefings during subsequent months suggested an atmosphere of perpetual crisis.

In addition to the six-point agreement, Kissinger and Sadat decided to raise the rank of the head of the US Interests Section in Cairo, and of his Egyptian counterpart in Washington. Both men became ambassadors, an extraordinary anomaly given that diplomatic relations had not yet been restored.‡

Realizing that this would be a shock to Egyptian and Arab public opinion, and to Moscow, Ismail Fahmy sent Sadat a memo suggesting

* The six points (summarized) were: 1) ceasefire to be observed; 2) immediate discussions on return to 22 October positions 'in the framework of agreement on the disengagement and separation of forces under the auspices of the UN'; 3) Suez [town] to receive food, water and medicine and wounded civilians to be evacuated; 4) non-military supplies to be permitted (by Israel) to reach east bank; 5) Israeli checkpoints on Cairo–Suez road to be replaced by UN checkpoints, but Israelis to be allowed to supervise non-military nature of supplies; 6) exchange of all prisoners of war.

† See *Years of Upheaval*, p. 831.

‡ Full diplomatic relations between Egypt and the US were restored six months later. Meanwhile Moscow replaced Vinogradov with a more senior ambassador who carried the rank of deputy foreign minister.

a way of presenting the move: 'Can you please allow us [meaning the Egyptian government] to say that this arrangement represents our limited response to the desire of the United States to have a high-ranking diplomat in Cairo?'

One of the guests at a dinner given in Kissinger's honour that evening (7 November) was Vladimir Vinogradov, who was smarting from the humiliation Sadat had delivered by accepting an American plan without prior consultation. When the Soviet ambassador asked: 'Is this plan going to bring peace, Mr Secretary?' Kissinger replied: 'Peace will come, Mr Ambassador, when you stop sending arms to the Arabs.'

In a conversation with Kissinger after dinner I tried to probe what role he was playing. 'The United States cannot be a negotiator, because it is not a party to the conflict. On the other hand the US cannot be an accepted mediator, because it is not neutral between Israel and the Arabs,' I pointed out. Kissinger looked irritated. After an easy ride with Sadat it was annoying to be asked awkward questions.

Early next morning I went to see the president and found him relaxing in what had once been the Queen's bedroom, a magnificent chamber hung with white curtains. Sensing that I had come to express reservations, Sadat played for time. 'You're like a horse at the start of a race scraping the soil with its hooves,' he said, and ordered vodkas. His glass was emptied and refilled twice before he came to the point.

'I want you to realize that I'm not having a disengagement with Israel, I'm having a disengagement with America,' the president said. 'Number two: Henry Kissinger is the only man on earth who can order that woman out, and make her obey.'

'Which woman?' I asked.

'Golda Meir.'

'Mr President, do you really believe that?' I asked in disbelief.

'Yes,' he emphatically replied.

Sadat's confidence was astounding. I reminded him that in any conflict where the two superpowers had an interest, the regional powers still retained room for manoeuvre. Sadat had been able, despite Egypt's dependence on the USSR for arms, to secure the withdrawal of all Soviet military experts from Egypt. If Egypt could make Moscow do its bidding, Israel's standing in Washington was ten times stronger. Israel exercised direct influence in US internal politics and would not withdraw from Egypt unless its own national interests dictated such a course. Sadat should therefore develop an Egyptian policy which did not depend on the ability of 'that man' to dictate to 'that woman'.

Egypt had no shortage of assets on which to base a negotiating position. In the interval since the ceasefire two reserve divisions had been moved from the east to the west bank to face Sharon's forces in case hostilities should resume. A shipment of 250 new TU62 tanks had arrived from the Soviet Union. Yugoslavia had provided a complete force with 110 tanks. Algeria had sent two tank brigades and Libya was providing large quantities of equipment, including Mirage fighter-bombers. The Arab world could count on Soviet support in the Security Council, and the oil producers' embargo was bringing economic pressure on the West. The fact that European countries and the Soviet Union wanted the Suez Canal reopened also tended to increase support for the Arab stand. Other important cards included thirty-six captured Israeli pilots, many other prisoners of war, and the presence of two Egyptian navy destroyers guarding the Strait of Bab el-Mandeb at the southern end of the Red Sea, preventing Israeli ships from reaching the port of Eilat. To complete its negotiating hand, Egypt had the advantage of legitimacy, as it was seeking to regain Arab territory.

Even with US support Israel was not necessarily better placed, because of overstretched supply lines, national exhaustion and difficulties in sustaining mobilization for long periods. Moreover, Israeli politicians were tearing each other apart in a row over responsibility for the failure to foresee the Egyptian–Syrian attack.

Sadat continued listening as I pointed out that the US secretary of state should not be considered impartial. During our after-dinner conversation Kissinger had made it clear that Israel's security was his first priority. He was not in favour of any Israeli expansion beyond the 5 October lines, but that did not mean he was committed to bringing about a complete Israeli withdrawal. After Israel's security, he had two strictly American priorities which were not helpful to Egypt. These were to persuade the oil producers to drop the embargo, and secondly to squeeze the Soviet presence in the Middle East.

Sadat tried to smother these objections with flattery, by reminding me of articles I had written in Nasser's day, when Egypt's relations with Washington were tense. My theme at the time had been that

Egypt should accept the fact that the US had interests, power and a presence in the region. 'I am trying to implement your policy, neutralizing the United States,' Sadat said. When I left him that afternoon it was clear that no amount of persuasion would change his mind.

Unknown to me at the time, Sadat had made a secret additional promise which was not committed to paper. The two Egyptian destroyers at Bab el-Mandeb were to be discreetly withdrawn from the strait and held off the coast of Djibouti, without any announcement that the blockade was over. Another matter which was not disclosed until later was a request by Sadat for US measures to improve his personal protection. This led to a team of three CIA agents being sent to Egypt to work out a security plan and to train Sadat's bodyguards, making Sadat physically as well as politically dependent on Washington.

Kissinger left Egypt on 8 November, having achieved more than he could have dreamt. Arrangements had been made with Israel for the six-point agreement to be signed by Egyptian and Israeli military delegations three days later. As the secretary of state departed, telegrams began to pour into Cairo from other Arab countries.

President Assad warned Sadat: 'You are moving towards making a separate peace with Israel,' and hinted that Egyptian–Syrian relations would suffer. As a former air force commander Assad understood the value of the thirty-six pilots Egypt had promise to hand over; in his view no prisoners should be exchanged except in the context of an overall settlement. He was astonished that Egyptian officers had agreed to talk to their Israeli counterparts.

Kuwait expressed surprise over the speed of Egypt's decision to exchange ambassadors with the US, asked what guarantees Washington had provided, and showed concern about the lack of coordination between Cairo and Damascus.

President Houari Boumédienne of Algeria said the agreement had caused him embarrassment in his own country.* 'You have fallen into an American trap,' Boumédienne said. 'What have you done to Syria? You must realize that it is Egypt which unites or scatters the Arabs.'

Before the Yom Kippur War, the Egyptian and Syrian leaders had

* Boumédienne was Algeria's second leader after independence, replacing Ahmed Ben Bella in 1964.

been on excellent terms, treating each other with affection and respect. The two men had spent a pleasant day together in September 1973 at Sadat's rest house at Borg el-Arab on the Mediterranean coast. When the main business of fixing a date for the attack and arrangements for the subsequent ceasefire had been settled, they turned to other subjects. Assad had a lively mind with a huge range of interests, the greatest of which was history. Later, after seeing the Syrian leader off at the rest-house helipad for the return flight to Damascus, Sadat remarked: 'Assad is different to all the other Syrians we have dealt with.' That bond was shattered by Sadat's political *coup de foudre* with Kissinger. From 8 November onwards communications between Assad and Sadat became stiff and formal, and they avoided speaking to each other until Kuwait arranged a meeting weeks later.

The six-point agreement was signed on 11 November at a spot on the Cairo–Suez road known as Kilometre 101 by military delegations led by General Mohamed Abdel-Ghany El-Gamassi for Egypt and General Aharon Yariv for Israel. The encounter was psychologically difficult for both sides, coming too soon after the fighting.

Sadat's instructions to Gamassi before the talks reflected another presidential flight of fantasy. The Egyptian leader was aware of the long-standing quarrel between Moshe Dayan and Golda Meir, and had also heard that General Yariv, the Israeli representative, was close to Dayan. These Israeli differences stemmed from ordinary rivalry, but were often described in journalistic shorthand as a battle between doves and hawks. Sadat took this over-simplification at face value and conceived a plan to use the Kilometre 101 talks to widen the split within the Israeli cabinet. The idea was not only unrealistic but counter-productive, distorting Egyptian policy for illusory gains.*

Sadat's plan was to show General Yariv that Egypt could be flexible and generous, giving him enough success in the talks to strengthen the Dayan faction in the Israeli cabinet. The idea of seducing the enemy with kindness was anathema to Gamassi, a disciplined professional soldier from a farming background who had agreed to head the delegation only after personal pressure from Sadat.

* Sadat's idea started a trend which continued as late as 1994. Egyptian attempts to exploit differences between the Labour Party and Likud, or between different Labour leaders such as Peres and Rabin, wasted much time and effort.

The talks began with an understandable feeling of awkwardness, which increased when Gamassi called for Israeli withdrawal. Yariv replied: 'This is a political matter, and we are both heading military delegations.'

Sadat's solution, when Gamassi made his report that night, was typical of his way of thinking. Gamassi's title was changed to 'assistant to the minister of defence for political affairs', and the Egyptian team was described as a 'military-political delegation'. The change was made in time for the second meeting.

Yariv realized that Gamassi was trying to make some kind of approach beyond the agreed terms of the talks, and saw an opportunity to gain a concession. In addition to the accepted list of prisoners to be exchanged, Yariv asked for an Israeli spy who had been arrested in Yemen several years earlier, and for a pilot who had been shot down in 1970, during the war of attrition. Releasing the spy would have been difficult for legal reasons, but Sadat decided to hand over the pilot as a special gesture, hoping that this would help Gamassi to gain Yariv's confidence. At the next meeting, Gamassi announced: 'I have a present for you,' and Lieutenant Dan Avidan, the Israeli pilot, was brought into the tent and handed over to Yariv.

For the first two weeks Sadat was optimistic that his strategy would succeed. Yariv responded to Egyptian gestures by putting forward proposals which, although far short of Egyptian demands, offered a basis for negotiation. The two sides appeared to be moving towards each other when Yariv suddenly took a harder line. It later transpired that he had come under criticism in Israel for widening the range of issues under discussion, and that Kissinger had advised Israeli leaders to reduce the pace of the talks. The secretary of state thought that undue speed would encourage exaggerated Arab expectations, and wanted Cairo to feel that nothing could be achieved without US help.

Meanwhile Kissinger announced plans to convene an international conference in Geneva in December under the auspices of the two superpowers. The need for a conference stemmed from item three of UN Resolution 338: 'immediately and concurrently with the ceasefire, negotiations [will] start between the parties concerned under appropriate auspices'.

Until the conference was announced Israel had always wanted talks with Arab governments, but the American invitation gave Israel an incentive to be difficult. An Israeli refusal would be humiliating for Nixon and Kissinger, which meant that concessions could be obtained in return for Israel's acquiescence.

Israeli leaders found a host of reasons to object. Israel did not like the Soviet involvement; Israel did not want a multinational forum; Israel rejected any prominent role for the United Nations; Israel would not attend if any Palestinians were invited; Israel would not sit in the same room as Syrian delegates unless Damascus provided a list of Israeli prisoners of war before the conference.

The Americans retreated before this barrage of protests. Kissinger decided that the conference should concentrate on the disengagement of Arab and Israeli armies, which meant that the causes of the dispute would not be addressed and the Palestinians need not be invited. His step-by-step approach consisted of breaking the problem into parts so small that the fundamental issues never had to be tackled. The Arab world began to split into those who understood and rejected the US strategy, and those who wanted to be closer to the Americans.

Sadat wrote to Assad explaining that Cairo had decided to attend the conference, and urged Syria to participate. Assad's reply began: 'My Brother the President [omitting the word 'dear'], I don't see any purpose in our going to a peace conference.' He argued that talk of peace was encouraging Israeli arrogance, and had no meaning without the rapid implementation of UN Resolution 242.

Sadat replied: 'But we cannot ask for a withdrawal before the conference. I hope that you are aware that the Soviet Union is repeating advice that there should be a peace conference . . . I don't think we can be absent . . . There might even be a deal between the two superpowers in our absence.' He again urged Syria to attend, but Assad remained sceptical.

Kissinger held further meetings with Sadat at the Barrages in the Nile Delta on 13 and 14 December. The conference was due to open on the eighteenth, and Israel had not yet given its consent. Sadat tried to help by giving the secretary of state a handwritten note to deliver to Golda Meir. He said he was serious in wanting peace and proposed that Egypt and Israel should communicate through Kissinger. The content of the message was less important than the fact that it was written, marking a further step in reducing the Arab taboo.

Sadat had been reflecting on a remark made by Kissinger during their first encounter immediately after the war. The secretary of state had said that the barriers between Israel and the Arabs were primarily psychological (70 per cent, in his estimation). That idea appealed greatly to Sadat, and came to influence all his subsequent thinking. After the meeting at the Barrages Sadat repeatedly used the secretary of state's comment (and estimate) in his own speeches and remarks.

Israel was still playing hard to get when Kissinger arrived in Jerusalem on 16 December, two days before the conference was due to open. Part of the problem was that the Israeli general election originally scheduled for the end of October had been postponed to 31 December, as a result of the war. The Israeli government wanted the conference to take place, to show voters that peace was at hand, but also sought to score political points through brinkmanship in negotiations with Washington.

Nixon's original intention was that if Israel refused to attend, the conference would go ahead as planned in its absence. Golda Meir and her colleagues called the US president's bluff by failing to come to a decision, forcing Nixon to announce a three-day postponement. It took five hours of talks between Kissinger and Golda Meir, and another US concession, before Israel relented. Not content with their victory in excluding Palestinians from the conference, the Israelis insisted that there should be no mention of the Palestinian issue in a letter of invitation to be sent by Washington and Moscow to the participants. In his memoirs Kissinger referred to this further Israeli victory as 'minor'.*

Matti Golan, a prominent Israeli writer closely connected with General Dayan, says that there was a strong feeling at the time that Israel should not give up any part of the occupied territories for less than full peace. Kissinger was seen as pressuring Israel to abandon that principle. During his visit on 16 and 17 December he urged the Israeli cabinet to offer Cairo more generous terms, and said he was amazed that Sadat had not used Egypt's strong negotiating position to force Israel to return to the pre-5 June 1967 lines.

The secretary of state's explanation was that Sadat had begun to imagine grateful crowds in the streets of Suez cheering him for bring-

* See *Years of Upheaval*, p. 791.

ing peace to the embattled town.* According to Golan, Kissinger's advice was accepted by hardliners, including Yigal Allon, who had been opposing any withdrawal from the west bank of the canal. This shift led to an improved offer to Egypt after the conference.

After leaving Israel, Kissinger visited Assad in Damascus and made a final attempt to persuade him to send a representative to the conference. The Israelis were still demanding a list of Israeli prisoners of war in Syrian hands as the price for any contacts with Damascus, but they also told Kissinger that if they received such a list they would be willing to start disengagement talks on the Golan Heights. The secretary of state passed this on to Sadat, asking him to use his influence with Assad, not realizing that the Egyptian and Syrian leaders were no longer on speaking terms.

The Egyptian participation in the conference was planned from the first as a charm offensive to woo the international media. A government planning document at the time said: 'We suggest that the president should appear in Walter Kronkite's programme on Sunday 16 December 1973 . . . We should try to make this conference look like the political crossing to follow the military crossing.'

When the conference convened at the Palais des Nations in Geneva on 21 December, the atmosphere reminded one of the Arab ambassadors of a scene from an Agatha Christie novel: 'Everybody was hiding, everybody was cheating, everybody was lying and everybody was looking for a body, but neither the corpse nor the criminal were to be found.' In the hours before the start half a dozen seemingly trivial squabbles betrayed the tension. There was a row over the shape of the conference table and who should sit next to whom. The Egyptian delegation became upset when Gromyko held a pre-conference meeting with Abba Eban, the Israeli foreign minister. Gromyko pointed out, not without justice, that Moscow had been kept in the dark while Cairo conducted secret negotiations with Washington. 'It is in Arab interests that the Soviet Union should have reasonable relations with Israel,' he insisted. Farouk Kaddoumi, the PLO officer responsible for foreign affairs, was shut out of the proceedings and had to wait in the lobby of a nearby hotel. Most Arab observers felt that the conference had been rushed to give the Israeli government a grandstand from

* See Golan, *The Secret Conversations of Henry Kissinger.*

which to garner votes at home. The suspense as to whether Damascus would boycott the conference or not was sustained until no one showed up to occupy a space set for Syria's delegate, complete with Syrian flag and nameplate. Those seated around the seven-sided table were Waldheim, acting as convenor, Kissinger and Gromyko, as co-chairmen, Ismail Fahmy, representing Egypt, Zaid Rifai, prime minister of Jordan, and Abba Eban. The parties to the dispute spoke not to each other but to domestic opinion in their own countries, and Jordan, which had tried to stay out of the war, made a tougher speech than Egypt which had fought all through it. A telegram from Fahmy to Sadat after the opening session said that Kissinger, who was sitting near him, came over and whispered: 'Look at them. Is this the Israeli delegation you used to see when you were based at the United Nations?' The Egyptian foreign minister stretched the point by telling Sadat that the abject countenance of the Israeli delegation reminded him of the Japanese officers who surrendered to the United States in 1945.

As in many international gatherings, the formal speeches meant less than the private contacts which took place outside. Kissinger used the occasion to strengthen his rapport with Arab delegates, especially by feeding the rumour-mill with comments, political insights, jokes and criticisms of both enemies and friends. The secretary of state was highly skilled in building intimate links through indiscretions which sounded more significant than they were. Kissinger quoted Nixon as saying that if the Israelis did not show more flexibility he (Nixon) would hold a personal meeting with the heads of AIPAC* (which meant nothing but gave an impression of firmness). The secretary of state entertained Fahmy with gossipy reminiscences of the difficulty he had had persuading the Israeli prime minister to accept his political advances. 'Imagine spending a whole night with one woman, and that woman is Golda,'† he said. He also worked to aggravate the dispute between Egypt and the Soviet Union caused by Gromyko's meeting with Eban. According to the Soviet foreign minister, Eban had suggested a resumption of Israeli–Soviet diplomatic relations, but

* AIPAC, the American Israel Public Affairs Committee, was an important factor in the Jewish lobby in the United States.

† Mrs Meir was seventy-five.

Kissinger claimed that the request had in fact come from Gromyko. 'Don't believe Gromyko, he is a liar,' Fahmy quoted Kissinger as saying. A further dispute arose over a statement issued by the Vatican asking that the conference should refrain from taking any steps which might affect the future of Jerusalem. Kissinger said he thought the Vatican interference was unwarranted, and Fahmy instructed the Egyptian ambassador to the Vatican to ask for a clarification.

Kissinger let Fahmy into the secret that Georges Pompidou was seriously ill with cancer and had an estimated six months to live. He said he wanted Sadat to know this so that Egypt could adjust its relations with France. What lay behind this was a private battle between Kissinger and Michel Jobert, the French foreign minister, who had described the conference as 'humiliating' and said that France would not participate if invited. Jobert's view reflected a French wish to remain in line with the Arab majority, which suspected a secret deal between Sadat and Kissinger.

In a meeting with other Arab ambassadors on 27 December Fahmy said he was amazed by their suspicions. 'I told them that Egypt does not have an open position and a secret position. What we do in secret is exactly what we say in the open,' he reported in a telegram to Cairo.

Another dispute during the conference arose from a decision to appoint a military commission to conduct detailed talks. The participants were to be the United States, the Soviet Union, the United Nations, Egypt and Israel. Kissinger and Israel were against Soviet participation, and Fahmy went along with Kissinger's view. Meetings were held secretly, involving Egypt and Israel under US supervision, which was part of Kissinger's plan to encourage direct talks on all levels between Egyptians and Israelis. Vinogradov, who was part of the Soviet delegation, learned of such a meeting from Waldheim, and was furious. He warned Fahmy that if any further secret meetings were discovered a Soviet military attaché would be sent in, using force if necessary.

The Israelis used one of these meetings to approach the Egyptian delegation with an extraordinary proposition. Colonel Dov Sion of the Israeli delegation suggested that Egypt was wasting its time concentrating on the wrong issue, and should turn its attention to Libya. By taking over its neighbour to the west and seizing the oil fields, Egypt could solve its economic problems and at the same time silence

Muammar Gadaffi. 'Go and take Libya and forget about all your problems with Israel,' Sion suggested, adding that Israel would not interfere with any Egyptian move to achieve that goal.

Ambassador Hussein Khallaf, coordinator of the Egyptian delegation, sent a telegram to Cairo on 27 December about the Israeli suggestion. Colonel Sion also casually provided a document elaborating the argument:

> For any country to advance it needs land, labour and capital. Egypt has plenty of the first two but its suffering has been due to its lack of capital; and Libya simply has it. At present Libya's cash reserves are in excess of $3.4 billion and in 1974 to 1980 oil income should be at least $36 billion or an average of $5.1 billion annually. With such a tremendous amount of capital, Egypt could buy all its military and industrial requirements; and it would not be long before Sudan joined such a union. The new nation could become a real power to be reckoned with.

Dealing with Israeli–Egyptian relations, the document said:

> Unity with Libya is more important than any other problem facing Egypt today. Neither Sinai nor any other issue will solve Egypt's problem as much as complete union with Libya . . . Naturally a strong Egypt will be a threat to US interests in the whole Arab world. Therefore the US will pay any price to delay such a union.

Egypt did not take Israel's bait at the time, but four years later, in the summer of 1977, the United States became aware that it was considering such a move. The US ambassador in Cairo warned Sadat that Washington would not permit an Egyptian invasion of Libya.*

Israeli diplomats also used the Geneva meetings to persuade Egypt to use its influence with Damascus, hinting that Israel would be more helpful to Cairo if Syria provided a list of Israeli prisoners of war. Cairo took this up with Damascus but made no headway.

As delegates returned home after the peace conference many must have wondered what, if anything, had been achieved. Two decades later that point remains controversial. What can be said for certain is that the conference became a model for subsequent attempts at peace-

* See also p. 247.

making. Although most Arab countries disagreed with the participation of Egypt and Jordan at the time, in later negotiations all Arabs wanted the Geneva conference to be reconvened as a way of giving international legitimacy to the peace process. The conference enabled Egypt to acknowledge publicly that it no longer considered direct contacts with Israel to be wrong. This weakening of the taboo was confined to Egypt, however, and specifically excluded the Palestinians and Syria.

The conference was also the beginning of a long, slow process of separating Egypt, the principal Arab military power, from the mainstream of Arab political opinion. Paradoxically, that divergence suited Sadat just as much as it did Kissinger and Golda Meir. Sadat had a theory that an assertive Egypt would inevitably cause trouble in the Middle East; if not with Israel then with traditional Arab regimes which would feel threatened. He wanted to create a situation in which Egypt would no longer be perceived by Israel or other Arabs as a threat. Participating in the Geneva conference went a long way towards achieving that aim, by forging a link which made it difficult to resume hostilities later.

Sadat was also in step with Kissinger's views on Soviet influence. Kissinger saw that if Moscow lost Egypt it would forfeit its position in the Arab world, because Syria alone was not sufficient.

He hoped that Sadat could help him secure the lifting of the Arab oil embargo, which was already having dramatic effects. In the scramble for dwindling supplies European countries were ready to pay more, and on 23 December the Organization of Petroleum Exporting Countries (OPEC), which included many non-Arab oil producers, announced a 100 per cent price increase. Two days later Arab oil ministers meeting in Kuwait decided to resume normal supplies (but at the new price) to Japan and certain European countries, while continuing the embargo against the United States.

The effectiveness of the Arab oil weapon was reflected in a letter which Nixon wrote to Sadat after the Geneva conference. The US president implied that Sadat would have to use his influence with the oil producers if he wanted US diplomatic efforts to continue.

> Relationships between our two countries have been put on a new basis of cordiality and understanding . . . [However] the ceasefire,

> the six point agreement, [and] the opening of the conference . . . are only beginnings. We are committed . . . to full support and implementation of the November 1967 Security Council resolution.
>
> Our two nations stand at the threshold of a great turning point in history [but] in order to make it possible for me to move decisively it is necessary that the discrimination against the United States which the oil embargo represents be brought to an end.

Nixon said he had noted 'with dismay' the decision of Arab oil ministers to continue the embargo against the United States while resuming supplies to other countries: 'It is essential that the oil embargo . . . be ended at once. It cannot wait the outcome of the current talks on disengagement.' The implied threat in this letter was not carried out. Both the embargo and Kissinger's mission continued uninterrupted.

The secretary of state's first task was to close the gap between Israel and Egypt over terms for a first stage of Israeli withdrawal. The Israeli government had fared badly in the 31 December election, but remained in office on a caretaker basis pending negotiations to form a new coalition.* Immediately after the election the cabinet approved a plan based on the ideas which Moshe Dayan had been putting forward for years. Dayan submitted the plan to Kissinger in Washington and he agreed to present it to Sadat. The details were kept secret, apart from speculative stories in the Israeli press, until a series of meetings three weeks after the Geneva conference. Kissinger held four sets of talks with Sadat in Egypt on 11–12 January, 13–14 January, 16 January and 18 January, and visited Israel between and after the sessions. Most of the discussions in the Egyptian part of the shuttle were held at Sadat's rest house in Aswan. Kissinger and his team, which included Ellsworth Bunker, former US ambassador to South Vietnam, and Joseph Sisco, assistant secretary of state, stayed at the Old Cataract Hotel not far from the high dam.

Sadat chose General Gamassi, third in command of Egyptian forces, to present the Egyptian army's case, as he had quarrelled with General Shazli, the chief-of-staff, and Ahmed Ismail was ill. Gamassi's argument was that neither Israel nor Egypt should gain any military advan-

* The Labour Party lost seven seats, reducing its strength from fifty-six to forty-nine seats in the 120-member Knesset.

tage as a result of disengagement and that any restriction on force levels in the Sinai should be mutual. Gamassi (representing the Egyptian command) wanted to retain at least two divisions and 200 tanks east of the canal, while Israel should withdraw to a point east of the mountain passes.

The proposal Kissinger brought from the Israelis was very different. Israel accepted the principle of giving up its bridgehead on the west bank, and was prepared to withdraw up to twenty kilometres east of the canal (remaining west of the passes), but attached tough conditions. Egypt would have to withdraw nearly all its forces from the east bank of the canal, reduce its forces on the west bank, and pull back most of its armour to a line thirty kilometres west of the canal. The area either side of the canal would be divided into sectors in which force limits and arms restrictions would be imposed, and there would be a United Nations buffer force on the east side to keep the respective armies apart. Israel also wanted Egypt to reopen the canal and allow Israeli shipping to use it, and to end the blockade of the Strait of Bab el-Mandeb (which had already been discreetly withdrawn, although this had not been declared). The proposal included another important demand which Kissinger held back until the second shuttle, not wanting to provoke an early crisis.

Sadat replied that the minimum Egyptian force he could accept on the east bank was one and a half divisions. He was prepared to end the blockade and allow non-Israeli ships carrying Israeli cargoes to use the canal, once a disengagement of forces came into effect.

In Kissinger's first round of talks in Jerusalem and Tel Aviv on 13 January the Israeli government demanded extra Egyptian concessions. Not only would Egypt be denied any tanks at all on the east bank, but only 300 would be permitted on the west bank, the remainder being pulled back thirty kilometres towards Cairo. These demands were met with astonishment and anger when Kissinger disclosed them at a meeting with Sadat at his rest house the next day. The mood grew darker still when Kissinger revealed an element of the Israeli package which he had concealed during the first visit: Israel wanted Egypt to guarantee that the destroyed Egyptian cities along the canal would be rebuilt immediately, to ensure that any resumption of hostilities would be immensely costly for Egypt.

The full import of Israel's demands was now clear. Egypt had 70,000 troops on the east bank, and Israel wanted 68,000 of them withdrawn. Egypt had nearly 1000 artillery guns and 700 tanks on the east bank, and all would have to go. All Egyptian surface-to-air missiles would have to be removed from their fortified positions on the west bank and transported out of range, so that they could not be used to protect the Egyptian front line on the east bank against aerial attacks.

Gamassi immediately showed his opposition and made it clear that such a scheme would be unacceptable to the Egyptian army. Sadat decided to have a closed meeting with Kissinger. Other members of the two delegations went to the Old Cataract Hotel to await the outcome of the leaders' deliberations. In the private talks with Kissinger Sadat agreed to make important concessions. The strength of Egyptian forces on the east bank could be cut to eight battalions (about 5000 men) with thirty tanks. No final decision on the missile screen was made, but Sadat felt the withdrawal should not exceed thirty kilometres from the Egyptian front line, rather than thirty kilometres from the canal.

Ambassador Ellsworth Bunker brought the first news from the rest house to the teams waiting at the hotel. After announcing the limits of eight battalions and thirty tanks he added that no guns exceeding 122-millimetre calibre would be permitted on the east side, and a no-fly zone would be established in a thirty-kilometre-wide strip east of the canal. Gamassi was bitterly upset when he heard of Sadat's concessions, in view of the heavy loss of life which had been needed to establish the two armies on the east side. Kissinger arrived soon afterwards. Feeling the tension in the Egyptian delegation, he approached Gamassi.

'Is there anything you want to say, General?'

'Nothing, sir,' Gamassi replied, but his face betrayed his feelings.

'Do you want to say something?' Kissinger asked again.

'I am a soldier, and orders are orders,' Gamassi replied. He then rose, went to a window, and stood looking out across the Nile, trying to hide his tears. Everyone noticed when he drew a handkerchief from his pocket.

Kissinger returned to Israel, and after nineteen hours of negotiations the government accepted the levels of eight battalions and thirty tanks, and said that Sadat's tentative offer on the missile pull-back was the minimum that it would accept. While Kissinger was in Israel Gamassi made a concerted effort to persuade Sadat that Egyptian missiles should not be withdrawn more than twenty-five kilometres from the Egyptian front line.

Back in Aswan on 16 January Kissinger held a further private meeting with Sadat while other senior members of the US and Egyptian teams waited in the rest-house garden. Sadat told Kissinger of Gamassi's objections to the thirty-kilometre missile limit and asked him to try again with the Israelis.

In a meeting at the hotel later between Kissinger, Bunker, Gamassi and Fahmy, Gamassi continued to demand the twenty-five-kilometre limit. The difference of five kilometres determined whether the missiles could be of any practical help to Egyptian soldiers who would be stationed east of the canal. Unknown to Gamassi, Sadat had privately intimated that he would settle for thirty kilometres if Kissinger was unable to obtain an improved Israeli offer.

Kissinger returned to Jerusalem that night and held further talks with Israeli leaders until the early hours of the morning. Knowing that Sadat would accept the thirty-kilometre limit, he made little effort to obtain the extra five kilometres when he met Israeli leaders the next day, 17 January. Instead he obtained Sadat's consent by telegram, completed the agreement, and returned to Aswan with a personal letter from Golda Meir to the Egyptian president saying that she was 'deeply conscious of the significance' of Sadat's message and hoped the contacts would continue. Sadat kissed the secretary of state on both cheeks in front of television cameras and referred to him as 'brother'.

The formal document was signed at Kilometre 101 the same day (18 January) by Gamassi and General David Elazar, the Israeli chief-of-staff. It was witnessed by UN representative General Ensio Siilasvuo, commander of the United Nations Emergency Force, which was to be stationed in the buffer zone between Israeli and Egyptian forces. To avoid big-power involvement the agreement specified that the UNEF should be composed of troops from countries which were not permanent members of the Security Council. Perhaps the most important part of the document was item D: 'This agreement is not regarded by Egypt and Israel as a final peace agreement. It constitutes a first step towards a final, just and durable peace.'

The more controversial aspects of the agreement were contained in a separate 'United States Proposal' signed on the same day by Sadat in Aswan and by Golda Meir in Jerusalem. Both sides were subject to force limits in the forward areas, in the zone between the canal and the Sinai mountains. Neither side could have more than eight battalions, thirty tanks, six batteries of small howitzers, no guns with a calibre of more than 122 millimetres, no weapons capable of shooting down the other side's planes flying over its own forces, and no permanent missile sites. The wording of the crucial point about the missile screen (point 3 in the US proposal) was: 'to a distance thirty kilometres west of the Egyptian line and east of the Israeli line, there will be no surface-to-air missiles'.* All other Israeli demands, including passage through the Suez Canal and rebuilding of Suez towns, were left to be included in a secret letter of intent sent by Cairo to Washington but not declared. Sadat agreed to make the lifting of the blockade of Bab el-Mandeb official, announcing it in a letter to Washington. Israel completed its withdrawal on the agreed basis by 21 February 1974.

From a military viewpoint, the first disengagement agreement left Egypt in a worse position than it had been before 6 October, in that resumption of the war of attrition became impossible. This was precisely Sadat's intention. He wanted to create an irreversible peace process which would eventually lead to full Israeli withdrawal from all occupied territories.

Sadat could not yet imagine formal peace between the two countries, and yet a small incident during Kissinger's shuttle diplomacy showed how quickly the mental barriers were crumbling. Kissinger's plane had been coming and going without any of the usual checks on those travelling with him. One of the passengers, I learned, was a Mrs Lea Rabin, who came from Israel to Aswan with Kissinger, travelled to Luxor to visit the temple of Karnak, and returned to Israel on Kissinger's next trip. The Egyptian minister of the interior went to Sadat and asked if he realized that Yitzhak Rabin's wife had visited Egypt. 'Yes, I know,' Sadat said, 'but don't be closed-minded. The woman had been dreaming all her life of visiting Karnak and she asked Henry to bring her here. What is wrong with that?'

After the first disengagement agreement Brezhnev and Gromyko felt slighted by Sadat and cheated by Kissinger. Apart from the Geneva conference all the talk of joint US–Soviet auspices had proved mean-

* This placed a greater restraint on Egypt than on Israel, because Israel had aircraft equipped to evade Soviet SAM-3 missiles.

ingless; Moscow had found itself excluded from real negotiations. Sadat knew that his dalliance with Kissinger had enraged Brezhnev, but felt that he should attempt to keep up appearances with Moscow. The United States was a far more valuable ally, he thought, but some sort of relationship with the Soviet Union could still be politically useful. In October 1973 Cairo had taken off with the Russians and landed with the Americans, a political feat it might want to repeat.

Egyptian policy was under daily attack by Soviet propaganda, and yet part of the Soviet military continued to want good relations with Cairo. This fact had been gleaned from a Russian officer who was being paid $500 a month for regular information. A Soviet document handed over by him gave instructions to political officers on what they should say to other Arabs. Item one from this document read: 'Attack Egypt vehemently and concentrate on the disengagement agreement as a betrayal of the Arabs and as a betrayal of the Egyptian army . . . Concentrate on the fact that Egypt deserted the Palestinian struggle which was the core of the Arab struggle. Do not attack Sadat by name; also avoid attacking Kissinger directly.'

Hoping to patch up the split, or at least to keep Soviet arms coming, Sadat sent Ismail Fahmy to Moscow in February 1974. The foreign minister found Brezhnev in furious mood. After listening to a three-hour tirade against Egypt's recent behaviour, he sent a telegram saying that Brezhnev 'was like an angry bull confronted with a red rag'. The Soviet leader had pointed out that in the past Moscow had advised Cairo to talk to the Americans, but Cairo had refused. 'What happened?' Brezhnev asked. 'Now you are not just talking to them, you are sleeping with them.'

Kosygin, who until then had kept quiet, complained that Suez reconstruction contracts had been awarded entirely to Western companies. 'It was our arms which fought and now all the benefits and dividends are going to the West,' he said. He made a pitch for Soviet companies to share in the billions of dollars Egypt had been given by other Arab countries to rebuild the destroyed towns along the Suez Canal.

Similar complaints about money and contracts were in the air when President Assad and Yasser Arafat made visits to the Soviet Union. It was during this period that the PLO chairman first realized that something deeper than anger over Egypt's ingratitude lay behind Moscow's ill-humour. Arafat was astounded to find himself summoned to see Boris Ponomarev, secretary of the Central Committee, who said that the Soviet Union had done much for the Arabs and it was time for the Arabs to reciprocate. Ponomarev asked if Arafat could arrange for a major package of Arab assistance for the Soviet Union. 'We are fed up with all the oratory you give us. It is time to show your friendship in a more substantial way,' Ponomarev said. Suddenly all was clear: the Soviet Union was facing a financial crisis.

The only country opposed to peace with Israel and able to pay the Soviet Union in hard cash was Libya. A huge deal for the purchase of Russian tanks at a cost of $3 billion was arranged. The Americans discovered that when payments for the tanks were made, the money remained in Soviet banks for only a few hours, and was then transferred to banks in the United States and used to pay for wheat shipments. 'They're hungry!' Arafat commented. 'How can the Russians help us when they're broke and hungry?' Both the Palestinians and the Syrians were alarmed by this discovery, while Sadat felt vindicated in his decision to switch alliances.

Meanwhile Kissinger had been exploring the prospects for arranging a disengagement of Syrian and Israeli forces on the northern front. He felt that the problems were substantially greater than those involved in the Egyptian–Israeli agreement. Unlike Sinai, the Golan Heights offered no expanses of empty territory which could be used as a buffer zone. Tel Aviv and Damascus were only 150 miles apart, making both sides understandably nervous about surprise attacks. The territory Israel had captured in 1967 had previously been dotted with Syrian towns and villages whose inhabitants had fled before Israel's advancing armies, and Israel had subsequently established settlements in the Golan Heights. Thousands more Syrian refugees had been produced by the Israeli conquest of additional territory in the October war. The greatest hurdle, from Kissinger's point of view, was a difference of attitudes. Assad, unlike Sadat, had no wish to make dramatic gestures towards Israel. If a disengagement agreement were to be achieved, the main concessions would have to come from Israel rather than Syria.

In talks with Assad in Damascus on 20 January Kissinger established that the Syrian leader wanted a substantial Israeli withdrawal as the price for disengagement. He then sought an Israeli counter-proposal, but was rebuffed, Israel insisting that Damascus should first submit a list of the Israeli prisoners of war held by Syria.

In early February Kissinger, now in Washington, was writing a note to Assad discussing his strategy for obtaining a counter-proposal from the Israelis when he learned of a new development. Assad had flown to Riyadh and had obtained King Faisal's agreement that there should be no lifting of the oil embargo against the US prior to Israeli–Syrian disengagement. Kissinger's anger is evident in a sudden change of tone in the letter:

> I have just been informed by the government of Saudi Arabia, that following your visit to Riyadh, and in response to your request, the Saudi government has taken the position that the oil embargo should not be lifted unless a disengagement agreement has been reached between Syria and Israel and is being implemented. We are informing the Saudi government that unless the embargo is lifted promptly, President Nixon will not authorize further efforts by the United States government to achieve Syrian–Israeli disengagement.*

Knowing that Faisal and Assad were planning a meeting with other Arab leaders on 14 February, Nixon stepped up the pressure. The US ambassador to Saudi Arabia informed Faisal on 6 February that if the boycott were not lifted before or at the 14 February meeting, the US would abandon its peace efforts. The ambassador added: 'If the boycott continues it will be taken in Washington as a sign that Saudi Arabia has lost confidence in the United States and faith in the promises of President Nixon.'

The Arab meeting, in which King Faisal and presidents Assad, Sadat and Boumédienne participated, reaffirmed the position already taken by the Syrian and Saudi leaders. This common stand was achieved despite the rift between Assad and Sadat. Nixon and Kissinger then backed away from their earlier statements and the secretary of state continued working for Syrian–Israeli disengagement. The Arabs had won a diplomatic battle, but the next round would go to the Americans.

During a shuttle trip at the end of February Kissinger obtained

* Kissinger's letter was to be conveyed to Assad orally by the US representative in Damascus. The two countries did not have diplomatic relations.

Israel's reply to Assad's proposals, and then personally delivered to Israel a list of the sixty-five prisoners held by Syria. The opening bids were far apart. Assad wanted Israel to withdraw from all territory seized in the Yom Kippur War and half the land taken in 1967, while Israel demanded that it should be allowed to keep all the 1967 ground and part of what it had seized in 1973. Kissinger arranged for Israeli and Syrian negotiators to travel to Washington for separate talks with US officials, without meeting each other. In the meantime, Israeli and Syrian forces carried out heavy shelling of each other's positions in March and April.

On 18 March most Arab oil producers decided, against Syria's wishes, to lift the embargo against the United States. With oil selling at three times the pre-October 1973 price, producers were no longer willing to put principle before profit. King Faisal was worried that Arabs would appear to be abandoning Syria, and announced that the move was provisional. If no progress were made on Israeli–Syrian disengagement, the ban could be reimposed.

A narrowing of the gap between Israeli and Syrian positions came about in March and April as a result of visits to Washington by Moshe Dayan and Brigadier General Hikmat Shihabi of Syria. By 28 April, when Kissinger began his next shuttle tour, the issue was whether the disengagement line would pass east or west of the Syrian town of Quneitra, which Israel had captured during the Yom Kippur War. In early May Israel again modified its demands, saying that it was prepared to give up the eastern half of the town but wanted to keep control of the western side. The sticking point proved to be three hills on the west side of Quneitra which Israel wanted to retain for strategic reasons. Finally, after Kissinger had shuttled back and forwards for thirty-four days, a disengagement agreement was achieved under which Israel gave up all land seized in 1973 and a few kilometres of the 1967 territory. The status of Quneitra was settled by placing it within a UN buffer zone separating Israeli and Syrian forces. Syrian civilians but not military personnel were allowed to return to the town. Israel was permitted to retain the three hills on condition that no forces or weapons would be stationed on the eastern slopes facing Quneitra. As in the Israel–Egypt agreement, zones of limited forces were established. In the ten kilometres of territory closest to the buffer zone, each party was limited to two brigades, seventy-five tanks and thirty-six artillery guns not exceeding 122-millimetre calibre. Other limits were placed on long-range artillery and surface-to-air missiles in zones further back from the front lines.

The main part of the agreement was signed in Geneva on 31 May 1974 by Major General Herzl Shafir for Israel and Brigadier General Hikmat al-Shihabi for Syria. The tone was significantly different to the Israeli–Egyptian document, which had emphasized a continuing peace process. Where the Israeli–Egyptian document said 'This agreement is not regarded by Egypt and Syria as a final peace agreement,' the wording of the Syrian–Israeli text was: 'This agreement is not a peace agreement.' Many of the controversial elements were in a separate 'United States Proposal'.

Throughout the diplomacy leading to the Syrian–Israeli agreement the Watergate scandal was steadily closing in around President Nixon, with talk of impeachment growing ever louder. Sadat was convinced that the US president was in no real danger but needed a political tonic to lift his morale. This led to an invitation to visit Egypt, which Nixon accepted. Kissinger called at Cairo to see Sadat at the end of the Syrian shuttle and asked what sort of reception Nixon could expect from the Egyptian people. Sadat assured him that the US president would be hailed as a hero.

As the visit drew close Sadat decided to authorize a US naval visit to Alexandria, an unprecedented gesture, as vessels of the US Sixth Fleet were normally barred from Arab ports. An aircraft carrier entered the port accompanied by escort ships, and a host of Egyptians went out in small boats to see the spectacle of US power. Suddenly the sailors began tossing cans of turkey down to the Egyptians, and word quickly spread that the Americans were coming laden with gifts. This was exaggerated, but Nixon did present his official helicopter to Sadat.

Sadat took Nixon on a journey in the former royal train from Cairo to Alexandria, knowing that people would flock to see the train even if they knew little about the visitor. Every station along the route was set with flags, with loudspeakers blaring music to draw the crowds. The television pictures of this extraordinary welcome, half stage-managed and half spontaneous, coincided in the United States with live television hearings of the US Judiciary Committee dealing with Watergate. The Egyptian visit proved to be the highlight of a Middle East tour designed to remind Americans that whatever his image in the United States, Nixon was seen abroad as a statesman. Two months later, after a further Watergate development, Nixon announced his resignation.*

His departure astonished Arab leaders, who had used censorship to prevent the word 'impeachment' being mentioned in Arab newspapers until it was clear that Nixon was about to resign. King Faisal suspected that the scandal was a Zionist–American plot to oust a pro-Arab president. The impact of the Watergate affair on the Arab–Israel conflict was that it distracted the attention of a US president who was willing, at times, to put pressure on Israel, and gave free rein to Kissinger, who was opposed to Israel being pressured.

When Gerald Ford succeeded Nixon in August 1974 little was known in the Arab world about the former vice president's views on the Middle East. Ismail Fahmy, the Egyptian foreign minister, went to Washington the same month to sound out Ford and to explain that Egypt was ready for a second disengagement agreement with Israel. After talks with other Arab and Israeli leaders Ford and Kissinger decided to explore the possibility of an agreement between Jordan and Israel first. King Hussein had been encouraged by the Egyptian and Syrian agreements to hope for recovery of part of the west bank of the Jordan. To demonstrate his flexibility, the king hinted that he would accept a limited Israeli withdrawal as a first step, involving Jericho and a ten-mile zone around the town. Even that was too much for Israeli hardliners who still dreamed of re-establishing biblical Eretz Yisrael.

An exploratory mission by Kissinger showed that the new Israeli government was divided on the west bank issue. Golda Meir had resigned in April 1974 amid a political storm caused by an official investigation into the failure to predict the 6 October attack by Egypt and Syria.† After a period as caretaker premier, Mrs Meir left office at the end of May and was replaced by Yitzhak Rabin, who had been chief-of-staff during the 1967 war. Rabin's main rival Shimon Peres,

* On 24 July the US Supreme Court ordered Nixon to hand over tapes of conversations recorded at the White House, leading to a discovery that on 23 June 1972 the president had given instructions that the CIA should be used to block an FBI investigation into the scandal. Nixon ceased to be president on 9 August.

† The investigation was carried out by the Agranat Commission, whose criticisms also led to the resignation of David Elazar, chief-of-staff.

leader of Rafi, a faction of the Labour Party,* became defence minister. Yigal Allon, previously deputy prime minister, was appointed foreign minister. The three leaders had little in common apart from their military background,† and disagreed on the future of the west bank. Pressure was growing in Israel to avoid any deal with Jordan and to allow time for settlements to be built on the west bank.‡

King Hussein felt that Kissinger's unwillingness to press the Israelis on the west bank showed that the secretary of state was avoiding the core of the Arab–Israel problem. A strong personal animosity developed between the two men, to the point of trading insults. Kissinger said some years later: 'I could destroy that little king in a day,'§ while King Hussein accused Kissinger of lying.

The outcome was that Kissinger shelved the idea of a Jordan–Israel agreement and gave priority to a second phase of the Egypt–Israel process. This had the advantage that all three parties, Egypt, Israel and Kissinger, knew what they wanted to achieve. Sadat was looking for control of the strategic passes in the Sinai mountains, Israel wanted to widen the split between Cairo and Damascus, and Kissinger hoped that a further negotiating success might persuade the oil producers to reduce their pressure on Western economies.

By the end of 1974 several main issues had emerged. Israel was unwilling to give up the passes unless Egypt agreed to end the state of war, whereas Sadat could not make that concession without achieving a complete settlement. The Egyptian leader knew that any agreement, even without talk of peace, would be unpopular outside Egypt. Damascus argued that a second Egyptian–Israeli agreement in the absence of an overall settlement would amount to abandoning the Arab cause.

Another important Egyptian goal was to regain the Sinai oil fields, which had been captured by Israel in 1967 and were providing a large proportion of its energy needs. A further Israeli demand was that the second stage of disengagement should last for twelve years, which was

* Rafi (Israel Labour List) had merged with the Labour Party in 1968.
† Peres had been director general of the ministry of defence, while Allon served as commander-in-chief of Palmah from 1946 to 1948.
‡ At the time only a handful of settlements had been constructed.
§ Kissinger made this remark to the author in 1980 at St Moritz.

unacceptable to Egypt.* Sadat wanted a short-term agreement as a further step towards a final accord.

The impasse was broken by an unexpected development. Sadat's effort to maintain appearances with Moscow while shifting alliances to Washington suddenly fell apart in February 1975 when Brezhnev angrily cancelled a visit to Cairo. Both Washington and Israel were pleased. Feeling that his goal of separating Egypt from the Soviet Union was coming to a critical phase, Kissinger made a second exploratory visit to the Middle East in February 1975, followed by a more formal negotiating effort in March. The second of these tours showed that Sadat was willing to be flexible on numerous points, because his primary aim was to maintain the peace and concentrate on the Egyptian economy. With the work of clearing the Suez Canal almost complete, Egypt could look forward to a resumption of shipping revenues.†

Kissinger concluded that while Egypt was ready for a deal, the political price demanded by Israel was unattainable. Sadat was prepared to declare that Egypt would not use military force and would not permit military operations by others operating from Egyptian territory, but Rabin continued to insist on a declaration that the state of belligerency had ceased. Kissinger repeated the 'flying State Department' approach and reduced the gap between the two sides on several points, but was unable to overcome the central problem: Israel would not give up the passes without the non-belligerency concession, and Sadat could not accept an agreement which left Egypt short of the passes.

The failure of Kissinger's efforts led President Ford to become more closely involved in Middle East diplomacy, and in June he held talks with Sadat in Salzburg and with Rabin in Washington. Sadat made a further concession on one of the secondary issues, a dispute over which side should control an intelligence-gathering station at Umm Khisheiba in Sinai. After a further two months of contacts it became clear that Israel was prepared to trade flexibility on certain points for a huge further increase in US economic aid.

After a further eleven-day shuttle trip by Kissinger in August, Israel

* Israel's demands formed part of a proposal which Allon submitted to Kissinger in December 1974.

† The canal was reopened in June 1975. Five years later revenue reached an annual rate of $1 billion.

agreed to give up the passes and the oil fields in return for comprehensive US commitments and minor Egyptian concessions. American aid to Israel rose to $2.25 billion in 1976 and Washington gave written assurances on supplies of oil and arms. The US also made political concessions, including an understanding that any further Egypt–Israel accord would be a peace agreement. The US agreed to man and supervise stations in the Sinai designed to provide early warning of plans by either side for an offensive. Sadat allowed Israel to keep the Umm Khisheiba station on the basis that a similar facility was built for Egypt with US assistance. Israel secured permission for ships carrying its cargoes to use the Suez Canal, but did not obtain an ending of the state of belligerency. The arrangements for limited forces zones were similar to those in the first agreement, though the figures for the numbers of men, tanks and short-range artillery guns permitted were slightly higher.

The second Israeli–Egyptian disengagement agreement, signed in Geneva on 4 September 1975, was widely unpopular in the Arab world. Most Palestinians and Syrians felt that Sadat had weakened the chances of regaining the other territories seized by Israel in 1967. Kissinger's step-by-step approach had eroded political assets the Arab world held in October 1973, leaving little to trade in any overall solution with Israel. In one of his early conversations with Kissinger in 1973 Sadat had said: 'Henry, you hold 99 per cent of the cards.' At the time that was an exaggeration, for Sadat's hand was stuffed with trumps. A year and a half later, during negotiations leading to the second disengagement agreement, Sadat repeated the remark in an interview with *Le Monde*. By then it was almost true.

After the second agreement US interest in the Arab–Israel conflict subsided and Kissinger became more involved with East–West diplomacy. Hoping to recapture American attention, Sadat announced the unilateral abrogation of the fifteen-year friendship treaty with the Soviet Union which he had signed with President Podgorny in 1971. Sadat's move, announced in a speech to the Egyptian parliament in March 1976, failed to bring Kissinger back to the Middle East. The only result was that the hot-line linking Abdin Palace in Cairo to the White House, which had been installed for Nixon's visit two years earlier, sprang to life for the first time. A message from President Ford to Sadat, sent on the hot-line teleprinter, said: 'My government and the American people have viewed this as a courageous assertion of self-respect and dignity . . . You can count on our strong support. The policy of moderation you pursued with us through so many difficult periods in recent years will, I am convinced, continue to bear fruit. I look forward to redoubling our joint efforts for a just peace in the Middle East.'

In his reply Sadat sought to engage US involvement by saying: 'I am sure that the present situation if left without serious progress may very well explode once again.' Nothing happened: Sadat had forgotten that US diplomacy in the Middle East usually comes to a halt in presidential election years. Washington was now accustomed to Sadat's sense of theatre, and knew that the friendship treaty had been a dead letter almost from the start.

This disappointment came at a time when Sadat was receiving advice on military operations by Israeli forces on the west bank against Egyptian forces while Egypt was not really an Arab country and should make a complete break with the Nasser legacy and with Arab nationalism. This would enable Cairo to settle its differences directly with Israel without depending on intermediaries. President Ceausescu of Romania had been pressing for direct Israeli–Egyptian contacts since Nasser's day. In the spring of 1976 King Hassan of Morocco was approached by Yitzhak Rabin, the Israeli prime minister. Rabin asked Hassan to tell Sadat that Israel was seriously interested in direct talks. The king sent General Ahmed El-Duleimi, commander of the Royal Guard,* to Cairo to inform Sadat of Rabin's approach. The general conveyed a message which Rabin had given verbally to the king in French. At Sadat's request, he wrote out the original words in French, and then translated them into Arabic. The message called for direct talks with the ultimate aim of achieving peace, stressing an Israeli commitment to maintain secrecy. King Hassan added his personal view that Rabin was serious and that Sadat should stop depending on the Americans and deal directly with the Israelis. Sadat did not take up the offer, and Jimmy Carter's narrow victory in the US presidential election on 2 November 1976 brought the Kissinger era, and the Kissinger–Sadat political partnership, to a close.

* General El-Duleimi later became the Moroccan minister of defence.

14

The Road to Jerusalem

On a cool morning in January 1977 President Sadat was sitting in the garden of his rest house at Aswan conducting an interview with a Lebanese newspaperwoman, when a glint of alarm appeared in the journalist's eyes. 'Mr President, something strange is happening behind you.' Sadat turned and saw a column of smoke arising from the town and a throng of protesters advancing across a bridge towards the house. He fled to the airport under the protection of his guards, using a back road, and flew to Cairo, unsure what was happening. Similar crowds were gathering in cities all over Egypt, growing into vast demonstrations which attacked police stations and offices of the Arab Socialist Union in protest against massive food-price increases. Slogans chanted in the streets showed that the protesters held Sadat personally responsible for their economic misery. The 'Hero of the Crossing' was no longer the hero of the people.

The demonstrations began immediately after an announcement on 18 January that subsidies which held down the prices of staple foods were being abolished and pay increases cancelled. As the crisis mounted Sadat summoned General Gamassi, who was now minister of defence, and ordered him to call out the army. Gamassi reminded Sadat of a promise the president had given never to use the army against Egyptians. In return for compliance, he insisted that Sadat should restore the subsidies and pay rises before the army took to the streets. Sadat accepted and radio stations announced the president's decision seven times before troops moved out of their barracks. Before calm returned to Egypt on 19 January 171 people had been killed and hundreds injured.

The causes of the uprising were obvious, but a group of senior advisers persuaded themselves that there had been a communist conspiracy. After wavering for some days Sadat accepted that advice and ordered the arrest of around 1200 activists of all political persuasions. It was easier to blame activists than to tackle social injustice, poverty, corruption in government and gross disparities between economic classes.

The food riots reflected not just the misery of the poor but a wider social, political and economic malaise. Years of mobilization had long since dissipated the excitement Egyptians felt after the 1973 canal crossing, and when the soldiers returned to their villages many faced unemployment. Far from lifting national spirits, the effect of demobilization was to deepen the moral and political vacuum and to unleash long-suppressed economic expectations. Other Arab countries contributed generously, providing Egypt with grants and loans estimated at between $16 billion and $22 billion,* but much of this was squandered because of a policy known as '*Infitah*' ('Open Door'), which gave free rein to commercial interests.

Sadat was unsure what to do next. The army had rescued his authority, but he dreaded the prospect of testing its loyalty in the streets again if further riots erupted. Some new goal was needed to keep the army busy, make the generals feel involved with the government, and divert public attention from economic problems. Three years earlier, during the Geneva conference, Israel had suggested that Egypt's problems could be solved by taking over Libya, with its rich oil fields (see pp. 227–8). That idea appealed to Sadat's wish to focus attention on himself, and to solve all his problems with a single dramatic move. There was no need, he reasoned, to occupy the whole of Libya; the eastern province of Cyrenaica, where most of the oil fields were located, would be sufficient. An invasion could be justified to the outside world and to other Arabs as punishment of a trouble-maker. If Gadaffi were separated from his source of wealth, he would be unable to continue sponsoring terrorist movements, and his radical influence on the peoples of the southern shores of the Mediterranean would decline. The United States, western Europe and the conservative Arab regimes would be in Egypt's debt, and the Soviet Union

* The Egyptian government estimate was $16 billion, while a study by Abdel-Latif El-Hamad, the Kuwaiti finance minister, put the total at $22 billion. These figures relate to total Arab grants and loans to Egypt between 1970 and 1977.

would lose one of its remaining centres of influence in the Middle East. Sadat even believed that Libyans would welcome such a move. This notion arose from conversations with his brother-in-law Mahmoud Abu-Wafya, who came from Egypt's western province, Beheira, and was in contact with leaders of the Awlad Ali and Bara'sa tribes in the border area. Sadat understood that these leaders would be glad to be rid of the revolutionary regime which had brought Gadaffi's tribe to supremacy in Libya.

In Sadat's mind, the 'Libyan solution' lacked nothing except a pretext for opening hostilities. In the late spring of 1977 the Soviet Union began delivering large quantities of weapons to Libya under a long-standing contract. Sadat had previously raised no objection to the deal, but now he began to claim that the deliveries were a threat to Egyptian security. Amid a propaganda campaign in the Egyptian press, Sadat mobilized thousands of troops and moved them from eastern to western Egypt. Hostilities opened on 21 July with a bombing raid against Libya's Nasser airbase in Cyrenaica, an ironic choice given that the base had been named in honour of the former Egyptian president. Almost immediately it became clear that Sadat had miscalculated: the expected upsurge of Egyptian nationalist feeling failed to materialize. Reports reaching Cairo from the Egyptian consulate in Benghazi spoke of Egyptian doctors weeping as they treated wounded Libyan soldiers. Neither the public nor the army saw any logic in disengaging forces with an enemy, Israel, only to attack an Arab neighbour. The fact that about a million Egyptians were living in Libya further strengthened feeling against the attack. If the Egyptian public was unenthusiastic, Washington was openly hostile. The US ambassador in Cairo conveyed a warning from Washington to forget any thoughts of invasion. Sadat was obliged to back down.

The failure of the Libyan adventure left Sadat deeper in difficulty than ever. In rash moments he had promised an 'Era of Plenty', but now he had no idea how the necessary economic conditions might be created. Like a man relying on winning a lottery to pay his debts, he began to dream of massive foreign aid. He convinced himself that, given the right conditions, the United States would provide a new Marshall Plan to assist recovery. The aid Egypt had already received from the Arab world was more than the Marshall Aid funds distributed by the US for the reconstruction of Europe after World War II,* but that fact did not deflect Sadat. In his mind, the top priority was to find the right political key to unlock Washington's generosity. If punishing Gadaffi was the wrong key, perhaps the right one was peace with Israel.

Thus it was that the food riots in January and a botched foreign adventure in the late spring led Sadat to the conclusion by mid-1977 that Egypt would have to negotiate a new relationship with Israel. He was therefore in a receptive frame of mind when the United States returned to active Middle East diplomacy after marking time throughout 1976 because of the presidential campaign.

The new US administration had taken office two days after the January food riots, amid concern in Washington that Egypt might drift back into Moscow's embrace. President Carter and Secretary of State Cyrus Vance decided to give urgent priority to the Middle East, and to adopt a new approach. Kissinger's step-by-step diplomacy was abandoned in favour of an effort to tackle the Arab–Israel problem at its roots, giving strong emphasis to the Palestinian issue. Two weeks after taking office Vance visited Middle East leaders and invited them to Washington for talks with Carter. The US proposed that all parties should try to agree on principles for a settlement, with the aim of reconvening the Geneva conference in the autumn and holding direct talks between Israel and individual Arab countries afterwards. Almost immediately the Americans faced a dilemma: Israel would not participate in a conference which included the PLO, while the Arabs could not accept the exclusion of the organization which they recognized as the 'sole legitimate representative' of the Palestinians.

In a meeting with Sadat on 15 February Vance suggested that the Israelis might agree to PLO participation in the peace conference if the PLO accepted UN Resolution 242, as this would amount to implicit recognition of Israel. Vance took this up with Yigal Allon, the Israeli foreign minister, who replied: 'A PLO which recognized Israel would no longer be the PLO.' Washington then began indirect contacts with the PLO through Sadat, with the aim of securing PLO acceptance of the resolution.

By March the outlines of Carter's policy were taking shape. The

* The US distributed $12 billion between 1948 and 1951.

new president advocated a comprehensive settlement involving a Palestinian 'homeland', Israeli withdrawal to the 1967 borders, and a clear definition of peace.

Sadat needed several months to come to terms with the change of US administration, feeling at first that the loss of Ford and Kissinger was a disaster. Any antagonism towards Carter melted away, however, when the Egyptian and US presidents met in April. The two men got on well, and Sadat made what the Americans considered a useful concession by telling Carter that if an overall solution could be achieved, Egypt would be prepared to have normal relations with Israel, including an exchange of ambassadors. This was a shift away from the standard Arab line of refusing to define the nature of peace until Israel had made a complete withdrawal. Carter said that there might come a point in the negotiations where he would have to call on Sadat to make a bold gesture towards Israel.

Prospects for Carter's new approach took a major step backwards in May as a result of an electoral earthquake in Israel. Yitzhak Rabin had resigned in April, and his Labour Party rival Shimon Peres was expected to be the next prime minister. Israeli voters, however, had grown weary of bickering among coalition leaders, and deserted the socialist group, which had dominated all governments since 1949, transferring their loyalties to the ideological right wing.*.

Menachem Begin, the new prime minister, was a Russian-born concentration camp survivor who had always supported extreme views. After serving as commander-in-chief of the Irgun terrorist movement during World War II, he founded Herut (Freedom), a party which reflected the hardline ideology of Jabotinsky's revisionists. Strong personal and ideological differences between Begin and David Ben-Gurion, leader of MAPAI, the core party within the socialist group, were a feature of Israeli politics for many years. Part of the reason for Begin's dislike of Israel's first prime minister was that Ben-Gurion had ordered the closure of Irgun and other terrorist groups.

In 1973 Herut merged with other right-wing parties, forming the Likud (Unity) electoral bloc to face the united socialist parties. The

* MAPAI (Workers' Party of the Land of Israel) had been the dominant socialist party since 1930. In 1968 MAPAI merged with two other socialist parties to form the Labour Party, which led coalition governments until Begin's victory in 1977.

result was that Israeli politics gained a second pole and a more even balance of strength. The scales began to tilt in Likud's favour in the 1973 election, and in 1977 Likud overtook Labour to become the largest group.*

There has been much debate as to whether ideological differences between the Israeli left and right are important to the Arab–Israel conflict. Some argued that the right was a greater danger to the Arab world because of its higher commitment to the 'Eretz Yisrael' concept. Matters were never that simple, because the two big political blocs contained overlapping currents of opinion. Israel's main periods of expansion (1948 and 1967) were carried out under socialist governments.

Although Labour governments were supposedly willing to trade land for peace, the party included important figures who favoured the construction of settlements in occupied territories. Moshe Dayan, leader of the RAFI faction until 1973, belonged to this tendency, and his views resulted in an important shift in official Labour Party policy before the 1973 election. The party adopted a compromise known as the Galilee Document, committing itself to settlement construction. That policy was implemented after the 1973 election, but at a slow pace because of opposition from prominent figures on the Labour left, including Abba Eban.

If both parties were in favour of settlements, why did the change from Labour to Likud in 1977 seem to Arabs to be a retrograde step? The difference was one of degree. Under Labour-led governments only about twenty settlements were built on the west bank during the decade after the Six Day War. After Likud's victory in 1977 the construction programme began in earnest. Secondly, the new government had different reasons for refusing to withdraw from the occupied territories. Labour governments had always insisted that withdrawal could take place only in exchange for peace, recognition and normal relations. The new Likud leaders were opposed to withdrawal from lands which they considered part of Eretz Yisrael. Arabs saw this as a dangerous development, because an ideologically motivated opponent would be more difficult to dislodge.

* The Sephardim, or Jews of oriental origin, voted mainly for Likud in the 1977 election, while the Ashkenazi, or Jews of European origin, continued to prefer Labour.

The Israeli system usually deprives any party of an absolute parliamentary majority, and long negotiations are needed to form coalitions. The combination which emerged in May 1977, with Begin as premier and Dayan as foreign minister, removed all inhibitions about building in the occupied territories. Immediately after taking office Begin visited the settlement of Elon Moreh and said he would like to see many more similar projects.

Sadat took the defeat of Labour as a personal blow, just as he had been upset by Gerald Ford's demise. Golda Meir and Yitzhak Rabin had been extraordinarily difficult to deal with, even with Kissinger's help, but at least their views were known to him. He had dealt with them through Kissinger and had written to some of them in his own handwriting. The new Israeli prime minister at first seemed an enigma, half religious fundamentalist, half ex-terrorist. This view of Begin was challenged in a message from Nahum Goldmann. The World Zionist Congress leader flew to Morocco in June and asked King Hassan to tell Sadat that Begin's victory should not be seen as the end of peace prospects.

Carter was not much more enthusiastic than Sadat about Begin's victory. The new prime minister lost no time in making clear his dislike of Carter's peace initiative, and especially the emphasis on an overall solution on the basis of pre-agreed principles and in the context of a Geneva conference. In a meeting with Carter and Vance in July the Israeli prime minister said that two of the five principles proposed by the US administration were unacceptable. Washington had suggested that Israel should withdraw in stages to the lines it had held before the June 1967 war, subject to minor border adjustments. Begin did not agree that the adjustments should be minor. Secondly, the US administration felt that the Palestinians should be allowed to decide their future status, which Begin rejected outright.*

Carter tried to persuade Begin to moderate his plans for constructing more settlements, but made no headway. This first meeting between Carter and Begin was deeply discouraging for Washington, but the

* The other three principles in the American plan were: 1) The Geneva conference should aim to achieve peace; 2) Resolutions 242 and 338 to be the basis for negotiations; 3) peace to be defined as a complete normalization of relations and not just cessation of the state of belligerency.

US president decided that peace could not wait until the Israelis elected a more amenable prime minister.

The attempt to organize a Geneva conference continued, and the secretary of state showed a willingness to cooperate closely with Arab governments. Vance supported a Saudi and Syrian proposal that all Arabs should be represented in a single delegation, including the Palestinians. Sadat initially opposed this idea, fearing that it would restrict his negotiating freedom, but later went along with it. He suggested that Israel's objections to PLO involvement could be overcome if the Palestinian representatives in an all-Arab delegation were not officials of the PLO.

Sadat drew up a secret draft to show Vance the kind of peace treaty which Egypt would be willing to sign, and asked him to obtain a counter-proposal from Israel, which Vance succeeded in doing. Another idea discussed at the time was that the west bank should be placed under the trusteeship of the United Nations.

While Vance was in the Middle East Carter announced that the United States was ready to hold direct talks with the PLO if they accepted Resolution 242. This infuriated Begin, who made a speech a few days later, during the secretary of state's next visit to Israel, comparing such contacts to Neville Chamberlain's attempts to appease Hitler in 1938. The Americans found this highly offensive; to the Arabs the comparison seemed strange and irrelevant.

Washington's energy and Israel's obstinacy created an odd brew. Dozens of ideas were circulating, but no one seemed capable of making them coalesce into something workable. The new Israeli government, moreover, was unconvinced of the need for a US role, and thought that direct negotiations with Arabs could be more productive. Soon after coming to office Begin visited President Ceausescu of Romania and asked him to make a further attempt to persuade Egypt to accept direct talks.

Begin complained to Ceausescu that Arabs were relying on American power to put pressure on Israel: 'I wish they would stop that policy. Please assure them in my name that Israel will decide for itself and no amount of American pressure is going to make her move one step more than she wants. Israel is not a banana republic to which the Americans can dictate. Please tell President Sadat that there is no other way but to deal directly with Israel.' Ceausescu conveyed this message to Sadat in July 1977, adding that Begin was indignant about the idea that Washington could 'deliver Israel to Egypt', as many (including US politicians) had encouraged Carter to believe. The Romanian president noted that Begin had repeated the phrase 'We are not a banana republic' three times during their conversation.

In a long message to Sadat, Ceausescu said that Begin wanted to be remembered as a peacemaker, not as a terrorist, and was no longer the diehard he had once been. Ceausescu considered Begin to be the only Israeli politician capable of emulating the role de Gaulle had played in bringing France to peace with Algeria. A peace treaty would have been impossible with Labour in power and Begin in opposition, but with the roles reversed the prospects were better. Ceausescu advised Sadat not to wait four years for a change of Israeli prime minister.

Sadat pondered these remarks during a holiday near Salzburg in Austria in August, but could not make up his mind whether to enter direct contacts with Israel. He was still undecided in October, when the shaky US initiative began to fall apart. A row had broken out over a US–Soviet joint statement of principles for the proposed peace agreement. The text infuriated the Israelis, because it contained a reference to 'Palestinian rights', and angered Sadat, who did not want the Soviet Union to be involved. 'We kicked the Russians out of the door and now Mr Carter is bringing them back in through the window,' he thundered. Several other Arab countries were equally critical of the Soviet involvement. The UN General Assembly was meeting at the time, and some Arab foreign ministers used the opportunity to express their displeasure to Cyrus Vance. He replied that the United States could hardly exclude the other superpower.

The text was also attacked by Henry Kissinger, who had involved the Soviets in the original Geneva conference. When asked by Ismail Fahmy about this apparent contradiction, Kissinger replied that he had given the Soviets a role before and after the disengagement talks, but not during the negotiating process. The former secretary of state added that the parties to the conflict had themselves insisted on limiting the Soviet role.

Three days after the US–Soviet joint statement, Dayan had a bruising encounter with Carter, speaking to the US president in harsh terms. The administration was left in no doubt that it had stumbled badly, and Carter seemed shaken.

The following month Sadat received a personal appeal from Carter, dated 21 October 1977, asking for help in unblocking the road to Geneva. The letter, written in unusual handwriting, sloping steeply to the right, recalled Sadat's visit to Washington earlier in the year.

> When we met privately in the White House I was deeply impressed and grateful for your promise to me that, at a crucial moment, I could count on your support when obstacles arose in our common search for peace . . . We have reached such a moment and I need your help . . . The time has now come to move forward and your early public endorsement of our approach is extremely important – perhaps vital – in advancing all parties to Geneva . . . your friend, Jimmy Carter.

The letter seemed to remove doubts which had been holding Sadat back for weeks. A plan had come into his mind, but he wanted to consult certain friends first. At the end of October he flew to Romania and asked President Ceausescu two questions.

> SADAT: Does Begin really want peace?
> CEAUSESCU: Yes, I can assure you of that.
> SADAT: Is he politically strong enough to push through a peace agreement?
> CEAUSESCU: If there is anyone who is strong enough it is Begin.

Sadat later disclosed that his decision to make a dramatic gesture to break the impasse was taken immediately after seeing Ceausescu.

After Romania the Egyptian leader flew to Iran to ask for the Shah's view, and received encouragement to negotiate with Israel. The Shah had been pressing Sadat for some time to turn his back on the Arab world and establish Egypt's separate identity. That advice had not entirely been ignored, for Cairo had begun to emphasize Egypt's Pharaonic past and its superiority over other Arab countries. This campaign was handled in an ugly and clumsy fashion, portraying Palestinians as sellers of sweets and desserts, and suggesting that there were two kinds of Arabs in the Arab–Israeli struggle: the fighters and the spectators. This absurd chauvinism fanned a bitter quarrel with the Saudis, Iraqis and Syrians.

After Iran Sadat flew to Saudi Arabia and explained to Crown Prince

Fahd that he felt American efforts were stuck and that some form of negotiation with Israel would be necessary. Not knowing what Sadat was planning, Fahd could only give general encouragement, wishing the Egyptian president luck in his efforts.

On his return to Cairo at the beginning of November Sadat found a message from King Hassan of Morocco saying that Dayan had visited him, bringing an offer from Begin. The Israeli prime minister was proposing secret face-to-face talks with Sadat on an exploratory basis. Having already made up his mind to enter into direct talks, Sadat accepted in principle, but was not prepared to take part in the first meeting himself. It was arranged that Begin would send Dayan secretly to Morocco to meet an Egyptian representative.

The envoy Sadat chose to represent Egypt was Hassan El-Tuhami, one of the original Free Officers, who had been involved with Nasser in an unsuccessful attempt to kill one of King Farouk's men before the revolution. Tuhami was a man of forceful personality and impressive appearance, with a healthy complexion, blue eyes and a silvery beard. He had undergone CIA training in 1953, and later served as ambassador to Austria and as Egyptian representative to the International Atomic Energy Agency.

Despite this background, Tuhami's suitability for so delicate a mission was open to question. During his spell in Vienna, staff at the Egyptian embassy had written to the foreign minister suggesting that the ambassador was unwell. He had been dining with colleagues when he stood up and said: 'What a pleasure. What a great honour to see you.' His colleagues asked: 'Who?' Tuhami replied: 'The Prophet Mohamed passed by.' After this incident Tuhami was brought back to Cairo. It was thought that his long stay outside Egypt, together with some personal problems, had affected him. He was appointed to a ministerial rank to boost his morale and allow him to regain his vigour. This therapy, however, did not work. Tuhami subsequently reported receiving visits from Sayyedna El-Khedr, a legendary figure in Islamic mythology who is regarded as a holy spirit roving the earth carrying inspiration and performing miracles.

The Tuhami–Dayan encounter was never intended to be a negotiating session, only a first contact under King Hassan's auspices. Dayan's account describes an elaborate deception to throw the press off his trail, involving a beatnik disguise and a complex route to Morocco via Brussels and Paris.* On the evening of 16 September King Hassan brought Dayan and Tuhami together. The Egyptian position, contained in a message from Sadat which Tuhami read out, was that Israel should withdraw from all occupied territories in exchange for peace. Sadat was willing to meet Begin, shake hands and hold talks, but only on the basis of a prior understanding that Israel would withdraw from all the territories. Egypt's position was presented as a take-it-or-leave-it offer with no room for negotiation.

Dayan stressed that he had come as Begin's emissary and could not react to Tuhami's points without instructions. However, no Israeli prime minister could give a prior undertaking to withdraw from all territories without consent from the Knesset.

Dayan returned to Israel, using his disguise and travelling via Paris, and reported to Begin. The two Israeli leaders agreed that Israel and Egypt should exchange proposals for a peace treaty. Begin was not prepared to give a prior commitment to withdraw from all occupied territories, but the Egyptians would understand Israel's position when they read the proposals.

Meanwhile Tuhami told Sadat that Dayan had said that everything was negotiable, and Egypt had no idea of the concessions Israel was prepared to make if it came to direct negotiations.† Exactly how Tuhami presented these points is unknown, but Sadat understood the message to be that Israel was prepared to withdraw from Egyptian territory.

Tuhami's memoirs give the impression that he thought the Israelis were in no position to bargain.‡ He recalls harsh comments which he made to the Israeli foreign minister, and implies that Dayan adopted a submissive manner. 'Moshe, I did not expect to meet you but on a battlefield,' Tuhami said.

According to Tuhami, Dayan replied that if the Egyptian army had advanced in the early part of the Yom Kippur War, the Israelis would have surrendered completely. 'We were ready to return to the original

* See *Breakthrough Moshe Dayan*, by Moshe Dayan, Weidenfeld & Nicolson, London, 1981.

† The first part of this was a standard Israeli position, while the second part was a familiar Israeli come-on.

‡ The memoirs were published in instalments in Kuwait in 1989, and in the Egyptian magazine *Al-Mussawar* in 1993.

land of Israel . . . without fighting, provided that you gave us a guarantee to spare our lives.' Tuhami also told Dayan: 'Moshe, you are the false prophet of Israel. There was a prophet before you who was one-eyed, and he was a false prophet.'

Dayan replied: 'Sir, I am not that man.'

Tuhami's account reads like the fantasies of a troubled man.

In the belief that Dayan had given Tuhami an assurance on withdrawal, Sadat was full of confidence when he replied to Carter's letter. He proposed a grandiose scheme involving the five permanent members of the UN Security Council, who were to assemble in Jerusalem and invite all parties to the conflict to join them in a peace conference. Sadat expected an enthusiastic response from Carter, and was disappointed when the US president replied in cautious tones, describing the idea as 'quite interesting'.

Carter pointed out that careful preparation would be needed to persuade the Soviet Union, China, France and Britain to take part, and to ensure that all Arab parties would accept. Sadat was planning to announce his initiative but Carter begged him to refrain, pointing out that premature publicity would offend the big powers. The US president thought that such an ambitious project could take a year to arrange.

The timing of Carter's reply influenced what followed. Sadat had told Carter that he planned to announce his proposal in a speech to the Egyptian parliament on 7 November. Carter's answer did not reach Sadat until that day, a few hours before the speech was due to be delivered. The reply came in the form of a phone call from US ambassador Herman Eilts, speaking on Carter's behalf, as it was too late to send a letter.

In response to Carter's request, Sadat felt obliged to postpone his speech, but he was annoyed, frustrated and worried. The reason for urgency was that Sadat feared the Israeli media might find out about Tuhami's meeting with Dayan. It would be highly embarrassing if Egyptians learned of the contacts from the Israeli press. That risk could only be neutralized by dropping a hint in a speech to parliament that something was afoot between Egypt and Israel.

Two days later Sadat hit on a way of pre-empting the feared media leaks without breaking faith with Carter. In a speech to the Egyptian parliament on 9 November he said nothing about his proposal for a five-power peace conference in Jerusalem, but made a more dramatic statement: 'I am ready to go to the ends of the earth for peace, even to the Knesset itself,' he announced, to the astonishment of members of parliament. Sadat mentioned the Knesset as an illustration of his eagerness for peace, not as a statement of intention, but he was well aware how this would be interpreted. Yasser Arafat, who had come to the parliament to hear the speech, walked out in disgust and immediately left the country. He stayed away from Egypt for years afterwards.

Such was the shock caused by Sadat's speech that Ismail Fahmy, the foreign minister, ordered newspapers not to carry headlines referring to the president's willingness to go to Jerusalem. Even Sadat's wife Jihan was stunned. The Egyptian president was digesting the unenthusiastic reactions when he received phone calls from the US television presenters Barbara Walters and Walter Kronkite. Reassured by the American media interest, he was astonished and angry when he received the first editions of the Cairo newspapers and found that his *coup de théâtre* had not been given prominence. He phoned Egyptian editors at 11.45 p.m., cancelled Fahmy's instructions, and ordered that his offer to go to Jerusalem should be the main front-page headline.

The remark was meant to make a splash and provide political cover in case the Tuhami–Dayan meeting became known, but the US media interest created a new situation.

Kronkite asked Sadat on the phone: 'Does this mean you are really ready to go to Israel?' In a moment of bravado Sadat replied, 'Yes, I declared that.' Kronkite asked: 'When are you going?' Sadat replied: 'When I receive an official invitation.'

Kronkite then spoke to Begin and told him what Sadat had said. Begin replied that he wholeheartedly welcomed Sadat, and an invitation would be sent through the US ambassador, but the Egyptian leader should be aware of Israel's conditions: 'Israel will not withdraw to the pre-1967 lines. Israel will not deal with the PLO. Israel will not accept a Palestinian state.'

Sadat paid no attention to these remarks because of his understanding from Tuhami that Israeli withdrawal from Egyptian territory presented no problem, and because the statement 'Israel will not withdraw to the pre-1967 lines' seemed to be a repetition of an old stand not yet adjusted to the new situation.

Egyptians learned of these developments mainly by listening to foreign radio stations, as the Egyptian press reported only Sadat's speech. Four years had passed since the taboo was first breached after the 1973 war, but the sense of shock and unease remained strong.

The following day Sadat called the six top members of the Egyptian National Security Council to his house to explain that his gesture was intended to break the impasse in peace negotiations. The US effort had virtually come to a halt, the Soviet Union was unacceptable to both Israel and the Arabs as a peacemaker, the Europeans were in no position to help, leaving only direct Arab–Israeli negotiations as a way forward. Sadat disclosed Tuhami's meeting with Dayan and gave a résumé of the points Ceausescu had made. He then drew out of his pocket a sheet of paper containing some points, attached to a hand-drawn map. Those present were not shown the map but were given the impression that a deal was virtually agreed. 'There is no problem at all on the Egyptian side,' Sadat said. 'The difficulties are psychological and the Israelis are the ones who need assurances. They are right when they ask how we can live in peace if we are not prepared to talk peace.' He then folded the map away, as if to imply that he had the solution in his pocket.

With the exception of Ismail Fahmy, who resigned, the government reluctantly went along with the president and concentrated on limiting the damage to Egypt's relations with other Arab countries. The most urgent need was to avert a break with Assad.

Two days before the visit to Jerusalem Sadat flew to Damascus in an attempt to mend fences, but found a frosty welcome. 'Brother Anwar, you are always in a hurry,' Assad told him. 'You wanted to have battle in 1972 earlier than necessary. You jumped into a ceasefire earlier than was necessary. You rushed into a first disengagement agreement earlier than you need have done. I understand your impatience, but please understand that you cannot go to Jerusalem. This is treason. You are forgetting the martyrs of the Egyptian army. The Egyptian people will not take it. The Arab nation will never forgive you.'

Sadat asked for a mandate to talk on behalf of both Egypt and Syria when he visited Jerusalem, which was unrealistic. Assad said that Sadat was lucky not to be under arrest. At a meeting of the Syrian high command that morning one of the options considered had been to detain the Egyptian leader in Damascus and prevent him from travelling to Jerusalem. This would have been explained to the Arab public by saying that Sadat had gone mad.

After a miserable meeting the two men parted. Sadat flew back to Egypt knowing that the Jerusalem trip would wreck what little remained of the Egyptian–Syrian relationship and might lead to Egypt's isolation from the rest of the Arab world. He sought to calm Arab anger by announcing in a television interview that he would resign if his trip failed to produce the results which every Arab desired, and by insisting that the differences with Israel were mainly psychological.

Assembling a suitable team to accompany Sadat to Jerusalem was not easy, as Fahmy had resigned, and Mohamed Riad, the deputy minister, was wrongly understood to be unwilling to go. This misunderstanding arose because Hosni Mubarak, the vice president, phoned Riad and asked: 'Are you ready to go?' meaning 'Are you willing to go?' In Arabic, as in English, the same words can also mean: 'Have you got everything ready to go?' Riad understood the question in this second sense and gave a truthful answer, as much preparatory work remained to be done. The following morning Riad read in the Egyptian press that he had 'resigned', meaning that he had been dismissed for being unwilling to accompany the president. 'I thought I was being asked whether all the position papers and memoranda were ready,' he said.

The delegation which went to Jerusalem on 19 November consisted of Sadat, Mustafa Khalil, a former minister, Dr Boutros Ghali, secretary of state in the foreign ministry,* Hassan El-Tuhami and Osman Ahmed Osman, a wealthy contractor and father-in-law of Sadat's daughter.

A few hours before Sadat left Cairo for Israel, an ancient tradition was performed at Islam's holiest shrine, in Mecca. On the day of Eid El-Adha, the Feast of Sacrifice, the ruler of Saudi Arabia unlocks the door of the Ka'ba and says a prayer. King Khalid, normally a devout man, later said that he prayed that Sadat's plane would crash before it reached Jerusalem, 'so that an Arab scandal might be averted by the will of God'.

* In the Egyptian government a secretary of state is junior to a minister (unlike the American and British systems).

The Israeli government doubted until that morning that Sadat would go through with his grand gesture. One fear was that the Egyptian president would impose some condition which Israel would be unable to accept, and would then cancel the visit, blaming Israeli intransigence. There were also suspicions that the visit was somehow connected with a military scare which had occurred a few weeks earlier. The Egyptian army had informed the United Nations Emergency Force that routine training exercises would be held in the Sinai desert in October. The tense internal situation in Egypt after the January riots prompted speculation in Israel that Sadat would try to regain public support by provoking a fight with Israel. This led to fears that the Egyptian exercises were preparations for an attack.

A still more unlikely theory discussed in Israel was that the Egyptians might be planning to send a terrorist group with Sadat to kill the Israeli cabinet. A variation of that fantasy was that the Egyptian delegation might be led not by Sadat but by someone who looked exactly like him. The Israelis were jittery enough to ask the Americans for reassurance that Sadat's mission was indeed an innocent quest for peace.

These doubts cleared a few hours before Sadat's scheduled arrival time, and the Israeli cabinet met to consider the implications of receiving the Egyptian leader. They agreed that a visit at head of state level amounted to recognition of Israel and the beginning of normalization of relations. It was therefore in Israel's interest to accord Sadat the appropriate honours. Begin and other cabinet members decided to be at the airport to receive him.

If Israelis were incredulous, the mood in Egypt was hardly less turbulent. Whether they approved or not, Egyptians were unable to resist following the president's progress on live television, as if Sadat were travelling to a distant planet. The two countries had been at war for so long that very few Egyptians had ever seen Israel as anything other than an enemy on battlefields. Begin, Rabin, Meir and Dayan belonged to a puppet show of the imagination, not to the real world.

The strange atmosphere of that day was heightened by the music played by the Arabic service of Israel Radio in the hours before Sadat's arrival. As if welcoming the man who had been their most dangerous enemy like a returning lover, Israeli broadcasters played romantic Arab songs, including one whose opening lines ran:

O my love, so long have I awaited thee;
O my love, come see what has become of me;
O my love, open-armed I await thee.

Many Egyptians wept in anguish as Sadat's plane flew over the second disengagement frontier in the Sinai desert, crossing a line in the mind as much as in the sand. The sacred trust between Arabs, already eroded to the core, had finally parted. Never again would Egypt stand shoulder to shoulder with other Arabs against the invader. The aircraft was picked up by four Phantoms as it entered Israeli-controlled airspace, and was escorted to Lod airport near Tel Aviv. For the first time in his life Sadat put on a bulletproof vest, and went to the door of the aircraft. As television cameras followed him down the steps the guilt felt by millions of Egyptians was replaced by a sense of participation. Right or wrong, Sadat's political and physical courage was beyond dispute. His arrival on forbidden territory enthralled many Egyptians and appalled the rest of the Arab world.

The various members of the Egyptian delegation were paired off with Israeli counterparts for the thirty-five-minute journey from Lod airport to Jerusalem. The strained atmosphere showed as they struggled to find words to say to each other. Boutros Ghali, travelling with Dayan, began to talk about the conflict in general terms, and was surprised by Dayan's reaction.

'Mr Minister, you are a professor and academic, I am only a simple farmer. I have tried to educate myself, but please remember the difference between our levels when you speak to me.' Boutros Ghali was lost for words: how to respond to such self-abasement by a man of arrogance?

When the two sides reassembled in Jerusalem they discovered that the whole visit was built on misunderstanding. Sadat began saying that Egypt had received a message (through Tuhami) that Israel was ready to withdraw, and Begin instantly interrupted: 'Mr President, we did not say that.' Dayan recounted his meeting with Tuhami, pointing out that he had explained that his only role was to report back to Begin, not to negotiate. 'But Tuhami said you were ready to withdraw,' Sadat objected. 'Mr President, I did not say that,' Dayan insisted. Begin reminded Sadat that he had publicly announced Israel's conditions for the visit: no Israeli withdrawal to the 1967 lines, no dealings with the PLO, and no acceptance of a Palestinian state. It then became clear that Sadat had disregarded Begin's conditions because of Tuhami's report.

Sadat felt that Dayan had deceived Tuhami, and avoided talking to the Israeli foreign minister for the rest of the visit. When the teams held a second round of talks Dayan remarked: 'If Tuhami said we were prepared to withdraw, he is a liar.'

If the misunderstanding had become public knowledge while Sadat was in Jerusalem, the Egyptian government would have lost all credibility. Fortunately for Sadat, most Egyptians were captivated more by the spectacle than the politics of the visit. During the forty-eight hours Sadat spent in Jerusalem, ghosts of the Egyptian subconscious made a passage to the conscious mind. The wizened old woman and the one-eyed man (Meir and Dayan) who had seemed the embodiment of evil in 1973 began to look like a doughty Jewish grandmother and an injured war veteran. Yitzhak Rabin and Shimon Peres were seen talking with members of the Egyptian delegation. Sadat made a point of asking after Ezer Weizman, the Israeli defence minister, who had been injured in a car accident.* Weizman was touched by Sadat's concern, and hobbled on crutches to see the Egyptian president. Each encounter with flesh-and-blood reality cancelled a corresponding image stored in the Arab mind, affecting the way Egyptians looked at their dispute with Israel. If there was a peacemaker in Jerusalem, it was the medium of instant communications.

The political highlight of the visit was to be an address by Sadat before the Knesset and a reply by the Israeli prime minister. Before the speeches Dayan pressed Boutros Ghali to allow the Israeli government advance sight of Sadat's text, so that Begin could adjust his own remarks accordingly. When Sadat refused, Dayan urged Boutros Ghali to persuade Sadat not to mention the PLO.

'We fully realize that the president will talk about withdrawal,' Dayan said. 'Maybe we will understand if he talks about Palestinian rights. But if he mentions the PLO, that will have the effect of a mine exploding.'

Sadat's speech was crafted to give as much legitimacy as possible to his decision to visit Jerusalem, reiterating standard Arab positions

* Weizman was a nephew of Chaim Weizmann, the first president of Israel.

in terms familiar to the watching millions. He called for 'an overall peace based on justice', and said that this would involve full Israeli withdrawal to the 1967 borders and a just solution of the Palestinian problem. It was incumbent, he said, on 'those known for their wisdom and clarity of vision' to find a way forward. Begin's reply was notable for its harshness and lack of generosity, and contained nothing to encourage optimism.

Crown Prince Fahd of Saudi Arabia went to see King Khalid the same day and expressed approval. 'Maybe it was wrong to go to Jerusalem, but what Sadat said was right,' Fahd observed.

Despite his public remarks, Sadat took a step towards a separate Egyptian–Israeli agreement by accepting three principles for a future accord. He and Begin agreed that there should be no further wars between the two countries, that talks should aim for the restoration of Egyptian sovereignty over the part of Sinai which was still in Israeli hands, and that an agreement between the two countries should include demilitarization of Sinai, with only minimal Egyptian forces stationed near the canal and the Mitla and Giddi passes.

As the Egyptian delegation flew home, the world's media tried to make sense of the visit. Sadat had taken a step towards Begin, but Israel had made no corresponding move in Egypt's direction. Some of the Egyptian delegation felt that the misunderstanding over Tuhami's meeting with Dayan had been a catastrophe, but Sadat remained sanguine, arguing that the trip had been intended only as a first step.

The Egyptian leader summoned prominent media editors for an off-the-record briefing, and surprised them with his opening remarks. 'I pity you men of the press,' he said. 'All these years you have been writing about the Arab–Israeli dispute, and now you are going to have to find another issue.' One of the editors asked: 'You mean they are going to agree to . . .'

'Everything,' Sadat interrupted. 'They are going to agree to everything.'

'Even Jerusalem?'

'I said everything,' Sadat replied.

Some editors were astonished, but they had no option but to believe the president. Sadat did not disclose the three-point agreement because that would have shown that he was edging towards a separate peace with Israel. The implication that he had an understanding on Jerusalem and the west bank which would be acceptable to Arabs was entirely false. Begin was prepared to discuss these issues, but had given no hint of accepting Arab demands. Other members of the Egyptian delegation were worried when they heard of Sadat's comments, but all remained silent.

After the visit a Scandinavian ambassador was reported to have asked Dayan: 'I hope you are going to compensate Sadat for the political risks he took?' Dayan replied: 'I don't see why we should pay a political price for every event. The guests invited themselves to a party on our territory, and we welcomed them. They brought their own food and drink and music. They should be the ones who thank us because we opened our home for their party.'

Begin ordered an evaluation of Sadat's motive for the visit and intentions for the future. He must have been sceptical about the explanation that there had been a misunderstanding, because the investigation was extraordinarily thorough. Even staff at the King David Hotel, where the Egyptian delegation stayed, and chauffeurs who took them to appointments, were questioned for snippets of conversation they might have overheard. Nothing useful was learnt, because the Egyptians had assumed that all rooms and cars would be bugged, and had been careful not to discuss sensitive matters.

In late November Sadat requested a further secret meeting in Morocco between Dayan and Tuhami to clear up the previous misunderstanding, under the auspices of King Hassan and with his participation. The need for secrecy was difficult for the Israelis to comprehend, but Sadat remained vulnerable to Arab suspicions. Describing this second meeting, held at Marakesh on 2–3 December, in his memoirs, Dayan says that concern about Arab suspicions that Egypt was preparing to make a separate deal with Israel was the principal worry expressed by Tuhami. The Egyptian envoy begged Dayan not to inform Washington about the secret talks until all differences had been settled. Sadat felt that it would only be possible to move ahead in bilateral talks if Israel held similar discussions with the other Arab countries.

Tuhami read from a handwritten document in Arabic setting out a four-point message from Sadat. The main demand was that an Israeli–Egyptian agreement should include a section dealing, in general terms, with the main points which worried other Arab states. Israel should guarantee to return the occupied territories and to provide an independent status for Palestinians. The other three points dealt with detailed Egyptian–Israeli issues.

In his memoirs Tuhami writes of the second meeting with Dayan in a similar vein to his description of the first, dwelling on what he supposedly said to the Israeli foreign minister. 'Liar, I will drag you to the ground and force you to confess your guilt. You will go to your knees before the whole world and confess your foul deeds,' Tuhami quotes himself as saying. Such remarks, whether fantasy or fact, raise questions about their author's mentality.

Describing his own reactions, Dayan wrote: 'I . . . had an unhappy feeling about Sadat . . . I did not think he would retreat from the course of peace on which he had embarked, but I suspected that he did not quite know how to advance.' The observation was accurate. Sadat was in a quandary, his chosen path blocked by the political and psychological difficulty of making a final break with other Arabs.

At the same time (about two weeks after the Jerusalem visit) Washington began to understand what Sadat was trying to achieve. Carter had previously assumed that Egypt would never make a separate peace with Israel, but now realized that Sadat was offering Israel and the United States a political gift of great value. Much of the US president's time during the next ten months would be devoted to persuading Israel to accept.

15

Camp David

In the weeks after the Jerusalem visit many world leaders urged Menachem Begin to pick up Sadat's roses, and none more insistently than the matchmaker in the White House. Carter feared the opportunity for peace would be lost unless Sadat's overture received a positive response before disillusionment took hold of Egyptian public opinion. Cyrus Vance set off for the Middle East in mid-December 1977 to find out what Washington could do to help, while at the same time the Jewish lobby in the United States provided unexpected political support.

Edgar Bronfman, leader of the World Zionist Congress, was among those who pressed Israel to respond to Sadat. American Jewry found itself in the unusual position of seeming pro-Egyptian, and of lacking the usual intimate bonds with the Israeli government. After thirty years of links with Israeli socialist governments time would be needed to build a close rapport with Likud.

At the same time Helmut Schmidt, the West German chancellor, Bruno Kreisky, the Austrian chancellor, and other Socialist International leaders were doing all they could to boost the Egyptian president's prestige.

Begin did not take kindly to being hustled towards a quick engagement, nor to the international flattery Sadat was enjoying. Addressing cabinet colleagues he said: 'Carter thinks he opened the door [to peace] . . . It was our pressure on Egypt that opened the door . . . so we should not be rushed into anything.'

Hopes began to focus on a return visit which Begin was due to pay to Sadat on 25 December at Ismailia, one of the canal-side towns which had been destroyed and rebuilt. The Israeli leader prepared a plan and flew to Washington in mid-December to seek American backing before presenting his proposals to Egypt. Some members of the US administration realized, but failed to say, that Begin's scheme consisted of several steps forwards and a bigger pace backwards. Positive elements included acceptance of eventual Palestinian self-administration in Gaza and on the west bank (referred to in the plan as 'Judea and Samaria'), and an offer to delay Israel's claim to sovereignty over these areas for five years. The pace backwards was a proposal that self-administration should be a permanent arrangement, not a transitional stage towards independence. This could only mean that Israel had no intention of letting go of the occupied territories, whatever the talk of putting off the sovereignty question for five years.

Begin also wanted to exclude Israeli settlements in Sinai, near the town of El-Arish, and the strategic area of Sharm El-Sheikh from territory to be returned to Egypt under the treaty. President Carter understood how these ideas would be seen in Egypt but did not express himself clearly, which enabled Begin to give the impression in a public statement that the plan had US support.

Before the 25 December meeting Sadat decided to appoint a replacement for Ismail Fahmy, who had resigned as foreign minister. Boutros Ghali would have been well qualified, but was not chosen because he was a Coptic Christian married to a Jewess, and because he was from a family known for collaboration with the British during the colonial era. Many considered that Ghali had been unjustly passed over.

The president's choice was Mohamed Ibrahim Kamel, who had shared a prison cell with Sadat in pre-revolutionary times. As Kamel came from a wealthy family he had been able to have food sent into the jail, and he gave some of it to Sadat. Kamel became a diplomat and was serving as ambassador to Bonn when his appointment was announced on radio shortly before the second Sadat–Begin meeting. He was taken by helicopter to Ismailia and arrived at Sadat's rest house just before Begin arrived. He was dreading the prospect of meeting the Israeli prime minister on his first day as foreign minister.

Mamdouh Salem, the Egyptian prime minister, had already gone to the airport to await Begin, but for protocol reasons Sadat stayed behind.* The Egyptian leader realized that the Israeli prime minister

* When Sadat visited Jerusalem in November 1977, Begin was among the reception party at the airport. Egyptian protocol officials argued that Sadat could not return this gesture when Begin visited Egypt, because Sadat was a head of state and Begin a head of government.

might be upset by the protocol, and wanted to show that no offence was intended. Meaning to accord Begin an unusual honour, Sadat arranged for him to be present when Kamel took the oath of office as foreign minister. Kamel was horrified by this plan and begged Sadat to relent. 'Why?' Sadat asked.

'Because I would be branded as a traitor by everyone I know, even my own children,' Kamel replied.

Sadat compromised to the extent of holding the ceremony in one corner of a large room with Begin sitting in the opposite corner. The first person to congratulate the embarrassed foreign minister afterwards was the Israeli prime minister.

Sadat and Begin held a preliminary talk before the negotiations and agreed that two committees should be formed. A political committee was to be headed by the two foreign ministers, Moshe Dayan and Mohamed Ibrahim Kamel, and a defence committee by Weizman and Gamassi. Other members of the Egyptian delegation were upset by Sadat's move in settling this privately with Begin, as it would have been logical for the matter to be decided by the full delegations.

The mood of the Egyptian delegation became tense as Begin outlined his proposals on the Palestinians and on permanent Israeli areas in Sinai. Realizing the sense of shock Begin's scheme would cause if it were published, the Egyptian team tried to limit what was said at a press conference afterwards, but to their embarrassment nothing was held back. Until then many in Egypt had assumed that Sadat must have some secret understanding with Begin, but when the plan appeared in the newspapers Sadat was left politically naked. The disillusionment Carter had feared was beginning to take hold.

Seeking a way out of his dilemma, Sadat asked Ezer Weizman, the Israeli defence minister, to meet him. Following their encounter during Sadat's visit to Jerusalem, Sadat felt that Weizman might be more reasonably-minded than Begin. This impression was strengthened when Sadat and Weizman held discussions on 11 January 1978, and a close understanding began to develop.

Sadat valued his relationship with Weizman highly, because the defence minister had been the mastermind of Begin's election victory, giving him a special standing with the prime minister. By the early spring of 1978 Weizman was acting as the primary high-level link between the two governments. As Sadat came to know Weizman better he realized that the defence minister's reputation as a military hawk was based on out-of-date information. A major change of outlook had occurred as a result of a family tragedy a few years earlier, when Weizman's son was hit by a bullet during the war of attrition, leaving him permanently handicapped. The sorrow of this event seemed to have converted Weizman into an ardent advocate of peace.

Weizman was to prove a stabilizing influence during the roller-coaster ride which relations between the two countries followed during the next nine months.

The first meeting of the political committee was held in Jerusalem on 17 January 1978, and resulted in another setback. The working relationship between the two foreign ministers was not bad, and progress was made on a set of principles for an agreement, but a speech by Begin at a dinner in Kamel's honour wrecked the atmosphere. Begin began reasonably enough by saying: 'The foreign minister of Egypt was still very young when the Holocaust was inflicted on the Jews by the Nazis, so he does not realize how badly they needed the return to the safety of their historical home.' His tone then changed: 'The Arabs have enjoyed self-determination in twenty-one Arab countries for a very long time. Is it too much for Israel to have one country among twenty-one? NO, I declare in my loudest voice, NO to withdrawal to the 1967 lines, NO to self-determination for the terrorists.'

This declaration embarrassed both the Egyptian foreign minister and Cyrus Vance, who was present. Begin's words were broadcast by the Israeli media, putting Sadat in a still more difficult position. The Egyptian president phoned Kamel and summoned him home with his delegation. Further committee meetings were suspended, and deadlock seemed imminent.

In the first week of February 1978 Sadat and Carter spent a weekend together at Camp David, the presidential retreat in Maryland, considering what to do next. Carter's attitude was that Sadat had been bold and courageous, but the decision to venture everything on a political gamble had been made alone, without consulting Washington. This was depressing for Sadat, who knew that the Egyptian public had not forgotten his promise to resign if the negotiations produced no results. Nothing had yet been achieved: if Carter could not help, Sadat's position would be impossible.

The American president did not disappoint his guest. The two men agreed that Sadat should resume the Egyptian–Israeli committee meetings, adopting a firmer tone on Resolution 242, Palestinian self-determination and Israeli settlements. The assumption was that the talks would come to a crisis, giving the US administration an opportunity to step in as a mediator with an American compromise proposal.

Although elated by Carter's interest, Sadat felt as he returned home that the American plan would take too long to reduce the political pressure he was feeling in Cairo. Instead of following the agreed strategy of firmness on essential issues, he adopted different postures at different times, alternating tough political statements with visionary ideas for the future. In his visionary mode, Sadat proposed building a complex dedicated to the unity of the sons of Ibrahim/Abraham, incorporating a mosque, a synagogue and a church. The complex was to be constructed on Mount Sinai where Moses was said to have received the ten commandments. Most Egyptians felt that Sadat was jumping ahead too quickly.

Months passed and many meetings were held, but no way of overcoming the deadlock emerged. Begin's three refusals (no return to the 1967 borders, no dealings with the PLO, and no acceptance of a Palestinian state) left little room for negotiation on major issues.

Sadat poured out his frustration at a meeting in Austria in mid-July 1978 with leaders of other socialist parties, at which Shimon Peres was present in his capacity as chairman of the Labour Party.* The two men got on well, and Sadat told Kamel that Peres made a refreshing change after the closed-mindedness of Begin.† If Peres were prime minister of Israel it would be easy to reach an agreement which met the needs of both countries. Willy Brandt, chairman of the West German Social Democrats, and Chancellor Kreisky of Austria also took part in the discussion.

At a dinner party later Kreisky said that it was time for King Hussein to join the negotiations, so that an overall settlement could be achieved. Sadat objected that Hussein was an opportunist who did not want to take risks. 'He wants to sit in his palace and let others bring him the west bank as a gift,' Sadat claimed, recalling that Hussein's father had

* Peres held the party chairmanship from April 1977 until February 1992, when he was defeated by Yitzhak Rabin.

† See *The Camp David Accords: A Testimony*, by Mohamed Ibrahim Kamel, KPI, London, 1986.

been a schizophrenic. Kreisky and Brandt defended Hussein, expressing admiration of his courage and intelligence.

While in Austria Sadat hit upon an extraordinary scheme to turn public opinion in Israel against Begin by showing that the prime minister was being unreasonable. The plan was prompted by Sadat's meeting with Peres, which had received some publicity; if another encounter between Sadat and Weizman could be arranged quickly, media interest was sure to quicken. Sadat imagined that by forming relationships with Begin's chief opponent and closest aide, he could begin a political encirclement of the Israeli prime minister. Kamel objected that while Weizman might seem more moderate than Begin, he was nevertheless a senior minister and could not be expected to take sides against Begin. Hassan Tuhami, on the other hand, supported Sadat's scheme, and Weizman was invited to Austria.

On 13 July 1978 Sadat and Weizman spent three hours together in an Austrian castle discussing all aspects of the problem. The talks went well, but the supposed effects on Israeli public opinion remained a figment of Sadat's fantasy. He later recounted the conversation to Kamel: 'I told Weizman that Begin was wasting the opportunity for peace . . . he [Begin] does not understand anything about politics. Had he been a real politician he would have responded to my initiative. But he is a small man.' Six days later Kamel held talks with Dayan at Leeds Castle in England, but nothing emerged to break the deadlock.

Meanwhile the Carter administration was anxiously watching the situation in Iran, where mass discontent with the Shah's rule was developing into demonstrations, strikes and riots. The roots of the malaise lay partly in the Shah's authoritarian style of government and partly in rapid changes of economic policy. The vast rise in oil revenues of 1973–74 had been used to finance an even bigger increase in government spending, with the impossibly ambitious target of making Iran one of the world's six leading industrial nations by the end of the century. The result was rapid inflation, and when oil prices began to slacken the government was obliged to apply economic brakes, causing a switch from boom to recession. A strange coalition of left-wing elements and Islamic mullahs gave powerful expression to the people's anger. Ayatollah Khomeini, who was living in exile in Paris, began to issue statements calling on the Shah to abdicate. The Shah tried to shore up his crumbling authority with a combination of police repression against the left and economic concessions, but was reluctant to use the army against the people. This approach alarmed Washington, which had expected the Shah to exercise his military power to restore order. Since the 1950s, when the United States assembled a ring of alliances around the Soviet Union, Washington had felt that it was vital to have a strong pro-Western leader in Iran. Stunned by his unpopularity and weakened by cancer, the Shah could no longer be relied upon to act as regional policeman in the event of some emergency. Casting about for alternative security arrangements, the Carter administration felt that Israel and Egypt could act as the anchors of Middle East stability. That, however, depended on bringing the two countries to peace.

Carter asked Cyrus Vance to go to the Middle East and invite Begin and Sadat to a summit at Camp David under US auspices. The US president's hope was that once the two leaders came together neither would be able to walk out without losing political face. The summit would begin on 5 September and continue for as long as necessary. Both leaders accepted immediately.

Before setting off for America Sadat was in a dramatic mood, insisting that he was going to take a tough line with Begin. In a meeting of the Egyptian National Security Council he said that if the summit failed he would address the US Congress and put all the blame on the Israeli prime minister. If Congress and Carter were still unable to help after that, Sadat would resign. By now the whole Egyptian government was accustomed to such remarks.

Another of Sadat's strange ideas involved sending two emissaries to Paris and London with sealed envelopes. If the summit failed the envoys would open the envelopes, containing instructions to deliver protests to French and British leaders, hold press conferences and arouse as much indignation as possible against Begin. Everyone who knew Sadat understood the emptiness of these dreams, yet the Egyptian leader invariably made a favourable impression on visitors and the media. During the build-up to Camp David Sadat became a media star, gaining more favourable attention than the less attractive Begin.

The three leaders assembled at Camp David on 5 September and were accommodated in cabins named 'Aspen', 'Dogwood' and 'Birch', set less than a hundred yards apart. The Americans tried to promote harmony by asking the Egyptian and Israeli teams to mix at meal times and rest periods. Everyone was expected to dress casually, and the Americans distributed special Camp David windcheaters. Carter was cycling to 'Aspen', the presidential cabin, when he spotted some junior Egyptian typists and dismounted to ask them why they were not wearing the windcheaters. The typists were astounded to be addressed personally by a US president. Some of the American efforts to create a conducive atmosphere were devised by Rosalynn Carter, who was the only first lady present.

Apart from the three leaders, none of the ministers attending the talks was housed in comfort. The Americans were put up in a military barracks, while senior Israeli and Egyptian advisers were crammed two to a room in small cabins. Boutros Ghali, who was prepared to share with anybody except Hassan Tuhami, found himself sleeping next to Mohamed Ibrahim Kamel, the foreign minister. 'We came here in peace. I hope we will still be at peace when we leave,' Kamel remarked.

Before the first joint session Sadat and Carter had a private meeting. Sadat said he had brought two proposals, one of which was relatively tough, the other a compromise which could be used as a fall-back position later in the talks. Carter begged Sadat not to read the first proposal in the meeting with Begin, but Sadat insisted on doing so.

As Carter had feared, Sadat's remarks, which were no more than the standard Arab position, infuriated Begin, who kept interrupting and objecting, and made an equally tough reply. After the first meeting Carter told Sadat: 'My God, you were roaring like a lion.'*

The roars were strictly for Arab public consumption. Carter had hoped to avoid such posturing by secluding the leaders beyond the reach of the media, but he had limited success, as Sadat and Begin had direct-line phone links to their respective countries and could not be prevented from leaking whatever they wished. The US president decided after only two joint sessions (on 6 and 7 September) to suspend direct talks and to adopt a system similar to Ralph Bunche's negotiations of 1949. Carter and Vance shuttled continuously between the Egyptian and Israeli delegations carrying American proposals which were constantly revised.

Most members of the US delegation thought that the gap between the Israeli and Egyptian positions was too great to be bridged, and

* This was Sadat's version of what Carter said, as recounted by him to Kamel.

that Camp David should be seen as part of a process rather than as an opportunity for a solution. This idea was resisted by Carter, who was more optimistic, and by presidential image-makers, who felt it was vital to score an American foreign policy success, to help the president's domestic position.

The differences had changed little since Sadat's trip to Jerusalem, but Begin seemed more intransigent than ever. He was almost abusive in his insistence on keeping parts of Egyptian territory, including settlements in Sinai and the strategic point of Sharm El-Sheikh. Dayan had once said: 'If I have to choose between peace without Sharm El-Sheikh, and Sharm El-Sheikh without peace, then I prefer the latter,' and this now became Begin's theme.

Had the argument been solely about the future of the west bank and Gaza, Sadat would have felt less under pressure. Carter sided with Sadat on this matter and put strong pressure on the Israelis to accept full withdrawal from Egyptian territory.

An effort to improve the atmosphere was made by Weizman, who felt that the origin of the bitterness was the misunderstanding over Tuhami's first meeting with Dayan. The Israeli foreign minister had been telling anyone who would listen that Tuhami was a liar, and Tuhami was no less angry with Dayan. Sadat continued to feel that Dayan had tricked his emissary into believing that Israel was prepared to make a full withdrawal from Egyptian territory. Weizman persuaded Sadat to invite Dayan to tea at 'Dogwood', the Egyptian president's cabin, as a gesture of reconciliation. The two men spent an hour and a half together and patched up their quarrel, though the ill-feeling between Dayan and Tuhami continued.

As the summit progressed it became clear that Carter felt comfortable in Sadat's company, but found Begin touchy and unreasonable. One of the most sensitive issues was Begin's refusal to accept that UN Resolution 242 applied to the west bank and Gaza, a matter of crucial importance to the Palestinians. Carter reached the point of near despair on the night of 11 September after Begin had refused to agree to phrases from Resolution 242 being included in a draft agreement, even though Israel publicly supported the resolution. Rosalynn Carter records in her memoirs that her husband was furious.* 'If you won't

* *First Lady from Plains* by Rosalynn Carter, Ballantine Books, New York, 1984.

accept past agreements then we are wasting our time here,' Carter told Begin. He told his wife that the Israeli prime minister was 'completely unreasonable', and that it would be a miracle if the summit accomplished anything.

Sadat became so exasperated with Begin that he ordered the Egyptian delegation to prepare for departure. As they were packing Cyrus Vance dropped in to see Sadat and realized what was happening. He called Carter, who rushed over to 'Dogwood'. 'I am leaving and I am going to Washington to address Congress,' Sadat said. Carter spent fifty minutes persuading Sadat not to abandon a summit in which so much hope had been invested.

The Egyptian president's version of the meeting, recounted to his aides later, was that Carter thought his prospects of winning the 1980 presidential election could be affected by the outcome. 'Help me win the election and I promise that in my second term I will really try to help,' Sadat quoted Carter as saying. In the meantime Carter promised to exercise the maximum pressure on Begin to come to an agreement at Camp David.

Carter's own version was different. He said that if Sadat wanted to leave in a huff, that was his right, but he would lose his case in the eyes of American public opinion. The idea of complaining to the US Congress was unrealistic, because Congress could do nothing to help. If Sadat stayed and showed patience, an agreement might yet be achieved, allowing him to return to Egypt with a success. Carter also pointed out that Sadat's departure would cause considerable embarrassment after the US president had abandoned all other world and domestic problems for ten days to bring Egypt and Israel together.

Sadat agreed to stay, and efforts continued to draft a statement of principles which both sides could accept. Dr Ossama El-Baz, an under-secretary at the Egyptian foreign ministry, was invited by Carter to work with Aharon Barak, the Israeli attorney general, on an outline agreement. The Americans correctly believed that Begin would eventually give way on complete withdrawal from Egyptian territory, but not on the west bank.

It was agreed that Egypt, Israel, Jordan and Palestinian representatives should hold talks on the Palestinian problem, and that negotiations on the west bank and Gaza should proceed in stages. During the first period, lasting not more than five years, the Palestinians would be granted self-government. Once an elected authority had been set up, Israeli armed forces would withdraw from the territories. Talks on the final status of the west bank and Gaza would begin not later than the third year of the five-year transitional period. The aim was to put off the most difficult issue for several years.

Two key sticking points remained: an Egyptian demand that Israel should stop building settlements on the west bank during talks on implementing Palestinian autonomy, and Israel's insistence that the text should be worded in a way which did not prejudice Begin's claim that Resolution 242 did not apply to the west bank and Gaza.

The Americans eventually gave in on the latter point and allowed the US draft to be altered as the Israelis wished. This turning point occurred on the twelfth day, 16 September, when Carter and Sadat seemed to reach exhaustion. A few hours later Carter also agreed that the freeze on settlement construction during the Palestinian autonomy talks would not be part of the text, but would be expressed in a letter from Begin to Carter. Carter informed Sadat, and soon afterwards the Egyptian leader summoned Kamel to his cabin. The foreign minister found Sadat in pyjamas lying on a chaise longue watching television while the delegations began packing up.

Kamel told Sadat: 'I would have agreed with you had you been able to get something concrete.'

Sadat replied: 'I accepted some concessions to help Carter. I will sign anything President Carter puts in front of me before reading it.'

'Why, Mr President? Why should we sign blindly?'

'Mohamed, don't you trust me?'

'I am ready to trust you, but there is nothing in this agreement which we can accept. We are doing this for Carter. To hell with Carter.'

Kamel stormed out, and submitted his resignation the same morning. Sadat responded: 'Do you want me to leave here as a failure? Do you want the Soviet Union to say that I failed? And Gadaffi? And Assad?' The exasperated Egyptian leader asked other members of the delegation what they thought of the agreement. Ossama El-Baz replied: 'One word is missing. Had we included self-determination for the Palestinians, it would have been perfectly all right.'

Sadat answered: 'I suggested that to Carter but he said it would cost him his chair.'

Kamel again exploded with rage. 'Just because he wants to be the president of the United States for eight years instead of four, we sacrifice the whole nation.'

There was silence, and then Sadat said: 'Mohamed, you will never be a politician.'

Kamel: 'If this is politics, I don't want to be a politician.'*

Kamel was left to pack his belongings and make his own way back to Egypt while the rest of the delegation accompanied Sadat to Washington for the signing ceremony.

Meanwhile Begin had written a letter to Carter to be appended to the text, dealing with the freeze on settlements. Carter read it and found that the Israeli prime minister had gone back on his word. Instead of stopping construction for the duration of the autonomy talks, Begin agreed only to a pause for three months. Carter rejected this and asked for a new draft, but allowed the signing ceremony to go ahead in the meantime. Begin then sent Carter a 'revised' letter which left the vital point unchanged. Carter felt deceived, and tried for weeks afterwards to persuade Begin to provide another letter following the original understanding, but he had been outmanoeuvred by a more devious politician.

Another extraordinary aspect of the agreement was that a fundamental disagreement about Jerusalem was papered over by allowing each side to state its position in a letter to Carter. In effect Sadat agreed to disagree on an issue which, from an Arab viewpoint, was not open to compromise. The first two points of Sadat's letter to Carter said: '1) Arab Jerusalem is an integral part of the west bank. Legal and historical Arab rights in the city must be respected and restored. 2) Arab Jerusalem should be under Arab sovereignty.'

Begin's letter to Carter referred to a law passed by the Knesset on 28 June 1967 giving the government power to apply Israeli law, jurisdiction and administration to any part of Eretz Yisrael. The letter continued: 'On the basis of this law, the government of Israel decreed in July 1967 that Jerusalem is one city indivisible, the capital of the state of Israel.'

* See *The Camp David Accords: A Testimony*. Sadat later offered to restore Kamel to his former status as an ambassador, but Kamel refused and instead wrote his memoirs.

The two letters were simply appended to the text without comment, an innovation in diplomacy which allowed the Americans to claim that the summit had been a success. The accords were signed by Sadat and Begin in the East Room of the White House on 17 September, with Carter acting as witness. In an address to a joint session of Congress in the presence of both Sadat and Begin the US president praised 'the two men who have made this impossible dream now become a real possibility'. Carter pointed out that it was the first time an Arab and an Israeli leader had signed a comprehensive framework for peace, but acknowledged that many obstacles remained unresolved.

During their isolation at Camp David the three leaders had had little time to follow the deteriorating situation in Teheran. The Iranian people were now in open revolt against the Shah, with the capital and many other cities in uproar. The army remained loyal to the Peacock Throne, and yet the besieged emperor continued to use only a fraction of the force he could have summoned to put down the uprising. When the fanfare of 18 September was over Begin talked to Carter about the need to boost the Shah's self-confidence, and said that his advice would be to throw the full weight of the Iranian army against the revolution. Carter phoned the Shah in the presence of Begin and Sadat to offer encouragement, but there was little else the US could do.

Meanwhile the Arab world ignited in anger against what it saw as Sadat's betrayal of the Palestinians, with even traditional friends of Washington expressing reservations. Vance made an immediate tour of the Middle East to explain that the accords did not mean abandonment of the Palestinian cause. In a speech to the United Nations at the end of September the secretary of state said: 'No peace agreement will be either just or secure if it does not resolve the problem of the Palestinians in the broadest sense.'

Sadat returned to a subdued welcome in Egypt, where many were shaken by the strength of criticism from other countries. He announced the demobilization of some army units 'because the battle of liberating [occupied] lands is over'. Feeling a need to give the government a fresh look, Sadat dismissed prime minister Mamdouh Salem and his team and initially asked vice president Hosni Mubarak to form a government. Mubarak accepted and began assembling a cabinet, but within twenty-four hours Sadat changed his mind and offered the prime ministership to Mustafa Khalil, deputy chairman of the party.

Khalil was a latecomer to politics, having made a career as a professor of railway engineering. That experience helped in his first government post as transportation minister under Nasser. He had been educated in the US and believed strongly that Egypt's interests lay with the West, making links with Israel necessary. It was for this reason that he volunteered to accompany Sadat on the visit to Jerusalem in 1977, at a time when most colleagues regarded the trip as a risky political adventure.

After taking office as premier, Khalil decided to keep the foreign ministry portfolio in his own hands, on the grounds that solutions to Egypt's problems depended on success in turning the Camp David framework into a peace treaty. The new prime minister also felt that Egypt's negotiating position was in disarray and needed a more orderly approach. In many subsequent negotiations Khalil headed the Egyptian team himself, with help from Boutros Ghali, secretary of state for foreign affairs.

If Camp David had been slow and difficult, the process of converting the framework into a peace was to take much longer. Sadat had spoken confidently of signing a treaty within two months, and Carter was equally anxious for rapid progress, but Begin felt that time was on his side. 'We need some dramatic effort to unblock the talks,' Khalil told Sadat.

'Don't worry, I have got the solution in my pocket,' Sadat replied.

Soon afterwards another futile Egyptian–Israeli meeting was held in Alexandria, and Khalil again pressed Sadat to find some way of breaking the impasse.

'I don't know why you are worrying so much,' Sadat said. 'I told you I had the solution in my pocket.'

'Mr President, if you have something in your pocket, why do you leave us spinning in circles?' Khalil asked.

'Don't push me. The Israelis know what I can offer, and at the right moment I will tell you.'

Soon afterwards Boutros Ghali had a further meeting with Dayan in Israel. On his return Ghali went to see Khalil and recounted something Dayan had told him while they were dining together. The Israeli foreign minister said that Begin had been in a furious mood the previous day, and had shouted that he was not prepared to sell the security of Israel for water. Boutros Ghali asked what this meant, but Dayan knew no more.

Suspecting that Sadat was thinking of exchanging Nile water for political concessions, Khalil went straight to the president, taking Boutros Ghali with him, and asked the secretary of state to repeat his story to Sadat.

Sadat replied: 'Why not? Don't we have Nile water which we discharge into the sea?'

Khalil agreed that Egypt discharged about 800 million cubic metres of Nile water into the sea each year, but reminded the president that this was necessary in order to keep the hydroelectric turbines operating, and to control the river level for navigation.

'Right, we'll give them that water,' Sadat shouted.

Khalil said this was impossible, because the electricity generating system depended on water being discharged through the turbines. Seeing that Sadat was not convinced, Khalil ordered a report from the minister of irrigation and the legal department of the foreign ministry. The report said that Egypt's share of the waters of the Nile was fixed under treaties with other Nile-basin countries negotiated during the British colonial era. If water were diverted to a third party a new legal situation would be created and the treaties would have to be renegotiated. Some of the other countries were already secretly pumping more than their share, and were sure to make steep demands in the event of renegotiation. As Egypt lay at the end of the river basin, and was dependent on rainfall in East African countries to maintain the river level, its negotiating position was not strong. Egypt's share under the treaty was 55 billion cubic metres a year, which was almost exactly what the country needed.

Sadat replied: 'Then let us give the Israelis at least some water. We can say that it is drinking water for Palestinian Arabs.'

Khalil replied: 'Mr President, it is my duty to you and to the country to say no.' He pointed out that Egypt could not afford to make gifts to Israel of a precious resource, and that Egypt currently owed Sudan 14 billion cubic metres of water which had been accepted on a loan basis. Any water given to Israel would increase the difficulty of repaying the Sudanese loan. Existing water supplies were just sufficient in normal years, and a prolonged drought upstream could cause serious difficulties. It was true that Nile water could be used more efficiently, but that would require a huge investment in modern irrigation and treatment systems. Sadat gave the impression of accepting these points, and Khalil thought that he had won the argument.

In the next session of the Israeli–Egyptian political committee, Khalil called for a fresh start. Seeking a more constructive atmosphere, he proposed efforts to build confidence, treating each other not as enemies but partners in search of a solution. The practice of dining separately during committee-meeting breaks should be stopped, with the aim of creating relationships between those involved. Meetings should be conducted in a disciplined, polite manner. Both sides should refrain from oratory and neither should quote from any sacred text. Arguments based on religion and biblical history should have no place at the negotiating table. Finally, Khalil suggested that the two sides should agree on what to say to the press after meetings, and should stop unauthorized leaks.

Talks on implementing the accords began at Blair House in Washington on 12 October 1978, with Cyrus Vance acting as the principal US negotiator. The Egyptian delegation was led by Kamal Hassan Ali, assisted by Boutros Ghali and Ossama El-Baz, while the Israeli team included Dayan, Weizman and Barak. Discussions on an American draft treaty showed several areas of strong disagreement. The Israelis insisted that the treaty should have precedence over any commitments between Egypt and Arab countries, if conflicts between the two sets of obligations should arise. This was unacceptable to Egypt. Another sensitive issue was whether diplomatic relations should be established before Israeli withdrawal from Sinai (as the Israelis wished), or after the Palestinians had elected a self-governing authority (as Egypt demanded). Boutros Ghali was worried that Israel would refuse to carry out its commitments to the Palestinians, implementing only the parts of the treaty that affected Egypt. The Israelis were reluctant to discuss how elections for a Palestinian authority would be held, arguing that detailed matters should be left to Israeli–Palestinian talks. Mutual suspicions fuelled disputes over numerous secondary issues.

In addition to the US-organized negotiating process, the two parties held direct talks at various levels. Weizman advised Sadat and Khalil to give special attention to Dayan, because the foreign minister could influence Begin on security matters. 'What Dayan accepts, Begin will accept,' Weizman said. Begin, however, was edging away from the limited commitments he had made at Camp David, while Sadat remained under strong Arab pressure and criticism. When the Nobel Prize Committee announced on 27 October 1978 that Sadat and Begin were to share the peace prize, many feared the committee might come to regret its decision.

An Arab summit in Baghdad on 5 November passed a resolution criticizing the Camp David accords, and sought by a mixture of threats and incentives to make Sadat change course. The leaders, meeting in Sadat's absence, threatened to move the headquarters of the Arab League from Cairo to Tunis if Egypt made a separate peace treaty with Israel. A delegation of three foreign ministers was sent to offer Egypt $5 billion a year for ten years in return for staying within the Arab fold. Sadat refused even to meet the delegation. He asked Ahmed ben Souda, King Hassan's envoy: 'Who told those mentally retarded idiots that I wished to stay with them?'

Cyrus Vance, who carried out another Middle East tour in mid-December, felt that the main problem was Begin's intransigence. The US secretary of state also held a joint meeting with Khalil and Dayan in late December.

On 16 January 1979 Mohamed Reza Shah Pahlavi left Iran for what was described as a holiday, but was in fact a journey into exile. Harold Brown, the US defense secretary, made a tour of the Middle East to assess how US security policy in the region could be reorganized after the loss of its eastern pillar. His main recommendation when he returned to Washington in February was that Carter should accelerate efforts to conclude an Israeli–Egyptian peace treaty.

At the same time Democratic Party managers were watching the electoral clock. The Camp David accords had been sold to the US public as a success, and it was vital to transform hopes into reality before the election. The treaty needed to be concluded in 1979, because in 1980 the president would be too busy campaigning to conduct Middle East negotiations personally. This combination of pressures, Iran and the electoral cycle, prompted Carter to give the Middle East his almost undivided attention for the next two months.

His first idea was that Vance should hold fresh talks with Khalil and Dayan at Camp David. These discussions, held from 22–25 February 1979, proved fruitless because while Khalil had a full negotiating mandate from Sadat, Dayan was unable to make decisions without referring back to Begin. Washington then asked Begin to join the talks, but received a sharp rebuff. The Israeli cabinet voted by fourteen to two against Begin attending talks with Khalil (the dissenters being Dayan and Weizman). An Israeli cabinet statement claimed that Khalil had presented 'a more extreme position' during the talks with Dayan and Vance at Camp David. Begin told a Zionist meeting that it was beneath his dignity to negotiate with an unelected Egyptian prime minister. Khalil was offended and went to Cyrus Vance to complain that Begin's statement was an interference in Egyptian internal affairs. 'Egypt has a history of 7000 years behind it and it is I who refuse to negotiate with him, and not him with me,' Khalil said.

Begin agreed, however, to go to Washington to see Carter. The US president felt that the outstanding issues were minor points. 'Only very small insignificant things separate [Egypt and Israel] . . . it is just disgusting . . . . to feel that we are that close and can't quite get [an agreement],' he said on 27 February. The following day Begin refuted Carter's analysis, describing the remaining points as 'grave issues'. According to testimony given by Dayan to a Knesset committee on 28 February, the points of deadlock were a demand by Egypt that Palestinian autonomy in Gaza and the west bank should be established within a year of the treaty being signed; the continuing dispute over whether diplomatic links should come before, after or during Israeli withdrawal; the row over Israel's insistence that the proposed treaty should take priority over Egypt's treaties with other countries; and the question of oil supplies to Israel from the Sinai oil fields.

The three days of talks which Carter and Begin held from 2–4 March were exceptionally tense. Begin knew that the Iranian revolution had increased the strategic importance of Israel as a bulwark against Soviet expansion. It was clear that the United States could be made to pay a high price for a peace treaty if Israel played its cards with cunning. Begin's tactic was to argue the minutiae of every issue to the point where the US president became exasperated. Following tactics which might have been taken from a military textbook, he sustained his assault for two days and then made a false retreat, accepting American proposals on certain points of detail. The effect was to lead Carter, who was perpetually over-optimistic, to think that a presidential visit to Egypt and Israel could settle the remaining points.

Less than a week later Carter discovered that his anxiety to clinch a deal had drawn him into a trap. The talks with Sadat in Cairo went well, but when Carter arrived in Israel on 10 March 1979 Begin declared that the treaty negotiations could not be concluded while the US president was in the Middle East. His argument was that the Knesset would need time to debate the proposed treaty. Carter failed to realize that this was psychological warfare. Begin knew that the US president had put his prestige at stake and would look foolish if he returned to Washington with nothing achieved.

The Israeli prime minister then subjected the American delegation to three days of exhausting talks, mainly on legalistic matters of limited importance. The aim was to divert Carter and his aides from the remaining issue of substance: a request by Sadat for Egyptian liaison officers to be stationed in Gaza. The Egyptian president felt that this would help him defend the treaty against Arab critics. Begin was determined that Sadat should have no such figleaf.

The Israelis also wanted changes dealing with the timing of withdrawal from Sinai, and an improved US guarantee of oil supplies for Israel. On the evening of 12 March Begin abruptly declared that the talks were concluded, and Carter despondently prepared to return home.

Later the same night Begin, clearly following a prepared strategy, used his more moderate ministers to suggest to Carter that a deal could still be reached before his departure if the demand for Egyptian liaison officers were dropped. Carter fell for Begin's trick, accepted the suggestion, and the treaty was agreed in a few hours. The US president returned to Cairo the following day, obtained Sadat's acceptance of the revised treaty, and flew back to Washington with an apparent success.

The main elements of the treaty were that Israel would withdraw its forces and settlements from Sinai within three years, UN forces would be deployed in border areas, ambassadors would be exchanged ten months after ratification of the treaty, Israel would have the right to use the Suez Canal, Egypt would end its economic boycott of Israel, and Israel and Egypt would start negotiations on Palestinian self-rule in Gaza and the west bank a month after the exchange of ratification documents. Sadat and Begin also agreed that the Sinai oil fields would be returned to Egypt seven months after ratification of the treaty.

On 26 March 1979 Begin and Sadat signed the treaty in a ceremony attended by 1400 guests on the north lawn of the White House, with Carter acting as the witness. In his speech Carter referred to the treaty as 'a victory, not of a bloody military campaign, but of an inspiring peace campaign', and said that the Israeli and Egyptian leaders had 'conducted this campaign with all the courage, tenacity, brilliance and inspiration of any generals leading men into combat'.

Sadat, in his reply, said: 'Let there be no more war or bloodshed between Arabs and Israelis. Let there be no more suffering or denial of rights. Let there be no more despair or loss of faith.'

Begin described the occasion as 'a great day in the annals of two ancient nations . . . whose sons met in battle five times . . . It is thanks to our fallen heroes that we could have reached this day.' The signing ceremony was, he said, the third greatest day in his life, the other two being the declaration of Israel's independence in May 1948 and the day when Jerusalem 'became one city' under Israeli rule in 1967. This last comment showed the gulf between rhetoric and reality. The status of Jerusalem remained a bone of contention in 1994, fifteen years after the three men made their comments.

President Carter's moment of triumph was purchased at a price of $3 billion of US aid for the construction of Israeli airfields in the Negev desert to replace the ones given up in Sinai, and $1.5 billion in military aid to Egypt. Washington also increased its political commitments to Israel. In a memorandum of understanding on 26 March, the US pledged that in the event of Egyptian violation of the treaty the US would 'take such remedial measures as it deemed appropriate, which may include diplomatic, economic and military measures'. In a letter of protest to Vance, Khalil said that the memorandum was 'contrary to the spirit' of US–Egyptian relations.

The ceremony at the White House was the logical destination of a journey Sadat had begun on 7 October 1973 with the telegram to Kissinger which disclosed his intentions for the conduct of the Yom Kippur War. In the six years between those two events Sadat's actions had shattered the taboo in the Egyptian mind, but not that of other Arabs.

The treaty cost Egypt the last shred of its standing in the Arab world. At a meeting in Baghdad, eighteen Arab League countries and the PLO announced that diplomatic relations with Cairo would be cut and an economic boycott imposed. The PLO had also demanded an economic boycott and oil embargo against the United States. Two Arab League countries, Oman and Sudan, supported Sadat's decision to make peace but stayed away from the Baghdad meeting. Cairo responded by 'freezing' its relations with the Arab League.

After the Washington ceremony many points remained to be settled between Israel and Egypt on implementation of the treaty. It was agreed that Weizman would visit Egypt for preparatory discussions, leading to a Begin–Sadat summit to be held in Cairo in April. In the meantime Sadat had gone to his rest house in Aswan, while Khalil remained in the capital. The Egyptian prime minister naturally assumed that Weizman would hold two sets of discussions, one with himself in Cairo and the other with Sadat in Aswan. Instead the Israeli defence minister went straight to Aswan, saw Sadat, and returned home without phoning Khalil. The prime minister realized that Weizman was avoiding him, and discovered why soon afterwards, when Sadat called a meeting of the National Security Council. On arrival in Aswan Khalil was astonished to find that the agenda consisted of three highly controversial items: Nile water, sharing the oil resources of the Sinai desert, and abolition of the Arab League.

Sadat opened the meeting by saying: 'Weizman brought me a wonderful message when I saw him. He told me that we would find Begin a completely different person at the next meeting.'

'Different in what way?' Khalil asked.

'He said we would find Begin ready to reach solutions on all the remaining problems.'

Dealing with the agenda items, Sadat argued that the Arab League had proved useless, and proposed either straight abolition or a radical change, opening the organization to the Arab masses and eliminating the involvement of governments. He then talked briefly about oil and water, proposing the sharing of both resources with Israel. When he stopped speaking there was a stunned silence among the sixteen National Security Council members, until Khalil raised his hand.

'You are the president and the decision is yours, but this is a matter of conscience. I want to defend your position and your image in the country, and it is our duty now to tell you what we think.' Khalil reminded Sadat of their previous discussion on sharing Nile water, insisting on the legal and technical problems. Many present must also have realized that any sapping of the Nile's strength for such a project would have deep psychological implications. For thousands of years the changing states of the Nile had regulated the lives of all who lived on its banks, from the beginning of recorded history until the construction of the high dam. The special problems and advantages of proximity to the river had made a strong central authority necessary, a fact accepted by Egyptians since the late pre-dynastic period (about 3100 B.C.) and still reflected to this day in the Egyptian style of government. Links between rulers and the ruled depended on the river as a means of communication until the invention of railways. The river was a longitude of psychological reference for every Egyptian, defining his physical and social location, and the continuous thread between the present world and the afterlife. When the Nile ran strong, the country prospered, while low Niles coincided with civil wars, economic misery and foreign aggression. These ancient associations remain latent in the Egyptian mind even in the twentieth century; any tampering with the fount of Egyptian culture risked slackening the fabric of Egyptian society.

Turning to the Arab League, Khalil said that Egypt could withdraw if it did not like the organization. There was no reason to abolish a body which represented hope for millions of Arabs, and in any case Egypt could not take such a step without support from other countries.

The oil issue was just as controversial. Israel had insisted at the time of the second disengagement agreement that Egypt should provide a regular supply of 2 million tons of oil a year (about 14 million barrels), at a special price. Khalil did not argue against Israel's priority of supplies, but said that the price should be the market rate, established by open bidding.*

Sadat listened in silence to Khalil's objections, which were supported by others present. No deal on Nile water was made at the time, although the Israelis continued to press the issue and schemes were drawn up for a 'Peace Canal' linking the Nile to the Negev desert.† The project was still being debated as recently as 1994. On the oil question, four companies were formed to specialize in purchasing supplies, and these firms were given preferential treatment when they

* Egypt is not a member of OPEC, and sells its oil on an auction basis.

† The intention was that the 'Peace Canal' should be partly covered, and that pipes should carry it under the Suez Canal.

submitted bids for oil produced in the Sinai. Sadat abandoned the idea of abolishing the Arab League but later in the year Cairo withdrew from the organization and at the same time the other members announced Egypt's expulsion. The headquarters was transferred from Cairo to Tunis.

Sadat was thus unable to make the grand gestures he had planned at his summit with Begin on 2–3 April. The two men nevertheless announced accords on several other points, including an acceleration of the timetable for El-Arish to be returned to Egypt, the opening of the border between the two countries, the establishment of air links, a hot-line connection between the two leaders, and practical arrangements for the talks on Palestinian autonomy.

Carter's hope that bringing Israel to peace with Egypt would help him in the 1980 presidential election was overtaken by events. From November 1979 onwards the only test of his skill in foreign affairs which mattered to US voters was progress in securing the freedom of fifty-four American hostages who had been seized when the US Embassy in Teheran was occupied by Iran's Revolutionary Guards. Carter failed that test and lost the election. Iran did not set the hostages free until Ronald Reagan came to office in January 1981.

PART II

Truth has Two Faces, and the Snow is Black

Truth has two faces, and the snow is black over our city.
Our cup of despair flows over as the End approaches our walls
with a sure-footed tread,
Along stones slippery with tears, sure-footed.
Who will lower our flags: Us or them? And who
will intone the 'Peace Treaty' to us, o harbinger of death?
Our fate is sealed in advance: Who will wrest our names
from our identity: You or they? And who will implant in us
The discourse of our dispersal: 'We could not lift the siege
So let us deliver the keys of our haven to the Vizier of Peace,
And save ourselves . . .'
Truth has two faces . . . the sacred cause was a two-edged sword,
so what have you done with what was our citadel before this day?
You did not fight for fear of martyrdom, but your throne is your
coffin.
So carry the coffin to save the throne, o master of procrastination.
This peace will render us but a speck of dust . . .
Who will bury our days after we are gone: You . . . or they?
And who will raise their flags over our wall:
You . . . or a knight bereft of hope?
Who will hang bells to mark our journey . . .
You . . . or a wretched sentry? Our fate is sealed in advance –
So why do the negotiations drag on, o harbinger of death?

MAHMOUD DARWISH

1

The Emergence of the PLO

It is a paradox of the Arab–Israel conflict that the central issue, the plight of the Palestinians, was long regarded by much of the world as peripheral. That attitude manifested itself as soon as the Arabs had been defeated by Israel in 1948. The United Nations considered the outcome irreversible and made no attempt to enforce the creation of a separate Palestinian state. The General Assembly resolution of 29 November 1947, calling for the partition of Palestine into Arab and Jewish states, with Jerusalem to be part of an international enclave, was treated as a dead letter. From then on the UN showed concern for the suffering of the Palestinians, but not for their sovereignty. A General Assembly resolution stating that the displaced population should be given a choice between repatriation and compensation was passed on 11 December 1948 and repeated on an annual basis afterwards. The most important UN Security Council pronouncement on the conflict, Resolution 242 of 22 November 1967, referred only to 'a just settlement of the refugee problem', without even mentioning the Palestinians. The second most important UN resolution, number 338 of 22 October 1973, was equally vague.

The failure to insist on Palestinian sovereignty may be ascribed largely, but not entirely, to US domination of the United Nations. Another factor was that many in the West tended to sympathize with the Zionist wish to recreate 'Eretz Yisrael'. A glance at the religious history of Palestine will show, however, that the question 'Who are the rightful inhabitants of Palestine?' cannot be answered by recourse to religion.

Canaan (the ancient name for Palestine) was populated from 3000 B.C. or earlier by a Semitic people who worshipped a pantheon of gods and goddesses, the most important of whom were the gods

El and Baal and the goddesses Asherah, Anat and Astarte. The Canaanites were joined by the Amorites, another Semitic group which had ruled in Babylon in the second millennium B.C. The Canaanites and Amorites together became an important power in the region between 1800 B.C. and 1600 B.C., but were then subdued by the Egyptian eighteenth pharaonic dynasty. Egyptian power introduced the Egyptian religion, with its own system of deities and beliefs, while the Canaanites retained their own faith.

The area which is now Israel, the occupied territories and Lebanon was then the home of numerous tribes and peoples in addition to the Canaanites. Some, like the Philistines, who arrived in the thirteenth century B.C. and lived along the coast between Jaffa and Egypt, adopted parts of the Canaanite religion. The Philistines gave paramount importance to Dagon, the ancient west Semitic fertility god, and worshipped at temples in Gaza and Ashdod. Among other groups were the Hittites, remnants of an ancient empire in Asia Minor which again briefly flourished in the thirteenth century B.C. The Hittites had their own religion, with some 600 gods. The Exodus of the Jews from Egypt is commonly put at around 1200 B.C.

The religious map was thus immensely complicated when Joshua crossed the Jordan and introduced monotheism to Palestine. What the Jews considered the 'promised land' was in fact a country or a group of city-states in which the Canaanite religion had been established for at least 1700 years, and where other religions were competing for attention. No valid claim can be made that Judaism was the 'original' faith of the area now in dispute.

If the claim is based on ancient military conquest, history shows that the Jewish period of dominance was intense but comparatively brief. Like other tribes who emerged from the desert to seize the fertile land of Palestine, the Jews were described by the Canaanites and other indigenous people as '*habiru*' (passers-by). Tablets discovered at Tell El-Amarna in Egypt in 1887 record that the inhabitants of the Sham appealed to the Pharaoh for reinforcements to face invading *habiru*.

The first centuries after Joshua's arrival were marked by constant struggles between Jews, Canaanites and other groups. It was not until the thirty-three-year reign of King David in the eleventh century B.C. that the Jews managed to subdue the indigenous peoples of Palestine. The Jews remained dominant and relatively united throughout the reign of King David's son and successor Solomon (968–928 B.C.), but then split into two kingdoms, Judah and Israel, which were often at war with each other. Israel ceased to exist in 721 B.C. when the Assyrians deported most of the Jewish population, while Judah lost its independence 130 years later, falling under the tutelage of first Assyria, then Egypt, and then Babylonia.

Any Jewish claim based on past domination can thus only refer to a short period – a few centuries at most. The exploits of kings Saul, David and Solomon would have no relevance now but for the fact that the Jewish version of military history was included in the Bible.

After the fall of Israel, the Jewish presence in Palestine was eroded by one wave of conquerors after another. The Babylonians destroyed Jerusalem and carried off the king of Judah and most of his subjects in 586 B.C. The area passed into the hands of Persia and then Greece before returning to the Ptolemies of Egypt in 323 B.C. After alternating periods of Egyptian and Syrian rule, the Maccabean revolt of 167 B.C. marked the start of a century in which the Jews attained first religious and then political independence. This ended in 63 B.C. with the Roman conquest of Syria and Pompey's occupation of Jerusalem. After a Jewish uprising the Romans destroyed Jerusalem in 70 A.D. and Palestine became a Roman province. According to Zionist records some 600,000 Jews were slaughtered in a revolt against the Romans in 135 A.D. Others were sold into slavery, Judea was devastated, and Jews were barred from Jerusalem.

From then on the Jews were a minority in Palestine and were permanently under the rule of others. After the conversion of Emperor Constantine to Christianity in 312 A.D. efforts were made to christianize Palestine, and this resumed in a more energetic way under Byzantine rule in the fifth century. Synagogues were converted into churches and the practice of the Jewish faith was restricted by law.

After the Arab conquest of 640 A.D. much of the non-Jewish population converted to Islam, including some of the Christians. The Jewish minority was permitted to practise Judaism throughout the next 459 years, in which three successive Islamic empires (the Umayyads, the Abbasids and the Fatimids) ruled Palestine. During the Crusades (1099–1291) the Jews fought alongside Arabs in defending cities against Christian invaders. Saladin, the Egyptian Mamluke leader, drove the Crusaders out and permitted Jews to return to Jerusalem. However the city was destroyed during a brief invasion by the Mongols in 1260, and only two Jews were living there in 1267.

During the Mamluke era (1291–1516) and the Ottoman empire (1517–1918) Palestine was continuously under Islamic rule, and Arab Muslims and Christians made up the majority of the population. By the beginning of the 1880s the total Jewish population was not more than 25,000 people concentrated in Jerusalem, Hebron, Safed and Tiberias.

As this brief outline shows, the Zionist attempt to recreate 'Eretz Yisrael' can claim no justification in religious, military, administrative or demographic history. Moreover, if the dispute is regarded as primarily a legal issue, the scales come down clearly on the Palestinian side. The fact that until 1948 the Palestinians (Arab Muslims, Arab Christians and Druze) were a majority of the population and owned more than half the land is beyond question. The Zionist seizure of their homes and lands was against all legal principles.

The Zionist claim that the Palestinians were a non-existent people was and is simply untrue. The Palestinians are the descendants of the Canaanites and many other non-Jewish peoples, as well as more recent Arab immigrants. In a broad sense the population of the disputed area has been mainly Palestinian rather than mainly Jewish for most of the last 5000 years.

The Palestinians have never suggested that they should have sole occupancy rights, to the exclusion of Jews. The PLO's official goal until 1988 was the creation of a secular state in the whole of pre-1948 Palestine, in which people of all faiths would be equal. Since 1988 the PLO has accepted the irreversibility of Israel's existence and has concentrated on seeking a non-sectarian state in Gaza and the west bank.

In view of the long history of links with Egypt, it was natural that Palestinians looked to Cairo for support after the 1948–49 war. The Egyptian revolution of 1952 provided the Palestinian *fedayeen** with an ally, and the importance of that link grew as Nasser ascended the ladder to moral leadership of the Arab world.

In the early 1950s young Palestinians began conducting attacks against Israeli targets, operating from refugee camps in Gaza. The

* *Fedayeen* is an Arabic word meaning guerrilla fighters, or commandos.

Egyptian authorities, who then controlled Gaza, supported the attacks to the extent of providing training and arms. Some of these Palestinians came together and considered calling themselves the 'National Liberation of Palestine'. That name was dropped when they realized that the acronym in Arabic would spell '*hatf*', which means death. Rearranging the same letters they came up with '*fatah*' (conquest, or victory).

Fatah's founders included Yasser Arafat, a successful engineer working on construction projects in Kuwait; Salah Khalaf, a mathematics teacher with the ministry of education in Kuwait; and Khalid El-Hassan, an agent for the Sony company. Arafat, born in 1929, graduated from Cairo University, where he was president of the Palestinian Students' Federation. Khalaf, born in 1933 at Jaffa, also went to Cairo University and acted as Arafat's deputy in the Students' Federation. Khalil El-Wazir, another founder member, was born in Gaza and educated in Damascus.

The founders of Fatah were united in their desire for a more combative approach to the struggle, but otherwise had no common ideology. Three main influences can be detected in the ideas they expressed at the time. One was the Muslim Brotherhood, to which Arafat belonged while studying at Cairo University. When Nasser suppressed the Brotherhood after an assassination attempt during a public meeting in October 1954, Arafat left Egypt, but returned in 1955. The second influence was the Ba'ath (Resurrection) Socialist Party, which had strong followings in Syria and Iraq. Farouk Kaddoumi, who later became the PLO official responsible for foreign affairs, was originally a Ba'ath Party member. The third influence was President Nasser, whom many Palestinians regarded as their leading champion. This perception was not wrong, but other matters were competing for Nasser's attention.

The Lavon affair of 1955, in which two Israeli agents placed bombs in Egyptian cinemas and other public places, prompted Nasser to authorize greater Egyptian aid for Palestinian commandos.* This led to further Palestinian–Israeli fighting, culminating in a massive Israeli raid on the Egyptian headquarters in Gaza, with heavy military and civilian casualties. The raid can be regarded as the start of the cycle of events in 1956 which culminated with the plot by Britain, France and

* See p. 106.

Israel to seize the Suez Canal. The Israeli invasion of Sinai on 29 October 1956, which marked the start of the Suez crisis, was accompanied by simultaneous attacks against Palestinian groups in Gaza. Arafat had by this time joined Arab volunteers attached to the Egyptian National Guard.

The difficulties experienced in recovering Sinai from Israel after the 1956 crisis restrained Egypt's enthusiasm for further Palestinian raids from Gaza into Israel. Nasser's priorities were to strengthen the Egyptian economy and extend social programmes which had begun before the crisis, and he wanted to avoid the diversion of economic resources which continued hostilities would have entailed. This was resented by Fatah and other militant groups, which felt that not only Egypt but every other Arab government was absorbed in domestic problems. None wanted to take risks before being ready for the consequences.

President Nasser was nevertheless the first Arab leader to realize that Hashemite rule on the west bank could not be a permanent solution. By the early 1960s Palestinians on both sides of the river Jordan were beginning to recover psychologically, and were making their discontent felt. A desire to allow Palestinians to express their own identity was high among Nasser's priorities when he called an Arab summit on 13 January 1964. It was at this meeting that the PLO was created.

Gathering in Cairo, Arab leaders chose the PLO's first leader, Ahmed Shukairy, a respected Palestinian lawyer. Shukairy had made a reputation for himself at the UN, serving at times as chief delegate for Saudi Arabia, and at other times in the same capacity for Syria. This made him acceptable to the two poles of Arab leadership, the monarchs and the revolutionaries. Fatah leaders considered Shukairy too conservative and thought the PLO needed a commander rather than a lawyer at the helm.

The PLO leader was given facilities and financial aid to look after Palestinian interests in the Gaza strip, which was still under Egyptian administration, and on the west bank, which had not yet been occupied by Israel. A political and administrative headquarters was set up in east Jerusalem, and the organization began to form military units, which were attached to the regular armies of Egypt, Syria, Jordan and Iraq, with Egypt providing most of the training.

The risk of friction between the new Palestinian entity and the Jordanian government was apparent from the earliest days. When a further Arab summit was held in Alexandria in September 1964, Shukairy made two complaints. The first was that donor countries had not lived up to their promised financial commitments, a problem similar to that faced thirty years later by Yasser Arafat in launching the Gaza–Jericho entity. The second was a lack of cooperation from Amman, which felt threatened by the fact that half the Jordanian population now looked to Shukairy's team for inspiration.

The PLO as originally conceived was not to the liking of all Palestinians. Many, including Fatah, wanted a more independent and militant organization free of the tutelage of powerful Arab neighbours. In 1965 George Habash, a doctor who had studied at the American University of Beirut, sent President Nasser a memo saying that another Palestinian organization was emerging, made up of young men who wanted to carry out *fedayeen* operations against Israel, to keep the Palestinian torch burning. Nasser wrote a handwritten addendum to Habash's message: 'This is not the right time.' He felt that such operations could cause grave complications at a time when a third of the Egyptian army was serving in Yemen. It appears that Nasser's comment was never passed back to Habash. The Egyptian president's point of view was understandable, but others felt that Arab governments were preoccupied with their own concerns, and that armed struggle was the only language Israel would understand.

Fatah carried out its first sabotage attack and issued its first military statement on 1 January 1965. In November 1967 Habash changed his Arab Nationalist Movement into the Popular Front for the Liberation of Palestine, which brought a Marxist-Leninist element to the Palestinian struggle. The two organizations were never close.

All *fedayeen* groups felt that while they could achieve certain operations with limited military resources, Palestine could not be liberated without drawing in Arab armies. This led to the strategy known as 'the battle of *tawreet*', which in this context meant 'dragging them feet first', to involve Arab neighbours in the struggle against their will.* These young men had no idea of the real balance of military power, and gained an unrealistic impression of Arab strength from the proposal made at Arab summits in 1964 and 1965 by General Amin

* See p. 125.

El-Hafiz of Syria for a massive coordinated Arab attack against Israel.*

The '*tawreet*' strategy lay behind *fedayeen* attacks in March and April 1967, which contributed to the escalation of tension in May that year and the devastating Israeli attack in June. The outcome of the Six Day War made Arab governments far more cautious about permitting *fedayeen* movements to operate from their territory. Stunned by the Israeli occupation of the Golan Heights, Damascus ordered the Palestinians to stop all activities on its front with Israel. Arafat was detained for two months in Mezza, a prison with an unsavoury reputation in a military area near Damascus international airport.

Alarmed by Syria's attitude, Fatah sent Khalid El-Hassan, one of the founder members, to Cairo to sound out those close to Nasser. El-Hassan saw me in September 1967 and explained that the organization was looking for cooperation with Egypt. Nasser listened with interest when I told him of this approach. He had realized that something was needed to rally the spirits of Palestinians living under Israeli occupation, many of whom were showing disturbing signs of apathy, accepting the conquest as a *fait accompli*.

Khalid El-Hassan made another visit to Egypt soon afterwards accompanied by Kaddoumi and Khalaf, who explained that Arafat would like to meet an Egyptian government official. I had not heard of Arafat before; at the time none of these men was known outside the *fedayeen* movement.

They returned with Arafat in October expecting to see an Egyptian official, and I took them in my car to the appointment, without disclosing at what level they would be received. As the car approached Nasser's home they assumed that they were to see his secretary. Nasser had phoned me that morning to say that he would see the visitors personally, despite misgivings expressed by the intelligence service. 'Some information has arrived from Beirut warning me against receiving your friends,' he said. 'It seems that all the warring Palestinian factions are fighting among themselves more than against the Israelis, and these people are coming to Egypt with a plot to assassinate me.'

'I think the intelligence people must get their information from some street-corner tobacconist,' I replied.

* See pp. 143–4.

As we entered Nasser's home the presidential guards noticed that Arafat was wearing a revolver. Without waiting to be asked he unbuckled his gunbelt and left it at the door. The visitors were overwhelmed to find themselves in the presence of the man who was still a legend in the Arab world despite the 1967 defeat. If kisses had been bullets, Nasser would have died a dozen times that morning.

'I decided against the advice of everybody in the Egyptian government to see you,' Nasser said. 'I have lost confidence in the PLO leadership. The Palestinian cause does not now need people who can give good speeches. It needs people who can mobilize the resistance of the Palestinian people against occupation. I want you to fire one bullet every day in the occupied territories. Even if you only fire a shot in the air, that report will be a symbol that the Palestinian people do not accept Israeli occupation as their final fate.' Nasser hoped that continuous low-level attacks inside the occupied territories could proceed at the same time as the war of attrition across the Suez Canal, which had already begun.

Part of the reason for Nasser's displeasure with the PLO leadership was that the organization was becoming too bureaucratic. Generous funding had been voted by Arab heads of state at the Khartoum summit in August 1967, and Shukairy was assembling a substantial staff. The organization's military aspects were not his first priority.

It was agreed that Fatah would receive Egyptian financial and military aid and training. Within a few months the organization began carrying out successful operations against Israel, and in March 1968 it took part in the battle of Karamah in Jordan, fighting alongside regular Jordanian army troops against an Israeli raiding force. Karamah is a place but also an Arabic word meaning dignity, which was what Fatah was struggling to achieve for the Palestinians.

In the summer of 1968, at a time when the four-power peace talks were stalled, Nasser decided to visit Moscow to discuss the next steps with the Soviet leadership. The war of attrition was continuing steadily, and Egyptian defences on the west bank were in sound condition. The time had come, Nasser felt, to seek Moscow's help in stepping up the pressure on Israel. Egypt needed more Soviet arms and bolder Soviet political support.*

* See pp. 136–8.

At the same time Fatah's military activities were expanding rapidly. I suggested to Nasser that we should use the opportunity to introduce Arafat to Soviet officials, in the hope that Moscow would recognize that Fatah was a national liberation movement, and provide some assistance.

Arafat was attached to the Egyptian delegation which flew to Moscow in July 1968, travelling under the assumed name of Abdul Fatah Ibrahim, with the rank of counsellor. When Nasser told Brezhnev and Kosygin on the first day of talks that there was a Palestinian in the delegation, their reaction was swift and sharp. They said that the *fedayeen* represented two things they did not like, adventurism and terrorism. Nevertheless, an opportunity arose on the last day when Nasser gave a reception in honour of the Soviet hosts. Arafat was able to shake hands with Brezhnev and Kosygin, who advised him to talk to Pyotr Mazerov, the member of the Politburo responsible for liberation movements. Mazerov was too busy to see Arafat but referred him to Boris Ponomarev, secretary of the Soviet Central Committee.

The encounter with Ponomarev was more like an interrogation than an interview. The Central Committee secretary and two assistants bombarded Arafat with questions on his political views, his attitude to UN Resolution 242, the relationship between Fatah and the Arab frontline states, and many other matters. Eventually Ponomarev seemed satisfied, and the Soviet Union decided to give Fatah weapons worth up to 500,000 roubles, to be delivered through the Egyptian army.

After our return to Cairo the Soviet ambassador Alexei Vinogradov* gave me a typed list of the weapons Moscow was prepared to let Fatah have. Arafat needed these supplies urgently, so I persuaded General Mohamed Sadek, the Egyptian chief-of-staff, to hand over equivalent items from Egyptian army stores, on the basis that Cairo would take the new equipment when it arrived from the Soviet Union. This arrangement suited both Arafat and Sadek.

Fortified by the weapons, the victory at Karamah and its relationships with Moscow and Egypt, Fatah became the most powerful of the many Palestinian organizations resisting Israel. Arafat was now

* There were two Soviet ambassadors to Cairo with the same surname at different times. The other, Vladimir Vinogradov, played a role during the Yom Kippur war. See Part I, Chapters 12 and 13.

strong enough to challenge Shukairy's leadership of the PLO. When the Palestine National Congress assembled at the Arab League building in Cairo in February 1969, *al-Ahram* carried a front-page headline predicting that Fatah would win a majority of seats in elections to the Executive Committee.

Realizing that the headline represented Nasser's will, Shukairy stepped aside to make way for Arafat, who was elected chairman of the Executive Committee. With Arafat leading both the PLO and Fatah, the distinction between the two became blurred, and the PLO took on a more radical character. Although Fatah representatives were dominant, the Executive Committee included most other Palestinian groups, with one important exception. The PFLP kept itself apart, emphasizing its differences with Fatah over the role ideology should play in the struggle. George Habash thought the Palestinians should follow Fidel Castro's example, giving the revolution a clearly communist identity, as a means of gaining full Soviet support. Fatah, on the other hand, had no strong ideological leanings and felt an affinity to Egypt. The effect of this link, coupled with Nasser's personal support of the Palestinian cause, was that the PLO came to look to Egypt as its main source of moral and political support.

During the three years between the Six Day War and the September 1970 civil war, Jordan became the centre of operations for virtually all *fedayeen* movements. Attacks against Israel across the border from Egypt were impossible after June 1967 because of the Israeli occupation of Sinai, and at the same time Syria continued to forbid guerrilla operations on its borders. Many attacks were carried out by commando groups slipping across the Jordan river to infiltrate the occupied territories. Israel began to take tough reprisals against Jordan.

King Hussein was prepared to tolerate Israel's raids but not the verbal attacks of his Palestinian 'guests'. Some of the smaller Palestinian groups wanted the movement to follow the Vietnamese example, with Amman playing the role of Hanoi. This presupposed an insurrection by Palestinians living in Jordan against the Hashemite monarchy. The Egyptian and Jordanian governments pointed out that the Palestinian struggle could not be conducted like the Vietnam War, because the Viet Cong's tactics required jungle rather than desert terrain, but these objections were ignored. King Hussein increasingly feared that the *fedayeen* were trying to create a state within his state.

Tension between the *fedayeen* and Hussein soared when Jordan and Egypt accepted the Rogers Initiative and the three-month ceasefire which began on 7 August 1970. All *fedayeen* groups were opposed to the initiative as violently as they had been to the earlier Rogers Plan, refusing to distinguish between them.* Nasser explained that he had accepted because there was no hope of liberating Palestine by military or diplomatic means, and the least of the evils seemed to be a middle road, based on the Rogers Initiative and the use of military power at an appropriate moment, to create pressures leading to a solution. This was a rude political awakening for the PLO. To be told by Nasser, champion of the Palestinians, that the liberation of Palestine was in present circumstances out of the question, was hard to take.

The *fedayeen* tended to underestimate Israel's military strength and to overestimate their own political power, thinking that as they represented a sacred cause they could say whatever they wished. Egypt's acceptance of the Rogers Initiative was attacked as 'treason' by Palestinians broadcasting from the radio station which I, as minister of information, had handed over to them. As a cabinet minister it fell to me to convey a message to them from the president: 'You have every right to refuse the Rogers Initiative and Resolution 242, but you cannot accuse those who accept of treason.' The Palestinians promised to moderate their language, but the following day they repeated the same accusations. There was no alternative but to close them down. The broadcasters were surprised, knowing that Fatah had been introduced to Nasser through me, but left without argument.

It was for this reason that King Hussein thought that Nasser would not object if Jordan liquidated the PLO,† an incorrect assumption which lead to the bitter fighting of 'Black September', and to Nasser's warning to Hussein not to misunderstand the reasons for Egypt's acceptance of the Rogers Initiative.

At the height of the fighting, when the *fedayeen* were facing destruction and Nasser was trying to mediate, it became important to evacuate Arafat to attend the peace summit which Nasser had called in Cairo. The PLO chairman was holed up in a building near the office of the Egyptian military attaché in Amman. A Kuwaiti delegation led by

* See p. 157.
† See pp. 157–9.

Sheikh Sabah El-Ahmed El-Sabah, a member of the ruling Sabah family and deputy foreign minister, went to Amman and obtained King Hussein's permission to talk to Arafat. As the delegation entered the building where Arafat was sheltering, Jordanian troops counted the delegates. Once inside, Sheikh Sabah asked his private secretary to undress and hand over his *dishdasha* (an ankle-length garment) to Arafat. The delegation then emerged with Arafat disguised as the private secretary. The Jordanian troops counted the delegation as they left and noticed no change. Arafat was then taken to Cairo for the Arab League summit at which Nasser negotiated a Jordanian–PLO agreement to stop the fighting. Nasser also intervened to prevent the execution of Salah Khalaf (Abu Iyad), who had been arrested in Jordan during the fighting.

Nasser's death on 29 September 1970, the last day of the summit, brought a vast outpouring of grief from Palestinians, as well as Egyptians and other Arabs. The Palestinians knew that whatever their differences with Nasser over the Rogers Initiative, they had lost their greatest defender.

2

An Ambiguous Relationship

After the loss of a leader of towering stature, it was perhaps inevitable that Nasser's successor, Anwar Sadat, became the butt of unflattering comparisons. Arafat, like many prominent Palestinians, regarded the new president as a political lightweight, not to be taken seriously. Although that assessment was modified later, the relationship between the PLO chairman and Sadat never acquired the political depth and intensity he had experienced with Nasser.

One of the reasons for Arafat's attitude was that Sadat lacked Nasser's voracious appetite for detail. The first Egyptian president had read more than necessary, while the second found it tedious to spend long hours at a desk. Sadat was not by nature a hard worker.

Abu Iyad (Salah Khalaf) was unable to hide his disappointment after a ninety-minute conversation with Sadat in October 1970. 'Do you think the office will change him? Make him get to grips with the issues?' he asked me. 'Definitely,' I replied, sounding more confident than I felt. Abu Iyad looked unpersuaded. 'He's still strange,' the PLO official said, 'just as he always was.'

Strange perhaps, but the new leader was also intelligent and quick to absorb oral information, and fully understood the political importance of the Palestinian cause. In his capacity as vice president Sadat had taken part in the September 1970 summit, which served as a crash course on that issue. In the space of three days he saw the restoration of order between the PLO and Jordan, the death of Nasser, and his own nomination as acting president.

Perhaps because of that episode, Sadat continued afterwards to think of the Palestinian issue as an aspect of inter-Arab rivalry. Not having Nasser's first-hand experience of Palestinian suffering during the 1948 war, Sadat was less concerned with the rights and wrongs of the conflict and more with managing and using the emotions it had aroused.

While Nasser was alive, most Palestinians were content to subsume their national feelings within the wider Arab nationalism which Nasser championed. After his death no one had the exceptional status necessary to act as moral leader of the Arab world as a whole. Arab unity was a goal so amorphous that no one knew how to approach it. The liberation of Palestine was just as daunting, but at least it had the appeal of clarity. A race developed in the early 1970s to inherit that part of Nasser's mantle.

One of the contenders was Sadat, who hoped to gain credibility with the Egyptian army and people by continuing Cairo's support for the Palestinian cause, while steering a moderate course internally. Another was King Hussein, who sought to regain ground lost to the Palestine national movement, and to make up for 'Black September'.

The king's position was difficult. Acting as host to the Palestinians had enhanced Jordan's prestige in the Arab world, and earned subsidies from Libya and Kuwait, but had also brought the rule of the Hashemites into question. The fear that the *fedayeen* wanted to establish a state within a state was not entirely dispelled by the settlement Nasser had negotiated. In the spring of 1971 Hussein resumed attacks against what remained of the PLO's presence in Jordan, and eventually destroyed the last guerrilla bases on his territory. This gave Sadat a pretext to interfere politically, and he succeeded, at least briefly, in snatching the moral banner.

The Palestinian leadership did not regard Sadat as an ideal sponsor, but it had little option at the time, because other Arab doors were closed or only half open. Many of the *fedayeen* had fled from Jordan to Damascus, assuming that Syria's intervention on the Palestinian side during the civil war in Jordan showed a changed attitude.* That hope was quickly extinguished by a military coup in Syria in which the faction of the Ba'ath Party which had authorized intervention was ousted by opponents within the same party. General Hafez Assad came to power and restored the previous policy of prohibiting *fedayeen* activities on the Syrian–Israeli border. Facing tough repression in Damascus, the PLO again moved on, this time settling in Lebanon, which had been growing in importance as a centre of guerrilla activity.

* See p. 158.

In November 1971 four Palestinians assassinated Wasfi El-Tal, prime minister of Jordan, in the lobby of the Sheraton Hotel in Giza, as a reprisal for King Hussein's actions against Palestinian guerrillas. The fact that the killing happened in Egypt, and that the PLO was under Egyptian political patronage, led to an assumption that Sadat had given approval. King Hussein considered security in Cairo to be tighter than in any other Arab country, and suspected that someone had ordered the armed guards in the hotel lobby to stand aside. I was with Sadat when he received the news of the killing, and am sure from his reaction that it was a surprise to him, though not necessarily a disagreeable one. Anything which inflamed acrimony between the PLO and Jordan strengthened Sadat's hold on Palestinian loyalties. The tone of Egyptian press reports of the assassination was far from sympathetic to Amman.

As an open row between Jordan and Egypt would not have been in Cairo's interests, Sadat quickly sent a warm telegram of condolences to Hussein. Soon afterwards the Egyptian ambassador in Amman received a call from the head of the royal cabinet, who said that the telegram had saved relations between Egypt and Jordan, but added that the king was upset by the way the Egyptian press was covering the assassination. 'The King is really sad if this is the reward for all the efforts they [the Jordanian government] are making to control feelings between the Jordanians and the Palestinians,' the head of the royal cabinet said. 'He is sure that there are elements who are against any rapprochement between Amman and Cairo and whenever the relations get better they do something to destroy them.'

Hussein then sent Sadat a letter which maintained the pretence of cordial relations but also contained an implicit warning. 'My dear brother President Sadat, I send your excellency our love,' the letter began. 'When I received your telegram I felt it reflected . . . your sincere feelings and the deep grief of the Egyptian people over this horrible crime which occurred in the glorious land of Egypt, which is a refuge for everybody . . . I talk to you, my dear brother, with a wounded heart, so please accept my frankness. I hope that those betraying bullets will not find other targets.'*

The reference to 'other targets' was ambiguous, but may have been

* The king's letter was dated 3 December 1971.

a way of warning Sadat that if he played host to the Palestinians, his own life or those of his ministers would be in danger from the PLO. The king may also have meant to imply that feelings aroused during the trial of the four Palestinians accused of assassinating El-Tal could further damage Egyptian–Jordanian relations.

The assassination occurred at a time when Arab leaders were jockeying for position in the redistribution of influence which took place after Nasser's death. King Hussein was trying on one hand to improve his standing with other Arabs, and on the other to reach understanding with the Israelis. The tempo of his secret contacts had increased, with a meeting in London in November 1970 with the Israeli foreign minister. A month later Hussein met an Israeli delegation in Teheran, and during the talks the Shah of Iran encouraged him to face what he called 'your examination by history'. In January 1971 there was a meeting in Aqaba attended by Israeli prime minister Golda Meir, who urged the king to 'seize the moment by opting for an agreement with Israel'.

There was much in Mrs Meir's arguments to tempt Hussein. She pointed out that Israel was not and never had been his enemy; on the contrary, it had proved to be a guarantor of Hashemite rule in Jordan. The real threat was Palestinian militancy, as the events of August and September 1970 had demonstrated. The king had faced a direct challenge for the loyalty of his people, and the PLO had shown itself to be as much a threat to his kingdom as to Israel. The 1970 crisis had also underlined the inability of the United States to assist Jordan at short notice. The incursion of a column of Syrian tanks into Jordan to show support for the Palestinians had been a reminder that a threat could emerge suddenly and from an unexpected quarter. Israeli forces had been on standby to intervene on the king's side, with the knowledge and approval of Washington. As it turned out Hussein's air force had been able to beat off the Syrians.*

Jordan's victory in the civil war had reduced these dangers, leaving the PLO scattered, divided and disillusioned. Mrs Meir felt that if Hussein seized the opportunity to build a political bridge to Israel, no Arab leader or organization would be able to block his path. Egypt was absorbed in an internal squabble among Nasser's heirs, Syria and Iraq were caught up in rivalry between their respective branches of

* See p. 158.

the Ba'ath Party, and Gulf rulers would be glad to be rid of the economic and political costs of the conflict. Even the Arab masses, once a force to be reckoned with, no longer constituted a great obstacle. The mood had changed considerably since Nasser's death.

King Hussein understood Mrs Meir's arguments, which were not far from his own way of thinking. After two decades in office the king was among the most experienced, astute and intelligent leaders in the Middle East, and within the limits of his situation he had shown courage. At the same time he was also prudent and keenly aware of the delicate balance of forces in a turbulent region. The advantages of an agreement had to be weighed against the fragility of his kingdom, suspicions in Arab minds stemming from Hashemite history, and the need to maintain a line of political retreat.

On a human level the Hashemites had always suffered from a martyrdom complex, feeling that the family had made great sacrifices for Jordan and for peace. The assassination of Hussein's grandfather King Abdullah by a Palestinian had left them feeling under-appreciated by those they sought to help, and King Hussein longed to amend what he saw as an unfair perception of his family's role. His dream was an Arab consensus according him a fair measure of acclaim, or at least acceptance.

Wasfi El-Tal, the slain prime minister, had been in favour of taking a daring step with the Israelis, which made the blow of his assassination even greater. The king was in an angry, disturbed mood, feeling under pressure from all directions. His relationship with Sadat was unsettled, the Israelis were still pressing, and Joseph Sisco, US assistant secretary of state, was urging him to wait no longer. Between December 1971 and February 1972 the king held four meetings with Richard Helms, director of the CIA, and one further encounter with Israeli leaders at Wadi Araba near the shores of the Dead Sea.

As a result of his contacts Hussein knew that the Israelis would not accept any settlement which gave the Palestinians an independent state, but were prepared, given advantageous terms, to return the west bank to Jordan. The conditions for Israeli withdrawal could be created, he thought, if the Palestinians were granted self-rule on the west bank within a Jordanian federation. This called for a change to the Jordanian constitution, creating a two-part kingdom under Hussein's throne. The scheme could only work if it obtained big-power support as well as the acquiescence of Israel, the Palestinians and the Arab world as a whole.

King Hussein launched his project on 13 March 1972 by briefing the ambassadors of the four big powers, followed by the Egyptian ambassador. Jordan, he said, had been one of the Arab countries which voted in January 1964 for the creation of the PLO, but now felt that decision had been a mistake. The PLO had imported dangerous ideologies, nearly causing the collapse of Jordan. Meanwhile Israel was moving towards the creation of a weak puppet Palestinian entity on the west bank 'so that they can swallow it when they wish'. Hussein felt that municipal elections recently conducted by Israel on the west bank formed part of that plan. He proposed the creation of a United Hashemite Kingdom on a federal basis, and suggested that the PLO could be absorbed into the Jordanian army.

In a separate letter to Sadat, King Hussein recalled Nasser's fears that Israel would try to change the nature of the west bank,* and Nasser's insistence that a solution should be found before the changes reached a point of no return. The municipal elections, Hussein told Sadat, had been part of a plan to 'put the Palestinian man into a small jar so that he could be used or broken at any time'.

The king proposed that the western part of the United Hashemite Kingdom should have Jerusalem as its capital and would consist of the west bank 'and any other parts of Palestine which can be liberated' (a reference to Gaza). The eastern part would consist of Jordan with Amman as its capital. Each part would have its own executive council and legislative authority, and would run its own affairs, while the central authority would deal with international relations and national security.

Hussein then appealed to 'my dear brother president Sadat' for political and financial support to bring the project to realization. The request did not suit the Egyptian leader's plans. His secret wish was to reach an agreement between Egypt and Israel, but that was not politically feasible at the time. While waiting for the right circumstances, Sadat wanted to keep the Palestinian card in his own hands. Egyptian sponsorship of the cause was an important political asset,

* See p. 132.

maintaining his credibility with Arab masses and governments. Sadat therefore rejected King Hussein's proposal outright.

In a letter to Hussein Sadat said: 'This is a way of robbing the Palestinian people of their right to self-determination.' The Egyptian leader's stand put paid to the king's venture and earned Sadat much public support. Sadat was in fact concerned less about Palestinian self-determination than Egyptian–Jordanian rivalry. Had the United Hashemite Kingdom succeeded, Hussein would have gained prestige at Sadat's expense.

After the assassination of Wasfi El-Tal, Black September made an unsuccessful attempt the following month to kill the Jordanian ambassador to London. According to US intelligence, some 300 Fatah guerrillas were now operating under the Black September name. In May 1972 the group seized command of an El Al airliner flying from Brussels to Israel. When the plane landed at Tel Aviv four commandos armed with hand grenades and pistols held the 110 passengers and crew hostage and demanded the release of 317 Palestinians from Israeli prisons, and safe passage to Egypt. A deadline was set but extended during lengthy negotiations. Some twenty-three hours later twelve Israeli paratroopers stormed the plane and two Palestinian commandos and one hostage were killed, while two commandos and four hostages were wounded.

Four months later Black September hijacked the attention of the world's media during the Olympic Games in Munich. On 5 September 1972 eight commandos stormed the Israeli compound at the Olympic village, killing two Israelis and capturing nine others. The commandos demanded the release of 200 Palestinians from Israeli prisons and safe passage to Egypt, in return for release of the hostages. Both the commandos and the hostages were transferred to Furstenfeldbruck airport by bus and helicopter, but while negotiations were under way Munich police attempted a surprise assault. In the shoot-out and explosions which followed all the hostages and five of the commandos were killed, the other three being wounded and captured.

The following month Black September hijacked a Lufthansa jet and threatened to blow up the plane and its passengers unless the three Palestinians captured during the Munich operation were released. The West German government agreed to free the prisoners, and the hostages were eventually released unharmed in Libya.

In December 1972 Black September seized the Israeli embassy in Bangkok, taking six hostages. The operation ended without bloodshed, the hostages being released unharmed, while the commandos were flown to Egypt. Another Black September operation followed in March 1973, when the Saudi Arabian embassy in Khartoum was occupied, followed by the assassinations of one Belgian and two American diplomats in the Sudanese capital.

These operations and others had both positive and negative effects. The world became more aware of the Palestinian grievance, but it also associated the cause with terrorism rather than armed struggle. If the intention was to force the West to put pressure on Israel, terrorism was not successful. Washington's support for Israel became firmer than ever, and American diplomatic efforts fell to an unusually low level. No prospect of radically changing the Middle East equation emerged until Sadat told Arafat that he wanted to 'light a spark to create a solution'.*

During the Yom Kippur War the PLO asked to be given duties in the battle but was offered only vague missions, such as trying to disrupt Israeli communications in the central area facing Jordan, without compromising King Hussein's wish to keep the Jordanian border quiet. After the war the Palestinians again found themselves pushed aside as Sadat and Kissinger began arranging a new relationship between Egypt and Israel. Kissinger's decision not to invite the Palestinians to the Geneva conference was seen as an affront to the Arab world as a whole. Arab heads of state, meeting in Algiers from 26 to 28 November, called for the restoration of the 'full national rights' of the Palestinians and for Israel's immediate withdrawal from all occupied territories. The summit, which was attended by Arafat and boycotted by King Hussein, issued a communiqué whose tone implied more enthusiasm for the Palestinian cause than many Arab leaders felt. As on many previous and subsequent occasions, the leaders tailored their remarks to suit the popular mood of the Arab world.

When Kissinger next visited Egypt,† Sadat appealed to him to make some kind of concession to the Palestinians to restrain them from

* See p. 178.

† Kissinger had two meetings with Sadat at the Barrages in the Nile Delta on 13 and 14 December.

joining those in Damascus and Baghdad who were attacking Cairo for its decision to attend the conference. Kissinger replied that he had no intention of ignoring the Palestinians, but wanted to bring about disengagement agreements first. He gave Sadat a memorandum to pass on to Arafat setting out US views on talks with the PLO. The document, something of an innovation in the art of diplomacy, began with an invitation:

1. Establish direct contact with HK [Kissinger] soon.
2. Be specific and realistic in stating what is wanted from US.
3. Be prepared to explain further views on following:
   – Resolution 242 – what parts, if any, are acceptable?
   – Arab–Israeli peace settlement.
   – Existence of Jewish state in Palestine.
   – Jordan and King Hussein.
4. What practical first steps can be taken to establish framework and momentum for later steps?
5. What coordination is desirable with Sadat, Asad, Boumediene, Faisal?

General Points to note:

1. US is open minded. No particular outcome has been precluded, no secret commitments have been made.
2. US is willing to engage in serious dialogue in near future.
3. US has no intention of abandoning Israel or King Hussein, but this does not mean that it will support them on all points.
4. US will be attentive to any position supported by major Arab countries, especially Egypt, Syria, Algeria, Saudi Arabia.
5. US is strongly opposed to further 'terrorist spectaculars.
6. US is serious when it says P [Palestinian] interests must be met in any comprehensive peace settlement. This is not just a matter of refugees. US is ready to discuss further how these interests can be met.
7. US has no abstract peace plan. US will pursue step-by-step process, promising no more at any given stage than it is sure it can produce. Will be short on rhetoric, but will deliver on any commitments undertaken.

The memorandum contains two points of special interest. Item three in the first group ('Be prepared to explain further views on . . . Resolution 242 – what parts, if any, are acceptable') implies that the US was willing to enter into talks without a prior PLO statement accepting Resolution 242 in full. Kissinger had always been sceptical about the resolution because of its deliberate ambiguity, but he knew that its full acceptance by the PLO would imply recognition of Israel. The second point of interest is the statement in item six in the second group 'This is not just a matter of refugees.' While this was not new, the fact that Kissinger was prepared to make such a statement in a memorandum intended for the PLO chairman was important.

Sadat passed the memorandum to Arafat and meetings were arranged between a PLO representative and a CIA agent in Cairo. The discussions were meant to establish whether a basis existed for more formal meetings, but the PLO official gained the impression that the CIA agent was merely fishing for information, and wrote an unenthusiastic report to Arafat.

Sadat pressed Arafat to cooperate and assured him that Kissinger would turn his attention to the Palestinian people once disengagement agreements had been achieved. In view of Kissinger's warning about 'terrorist spectaculars', the PLO chairman reluctantly decided the following year to suspend major commando operations. A US intelligence summary of this period, written in 1978, said that Arafat gave orders in September 1974 that Black September should cease operations. The report also claimed that the Fatah Central Committee ordered Khalaf, who had organized the Munich operation, to be suspended from any role for six months.

Another effect of the October war on the PLO was that Arab financial assistance grew at an unprecedented rate. The oil price explosion of 1973–74 vastly increased the wealth of the Gulf countries, but carried a high price in guilt. There was a feeling that Egypt's disengagement with Israel had been bought at the expense of the Palestinians. Conscience money flowed into the PLO's coffers, coming not only from monarchies and sheikhdoms in the Gulf but also from the growing Palestinian bourgeoisie. The PLO was becoming rich, and yet its capacity for military action was limited to guerrilla actions across the Lebanese–Israeli border. One result of this dilemma was that the PLO used its resources to set up a parallel state within Lebanon.*

The exclusion of the Palestinians from the Geneva conference, fol-

* See pp. 335–7.

lowed by the first disengagement agreement between Egypt and Israel, was deeply depressing for all the Palestinian organizations. The entire Arab world understood that feeling, and no Arab leader could afford to appear indifferent to the cause. This was the political atmosphere in which an Arab summit of crucial importance was held at Rabat in October 1974. A resolution was passed supporting the right of the Palestinians to establish, in any liberated territory, an independent national authority led by the PLO 'in its capacity as the sole legitimate representative of the Palestinian people'. The resolution was to some extent influenced by a decision taken by the UN General Assembly the previous month to invite Arafat to participate in a debate on the Palestinian question.

After the two Egyptian disengagement agreements with Israel, Sadat was under constant attack from Palestinian groups, yet he continued to seek Palestinian support or understanding. In mid-1976 he received intelligence reports showing that a major hijacking operation was being prepared by the PFLP. He was in a position to stop the action, but did not want to give the impression that he had abandoned the Palestinian cause.

Five commandos took over an Air France plane en route from Tel Aviv to Paris and diverted it to Benghazi, Libya, where more commandos boarded the plane and forced the crew to fly to Entebbe airport outside Kampala, the capital of Uganda. With the complicity or acceptance of the Ugandan leader Idi Amin, the group demanded the release of fifty-three members of Palestinian organizations imprisoned in Israel, France, Kenya, Switzerland and West Germany in exchange for the plane's 257 passengers and crew.

On the night of 3/4 July 1976 Israeli paratroops and infantrymen staged an early-morning raid and rescued the hostages. The commander of the Israeli operation, Colonel Netanyahu, was killed, along with seven PFLP commandos and three hostages. Twenty Ugandan soldiers were killed and many wounded. The raid on Entebbe gave Israel an immense propaganda coup, striking as it did at two targets especially disliked by the West – hijackers and Idi Amin. As a matter of principle Egypt never supported hijackings.

Part of the reason for Sadat's decision not to block the hijacking was that 1976 was a US election year, and the Ford administration had put its Middle East diplomacy into hibernation to avoid upsetting

Jewish voters. Sadat, who was feeling frustrated by the lack of US involvement, thought that a spectacular event might shake the State Department from its slumbers. As it was, he had to wait until early 1977, when the new Democratic president, Jimmy Carter, entered the White House.

The new administration came to office with fresh energy and a different approach.* One of the ideas put forward by Kissinger's successor as secretary of state Cyrus Vance during a visit to the Middle East was that the Palestinians should initially be granted self-rule in Gaza and Jericho. This was a forerunner of the concept at the heart of the Oslo agreement of August 1993.

Vance raised the proposal in talks with Sadat in Alexandria at the beginning of August 1977, and received an enthusiastic response. The secretary of state asked Sadat to obtain a quick reply from the PLO, and said he would return to Egypt in a few days. Meanwhile Carter announced that the United States was ready to hold direct talks with the PLO if the organization accepted Resolution 242.

Two days later Sadat briefed Arafat and Abu Iyad (Khalaf) on Vance's proposal. After their meeting with Sadat the two Palestinians came to my home. Arafat was in the best of spirits, but Abu Iyad seemed worried. Just before lunch Arafat left the room for a few minutes and Khalaf seized the opportunity to explain that Sadat's briefing had been over-enthusiastic. Jumping ahead in his thoughts, the Egyptian leader had asked Arafat to consider which Palestinian figures would be suitable to serve on the Palestinian interim authority which would administer the autonomous territory. Sadat wanted to ease Israeli anxieties by choosing two Palestinians who held American passports and lived in the United States, men with no terrorist links. The names discussed were Professor Edward Said of Columbia University and Professor Ibrahim Abu-Lughod of Georgetown University.

Arafat had emerged from the meeting brimming with enthusiasm, and during the journey to my home he began dreaming aloud of leading an embryo Palestinian state based on Gaza and Jericho. In his imagination, the Palestinian colours were already fluttering in the air.

'The chairman should be rescued from himself,' Abu Iyad pleaded

* See p. 248.

with me, pointing out that Israel had always wanted to be rid of Gaza and that Jericho was being thrown into the proposed bargain as a sweetener. After lunch and much debate Arafat's fantasy began to fade. When Vance returned to Egypt Sadat told him that the PLO had rejected the offer.

Three months later, when Sadat made up his mind to break the deadlocked peace process with a dramatic gesture, it became important to secure a favourable or neutral PLO reaction. The president sent a message to Arafat, who was in Libya, asking him to fly to Egypt to hear a speech of great importance. A special plane was sent to Libya to collect him, and Arafat was present in the Egyptian parliament on 9 November 1977 when Sadat announced: 'I am ready to go to the ends of the earth for peace, even to the Knesset itself.' Arafat realized that his presence might give the impression that the PLO approved of Sadat's offer, and that this was why he had been summoned from Libya. As soon as Sadat left the rostrum Arafat hurried out of parliament and went straight to the airport. Before boarding his plane he phoned to tell me what had happened. 'Sadat put the turban on my head,' he said, using an Arabic expression meaning that the Egyptian president had made a fool of him.

Arafat stayed away from Egypt for eight years after this incident, but despite his anger he usually refrained from strong personal criticism of Sadat. A US State Department analysis said that Arafat was 'exceedingly restrained' long after others in the movement and the Arab world had taken a hard stand against the Egyptian leader.*

The same document gave an assessment of the PLO chairman:

> Arafat is a survivor. Because of his diplomatic and political adeptness, he has endured as the leader of the Palestinian resistance . . . He is essentially a non-ideological pragmatist or opportunist, seeking to facilitate good relations with all Arab countries, whether conservative or progressive, in order to accrue the benefits of financial, moral, diplomatic and arms support necessary to advance the national cause.

Criticisms of Sadat issued by the PLO as an organization were gener-

* This analysis formed part of a document marked 'Secret' found when the American Embassy in Teheran was occupied in November 1979. See pp. 331–2.

ally sharper than those made by Arafat personally. Nevertheless, the PLO was not as harsh as some Palestinian organizations, because its finances depended on donations from Arab governments. When the PLO issued a tough statement after Sadat's visit to Jerusalem, Farouk Kaddoumi, the PLO official in charge of foreign affairs, was asked to visit King Hassan of Morocco. The king's displeasure was clear when Kaddoumi arrived in Rabat a month after the Jerusalem visit. It was time, King Hassan said, for the PLO to learn the discreet manners of diplomacy, and to abandon its habit of reacting instantly to events. 'You are always nervous and you are always the losers,' the king said. 'Let me give you a lesson.'

King Hassan said that when the PLO found that the actions of a king or president raised a problem, certain conventions should be observed:

1. Wait two days before reacting.
2. Your first reaction should be to ask permission to send a delegation to explore the facts.
3. You should send the delegation with a list of at least two dozen questions to be answered, and allow time for those answers to reach you.
4. Never forget that you are dealing with states, and states have prestige and interests.
5. Try to initiate formulas which can bridge the gap between what you think is right and what others legitimately consider matters of prestige, or matters affecting their interests.

The king offered to place a plane at the PLO's disposal whenever the organization needed to send a delegation to an Arab country, and concluded his 'lesson' by admonishing the PLO for criticizing the Egyptian president's trip to Jerusalem. 'What you did to Sadat was completely wrong. Try to learn your lesson,' he said.

The PLO was now being asked to behave like part of the Arab establishment, accepting shackles of the mouth and the mind.

3

1974–1978
The First Peace Feelers

The moment when the world realized that a deal between Israel and the Palestinians might be possible can be precisely dated. Yasser Arafat's dramatic speech to the United Nations General Assembly on 13 November 1974 showed that the organization, or at least its leader, was prepared to consider a non-military solution.

The invitation to Arafat to address the United Nations was a consolation after a year in which international attention had been focused on every aspect of the Arab–Israel conflict other than the Palestinian cause. Media attention had been dominated by the Geneva conference, the Egyptian and Syrian disengagement agreements, the tripling of oil prices, and the Arab decision to drop the oil embargo. Apart from Kissinger's note to Arafat in December 1973 (see previous chapter) and secret discussions between a PLO representative and a CIA agent, the Palestinian cause had been pushed aside. The UN General Assembly's invitation expressed a feeling that the Palestinians' turn for attention was long overdue. Kissinger understood the need to make the Palestinians feel that their turn would come. At the time of Arafat's speech the secretary of state had virtually made up his mind that the next step should be a second agreement between Egypt and Israel. It was important, from his point of view, to keep Palestinian criticism of that decision within bounds.

Arafat was treated almost as a visiting head of state when he arrived at the UN. The pomp reflected the decision of the Arab League summit in Rabat a few weeks earlier to recognize the PLO as the 'sole legitimate representative' of the Palestinian people. His appearance at the rostrum wearing a military uniform and a holster* brought a buzz of excitement. In a speech which made headlines around the world, the PLO chairman looked forward to a time when people of all faiths could enjoy equality within Palestine.

'I have come bearing an olive branch and a freedom fighter's gun. Do not let the olive branch fall from my hand,' Arafat said. The phraseology avoided the word 'peace', which remained politically sensitive, but the intention was clear. Arafat was taking a risk, knowing that there was not yet a consensus in the PLO for the change of policy which his words implied.

The speech was the first public hint that a a debate had begun within the top PLO leadership about alternatives to armed struggle. The timing was important, reflecting new realities created by the Egyptian and Syrian disengagement agreements. Arafat and some of his colleagues recognized that Egypt and Syria would neither enter into another war with Israel nor allow Palestinian groups to conduct attacks from their territory.

Among the first to suggest a reassessment of PLO policy was Abu Mazen (real name Mahmoud Abbas), a Palestinian teacher who had worked in Qatar before becoming fully caught up in the cause. Abu Mazen remained in Syria when most PLO officials moved to Beirut in the early 1970s. This gave him more time to read and think than colleagues embroiled in the turmoil of Lebanon. The works of Eliahu Sasson, the former Jewish Agency official who had been active in secret contacts with Egypt and Jordan in the 1940s, provided fuel for Abu Mazen's ideas, as did the 'Peace Now' movement in Israel, which was beginning to gain international attention. Most PLO members suspected that 'Peace Now' was a ploy to lure the Arabs into a dialogue, but Abu Mazen felt that there were elements in Israel and among world Jewry generally with whom the Palestinians could talk.

The more Abu Mazen pondered events since 1948, the more convinced he became that refusing to talk was a mistake. An absence of dialogue played into Israeli government hands, making it easier to pretend that the Palestinians did not exist. The Israeli strategy, Abu Mazen suspected, was to drown the Palestinian issue within the Arab–

* Arafat pointed to the holster during his speech, but it was empty. He had left his pistol outside the hall of the General Assembly.

Israel conflict, so that the outside world would forget how the conflict had begun. Had the Palestinians been left alone by Arab states to manage their own affairs, a way might have been found to reach agreement with the Israelis, or failing that to resist them more successfully. On the battlefield as at the negotiating table, the relationship had always been between Israel and its Arab neighbours, while the Palestinians were overlooked.

The risks posed by the Arab taboo remained substantial, but a path through that minefield could be discerned by studying Egypt's experience. The procedure the PLO would need to follow in order to build a relationship with Israel involved seven stages. The first and least controversial phase would consist of meetings between intellectuals and academics. Palestinians, Europeans and non-Jewish Americans could take part in early discussions, which would later be expanded to include Jewish Europeans and Americans. When Palestinian opinion grew accustomed to such contacts, Jews holding dual Israeli–American or Israeli–European nationality could be invited to join in. By confining the discussions to non-political matters (especially science) the risks could be minimized.

The next step would be secret meetings between PLO ambassadors or senior aides with prominent US and European personalities known to sympathize with Israel. If news of these meetings leaked out the organization could say that it was trying to use Israel's friends to bring political or economic pressure on the Israeli government.

The Egyptian experience suggested that step three should consist of contacts with Israeli Arabs, including Arab members of the Knesset such as Abdel-Wahab Darawsha. These representatives of Arabs who remained in Israel after the 1948 war should not be regarded as collaborators. They could be expected to urge the Palestinian leadership to distinguish between good Israelis and bad Israelis, between liberals and fanatics, and between hawks and doves. The aim, in their view, should be to establish dialogue with the doves and to isolate the hawks.

The fourth step would consist of secret meetings with Israeli doves. If word of these talks leaked out, it could be argued that the contacts were a manoeuvre to cause internal divisions in Israel.

Step five would consist of meetings with middle-ranking Israeli officials, including under-secretaries and ambassadors. When Egypt took the road to peace this phase brought the first practical benefits, as Sadat received Israeli intelligence warnings of plots against him.

The sixth and seventh steps, which lay beyond the range of PLO–Israeli contacts then imaginable, would consist of regular channels leading to new attitudes on both sides. When the Egyptians reached step seven they realized that the strategy followed by Sadat in 1973/74 had been based on a misconception. The Egyptian leader then thought that Washington could be used to influence Israel; later he learned that Israel could be used to influence Washington. An example of this was that after making peace Sadat used Israel to persuade Washington to increase US aid to Egypt.

Abu Mazen had studied Egypt's experience carefully and realized that it offered a planned, tested and reasonably safe route to a PLO–Israel relationship. In addition, he added an innovation of his own based on a thesis he had written while at university in Moscow. His idea was that differences between the Ashkenazim and the Sephardim, the Jews of European and Oriental origin, could help create pressure for peace inside Israel. The thesis was a study of the attitudes of Jews who had emigrated to Israel from Arab countries between the late 1940s and the Suez crisis. About 400,000 of these Sephardic Jews came during that period, swelling Israel's population by nearly 40 per cent. Abu Mazen believed that many retained happy memories of life in Egypt, Iraq or Syria and were eager for contact with Arab friends they had left behind.

If contacts could be opened with Israeli 'peaceniks' and Jews in the United States, perhaps with the help of Palestinian academics resident in America, a momentum for peace might be created. The Sephardim would then feel free to voice their desire for better relations with Arabs. Abu Mazen also suggested that the PLO should join the Socialist International and become involved in a broad front of organizations interested in peace.

Abu Mazen's views were not representative of the PLO as a whole, but the fact that such thoughts could be discussed showed that a shift had begun. The PLO applied successfully to join the Socialist International, and by the mid-1970s several informal links had been established.

Some of the most important connections were made by Dr Essam El-Sartawie, a prominent Palestinian intellectual who had received permission from Arafat to talk to Israelis. The authorization extended only to contacts with Jews who might be well-disposed towards setting up a Palestinian entity in the occupied territory, and did not include authority to negotiate. Sartawie worked from a flat in Paris and made his first contacts with the help of Tahseen Bashir, one of President Sadat's aides.

Membership of the Socialist International opened many doors, not least because Sartawie got on well with the Austrian chancellor Bruno Kreisky. Kreisky was Jewish, but he was not a convinced Zionist. Although close to many Israeli figures, including Shimon Peres and Teddy Kollek, mayor of Jerusalem, he tried to be fair to both sides. As a natural conciliator the chancellor felt that there was right on both sides of the Israeli–Palestinian dispute.

Kreisky had a lever of influence with Israel, because Jews emigrating from the Soviet Union were sent first to Austria, where they were processed before continuing their journey. In the 1960s the Jewish Agency had asked to be allowed to take over processing and transport arrangements at the transit camps, but Kreisky, who was then foreign minister, insisted on keeping control in Austrian hands. When he reached the highest office in 1970 he was thus in a position to control the immigrant flow.

From 1974 onwards Kreisky began urging Palestinians to make themselves acceptable to Israelis, but also to proclaim the existence of a state in the occupied territories and to set up a government in exile. 'It is unrealistic to expect Israel to create a Palestinian entity,' he told Sartawie. 'The Palestinians should take the initiative by offering a programme based on peace and co-existence.'

Kreisky also had much influence with Willy Brandt, François Mitterrand, Pierre Mendès-France, the former French prime minister, and other prominent European socialists. These friendships opened up many possibilities for contact with Jewish opinion-makers.

A further stage of the PLO's internal debate arose from the second disengagement agreement between Egypt and Israel in September 1975. One of the secret terms of the agreement was a pledge by Egypt not to permit terrorist groups to work from its territory, nor to allow itself to be a base for anti-Israeli propaganda attacks. Arafat and others had foreseen such a move at the time of the first disengagement agreement.

Syria and Jordan had long been closed to guerrilla activity, and now

Egypt was just as restrictive. These realities led to the first open attempt to change PLO policy. A resolution was submitted on 12 March 1977 to a meeting of the Palestine National Congress in Algiers inviting the PLO Executive Committee to explore the possibilities of contacting Jewish groups to discuss a framework for a settlement. The leaders knew that Abu Mazen and Sartawie were already engaging in contacts, and that the resolution was really a way of legitimizing what Arafat had authorized. The resolution was approved, and many who might have been expected to object remained silent; but that did not mean that no one was opposed. A great many Palestinians still felt that any kind of non-military contact with Israel was a betrayal of the cause.

The strength of those feelings soon became clear, with the first two assassinations of PLO officials involved in contacts. Sa'id Hammami, the PLO representative in London, was killed on 4 January 1978 after beginning serious contacts with British Jews, but not with Israeli officials. Seven months later, on 2 August, Dr Ezzedin Kalak, the PLO representative in Paris, met the same fate. Many more were to die as contacts progressed.

The PLO was thus in a highly confused state as it approached the end of the 1970s. One part of the organization was groping in the dark for an unknown partner in Israel, another part was trying to thwart the efforts of the first, while a third and larger element was looking about for some alternative way forward. This third element, which at the time included Arafat, felt that negotiations alone could not be the answer. The PLO needed to be in a position of strength to achieve an acceptable deal, and that meant securing the firm friendship of a local power. Egypt was no longer a candidate after its two agreements with Israel. Syria seemed to want to lead the Palestinian cause as the master rather than the partner of Palestinian fighters. Lebanon was still open, but only because its central government was too weak to keep the PLO out. Southern Lebanon was a useful base, but Beirut provided no political, moral, economic or military support.

If the PLO was to acquire the strength necessary to secure fair terms from Israel, it needed a strong sponsor, a country able to serve as both backer and base. That perception guided Arafat in a series of experiments between the late 1970s and the early 1990s, involving a quest for partnership with Iran, a deep involvement in the internal politics of Lebanon, and finally a bid to secure the sponsorship of Iraq.

4

The Iranian Opportunity

During its long sojourn in southern Lebanon the PLO forged a link with young Iranians inspired by the mullahs of Kom, the city in west central Iran where Ayatollah Ruhollah Khomeini had taught before his arrest and exile in 1963. Tremors of spiritual energy from Kom were beginning to reach Shi'ites throughout the Islamic world.

Before the advent of air travel, the 900-mile journey between Kom and southern Lebanon involved crossing the mountains of western Iran, the fertile lands of Iraq, and the Sham desert of Syria. Despite the natural barriers strong religious associations have existed between Persia and the Levant for at least a millennium.

The origins of this link can be traced to a period about 300 years after the schism between the Sunni and Shia branches of Islam.* Differences had emerged among Shi'ites as to which of the descendants of Ali, the Prophet's son-in-law, should be recognized as imams. The main branch of Shia Islam gave special reverence to the first twelve descendants, the last of whom mysteriously disappeared in the ninth century and became known as the Absent Imam. Another Shia branch

* The schism arose from events a quarter of a century after the death of the Prophet Mohamed in 632 A.D. The prophetic role could not be inherited, but successors known as caliphs were chosen to perpetuate the Prophet's temporal and spiritual authority. Ali, the fourth caliph and son-in-law of the Prophet, was assassinated during a long dispute over the succession. The word 'Shia' meant the partisans of Ali. After his death in 661 the Shi'ites gave reverence to Ali and his descendants as imams, or legimitate heads of the community. The caliphate system continued after Ali's death and remained the main form of religious authority for Sunnis, who account for 80 per cent of all Muslims. Sunnis recognize the first four caliphs, Abu-Bakr, Omar, Uthman and Ali, as being 'rightly guided', and give strong emphasis to the Sunna, the customs and usage of the Prophet as found in his deeds and sayings.

with different views grew up in south-western Persia and the Levant, strengthening the bonds between the two areas.

From the year 910 A.D. much of the Arab world was ruled by the Fatimid dynasty, which adhered to Shi'ism. Their empire endured for 262 years, and included Egypt,* which was predominantly Sunni, and the Levant, whose population was of mixed faith. In 1171 the Fatimids were ousted by Salah El-Din (Saladin), who was a Sunni. Remnants of the Fatimids fled from Egypt to the Levant to join other Shi'ites, and found refuge in the mountains of Lebanon. The links between Shi'ites in the Levant and those in Persia continued, and gave rise to a more general tradition of connections between the two areas.

The importance of these links increased after 1501, when Shah Ismail I of Persia established Shi'ism as the state faith. As the Persian population was then equally divided between Sunnis and Shi'ites, Shah Ismail's decision created a need for more Shia sheikhs and teachers.† One of Shah Ismail's successors, Shah Abbas the Great (1587–1629), sent emissaries to southern Lebanon to recruit religious teachers to work in Persia.

The connection gained a political dimension in the twentieth century when Reza Khan, a Persian army officer, overthrew the Kajar dynasty and became emperor.‡ The new Shah and his son Mohamed, who succeeded him in 1941, had dreams of establishing a wider sphere of influence, and wanted the Shi'ites of Lebanon to act as Iran's§ window on the Mediterranean.

In the 1960s an Iranian religious figure, Imam Mousa El-Sadr, born in Kom in 1928, arrived in Tyre, the ancient port in southern Lebanon, and began to gain a following among Lebanese Shi'ites. The Shah's known ambitions gave rise to a rumour that El-Sadr was some kind of imperial envoy. This proved to be incorrect: the imam had been sent by the religious establishment of Kom to lift the spirits and self-

* One of the achievements of the Fatimids was the founding of Cairo.

† 98 per cent of Iranians today are Shi'ites.

‡ Reza Khan toppled the Kajar dynasty in 1921 and established the Pahlavi dynasty in 1925.

§ Persia was renamed Iran in 1935.

awareness of Shi'ites in Lebanon. Despite their substantial numbers,* the Shi'ites were the poorest segment of the population, ignored by the wealthier and more powerful Sunnis and Christian Maronites, and even by the Druze.† The Shi'ites, feeling dejected and undervalued, were natural ammunition for revolutionary movements.

Imam Mousa El-Sadr started a Shia movement called 'The Deprived' and began to shake the fragile web of Lebanese society, attacking the Christians as rightists and the Palestinians as nihilists, while accusing the Syrians of wanting to swallow Lebanon. He maintained contacts with the PLO but regarded the organization's growing military power with suspicion.

The imam's influence gave the Shi'ites greater self-confidence, and within a few years they became a highly active element in Lebanese politics. Meanwhile tremors emanating from Kom were beginning to rattle the imperial crockery in Teheran. The mullahs made no secret of their opposition to the Shah, and their followers began to prepare themselves to carry out what they saw as God's work. Lebanon, with its large Shia population and weak central government, was the obvious place to prepare for the overthrow of the Pahlavi dynasty. Despite the imam's suspicions of the Palestinians, Iranian revolutionaries began receiving instruction at Palestinian training camps.

The situation took an ironic turn in 1975 when President Sadat persuaded the Shah to help the Palestinians. The Shah received a PLO delegation and agreed to donate $50 million. The PLO, for its part, promised to close a camp where Iranian revolutionaries were being trained. Both parties deceived each other: the camp was closed but training of the Iranians continued at another centre, and the Shah paid only one fifth of the promised sum.

On 3 August 1978, six months before the Iranian revolution, El-Sadr disappeared in mysterious circumstances. The imam had been visiting Libya, and according to the authorities in Tripoli had set off for Rome. He never arrived in the Italian capital and no trace of him could be found. Some of his followers drew parallels with the strange disappearance of Mohamed, the twelfth imam, who vanished in the year

* The precise total was unknown, as no census had been taken since 1932.

† The Druze broke away from the Ismailis in the eleventh century. They believe that the Fatimid caliph El-Hakim (996–1021) will eventually return from divine concealment. They are found mainly in Lebanon, Jordan and Syria.

873 A.D. Others pointed out that many parties had motives for wanting the imam dead.*

Meanwhile Ayatollah Khomeini, then aged seventy-six, was acquiring ever greater influence through declarations issued from Paris, his home in exile. The ayatollah addressed not just the Shi'ites of Iran but the entire Muslim world, on both sides of the schism, and was ready to embrace the Palestinian cause. The holy city of Jerusalem was a shrine for all Muslims on an equal footing with Mecca and Medina, quite apart from its role as the Palestinian capital.

After the Shah's departure into exile in 1979† Khomeini returned in triumph from Paris and was given an ecstatic reception. Under the ayatollah's austere guidance Iran became a republic with a strong fundamentalist personality and pronounced anti-Western views. Hundreds of the old regime's supporters were tried and executed. Western habits and clothes gave way to a new code of disciplined behaviour and dress. Most women adopted the chador.

The new government included among its prominent members some of the revolutionaries who had trained at Palestinian camps in Lebanon. Abol-Hassan Bani-Sadr, the first president of the Iranian republic, Mustafa Shamran, the first minister of defence after the revolution, Ibrahim Yazdi, deputy prime minister, and Sadek Kotb Zadeh, foreign minister, had all learned their fighting skills from the PLO.

The PLO was handsomely rewarded for its training role. Khomeini ordered that the office of the Israeli delegation in Teheran should be seized and given to the PLO, and that the balance of the $50 million promised by the Shah should be paid.‡ Another of Khomeini's early decisions was that Arabic, the language of the Koran, should be taught in schools as a second tongue after Farsi.

In the spring of 1979 the PLO found itself the pampered friend of Iran precisely at the moment when Egypt finally slipped from the organization's grasp, with the signing of the Egypt–Israel peace treaty. The PLO leadership saw Teheran as a regional ally to compen-

* After the imam's disappearance the Shia movement in Lebanon divided into two groups, Amal (Hope) and Hezbollah (Party of God), both of which had political and military aspects. The groups became important in the 1980s. See pp. 341, 360.

† See p. 283.

‡ Ayatollah Khomeini confirmed in an interview with the author that he had given these instructions personally.

sate for the loss of Cairo, and began to dream of escaping from the restraints which had forced it to suspend major military actions since 1975.

The honeymoon proved short-lived. Forgetting the lesson which King Hassan had given Farouk Kaddoumi,* the PLO behaved as if the new Iranian leaders were still fellow-revolutionaries. However close the relationship, a degree of respect and reserve was needed when dealing with ministers of an important country. Palestinian leaders assumed that the effective leaders of the revolution were those they had known in the training camps, which was wishful thinking. The real core of the revolution had remained inside Iran, and these men felt less natural empathy with the Palestinians. While PLO representatives spoke the language of revolution, the key Iranian leaders were Shia intellectuals, men inspired by visions of social justice, with little patience for radical jargon.

The PLO also caused irritation by trying to continue a master–pupil relationship. Some of the PLO's assistance in military training was helpful while the new government was setting up Revolutionary Guards units, but the organization also wanted to offer advice in areas where the Iranians had expertise, such as the oil industry. In the early days after the Shah's fall the PLO supplied the new regime with information about the outside world, but that arrangement proved short-lived. The new Iranian leaders found that the information was coloured by PLO views, and that the apparatus of state now at their disposal could do better.

A further mistake was that the PLO appointed itself as a messenger of the anti-Israel cause. The Kom theocracy was already committed to the cause for religious reasons, and could hardly accept lessons from a *fedayeen* organization, while the secular elite needed no guidance on Israel's iniquities, having reasons of its own to be fiercely opposed to the Zionist state. Israel had worked hand in glove with the Pahlavi regime, and especially with the hated SAVAK secret police. The files of SAVAK were found to contain information supplied by Israel on the Shah's opponents inside and outside Iran. Before the revolution SAVAK had been in the habit of torturing those suspected of revolutionary sympathies.

* See p. 319.

The PLO further overplayed its hand by asking Teheran to give the organization a base on an island in the Strait of Hormuz, controlling the entrance to the Persian Gulf. The intention was to use the position as a potential threat to ships carrying oil to the West, as a way of raising the political stakes with Washington. The organization had already asked Yemen to let it set up a base on an island called Dahlak in the strait of Bab El-Mandeb at the entrance to the Red Sea. The request was granted, giving the PLO a potential ability to harass Israeli shipping heading for Eilat. The organization thought that the two islands could become strategic keys to the gateways to the Gulf and the Red Sea. Such notions would have been ambitious even for a major regional power. Teheran did not comply with the request.

All these developments were followed by informers working for the US embassy in Teheran, and the information was passed on to Mossad under a US–Israeli intelligence cooperation agreement. The extent of the US spying network came to light after the occupation of the embassy by Revolutionary Guards in November 1979. Although embassy staff shredded most of the documents before being taken hostage, Iranian students patiently reassembled the thousands of slivers of paper into complete reports. The documents showed, among other matters, that the Americans were aware of the request for a base at Hormuz and were monitoring the role of Palestinians in training the Revolutionary Guards.

A document marked 'Secret', dated 22 May 1979, said that large numbers of Iranians had approached the PLO office in Teheran offering to go to Palestine to fight. The volunteers had been registered but there were no current plans to send them to Palestine. Precise locations were given of three places where a PLO team was carrying out training. The informer, referred to as B/1, also said that efforts were being made to lobby Khomeini to cut diplomatic relations with Egypt. Another document dated 6 September 1979 said: 'The PLO is able to play an important role in current events in Iran.'

The students also found internal warnings to US staff to be on guard against possible Palestinian attacks. One such telegram referred to a statement made by Arafat after the Camp David accords of September 1978. 'Carter's signature will cost him his interests in the Arab region,' Arafat was quoted as saying on 19 September. A statement two days later by George Habash was more direct: 'All American interests in the

Arab area [are considered] as legitimate targets for Arab and Palestinian revolutionary movements.'

Another document, marked 'Secret' but not shredded, gave a US assessment of the relative strengths of the various Palestinian movements at the end of 1978. It said that Fatah had 8000 to 10,000 members and was about four times as big as the next largest Palestinian organization.

> Fatah's . . . extensive military and political training programme has a broad curriculum covering everything from military to commando to terrorist subjects. Fatah has access to training by a variety of Arab and Warsaw Pact countries, including helicopter and fighter-plane pilot training, underwater instruction, [and training] in security and intelligence.
>
> Fatah's arsenal, the most sophisticated in the Palestinian resistance movement, possesses a wide range of weaponry from . . . Kalashnikov rifles and hand grenades to 155-millimetre towed field artillery, surface to air missiles and high-grade explosives. Reports in late 1978 indicate the possibility that Fatah soon might have access to transport aircraft and a small submarine.

The US assessment also said that Black September at its height in 1972/73 had about 300 people, but had been dormant since 1975.

By the spring of 1980 it was clear that the prolonged captivity of American hostages in Teheran could cost President Carter his chances of re-election.* The PLO attempted to exploit Carter's weakness by offering to use its influence with Teheran in return for US recognition of the PLO. Arafat visited Khomeini and sought to persuade him to allow the organization to gain acceptance with the Americans in this way. Khomeini, who regarded the United States as the 'Great Satan', was deeply angered by the PLO chairman's approach. He later told me that he felt the Palestinian revolution was trying to sell the Iranian revolution.†

Khomeini was also shocked by the excesses of Palestinian diplomats in Teheran, whose behaviour was no more abstemious than that of some Western envoys. The fact that Palestinians drank whisky and

* See p. 289.

† The hostages were held for 444 days in all, and were only released in January 1981, when Ronald Reagan came to office.

frequented women would not have caused offence in most capitals, but in Teheran higher standards were expected. The imam realized that the PLO representatives were guerrillas, not sheikhs, but felt that allies of the Iranian revolution should be more discreet.

In September 1980 Iraq's Saddam Hussein launched a massive attack against Iran, precipitating a devastating eight-year war. The following year, when thousands of young Iranians were dying in the defence of their country, Arafat attempted to mediate between the Iraqi and Iranian leaders. His involvement infuriated Khomeini, who felt that Arafat had no right to remain neutral in what the Iranian leader considered to be a struggle between good and evil.*

By 1981 nearly all the Iranians trained by the PLO before the revolution had been squeezed out of office or killed. The PLO's failure to build relationships with other Iranian leaders, and its lack of respect and diplomacy, cost it all the goodwill which had been earned before 1978. Once again the Palestinian leadership felt isolated and rejected, with no country in the region willing to provide the political, military and moral support they needed. Lebanon, where the PLO had made its headquarters since 1970, was an ever more unwilling host, tolerating the organization's presence only because central government had almost collapsed. The lessons of Black September had not been learned: the PLO was now a state within the Lebanese state, and therefore a threat to forces more powerful than itself.

* Arafat later sided with Iraq (se p. 365).

5

The PLO in Lebanon

When Mark Sykes and Georges Picot redrew the map of the Middle East in 1916, what is now Lebanon was shown as part of a larger area which France would administer as it wished. After World War I the Sykes–Picot agreement was modified,* but France kept the right to reorganize that part of the defunct Ottoman empire. The borders which emerged during the French mandate were intended to suit the Maronite Catholic population, which mostly lived in the Mount Lebanon region.† Had the state of Lebanon been confined to that area, many subsequent problems might have been avoided, but the French decided to add on four Syrian districts with mainly Shi'ite, Sunni or Druze populations. The outcome was a country 120 miles long and thirty to thirty-five miles wide, smaller than Connecticut, which the French considered 'le Grand Liban'.‡

Despite the reckless French disregard for homogeneity, this Maronite island in a sea of Islamic sects had positive aspects. In time a distinctive Lebanese national character developed, an amalgam of different but not necessarily contradictory identities, Arab by affiliation yet Mediterranean in outlook. A country which might have been just a crossroads between Islamic and Christian peoples found itself developing more useful roles. For some, Lebanon

* See p. 38.

† Lebanon as designed by the French was mainly drawn from three of the six small coastal provinces which made up the 'Vilayet of Beirut' under the pre-1918 Turkish administration.

‡ The shape of Lebanon was also influenced by the fact that after Saladin's victory over the Crusaders, the European invaders were confined to a coastal strip. This arrangement became formalized in 1192 under a treaty between Saladin and Richard Coeur de Lion (Richard I of England). The result was that a substantial Christian population remained in coastal areas.

served as Christendom's peephole into the Islamic mind; for others, Lebanon was the Arab world's window on the Mediterranean. As the decades passed the latter became the majority, and that majority increasingly wanted the Arab window to be firmly set in an Arab wall.

Lebanon was above all a country of vitality and excitement. When the economy functioned well, as it did for many years, the ethnic, cultural and religious mix made for a lively society. In those happy years the Lebanese could think of their country as a golden bridge between cultures. When the economy spluttered, as it did when the rich tried to hold back the aspirations of the poor, Lebanon could be the most unruly of colonialism's children.

An agreement was reached during the French era that the Lebanese president should always be a Maronite Christian, as the Maronites were then the majority. The prime minister was invariably to be a Sunni, and the speaker of the National Assembly a Shi'ite. At least one government post was always given to the Druze, and one to the Greek Orthodox community. By the time the French departed in the 1940s, it was clear that the Muslim population was growing faster than the Christians. Because of the political sensitivity of relative population strengths, no further census was taken, and the political system remained unchanged. The arrival of hundreds of thousands of Palestinian refugees after the 1948–49 war altered the balance. By the early 1970s, when the *fedayeen* moved to Lebanon after being chased out of Jordan, the Muslims were almost certainly in a majority, with Shi'ites outnumbering Sunnis.

The Lebanese government was in no position to prevent Palestinian organizations from operating on its territory, because leaders of the various Lebanese communities disagreed on what attitude to take. Within three years the PLO had formed alliances with Lebanese Muslim groups and was beginning to rival the military strength of the Lebanese government. The main Christian party, the Phalange (Kata'ib in Arabic), felt its former dominance being submerged by the increased strength of the Muslims, and was also worried that attacks against Israel from Lebanese territory could give Israel an excuse for occupying rich agricultural areas near the Litani river.

In an interview with Phalange founder Pierre Gemayel in 1975 I asked about rumours of contacts between the party and the Israelis.

He replied: 'I am ready to cooperate with the Devil for the sake of Lebanon.' That cooperation was to have major consequences for his country seven years later.

The fact that Lebanon would have been part of Syria but for the French decision to create a Christian state caused endless complications. Damascus felt it had a right to intervene if events in Lebanon threatened its national security. The destabilizing effect of the PLO's presence made the Syrian government edgy.

By the mid-1970s much of southern Lebanon was under PLO military control, and the organization had a substantial headquarters in Beirut. Several other Palestinian organizations were located in Beirut at the time, with the result that the most right-wing capital in the Middle East became the centre of the most left-wing and adventurist forces.

Meanwhile Lebanon's inherent religious and ethnic tensions were exacerbated by economic factors. The gap between rich and poor in the capital was heightened by an influx of hundreds of thousands of Shi'ites migrating from the south and by large numbers of Palestinian refugees. These groups lived in belts of poverty close to the wealth and luxury of the business districts and smart residential zones.

During a lunch with Lebanese president Suleiman Franjieh at the presidential palace in 1975 the topic of conversation was how much longer the unique Lebanese system could survive. The answer came days later. On 13 April gunmen opened fire on a bus passing through a Christian quarter of Beirut. Twenty-two Palestinian passengers were killed, leading to a spiral of reprisals, followed by further provocations from Christian forces. From the beginning many suspected that the attacks formed part of an Israeli plot to root the Palestinians out of Lebanon.

A coalition of progressive groups, including the PLO, fought back fiercely and achieved major gains against right-wing Christian militias, bringing much of the country under their control by early 1976. Both sides were now taking heavy casualties.

The struggle was watched with concern by Damascus, which understood how easily Lebanon's delicate balance could be upset. If one group succeeded in gaining clear dominance over the others, Lebanon could become an uncomfortable neighbour. In the early stages, when the Maronites appeared stronger, Syria helped the progressives. Later, when Druze leader Kamal Jumblatt* announced that the progressives were close to victory, President Assad felt obliged to rescue the Christians. Assad consulted King Hussein by phone, and the Jordanian monarch begged him not to send troops into Lebanon: 'Please don't get into that political swamp', he said, but Assad felt he could stand aside no longer. From the spring of 1976 Syrian forces began building up a major military presence in Lebanon to prevent the defeat of the Maronites.

The Syrians gained control of most of the country, but heavy fighting continued in Beirut. By late summer the progressives appeared to be losing, and large numbers of Palestinian civilians in a refugee camp were killed. Arafat began to accuse President Assad of responsibility for these reverses. Saudi Arabia then stepped in as a conciliator, and an Arab summit was held in Riyadh in October, followed by a more restricted meeting in Cairo. It was agreed that an Arab peacekeeping force would be established in Lebanon immediately, and that this would include Syrian forces already there. However, no other Arab country sent troops, and the effect was to give Assad's intervention the legitimacy of general Arab approval.

The nineteen-month civil war eased in November, but Lebanon's cohesion as a country had been shattered, more than 50,000 people had been killed, and hundreds of thousands were homeless. The war had not settled the question of Palestinian attacks into Israel from Lebanese territory, which Syria did not want but was unable to prevent. The PLO remained dominant in the border area and in west Beirut, while the Christians retained their strongholds in northern Lebanon and in east Beirut, and Syrian forces kept the balance.

The violent 'truce' thus established was to last for five years, providing a tense peace in central and northern Lebanon, while cross-border attacks and reprisals continued in the south. It was a period of transition for the PLO in which some of the organization's attitudes started to change. Beirut provided a stimulating atmosphere for debate, with commandos mixing freely with intellectuals, poets and anti-war doves. The PLO's internal debate began to breathe more freely, even if the leadership still had to show caution.

At the same time the PLO was becoming financially and physically

* Jumblatt was assassinated in March 1977.

established, and the distractions of city life were making inroads into the organization's guerrilla ethos. The pleasures of war now had to compete with the gentler attractions of Beirut's highly Westernized womenfolk. Many a dashing fighter caught the eye of some equally attractive lady during the Lebanese sojourn. Hassan Salama, one of the most important PLO commanders and son of an important sheikh, fell in love with the Lebanese beauty queen Georgina Rizk and married her.*

The moderating effects of being settled and relatively comfortable were accentuated by contacts with the worlds of big business and merchant banking. Haseeb Sabbagh, chairman and owner of Consolidated, one of the most important contracting companies in the Arab world, was among important businessmen who offered advice during that period. Sabbagh helped the PLO in investing money received from Arab donors,† and his influence tended to strengthen those who favoured contacts with Israel. He was a Christian who dreamed of being buried in Jerusalem, and who wanted to make some contribution to peace as a form of homage to his late wife Claudia. Sabbagh was not in favour of abandoning vital Palestinian aims, but supported a search for peace on fair terms. Apart from advice and financial contributions, he made his personal jet available to carry PLO officials and visitors.

Consolidated worked closely with the large American corporation Bechtel and included a Bechtel representative on its board of directors. That representative was George Shultz, who later became secretary of state in the Reagan administration.‡

Other Palestinian businessmen who assisted the PLO included Abdel-Meguid Shouman, head of the Arab Bank Ltd, Abdel-Mohsen El-Kattan, one of the top contractors in Kuwait, Zein Mayyassi, another big contractor, and several other millionaires. All these men came to the PLO to offer help, to advise on the use of money, and to avoid waste. They also believed that Palestinian big business could have political influence in the West, just as Jewish capitalism had

* Hassan Salama was assassinated by Mossad in 1979.
† The PLO had received between 3 and 5 billion dollars in donations since its creation in 1964.
‡ Caspar Weinberger, Reagan's defense secretary, was one of Shultz's subordinates at Bechtel.

financed the Jewish lobby in the United States. Such men contributed a total of $50 million to a fund which was set up to promote the Palestinian cause, and Sabbagh made a gift of a million dollars to ex-President Carter's Center for Peace in Atlanta, Georgia.

Arafat welcomed the help of Palestinian businessmen, but at the same time he took care to limit what he called their 'trusteeship' of PLO business dealings. The chairman was determined to keep the organization's money under his own control, and succeeded in doing so.

Another development during the 1977–1981 period was that intelligence-gathering became one of the largest aspects of the PLO's operations. Abu Iyad (Salah Khalaf), the PLO intelligence chief, ranked second in the organization after Arafat, and established links with intelligence agencies of other countries, including France and the Soviet Union. Khalaf had contacts with Vincent Canistraro, head of the CIA's anti-terrorist department, including two face-to-face meetings in Italy and Spain.

Every intelligence organization in the region was spying on the Palestinians, and different Palestinian groups were trying to infiltrate each other, creating an atmosphere of mutual suspicion. The PLO intelligence chief succeeded in planting his own agent inside one of the cells of Abu Nidal, the hard-line group which had been set up when Sabri El-Banna broke away from Fatah in 1973.* As a result of Khalaf's triumph El-Banna tried thirty-two of his followers in southern Lebanon and had them executed. The PLO agent who had penetrated the organization later arrived in Egypt seeking asylum. The Egyptian authorities were surprised to find that the request was backed by the CIA representative in Cairo. Egypt refused, but the man was given a cosmetic operation to change his appearance, a new identity, and a change of nationality.

The PLO also found itself being asked to carry out secret missions which had nothing to do with the Palestinian cause. Libyan intelligence asked Khalaf to send a hit team to assassinate a former member of the Libyan Revolutionary Council who had been minister of the interior. Khalaf refused, and complained to Muammar Gadaffi personally. He

* Abu Nidal was both Sabri El-Banna's *nom de guerre* and the name of the group.

managed to convince the Libyan leader that the Palestinian resistance should not be used as a hired gun.

El-Banna (Abu Nidal) was once asked to arrange an arms deal for Iraq involving 700 armoured cars, and succeeded in doing so. Most of the Palestinian groups became involved in terrorism against non-Israeli targets, which did nothing to help the cause. Bit by bit the movement was becoming sucked into diversions, and the submerged part of the PLO involved in unnecessary activities was outstripping the more visible part in southern Lebanon.

The collapse of Lebanese central authority made Beirut a magnet for terrorist organizations and liberation movements from all over the world. The Palestinians found themselves cooperating with the Baader Meinhof gang from West Germany, the Red Brigades from Japan and Italy, and the Irish Republican Army. Some of these organizations established links with each other and even exchanged personnel. The PFLP team which carried out the hijacking of an Air France plane to Entebbe in 1976 included two Germans.*

By the late 1970s Palestinian organizations were devoting as much effort to spying, liaising with other organizations and plotting terrorist spectaculars as to their more traditional activities. *Fedayeen* attacks against Israel continued, but at a slower pace because the Lebanese–Israeli border was now more difficult to penetrate. After the 1975–76 civil war Major Saad Haddad, a Lebanese Christian, had established a militia to control the border area, with finance and political backing from Israel. Palestinians still managed, however, to slip through Haddad's lines and conduct small operations, and the Israelis were determined to stop these attacks. Several Arab countries were given advance warning in discreet ways that a major operation to purge southern Lebanon of *fedayeen* was being planned. An attack on an Israeli bus in March 1978 provided a pretext, and Israeli forces poured across the border.

When Ismail Fahmy, the Egyptian foreign minister, phoned Sadat in the early morning to tell him that news agencies were reporting a large-scale operation, Sadat sounded irritated. 'You wake me up to tell me that the Palestinians got spanked in southern Lebanon? You should have left me to sleep,' Sadat laughed before putting down the

* See p. 316.

receiver, leaving his foreign minister open-mouthed in astonishment. Someone must have tipped off the president in advance. Operation Litani, as the Israelis called their first major invasion of southern Lebanon, destroyed hundreds of homes and killed many civilians, but did not achieve its main aims. The PLO moved further north and waited until June, when the Israelis withdrew and were replaced by the UN Interim Force in Lebanon (UNIFIL). The situation was not suited to effective UN peacekeeping, and soon southern Lebanon reverted to the pre-March pattern, with Haddad's forces acting as the buffer between the Palestinians and Israel.

In the early 1980s Hezbollah and Amal, the two Lebanese Shia groups which had been formed after the disappearance of Imam Mousa El-Sadr,* became highly active in southern Lebanon. This alarmed the Christian population and President Elias Sarkis, who had succeeded Suleiman Franjieh after the 1975–76 civil war. Looking for an explanation of the phenomenon, Christian leaders came to the facile conclusion that Iran was using its links with Lebanese Shi'ites to export the revolution to Lebanon.

Several other developments during the period 1979–81 added to the confusion. The PLO fell out with the Druze and Lebanese Muslim militias with which it had been in alliance in 1975–76. The Christians turned against the Syrians and demanded their withdrawal from Syria. Meanwhile a serious dispute arose between the Phalange and another major Christian party led by former president Franjieh. The disintegration of order was exploited by gangs of heavily armed bandits who sacked shops and banks for purely monetary gain.

Feeling the chaos of 1975–76 returning, the Christian population began casting about for a tough leader who would be willing to work with Israel to neutralize what they saw as the Iranian and Palestinian threat. Despite the row between the rival Christian parties, the Christian militias, totalling about 30,000 men, had been united since 1976. The combined units, known as Lebanese Forces, were led by Bashir Gemayel, younger son of the Phalange leader Pierre Gemayel. By 1981 Bashir Gemayel was emerging as a candidate to succeed President Sarkis, whose term had only one more year to run. The Lebanese Forces chief had the image of personal toughness which the Christians

* See pp. 328–9.

were looking for, and he was also the candidate who appealed to Israel, because of long-standing contacts with the Phalange. Menachem Begin felt confident that if Gemayel won the election, relations between Israel and Lebanon could be conducted on a new basis. Since the time of David Ben-Gurion, Israel had dreamt of cooperating with a strong Christian government in Lebanon, but no suitable partner had emerged. Now, it seemed, a prospect was emerging of a Jewish–Christian alliance on the eastern shores of the Mediterranean.

6

Unheeded Warnings

Towards the end of the PLO's stay in Lebanon several channels of contact with Jewish figures were in progress. The Socialist International link, in which Austria's Chancellor Bruno Kreisky and Dr Essam El-Sartawie* played leading roles, was continuing to expand. Kreisky sought to create a wide base for contacts by introducing Sartawie to as many European leaders as possible, including Willy Brandt, François Mitterrand and several Scandinavian leaders, who were well placed to act as intermediaries without attracting international press attention. He also arranged for Arafat to attend a Socialist International meeting, but insisted that this should be done without publicity, not wanting to offend Sadat, who was still continuing his peace efforts but had nothing further to offer Israel.

After laying this basis Kreisky began trying to arrange for Sartawie to meet Israeli opposition leaders. This was difficult, because of an Israeli law making contacts with the PLO a criminal offence. The price of negotiations could be a fine and imprisonment for the Israeli party and death for any Palestinian representative, as the assassinations of Hammami in London and Kalak in Paris in 1978 had shown.† Despite these warnings Sartawie took few precautions, and his growing web of links began to attract attention. Farouk Kaddoumi made a stop in Paris on the way to a UN meeting in 1981 and used the opportunity to warn Sartawie to be careful. Arafat had given authorization for the contacts, but this did not mean that he would provide political support if word leaked out. Sartawie received a similar warning about the need for precautions from Kreisky, who added that the Palestinian academic

* See pp. 323–4.
† See p. 325.

could always seek the help of Austrian embassies wherever he was, if he were in danger. Sartawie, who was a member of the PLO Executive but had no official post in Paris, felt entitled to meet anyone he wished, and did not take the warnings seriously.

Early in 1981 Kreisky arranged a meeting in Paris between Sadat and a group of influential British and French Jews. 'Every one of them feels he is a King David, so I think you should see them,' Kreisky explained. Those present at the meeting at the Palais de Marny on 12 February included Sir Siegmund Warburg, the British merchant banker, Baron Alain de Rothschild, the French banker, and Lord Goodman, the lawyer and Master of University College, Oxford. They listened and asked questions, with the exception of Siegmund Warburg, who said little. Afterwards one of Sadat's aides asked Warburg why he had remained silent. 'Because when you are in the presence of people who make history, you only listen,' the aide later quoted Warburg as saying. An idea raised during the meeting was that the prominent Jewish figures should visit Israel for talks with Begin. When Warburg was asked whether he would be prepared to join such an expedition he replied: 'I don't want to talk to a man who has forgotten how to listen.'*

Five days before flying to Paris, Sadat asked Said Kamal, the PLO ambassador to Cairo, to come to the presidential palace. The invitation came as a surprise, because although Kamal held several important posts he was rarely granted an audience.† The rift between Arafat and Sadat probably lay behind the low level of contact.

The president drew the ambassador's attention to a propaganda campaign which the PLO had been waging against Egypt since the 1979 Egypt–Israel treaty. 'My son, you are giving me hell, but some day you will be obliged to do the same thing,' Sadat said. 'I don't know whether I will live long enough to give you advice at the proper moment on how to deal with the Israelis. In case something happens to me, I want to give you some clues.'

Sadat's advice was not to try to deal with Israel through Washing-

* A meeting between the same group of leading Jewish figures and Dr Sartawie was held afterwards.

† In addition to being ambassador to Egypt, Kamal was also a member of the Palestine National Congress and of the PLO Executive Committee, and assistant secretary general of the Arab League.

ton, and not to go directly to the Israeli government. The best way, he said, was to approach the Jewish establishment, which would know what to do. Sadat instructed Kamal to make a note of an important contact: Stephen Cohen, director of an American academic institute dealing with Middle East studies, a body which had links with all the major Zionist and Jewish organizations in the United States.* The president felt that Cohen was best placed to put the PLO in touch with appropriate Jewish people who were not members of the Israeli government. Any approach to Washington should come after, not before, entering into contact with the Jewish establishment.

Soon after receiving this advice, Kamal was invited to an academic discussion in Cairo and found that Cohen was present. The two men were introduced and held several meetings. News of these contacts quickly leaked out and there was a row within the PLO leadership. Arafat felt obliged to dissociate himself and to dismiss Kamal from his ambassadorship, but first he contacted Kamal and agreed on a damage-limitation strategy. It was arranged that the ambassador would be summoned to Beirut for an investigation of the facts, and would refuse to go, so that he could be dismissed for disobedience rather than for the contacts. After Arafat's announcement the contacts resumed, but Kamal no longer officially represented the PLO.

Cohen invited Kamal to a meeting between Arab and Israeli academics in New York and hinted on the phone that there was a good chance of useful exchanges. Kamal suggested that Cohen should redirect the invitation to Sartawie, who had more experience of such contacts, but Cohen objected that Sartawie's activities had become too widely known. Cohen said that the situation in Israel was not ripe for the high-level contacts Sartawie was attempting to arrange, but prospects were opening at other levels. Kamal replied that he would have to seek authorization from the PLO chairman.

Kamal phoned Arafat in Beirut, but was unable to speak to him without being overheard by others. Arafat tended to surround himself with officials and advisers and conduct his business openly, with the idea that no one could accuse him of hiding anything. Realizing that the conversation was being overheard, Kamal said: 'I have been invited

* In 1994 Stephen Cohen was the director of the Montreal Center for Middle East Peace.

to a congress which is not really a congress,' and then gave a code name for Cohen. Arafat was silent for some minutes. Then he shouted down the phone: 'God is Great. Apply the rule of the commander and soldier.' This was a way of saying that Kamal was free to attend the New York congress, but on his own responsibility, not Arafat's. If the contacts bore fruit Arafat would provide political support; if not, Kamal would be on his own.

Kamal also consulted Kaddoumi, who advised him to attend the conference in the company of another PLO official, so that the responsibility would not fall on Kamal alone if word of any contacts got out. Kamal felt, however, that this would increase the risks of being discovered. Kaddoumi also advised him not to put anything in writing, and especially not to write to Arafat. Egyptian officials urged Kamal to accept Cohen's invitation, and eventually he did so.

The effort expended in deciding whether to attend was scarcely repaid by the results. Despite much talk about peace no serious contacts with Israelis took place in New York, and Kamal returned to Egypt convinced that Israel was not yet ready to do business. This perception proved to be accurate, for Israel was secretly planning an invasion of Lebanon with the aim of destroying the PLO or forcing it to leave the country.

An important factor in the timing of the invasion was the completion of Israel's withdrawal from Sinai under the three-year timetable set by the Egypt–Israel treaty of 1979. Begin realized that an invasion of Lebanon prior to withdrawal from Sinai might arouse suspicions that Israel did not plan to leave Egypt. The treaty was a political prize of great value to the Israeli prime minister, and the neutralization of Egypt would not be complete until the treaty's terms had been implemented. A dispute remained over the Taba area, but that matter was small enough to be dealt with separately.

The last Israeli troops left Sinai on 25 April 1982 and were replaced by a US-led multinational peacekeeping force. To the surprise of many of his supporters, Begin also implemented the agreement to dismantle settlements at El-Arish, the 15,000 settlers being relocated in Israel or in other occupied territories. This aroused strong opposition in Israel, but Begin thought the price worth paying.

Long before withdrawal from Sinai was completed, Israel began passing messages to Egypt to expect an operation against the PLO.

The purpose of these warnings was to reduce the risk of any Egyptian military intervention to rescue the PLO. By the early autumn of 1981 Sadat knew that an invasion of Lebanon was likely, but understood that Israeli forces would not penetrate more than forty kilometres into Lebanese territory. He was also receiving advice from the United States that Israeli patience was near breaking point. Wanting to advise Arafat of the danger, Sadat summoned Kamal and asked him to convey an urgent message to Beirut. Without mentioning the specific information about a forty-kilometre invasion, Sadat pointed out that the PLO was surrounded by hostile Israeli, Syrian and Christian forces, and would inevitably be squeezed between them. 'I can foresee lots of bloodshed in Lebanon. Get out while you can,' Sadat warned. The warning was not heeded, and Sadat did not live long enough to repeat it.

Egypt was passing through a tense, unhappy period. A law had been passed limiting free speech, and many felt that a police state was emerging. Sadat ordered the arrest of hundreds of intellectuals, journalists and politicians in 1981,* and a fierce campaign was conducted to stamp out certain Islamic fundamentalist groups. The Arab rumour-mill was rife with whispers of plots to assassinate the president, some of which were well-founded. It was later established that eleven different groups had been looking for ways of killing Sadat.

Arafat was aware of the rumours, most of which originated in Beirut, and realized that if Sadat were killed, the organization would be blamed. The PLO had been accused of involvement in earlier conspiracies. Arafat, Abu Iyad and other members of the PLO Executive Committee felt that Sadat should be told of the rumours, and that the PLO should show that it was not involved in any plots.

Arafat instructed Kamal to approach Osman Ahmed Osman, father-in-law of Sadat's daughter, who had accompanied the president on the visit to Jerusalem, and pass on the information. Kamal decided, however, to approach Sadat directly. This was not easy, because the president's staff were reluctant to give an appointment, and demanded to know why the ex-ambassador wanted to see the president. Said Kamal insisted that his information could only be given in person, and eventually obtained a five-minute appointment at 8 a.m. the following

* The author was among those imprisoned without trial on suspicion of opposing government policy.

morning at the president's home. Sadat was in a brisk mood and did not invite Kamal to sit down. 'What is it, Said?'

Kamal showed him the message from Beirut. Sadat glared at it with contempt.

'Ha! Tell Arafat to look after his own safety.' And the audience was over.

A few days earlier an army lieutenant named Khaled Ahmed Shawki El-Islambouli had been ordered to lead a detachment of twelve artillery guns and their trailers in a military parade on 6 October to mark the eighth anniversary of the crossing of the Suez Canal at the start of the Yom Kippur War. Islambouli was a member of a small group of Islamic fundamentalists which was loosely connected with many similar cells. These groups had secretly agreed earlier in the year that Sadat should be condemned to death. A sheikh was asked whether it was lawful to shed the blood of a ruler who did not rule according to God's ordinances, and had replied affirmatively. This was taken as a '*fatwah*', or religious ruling, conferring legitimacy upon any assassination attempt.

Islambouli knew that a *fatwah* placed a special responsibility upon anyone who might have an opportunity to implement it. 'Let God's will be done,' he said when ordered to take part in the parade. During the thirteen days between that decision and 6 October, Islambouli devised a complicated plot. Three members of his gun crew were released on various pretexts and replaced with three 'security officers', who were in fact members of Islambouli's fundamentalist group. On the morning of the parade an officer of the Presidential Guard ordered that all strikers and firing pins should be removed from weapons carried by soldiers in the parade. Each unit commander would be personally responsible for the safekeeping of these items. As the commander of his unit, Islambouli was able to put his 'security officers' in charge of collecting and guarding the firing pins and strikers, and of smuggling some of them into the parade, so that the conspirators would have fully operational sub-machine guns.

When Islambouli's truck drew level with the reviewing stand where Sadat was sitting among his generals and foreign ambassadors, the lieutenant drew a pistol and forced the driver to stop. The four conspirators then leapt out and began firing and hurling grenades. Islambouli rushed into the stand and slaughtered Sadat at point-blank range with a long burst of sub-machinegun fire. Seven other people were killed and 28 wounded.

An analysis of the interrogation of Islambouli and his colleagues uncovered three reasons for the assassination. The first was that existing Egyptian laws were not consistent with Islamic law. Secondly, peace had been made with the Jews, a reference to the Egyptian–Israeli treaty. Thirdly, many Muslim leaders in Egypt had been arrested, persecuted and humiliated. In Western thought this would be considered a mixture of religious and political motives, but Islam accepts no such distinction. The four conspirators were tried and executed.

The assassination of Sadat sundered an Egyptian mental barrier which had protected every previous Egyptian pharaoh, ptolemy, king and president against assassination by ordinary mortals. Menachem Begin, whose lack of generosity had deprived Sadat of concessions which might have saved his life, attended the funeral. Jimmy Carter, Richard Nixon and Gerald Ford were present, but the millions who had mourned for Nasser in 1970 stayed away. Sadat had been popular with the White House and the Western media, but not with his own people.

Six months after Sadat's death, Kamal received another phone call from Stephen Cohen. Cohen said he was coming to Cairo and wanted to discuss an important matter. Kamal informed Egyptian intelligence and sought clearance from Beirut to meet the visitor. Cohen arrived in Cairo and stayed in a small hotel, to avoid drawing attention to himself. When the two men met, Cohen asked Kamal to take him to a modest restaurant, as a further precaution against being noticed. Over lunch Cohen explained that he had come to ask for an appointment to see Arafat and Khalaf in Beirut. Despite his lack of official status, Kamal felt that this might be possible, and asked whether Cohen would like to see Abu Jihad (Khalil El-Wazir) as well. Cohen replied: 'No, I have explored his ideas.' Kamal was astonished to realize that Cohen had already had contacts with Abu Jihad, who was then Arafat's deputy.

'What would be the purpose of a meeting with Arafat and Abu Jihad now?' Kamal asked. The reply came in the form of another question:

'If Sharon [the Israeli defence minister] attacked Lebanon and pressed the invasion as far as Beirut, how much resistance could the PLO put up?'

'I am no military man, but it would depend on the size of Sharon's forces and the extent of Arab and international reaction to such an attack,' Kamal replied.

Cohen said that Sharon would probably attack with eleven battalions in the near future. This was not privileged information, but reflected speculation which had been appearing in Israeli newspapers. However, the newspapers had spoken of a forty-kilometre invasion, and Cohen's suggestion that Sharon's forces might reach Beirut was new to Kamal.

The most important part of Cohen's analysis dealt with international reaction to the Israeli raid: 'I can tell you right now that neither the Arab countries nor the Soviet Union will do anything. The attack has been agreed at the highest levels, including the Arabs and Moscow. Everybody is fed up with you and what you are doing. They are all convinced that there is no solution unless you get out of Lebanon and recognize Resolution 242,' Cohen said.

After the meeting Kamal consulted the director of Egyptian intelligence, to ask what he thought of Cohen's remarks. The director, who held the rank of general, confirmed that Egyptian intelligence was aware that Sharon's attack might be carried as far as Beirut. Kamal immediately sent a message to Arafat through an Egyptian academic. The reply arrived the same day, and consisted of only three words (four in English): 'Let the guest come.' Kamal was again astonished when the Egyptian authorities instantly provided a plane to fly Cohen to Beirut. The plane then waited in Beirut to fly him straight back to Cairo afterwards.

In a meeting in Arafat's bunker, Cohen asked the PLO chairman and Salah Khalaf how long the PLO could resist the kind of attack Israel was contemplating. Both men were of the opinion that the PLO could hold out for six months, and said they would not mind if Israel went ahead because such an operation would lead to pandemonium throughout the Middle East.

Cohen made it clear that the Israelis were not worried about the regional reaction, and added: 'I doubt if you can stand up to an attack for six months.'

Arafat replied: 'We can unless we are stabbed in the back by the

Lebanese. In any circumstances, it will not be less than three months.'

Hosni Mubarak, who had succeeded Sadat as president, sent Arafat a further warning on 28 May 1982. The message said that Sharon would enter southern Lebanon within a few days and would not limit the invasion to forty kilometres.

'Maybe you would find it best to avert the attack now by making a political move,' Mubarak suggested. 'The time has come to put your sword in its sheath, before it is too late.' The warning went unheeded.

7

Last Stand in Beirut

Throughout the early months of 1982 General Ariel Sharon, the Israeli defence minister, sought to prepare Washington for the coming explosion in Lebanon. Numerous Israeli–US meetings were held, and Sharon gained the impression that Washington would not object too strenuously to an attack on Beirut with the aim of crushing the PLO. The Egyptian ambassador to Washington was among many who later felt that Sharon had reached a secret deal with Alexander Haig, the US secretary of state. According to Shamir's memoirs,* Haig was mainly concerned that the invasion should be seen to be justified by some major provocation. At the time nothing major was happening, as the Israeli–Lebanese border had been mostly quiet since a ceasefire arranged by American negotiator Philip Habib in July 1981.

On 3 June 1982 an Abu Nidal hit squad gunned down Shlomo Argov, Israeli ambassador to Britain, in front of the Dorchester Hotel in London. Argov survived, and Abu Nidal (Sabri Banna) had long since severed his links with the PLO, but the Israelis decided they had the necessary pretext. The attack began with bombing raids against PLO positions in Beirut on 5 June, in which 150 people were killed and forty-five injured. The PLO responded with a cross-border artillery bombardment, and on 6 June Israel sent six divisions into Lebanon, supported by air strikes and landings from the sea. The advancing tanks and infantry attacked not only Palestinians but also some Syrian units. The aims were to demonstrate Israel's supremacy in the region, to break the fighting power of the PLO and reduce its political influence, and to reorganize Lebanon politically, installing a puppet government under a pliable president.

* *Summing Up: An Autobiography*, Weidenfeld & Nicolson, London, 1994.

As Israeli forces swept northwards President Ronald Reagan sent a stiff note to Israeli prime minister Begin calling for a ceasefire to begin the following day, 10 June, and warning that refusal by Israel would pose a serious threat to world peace. The US president's letter was sent against the advice of Haig, who felt that Israel should be allowed to complete the destruction of the PLO. This brought to a head differences between Reagan and the secretary of state, who some regarded as a potential future president. Haig overplayed his hand and was replaced during the crisis by George Shultz. Meanwhile US diplomats sought to convince Egypt and Saudi Arabia that 'Operation Peace for Galilee', as the Israelis called the attack, was an understandable response to a long period of PLO harassment.

The rapid Israeli advance continued and Sharon's forces laid siege to Beirut for two and a half months, with massive shelling and aerial attacks on PLO and Amal positions and on Palestinian and Shia residential areas. At one point General Sharon's command tent was only a few hundred yards from the presidential palace. Sharon sent a message asking President Sarkis to come and see him. Sarkis replied that he would not go voluntarily, and Sharon would have to take him by force. The Lebanese government asked Washington to organize a multinational force in Lebanon to enable the PLO to depart. Israel was prepared to go along with this arrangement provided the United Nations was not involved. Contacts continued throughout July, with President Sarkis acting as an intermediary between Arafat and American negotiator Philip Habib. Meanwhile the fighting continued.

Arafat's forces and Shia groups resisted the Israeli offensive bravely, but received no help from the Druze militia and Lebanese Muslim forces, which were now opposed to the PLO's presence in Lebanon. Syria was in a position to help the PLO but remained on the sidelines. Television coverage of the fighting had a political impact in the United States, where support for Israel's action plummeted. The publication of pictures of a Palestinian child being hit by bomb shrapnel brought shocked reactions, and Senator Charles Percy of Illinois said that US aid to Israel was being used to finance the slaughter. Ripples of these criticisms reached Israel, where Begin eventually felt obliged to dissociate himself from Sharon's handling of the war.

Stephen Cohen phoned Said Kamal in Cairo on 25 July and told him that PLO resistance was much stronger than the Israelis had expected.

Cohen, who appeared to be acting for the Israeli government, asked Kamal to fly to the United States for talks. As Kamal was no longer the PLO's ambassador he felt a need for authorization, and consulted a colleague who had been nominated to replace him. The colleague's advice was to speak to Arafat in Beirut, but the PLO chairman could not be reached by phone. Kamal spoke instead to Hani El-Hassan, a counsellor to Arafat, who gave him the blessing of those who could be contacted. 'Our brothers say "God speed." Go if you wish, and keep in touch by satellite.' Hassan also asked Kamal to contact Esmat El-Meguid, the Egyptian permanent representative to the UN.*

Before Kamal's arrival in New York at the beginning of August, Cohen spoke to Meguid and put forward what was apparently an offer from Israel. Cohen proposed direct contacts between the PLO and Israel, and said that if the PLO recognized UN Resolution 242, face-to-face talks between Israeli and PLO liaison officers could take place immediately, on the lines of the Kilometre 101 talks between Israel and Egypt held immediately after the Yom Kippur War. The offer seemed to reflect Israel's embarrassment over the unexpectedly long time Sharon was taking to break the PLO, and over the international outcry against the rape of Beirut.

Meguid replied that he had no authority to negotiate and had only been instructed to facilitate contacts. However, over lunch at Meguid's home in New York Cohen repeated the offer of direct talks to Kamal, who had just arrived from Cairo. A misunderstanding arose at this point, in that Kamal was not aware that the offer of talks similar to Kilometre 101 was conditional on PLO acceptance of Resolution 242.

After lunch the three men used a satellite link from the Egyptian mission in New York to contact Arafat's satellite station in Beirut.

'Which of our brothers is there?' Kamal asked.

'Nobody from the command,' the operator shouted. Kamal could hear the roar of gunfire in the background.

'I've got a very important message,' Kamal told him.

'All right. Stay where you are and we will call you back.'

Half an hour later the phone rang in the Egyptian mission. Abu Za'im, the PLO security chief, was calling from the satellite station,

* Esmat El-Meguid was later foreign minister of Egypt. In 1992 he became the secretary general of the Arab League.

and Arafat could be heard talking in the background. Kamal heard Arafat say to Abu Za'im: 'Tell him to speak quickly because we cannot stay in one place for more than ten minutes.' The Israelis were using radio direction-finders to follow Arafat's movements through his telephone calls, with the aim of scoring a direct artillery or bombing hit. The time needed to identify an exact position from a phone call was less than a quarter of an hour.

Kamal explained the Israeli proposition, and could hear Arafat discussing it with other leaders whose voices he recognized. It appeared that several members of the PLO leadership were in the room listening to the call. 'But we have heard all this before,' Kamal heard one of them say.

Not realizing that the Israeli offer was conditional, Kamal tried to persuade the PLO leadership to agree to the talks, arguing that this would amount to Israeli recognition. Secondly, the talks would take several days, delaying the moment of PLO withdrawal and allowing time for an orderly evacuation. Abu Za'im promised a quick decision and asked where he could contact Kamal.

An hour later Kamal received a further call, this time at his hotel on 42nd Street in Manhattan. Abu Za'im told him that the proposal had been rejected, but gave no explanation. Later it emerged that the PLO leadership had received the same offer previously through another source (probably Habib), together with the condition about Resolution 242. Arafat is also thought to have received a message from the Egyptian government saying that the Israeli offer was serious.

Some PLO officials subsequently recounted the story omitting the condition about Resolution 242, implying that at that stage the Israelis were ready to concede implicit recognition of the PLO. This was not a true reflection of the Israeli offer. The proposal for meetings between PLO and Israeli liaison officers was solely a practical arrangement to facilitate PLO withdrawal after the organization had recognized the UN resolution.

The fighting continued and American media coverage of the battle became steadily more hostile to Israel, putting President Reagan under pressure to distance himself from Begin. Three senior members of the World Zionist Congress flew to Jerusalem to see the Israeli prime minister and told him that the invasion had caused severe embarrassment for the Jewish lobby in the United States in its relations with the White House.

'You misled us and you misled the US administration,' the Jewish leaders told the prime minister. Begin blamed Sharon and suggested that the defence minister had taken Alexander Haig's lack of objection to the invasion plan as a form of consent. He also said that the operation had required a bigger military commitment than expected.

On 1 August Israeli forces stepped up their artillery and aerial bombardment of Beirut with massive intensity, while Israeli tanks entered the southern outskirts of the city. Reagan told Israeli foreign minister Yitzhak Shamir that he was losing patience, but this warning made little impression on the Israeli government. When Philip Habib tried to set up proximity talks, with different parties on different floors of a building and US coordinators shuttling between them, Begin rejected the arrangements as 'totally unacceptable'.

Israeli gunners were shelling Beirut day and night, but the PLO and Amal continued to fight back, and pressures grew in the Arab world for Syria to intervene on the PLO's side. Just when Syrian and Israeli forces seemed on the brink of engagement, Israel launched a pre-emptive air strike and destroyed seventeen Syrian missile batteries. Syria stuck to its former stance of non-involvement.

The PLO's withdrawal was now only a matter of time, but they had nowhere to go. Sharon asked an Egyptian intermediary to persuade Arafat to lead the PLO back to Jordan, and said that if he accepted Israel would force King Hussein to make way for the organization.

'One speech by me will make King Hussein realize that the time has come to pack his bags,' Sharon said.

The message was passed to Arafat, who asked the intermediary to give Sharon an immediate reply:

1. Jordan is not the home of the Palestinians.
2. You are trying to exploit the agony of the Palestinian people by turning a Palestinian–Lebanese dispute into a Palestinian–Jordanian contradiction.

Arafat also suggested that Sharon hoped to ignite a Jordanian–Palestinian conflict to give Israel an excuse for occupying the east bank of the Jordan. The intermediary read Arafat's reply to Sharon, who responded with an obscene phrase in Arabic.

An arrangement was eventually negotiated by Philip Habib for the PLO to withdraw to Tunisia. A first contingent of fighters left by sea on 21 August 1982, and in the next four days most others followed. The withdrawal of Arafat was delayed until 30 August, when he boarded a Greek merchant ship escorted by a Greek warship, with air cover provided by the US Sixth Fleet. Two days later a final PLO contingent departed on another ship, bringing the total evacuation by sea to 8500 men. In the meantime 2500 more had made the overland journey to Syria and Iraq. Yemen also offered to accept PLO evacuees, but Egypt, Saudi Arabia and the Gulf sheikhdoms refused.

After seventy-seven days of heavy fighting the PLO found itself banished from the frontline states to the periphery of the Arab world, 800 miles from Israel. The organization's military strength was shattered, but its pride remained intact. No one had expected an army without a state to stand up to the might of Israel for so long. As Stephen Cohen had predicted, not one Arab state had lifted a finger to help the PLO.

One of the aims of the invasion, apart from crushing the PLO, was to create a climate of fear to coincide with the Lebanese presidential elections. The Israelis wanted the Lebanese parliament, which elects the president, to feel that national survival depended on choosing a president acceptable to Israel. When the parliament met on 23 August to make its choice, the PLO evacuation had begun, but successful completion depended on Israeli cooperation. Parts of Beirut were in ruins and casualties were estimated at 35,000 to 38,000 dead, mostly civilians. Enough deputies were intimidated to bring about the election of Israel's preferred candidate Bashir Gemayel, though only by a majority of a single vote.

Gemayel, a ruthless young man, was very different to his experienced father Pierre, founder of the Phalange. Pierre Gemayel had had contacts with Israelis for years but had not met them personally until the war. Bashir Gemayel, on the other hand, had been working closely with Mossad through the intelligence arm of Lebanese Forces. At the height of the fighting Bashir Gemayel persuaded his father to hold talks with General Raphael Eitan, commander of 'Operation Peace of Galilee' and chief-of-staff of Israeli forces.

Under the Lebanese system a president is elected in August but takes office in September. In the interim, Bashir Gemayel was summoned to see Begin, Shamir and Sharon at Nahariya, a coastal resort in northern Israel. After exchanges of mutual congratulations, Begin began talking about the Israeli army's sacrifices in Lebanon. He claimed that Israel had carried out the operation for the sake of peace in Lebanon and to bring about solid relations between Israel and the Christian Maronites. Begin then proposed a peace treaty between Israel and Lebanon on the lines of the Egyptian–Israeli treaty of 1979.

Bashir Gemayel said that he would need time before he could persuade the Lebanese parliament to accept such a move. There were formalities to be observed, including swearing the oath of office and the formation of a government. Begin listened to these objections with impatience. Israel, he said, wanted a treaty to be signed immediately, without delay. The urgency stemmed from international pressure on Israel to withdraw its forces from Lebanon.

Gemayel, showing more sense than his previous behaviour would have suggested, was reluctant. Begin no longer hid his anger: 'I am astonished that you are hesitating to sign a treaty. I expected you to come to us full of thankfulness and gratitude and instead I find that you are hesitant.'

'I come to you in changed circumstances', Bashir Gemayel replied. 'Now I am president of Lebanon and am tied by institutions.'

Apart from a peace treaty, Begin also wanted a recognized role for Major Saad Haddad, the Christian officer who had been financed by Israel to establish a militia to control the southern border areas of Lebanon.

'Give me a chance to talk to the old folk,' Gemayel said, referring to his father and others of the same generation.

'Our forces are in the heart of Beirut. What you will not give us voluntarily we can take by force,' Begin snapped.

Feeling threatened, Gemayel again pleaded for time to talk to his father and his party, and requested that the meeting with Begin be kept secret. Despite this request the encounter was leaked to Israeli newspapers, which published details as Gemayel returned to Lebanon, placing the president-elect in a difficult situation.

Sharon visited Gemayel and apologized for the leak, but said he wanted a reply to Begin's requests for a treaty and a role for Haddad. Gemayel did not answer immediately. Sharon insisted on having a decision before Gemayel entered the presidential palace. He also discussed an Israeli plan for the expulsion of the 400,000 Palestinian refugees in Lebanon.

Sharon never received answers, because Bashir Gemayel was killed on 14 September by a bomb planted in the home of the Kata'ib (Phalange) Party, where he was meeting with his top aides. Israeli forces used the assassination as a pretext to occupy west Beirut, taking control of areas formerly held by the PLO. Two days later the Lebanese Forces militia, which Gemayel had led, moved into the areas newly seized by Israeli forces and slaughtered 800 Palestinian civilians in two Palestinian refugee camps. The camps, Shatila and Sabra, on the south side of Beirut, came to be seen throughout the world as symbols of Palestinian suffering. The international outcry which followed was accompanied by a sense of shock and revulsion in Israel, where a commission of inquiry was set up under Supreme Court justice Yitzhak Kahan.

After Bashir Gemayel's death the Lebanese parliament elected his elder brother Amin as president. In a position paper dated 10 October 1982 the Israeli cabinet set out terms for withdrawal from Lebanon, and contacts between the two governments began immediately. Amin Gemayel and most of the Maronites were ready to enter into peace with Israel, but understood the difficulties of persuading the Sunnis, Shi'ites and Druze to go along with a treaty. Gemayel contacted President Mubarak and requested Egypt to put its negotiating experience at Lebanon's disposal. The Egyptian government was eager to help, feeling that a Lebanese–Israeli treaty would ease Egypt's isolation as the only Arab country to have made peace with Israel. Many Egyptians continued to regard the late President Sadat as a pioneer rather than a defector from the Palestinian cause, and felt sure that other Arab countries would eventually follow his example. Lebanese negotiators flew to Cairo and were given a crash course in everything the Egyptians had learned while negotiating the 1979 treaty.

Agreement between Lebanon and Israel did not come easily. However much some Maronites might want peace, the need to rebuild a workable consensus between the different Lebanese groups was more important. Gemayel was beginning to realize that no internal reconciliation would be possible if Lebanon entered into a full peace treaty.

While the Lebanese–Israeli negotiations continued, American forces, which had been withdrawn after the PLO's departure, were sent back to resume peacekeeping duties alongside French, British and

Italian troops. The Israelis, meanwhile, ejected the remaining PLO forces who had stayed behind in Tripoli, the Sunni-dominated port in northern Lebanon. The United States then began to expand its role into a more general attempt to put President Gemayel's government firmly in control, but ran into strong resistance from Amal and Hezbollah. In April 1983 a Shia commando drove a lorry loaded with explosives into an American barracks and killed 241 US servicemen, leading to domestic pressure on the Reagan administration to withdraw from Lebanon.

A compromise between Lebanese and Israeli positions was eventually found with American help. The word 'peace' being too sensitive, the two sides entered into a 'non-belligerency' agreement, declared the international boundary between the two states to be inviolable, and agreed on arrangements for Israeli withdrawal. The accord was signed by both countries on 17 May 1983, but contained an inherent flaw. Israeli withdrawal was conditional upon Syria removing its own forces from Lebanon, which Damascus was not prepared to do. The treaty therefore lapsed, and Israeli forces remained. Attacks by Amal and Hezbollah intensified, Reagan decided to withdraw American peacekeeping forces for a second time, and world opposition to Israel's occupation mounted. Inside Israel criticism of the way Sharon's forces had behaved came to a climax in February 1983, when the Kahan commission issued its findings. Sharon and some of his officers were censured by the commission for not having prevented the Shatila and Sabra massacres. The defence minister was forced to resign and was replaced by Moshe Arens.

Sharon was followed on 16 September by Begin, who unexpectedly announced his own resignation. The prime minister was depressed after the recent death of his wife, and the barrage of international and domestic criticism had left him feeling unappreciated.

The war had been a bitter experience for all concerned, leaving deep scars on the Palestinian mind and permanent damage to the PLO's fighting ability. In two years, 1981 and 1982, the organization had lost its relationship with Iran and its position in Lebanon, while its uneasy links with Syria had been further soured. Israel had achieved one of the invasion's three objectives, at a political price which most Israelis considered unacceptably high.

The Lebanese tried to pick up the pieces of their shattered country, and in November 1983 a reconciliation conference was held in Geneva. Although not all parties attended and the atmosphere was far from warm, the conference was a reminder that the Lebanese had a distinctive personality, unlike any other country and yet undeniably Arab in character. That Arab identity was the one point on which all at the conference could agree.

8

1982–1985
Years in Limbo

The Mediterranean city of Tunis, with its palm trees and sea breezes, its tourists and Phoenician ruins, was a hospitable and yet depressing place of exile. Separated by expanses of sea from their roots in Gaza and the west bank, Arafat and the 8000 PLO fighters who had come from Lebanon felt marooned on an Elba of the Arab world. It would henceforth be impossible for them to move a muscle without being observed by the American embassy in Tunis and its omnipresent informers. Habib Bourguiba, the elderly, dogmatic president of Tunisia, regarded the Americans as friends and tended to understand Washington's point of view on the Arab–Israel conflict. Arafat and his men could hardly avoid feeling that their place of exile had been chosen to suit Washington.

The most urgent question was what to do next. Those who, before the expulsion from Lebanon, had wanted contacts with Israel now felt that a negotiated solution was more necessary than ever, but also more difficult, because the PLO had less to offer Israel. Those who had been against contacts felt that Israel should not be rewarded for its aggression. The result was that during the next few years the organization followed two different paths at the same time, neither of which was linked to the American-driven peace process.

The 'doves' made their first open move at a meeting of the Palestine National Congress, held in Algiers just after the expulsion from Lebanon. Dr Essam Sartawie, who had been continuing his contacts in Paris, said that if the PLO continued as before it would be expelled not just to Tunis but to Timbuktu. The time had come to sue for peace, and the PLO should enter into talks with Israel and recognize Resolution 242.

Arafat, who was chairing the meeting, interrupted with shouts of 'Shut up!' but Sartawie continued: 'I am afraid that if my advice is not taken, the present policy is going to lead us to destruction and complete surrender.' Worried that the discussion might lead to disclosure of the secret contacts, Arafat ordered Sartawie's arrest and forcible removal from the meeting.

As Arafat had personally but secretly authorized Sartawie's contacts, this was an injustice. The PLO chairman asked his security chief Abu Za'im to hold Sartawie under house arrest in Tunis, but within two months Sartawie managed to convince Abu Za'im that he should be freed. Za'im interceded with Arafat, who relented, and Sartawie returned to Paris and resumed his contacts.

Encouraged by Bruno Kreisky and others in the Socialist International, Sartawie arranged meetings with members of the Israeli 'Peace Now' movement, including Matityahu Peled, a former air force general, Yuri Avneri, editor of the newspaper *The World Today*, and Yehoshafat Harkabi, an academic and former director of military intelligence.

While these contacts continued, two other important strands in the situation were developing. The Reagan administration, which had produced no important Arab–Israeli peace initiatives during its first year in office, began preparing a new policy.

Meanwhile Arafat was looking for another strong regional partner, feeling that there was no hope of securing justice without military strength. As Egypt had made peace with Israel and relations with Iran and Syria remained tense, the only other country with the right combination of military power and radical ideas was Iraq. Arafat therefore began to build on the relationship he had struck up with President Saddam Hussein two years earlier, at the start of the Iran–Iraq War, hoping to engage Baghdad's commitment as a political and military sponsor of the cause. The PLO chairman made numerous visits to Iraq, and became increasingly involved in the complex relationships between Iraq and its neighbours.

The Iran–Iraq War had transformed the attitudes of Arab sheikhs and kings on the western shores of the Gulf. Before 1980 many had been nervous of Baghdad's military power, but now they looked to

Saddam Hussein as a bulwark against the revolutionary fervour of Iran. Their support for the Iraqi leader was encouraged by Washington, which was clearly on Baghdad's side in the early stages of the war. American policy later became more complicated.*

American officials were not just supportive of Saddam Hussein but seemed willing, within limits, to show an understanding attitude towards Iraqi wishes for territorial adjustments. This emerged when a meeting took place in Madrid between William Casey, director of the CIA, and General Fadel El-Barrack, chief of Iraqi intelligence. The year was 1981, and the Iraqi army had advanced deep into Iran, occupying the whole of Khuzestan, the Iranian province adjacent to south-eastern Iraq and the Iraqi city of Basra. General Barrack told Casey that Baghdad was thinking of annexing the province, which had been part of the Arab world until the end of the nineteenth century.† Two US experts assisting Casey in the meeting objected to this plan, pointing out the risk of causing a regional imbalance. The effect, they said, would be like taking Kurdistan away from Iraq and giving it to Turkey.

General Barrack pointed out that Iraq was almost cut off from the Persian Gulf, having only a short stretch of coastline and no deep-water port. This led the discussion to Kuwait and to Iraq's historical claim. Barrack reminded the Americans that his country considered Kuwait to be a part of Iraq which had been lured away by the British at the end of the nineteenth century. At the time Britain was assembling a ring of dependencies around the Persian Gulf as part of its strategy of controlling waters near the route to India. When the Ottoman empire collapsed at the end of World War I, Britain rewarded the ruling Sabah family of Kuwait for their loyalty by allowing the enclave to remain separate from Iraq.

The CIA director and his assistants listened to General Barrack's

* The US decision to provide Iran with weapons, in the hope of securing the release of US hostages, did not come until the seventh year of the war. In May 1986 Robert McFarlane, the US national security adviser, made the journey to Teheran which marked the start of the 'Iran–Contra' affair.

† The border area between Iraq and Iran marks the meeting point between two distinct cultures. Although linked by a common religion, the Iranians (Persians) belong to a different ethnic and linguistic stock. Arabic, like Hebrew, is a member of the Hamito-Semitic group of languages, while Persian, or Farsi, is an Indo-European language.

remarks about Kuwait without raising objections. They gave the impression of being more concerned about Khuzestan, and mentioned that the US had no treaty obligations to Kuwait. General Barrack emerged from the meeting convinced that Iraq had been given a green light to take over Kuwait.

Later in the decade, when the war turned in Teheran's favour, Kuwait was at constant risk of being overrun by Iranian forces, and there were moments when the Kuwaitis seemed ready to accept Iraqi protection. There is no evidence that the ruling family was aware of the talks between General Barrack and William Casey, but at least two other Gulf rulers knew of them.

The idea that Washington would not really object to the annexation of Kuwait remained in the background of Baghdad's thinking and seeped into subsequent plans. Nine years later that seepage contributed to miscalculations which led to the Gulf War, and to the greatest setback in Arafat's career.

In the early 1980s, however, Arafat saw links with Iraq as a solution to his problems, especially after the withdrawal from Beirut. Saddam Hussein was now the strongest Arab leader with the most powerful army, a man treated with respect by Washington. The PLO chairman could hope that some day Iraq might help the PLO regain the strength it had enjoyed before the fall of Beirut.

At the time there was no contradiction between links with Iraq and a better understanding with Washington, which was Arafat's next most important goal. Although the PLO had been in contact with CIA representatives since 1973, Arafat wanted the legitimacy of an acknowledged relationship. He thought he had taken steps in that direction, first by trying to intercede with Ayatollah Khomeini to obtain the release of US hostages in Iran,* and then by protecting American subjects in Lebanon, firmly opposing the taking of US hostages.

This was an illusion, as Washington had no interest in a relationship with the PLO. Ronald Reagan barely hid his pleasure at the PLO's expulsion from Lebanon, and thought that this had enhanced prospects for peace.† George Shultz had worked out a new approach to Middle

* See p. 332.

† Reagan, in his speech on 1 September 1982, said: 'The Lebanon war, tragic as it was, has left us with a new opportunity for Middle East peace.'

East peace, which became known as the 'fresh start', but he had no intention of involving the PLO. The fresh start formed the basis of a major speech given by Reagan on 1 September 1982, in which the US put forward clear lines of policy on some of the controversial points which had remained unsettled since the 1978 Camp David accords.

One of these issues arose from the deliberate ambiguity of Resolution 242, which called for the 'withdrawal of Israeli armed forces from territories occupied in the recent conflict'. The lack of the word 'the' or 'all' before 'territories' allowed Israel to argue that the UN had not demanded Israel's complete departure. Israeli prime ministers Begin and Shamir refused to accept that the resolution meant that Israel should withdraw from the west bank and Gaza. Reagan rejected the Israeli interpretation: 'It is the United States' position that – in return for peace – the withdrawal provision of Resolution 242 applies to all fronts, including the west bank and Gaza,' he said.

Reagan strongly supported the five-year transitional period envisaged in the Camp David accords, to begin after elections for a self-governing Palestinian authority. The aim, he said, was 'to prove to the Palestinians that they can run their own affairs, and that such Palestinian autonomy poses no threat to Israel's security'. Another question which had remained controversial since the Camp David summit was what the ultimate status of the Palestinians should be at the end of the transitional period. The Palestinians insisted on a Palestinian state, while the 'Eretz Yisrael' lobby continued to want Israeli annexation of the west bank.

Reagan's position was different: 'The United States will not support the establishment of an independent Palestinian state, and we will not support annexation or permanent control by Israel . . . it is the firm view of the United States that self-government by the Palestinians in association with Jordan offers the best chance for a durable, just and lasting peace.'

Reagan called for an immediate freeze on the building of Israeli settlements in the occupied territories, and said that the US would not support the use of any additional land for settlements during the transition period. However, in notes of clarification sent to Begin afterwards, Reagan said: 'We will oppose . . . dismantlement of the existing settlements.'

Shultz mentions in his memoirs* that he 'encouraged' Reagan to make the speech. It is widely believed that the secretary of state wrote it himself.

The Reagan Plan, as it came to be known, was rejected outright by the Israeli government. The Arab world neither accepted nor rejected it, but replied with a counter-proposal which emerged from an Arab summit held at Fez, Morocco. The main element of this plan, known as the Fahd Initiative, was that the Arab world accepted UN Resolution 242, including the right of every country in the region to live in peace. This was an implicit recognition of the state of Israel.† The plan also called for the removal of Israeli settlements, a transitional period of one year (instead of five), and a superpower guarantee of an Arab–Israel agreement.

The Arab world reacted cautiously to Reagan's view that Palestinians should have self-government in association with Jordan. The US president seemed to be reviving the Hashemite claim to the west bank, which had last surfaced in March 1972, when King Hussein proposed that the west bank should be a self-governing sub-state within a United Hashemite Kingdom.‡ That idea had been roundly condemned by Sadat and others. King Hussein was not unhappy with Reagan's remarks, but had to be wary in his own public response. It was important that Washington and not Amman should be seen to make the running.

During talks in Washington in December 1982 Reagan urged King Hussein to enter into talks, and offered the inducement of US military aid. The king then began discussions with Arafat aimed at patching up their dispute and exploring the possibility of a solution based on Reagan's proposal. Arafat was prepared to consider a confederation, in which the west bank and Gaza would be a sovereign state of Palestine linked to Jordan. Hussein, however, wanted a federation, in which Palestine would be subject to Jordanian sovereignty. A federation was more likely to be acceptable to the United States and Israel.

After months of unsuccessful efforts to bridge this gap the king informed President Reagan in April 1983 that the talks had failed, and

* *Turmoil and Triumph: My Years as Secretary of State*, Charles Scribner's Sons, New York, 1993.

† Egypt and Jordan had accepted Resolution 242 in 1967. See pp. 133–5.

‡ See p. 311.

that without agreement with the PLO Jordan could not support the Reagan Plan. This forced a suspension of American efforts.

Meanwhile Dr Sartawie had been continuing his attempts to talk to high-ranking Israelis. Senior figures in the Socialist International believed that Shimon Peres, the chairman of the Israeli Labour Party, would be prepared to talk to Sartawie if adequate secrecy could be arranged. Sartawie, however, continued to see no need for furtiveness. In late March 1983 it became known that both Sartawie and Peres would be attending a meeting of the Socialist International in Portugal the following month.

The day before Sartawie was due to fly from France to Portugal, Egyptian intelligence got wind of an assassination plot. The head of intelligence asked a Palestinian contact to warn Sartawie not to go to Lisbon but to take refuge in Egypt and keep a low profile for a while. The Egyptian embassy in Paris was instructed to issue immediate visas so that Sartawie and his family could leave Paris on a plane the same night.

The Palestinian contact phoned Sartawie and said in Arabic, 'I heard it from the Sparrow,' which is similar to the English phrase 'a little bird told me'. Sartawie would have understood that 'the Sparrow' was a friendly intelligence service.

'Nonsense,' Sartawie said on the open phone line. 'My meeting in Lisbon is very important.' Then he added: 'God save me not only from my enemies but my friends.'

Sartawie flew to Lisbon as planned and then travelled to a hotel in Albufeira, on the Portuguese coast, where the congress was being held. On 10 April 1983 he was assassinated as he emerged from the hotel. Peres was only five metres away from the gory scene.

Among the witnesses was Thorvald Stoltenberg, the Norwegian foreign minister, who had been trying to help Sartawie in his efforts to talk to Peres. The incident profoundly affected Stoltenberg and probably contributed to the highly active peace policy which Norway followed a decade later.

The assassin was a member of Abu Nidal, but many in the Arab world suspected that Mossad was somehow involved. This suspicion sprang from links between the Israeli secret service and those Zionists who wanted to avoid peace with Arabs until the rebuilding of 'Eretz Yisrael' had been completed. Senior Mossad officers had close personal contacts with the Labour Party leadership, but were considered ideologically closer to Herut, the core bloc within Likud. Yitzhak Shamir, the Israeli foreign minister, had been a senior Mossad officer before entering politics.*

Shamir became prime minister in October 1983 after a turbulent period of Israeli politics which began with the Kahan report in February and continued with the resignations of General Sharon and Menachem Begin.

Begin's departure encouraged Washington to hope that the Reagan Plan, which had been shelved a year earlier, might have some chance of success. King Hussein, too, felt more confident, and decided to make another attempt to reach a rapprochement with the PLO. The mood among Palestinians had changed since the failure of the earlier Arafat–Hussein talks, and anxiety to reach a solution seemed stronger. In a speech to the Jordanian parliament on 9 January 1984 King Hussein expressed readiness to work with the PLO in reaching a solution. This led to discussions on forming a joint PLO–Jordanian delegation to negotiate a peace agreement.

One early outcome of this process was that Egypt was partly readmitted to the Arab fold, from which it had been excluded in 1979. King Hussein, needing Egypt's moral support for his project, was instrumental in securing an invitation for Cairo to return to the Islamic Conference from the spring of 1984, despite objections by Syria. Arafat was also in favour of Egyptian involvement, partly as a counterweight to the king's influence, and partly because the PLO needed as much political company as possible. Undertaking negotiations with Israel, even within the framework of an international conference and as part of a joint delegation with Jordan, was bound to anger Palestinian hardliners and Arab radicals. A further reason for Egypt's reacceptance was that President Mubarak, who had been in office for two years, was following a careful policy, aimed at returning to Arab ranks.

Although most Arab countries had broken links with Egypt in 1979,

* Shamir, born in Poland in October 1915 as Yitzhak Jazernicki, was involved in two terrorist movements, Irgun and Lehi, during the British mandate (see p. 62). After being arrested and exiled by the British authorities, he returned to Israel in the 1950s. During his service with Mossad, Shamir was in Paris for several years. He entered politics in 1970 as a member of Herut and served as speaker of the Knesset and as foreign minister before succeeding Begin.

Cairo's exclusion was never as complete as it appeared. Most Arab countries retained informal contacts, and Said Kamal, Arafat's accredited representative in Cairo, continued to send Arafat reports from Cairo on an almost daily basis. Iraq, too, remained in constant touch, and bought arms from Egypt for the war against Iran.

The attempts to work out a Jordanian–PLO accord continued all through 1984, with guidance from the US State Department. As in the earlier talks, the difference between federation and confederation was the main stumbling block. Doubting the ability of the two parties to find a middle line, George Shultz began to advise King Hussein to prepare a fall-back option in case agreement with Arafat proved impossible. That option, according to Shultz, should be a direct agreement between Jordan and Israel, without PLO involvement.

Arafat got wind of this possibility and realized that the consequences could be disastrous for the PLO, which might find itself stranded without a role in a peace negotiated between Jordan and Israel. If Amman was prepared to negotiate directly with Israel, perhaps the time had come for the PLO to follow the same course. In Arafat's mind (but not yet in reality) a race was developing between Jordan and the PLO to come to terms with Israel.

The prospects for peace improved in July 1984, when elections in Israel produced an even balance between Likud and Labour. This led to a government of national unity with a rotating premiership. Shimon Peres was appointed prime minister for two years, on the basis that he would hand the post back to Shamir in October 1986. The post of foreign minister was to be held first by Shamir and then by Peres, while Yitzhak Rabin became defence minister for the full four-year term.

The effect of these changes was soon noticed. Within weeks of taking office Peres ordered the withdrawal of the remaining Israeli troops in Lebanon, despite objections by Likud. Relations with Egypt, strained by the occupation of Lebanon, were patched up, but the Egyptian ambassador to Israel, who had been withdrawn in protest against the invasion, could not be sent back to his post immediately because of another Egyptian–Israeli dispute over the status of Taba.

The formal programme drawn up by the national unity government stated that Israel should try to engage Jordan in direct peace talks. Labour and Likud agreed on that much, but differed on the terms of reference of any such talks. Because of Likud's objections, Peres could not offer King Hussein anything which was not in the Camp David accords. Despite this drawback the Reagan administration quickly sensed a more flexible mood.*

A feeling that peace was now possible began to emerge in a confused way, though no one was yet sure how best to achieve it. In a highly complicated situation all the parties involved looked to the United States for guidance, even if many did so reluctantly. The result was that unofficial contacts arranged through Washington, or through academic groups or private individuals who were in contact with the Reagan administration, began to assume great importance. It was often difficult to tell whether the Americans involved in this process were acting as intermediaries or merely expressing personal opinions.

One of the colourful characters who gained prominence during this period was Judith Kipper, a fellow of the Brookings Institute in Washington. Ms Kipper had been well connected with upper echelons of the Arab world for several years, especially during the last part of the Sadat era. Although she neither had nor claimed to have any official position, many thought of her as a special representative of George Shultz. During the attempts to bring Jordan and the PLO together in a joint delegation, her opinions were often taken as a guide to official US views. Ms Kipper, however, insisted that her sole interest was to help the cause of peace. Her contacts included King Hussein, Said Kamal, and previously Dr Sartawie. None of this would have been surprising but for two other facts: Ms Kipper was Jewish (though not Israeli), and was also a remarkably attractive woman working in a field where virtually all the other players were men. At a time when contacts between Israel and PLO figures were still difficult to arrange, she helped to set up meetings for an American pressure group, some of whose members were Jewish, which travelled around the region meeting Israelis and Palestinians.

Said Kamal questioned whether this indirect method of bringing the parties together was still necessary. 'Why don't we just meet the Israelis directly instead of going about it in this way?' he suggested. Ms Kipper replied that the Israelis understood the need for contacts,

* Reagan's victory over Walter Mondale in November 1984 assured Shultz a further four years in office as secretary of state.

but it was still impossible for them to meet Palestinians not resident in the occupied territories. Her advice to Kamal was to concentrate on links with American Jews.

In mid-February 1985 Jordan and the PLO found a way of papering over the unsettled dispute about confederation or federation. The agreement was that after Israeli withdrawal the state of Palestine would emerge in the west bank and Gaza, linked to Jordan in an alliance described as a confederation but operating more like a federation. This was an ingenious compromise which preserved the Palestinian need for statehood but at the same time reassured Israel, by vesting Amman with control of defence and foreign affairs.

Both parties were prepared to work together in a joint delegation at an international conference to find a solution. Jordan and the PLO, supported by Egypt, pressed this idea in their contacts with Washington, but Shultz was unenthusiastic. Some assumed that he was worried that an international conference would give the Soviet Union an opening. That seems unlikely, because by March 1985, when Mikhail Gorbachev was appointed general secretary of the Soviet Communist Party, Soviet power was already in decline.

Shultz seemed to think that an international conference was unworkable because of Israeli objections, but the Israeli government was in fact divided on this issue, Shamir expressing strong opposition and Peres cautious approval. Israeli public opinion as a whole was sceptical, but the prime minister argued that setting peace talks in the framework of an international conference could overcome King Hussein's anxiety that Jordan might appear to be out of step with the Arab world.

King Hussein held a secret meeting with Peres in London on 19 July 1985 and suggested that peace talks should begin with a meeting between a US representative and a joint Jordanian–PLO delegation. This proposal had the effect of sharpening differences between Peres and Shamir on the conduct of the peace process. Shamir did not want the American government to hold an official meeting with Palestinians, whether members of the PLO or not. Peres, on the other hand, thought that such a meeting would do no harm provided the Palestinians were not PLO members.

Faced with two different Israeli positions, Reagan wavered, giving confusing instructions. A meeting between a joint PLO–Jordanian delegation and Richard Murphy, assistant secretary of state, was arranged in Amman, but had to be cancelled at the last moment when Reagan suddenly withdrew permission. This fiasco and subsequent events put the Jordanian–PLO agreement under severe strain. Sensing that Arafat's relationship with King Hussein was again crumbling, Damascus felt that the time had come for Syria and Jordan to work together to bring about an international conference. Over the next few months the two countries, which had been in dispute over other matters, quietly patched up their differences.

President Assad had realized that the real reason for Shultz's objections to an international conference was that the United States wanted direct talks between Israel and Jordan to be conducted under US auspices. This arrangement was bound to favour Israel, just as Carter's sponsorship of the Camp David Accords had worked to the advantage of Begin. However, when Assad drew attention to this risk, Arafat felt that the Syrian leader was interfering.

The PLO chairman then made an extraordinary attempt to confront the Syrian leader in his own country. Arafat travelled by sea to Tripoli in Lebanon, then went overland to Syria, where he made a speech implicitly attacking the president. Without mentioning Assad by name, he said that some people were trying to take the Palestinian card and use it for their own purposes. The Palestinian card, Arafat argued, belonged to the Palestinians alone.

Arafat thought that this would force Assad to grant him an audience. Instead the head of Syrian intelligence was sent to escort Arafat out of the country, an embarrassing rebuke. Arafat's speech was by no means the first time he had attacked Assad. After the PLO's expulsion from Lebanon, he had implied that Syria's refusal to enter the fight against Sharon's forces showed either cowardice or complicity with Israel.

Arafat also funded attacks against Syrian forces in Lebanon by PLO fighters who had slipped back into the country after Israel's withdrawal. Some of his advisers began to feel worried about the outpouring of effort and money involved in these operations. One financial counsellor estimated that over $100 million had been spent in a single year. Feeling that this was both wasteful and dangerous, political counsellors asked Arafat what he was trying to achieve. 'Who is the real enemy?' was a question often posed but rarely answered.

'It is Israel, but our road to Jerusalem goes via Damascus,' Arafat replied on one occasion.

The PLO chairman was reminded that Damascus was the most important strategic partner against Israel. If Arafat accepted that undeniable fact he should cooperate, not fight, with those who ruled Syria. Anything else was beyond his means. In his frustration Arafat was unable to accept the realities of power.

By late summer 1985 there was widespread speculation that the PLO–Jordanian agreement had come to nothing. An incident which seemed to reflect PLO frustration with the general lack of progress occurred in September, when three commandos, later identified as members of Force 17, Arafat's security unit, attacked an Israeli yacht at Larnaca in Cyprus, killing three Israelis. Israel hit back on 1 October with a massive bombing attack on the PLO headquarters in Tunis, in which seventy-three people were killed. Arafat survived only because he was late for a meeting.

A week later the Palestine Liberation Front (one of the smaller PLO factions) hijacked an Italian cruise ship, the *Achille Lauro*, murdered an elderly American passenger named Leon Klinghoffer, and dumped his body overboard. The PLO said it would try the hijackers, but an Egyptian airliner carrying the three men to Tunis was intercepted by US fighters and forced to land in Sicily, where the men were arrested. The PLF action aroused US public indignation against Palestinian organizations generally and exacerbated Reagan's obsession with terrorism.

Realizing that such incidents were harming rather than helping the Palestinian cause, President Mubarak arranged a meeting with Arafat and urged the PLO chairman to make a clear break with terrorism. Mubarak pointed out that Washington would continue its refusal to hold official talks with the organization until such a pledge was given.

At the end of this meeting, on 7 November 1985, Arafat appeared before television cameras, with Mubarak at his side, and declared that while the PLO reserved the right to resist Israel in the occupied territories, it would neither carry out nor encourage acts of terrorism in other countries. This statement, known as the Cairo Declaration, took the PLO more than halfway towards conditions Washington had set for talks, the remaining step being acceptance of UN Resolution 242, which Arafat was not yet ready to take.

The Cairo Declaration was a reflection of pressure on Arafat not just from Egypt but from most of the non-radical Arab governments.

Many of the sheikhs were by now exhausted with the seemingly endless setbacks of the struggle with Israel, and tired of facing criticism when they travelled in the West. Another factor was the massive pace of settlement construction in the occupied territories, which had accelerated during the Begin and Shamir administrations and continued unabated even after Reagan's warning of September 1982. There were now 120 settlements and more than 60,000 Israeli settlers on the west bank, and a further twenty-one settlements and 2500 settlers in Gaza. The settlements included about half the cultivated land in the west bank and about 40 per cent in Gaza. The Gaza settlements were already taking a third of the available water, leaving inadequate supplies for Arab lands. Fears that nothing would be left of the west bank if the Palestinians did not come to terms with Israel soon contributed to an attitude of defeatism in much of the Arab world.

Meanwhile Shimon Peres forged ahead with his attempts to reach agreement with Jordan, holding another secret meeting with King Hussein in London on 5 October 1985. The Jordanian monarch was increasingly leaning towards Shultz's view that a deal with Israel without PLO involvement would have more chance of success. At the same time Peres was growing more confident that Israeli public opinion would support a change of policy, abandoning Israel's objections to an international peace conference.

In a speech to the United Nations the same month, Peres proposed that an international conference should be followed immediately by direct talks between Jordan and Israel. He insisted, however, that the PLO and those Arab countries which had no diplomatic relations with Israel should be excluded from the conference. The Knesset subsequently endorsed Peres's proposal, which was unacceptable to the Arab world.

The year ended with relations between Jordan and the PLO becoming steadily more strained and the rapprochement between Jordan and Syria growing stronger. King Hussein visited Assad on 11 December and the two men agreed that an international conference represented the best way forward.

A final attempt to save the Jordanian–PLO agreement was made at the beginning of 1986, when American contacts urged the PLO to accept UN Resolution 242, in order to enable Israel to drop its objections to PLO involvement. Arafat was prepared to take this step if the

United States, in return, issued a statement supporting the Palestinian right of self-determination (Reagan had supported only Palestinian self-rule). The United States, dealing with the PLO through Jordan, rejected this demand, resulting in an argument between Arafat and King Hussein. On 19 February 1986 the king declared that the Jordanian–PLO agreement had come to an end, and blamed the PLO for the failure.

Three of the four frontline states, Lebanon, Syria and Jordan, were now closed or unwelcoming to the PLO chairman, leaving only Egypt, the country which had made peace with Israel, to offer moral and political support. Egypt also continued to act as a home for some 12,000 Palestinian soldiers, though not as a base for operations against Israel.

Beyond the frontline states the PLO still had friends among the radical countries, and especially Iraq, but the richer countries kept their distance. The Gulf states continued to contribute to PLO funds and to support pro-Palestinian resolutions at Arab summits, but wanted no other involvement. Saudi Arabia, like several wealthy countries, limited the PLO's presence on its territory to an ambassador and a handful of diplomatic staff.

While the exasperation of Arab leaders with the PLO was understandable, these disputes served only to strengthen right-wing opinion in Israel and the United States. Divisions within the Arab world encouraged those who wanted only to subdue the Palestinians, not negotiate with them.

The Reagan administration, which never had much patience with the Palestinians, failed to realize that an opportunity for stable peace had been lost with the collapse of the Jordanian–PLO agreement. A rational analysis would have shown that an agreement which excluded the PLO was worthless. The United States, however, was still treating the PLO as part of a problem of world terrorism, connected in a general way with many shady organizations.

In the spring of 1986, nearly four years after its arrival in Tunisia, the PLO found itself as far from the centre of events as in 1982, both physically and politically. The frustration of being shut out of the peace process by Israel and the United States and marginalized by Jordan and Syria was about to produce a radical change in direction.

9

The Intifada

An important signal that 'doves' within the PLO were gaining the upper hand emerged at a meeting of the Palestine National Congress in Algiers in 1986. All groups within the organization approved a resolution inviting the executive committee to open contacts with Jewish circles 'which look with sympathy to our cause, and to the idea of an independent Palestinian state'. In a sense the resolution was ill-founded, because no Jewish groups were known to favour an independent Palestinian state, but the fact that the resolution was passed unanimously suggested a new mood. Nine years had elapsed since the more cautiously-worded resolution of March 1977 which invited the executive committee to 'explore possibilities of contacting' Jewish groups.* The taboo in Palestinians hearts had weakened during that time, but still remained a force to be treated with respect. The assassinations of the PLO representatives in Athens, Nicosia and Amman, all of whom had been engaged in contacts, were reminders that some still regarded talks as a form of surrender. On 22 June 1986 the new PLO representative who had been sent to Athens to replace the one who had been assassinated was himself killed.

These warnings did not stop the contacts. Said Kamal, Arafat's accredited representative in Cairo, saw most of the official Israeli delegations which visited Egypt. Egyptian ministers, who were keen to encourage these meetings, provided facilities to ensure that Kamal could talk to the visitors in secret. Reports of these meetings were sent regularly to Farouk Kaddoumi and Khalid Hassan in Tunis. Meanwhile Abu Mazen kept up the link through the Socialist International, meeting a wide range of figures on the Israeli left, including General

* See p. 325.

Abraham Sneh, Uri Avneri, Shulamit Alloni and others.

Some of the Palestinian millionaires who had begun years earlier to advise the PLO on its funds* were now involved in contacts with American Jews. Another channel consisted of volunteers and intellectuals who had links with Jews in the United States and other countries and who passed on anything they picked up to Arafat.

The most important contact during this period was made by Walid Khalidi, a descendant of a noted Palestinian family, who had graduated at Harvard and subsequently became a Harvard professor. Some years earlier Sadat had suggested that Khalidi should be included as a Palestinian representative in a Jordanian delegation, in the event of the Geneva conference being reconvened.

Khalidi was introduced by American contacts to Abba Eban, the former Israeli foreign minister, who was now chairman of the Knesset Foreign Affairs and Defence Committee. Eban had been pressing Peres to introduce immediate autonomy on the west bank and Gaza, but this view was not accepted by the Labour Party as a whole.

The meeting between Khalidi and Eban, held in Washington on 13 May 1986, was the highest-level contact achieved up to that point. Eban criticized the negative attitude the United States had adopted towards attempts to set up a joint PLO–Jordanian delegation to an international conference. Washington, he said, had failed in its role as a friendly mediator in not deviating from the Israeli position.

He also felt that the Israeli government had been wrong to withhold permission from a Palestinian delegation which had wanted to travel from the occupied territories to meet King Hussein and Arafat in Amman during their talks.

Khalidi was pessimistic about prospects for any change of view by Washington, and felt that the main problem was that the US political elite saw no reason to challenge the American Jewish lobby. The State Department, too, was paralyzed by similar attitudes. The initiative, Khalidi said, could only come from the parties themselves.

'We need to have an encounter,' Eban said. 'We have never reached the table.'

Eban urged Palestinians not to be put off by what they read in Israeli

* See pp. 338–9.

newspapers. 'Arabs pay too much attention to our semantic obduracies – these are for domestic consumption, not for negotiation. There is too much use of words – all of which is done for the sake of image to prove that the other side is culpable.'

After the Walid Khalidi–Abba Eban meeting there could be no further doubt that doves on both sides were working for a settlement. The Cairo Declaration of 1985 renouncing attacks outside the occupied territories, followed by the resolution at the 1986 Palestine National Congress meeting, was a clear signal of a wish for peace. Arafat was receiving warnings, however, that these moves would not be sufficient to gain Washington's involvement as a peacemaker between the PLO and Israel. A further dramatic step, recognizing Israel and accepting Resolution 242, would be needed first. The PLO chairman began preparing Palestinian opinion.

Peres, for his part, made further efforts during his final months in office to improve the atmosphere. Arab mayors were appointed in Hebron, El Bireh and Ramallah, and Israeli officials began to drop hints that Israel and Jordan were coordinating their policies for management of the territories. Israeli and Jordanian officials held talks on the west bank covering issues ranging from education to agriculture. When King Hussein announced a five-year development plan for the west bank involving expenditure of $240 million a year, Peres voiced strong support. In July 1986 Peres made an official visit to Morocco and was welcomed by King Hassan in a move intended to pave the way for introductions to other Arab leaders. At the same time King Hussein and Peres began working on George Shultz to drop his objections to an international conference, and the secretary of state showed signs of accepting this point of view.

Meanwhile in September 1986 the long-running dispute between Israel and Egypt over the status of Taba on the border near Eilat was finally settled. President Mubarak felt able to send the Egyptian ambassador back to resume his post in Tel Aviv after a four-year absence. Egypt was now poised to play a role in passing messages between the PLO and Israel.

All these moves gave an impression that the peace process was acquiring an unstoppable momentum, and yet the hopes were premature. Even if Peres had been able to continue in office, the policies he and King Hussein were pursuing could not have led to peace. An international conference held in the absence of the PLO, followed by direct Jordanian–Israeli talks, was a 'peace' formula guaranteed to prolong conflict.

This period of unrealistic hopes came to an end on 20 October 1986 when Peres and Yitzhak Shamir exchanged roles, as had been agreed two years earlier. Shamir promised to adhere firmly to the Camp David framework, which meant in practice that the new prime minister would use the Sadat–Begin–Carter accords to prevent, rather than promote, peace.

Peres, however, continued pursuing his uncompleted mission in his new capacity as foreign minister. On 10 April 1987 he and King Hussein met in England, at the king's country house in Sussex, and worked out a framework for convening an international conference. The document, finalized the following day in London, proposed that Javier Pérez de Cuéllar, the UN secretary general, should invite the five permanent members of the Security Council and the parties to the Arab–Israel conflict to negotiate a comprehensive solution based on UN resolutions 242 and 338 'for the purposes of obtaining comprehensive peace in the region and security for the countries in the area, and granting the Palestinian people their political rights'.

The role of the five powers at the conference would be limited to convening direct talks between the parties, and the conference would have no authority to impose a solution or veto anything the two parties might decide. Peres was particularly keen on this point as a means of limiting the role of the Soviet Union.

The key section of the document was item C, which said in part:

> C3. The Palestinian issue will be discussed in a meeting of the Jordanian, Palestinian and Israeli delegations;
>
> C4. The representatives of the Palestinians will be included in the Jordanian–Palestinian delegation;
>
> C5. Participation in the conference will be based on acceptance of UN resolutions 242 and 338 by the sides and the renunciation of violence and terror.

The PLO was not mentioned, but its participation clearly depended on acceptance of the conditions in item C5. Such a formula was bound to upset Palestinians, but would be less difficult for King Hussein to sell if it appeared to come from the United States. The preamble therefore stated: 'Part C is to be treated with great confidentiality, as commitments to the United States from the government of Jordan to be transmitted to the government of Israel.'

The intention was to pretend that the United States had proposed these provisions and had persuaded Jordan to accept them. King Hussein contacted Shultz and explained what had been agreed, urging the secretary of state to give his blessing. Shultz, however, suggested that the king should present the plan boldly as a Jordanian–Israeli initiative, without hiding behind the United States. Hussein was reluctant to take such a step.

Peres was just as anxious as the king to have American political cover, though for different reasons. The Israeli foreign minister knew that the document had no chance of being approved by Shamir unless it was presented as an American proposal. As soon as the meeting with King Hussein was over, Peres sent his assistant Yossi Beilin to Helsinki, where Shultz was attending a conference, and pressed him to adopt the document as an American plan. Beilin brought a message from Peres saying that this was the most important event in the history of Israel since the Biltmore Conference of 1942.*

Neither Peres nor Hussein had signed the document, partly because of its sensitivity and partly because Peres would have needed authority from the ten-member Israeli inner cabinet, which was evenly balanced between Likud and Labour ministers.

Shultz, however, refused to be used by one element of an Israeli government to twist the arm of the other, and Peres was left politically naked. As he had feared, Shamir was opposed to the entire concept and angry that Peres had acted behind his back. Peres could have put the matter to a vote in the inner cabinet, but decided not to do so as the outcome was certain to be an exact five–five split. It was clear that the agreement with King Hussein could not be implemented unless and until Israeli voters returned a Labour-led government to power.

In his book *The New Middle East*,† Shimon Peres looked back at the 1987 agreement as a lost opportunity. 'We could have saved ourselves and the Palestinians six years of Intifada ['Uprising'] and the loss of so much human life, had the former head of the Likud-run

* See pp. 58–60.

† Henry Holt & Company, New York, 1993.

government not undermined the agreement I had worked out with King Hussein of Jordan.'

Arafat was by this time moving towards acceptance of Resolution 242. Had Shamir accepted the London agreement, it seems possible that the PLO would have made the changes necessary to qualify for participation. The PLO chairman was also now prepared to deal directly with the Israelis, as the earlier attempts to coordinate with the Jordanians had failed. In the past the PLO and Israel had been equally determined not to talk to each other, but now the refusal was one-sided. Arafat was open and eager for discussions.

Between June and August 1987 Shamir explored the possibility of reaching a new deal with King Hussein on different terms. The prime minister sent an emissary to see Shultz and held a meeting with King Hussein, but no basis for agreement was found. King Hussein felt that with Shamir in power the situation was hopeless.

Over the next six months Palestinians in the occupied territories realized that all the hopes raised during the Peres years had come to nothing. A feeling of hopelessness turned to desperation, and desperation turned to anger. Palestinians watched their remaining land disappearing into Israeli settlements, while life in the slums of Gaza remained as violent and miserable as ever. According to an account later distributed by the Palestinians in London,* seventeen Palestinians were murdered during the first nine months of 1987, 129 seriously injured, seven expelled, seventy-seven imprisoned without trial and forty-eight prohibited from leaving the areas where they lived. As the tension mounted the territories became a tinderbox awaiting a spark.

On the evening of 8 December 1987 the 100,000 Palestinians who had regular jobs in Israel were returning to their homes after a normal day's work. A vehicle carrying some of them to Gaza was suddenly rammed at high speed by an Israeli army truck. There are differing versions as to what happened next, but some said that an Israeli soldier in the truck got out and opened fire at point-blank range, killing four Palestinians and injuring nine others. The next day 3000 people attending the funerals were surrounded by Israeli troops who attempted to disperse them. A boy threw a stone at a soldier, the troops

* 'The Intifada: A Message from Three Generations of Palestinians', Knight Financial Services, 1988.

opened fire, two Palestinians were killed and thirty more injured. The killings sparked immediate protests and demonstrations throughout Gaza and the west bank, leading to tough Israeli repression, followed in turn by a still greater explosion of Palestinian anger. Every man, woman and child with the courage to risk martyrdom became an autonomous fighter, resisting occupation with any weapon that came to hand. Children with stones achieved more to arouse world sympathy for the Palestinian cause in eighteen months than the PLO could ever do with machine guns and artillery. The use of stones carried an unconscious symbolism, recalling the Islamic ritual of '*rajm*', in which pilgrims on the Hajj to Mecca throw forty-nine stones at the Devil. The Intifada was the biggest Palestinian protest movement since the 1930s.*

Yitzhak Rabin, the Israeli defence minister, responded with massive severity, ordering his troops to 'break their bones' to restore order. Among the estimated 300 Palestinians shot dead by Israeli troops during the first year of the uprising was Najwa Hassan El-Masri, a girl of seventeen killed while marching in a demonstration at Beit Hanoun. While live ammunition was the main cause of death, many a demonstrator lost an eye when hit by rubber bullets, and hundreds suffered broken limbs when beaten or clubbed by Israeli soldiers. The massive use of tear gas was a further cause of casualties, and there were reports of women suffering miscarriages. Some of the gas victims were elderly, such as Khalil Hassan Saadeh, a man of seventy who died on 18 December 1987 when gas grenades were hurled into al-Aksa mosque in Jerusalem, where he was praying. Amnesty International later issued details of more than forty deaths, including eighteen babies, caused by gas. Amnesty said: 'There has been at least one instance in which an individual was deliberately shut in a room which was then sprayed with tear gas.'

More than 300 Palestinians were arrested without trial in a single week in March 1988, and thousands more would follow them into 'administrative detention' before the Intifada was over. In April an Israeli team assassinated Abu Jihad (Khalil al-Wazir), the PLO's deputy military commander with special responsibility for the occupied territories and one of Arafat's closest colleagues, in his home in Tunis.

* See pp. 44–8.

The role of the media in the Intifada proved crucial. Pictures of Israeli troops firing at stone-throwing children brought outrage in the United States and Europe. Under pressure from public opinion, the Reagan administration expressed dismay and supported a UN resolution calling on Israel to desist from 'such harsh measures'. The United States normally vetoed UN resolutions critical of Israel or abstained, and had not voted in favour of such criticism since 1981.

The courage of the young Palestinians inspired the Arab world and surprised the Israelis. Even Yitzhak Rabin confessed, in a conversation with former Egyptian prime minister Mustafa Khalil, that he had been forced to rethink his attitudes: 'There was a time when I thought that we Israelis and the Palestinians could live together, but now I see that it is impossible,' he said. 'As a soldier I feel that these people have fought with a courage that deserves respect. They deserve to have an entity. Not the PLO, not a state, but a separate entity.'

Stephen Cohen realized that Rabin was undergoing a mental transition and urged the Egyptian government to encourage the process. It would be helpful, he advised a PLO contact, if President Mubarak invited the Israeli defence minister to Cairo. Soon afterwards Arafat passed through Cairo for talks with Mubarak and made an identical suggestion. The Egyptian president immediately phoned Mohamed Bassiouni, his ambassador in Tel Aviv, and asked him to deliver an invitation.

In his talks with Rabin, Mubarak explained that the PLO was moving towards acceptance of UN Resolution 242, and suggested that the time had come for Israel to talk to the organization. Rabin said that that was out of the question so long as Shamir remained prime minister. However, Arafat could delegate people in the occupied territories to act as his representatives in discussions with the Israelis, and some sort of administrative entity run by Palestinians might be possible.

Rabin's views seemed to suggest a shift towards moderation rather than any dramatic change. There was always a risk of overemphasizing the divisions between the two big Israeli parties. Whatever their rivalry, Likud and Labour agreed that order had to be restored before any negotiations, that the PLO should be excluded from talks, that the main negotiations should be with Jordan, and that no independent Palestinian state could be permitted. Any dispassionate analysis by Arabs would have shown that no lasting peace could be negotiated so long as such views persisted.

In February and March 1988 George Shultz made two tours of the region in search of fresh ideas, and produced a package which became known as the Shultz Initiative. The secretary of state hoped to persuade the Israelis to suspend the settlement programme and the Palestinians to suspend the Intifada, on the basis that negotiations would begin the same month (March 1988), with the aim of achieving Palestinian self-rule by February 1989. The negotiations were to be conducted on the basis foreseen in the Camp David accords, but with a faster timetable. Begin, Sadat and Carter had agreed that the final status of the occupied territories should be decided within five years of elections for a self-governing Palestinian authority. Shultz felt that this was too long, and suggested a target of one year. The package also reflected the Peres–Hussein agreement of 1987, proposing that a joint Jordanian–Palestinian delegation should negotiate all Palestinian matters with Israel. Another idea, perhaps the most radical in the package, was that the concept of sovereignty should be blurred by instituting shared Israeli–Palestinian authority over certain administrative functions.

The Shultz Initiative was the first major US effort since the 1982 Reagan Plan (which was in fact a Shultz plan). Peres praised the initiative and King Hussein, despite many reservations, appealed to other Arabs not to reject it out of hand. Most Arabs felt that the plan was flawed in tying the Palestinians too strongly to Jordan. Shamir, not surprisingly, was adamantly opposed, and two further trips by Shultz failed to overcome his objections.

Shultz believed that after the Intifada the PLO would never again enjoy a near-monopoly of Palestinian politics.* One of the important lessons of the Intifada was that Palestinians were no longer prepared to take orders from a remote leadership. Street leaders came together in a new body known as the Unified National Leadership of the Uprising. This temporary organization acknowledged the overall leadership of the PLO but at the same time retained local control. Some of the demonstrators emblazoned portraits of Arafat on the red, black, white and green flag of Palestine.

In the early stages of the Intifada Arafat said that orders for the

* See Chapter 47 of *Turmoil and Triumph*.

uprising had come from himself, a claim which was not well-received. When the PLO chairman next visited Cairo President Mubarak offered some advice. 'Abu Ammar, I doubt that you gave the orders, but even if you did you should not say so openly. Let the people take the credit.'

Later the men and women of the Intifada found that they needed the PLO because of severe financial hardships arising from the Intifada. The cost of funerals and medical treatment, the destruction of homes and sometimes the loss of the only member of a family with a paid job brought new burdens which could only be relieved by turning to the PLO.

The financial difficulties gained another dimension on 31 July 1988 when King Hussein unexpectedly announced that Jordan was cutting its legal and administrative ties with the west bank. The move was seen by some as an acknowledgement that after the Intifada Jordan could never again hope to rule the west bank, and that the Palestinians had achieved a kind of secession while still under Israeli rule. That interpretation was over-generous. It would be closer to the truth to say that the king's announcement was meant to show the Palestinians that it would be difficult to manage without Jordan. Many in Amman were exasperated with what they saw as the ingratitude of the Palestinians despite Jordanian efforts to improve their lot. Jordan had continued to pay the salaries of about a third of all Palestinian civil servants throughout the two decades since the Six Day War. In future, the king said, the PLO would be responsible for all Palestinians.

The announcement caused panic on the west bank, where Palestinians rushed to withdraw their savings from Jordanian banks, and the value of the Jordanian dinar dropped. On 7 August the king added that Jordan would never again assume the role of speaking on behalf of the Palestinians. This statement, which was probably not meant to be as final as it sounded, was seen in the US as a blow to the Shultz Initiative, because Jordanian–Palestinian cooperation was central to the secretary of state's proposals.

The PLO, whose offices in Amman had been closed by the Jordanian authorities, was not consulted on the transfer of responsibilities. Realizing that the change would cause many families severe hardship, the organization began smuggling large sums of money into the occupied territories. Much was lost as a result of greed or theft on the part of the couriers. An Israeli officer on the Lebanese front was offered a 10 per cent commission to deliver $500,000 to contacts on the west bank. The officer accepted but in fact took $150,000 dollars, three times the agreed amount. Prince Salman, brother of King Fahd, who carried out a collection on behalf of the Intifada, was determined to avoid such problems. He raised $5 million and transferred the money to the Palestinians without it passing through the PLO.

Another consequence of the Intifada was that Hamas, a local Islamic party, began to gain stronger support. The name is an Arabic word meaning enthusiasm, and also an acronym for 'Islamic Organization for Palestine'. In order to obtain authorization from the Israeli authorities, the party was obliged to pledge that its fight for Palestinian rights would be conducted within constitutional and legal constraints, without the use of arms. Ironically, the Israeli government initially encouraged Hamas, thinking that a religious party could provide a counterweight to the nationalism of the PLO. When Hamas members became involved in the Intifada, the initial feeling was that stones were not really 'arms', and thus the organization was still within its remit. Soon, however, the desire to stay within the law was abandoned and Hamas gained wide popular support. The Intifada thus changed the nature of Hamas, making it much more radical. The party's founder, Sheikh Ahmed Yassin, a paralyzed religious teacher, was arrested during the uprising and was still in prison at the time of writing in 1995.

Another Palestinian leader who was repeatedly arrested for periods of weeks or months during the Intifada was Faisal Husseini, grandson of Hajj Amin El-Husseini, the former Grand Mufti of Jerusalem.* As head of the Arab Studies Centre in Jerusalem Husseini enjoyed respect not only among Palestinians but also with Israeli journalists, who frequently consulted him. In July 1988 he was invited to address an Israeli Peace Now rally and made a speech proposing peace and justice. Three days later he was arrested and imprisoned for six months without charges or trial.

* See pp. 43–7.

10

The Geneva Statement

By the spring of 1988 the philosophical journey which had begun three years earlier with the PLO's renunciation of violence outside the occupied territories was approaching its logical conclusion. Arafat was now ready, in the context of a full settlement, to accept Israel's 'right to live in peace', but he knew that these and other words from UN Resolution 242 still represented a hurdle for some of his colleagues.

In his customary style, Arafat tested internal opinion with caution. His press secretary Bassam Abu Sharif was given authorization to write a position paper hinting at a willingness to remove the remaining obstacles to negotiations. This paper, entitled 'PLO View: Prospects of a Palestinian–Israeli Settlement', was distributed to delegates at an Arab summit in June 1988, and went far beyond any previous statement issued by the organization.

The document was unsigned, and when delegates asked whose views it represented Sharif said he was the author. The result was a blaze of publicity in the Western and Israeli media, promoting Sharif as a new star and as the centre of discussion in the Arab world. In the past such views would have brought denunciations from many Palestinians, but now the criticism was muted. The fact that Sharif worked directly to Arafat prompted questions as to whether the PLO chairman was the real originator of the document. Many expected Arafat to issue a categorical denial, but he said nothing. Egypt warmly welcomed the paper, while US officials were unsure whether to believe it. Reaction in Israel was positive, and General Abraham Tamir, Israel's former liaison officer with Egypt, sought a meeting with Sharif. The encounter did not materialize, but the fact that Tamir had been willing to meet a PLO official was a step forward.

The success of Sharif's trial balloon gave encouragement to two new channels of contact which had begun a few months earlier. One channel consisted of efforts by Sten Andersson, the Swedish foreign minister, to set up a discussion group involving PLO officials and American Jews. The other involved a Palestinian economist and author, Mohamed Rabie, who was on good terms with Arafat and who believed that talks between Washington and the PLO were within reach. Rabie had already begun contacts with William Quandt, a former staff member of the US National Security Council and fellow of the Brookings Institute of Washington. Rabie and Quandt worked out drafts of a statement which Arafat could make to remove US objections to dealing with the PLO.* Quandt passed word from the State Department that talks could begin right away if the PLO made the kind of statement the US required.

Washington's terms for talks with the PLO had not changed since 1975, when Kissinger said that the organization would have to acknowledge Israel's right to exist and accept Resolution 242. Arafat felt that any PLO statement making these points should be answered by a US declaration endorsing the Palestinian right to self-determination. No official US declaration had gone beyond supporting self-government.† Quandt says that Shultz showed interest in the PLO reply but was not prepared to endorse Palestinian self-determination. The secretary of state's argument was that the final status of the Palestinians had to be settled by negotiation, not by prior US approval of a Palestinian state.

Shultz says in his memoirs that in early September 1988 Quandt went to see Richard Murphy, assistant secretary of state, with a document approved by the entire PLO executive committee. Shultz decided that the document fell short of US conditions, but was informed on 12 September that the PLO leadership had adopted another version which met the conditions. The secretary of state would have been prepared to open a dialogue at that stage, but ran into opposition from Ken Duberstein, the White House chief-of-staff, and from Shamir. Republican campaign managers feared that anything which upset American Jewish opinion could work against Vice President George

* See pp. 573–4 of William Quandt, *Peace Process*, Brookings Institute, Washington D.C. and University of California Press, 1993.

† See p. 366.

Bush, the Republican candidate to succeed Ronald Reagan. Shultz therefore delayed his reply to the PLO initiative until after the presidential election.

Meanwhile Arafat began planning for a meeting of the Palestine National Congress in November, at which he hoped to secure approval from Palestinian parliamentarians for accepting the UN resolutions. In preparation for the Congress he invited a small working group to take part in discussions on the resolutions he planned to introduce. The group, coordinated by Haseeb Sabbagh, chairman of Consolidated (a large Arab contracting company), included Abd El-Meguid Shouman, Abdel-Mohsen El-Kattan and Zein Mayyassi, all prominent and reputable financial backers of the PLO. Also included were Edward Said, professor of comparative literature at Columbia University, New York, Basil Akl, one of the PLO representatives in London, distinguished writer Ahmed Bahaa' El-Din, and myself.

Discussions were held for two days at the Richmond Hotel in Geneva, and a private plane then took half the group from Geneva to Tunis. Abdel-Hakam Bal'awi, the PLO ambassador in Tunis, made his French-colonial residence on the seafront available for discussions with Arafat, which went on for ten hours in the bomb-protected basement. There were differences of opinion, but the PLO chairman seemed determined to follow his chosen course.

Arafat planned to put to the congress a resolution based on accepting UN Resolution 181, the original UN partition plan of 1947,* as well as resolutions 242 and 338. As all Arabs had rejected resolution 181 in 1947, and as the PLO had always opposed the other two resolutions, these were daunting concessions to make. Acceptance of Resolution 242 was contrary to the spirit of many provisions of the Palestine National Covenant, drawn up in 1964. Article 21, for example, said: 'The Palestinian Arab people, expressing themselves through the Palestinian armed revolution, reject all alternatives to the total liberation of Palestine.' Only six months earlier Arafat had told me that he would sooner cut off his right hand than accept Resolution 242.

Wanting to avoid an impression of retreat, Arafat proposed that the concessions should be accompanied by the declaration of an independent state of Palestine in the west bank and Gaza. This was essentially

* See p. 73.

the idea which Bruno Kreisky had suggested in 1974.* Arafat thought that the declaration of a state, with himself as president, would overshadow acceptance of the resolutions, because the attitudes of most PLO members had already changed.

A change in the Israeli mood was clear to all. The Intifada was becoming an unbearable burden, harming Israel's image in the Western media, costing the Israeli army its self-esteem and the admiration of Jews the world over. An efficient fighting army was being transformed into an exhausted, repressive police force. The economic costs were also considerable. Israel seemed likely to hand over several densely populated centres, notably Gaza but also rebellious west bank cities like Nablus and Ramallah, if an acceptable Palestinian administration could be arranged.

One of the risks considered during our discussions in Tunis was that the PLO might find itself in a political trap. What if Israel handed over Gaza and then refused to budge from the west bank? No one doubted Israel's willingness to leave Gaza, because the strip had become uncontrollable. With 750,000 people crammed into a sliver of territory twenty-six miles long by six miles wide, Gaza was among the most densely populated places on earth. Yitzhak Rabin once told François Mitterrand that he would like to be rid of Gaza at almost any price: 'Sometimes I dream that Gaza had sunk into the sea, and wake up to find that it is still there. I wish my dream were true.'

The concern I expressed to Arafat was that if Israel handed over Gaza but not other areas, the PLO could find itself involved in clashes with Hamas. Any bloodshed between the two groups would give the Israelis a pretext to interfere. Arafat, however, was not prepared to wait. In his scheme for the coming months, the congress was a stepping stone to Washington, which would carry the PLO to talks with Israel.

On the second day we were invited to a lunch at which the other guests included George Habash, leader of the PFLP, and Nayef Hawatmeh, leader of the Popular Democratic Front for the Liberation of Palestine. Both leaders tended to take a harder line than Arafat, and the attitudes they expressed at the congress could be of decisive importance.

* See p. 324.

The PLO chairman was particularly keen to enlist the support of Habash because of his high reputation in the movement as a man of wisdom and dedication. 'Hakim' (the Wise), as he was known, had remained true to his ideals, maintaining an unpretentious lifestyle. During a long conversation after lunch Habash seemed resigned to acceptance of the UN resolutions, not least because Arab countries, including Saudi Arabia, had made their views clear. 'If this is what all our Arab brothers are asking us to do, so be it,' he said. 'I don't think it will bring us any benefits, but on the other hand we have little choice. I don't mind recognising Resolution 181 and I hope and I pray that it [a Palestinian state] may come true. Arafat will not find an obstacle in me.'

Meanwhile the Rabie–Quandt channel had kept Washington informed of Arafat's intentions. Although Shultz felt that the PLO chairman was moving towards US terms for talks, certain aspects of the proposed declarations were not to Washington's satisfaction. Arafat was ready to condemn terrorism, but Shultz wanted a specific statement renouncing violence, and a specific rather than implicit acknowledgement of Israel's right to exist.

In Israel, meanwhile, the excitement of impending elections was beginning to overshadow the daily headlines connected with the Intifada. The Palestinians and the Arab world followed Israel's internal politics with anxiety, knowing that the outcome would determine prospects for peace. Some Arab countries had been ready for years to contribute to the finances of the Labour Party. There was a longstanding plan for infusing funds through the Socialist International, and in the 1988 election Arab money became a significant factor.

More than financial help was needed. Mustafa Khalil, the former Egyptian prime minister, visited Arab mayors and dignitaries in Israel and tried to persuade them to vote Labour. Many were primarily concerned with local issues, on which Likud's platform was sometimes more attractive. Khalil also urged Arab Israelis to vote as a bloc, pointing out that with up to seven deputies in the Knesset they could be an important coalition element.

Labour's election platform included a four-point plan for peace. This called for a period of calm in the occupied territories to pave the way for elections in which Palestinians would choose peace negotiators, leading to a five-year period of Palestinian autonomy, followed by a final peace settlement under which the autonomous Palestinian region would be linked to Jordan.

In the election on 1 November Israeli voters seemed disillusioned with both Likud and Labour, both of which were returned with fewer seats than in the 1984 elections. Likud was nevertheless marginally ahead, with forty deputies to Labour's thirty-nine, and President Herzog gave Shamir the mandate to form a government.

In the same week George Bush won the US presidential election with an easy victory over Democratic candidate Michael Dukakis. This removed the constraints which had prevented Shultz from responding to the PLO's initiatives, but the day after the election events took a fresh twist. The PLO applied for a visa for Arafat to attend the General Assembly, at which it had status as an observer delegation.

Shultz pointed out that under US law the PLO was considered a terrorist organization, and members could be admitted only if the secretary of state recommended the attorney general to issue a waiver. Shultz delayed his decision, apparently awaiting the outcome of the Palestine National Congress.

The congress, which met from 12 to 15 November in Algiers, passed the resolutions recommended by Arafat, and Habash, true to his word, supported the PLO chairman. The declaration of a Palestinian state with Jerusalem as its capital and Arafat as president made headlines around the world, although the West and Israel gave greater attention to the concessions.

Shultz discussed the Algiers meeting with George Bush and Gerald Ford, and all agreed that the PNC had shown moderation. Prince Bander, the influential Saudi Arabian ambassador to Washington, also commended the PNC resolutions. Shultz concluded, however, that the PLO had not met American conditions for talks, and that the organization was still trying to conduct a trade in statements, wanting the US to commit itself to Palestinian self-determination. The secretary of state was under pressure from many quarters, including former president Jimmy Carter, to grant Arafat the visa to attend the United Nations.

Meanwhile Sten Andersson had been continuing his discussions with American Jewish academics, attorneys, economists and others, including the New York lawyer Rita Hauser. On 21 November 1988 Andersson brought this group together with Khalid Hassan and other

Palestinian parliamentarians to discuss the meaning of the PNC resolutions. The two sides agreed that the PNC had in effect recognized Israel's right to exist.

After this meeting Andersson and his contacts carried on the work which had been begun in the Rabie–Quandt channel of elaborating a public statement to meet US demands. The pace was now faster, as Andersson was able to communicate directly with Shultz, and because the outgoing Reagan administration had arranged with the incoming Bush team to settle the matter before the new president took office in January.

Despite the progress, Shultz decided on 26 November not to recommend the US attorney general to issue the waiver for Arafat to enter the United States. The secretary of state said that the US had 'convincing evidence' of PLO terrorism against Americans (presumably meaning Leon Klinghoffer*). The decision was denounced by UN secretary general Javier Pérez de Cuéllar, and on 2 December the General Assembly voted by 154 to 2 to hold a special session in Geneva so that Arafat could attend and speak.

Sten Andersson arranged a further meeting between Jewish Americans and Palestinian leaders on 6 December, this time in the presence of the PLO chairman. On his arrival at Stockholm airport Arafat was accorded honours appropriate to a visiting head of government, causing much annoyance in Israel. The American Jewish side was led by Rita Hauser, representing the International Peace Institute of the Middle East, while Stephen Cohen was seen as the motivator behind the conference.

The Swedish government informed Washington that Arafat would make a statement the next day meeting the US conditions for talks with the PLO. This proved to be premature, because although Arafat signed a document which became known as the Stockholm Declaration, he did not read it at a press conference as expected, as the approval of the PLO executive committee was needed first.

The statement, marked 'Secret', contained only three points:

1. That it [the PLO executive committee] is prepared to negotiate with Israel within the framework of the international conference

* See p. 374.

a comprehensive peace settlement of the Arab–Israeli conflict on the basis of UN resolutions 242 and 338.

2. That it undertakes to live in peace with Israel and other neighbours and respect their right to exist in peace within secure and internationally recognized borders as will the democratic Palestinian state which it seeks to establish in the Palestinian occupied territories since 1967.
3. That it condemns individual and state terrorism in all its forms and will not resort to it.

Signed: Y Arafat 7.12.88

The declaration astonished Egypt and Saudi Arabia, which had not been informed in advance. When a Palestinian envoy brought the text to Cairo, Dr Ossama El-Baz, President Mubarak's acting national security adviser, exploded in anger: 'You sons of —, how can you do this after all our efforts to help you?' The annoyance was not over the content but the lack of consultation.

Arafat found a mixed response when he sought the reactions of colleagues at a meeting held at Abu Mazen's home in Tunis. Mahmoud Darwish, the celebrated Palestinian poet, said he felt the PLO had paid a high price to draw the United States into talks, and pointed out that there was no guarantee that Israel would accept anything the PLO might agree with Washington.

'Praise the Prophet,' Arafat shouted in anger. 'We have always wanted talks with America.'

Darwish replied: 'I have lived in Israel for a long time. Israel is ready to deal with any Arab country, but we should ask ourselves whether it is ready to deal with us.' He called for caution and warned that the only type of agreement Israel would sign with the PLO was one which led to the organization being swallowed by the Zionist state.

When asked who had arranged the Stockholm encounter, Arafat deflected personal responsibility by pointing to the roles of Bassam Abu Sharif, the American Jewish lobby and Palestinian businessmen.

Arafat then flew to Baghdad, but was pursued by the waves he had stirred up in Stockholm. Said Kamal, who had recently been reinstated as the PLO's ambassador to Cairo, arrived in Iraq with a message for Arafat from Mubarak. Fearing that their conversation was being monitored, Arafat escorted the envoy to a swimming pool, where they were less likely to be overheard. Kamal explained that Mubarak was surprised that the PLO had not consulted the Egyptian government, but accepted the situation and wanted to know what Arafat planned to do next.

Mubarak's question reflected concern in the Arab world as to what Arafat might say in his speech to the United Nations. Many felt that the Stockholm Declaration had stretched the meaning of the PNC resolutions, and feared that the Geneva speech might go further still.

Arafat knew exactly what Shultz wanted him to say, because Andersson had passed on a draft prepared by the State Department. The Swedish foreign minister encouraged Arafat to follow the American draft, but strong opposition to that idea arose within the PLO. The result was that Arafat modified the speech he had planned to make to the UN, trying to satisfy both his PLO opponents, led by Nayef Hawatmeh, and the American secretary of state.

Before Arafat's appearance in Geneva on 13 December, Yitzhak Shamir sent Shultz a message asking him not to react to the speech until he had heard Israel's response. The Israeli prime minister warned that there would be 'great difficulty' in the US–Israeli relationship if Washington opened a dialogue with the PLO. Shultz replied that if Arafat met the US conditions, Washington would keep its word.

The secretary of state had understood from Stockholm that Arafat planned to follow the exact words of the US draft. Instead the PLO chairman used different words, whose meaning was close to what Shultz had wanted, and dispersed the various ideas within a long speech. Shultz decided that this was not good enough. One of the objections was that Arafat 'condemned and rejected' terrorism rather than renouncing it.

In the hours after the speech Arafat was approached by a succession of envoys pleading with him to say exactly what the Americans wanted to hear. The following day at a press conference in Geneva he 'clarified' these points, using the magic words 'we totally and absolutely renounce all forms of terrorism'. Arafat also referred to the right of Israel and Palestine to live in peace and security.

Shultz was at last satisfied and announced that a dialogue could begin through the American ambassador in Tunis, adding: 'Nothing here may be taken to imply an acceptance or recognition by the United States of an independent Palestinian state. The position of the United States is that the status of the west bank and Gaza cannot be determined by unilateral acts of either side, but only through a process of negotiations.' Shultz's memoirs show that he remained sceptical about the PLO, despite Arafat's statement.

The American decision brought reactions of anger and disbelief from Israel, which was now isolated in its refusal to talk to the PLO. On 22 December Shamir presented another national unity coalition to the Knesset for approval, with himself as prime minister and his Herut colleague Moshe Arens as foreign minister. Peres was relegated to the post of finance minister, while Rabin retained the defence portfolio.

The Israelis faced a further shock three months after the inauguration of the Bush administration. James Baker, the new secretary of state, said in a speech to AIPAC (American Israel Public Affairs Committee) on 22 May that the time had come for Israel 'to lay aside, once and for all, the unrealistic vision of a greater Israel . . . Forswear annexation. Stop settlement activity. Allow schools to reopen.'

Baker said, however, that Israel had made a positive start towards negotiations. This was a reference to a decision by the Israeli cabinet on 14 May to adopt part of the plan which Labour had put forward in its election manifesto. Labour's concept of a period of calm leading to Palestinian elections, followed by negotiations on transitional arrangements, was rewritten and became known, ironically, as the 'Shamir Plan'. The plan had only majority, not unanimous, support and was strongly attacked by Ariel Sharon, now minister of trade and industry. Sharon rejected any elections in the occupied territories and called for the construction of further settlements to strengthen Israel's control.

The Shamir Plan in no way modified Israel's refusal to talk to the PLO, nor did it envisage Israeli withdrawal from the occupied territories. Despite Baker's polite remarks, the plan offered no basis for a solution.

While Israel's intransigence was attracting international criticism, Arafat found himself the centre of flattering attention. Once the Western media had portrayed the PLO chairman as a gang leader; now he was lauded as the leading moderate of a noble cause. The habit of treating him as a head of state or government began to spread beyond the Arab world. Five months after the Geneva Declaration, France accorded Arafat unusual honours. On the first day of a visit to Paris in May 1989, Arafat was received personally by François Mitterrand at the Elysée Palace. The two men had met on one previous occasion, before Mitterrand became president, when the French Socialist Party leader was my guest during a visit to Cairo, and I took the opportunity to introduce him to the PLO chairman.

Mitterrand's decision to take a European lead in boosting Arafat's image followed persuasion by Marie Claire, widow of former socialist prime minister Pierre Mendès-France, who was Jewish and had been involved in peace efforts by the Socialist International.*

On the second day of his visit Arafat held talks with Alain Dumas, the French foreign minister, at the Quai d'Orsay. Dumas urged Arafat to repay the president's hospitality with some form of political gift: 'You gave the Americans a lot in Geneva, now it is time to give President Mitterrand something.'

This was not easy, because Arafat had already conceded the main points. The most controversial remaining issue was the Palestine National Covenant. Israeli journalists had cast doubt on the value of Arafat's Geneva Declaration by pointing out that the covenant had not been altered or withdrawn. This was a spurious issue, as the covenant had been superseded by the PNC resolutions at the Algiers summit in November. Nevertheless, the Israeli media drew attention to Article 9, which said: 'Armed struggle is the only way of liberating Palestine and is thus strategic, not tactical,' and Article 10: 'Commando action constitutes the nucleus of the Palestinian popular war of liberation.'

Arafat solved two problems at once, replying to Israeli propaganda and repaying Mitterrand's hospitality, by saying at a press conference that the covenant was now '*caduque*' (null and void). The *Jerusalem Post*, in its report of the visit, noted that Arafat refused to translate the French word '*caduque*' into Arabic or English. The article was headed: 'Arafat saves Mitterrand with a word'. That word had in fact been personally suggested to Arafat by Dumas.†

The PLO chairman was thinking of going on to London, and sent Bassam Abu Sharif to seek a meeting with Prime Minister Margaret Thatcher. I was in London while Sharif was trying to make arrangements through Jeffrey Archer, the novelist and former deputy

* See p. 324.

† Before Arafat's use of '*caduque*', the strongest previous statement on the covenant had been made by Ibrahim Souss, the PLO representative in Paris, who said that the PNC resolutions in November amounted to '*de facto* abrogation of the covenant'.

chairman of the Conservative Party, and Arafat phoned to ask what I thought of the chances of success. He hoped a meeting with the 'Iron Lady' would consolidate his triumph in Paris. I was doubtful. Shortly afterwards Bruno Kreisky died, and Arafat went to Vienna instead to attend the funeral.

The former Austrian chancellor had been one of the most persistent champions of peace since 1959, when he became foreign minister. Kreisky tried to assist Sadat's attempts to reach an understanding with Begin,* and later played a leading role in efforts by the Socialist International to build bridges between the PLO and its adversary.† He would have been given much credit in the Arab world but for a misjudgement over an unrelated matter in the late 1970s when, as Austrian chancellor, he was looking for a way of disposing of radioactive waste from nuclear reactors. He told Sadat that studies had shown that old salt mines in Egypt would be suitable as storage depots. The Egyptian president accepted this request, and plans were made to bury the waste deep underground in the eastern Egyptian desert near the Red Sea. These arrangements were well advanced when environmentalists brought the potential hazards to light, resulting in a scandal which tarnished the reputations of both Kreisky and Sadat. Sadat sought to justify his decision by saying that Kreisky was trying to help Egypt, but found no acceptance, and the agreement was cancelled. Sadly, the constructive role Kreisky had played was overshadowed.

* See p. 271.
† See pp. 324, 343, 363.

11

The Madrid Conference

After the exhausting process of making itself acceptable to Washington, the PLO discovered during the second half of 1989 that there was still no place at the negotiating table for the 'sole representative' of the Palestinians. Instead of pressing Israel to reconsider its refusal to talk to the PLO, the United States attempted to adapt the Shamir Plan into a basis for a settlement. This could only be achieved if the PLO agreed to stay out of a delegation representing the Palestinians in talks with Israel. The US attitude caused much anger within the movement, and many questioned whether the dialogue with the American ambassador in Tunis was worth the political price which had been paid.

In October 1989 James Baker proposed that the Israeli–Palestinian talks should take place in Cairo, and put forward a five-point proposal covering the scope of the dialogue and a procedure for selecting Palestinian participants. Neither the PLO nor Egypt was happy with Baker's ideas, but by the beginning of 1990 US officials felt that a compromise was emerging. The Palestinians selected would be people acceptable to the PLO, but would not say openly that they supported the organization. It was important to the PLO that the list should include Palestinians from east Jerusalem, because of the disputed status of the capital. Baker supported this demand.

If the Palestinians and Egyptians gave the impression of being prepared to go along with Baker, albeit reluctantly, the reaction in Israel was much sharper. The proposal to hold Israeli–Palestinian talks sparked months of infighting between the Israel right and the far right, overshadowing the relatively favourable attitude shown by the Labour Party. Shamir found himself under fierce attack from Ariel Sharon, David Levy (Herut) and Yitzhak Modai, the Liberal leader. The three ministers insisted that the 140,000 Palestinians living in east Jerusalem should be excluded from elections to select a Palestinian negotiating delegation. Palestinians who had been deported from the occupied territories should also be ineligible, and the cessation of the Intifada should be a precondition for elections. The aim of these ministers was to block the peace process.

In February the row developed into an open power struggle when Sharon resigned after accusing Shamir of giving free rein to Palestinian terrorism, and announced that his aim was to take control of Likud. Six Likud deputies resigned and set up a new party, and on 15 March the government fell on a sixty to fifty-five vote of no confidence.

The motion was sponsored by Labour, but proved counter-productive. President Herzog gave Peres a mandate to form a new government, but on 26 April the Labour leader was forced to confess his inability to put together a coalition. Shamir then accepted a new mandate, and formed a government composed of Likud and other right-wing parties, and excluding Labour.

Presenting the new government to the Knesset on 11 June 1990, Shamir said it was composed of those who had 'fought and worked for the sake of Eretz Yisrael'. The Arab world was now facing a government with a strong ideological commitment to annexation of the west bank, even if this was not openly stated. At the same time Moscow relaxed emigration restrictions and Soviet Jews began arriving in large numbers, swelling Israel's population by 350,000 over the next two and a half years. This combination of Zionist ideology and population pressure alarmed not only Arabs but also the Bush administration.

The frustration of the PLO was aggravated by further killings of Palestinian civilians by Israeli soldiers. Arafat wanted to address the United Nations to call for international action to protect Palestinians, and ran into another wrangle with Washington over whether he should speak in New York or Geneva.

On 30 May a group of Palestine Liberation Front commandos attempted to attack an Israeli military target near Tel Aviv, but were intercepted by Israeli forces. No civilians were killed in this incident, but Israel argued that the PLO had broken the pledges which Arafat gave in December 1988, and urged the United States to stop the Tunis talks. Bush demanded that Arafat should condemn the raid and take action against Abul Abbas, leader of the PLF, but the PLO chairman was facing an internal balance of power which made it impossible to adhere to US conditions. The entire Palestinian movement was now disillusioned with the US–PLO dialogue and unwilling to pay a further political price. By 20 June 1990, when Washington broke off the talks, the peace process was back to where it had been before 1988.

The lack of impartiality by Washington, the intransigence of a fundamentalist Israeli government, the territorial erosion of the west bank and the flood of Soviet Jews contributed to a feeling among Palestinians that the declarations made by the PNC and Arafat in 1988 had been premature.

Throughout the five years of his active quest for peace, from the Cairo Declaration of 1985 to the rupture of US–PLO talks, Arafat had maintained close links with Saddam Hussein in Baghdad. The importance of these connections increased after Ayatollah Khomeini's declaration in July 1988 that the time had come to 'drink poison' by accepting UN Resolution 598, the international formula for ending the Iran–Iraq War.

The ceasefire of August 1988 allowed Iraq to claim victory, though the true result was a stalemate. By 1990 Baghdad was returning to a peacetime economy and found itself in urgent need of funds for reconstruction. Fifteen years earlier the problem could have been solved through oil exports, but prices had slipped from the heights of 1974.

Iraq and other countries obtained an OPEC agreement to cut production in the hope of boosting prices, but some Gulf countries, including Kuwait, refused to respect the new quotas. Overproduction continued, prices remained low, and Iraqis found their economic expectations frustrated. Anger against the ruling Sabah family of Kuwait fuelled nationalist feelings in Baghdad, and fresh calls were heard for the 'nineteenth province' to be reincorporated in Iraq.

The Iraqi leadership had not forgotten the discussions conducted in 1981 between William Casey, director of the CIA, and General Fadel El-Barrack, chief of Iraqi intelligence.* At that time Washington was strongly against annexation of Khuzestan, but showed less opposition to Iraq's claim to Kuwait. Nine years had passed, but Baghdad still felt that Washington had a moral duty to respect the understanding.

* See p. 364.

The war against Iran, applauded by Washington, had prevented the Middle East from being overrun by Iranian fundamentalism, thus securing vital Western oil interests. Baghdad realized that Washington was now opposed to annexation of Kuwait, but guessed, in view of all that had happened, that the US would stop short of using force.

At the same time there was growing anger in Baghdad over encouragement Washington was giving Kuwait to maintain oil production. A suspicion that Washington favoured Kuwait more than Iraq had been aroused a few years earlier, when the US allowed Kuwait to fly the American flag from eleven of its tankers, which thus qualified for US naval protection. The result of this 'reflagging' was that Kuwait maintained its oil exports at a high level throughout the Iran–Iraq War, while Iraq suffered a loss of exports.

During the late 1980s Saddam Hussein expressed the anger and frustration of the Iraqi people against both the United States and Kuwait. Throughout the same period he made strong statements against Israeli intransigence, emerging as the foremost Arab champion of the Palestinian cause. Saddam Hussein's boldness delighted the Palestinians, who felt that at last an Arab leader was standing up to oppression. Arafat began to spend increasing amounts of time in Baghdad, and there was talk of moving the PLO headquarters from Tunis. Baghdad contributed $40 million a year towards the PLO's costs arising from the Intifada.

The crumbling of East European governments during the autumn and winter of 1989 had shown that the Soviet Union's days were numbered. The US would soon be the sole superpower, but it could not hope to dominate every region of the world. Iraq, with an army of fifty-five divisions, began to look like a powerful counterweight to US and Israeli influence in the Middle East. The Iraqi artillery was renowned as the best-equipped and most battle-experienced in the region. All these points made a close relationship with Baghdad attractive to the Palestinian leadership.

One of the causes of the Iraqi leadership's anger in the late 1980s was the Iran–Contra affair, and Israel's role as conduit and participant. The disclosure of Washington's duplicity in applauding the war against Iran while simultaneously flirting with the enemy aroused indignation. Iraq had stood alone against the might of Iran, unaware that at a critical point in the conflict US aid was flowing to Teheran. Some in Baghdad felt that Iraq should be compensated for this injustice. Previously there had been a feeling that Washington would not strongly oppose Iraqi annexation of Kuwait, but after the Iran–Contra revelations an attitude grew that the US had forfeited any say in the matter. If the administration would not compensate Baghdad in a material sense, Iraq would take its own compensation through a military-political move. This complicated logic was leading Baghdad down an ever more dangerous path.

Saddam Hussein and other Iraqi leaders made indirect references in speeches to the Casey–Barrack discussion. 'The United States knows what we are talking about' was a hint dropped more than once. Arafat did not know the details of the earlier contacts, but picked up enough to realize that Baghdad was confident that it could get away with the annexation of Kuwait. As late as 24 July 1990 the US ambassador to Baghdad, Miss April Glaspie, told Saddam Hussein that the United States had 'no opinion' about the border dispute between Iraq and Kuwait.

After Iraq's invasion on 2 August 1990 the US issued an ultimatum to Baghdad to withdraw. Most in the Arab world and the West quickly realized that Washington was in earnest, but Arafat continued to think the US would stop short of armed intervention.

The defeat of Iraqi forces in March 1991 left Arafat and the PLO with few friends in the region. Arab countries which had supported the US-led military coalition against Iraq wanted nothing to do with the PLO chairman. Kuwait and Saudi Arabia, which had been the organization's most important backers before 1989, cut off all financial and political support, as did the smaller Gulf producers. The Intifada continued but no longer gained as much attention as before the Gulf War, and Israeli occupation was no longer the sole target. An increasing number of executions by Palestinians of other Palestinians suspected of collaboration with Israelis gave the struggle a different tone, and at the same time the PLO was steadily losing ground to Islamic fundamentalist groups. The organization had also been weakened by the loss of two of its key members, Salah Khalaf (Abu Iyad), the intelligence chief, and Hayel Abdel Hamid (Abu El-Hol). A Palestinian reportedly acting on orders from Abu Nidal assassinated both men on 14 January 1991.

After the Gulf War Washington felt in debt to Shamir, who had accepted requests by President Bush to stay out of the fight, showing restraint when Israel was attacked by Iraqi Scud missiles. Washington also owed gratitude to Saudi Arabia, Egypt, Syria and other countries which had supported the coalition. During the four crucial months at the end of 1990, when the coalition assembled its forces in Saudi Arabia, Washington gave commitments that it would resume the Arab–Israeli peace process once the conflict with Iraq was over. In a speech to the UN General Assembly in October Bush said that when Iraq withdrew from Kuwait there would be opportunities 'for all the states and the peoples of the region to settle the conflicts that divide the Arabs from Israel'.

Whatever their reservations about the PLO, all Arab countries wanted justice for the Palestinians, and pointed out the disparity between the swift enforcement of UN resolutions against Iraq and the fact that nothing had been done to make Israel respect resolutions 181, 242 or 338. The same Arab coalition partners were equally worried about the continuing influx of Soviet Jews and the construction of Israeli settlements.

The need to reconcile US political debts to Israel and to Arab countries brought the Bush administration to a less one-sided attitude than it had shown before the Gulf War. In a speech to a joint session of Congress on 6 March 1991 Bush said: 'A comprehensive peace must be grounded in . . . resolutions 242 and 338 and the principle of territory for peace. This principle must be elaborated to provide for Israel's security and recognition, and at the same time for legitimate Palestinian political rights.' If the administration had applied those principles more vigorously at the beginning of its term, Arafat might not have been driven into Saddam Hussein's arms.

Before the Gulf War Bush expressed opposition to Israeli settlement construction in speeches; after the war he backed words with pressure. In May 1991 Shamir's government asked Washington to guarantee loans of $10 billion to pay costs arising from the influx of Soviet Jews. The Bush administration soon dropped hints that the answer would depend on the Israeli government stopping the construction programme. A decision on the loans was delayed, and Washington stepped up its attacks against settlements. On 22 May James Baker told the Subcommittee on Foreign Operations (part of the House Appropriations Committee): 'I don't think that there is any bigger obstacle to peace than the settlement activity that continues not only unabated but at an enhanced pace.' These remarks were attacked by Israeli and American Jewish spokesmen, but Bush defended his secretary of state: 'Secretary Baker was speaking for this administration and I strongly support what he said.'

James Baker made eight tours of the Middle East between March and October 1991. The negotiating concept he followed was the same as in 1990, but the atmosphere was different. Israel was now under financial pressure, the PLO was in disgrace, Bush was riding high, and Baker was prepared to take a firmer line. He made a point of talking to Palestinians resident in the occupied territories who had known links to the PLO, including Hanan Ashrawi and Faisal Husseini. No previous secretary of state had taken such a step.

The PLO was in no position to improve the indirect role in peace talks which had emerged in the 1990 discussion. Given the organization's weakened position, Arafat had to accept that no member of the PLO would be included in a joint Jordanian–Palestinian delegation for peace talks with Israel. The organization would, however, be allowed to select the delegation. This arrangement saved face for Shamir, but was plainly unjust. The categories of Palestinians ineligible for the delegation were to be those on which Sharon and right-wing colleagues had insisted at the end of 1989.

Between June and August 1991 Syria, Jordan and Israel agreed to a US proposal that a peace conference should be held in October in Madrid. The invitations were to be issued by Washington and Moscow as joint sponsors, but the Soviet role was mainly symbolic. Gorbachev was now in Bush's pocket and had cooperated in the UN resolutions which allowed Iraq to be crushed. After a failed coup attempt in Moscow by old-guard elements in August the collapse of Soviet communism was imminent.

In September Bush stepped up financial pressure on Israel by asking Congress to delay consideration of the loan guarantee issue, and by making further attacks on the settlement programme. Meanwhile Baker, helped by Egypt, oversaw the complex process by which the Palestinian–Jordanian delegation was selected. In order to persuade the PLO to cooperate, it was necessary to say that Israel had no power of veto. At the same time, Israel had to be assured that it was not obliged to negotiate with anyone it considered unacceptable.* These incompatible assurances were reconciled by persuading the PLO to accept delegates who met the Israeli rules. However, the PLO found ways of preserving essential Palestinian positions. The principle that east Jerusalem Palestinians should be represented was upheld with the help of Amman, which included in its team a Palestinian Jordanian whose family lived in Jerusalem. Israeli restrictions were further bypassed by attaching a 'steering committee' to the Palestinian delegation, composed of people with known PLO links, including Faisal Husseini and Hanan Ashrawi.

The letter of invitation sent by the co-sponsors proposed that the opening session should be followed by direct talks between Israel and the Jordanian–Palestinian delegation, and between Israel and other neighbours (Syria and Lebanon). The parties invited were Israel, Syria, Lebanon, and the Jordanian–Palestinian delegation. Egypt was not a party, but was invited as a participant, as was the European Community. The Gulf Cooperation Council and the United Nations were invited to send observers.

The aim of the talks between Israel and the Jordanian–Palestinian delegation was to reach agreement within a year on arrangements for a five-year interim period of Palestinian self-government. During the third year of the interim period negotiations were to begin on permanent status on the basis of resolutions 242 and 338.

Faisal Husseini replied to the invitation on behalf of the fourteen Palestinian members of the Palestinian–Jordanian delegation. In a letter to the American and Soviet consuls in Israel on 25 October he said: 'During the conference and the negotiations the Palestinians should have the right to raise any issue they feel important.' This understanding had been negotiated with Washington through Arab intermediaries as the key PLO condition for accepting the arrangement.

Husseini also spelt out the Palestinian position that accepting the

* The mutually contradictory assurances were set out in a US letter dated 10 October 1991: 'Only Palestinians can choose their delegation members, which are not subject to veto from anyone. The United States understands that members of the delegation will be Palestinians from the territories who agree to negotiations on two tracks in phases, and who are willing to live in peace with Israel. No party can be forced to sit with anyone it does not want to sit with.'

exclusion of the PLO did not affect the organization's status as the 'sole representative' of the Palestinians. 'We expect the full participation of the PLO in all the later parts of the process.'

The letter implied that a meeting on 17 October of the PLO executive committee had decided only with reluctance to go along with the arrangements: 'We protest against the unfair form of our representation in the conference. It is unfortunate that the two sponsors have accepted the pre-set Israeli conditions. But that should not be a precedent . . . and we hope you know that our acceptance was difficult and painful.'

Before the delegations went to Madrid the Egyptian government arranged a seminar to share Cairo's experience of negotiating with the Israelis. The top floor of a Cairo hotel was turned into a college and almost the entire Palestinian group attended lectures given by Boutros Ghali (then minister of state at the Egyptian Ministry of Foreign Affairs), Mustafa Khalil, the former prime minister, Amr Moussa, foreign minister, and Mohamed Bassiouni, ambassador to Israel. The lectures sought to acquaint the delegation with the Israeli style of negotiating, which differed from that of the Arab world in its emphasis on the precise meanings of words, rather than on the broad meaning of statements.

The Egyptians pointed out that when the Camp David accords of 1978 and the Egyptian–Israeli peace treaty of 1979 were negotiated, the relationship between the United States and Israel differed in an important respect. Two years after the treaty, in November 1981, President Reagan entered into a strategic cooperation agreement with Prime Minister Begin. A month later Begin extended Israeli law, jurisdiction and administration to the occupied territories in the Golan heights. The United States showed its opposition to this move by voting in favour of a UN resolution of condemnation, and by suspending the strategic cooperation agreement. In October 1983, however, Washington felt in need of Israel's help after the attack by a Shia suicide bomber on the US military compound in Beirut. A few days later Reagan reactivated the agreement, and since then regular joint military-political meetings had been held. Israel thus became more than ever the eyes and ears of the US in the Middle East.

Other significant differences between 1978/79 and 1991 were the increased number of Jewish settlements, the Intifada, the political aftermath of the Gulf War, and the collapse of the Soviet Union. Moreover,

Israel had a strong motive for negotiating peace with Egypt, because the neutralization of its largest Arab neighbour would remove the main risk to Israel's security. In negotiating with the Palestinians, Israel had less to gain and more to give up.

The Egyptians advised the Palestinians that no delegation in the talks would be able to outmanoeuvre other participants, because anything confided to Israeli negotiators would quickly become known by all other parties. It was suggested that the Palestinians should take the self-rule elements of the Camp David accords as a basis for negotiations and try to reach a declaration of principles with the Israelis.

One of the sensitive points which arose during the Egyptian–Israeli negotiations concerned arrangements for holding elections on the west bank. Egypt insisted that the Israeli military administration should be removed during the elections. Israel was willing to withdraw (rather than remove) the administration, but that implied that the military governor might return after the elections. The Egyptian lecturers therefore advised the Palestinians to insist on cancellation of the authority of the military administration prior to the elections. The Palestinians could also seek international supervision of the elections, or the presence of foreign observers. Israel had always shown a strong distrust of the United Nations, but the Palestinians could propose supervisors or observers from countries such as the United States, Egypt or Jordan.

A further issue was whether candidates in the elections should stand as independents or as party representatives. If parties were to be involved, an agreement would be needed on Palestinian rights in forming parties. Existing Israeli rules for the formation of parties were highly restrictive, prohibiting any group inspired by the Palestine National Charter, and requiring that parties recognize the state of Israel.

Another important aspect of the electoral system was the choice between a list system, as used in Israel, and the constituency system. The Egyptian advice was to press for the latter, because the attachment of the Palestinians to their land would be more strongly emphasized if candidates represented constituencies. If the Israelis refused a constituency system, the Palestinians could ask for an amalgamation of the two systems, as used in Germany.

Before the conference the United States presented the Palestinian delegation with a set of proposals. The key element was the establishment of a Palestinian Preparatory Authority (PPA) and a Middle East Development Fund (MEDF), with a related timetable and a working programme. The paper said that a PPA would secure international recognition and would mark the start of 'the countdown towards the beginning of final status negotiations'. The aim of the MEDF was to obtain substantial international backing from OECD countries, undertake economic planning, finance projects, promote investment and provide insurance for foreign investors.

The Madrid conference, which opened on 30 October 1991, was intended as the beginning of a long process, not as an end in itself. For the first time in forty-three years of conflict Palestinians sat at the negotiating table with Israelis, even if no progress was made, or expected, on what was mainly a symbolic occasion.* The presence of Syrians, who had negotiated with Israelis only through Henry Kissinger, was almost as remarkable. There was no sense of reconciliation and no particular reason for optimism, but the occasion generated high expectations of progress. Another minor triumph was that Shamir and Gorbachev could sit at the same table. Relations between their countries, broken off in 1967, had not been restored until 18 October.

President Bush called on Arabs to answer Israel's sense of insecurity, and on Israelis to show fairness, respect and cooperation in dealings with Palestinians:

> Now is the ideal moment for the Arab world to demonstrate that [it] is willing to live in peace with Israel and make allowances for Israel's reasonable security needs.
>
> We know that peace must be based on fairness. In the absence of fairness there will be no legitimacy, no stability. This applies above all to the Palestinian people, many of whom have known turmoil and frustration above all else. Israel now has an opportunity to demonstrate that it is willing to enter into a new relationship . . . predicated upon mutual respect and cooperation.

Prime Minister Shamir did not rise to that invitation. Instead he reiterated his rejection of the principle of land for peace and of demands for a halt to settlement construction, and his refusal to negotiate with PLO representatives. He implied that if any member of the Palestinian

* After the opening session the first bilateral talks between the parties were held while they were still in Madrid.

delegation so much as hinted at links with the PLO he would walk out. Saeb Ereikat, an American-Palestinian professor, showed the futility of Shamir's ban by appearing on television after the opening session wearing an Arafat-style *kaffiyeh* (a headscarf with a black and white design).

For the Palestinians the occasion was above all a public-relations triumph. Hanan Ashrawi became an instant media star, and for the first time millions of people in the English-speaking world saw the PLO represented by someone who was articulate, photogenic, reasonable-minded and well-educated. Few would claim those qualities for Shamir.

For Palestinians in the occupied territories the Madrid spectacular was crucial in breaking the taboo. The effect on residents of Gaza and the west bank was similar to the impact Sadat's visit to Israel had on Egyptians in 1977. Seeing people they knew sitting at the negotiating table with Shamir in the presence of the two superpower presidents brought a sense of wonder. The fact that the Palestinians and other Arab delegates talked sensibly and behaved in a civilized fashion, while Shamir hurled accusations of terrorism, afforded a new measure of comparison. A comment which circulated among Palestinians watching the event on television was that Ashrawi was like a butterfly fluttering just out of reach of a spider. Palestinians were thrilled, too, to see their representatives appearing as equals alongside other Arab leaders.

A report to the Egyptian government on the impact of the conference written by Mohamed Bassiouni, Egyptian ambassador in Tel Aviv, pointed out that acts of violence almost completely stopped in the occupied territories during the conference, reflecting a feeling of optimism. When the delegation returned from Madrid to the occupied territories a large crowd turned out to welcome them, but Israeli forces broke up the demonstration with great violence.

Bassiouni added that the fact that all Palestinian factions were represented through the delegation led to an increase in Fatah's popularity. This became clear in elections to the Board of Trade in Gaza, in which thirteen Fatah representatives were elected against only three from the Islamic bloc. When the euphoria of Madrid faded and the Israeli army resumed its provocative ways, violence returned to the territories.

12

The Washington Talks

Among the words of caution in President Bush's speech to the Madrid Conference was a warning against hopes of rapid progress: 'We don't expect peace to be negotiated in a day, or a week, or a month, or even a year. It will take time.' That would have been reasonable if the Israelis had intended to negotiate in good faith. It soon emerged, however, that time was the only thing the Shamir government wanted from the negotiations. Time to build more settlements, time to quell the Intifada, time to wear down Arab expectations. The Israeli prime minister hoped to delay as long as possible the moment when 'interim' self-rule would have to be granted, and then ensure that the interim situation became permanent.* For the Shamir government, the passing of time was an end in itself.

The Washington talks were rich in opportunities for procrastination. The first round was frittered away in squabbles about who should talk to whom. The Israelis would not go into a negotiating room with Palestinians alone, even to talk about solely Palestinian issues. Nearly a month was spent arguing in the corridors of the State Department, with the Israelis insisting that the Jordanian–Palestinian delegation should sit as a single body, while both Palestinians and Jordanians wanted separate sessions, their interests in relation to Israel being different.

During the so-called 'corridor talks', Eliakim Rubinstein, head of the Israeli delegation, overheard Dr Haidar Abdel-Shafi, leader of the Palestinian group, saying that the Palestinians had a historical right to

* The idea that the 'interim' period could last indefinitely was indicated by Shamir himself in remarks after his election defeat in 1992. He was also quoted as saying that if re-elected he would have made the negotiating process last another decade, but later claimed that he had been misunderstood.

have a separate delegation. Rubinstein, who was talking to Dr Abd El-Salam El-Majali, head of the Jordanian–Palestinian delegation, remarked: 'What historical rights? Please tell him that in the whole history of the region there has never been a state called Palestine. What he calls Palestine has been occupied territory ever since the Roman empire. So what country is he talking about? We consider the Palestinians to be refugees who have stayed in our country since the time of the Jordanian occupation. We are ready to give them human rights, but not political rights.'

Rubinstein said that if the Palestinians wanted to talk about political rights, they should talk to Jordan, because that was their own country. Israel, he said, would be happy to see them depart for Jordan, but neither Amman nor any other Arab capital wanted them, 'So we are obligingly keeping them in Judea and Samaria.'

'What arrogance,' Majali exclaimed in Arabic, which Rubinstein understood perfectly.

The Palestinians had accepted a joint delegation with Jordan only as a means of reaching the negotiating table. Now they found the Israelis attempting to transform the Palestinian–Jordanian relationship from reluctant cohabitation into wedlock. The Israelis were attempting to revive and impose what Peres had called 'the Jordanian option'.

These tactics were far too blatant for King Hussein's liking. A Jordanian solution with Palestinian consent was one thing, a shotgun wedding quite another. The king had ridden the roller-coaster of Jordanian–Palestinian relations long enough to know that constitutional links between his country and the west bank could be resumed only if the Palestinians came, through an evolution of ideas, to see that as the best solution.

The king's view of prospects at Washington was far from optimistic, and reflected much bitter experience. Hussein had never ceased to regret the decision taken at the Arab League summit in Rabat in 1974 to endorse the PLO as the sole representative of the Palestinians, even if he had reluctantly voted in favour at the time. That decision had seemed a poor reward for the six fruitless years Hussein spent chasing peace on the Palestinians' behalf, from the autumn of 1967, when Nasser asked him to seek a deal with Washington, until 1974, when Kissinger declined to negotiate a Jordanian–Israeli agreement.

In a conversation soon after the Rabat summit the king poured out his dismay over the 'sole representative' decision: 'From now on Abu Ammar is going to be responsible for the problem of the occupied territories. I am amazed that Arafat is taking it as a victory. He thinks that he has won something from me and that I was obliged in front of an Arab summit to surrender responsibility for Palestine. He does not know the facts.'

Hussein said that during his contacts with Israel through the Johnson administration, the Israeli government was never prepared to concede sovereignty of any part of the west bank: 'All the Israelis offered was that I should be the baker and cleaner and cobbler and teacher of the west bank. And frankly this is a role which I do not want. If Abu Ammar wants to take responsibility then welcome. The Israelis are not ready to give anything serious.'

Despite the many ups and downs which followed, the feelings the king expressed in 1974 still represented his viewpoint in 1991. The fiasco of 1986, when his short-lived agreement with Arafat fell apart, left a deep sense of being let down. The still greater disappointment of 1987, when Shamir refused to endorse the agreement which Hussein reached with Peres in London, brought feelings of hopelessness. A yet more discouraging factor was that figures on the Israeli right, including General Sharon, repeatedly argued that Jordan was the homeland of the Palestinians. Rubinstein's remarks to Majali during the 'corridor' talks were a variation on that theme. There were times when King Hussein felt trapped between the Israelis' determination that the Palestinians should have nothing, and the unanimity of other countries that they deserved something. That 'something' was apparently his kingdom. Hussein thus suspected that his throne was the sacrifice that some wished to place upon the altar of peace.

The king's announcement of July 1988 relinquishing responsibility for the west bank was an expression of frustration, not a statement of long-term intentions. King Hussein could not be immune from the dream which had impelled his grandfather to annex the west bank in 1950. The loss of importance and prestige his country had suffered in 1967, with the Israeli occupation of the west bank and east Jerusalem, continued to rankle. The king was justly proud of having maintained administrative and educational standards in the west bank under Israeli occupation, and of having continued for twenty-one years to pay the salaries of teachers and other public employees. Despite the 1988 declaration, permanent dissociation from the west bank was psychologically impossible.

This complicated blend of feelings and experience made the king deeply sceptical about the chances of success in Washington. The Americans had brought the parties together, but were offering no ideas or leadership to forge a solution. Without a strong and impartial mediator, the gap between Palestinian expectations and Israeli intransigence would remain unbridgeable.

A further reason for King Hussein's lack of enthusiasm about the talks was that the issues Jordan needed to discuss with Israel were of secondary importance. If the west bank problem were settled, all bilateral matters between Jordan and Israel would quickly fall into place. The matters included border rectifications, a dispute over some territory near the Dead Sea, and above all the sharing of water resources.

The king's instructions to his delegation were to bear in mind that Jordan could not afford to be the first party at the talks to enter into an agreement with Israel. It was in the state's interests to wait and watch the progress of other delegations.

Yasser Arafat's perspective was different. The whole Arab world was now following the State Department talks with excitement. Washington was developing into the best stage the PLO had ever enjoyed, and yet Arafat was not among the actors. He had been left in Tunis to pay the expense-account bills sent from Washington while 'his' delegation basked in media attention. The delegates were by now familiar faces to every Arab with access to television. The overall leader of the Jordanian–Palestinian delegation was the Jordanian prime minister Dr Abd El-Salam El-Majali, a member of a Bedouin family which had given Jordan three previous premiers and many military commanders. A jolly, stocky man with a pleasant personality, El-Majali had been head of the Jordanian army's medical services before entering politics.

The nominal leader of the Palestinian part of the delegation was Dr Haidar Abdel-Shafi, a studious man of seventy-five with a somewhat aloof manner. Abdel-Shafi was well respected as a physician and community leader in Gaza.

Paradoxically, the real stars were not permitted to take part in the negotiations. The 'steering committee' which had been sent as PLO hand-holders to keep the delegation in order included Hanan Ashrawi and Faisal Husseini. Ashrawi, professor of English literature at Bir Zeit University, was a highly effective communicator much sought after by the American media. Her skills relieved the Arabs of a depressing feeling that the Israelis were better communicators. Ashrawi personified the image of the new Palestinian woman, with the personality, education and assertiveness to stand up for herself in debate. The fact that she was a Christian underlined the nationalist and non-sectarian nature of the Palestinian cause. Faisal Husseini had special appeal for Palestinians as a scion of a family which had given the cause two of its outstanding figures, Hajj Amin El-Husseini, former Grand Mufti of Jerusalem, and Abdul-Kadr El-Husseini, martyr of the 1948 war. Faisal Husseini's own efforts as an activist, his repeated imprisonment by the Israelis during the Intifada, and his work at the Arab Studies Centre in Jerusalem had further boosted his image. Shimon Peres acknowledged in his memoirs that Husseini was the real leader of the Palestinian delegation, even though not technically a member of it.

The delegation was plagued by rivalry between the stars, giving an impression of disarray, to the annoyance of other members who received little attention from the media. With the exception of Haidar Abdel-Shafi, who had a following in Gaza, none of the delegates had a solid power-base in the occupied territories, although each enjoyed respectability within his or her social constituency.

The relationship between the delegation and Tunis was a mixture of interdependence and tension. While Arafat needed the stars, he felt that media attention had turned their heads and that the information they sent back to Tunis was inadequate. At the same time the delegation depended on the PLO for political protection and finance, but resented having to refer back to Tunis for decisions on every small point. When issues requiring expert knowledge were under discussion, Palestinians at the negotiating table would send points to PLO experts outside the hall, who would in turn obtain instructions from Tunis. Faisal Husseini described this process as '*fax politica*'. The PLO felt, however, that the delegation members either failed to explain clearly the points which were relayed to them, or gave themselves unwarranted negotiating freedom.

The Syrian delegation was led by Muwaffak Allaf, a retired ambassador who had served under a previous regime in Damascus, before

President Assad came to power. Allaf was chosen because he enjoyed prestige but no authority. Damascus wanted to make the point that no one directly connected with the Syrian Ba'ath Party would negotiate with Israel. Although Allaf had been a professional diplomat he was unable to call on the support of the ruling elite in Damascus.

Allaf and his delegation insisted from the start on establishing certain principles. The Israelis had been talking about withdrawing 'in', rather than 'from', the Golan heights, which left a doubt as to whether they intended to return all occupied territory. The Syrians were not prepared to proceed with other matters without confirmation that the withdrawal would be complete. A second dispute was that Israel wanted Syria to define the peace which would be granted in return for territory. Allaf replied that the Syrian definition would be given when Israel answered the question on withdrawal. As neither side was prepared to be the first to answer the other's question, little progress was made. Henry Kissinger encountered comparable problems when negotiating the Syrian–Israeli disengagement agreement in 1974.

The Lebanese delegation, led by ambassador Suheil El-Shammas, could only play the role of a small partner in association with the Syrian delegation. El-Shamaas was a professional diplomat who had served in the Lebanese delegation which negotiated the Lebanese–Israeli agreement of 1983.*

Eliakim Rubinstein, chairman of the Israeli delegation, had been a university lecturer in political science before becoming an adviser to Moshe Dayan during the Camp David negotiations. In June 1991 he was nominated as legal adviser to the prime minister, despite the opposition of the legal establishment, which considered him too young at forty-three, and not sufficiently experienced. Rubinstein was assisted by Eitan Bentsur, vice director general of the foreign ministry, responsible for North American affairs. Bentsur was a member of Peace Now and had reportedly refused to shake Shamir's hand at a public event.

A PLO paper on the Israeli delegation pointed out that several of its members had served with military intelligence, and some were believed to be senior Mossad officials.

The State Department team, led by Dennis Ross, played the role of coordinators but held back in the early rounds from making US

* See p. 360.

proposals. If Palestinian and other Arab delegates had hoped for American help in persuading Israel to make concessions, none was offered. There was also a lack of involvement by other Arab countries. Prince Bander, the Saudi ambassador in Washington, had close links with the White House and had attended the Madrid conference. When the delegations arrived in Washington they found bouquets of flowers sent by the prince, but when they subsequently tried to contact him they found him unavailable. Egypt, too, had taken part in the Madrid conference, and Ali Maher, the Egyptian ambassador to Washington, was considered a potential line of support. Maher was seen at the talks twice, but did not become involved. Delegates gained the impression that other Arab countries were keeping their distance.

At the end of 1991, after the second round of talks, Egypt, Jordan and the United States urged the Israeli government to reconsider its refusal to talk to the Palestinians other than as part of the joint Jordanian–Palestinian delegation. El-Majali told Rubinstein that any concessions the Israelis might give to a joint delegation would have less value, in Palestinian eyes, than concessions they negotiated themselves: 'If I brought them Haifa and Jaffa on a silver platter they would accuse me of treason and say that they could have negotiated a better deal themselves.'

King Hussein was particularly active in pointing out that it would be better for all concerned to separate the two halves of the delegation. The Israelis eventually accepted this argument, but would not abandon their refusal to talk to Palestinians alone, arguing that this was a matter of principle. An understanding was reached that the Palestinians would operate as a separate delegation under the political umbrella of Jordan, and that a few Jordanians would be attached to it. There then ensued a wrangle over how many Jordanians would be required to preserve the Israeli principle. Jordan thought one would be sufficient, but the Israelis wanted four. El-Majali was driven to the point of exasperation before a compromise was found. When the subject under discussion was mainly a Palestinian matter, the Israelis would talk to a delegation consisting of twelve Palestinians and two Jordanians. When the issue was mainly Jordanian, the proportions would be reversed. Agreement was reached at the beginning of the third round of talks, in January 1992.

This squabble over formalities became doubly ironic when the

Jordanians noticed that the Palestinians were more comfortable than themselves in talking to the Israelis. Before the Washington talks no Jordanian delegation had dealt with the Israelis, as contacts had always been conducted at a higher level. The Palestinians, on the other hand, were accustomed to dealing with Israelis every day in the occupied territories. El-Majali said later: 'At the beginning I was awed by the Israelis and felt inhibited talking to them. After some time I realized that they were no more intelligent or efficient than us, and their only area of superiority was greater discipline. They knew the limits of their authority and never exceeded them.'

After the separation of the Palestinian and Jordanian delegations, the Israelis began to adopt different forms of behaviour towards the two delegations. The aim seemed to be to differentiate between a collection of individuals with no status recognized by Israel (the Palestinians) and the representatives of a state (the Jordanians). The Israelis' tone was mostly civilized, but became rough if the Palestinians attempted to complain about their lot. On a day when four Palestinians had been killed by Israeli soldiers on the west bank, the Palestinian delegation stated that Israel was using terror as a weapon. Rubinstein replied: 'I will not allow such words to be used against us. This is not the place for complaints.' Agreement was later reached that complaints could be submitted in writing.

The first meeting of the Jordanian–Israeli track in the third round produced a surprise development. As the two delegations entered the negotiating hall Rubinstein handed an envelope to Majali. 'What's this?' Majali asked.

'It's a peace treaty.'

'This is crazy,' Majali objected. 'A peace treaty should come after we've talked, not before. What is the point of meeting if you do this? You might as well have sent it by post.' Majali said that he could not accept the document officially, but would take it for information only.

As the two sides got down to serious talks, it became clear that the path to Israeli–Jordanian agreement would not be easy, even if the issues were minor compared to Palestinian matters. Although accord was found on some points with little difficulty, real differences arose on others. It was not hard to agree that the borders drawn by Churchill in 1922 should serve as the reference base for discussing adjustments, and that international law should be the reference for settling refugee questions. However, when the Jordanian delegation tried to insert UN resolutions concerning the refugees, the Israeli delegation refused on the ground that such resolutions were not part of international law. When water resources were discussed the Israelis said that any accord should apply only to future projects, while the Jordanians wanted to discuss the unfairness of the existing situation. The Israelis were already taking three quarters of the water which should properly have been allocated to Jordan.

At the same time the Jordanians found that the Palestinian representatives in their delegation were refusing to discuss what the Israelis had said in Israeli–Palestinian meetings. It was essential to share information to prevent the Israelis playing one group off against another, but the Palestinians were silent. Majali complained to King Hussein, who raised the issue in a meeting with Arafat in Amman. 'We need some coordination,' the king said. 'The Israelis know what both sides are saying and can work out our plans. We've been surprised by some of the things they have said.'

This complaint failed to break the Palestinians' reticence, and eventually Majali was forced to take Dr Haidar Abdel-Shafi to task. The Palestinian delegation leader's reply was surprisingly frank: 'We are a delegation of fourteen people, right? On the face of it, that seems the situation, but in real terms we are fourteen different delegations. Each of us represents a group and each of us has his contacts.'

When King Hussein heard what Haidar Abdel-Shafi had said, his suspicion that the Washington talks would achieve nothing became stronger than ever. If Palestinians could not work with Jordanians, inter-Arab coordination was impossible. There was no question, however, of Jordan withdrawing from the talks. It suited Hussein to bide his time and wait for the parties to reach deadlock.

Meanwhile the Palestinian–Israeli track had at last moved away from procedural issues, and the delegations were discussing the proposed interim agreement on Palestinian self-rule. This was too much for two of the small right-wing parties in Shamir's coalition, which were opposed to any form of Palestinian autonomy. The five deputies of the Tehiya and Moledet parties resigned from the government in January 1992, leaving Shamir without a majority.

Elections were arranged for 23 June 1992, with the result that the Israeli campaign overlapped with the primaries of the US presidential election. Shamir and Bush thus found themselves running for re-election simultaneously, and each had some influence with the other's voters. The fact that Bush and Baker wanted Labour to win was an ill-kept secret. The unfavourable attitude of the Israeli government and the American Jewish lobby towards the Bush administration was no secret at all.

In February 1992 Yitzhak Rabin challenged his old rival Shimon Peres for the leadership of the Labour Party, and won. Rabin then campaigned vigorously on a platform combining a tough law and order stance with a limited offer to trade land for peace. Bush helped Rabin's prospects by announcing that if Israel wanted loan guarantees it would have to accept American conditions on settlements. Shamir then abandoned his request for guarantees, but Israeli voters understood that a Labour government, which would have less difficulty in accepting the conditions, would be able to reapply.

During the five months of the Israeli election campaign Israeli delegates in Washington became more cautious than ever, and the already slow pace of the talks slackened further. Apart from ruining what little goodwill remained, this led to mutual suspicions, jealousies and rumours. At one point Arafat began claiming that the Syrian–Israeli track was close to success, while in fact no progress was being made. The Egyptians took up the rumour and began encouraging the Jordanians and Palestinians to move faster, to avoid being beaten by the Syrians. The Palestinian delegation leader Haidar Abdel-Shafi also believed that the key to a solution lay with the Syrians. King Hussein realized that all this was nonsense, and hoped that when deadlock eventually came the Palestinians would see the merits of links with Jordan.

After complaints that the Israelis were not really negotiating, the Americans organized weekly meetings of all delegations, in the hope of breaking the impasse. This proved futile because no one said anything of substance. The gap between Israeli and Arab positions on all the main issues remained as wide as ever, and in some cases wider. In talks with the Lebanese delegation, for example, the Israelis demanded the removal of all Palestinians, Syrians and Iranians from the country, which was politically impossible.

Amid rumours that the talks were close to collapse the Americans urged all delegations to stay at the table, despite lack of movement.

Many of the Arabs, and especially the Syrians, were content to go along with the American request, feeling that if the talks ultimately failed the Americans would be held morally responsible. The Syrians thought Bush could ill afford such a failure during an election year, and would be obliged to put pressure on Israel to make concessions.

The Israelis were aware of the Syrian view, and replied that if Arabs were waiting for Washington to intervene they were deluding themselves. They also suggested moving the talks to the Middle East to reduce costs. Seeing that the Arabs were reluctant, the Israelis said it was a mistake to suppose that the State Department venue worked to the Arab advantage. The Arabs still refused to move the talks, but gradually realized that they had indeed overestimated the ability or willingness of Washington to pressure Israel.

Muwaffak Allaf, head of the Syrian delegation, said later: 'There was a time when we thought that the Americans influenced the Israelis. Now we feel that it is the Israeli foreign ministry that directs the State Department. The State Department coordinators have American faces, but their tongues are Israeli.'

A similar point was made by Majali in a report to King Hussein after he had stopped attending the talks personally, feeling that it was pointless to spend so much time in Washington. His report, entitled 'The Israeli Character of the American Coordinators', pointed out that many of the State Department coordinators were American Jews.

One of Majali's reasons for deciding not to attend further sessions was that attention was moving to trivial matters, because all important issues were deadlocked. One of the Israeli ideas was that Israel and Jordan should begin cooperating in a project to eradicate the mosquitoes of the Jordan valley. Another was a proposal for a scheme to stop Jordanian pigeons fouling the streets of Eilat. According to the Israelis, the pigeons went to the Jordanian port of Aqaba to feed at grain silos, and returned to Eilat to obey the call of nature. The Israelis also proposed building two canals, one from Aqaba to the Dead Sea, and the other from the Dead Sea to the Mediterranean. Although important, this proposal was ill-timed, as major capital projects could not be undertaken without first achieving political stability in the region.

On 23 June 1992 Likud was heavily defeated, winning only thirty-two seats (a drop of eight) in the Knesset against Labour's forty-four (an increase of five). The Tehiya Party, which had helped to precipitate the election, failed to secure the minimum 1.5 per cent of the votes necessary for representation, and disappeared from the Knesset. Soviet immigrants played an important role in the elections, punishing Likud for its failure to obtain the American loan guarantees, which would have eased problems of integration. It was estimated that 47 per cent of recent Soviet immigrants voted for Labour and only 18 per cent for Likud.

Fifteen years of Likud rule was at an end, and Arabs could look forward to doing business with a more amenable Israeli government. Rabin had promised, as part of his election manifesto, to reach an autonomy accord with the Palestinians within a year. Hopes rose in the Palestinian delegation in Washington that with new faces and attitudes on the Israeli side progress might at last be possible.

On 13 July 1992 Rabin presented a government with himself as prime minister and defence minister, while Peres once again took the foreign portfolio. The government had sixty-two seats in the 120-seat parliament, made up of Labour (forty-four deputies), the centre-left MERETZ bloc (twelve) and the Sephardi religious party Shas (six). The five Arab deputies were also likely to support the government, but were not part of it. A few days later Rabin announced the cancellation of 6000 houses and flats which had been planned for construction in the occupied territories. This made little impression on the Arab world because work continued on another 10,000 homes already under construction. President Bush considered, however, that Rabin had done enough to qualify for the $10 billion loan guarantees, and passed a recommendation to Congress.

Settlement construction had in fact begun to slow in the last months of the Shamir government, as supply was outstripping demand. Fewer homes were needed because the rate of immigration had dropped. The massive exodus from Russia which had begun in mid-1989 ran out of steam by the end of 1991. Many of the 350,000 new Soviet immigrants sent letters home warning their relatives of poor living conditions and a shortage of jobs in Israel. One measure of the socially depressed state of the immigrants was a survey showing that 70 per cent of Israeli prostitutes were Russian.

Shamir had nevertheless achieved his ambition of greatly extending the Israeli colonization of the occupied territories. The area between

Jerusalem and Ramallah was virtually saturated with settlements.

When the sixth round of talks began in Washington on 24 August the Arabs hoped for changes, but found that the Israeli delegation remained as before, with Rubinstein in charge. The American coordinators were more cautious than ever, not wanting anything to emerge which might unsettle Jewish opinion during the US election. Rabin began to speak of the need for quick agreement with the Palestinians, but no sense of urgency was felt at the negotiating table. A narrowing of differences was achieved in the Syrian–Israeli talks in the sixth and seventh rounds, but the Palestinian channel remained stalled. An impression was growing that the talks would continue to mark time until after polling day.

On 5 October, a month before the presidential election, Congress approved the Israeli loan guarantees. This improved the standing of the Republicans with American Jews, and ensured that neither the US–Israel relationship nor the Washington talks would loom large in the election. Voters were more concerned with the Gulf War, which had given Bush a massive popularity boost in 1991, but took on a different light in 1992. Attention was drawn to the fact that the Reagan administration, with Bush as vice president, had supported Saddam Hussein's military build-up in the 1980s. There were also accusations that the Bush administration, in the early part of 1990, had given confusing signals to Baghdad as to its attitude on the Kuwait issue. What voters did not know was that in 1981 the Reagan administration had failed to object to Iraqi intentions at a time when the future of Kuwait seemed negotiable.*

On 4 November 1992, however, all these arguments paled in comparison with domestic considerations, and Bush was punished by voters for having given too much attention to international matters and too little to the US economy. The president's defeat by Democratic candidate Bill Clinton dealt a further blow to the Washington talks, as the outgoing administration could not be expected to make further initiatives during its last two and a half months in office.

In early November Hezbollah forces detonated a bomb in the 'security zone' on the Lebanese side of the Lebanon–Israel border, killing five Israeli soldiers. Israel retaliated, and at the same time tension on

* See pp. 364–5.

the west bank rose, reflecting frustration over lack of progress in the talks. Rabin, who had promised voters a tough line on law and order, cracked down hard on protesters, and deaths on both sides rose to their highest level of the year. At the same time the government began making minor gestures designed to improve relations with the PLO. A front-page interview with Arafat in the Israeli newspaper *Y'di'ot Aharonot* in November was a signal that Israeli laws prohibiting contacts with the organization would no longer be enforced, although they were still on the statute books. From the eighth round of Washington talks in December the pretence that the Palestinian delegation had not been appointed by the PLO was dropped.

Any improvement in the tone was short-lived. On 17 December, near the end of the eighth round, Rabin deported 415 suspected Islamic activists, many of whom were members of Hamas or the smaller Islamic Jihad organization. The deportees were taken to the border with Lebanon, but the Lebanese government refused to allow them to enter, and they were left in freezing conditions in no-man's-land, with only tents for shelter. The Palestinian delegation suspended the talks in protest.

When the Bush administration left office on 20 January 1993, the Washington process had achieved nothing tangible. Bush's prophecy in his speech to the Madrid conference had been proved true in one sense, and wrong in another. 'It will take time,' he had said. 'Indeed it should take time – time for parties so long at war to learn to talk to one another, to listen to one another. Time to heal old wounds and build trust. In this quest, time need not be the enemy of progress.'

Fifteen months had passed, but wounds had not been healed. Time was indeed proving the enemy of progress.

13

A Refusal to Accept Failure

The ebb and flow of prospects for peace had come to seem as immutable as the tides, determined by mysterious forces beyond human control. When hope retreated once again in December 1992, many felt that agreement would never be achieved through the Washington talks. At the same time the prospect of failure was unacceptable to all concerned.

The search for Middle East peace had taken on a new light since the fall of the Berlin wall. The death of the twentieth-century dinosaurs, the Cold War, the division of Europe, and apartheid, made the Arab–Israel conflict seem a relic of the old order. Universities in the United States and Europe were pouring out papers on the implications of a world guided by only one superpower. The outcome of the Gulf War had left an impression that *pax Americana* might soon descend on other regional troublespots.

Despite the setbacks of December 1992, the wider political conjuncture offered the best prospects in decades. Israel was now ruled by a government which seemed willing to trade at least some land for peace, and in the United States a new administration was about to take office. Experience had shown that most US administrations, whether Republican or Democrat, made their major Middle East efforts at the beginning or middle of the electoral cycle. The coincidence of a Labour government with a new US presidency thus offered an opportunity.

Many of the Arab, Israeli and American leaders involved in the peace process were advanced in years. When the Clinton administration came to office Arafat was sixty-four, Rabin seventy-two, Peres seventy, secretary of state Warren Christopher seventy-one, Mubarak sixty-six and King Fahd seventy-one. All knew that their ability to shape the future would last only a few more years. If they wanted to set the course of the Middle East before leaving office, the opportunity for peace had to be seized.

The unacceptability of failure was also making itself felt in Israeli domestic politics. Rabin had won the June 1992 election on a promise to deliver an autonomy agreement within a year, and his performance was being assessed according to that measure. Meanwhile the part of the Israeli electorate which wanted expansion, regardless of the implications for peace, was quieter than usual. The Eretz Yisrael lobby could no longer make practical arguments for more settlements, because of the drastic slowdown of Soviet immigration.

Israel had many additional reasons for preferring to make peace sooner rather than later. Among the less obvious factors was the growing usefulness of the United Nations. For decades Israeli politicians had relied on Washington to prevent the UN from meddling in the Arab–Israel conflict, other than in token roles. The end of East–West tension and the growth of cooperation between Washington and Moscow had aroused fears that the Security Council might impose its own solution in the Middle East.

The Arab world was just as unwilling as Israel to accept failure in the peace process, but for different reasons. One important element was impatience among non-Palestinian Arabs, stemming from a loss of idealism experienced in most Arab countries during the two decades after Nasser's death. By the late 1970s the beating heart of Arab nationalism had fallen silent, giving way to a rush for collective and individual profit. The rise of the arms trade, drugs trafficking, land speculation, and the involvement of Arab governments in seedy privatization deals, contributed to a feeling that all noble values had been drowned by commercialism. In this ugly mood many regarded the Palestinian cause as an annoying distraction.

Another important factor was the unusual alliance between the sheikhs of the Gulf, the moderates of Egypt and the radicals of Syria, brought together by the shared experience of the Gulf War. The fact that Israel was part of that alliance, while the Palestinians were on the other side, created an extraordinary reversal of the usual alignments. Traditional attitudes to Israel were eroded when Saddam Hussein's call for a *jihad* went unanswered, and when Bush succeeded in restraining Shamir after Iraq's Scud missile attacks on Israel. Further evidence of change came in mid-1992, when some Arabs campaigned on behalf of

Labour in the Israeli elections. The Egyptian media and the PLO again urged Arabs living in Israel to vote for Arab parties which would support a Labour government.

A feeling was growing in all Arab countries that the Palestinian cause had for too long been a banner to be waved by politicians and carried into unrelated battles. The political costs of the PLO's flirtation with Baghdad showed the urgency of removing that temptation.

Another consequence of the Gulf War was that hundreds of thousands of Palestinians were dismissed from their jobs in Gulf countries and ordered to leave. This increased the financial strain on families in the occupied territories who had depended on remittances from relatives working abroad. At the same time the PLO stopped receiving funds from countries which had participated in the Gulf War coalition, and was obliged to reduce its own financial assistance to Palestinians on the west bank. Quite apart from their anger with the PLO, Saudi Arabia and Kuwait needed all available funds for their own reconstruction costs.

For west bank Palestinians these pressures came on top of the financial sacrifices necessary to sustain the Intifada. Even before the Gulf War, the PLO and the Arab world had contributed little, and now that little became nothing. The resulting bitterness accelerated the switch of allegiances from the PLO to Hamas, which in turn hardened the attitudes of the sheikhs.

At the end of 1992 fears were expressed in the West that the Islamic flood might overtake Egypt. A European ambassador said at the time that his government was convinced of this risk despite his advice to the contrary: 'They keep telling me that the Egyptian regime is about to collapse and that the Muslim Brotherhood will take over. I have sent them telegrams saying that this is not the case, but they seem sure of their information.' The ambassador began to think that his government must know something of which he was unaware, and he pleaded with President Mubarak's office for more information. The concern became so acute that the ambassador's government sent a joint team of intelligence and diplomatic experts to make a separate evaluation of the situation. During the same period several American universities announced that their programmes for the 1993–94 academic year would include studies of the threat facing Egypt.

The origin of this scare turned out to be Israeli defence under-secretary General Mordechai Gur, who was running day-to-day business at the defence ministry. In a meeting with a group of ambassadors Gur had predicted the fall of Cairo, and had said that this would invalidate the Israel–Egypt peace treaty. He further argued that the West could reduce the risks to Egypt by giving more financial aid. His views were given weight because of a Western tendency to assume that Israel understood the Middle East best.

Meanwhile the fundamentalist wave was sweeping through Algeria, Sudan and Yemen. In June 1990 the Islamic Salvation Front (FIS) took control of all the main Algerian cities in municipal elections. The Gulf War exacerbated anti-Western feelings in the spring of 1991, and the FIS was widely expected to win parliamentary elections in June, until President Chadli Benjedid altered the election rules and constituencies in ways which helped the National Liberation Front (FLN). This led to strikes and demonstrations which Chadli used as a pretext to postpone the elections indefinitely.

In Sudan, the power of Islamic elements had been felt much earlier. President Gaafar Mohamed El-Nemery began an attempt to extend Islamic Sharia law to the whole country in 1983, causing a renewal of civil war with the mainly non-Muslim south. President Omar El-Bashir, who came to power in a military coup in 1989, ensured that Sharia law was applied in all areas under the government's control. The National Islamic Front (NIF) was widely seen as the most powerful influence in shaping government policy.

In the Arabian peninsula, a puritanical form of Islam taught by Mohamed ibn Abd al-Wahhab was adopted as the official faith of the first Saudi kingdom as early as the eighteenth century. Despite this the Saudi royal family was as worried as all other Gulf rulers by the rise of Islamic fundamentalism in the 1980s and nineties. A videotape recorded by a fundamentalist sheikh achieved a sale of half a million copies in Saudi Arabia, and religious books enjoyed massive success throughout the Arab world.

As the fundamentalists advanced, the mood of the Arab ruling classes was deeply pessimistic. Many felt that Algeria, Sudan, Yemen, Egypt and perhaps even Tunisia were on the road to chaos. Iraq was in ruins, the Gulf countries were in a state of shock after the Gulf War, Libya was being bullied by the United States and Britain, and Lebanon was little more than a geographical term. These fears were exaggerated, but with most of the media under the control of governments, unbalanced ideas easily gained acceptance. Egyptian newspapers, which had once set standards of objectivity, came to be seen as organs of government. Arabs were now obliged to turn to foreign radio and television stations to discover what was happening in their own countries.

Yasser Arafat spent much of 1992 in Tunis brooding over the disastrous events of the previous year. With little new money coming in, the PLO had practically exhausted its savings and investments. Since its foundation the organization had received donations amounting to nearly $4 billion, but now only $150 to $180 million remained. Much of the money had been spent on imitating the trappings of statehood, with ninety-two embassies around the world and ambassadors who needed to maintain a certain image. When the Gulf countries resumed aid to the Palestinians, the money was given directly, without being channelled through the PLO. Prince Salman of Saudi Arabia said he would find a way of helping those affected by the Intifada, but would not assist Arafat.

Arafat struggled to gain reacceptance but found most doors closed. At the end of 1992 none of the Gulf states had yet agreed to receive him, and the Bush administration refused to communicate, other than through the Palestinian delegation at the Washington talks. King Hussein had long since been forgiven by Bush for having supported Saddam Hussein, but Arafat felt that his own repentance was being rejected.

Arafat asked President Mubarak to persuade King Fahd to allow the PLO to return to the Arab fold. Mubarak sought forgiveness and rehabilitation for the PLO chairman, but the Saudi king said that Arafat would first have to make a public apology. Fahd was prepared to set aside most aspects of Arafat's behaviour during the Gulf War, but he remained angry over an accusation by the PLO chairman that Israeli planes had participated in raids against Iraq from Saudi bases. The king considered this an insult to his family and an invitation to Arabs to assassinate him.

Arafat refused to apologize, but assured Mubarak that he had not made the alleged accusation. King Fahd insisted that Arafat should issue his denial in a clear public statement. This was too much for Arafat, though he began to make positive remarks about Saudi Arabia.

The PLO chairman's new tune worried Saddam Hussein, who inquired what had become of their friendship, and reminded Arafat that two brigades of the Palestine Liberation Army were still stationed in Iraq.

The Iraqi president felt that Arafat was wavering, trying to present himself in a new light to the Gulf states while at the same time seeking to remain on good terms with Baghdad. Saddam Hussein made a gesture to retain Arafat's loyalty when Arafat visited Baghdad at the beginning of February 1993. During a party given in the PLO chairman's honour, the Iraqi president presented Arafat with the Grand Order of Um El-Ma'arik (the 'Mother of All Battles Medal'), in recognition of his support for the Iraqi people.

Fearing that this would put paid to his chances of a rapprochement with Washington and the Gulf states, Arafat begged Mubarak to find a way of reducing the damage. The Egyptian president came to the rescue by declaring that he had sent Arafat to Baghdad on a mission of reconciliation, with a message from the Egyptian government to Saddam Hussein suggesting that they should readjust to new circumstances. At the same time the secretary of the Arab League, Dr Esmat Abd el-Meguid, submitted a motion calling for Arab reacceptance of Iraq as part of the fold. These moves were rejected by the Gulf countries, which argued that it was too soon for reconciliation.

Arafat thus found himself eclipsed at a time when a brighter star was rising. The media attention lavished on Haidar Abd El-Shafi, Faisal Husseini and Hanan Ashrawi made Arafat think that Americans were trying to promote an alternative leadership with more modern ideas. His patience snapped when Ashrawi told the media that she was not exactly a PLO member, just nominally attached to the organization. Arafat phoned and advised her to be more careful. 'I could bring you back to the west bank and make you stay at home,' he warned.

At the end of a miserable year and at a time of despair in the peace talks, Arafat was approaching a choice between unacceptable alternatives. Without some dramatic concession on his part, the Washington process seemed destined to fail. On the other hand, the Israeli price for peace involved abandoning essential Palestinian objectives. He could uphold the cause of Palestinian independence and remain an outcast at the head of a near-penniless movement, or he could accept the unacceptable and become a media prince of peace. The choice was to be admired by the West or to be vilified like Saddam Hussein and Gadaffi. The temptation to choose success and fame could not have been greater.

14

The Turning Point

At the darkest hour of Arafat's disquiet, fresh hope emerged from the least-expected quarter. Throughout the fifteen months since the Madrid conference, a second set of negotiations had been under way between Israel, the Arab states and Palestinian representatives. The talks had been held in Moscow, Rome, Ottawa and Brussels, but had attracted little media attention because the issues were practical and economic rather than political. In December 1992 a PLO representative involved in the multilateral talks was approached by an intermediary acting on behalf of an Israeli minister. A new secret channel, at first concealed even from Arafat and Rabin, began to take shape.

The new channel arose from a need to break out of the straitjacket of the Washington talks. Both Israel and the PLO were growing weary of the futile official talks, though the reasons for their scepticism were different. Israel's pretence that it was negotiating only with non-PLO Palestinians had collapsed, and yet it was still official government policy not to negotiate with the organization. This self-contradiction could only be overcome through secret contacts. The PLO, meanwhile, felt that it was not being taken seriously by Washington. The Americans continued to treat the PLO as a totem from the past whose blessing was needed to give a push to the future. This attitude was fuelled by the ambiguity in relations between Palestinian stars at the Washington talks and PLO headquarters in Tunis.

Apart from Washington, numerous other lines of contact were open, and yet none was producing results. No fewer than nine different secret channels ran through Cairo, where aides to President Mubarak were highly active in arranging meetings. David Kimche, under-secretary at the Israeli foreign ministry and former director of Mossad, was in charge of one of these channels. Among the Israeli personalities who participated in the Cairo contacts was David Levy, a senior member of Herut who had been foreign minister under Shamir. Secret messages exchanged during that period give the impression that the Israelis were using the contacts as a means of continuously probing Palestinian thinking at the highest level, but were not really negotiating.

A further reason for the lack of progress in Cairo was that Egyptian officials confined their efforts to bringing the parties together, leaving the Palestinians to speak for themselves. At the time the PLO needed more support. Indeed Arafat seemed to want Cairo to give a lead in proposing dramatic concessions, so that he could claim he had been obliged to accept an imposed solution.

Other secret links had been under way for years, especially in Europe. Shimon Peres and General Abraham Sneh, former commander of Israeli forces on the west bank, had met Palestinian representatives in Paris and Rome. Ezer Weizman had held two meetings with Nabil Ramlawi, the PLO representative in Geneva. Nothing had been achieved, and nothing seemed achievable. The White House was receiving advice from counsellors such as Richard Haas that the crisis was not yet ripe for solution. That view was understandable, and yet both sides had overwhelming reasons for wanting a settlement.

The PLO leadership felt under pressure from all directions. Palestinians in the occupied territories were demanding a solution, PLO funds were almost exhausted, and the organization was losing ground not only to Hamas but also to King Hussein, whose popularity was growing rapidly, especially in west bank cities. The Israeli wish to tie the Palestinians to Jordan had become stronger than ever after the Labour victory in 1992. The risk that Jordan and Israel might come to a deal without involving the PLO could not be dismissed. While the Palestinian delegation had suspended its participation in Washington, the Jordanian–Israeli talks were making progress. An agenda for a declaration of principles was ready to be signed as a first step.

The sense of urgency was just as strong in Israel because of the declining security situation. Gaza remained a living bomb, with riots continuing day and night, and Hamas soaring to ever greater prominence as a result of the deportations.

Six months earlier, in the last days before the June 1992 election, two academics, one Israeli, the other Norwegian, had discussed Gaza while lunching together at a restaurant in Tel Aviv. Neither had any idea that their casual conversation would lead to a new secret channel. The Israeli was Yossi Beilin, founder of a small research group called the Economic Cooperation Foundation. Beilin was also a Labour politician and had been Peres's assistant at the time of the 1987 agreement with King Hussein.* The Norwegian was Terje Larsen, founder of the Norwegian Institute for Applied Science, an organization involved in alleviating Gaza's chronic social problems. The two men were interested in Gaza from different angles. Beilin's priority was to solve one of Israel's biggest political and military problems, while Larsen was mainly concerned with relieving human misery.

Beilin explained that Labour was looking for ways of bypassing the Washington process, in the event of election victory. Larsen was in touch with influential Palestinians, including Faisal Husseini, as a result of his academic work. He offered to arrange a discussion between Beilin and Husseini, which although illegal was unlikely to be noticed if it were conducted on an academic rather than a political plane. The meeting was held shortly before the election.

After the election Beilin was appointed deputy foreign minister under Shimon Peres. Larsen offered to set up a further Beilin–Husseini meeting in Oslo, with help from the Norwegian government. The Norwegian academic had political contacts both through his institute and because his wife was a Norwegian foreign ministry official. Mrs Larsen, who used her maiden name Mona Juul, worked as an assistant to Thorvald Stoltenberg, the Norwegian foreign minister, and was also the sister-in-law of a Swedish government minister. The Larsens had previously spent three years in Egypt, when Mona Juul was attached to the Norwegian embassy in Cairo.

Larsen arranged for Beilin to meet Stoltenberg's deputy Jan Egeland. Stoltenberg had long been interested in the Palestinian problem, though his efforts tended until 1991 to be overshadowed by those of the better-known Swedish foreign minister Sten Andersson.† After a change of government in Sweden in 1991 Andersson left office and Stoltenberg's role gained in importance. The Norwegian government was willing to help Beilin on the basis that Norway would act as a

* See p. 381.
† See pp. 393–6.

facilitator of secret talks, but would not attempt to mediate. Knowledge of this role was restricted to a small group, including Norwegian prime minister Gro Harlem Brundtland.

A second Beilin–Husseini meeting had to be abandoned because of problems on both sides. As Beilin was now a junior minister, the chances of escaping media attention were remote. Husseini, too, was always under foreign media scrutiny because of his role in the Washington talks. A further complication was that if a Beilin–Husseini channel proved successful, the result would be a further rise in Husseini's already considerable glamour. Arafat was nervous about the prominence of his Washington stars, and could not be expected to welcome such a channel. The talks would have more chance of success if the Palestinian negotiator was under his direct authority, and if the interlocutors on both sides were people whom the media did not consider newsworthy.

The unknown actors needed for this new stage were found when Larsen attended a round of the multilateral talks in London on 3 and 4 December. Larsen was acquainted with the coordinator of the Palestinian delegation, Ahmed Kore'i, better known as Abu El Ala, and had already arranged to discuss the financing of refugee operations with him.

Abu Ala, a fifty-eight-year-old economist from a village called Silwan, between Jerusalem and Ramallah, had worked as a mathematics teacher in Kuwait before joining Fatah, and later became a full-time official in the PLO's economics department. One of his responsibilities was a PLO department called Samed ('Steadfast'), which supported Palestinians who had no other sources of assistance.

The two men compared notes on the harmful social effects of Israeli policies in Gaza. Both were concerned about the rising influence of Hamas, which was proving to be the most efficient Palestinian organization at running hospitals and social services. Favourably impressed by Abu Ala's attitudes, Larsen felt he had found a man who was intelligent, reasonable-minded and little-known, the qualities the new channel most needed.

One of the Israeli delegates at the conference was Yair Hirschfeld, a left-wing intellectual who participated in Beilin's academic group. Hirschfeld, a professor of Middle East history, was nervous about meeting Abu Ala, but eventually consented. After an initial session at

Hirschfeld's hotel in Piccadilly, Abu Ala reported to Abu Mazen, the PLO official responsible for contacts with Israelis, who was trying to build up a network of links with various parts of the Israeli establishment.

At that stage Abu Mazen asked few questions, wanting only to know whether the Norwegian government was involved in the channel. Abu Ala understood that there was a link, but had no proof.

'All right, go ahead,' said Abu Mazen, 'But don't tell Abu Ammar [Arafat] for the moment. Wait until we have something definite to say.' Abu Mazen was not particularly optimistic, because many previous contacts had ended without results. Neither Abu Ala nor Abu Mazen had any means of knowing that Larsen was acting for an Israeli government minister. Meanwhile Beilin gave Hirschfeld and his academic partner Ron Pundak, a history research fellow, approval to take part in further meetings.

In early January 1993 plans were made for the two sides to spend a long weekend together later in the month. Larsen arranged for them to stay at a private mansion at Sarpsborg, near Oslo, where they were unlikely to be noticed.

On 7 January Abu Mazen was present at a meeting between Arafat and Mubarak in Cairo. Knowing that Abu Mazen was responsible for contacts, Mubarak asked: 'What is new on your front?' Abu Mazen replied: 'Nothing important, but there are some new ideas.' In a résumé of recent developments he dwelt on other matters and gave only the smallest hint of the new connection. The Israelis had 'contacted one of our people', he said, and did not elaborate.

The Israeli law making contacts with the PLO illegal was repealed on 19 January, the day before the first fully-fledged meeting of the Oslo channel. Hirschfeld and Pundak flew to Oslo by an indirect route to avoid media interest. Abu Ala was accompanied by Maher El-Kurd, an economist who spoke excellent English, and Hassan Asfour, an assistant to Abu Mazen. The initial intention was that the encounter should be like any other discussion among academics, apart from the need for secrecy. By the end of the weekend it was clear that this was more than an academic exercise.

The Palestinian group put forward ideas radically different to those which were under discussion in Washington. The Washington talks had shown, they said, that a comprehensive settlement was unattainable, and that only an interim agreement had any chance of success. They proposed drawing up a declaration of principles for an interim accord based on the idea that Israeli withdrawal should begin with Gaza. This was a direct response to Israel's stonewalling in Washington, and a departure from one of the PLO's main demands.

The PLO's previous insistence on a comprehensive settlement was not without its internal critics. Some members, including Abu Mazen, had long favoured an interim settlement. In an internal PLO paper Abu Mazen argued that the organization should try to create 'facts on the ground', just as the Zionists had done in Palestine after the Balfour Declaration. Any starting point, even as small as Gaza, could be a basis from which to expand. This argument overlooked important differences. Zionist settlers were able to grow from small beginnings in Palestine because of British support and because of the wealth and political power of world Jewry. The Palestinians, on the other hand, had nothing but a defeated camp, an empty bank balance, and a worn-out population.

The majority PLO view was that if the organization accepted a 'Gaza first' settlement, Israel would have no incentive to cede other territory later. As early as 1977 Arafat had rejected a suggestion by Cyrus Vance that Israeli withdrawal should begin with Gaza, with Jericho thrown in as a sweetener.* Peres, too, proposed in 1980 that Israeli withdrawal should begin with Gaza.

After the 19 January meeting Abu Mazen felt that the channel was more promising than expected, and decided that Abu Ala, whose background was solely in economics, needed a thorough briefing on PLO political perspectives. The two men spent nine hours together in two sessions going over all aspects of PLO policy.

Abu Mazen also decided that the time had come to tell Arafat about the contacts. The PLO chairman's first question was: 'Did you assign Abu Ala for that role?'

'No,' Abu Mazen replied.

'Then the Israelis must have chosen him. They have picked a man of their own preference.'

Abu Mazen assured Arafat that there was nothing shadowy about Abu Ala, and suggested that the Israelis had probably wanted to avoid

* See p. 317.

dealing with any of the well-known PLO leaders because of the risk of leaks. Secondly, Abu Ala's rank was high enough to give him access to the leadership, even if he was not part of it himself.

After some discussion Arafat gave authorization for the contacts to continue, but insisted that Abu Mazen should check the extent of Norwegian government involvement. The PLO chairman knew that Norway had taken part in the earlier attempts to set up contacts through the Socialist International. If he could be sure that Oslo, rather than just Larsen, was backing the talks there would be more reason to take the channel seriously.

Meanwhile Hirschfeld and Pundak reported back to the Israeli government, and Peres decided that the matter was important enough to bring to Rabin's attention. The two academics had given the PLO no clue as to whether they were acting on their own behalf or had some kind of link with the Israeli government. Their reticence aroused the PLO's curiosity, and efforts were made to check through other sources. Abu Mazen asked Amr Moussa, the Egyptian foreign minister, to arrange a meeting with Israeli officials in Egypt, but this did not materialize. The PLO was thus still unsure at the end of January what to make of the Oslo channel.

A second meeting at Sarpsborg on 12 February marked an important step towards real negotiations, as opposed to exchanges of ideas. Abu Ala and his colleagues brought detailed proposals dealing with autonomy in the occupied territories during the interim period, the final status negotiations, and the Jerusalem issue. Hirschfeld came with a draft declaration of principles based on an Israeli withdrawal from Gaza, a gradual transfer of responsibilities, the building of institutions of self-government, and economic cooperation. The weekend encounter resulted in a joint declaration of principles which sought to blend the two sets of ideas.

An important element of this draft was that the future of Jerusalem would be decided as part of the final status talks on the west bank and Gaza, after a period of Palestinian autonomy. In accepting this concept the two academics departed from Labour Party policy. While Labour was willing to withdraw initially from Gaza and later from certain other parts of the west bank, the party did not want to discuss the status of Jerusalem.

When Arafat and Mubarak held another meeting in Cairo on 21

February, the PLO leader was mainly preoccupied with the PLO's financial crisis. The reduction in the organization's anti-poverty work was a serious source of concern, threatening long-term harm to the PLO's image in the occupied territories. Arafat asked the Egyptian president to persuade Saudi Arabia to come to the aid of Gaza: 'They promised Faisal Husseini that they would donate between $10 and $20 million, but they have sent nothing. All we have in the fund is $7 million which was given by Iraq in 1980,' he complained.

The Egyptian president, who was not yet aware of the Oslo channel, was anxious that Rabin should play a bigger part in peace efforts. Mubarak said he would send Dr Ossama El-Baz, his political adviser for foreign affairs, to Israel the same night to talk to the Israeli prime minister: 'It's important to get Rabin involved, but we mustn't forget that he is under attack from Netanyahu.' Binyamin Netanyahu, who succeeded Shamir as leader of Likud in 1992, had been making fiercely critical speeches against Rabin.

On 28 February Thorvald Stoltenberg left the Norwegian foreign ministry to become UN mediator in the former Yugoslavia, at the request of UN secretary general Boutros Ghali. Before taking up his new post Stoltenberg informed secretary of state Warren Christopher about the Oslo channel.

A third meeting in Sarpsborg was held in March, and this time Arafat's attention was fully engaged. He had always been aware of Abu Mazen's views but had not until now seriously considered accepting them in full. The idea that a small area of autonomy as a start might be better than nothing was beginning to find favour in the PLO chairman's mind. 'If the Israelis gave me one square metre of Palestine I would raise a flag on it and try to expand from there,' Abu Mazen argued.

After the March meeting Arafat decided that the Oslo team should be upgraded. Abu Ala was appointed a member of the central committee and head of the PLO economic delegation to the multilateral negotiations. Mahmoud Abu Kush, a former member of Fatah, was added to the team.

Arafat and Abu Mazen were still worried about a lack of certainty that the Israeli government was backing Hirschfeld and Pundak. At the same time they realized that if the Israeli government was involved, it would be sure to keep the United States and Egypt informed, and

King Hussein might also find out through his contacts. Arafat and Abu Mazen therefore felt that they should at least inform Egypt, to avoid the risk that Cairo might hear from Tel Aviv first. A message was sent from Tunis instructing the PLO ambassador in Cairo to inform 'the appropriate authorities'. The ambassador replied: 'There is nothing called the Egyptian authorities. You can't play with Egypt like this. If there is something to be said, it should be said to the president by Arafat in person.'

Arafat, Abu Mazen and Abu Ala went to Cairo in early April and were invited to the president's home, together with Amr Moussa, the Egyptian foreign minister, and Ossama El-Baz. Arafat was anxious, however, that Mubarak alone should hear about the talks. The PLO's ambassador had been instructed to say at a suitable point in the meeting: 'I think the chairman has something to say to the president.' Mubarak accordingly asked everyone but Arafat to withdraw, which annoyed the others. 'What's this? Has the chairman got a secret we can't hear?' the Egyptian foreign minister grumbled. After some time he and Ossama El-Baz were called into the room with the president and Arafat. The PLO chairman was illustrating his ideas with a map, but the ideas were not exactly those which had been discussed in Oslo. Instead of just Gaza, Arafat wanted the initial Israeli withdrawal to include Jericho as well. Arafat was in effect returning to the Cyrus Vance proposal of 1977.

Soon afterwards Mubarak visited Washington and held talks with President Clinton and Warren Christopher. With the exception of Dan Kurtzer in the State Department, the Americans gave no indication of being aware of any promising new channel. Meanwhile Arafat and Abu Mazen had discussed whether the PLO should inform Washington, and decided that it would be sufficient if Abu Ala mentioned to Hirschfeld and Pundak that the PLO did not want Washington to be left in the dark.*

The Washington talks had been stalled for four months because of the deportation of the Islamic activists from Israel, but in April some were allowed to return home. Rabin also dropped the Israeli objection to Palestinians from east Jerusalem taking part in the Palestinian

* Arafat also considered informing Syria, but decided that it might try to sabotage an agreement on the basis that was being contemplated.

delegation to the Washington talks. The State Department was thus able to schedule a ninth round of talks to begin on 27 April, and Faisal Husseini was permitted to head the Palestinian delegation, instead of remaining outside as head of the 'steering committee'.

On 29 April, two days after the resumption of talks in Washington, a fourth round of the Norwegian channel was held at a hotel just outside Oslo. Abu Ala and his team raised the demand that Israel's initial withdrawal should include Jericho as well as Gaza.

Two weeks before this meeting Johan Jorgen Holst had been appointed to succeed Stoltenberg as Norwegian foreign minister. Holst and his wife Marianne were on good terms with Larsen and Mona Juul, and became increasingly involved in the Oslo channel. This removed any remaining PLO doubts about the involvement of the Norwegian government, but Abu Ala and his team were still unsure whether Hirschfeld and Pundak had Israeli government backing. That concern was settled on 20 May, when the two Israeli academics arrived for another round of talks in the company of Yuri Savir, director general of the Israeli foreign ministry. Peres had wanted to attend in person, but met resistance from Rabin, and Savir was the compromise choice. Abu Ala immediately passed word back to Abu Mazen that the Oslo channel was a link with top levels of the Israeli government.

The timing of Savir's appearance in the Oslo talks was significant, as the ninth round of the Washington talks had proved disappointing for both sides. The Israeli delegation in Washington had made what Israel regarded as concessions, resulting in an agreement that the Palestinian interim authority would function more like a parliament than as an administrative body. The Israelis also proposed ideas on the sharing of water resources. These moves made little impression on the Palestinian delegation, which felt the progress was minimal in relation to the problems still to be overcome. Palestinians in Gaza and the west bank evinced no excitement about the prospect of having a parliament. It was the lack of positive reaction which made Peres lose interest in the Washington talks and turn his attention to the more promising discussions in Norway.*

* At one stage Peres entertained hopes of reaching an agreement by 14 May, the anniversary of the proclamation of Israel. That was impossible, as much negotiating remained to be done.

The Israeli foreign minister's special interest in the Oslo connection came to the attention of the Egyptian government, which was worried about a risk of confusion. It was felt that with so many different lines of contact operating, apart from the official talks in Washington, wires were bound to become crossed. Mubarak was not optimistic about the chances of success in Oslo, and was concerned that the channel might be merely a Peres sideshow, having more to do with Israeli politics than real negotiations. An opportunity to find out Rabin's attitude arose when Dr Ossama El-Baz, Mubarak's aide and chief foreign policy adviser, visited Israel for talks with the prime minister on other matters. At the end of the meeting El-Baz asked for a ten-minute private session with Rabin. His first question was: 'Are you in the picture about the meetings in Oslo?' Rabin confirmed that the foreign minister was 'keeping me in the picture'. El-Baz asked whether Rabin had any ideas about the remaining issues in Oslo. Rabin, slightly irritated by the questioning, replied: 'Am I under examination here?'

'No,' replied El-Baz, 'but we want to be sure of your view because that channel appears to be gaining momentum.'

'I happen to differ with you,' Rabin answered. 'I doubt if anything will come out of it.'

Rabin was perhaps not yet aware that important progress, from the Israeli viewpoint, had been achieved at the 20 May session of the Oslo talks. The Israelis had been worried that the future status of Jerusalem might have been jeopardized by the proposed declaration of principles. At the 20 May meeting Savir argued that the Jerusalem issue should be left on one side, as the aim was to achieve an interim agreement. Abu Ala consulted Abu Mazen, who gave authorization for the talks to proceed on that basis. After this major Palestinian concession all remaining issues were details. Some of these points were complicated, but the Israelis had already won the fundamentals. The proposed agreement left on one side not only the status of Jerusalem but also the final size and frontiers of the lands to be controlled by Palestinians, the future of Israeli settlements in occupied territories, and the fate of Palestinian refugees.

The difference between what the Palestinians were saying in Oslo and their official position in Washington was now immense. One delegation was ready to give the Israelis almost everything they wanted; the other was holding out for the original PLO demands.

Although Arafat and Peres were ready to go ahead, Rabin remained sceptical about the Oslo channel. He had made repeated statements opposing any direct deal with the PLO, and was not pleased to be presented by Peres with an outline deal. Rabin suspected that the foreign minister was chasing a spectacular political success without properly considering the consequences.

Throughout the eleven months since his election victory, Rabin's main priority had been to promote contacts with Syria. Egypt tried to assist Rabin in this enterprise, and Amr Moussa made two visits to Damascus, but President Assad was adamant that the Syrian government would not enter into discussions. Rabin sought to tempt him by saying that he did not rule out withdrawal from the Golan heights once peace with Syria was achieved, but to no avail.

Egypt learned of Rabin's reluctance to accept the tentative PLO–Israeli agreement at a time when Mustafa Khalil, the former Egyptian prime minister, was about to visit Israel to receive an honorary degree from the Weizmann Institute. President Mubarak asked Khalil to try to convince Rabin that there was no alternative to a deal with the PLO.

In his meeting with the Israeli prime minister, Khalil found that he was still fixed on his Syrian objective. Rabin wanted Khalil to arrange an Israeli–Syrian summit, and refused to accept Khalil's argument that this was impossible. The Israeli prime minister was under the impression that if he could achieve a deal with Syria, the PLO would cease to matter. Mustafa Khalil replied that if Israel made an agreement with the PLO, Assad would no longer be able to play the Palestinian card.

Rabin's refusal to deal with the PLO seemed to cut across the government's decision to allow Faisal Husseini to lead the Palestinian delegation in Washington. If an agreement were reached in Washington, Husseini and his colleagues would undoubtedly seek Arafat's permission before signing. An agreement signed by Arafat himself, on the other hand, would have far greater authority.

At the time of the Khalil–Rabin meeting there were indications that the Israeli public was coming round to the idea of a deal with the PLO. King Hussein's refusal to speak on behalf of the Palestinians and his insistence that the Israelis should deal with them direct in Washington had done much to change attitudes. Rabin's continuing resistance seemed out of step with the public mood. Opinion polls among Palestinians showed that the PLO remained the only organized Palestinian body with sufficiently wide support to enter into an agreement with Israel. Moreover, the Israelis had never been in a stronger position for such an agreement, because the PLO no longer had Soviet support, was desperately short of money, and felt under pressure from competitors. Rabin did not accept these arguments at the time, but a process of conversion had begun, and over the next three months his views slowly changed.

An analysis of the reasoning which brought the Israeli prime minister to accept a deal with the PLO was later made by an Egyptian government official. One of the clinching arguments was that Israel had failed to create a recognized alternative Palestinian leadership in the occupied territories. Arafat, on the other hand, had succeeded in bringing the Palestinian delegation in the Washington talks under his wing, whether by financial sponsorship or by political protection.

A further factor was that most of the continuing military resistance to Israel was religiously motivated. Israeli forces were under attack from Hezbollah in southern Lebanon and from Hamas in the occupied territories, both of which were backed by Iran. The PLO might prove the only organization capable of checking the fundamentalist trend.

Rabin was also influenced by the argument that a settlement with the Palestinians would leave Assad without a cause, apart from the recovery of Israeli-held territory in the Golan heights.

A sense that time was running out also contributed to Rabin's change of heart. He and Peres were among the last remaining powerful politicians who had been involved in the first Arab–Israel war. Now, in the dusk of his career, Rabin felt the need to achieve something for peace. 'I don't want at the end of my life to be a policeman chasing boys throwing stones,' he later said to Boutros Ghali.

The prime minister told a group of Knesset deputies: 'We must remember what our aims are. We did not set out to defeat Egypt or to occupy the Golan heights . . . our aim was to build a strong Israel. We wanted it to be strong politically and economically, to be part of the region, and to be able to set the agenda for the area. The conditions are right now to achieve those aims.'

By the end of May Rabin was on the road to acceptance of the tentative Oslo deal, Peres was full of excitement, and Arafat wanted to press ahead as soon as possible. The negotiations had reached a point where it was less difficult for the parties to go ahead than to turn back.

Arafat's sense of urgency can be traced to an event which occurred thirteen months earlier. On the night of 29 April 1992, the PLO chairman's plane crashed at a remote spot in the Libyan desert, and for a whole day, while rescuers searched for the aircraft, Arafat lay injured in the wreckage. Feelings of intense loneliness mingled in his mind with fears that he might die with his life's goal unfulfilled. Arafat had always been troubled by the example of Hajj Amin El-Husseini, who spent his life struggling for the Palestinian cause and kept the flame of resistance burning, but in the end left no monument.

After the Libyan crash Arafat became a man in a hurry. If the prize of Palestinian independence was unattainable, he was ready to accept something less, rather than end his days with nothing to show. 'I have the feeling that people expect me to be like a drone which fertilizes the queen bee and dies,' he said.

The crash occurred during the most difficult year of his career, at a time when the Gulf War rift remained unhealed, and when the media spotlight had passed to younger faces. The expulsion of the PLO from Lebanon a decade earlier had separated Arafat from the roots of his revolution, leaving him with no source of power other than patronage and his own personality. When funds from the Gulf states stopped, Arafat's power to exercise patronage was shackled. Nothing remained but the loyalty of his supporters.

Worries about his personal security added a further dimension to Arafat's sense of urgency. One by one his friends had been picked off by Mossad or Abu Nidal, including most recently Salah Khalaf, his closest colleague. Arafat had survived by keeping on the move, rarely sleeping in the same bed two nights running. During one of his many visits to Egypt I invited Arafat to take a short break from his travels. 'What's the hurry?' I asked. 'Why not spend a few nights here?'

He replied: 'They [the Egyptian government] don't want me here. As soon as I arrive they ask: "When are you leaving?" And yet Cairo is the only place where I can have a deep sleep. Everywhere else I sleep with one eye open, but in Cairo I feel secure.'

Thus it was that a lonely, worried man hemmed in by pressures came to regard the wretched offer Israel had made in Oslo as an escape from his troubles. In accepting the principle that the status of east Jerusalem could be set aside, Arafat had crossed a sacred line of trust.

15

The Oslo Agreement

Once Arafat had decided in principle to accept the outline Oslo agreement, there could be no turning back. Weeks of intensive negotiations lay ahead, and many a crisis would be reached, but the PLO chairman now had too much at stake to allow the channel to fail. The same was true of Peres, who had to prove to his sceptical prime minister that he could turn the outline into a workable deal. From the end of May the Israeli team gained a new member, a lawyer who was close to Rabin's way of thinking, and just as hard-headed. Joel Singer had been involved in the Camp David accords and later worked for Rabin for five years in the ministry of defence. His role initially was to assess the outline from a legal viewpoint. Singer was not impressed with the document, but felt that some of the points Abu Ala had made verbally to Hirschfeld were important. At the next meeting in Oslo on 11 June Singer questioned Abu Ala closely on the verbal points, and clearly wanted to include them in the written agreement. Abu Ala's replies found approval, and Singer left to report in positive terms to Peres and Rabin. Soon afterwards Bassam Abu Sharif sent a personal letter to Peres suggesting that the time had come for a high-level Israeli–PLO meeting. 'I am sure that Israelis want peace the same way Palestinians want it,' Sharif said.

Meanwhile the tenth round of talks had begun in Washington, and as yet no one in the Palestinian delegation was aware of the secret Oslo channel. Not a hint of the concessions Arafat was prepared to make had been disclosed to the Washington delegates, and with no movement on either side the talks were heading for deadlock.

The attitude among Palestinians in the occupied territories had changed from expectation to disillusionment. At the outset of the Washington talks in 1991 the Palestinian delegates had been local heroes, but by mid-1993 their credibility was spent. Hardly a week had passed without killings in Gaza and the west bank, while the Washington team droned on about matters that seemed arcane to people who simply wanted a solution. After twenty months of negotiations the two sides had still not reached agreement on a declaration of principles. The people were tired of the struggle, weary of polemics, and exasperated with a delegation which seemed unable to come to a conclusion one way or the other.

Sensing the risk of breakdown, the State Department submitted a compromise proposal at the end of June. The American paper was described as a synthesis of ideas raised by Israeli and Palestinian delegates and by US coordinators. The approach was the same as in October 1991: the two parties should agree on a declaration of principles to guide the negotiations, with the aim of achieving agreement in two phases. That much was non-controversial; the American proposals dealt with the difficult details.

While the delegates in Washington were digesting the US document, the talks in Oslo came to their first crisis. After two days together in Gressheim, north of Oslo, Abu Ala and Yuri Savir and their assistants found themselves in strong disagreement on numerous points of detail. The teams talked all night, but by 6 a.m. no progress had been made. It was too late to go to bed, and the atmosphere was too tense for them to take breakfast together. Both teams headed home wearily, thinking the negotiations had broken down.

Within days of reaching Tunis and Israel they were told to go back to Norway and try again. Both Peres and Arafat were determined to reach agreement, and a training course had already begun to prepare an initial batch of 1200 PLO commandos to serve as policemen when Israeli forces withdrew from Gaza and Jericho. Men from the Badr Brigade of the Palestine Liberation Army, based in Jordan, and from the Ain Jalut Brigade in Egypt were the first to be retrained for this role.

During the few days before the next round both teams were instructed to introduce additional points which had not been in the outline deal. Rabin wanted safeguards dealing with the security of settlements in the occupied territories and the safety of Israelis travelling through Palestinian areas to reach the settlements.

When Savir and Singer brought up these points in a meeting in

Oslo on 10 July, Abu Ala replied with new demands from Arafat. The PLO chairman wanted the organization to be mentioned explicitly rather than implicitly in the document, and insisted on measures to guarantee secure road communications between the two autonomous Palestinian areas. This could only be achieved, the PLO felt, if the area of Palestinian territory were extended to include a road running between Gaza and Jericho, 113 kilometres apart.

The Israelis felt that these were fundamental changes and had no chance of being accepted by Rabin. They therefore rejected Abu Ala's demands outright, and remained adamant even when the Palestinian negotiator produced a personal letter from Arafat expressing the importance he attached to the talks. The weekend ended with another crisis and more fears of breakdown.

Despite their reluctance to act as mediators, the Norwegians were equally unwilling to let the channel wither. On 13 July Larsen and foreign minister Holst went to Tunis to see Arafat, and found that the PLO chairman was upset about the proposals the Americans had made at the Washington talks. An analysis prepared in Arafat's own handwriting and coloured with red and yellow fluorescent markers showed that 65 per cent of the points in the US synthesis had been taken from an Israeli paper, 28 per cent from an earlier American paper, and only 7 per cent from the Palestinian delegation's paper. Fuming over this lack of even-handedness, Arafat said that the PLO was having to negotiate against not one but two delegations, the Israelis with Israeli accents and the Israelis with American accents. The Norwegians sought to assure him that the Israelis wanted a deal, and Larsen and Mona Juul then shuttled between Tunisia and Israel with messages. After a few days Peres and Arafat agreed to a resumption of talks, and Rabin reluctantly added his own endorsement.

Meanwhile Arafat sent his comments on the American paper to President Mubarak, to pass on to Warren Christopher. Although he was angry with the Americans, Arafat showed a willingness to accept concessions on certain points. These matters had not been discussed with the Palestinian delegates in Washington, who were surprised and angry when they learned of the concessions through the State Department. Although not yet aware of the Oslo channel, Haidar Abdel-Shafi realized that something important was going on behind their backs.

In an interview with the BBC Abdel-Shafi was asked whether the delegation planned to resign in protest. He replied that it was premature to talk of resignation, but that the delegation wanted changes. 'What we are asking for is democracy in the Palestinian decision-making process,' he said.

The delegation returned to the occupied territories on 15 July and spent several days writing a memorandum expressing unhappiness with Arafat's habit of taking decisions without consultation. Abdel-Shafi and others went to Tunis on 19 July to present their petition to the chairman. Arafat gave them the news of the agreement, and a lesson in modesty: 'It's time to throw away your chief negotiator's hat,' he told Abdel-Shafi. 'We don't need the Washington talks any more.'

Some time later I commented, in a lecture to the American University in Cairo, that the Washington delegates had been like canaries in a cage who knew how to sing but not how to sign. The remark amused Arafat, who added: 'Maybe some were canaries, but others were crows.'

After ten frustrating sessions in Washington, spread over twenty months, the delegates found themselves in bad odour both in Tunis and in the occupied territories. Such was the loss of faith in the delegation and in the PLO that many Palestinians now wished Jordanian rule could be re-established. An opinion poll in Nablus showed that King Hussein was the preferred leader, with a popularity rating of 70 per cent.

In mid-July attacks by Hezbollah and other groups killed seven Israeli soldiers in southern Lebanon, and Israeli villages were hit by Katyusha rockets. Israel retaliated on 25 July, using artillery, helicopter gunships and gunboats in a massive bombardment of southern Lebanon. These attacks were taking place while Savir and Abu Ala and their teams were holding further talks at Jevnaker, north of Oslo, but the fighting seemed not to affect the negotiating atmosphere. A serious effort involving a new negotiating strategy was made to find compromises on a raft of secondary matters, but despite many hours of talks nothing was achieved. Another crisis came and went, and this time the Israelis showed clearly that they were just as anxious as the PLO to close a deal. The turning point came when Savir told Abu Ala that Israel was prepared to include formal recognition of the PLO in the deal.

In a further meeting in Sarpsborg on 13 August the teams reached agreement subject to approval, but Abu Ala was unable to obtain consent from Abu Mazen by telephone for certain concessions and had to return to Tunis for consultations.

While these deliberations were under way, the Palestinian ambassador to Cairo was asked to contact certain Egyptian personalities known for their commitment to the Palestinian cause and to drop hints that something was afoot. It was important to prepare the announcement of the agreement with care, to reduce the risk of unfavourable reactions from people whose views might influence the Egyptian public. I was among those selected, but I was doubtful about the outcome. Many a false alarm had been raised before, and there was no reason to think that the Oslo channel would be different. 'Mmmm,' Said Kamal replied when I expressed my scepticism. 'In a few days we will know for sure.'

The ambassador's instructions were to ensure that I was not surprised by developments in Oslo. He had done his duty.

On 18 August Peres went to Stockholm on other business and was joined there by Larsen, Holst and most of the Israeli negotiating team. After discussing the remaining differences Peres felt that compromises could be reached by negotiating with Arafat on the phone, using Larsen as an intermediary. For several hours Larsen conveyed points from the Israeli team to Abu Ala, who discussed them with Arafat and gave immediate replies. By 4 a.m. on 19 August the two sides had settled all but a handful of matters, which could be left to a final meeting.

Two hours before dawn ambassador Kamal was awoken in Cairo by a phone call from Tunis. The agreement was almost ready to be initialled, but Arafat insisted that it should first be checked by Taher Shash, an Egyptian ambassador and legal expert. Shash had been a member of the Egyptian team at the Camp David talks and was assigned to the Palestinian delegation during the 1991 Madrid conference and the Washington talks. His knowledge of the issues was second to none.

Abu Mazen insisted that Said Kamal should try to arrange for Shash to board a plane for Norway immediately to check the document. Kamal phoned Amr Moussa, the Egyptian foreign minister, who was about to depart for a meeting of African ministers in Mozambique, and requested Shash's services. 'All right, I agree that Taher Shash should go, but the president ought to be informed immediately,' Amr Moussa replied. By 6 a.m. Kamal had sent a note to Mubarak, who was still sleeping, arranged a seat on a plane leaving Cairo at 9 a.m., and phoned the startled Mr Shash to break the news. Not delighted to be woken at that hour, Shash's first comment was: 'What the — was the point of all our work in Washington if you've come to an agreement in Oslo?' Kamal went to Shash's home to help him pack while Kamal's driver waited outside. Shash grumbled that a serious document should not be thrown together like vegetables in a pot. 'I'm not putting my name to it if it's a mess,' he warned. On the way to the airport the phone rang in Kamal's car. It was Abu Mazen calling from Tunis to ask Shash to phone Arafat as soon as he had seen the document.

By 4 p.m. the same day, 19 August, Shash had reached Oslo and read the proposed agreement. The problem, he realized, was not the legal language, which needed only minor corrections, but the political content. 'This is Camp David only even worse,' he told Arafat on the phone. 'But I don't think you could have got any more, and if you want to go ahead, I wish you God's blessing.'

Meanwhile Peres, the Israeli negotiating team and the Norwegians had flown from Stockholm to Oslo and set up a temporary headquarters at a hotel in the city centre. The last political points were settled between Savir and Abu Ala over dinner that evening and at a meeting afterwards, with the exception of the mutual recognition question, which was to be dealt with later. It had taken nine months and fourteen meetings since the first encounter in London to reach agreement. The 'Declaration of Principles on Interim Self-Government Arrangements', a nine-page document with seventeen articles, plus a further fourteen pages of annexes and minutes, was ready, but could not be signed without approval from the Israeli cabinet and the PLO executive committee. However, Rabin and Arafat had given permission for the document to be initialled.

In the early hours of 20 August the two sides conducted a small videotaped ceremony at the official guest house where Peres was staying. After initialling the document Savir and Abu Ala exchanged Arab-style kisses and sipped champagne. The presence of Peres was remarkable because official Israeli policy at the time was still to have no direct contacts with the PLO. The Norwegians present included Holst, Larsen and Mona Juul.

The agreement was arranged in two parts. Part one was a plan for Palestinian self-rule in Gaza and Jericho and a timetable for the handover, to be achieved within four months of the agreement being signed. The accord guaranteed safe passage between Gaza and Jericho, but the connecting road did not become Palestinian territory. As the Israelis withdrew from the autonomous areas they were to be replaced by Palestinian policemen and administrators. The Palestinians were already in control of their own social services, hospitals and schools throughout the occupied territories, and the agreement extended these areas of self-administration to include tourism and taxation. These first parts of the agreement were self-contained, but the rest was subject to further negotiations on details. The declaration of principles was thus a guide, not a blueprint.

Israeli forces were to remain in control of all parts of the occupied territories except Gaza and Jericho pending the election of a Palestine Interim Self-Government Authority (subsequently described as the Council). The timetable assumed that elections to the Council could be conducted nine months later. 'These elections will constitute a significant interim preparatory step toward the realization of the legitimate rights of the Palestinian people and their just requirements,' the accord said, without defining what these rights were.

The Council was to have jurisdiction over Palestinians in the west bank and Gaza generally, but not over Israelis or foreigners. 'After the inauguration of the Council, the Civil Administration will be dissolved and the Israeli military government will be withdrawn,' said Article VII. Israeli forces would then withdraw from the main towns and cities but would retain control of borders, main roads and Jewish settlements. Palestinian bodies under the Council's control were to be created to manage the electricity supply, water, ports, development and land. The Palestinian police force was to be expanded to assume responsibility for Palestinians in the whole of the west bank and Gaza. Israel was to retain responsibility for external security and for protection of Jewish settlers throughout the occupied territories. The declaration also provided for the return of displaced Palestinians, but did not define the numbers or terms.

The agreement was to last for not more than five years, and by the end of the second year negotiations were to start on final status.

The second part of the declaration was an agreement on mutual recognition and ending the state of war between Israel and the PLO, but at the time of the initialling ceremony that had been only partly negotiated. Although Savir had said that Israel was prepared to recognize the PLO, the commitment was not yet in writing.

Despite euphoria at the ceremony, both sides knew that agreement had been possible only because matters of principle had been set aside. The agreement gave the Palestinians no guarantee of an eventual state, failed to address the issues of Jerusalem, frontiers and settlements, and dealt with the crucial refugee question in an extraordinarily vague manner.

The PLO had also made major concessions limiting the autonomy of the Palestinian Council. The procedure for electing the Council, its structure, the number of its members, its powers and many other important details were to be negotiated with Israel. This ensured that only a Council broadly acceptable to Israel could emerge. Moreover, the Council's legislative powers were shackled by constraints. Most of the Israeli laws and military orders governing the occupied territories were to remain in force and could be changed only by agreement between the Council and Israel.

Another important limitation of the Council's powers stemmed from the establishment of four Israeli–Palestinian joint committees covering wide areas of responsibility. An analysis by Burhan Dajani, a Palestinian economist and intellectual pointed out that the Council would be largely ceremonial, and real power would lie in the hands of the joint committees.*

There was worse to come. The most disastrous PLO concessions were to be made almost by accident three weeks later, as a result of the sloppy drafting of a key letter.

After the Oslo initialling ceremony Abu Ala, Savir and their teams remained in the Norwegian capital to continue discussions on mutual recognition. Israel was holding out for a commitment by the PLO to halt violence in the occupied territories, as the price for recognition. These follow-up talks ended without agreement, but *de facto*

* Burhan Dajani, 'The September 1993 Israeli–PLO Documents: A Textual Analysis', *Journal of Palestine Studies* XXIII, No 3 (Spring 1994).

recognition had already taken place. Neither side could pretend not to recognize the other after initialling the agreement.

One of the issues discussed in Oslo was when and how the agreement should be announced. Both sides felt that the US should be involved in the announcement, but no details could be decided until the Clinton administration had been informed. That task fell to Peres, who immediately returned from Norway to Israel, and then set off again a few hours later for California, where Warren Christopher was spending a vacation. The Israeli foreign minister was accompanied by Holst, his Norwegian counterpart. They landed at the US naval air station at Point Mugu, near Santa Barbara, and the secretary of state came to see them, accompanied by Dennis Ross, the State Department's special coordinator for the Middle East. The Americans had been given only an inkling of what to expect and seemed astounded by the news. Rabin had betrayed no enthusiasm about the Oslo channel when he discussed prospects with the administration earlier in the month. 'Do you really mean you have signed a paper with the PLO?' Christopher asked Peres.

Peres opened a bag and produced the document with Abu Ala's initials on it. Christopher read it, scarcely able to believe his eyes, and commented that it was worth interrupting his vacation for news like this. Dennis Ross had mixed feelings, fearing that the accord would pump life into the PLO at a time when it might otherwise have faded away, and would weaken prospects for an Israeli–Syrian agreement. Peres sharply reminded Ross that Israel knew its own interests best. Meanwhile Christopher was wondering how the CIA had failed to keep the administration abreast of such an important development.

Peres and Holst raised the question of how the agreement should be presented. Abu Ala had suggested that it should be stage-managed to look like an American proposal. President Clinton could convene a gathering similar to Camp David and 'persuade' both sides to accept the deal. Abu Ala's proposal had received Arafat's backing and was also accepted by Rabin, as both felt equally in need of American sponsorship to shield them from critics at home. Rabin was also happy with the prospect that Peres would be forced to share the limelight with Clinton.

It was agreed that a month would be necessary to make all the arrangements in Washington. This supposed a need to maintain silence while preparations were made, but even as Peres, Holst and Christopher were talking the first media article was being prepared. A Jerusalem newspaper published the fact that a meeting between Peres and the PLO had taken place in Norway. Once the story began to leak, the information dam burst very quickly. Peres held a press conference in California, then flew back to Israel, where Rabin called a cabinet meeting to announce the deal. Holst returned to Oslo and held a press conference there with Jan Egeland.

Furious that the understanding about a one-month delay had not been respected, Arafat told colleagues that Peres was hogging the glory and running after the Nobel Peace Prize. The premature disclosure wrecked Arafat's hopes of using Washington to absorb or deflect Arab criticism. Hamas, Hezbollah, Syria and Iran were unanimous in denouncing the agreement as a sell-out. Dr Abdel-Aziz Rantisi, the chief Hamas spokesman, said: 'The "Gaza–Jericho First" plan is a catastrophe for the Palestinian people and generations of Muslims.' Rantisi predicted that the accord would provoke civil war among Palestinians, a possibility which was taken very seriously in Tunis. Ahmed Jibril, the radical Palestinian leader based in Damascus, said that Arafat would be risking assassination if he went ahead. Haidar Abdel-Shaffi said: 'The minority are accepting it and the majority are rejecting it. The agreement falls short of the minimum we expected.' Saeb Ereikat, a member of Abdel-Shaffi's delegation to the Washington talks, said: 'We [the delegation] were shocked. We were the appetizers. The PLO is the main course.'

Television coverage of the press conferences struck many Arabs as provocative and confusing. Hawks were seen borrowing dove feathers while doves behaved as if they were apologizing to hawks.

Members of the PLO executive committee expressed astonishment and anger over the lack of advance consultation. Only a handful of members and officials were told about the agreement before the Israeli and Norwegian announcements. Even Abu Lutf (Farouk Kaddoumi), a founder member of Fatah, was given only an inkling. A few days before the announcement Arafat showed Kaddoumi extracts from proposals made by the Israelis in Oslo. 'They are offering us a strange formula,' Arafat said. 'I don't take it seriously.' Then he added casually: 'I see the word "withdrawal". Any paper with that word in it is worth reading.'

Abu Lutf was shocked to learn soon afterwards that Arafat had allowed this 'strange formula' to be initialled. Feeling that he had been misled, Abu Lutf was on the point of resigning, but decided after much reflection that as he and Arafat were the last surviving founders of Fatah, he could not let the chairman down at such a time.

Mahmoud Darwish, the great poet of the Palestinian revolution, went to submit his resignation from the executive committee as soon as he heard the news. Arafat refused: 'It was not me who elected you to the executive committee. You were elected by the national congress. So if you want to resign you will have to tell the national congress.' Darwish, like Kaddoumi, felt pulled in two directions. 'I stood by him when the world thought he was an evil man,' he recalled. 'If I say goodbye when the world thinks he is wonderful, where does that leave me? Arafat has landed me in a mess; all of us in a mess.'

Arafat was not surprised by the negative reactions, but thought he could get away with the agreement because the Arab world was in disarray. Some Palestinians wanted peace at any price, while others were determined to resist. Egypt was eager that the PLO should go ahead, to reduce its own isolation. Syria lacked sufficient weight to rally a significant Arab bloc against the agreement. Algeria was absorbed in its own internal strife. The only serious doubt was whether the PLO executive committee would approve the deal at its meeting on 2 September.

Reaction in Israel was little more enthusiastic. Binyamin Netanyahu said that the deal would allow the PLO to attack Israel from forward positions, and called for a referendum. Addressing the Knesset, Netanyahu compared the Oslo agreement to Neville Chamberlain's appeasement of Hitler, and told Peres: 'You are even worse than Chamberlain. He imperilled the safety of other people, but you are doing it to your own people.' Rafael Eitan, former chief-of-staff and leader of the Tsomet Party, said that the government had signed 'an agreement with the greatest murderer of Jews since Hitler'. Major General Amnon Shahak told a Knesset committee that the war against terrorism after the agreement went into effect would be 'extremely hard'. In an interview on army radio Shahak added that the situation before the agreement was 'a comfortable situation for us', but that would change when Palestinian self-rule began.

An opinion poll showed that 44 per cent of Israeli Jews were against the agreement, and 53 per cent in favour. Eliakim Rubinstein, leader of the Israeli delegation to the Washington talks, was angry that he had not been consulted, and Peres was unable to placate him. Rabin himself referred to the PLO as a 'terrorist organization', but pointed out that a government could only make peace with enemies, not with friends. In a speech to the Knesset Rabin defended the agreement by pointing out its limitations: 'Jerusalem remains under Israel's sovereignty and is Israel's unified capital. The settlements remain . . . Security in everything that relates not only to settlements but also to Israelis wherever they may be in the area is in Israel's hands.'

Anxious that the plan should be well received in the occupied territories, the Israelis at first allowed demonstrators to let off steam. Until then anyone who waved a Palestinian flag or displayed a picture of Arafat had been liable to detention without trial, but these rules were relaxed. The result was an explosion of euphoria by some and demonstrations against the agreement by others, with clashes in some places between the two groups. The majority was clearly in favour, at first, and expectations were raised by reports that the West would help Palestine to establish itself. A premature public debate broke out over the composition of a future Palestinian government, and Arafat asked Hanan Ashrawi whether she would rather be ambassador to Washington or minister of foreign affairs. After twenty-four hours the Israeli authorities decided that the euphoria was running out of control and intervened in a heavy-handed manner to break up demonstrations. Many Palestinians suspected that the real purpose of the crackdown was to express Rabin's annoyance with Peres.

Mustafa Khalil told the Israeli foreign minister that the success or failure of the agreement would depend mainly on money. If resources to improve living standards were not made available promptly, disillusionment would set in, and the PLO would be unable to prevent attacks against Israeli targets. Peres was of the same opinion and took on the task of raising contributions from European countries to implement the agreement, including a $200 million pledge from the European Community.*

* The European Community commitment was later raised to $600 million. The US and the Soviet Union convened a forty-three-nation meeting in New York at the end of September 1993 to seek contributions to implement the Oslo agreement. Pledges totalling $2 billion were received, including $500 million from the United States, $200 million from Japan and $25 million from Israel.

Within days of the agreement, critics on both sides began to point out that the Oslo negotiators had left a vast range of points unsettled. Among the controversial issues was whether the Palestinian authority could be represented at crossing points from Jordan and Egypt into the occupied territories, especially at the vital King Hussein Bridge (previously called Allenby Bridge) across the Jordan river. Another serious omission was that Jericho had not been defined. It was unclear whether the area to be under Palestinian control was the town centre or the administrative district. The difference between these possibilities was immense. Jericho had a population of about 20,000 and an area, within the municipal boundaries, of twenty-seven square kilometres. The district of Jericho as administered under Jordanian law before the Six Day War encompassed an area of 378 square kilometres.

The agreement aroused controversy within Israel as to which government departments were responsible for certain questions. Lieutenant General Ehud Barack, the Israeli chief-of-staff, and Uzi Dayan, nephew of Moshe Dayan and director of planning in the Israeli defence ministry, complained to Rabin that the agreement treated the territorial question as a political issue rather than as a matter of security. Transferring areas to Palestinian control raised security questions, in their opinion, and was therefore within the competence of the ministry of defence. This was also Rabin's view.

King Hussein first learned of the agreement in a phone call from Warren Christopher, who asked him to give Jordan's support. The king was astounded that the PLO had made such concessions, especially as the deal was greatly inferior to the agreement which Peres and King Hussein had reached in 1987. 'If they accused us of treason over the London agreement, how can they accept something like this?' he wondered.

King Hussein had seen Arafat a few weeks before the agreement and they had discussed the vexed question of coordination in the Washington talks. Arafat had talked about the possibility of setting up a joint operations room in Amman to ensure coordination. The king was aware of the Oslo channel, and assumed that Arafat would tell him if there were anything to report. It had never crossed his mind that the PLO was about to abandon fundamental principles.

'What a world of wonders and strange events,' he commented when we next met.

'Or is it just political Disneyland?' I replied.

'A political Disneyland,' he agreed, repeating the phrase twice.

President Hafez Assad had always assumed that a deal between the PLO and Israel was out of the question, because any offer Israel might make would be far short of the organization's expectations. Assad also felt that Damascus was the last Arab capital truly upholding the Palestinian cause, and expected to be consulted on any important initiative. When he heard the news from Oslo and realized that the PLO had bypassed Damascus he exploded in rage, calling Arafat 'that old shoe'. Warren Christopher phoned asking for restraint, but the Syrian president could only promise to look at the agreement objectively. 'If it is damaging to us and the cause, we will oppose it; if it is helpful we will support it,' he said.

Christopher pleaded with him to keep the peace, and confessed that Washington was as surprised as Damascus. 'This is not something that has been hatched up behind your backs or ours, it has been hatched up behind everyone's back,' he said, adding that President Clinton had decided that the US would give the deal full support.

The Syrian leadership later issued a statement saying that the agreement was harmful to the interests of Syria and the whole Arab national cause.*

King Fahd was as surprised as President Assad and King Hussein, though his perspective was different. In the early decades of the conflict Saudi Arabia had been highly critical of Egypt and Jordan for accepting Resolution 242, and remained opposed (at least officially) to recognition of Israel until the early 1980s. Egyptian ministers accused the Saudis of struggling from afar, safe in their desert tents and happy with their oil wells, while others fought the battles.

The king recalled an opportunity for peace on fair terms which had arisen in 1977, when he stayed at the White House with President Carter. The US president was putting his daughter Amy to bed, and while the two men were chatting in Amy's bedroom Carter said: 'If Arafat accepted Resolution 242, I would receive him here at the White House as a head of state.' The king phoned Arafat and passed this on, and the PLO chairman gave the impression of being pleased. Later, however, Arafat sent the king a note expressing reservations. At the

* The Syrian statement was issued on 11 September.

time Arafat was based in Beirut and had formed a tactical alliance with Walid Jumblatt,* the Druze leader, whom Fahd regarded as a revolutionary. The king thought he detected Jumblatt's influence in Arafat's reservations, and felt that a historical opportunity for peace had been lost.

King Fahd also recalled the opposition of King Khalid, his predecessor, to Sadat's visit to Jerusalem in 1977, and the disappointment felt by the royal family that such a concession to Israel had been made without consulting Saudi Arabia. Fahd, who was then the crown prince, phoned Sadat and said: 'Mr President, we are astonished that you did not inform us of your intentions. We do not say, and God forbid, that you are a traitor, because it was you who fought and Egypt which gave its blood. But we would have been happier had you obtained something for the Palestinians.' Looking back at the Jerusalem visit from the perspective of 1993, Fahd felt that Sadat at least believed sincerely that he was doing the right thing. It was not clear to him whether the same could be said of Arafat.

Fahd also recalled his own peace plan of 1982, the year in which he came to the throne. The Fahd Plan, approved at an Arab summit in Fez,† marked the acceptance of Resolution 242 by most of the Arab world. The plan was an effort to make the best of an unusually difficult situation, and to respond to the less favourable Reagan Plan. King Fahd continued to feel even in the 1990s that Washington would have done well to take up his initiative.

The king recalled a remark made in 1982 by Arafat after the press conference at which the Fahd Plan was announced: 'Your Majesty, we find that the right door is closed and the wrong door is open.' Arafat thought that Egypt was best placed to help the Palestinian cause make progress, but was not prepared to do so because of its peace treaty with Israel. Syria considered itself the champion of the cause, and yet its own actions had, as Arafat put it, 'castrated the Palestinian independent will'.

All these memories returned to the king's mind while he sat with relatives and advisers discussing the surprise announcement of the Oslo

* The son of Kamal Jumblatt, the former Druze leader who was assassinated in March 1977. See p. 337.

† See p. 367.

agreement. 'I would never have thought Arafat could accept such a thing,' he said. 'My initiative [the Fahd Plan] was the first all-Arab plan for a settlement. When the whole Arab nation accepted it, my plan became the national plan. But what has Arafat obtained?'

In a conversation with former President Carter, who was touring the Middle East at the time, King Fahd added: 'Postponing the fate of Jerusalem is the only point which we understand, because we know how difficult that matter is. But the other concessions are a grave mistake. I have received many messages from Arafat and I have not replied to any of them.'

Within a week of the announcement of the Oslo agreement four members of the PLO executive committee had attempted to resign, and Arafat had refused to accept their resignations. In addition to Mahmoud Darwish, others who wanted to leave were Yasser Abd-Rabbo, political counsellor to Arafat, Shafik El-Hout, a journalist based in Lebanon who had been a PLO member even before Arafat ousted Shukairy in 1969, and, most surprisingly of all, Abu Mazen.

Although Abu Mazen had been the principal proponent of an accord based on limited beginnings, he was angered by the sudden concessions Arafat made in the final stages without consultation. The dispute between the two men was to continue for several months.

Objections to the agreement were debated at a meeting of the executive committee on 2 September in Tunis. Among the first to speak was Mahmoud Darwish: 'We the Palestinian people have given everything to Israel in return for one concession: that Israel recognizes the PLO. That recognition rescued Arafat at a very difficult juncture in his life. We should ask ourselves why Israel wanted to save him.' The poet felt that the PLO chairman was confusing his own political interests with those of the Palestinian people. 'With this agreement we have surrendered more than we have ever given up in the whole of Palestinian history. I feel as if we are a people who have lost their memory and no longer know who or where we are.'

There was a time when Darwish had thought that a poet could serve the struggle, but now his mission seemed useless. No poet could inspire the yearning of a people for their homeland with talk of caution and dry legal phrases. 'I feel that I have nothing further to offer,' he said. Then he turned to Arafat: 'I want only to say one thing before I leave, and that is that you are taking a very high risk, a historical adventure.'

Arafat replied: 'All my life has been a historical adventure; all our lives have been historical adventures.'

Darwish left the committee with sadness, convinced that Israel would give nothing of sufficient value to warrant the concessions Arafat had made. The agreement was bound to make other countries think the conflict was over, allowing the United States and Britain to forget their guilt and the rest of the world its sympathy for the Palestinian plight.

Arafat repeatedly drew the committee's attention to the PLO's deteriorating financial situation, in order to imply that the organization had no options. He had prepared the ground by stressing the financial problems at a previous meeting. At the time several members, including Darwish, protested and questioned how the situation could have become so grave. Now the matter was raised again as a central reason for accepting the Oslo agreement, but this time members hinted that Arafat was painting the picture darker than necessary.

The financial squeeze was extraordinarily tight, to the point that Abu Mazen had been unable to pay his home phone bill for six months. Shafik El-Hout, the executive committee member resident in Beirut, had been feeling the pinch for two years. The organization's financial relief work in the occupied territories had slumped to a fraction of former levels and was being overtaken by Hamas, which had support from Iran. Arafat had been telling those who complained about money that the PLO was almost bankrupt, which was an overstatement.

The executive committee had eighteen members, but only thirteen attended the meeting and some abstained when the matter came to a vote, resulting in approval of the agreement by a margin of one. Farouk Kaddoumi remained unhappy with the deal, but did not want to break ranks with Arafat and abstained.

After the executive committee meeting Abu Mazen felt that it was vital to restore links with Saudi Arabia, whose help would be needed to bring Palestinian autonomy to success. This was not easy, as Arafat had been unwelcome in all Gulf countries since the 1991 war. Abu Mazen contacted the Saudi ambassador in Tunis and sent a message to King Fahd asking for his blessing for the Oslo agreement. Three days later the ambassador brought Abu Mazen a polite refusal. A note from the Saudi foreign ministry said: 'We thank you for your message. Everybody is on holiday abroad. We wish you success.'

Meanwhile Saud El-Faisal, the Saudi foreign minister, flew to Alexandria to ask for more information about the agreement. Washington was bringing strong pressure on King Fahd not to express opposition, but the king wanted to stand firm at least on the principle of withholding financial support. Kuwait and other Gulf countries also continued their refusal to fund the PLO.

In the meantime King Hussein had been reassessing his attitude to the Oslo agreement. The initial shock had given way to a feeling that he should show restraint and bide his time. If Arafat managed to make something of the agreement, well and good; if not, Palestinians might again turn to Jordan for help. After encouragement from Washington the king phoned the PLO chairman and told him: 'Abu Ammar, we are going to give you our backing.' 'Your Majesty, back me in what?' Arafat asked. 'We are one party. We are one delegation.'

The PLO chairman was technically correct. The Oslo agreement maintained the pretence of the Washington talks that Jordan and the Palestinians were working together. The interim arrangements were matters for the PLO and Israel to settle, but once the talks on final status began, Jordan would enter the negotiations. At that point Jordan, the PLO and Israel would discuss whether Palestine should be linked to Jordan in a federation or confederation, or should be a fully independent state.

Israel and the PLO were now only ten days from the formal signing ceremony in Washington, and still there was no agreement on mutual recognition. During the weekend of 3–4 September Peres met Holst in Paris to discuss how this last hurdle could be overcome. The Norwegian foreign minister made a series of calls to Arafat on behalf of Peres, trying to bridge the gap. Some days later the PLO and Israel teams met at a hotel in the Rue Saint-Honoré in Paris and after talks which continued until late into the night reached agreement on a mutual recognition pact.

In Tunis Arafat signed a letter which said: 'The Palestine Liberation Organization recognizes the right of the state of Israel to exist in peace and security.' The letter formally renounced 'those provisions of the Palestine National Covenant which deny Israel's right to exist and the provisions of the Covenant which are inconsistent with the commitments of this letter' (something which Arafat did not have authority to concede, as any change to the Covenant required approval by a two-thirds majority of the Palestine National Council). On the same day, 9 September, Rabin signed a letter saying: 'The Government of Israel has decided to recognize the PLO as the representative of the Palestinian people and commence negotiations with the PLO within the Middle East peace process.'

The PLO chairman's letter amounted to the final abandonment of the Palestinian struggle. That much was clear immediately, but other implications were realized only later. Taken together, the effect of the letter and the declaration of principles was to make the proposed Palestinian authority responsible for protecting Israel against acts by Palestinians. Burhan Dajani pointed out in his analysis that in recognizing the state of Israel, the PLO had accepted the Israeli laws which had been used to legalize the expulsion of Palestinians from their homes and land, which the PLO had always resisted.

Arafat's letter contained no definition of the Israel which the PLO was recognizing, despite the fact that Israel had always refused to define its borders. The effect of this unspecific recognition was to leave Israel free to claim that its sovereignty extended beyond the 1967 borders. All these concessions were traded for a brief note by Rabin accepting that the PLO could serve as a negotiating partner. Dajani also drew attention to the legal significance of Rabin's omission of any mention of the declaration of principles in his letter. All references to Palestinian rights were in the declaration, which carried less weight than the letter, from a legal standpoint.

Arrangements for the Washington ceremony were now well advanced, but it was still unclear who would represent the two sides. Yitzhak Rabin was in a quandary. Whatever his reservations about the agreement, there was no doubt that his old rival Peres had scored a publicity coup. Arafat was known to want a ceremony involving himself and Rabin, but the prime minister was reluctant to sign any document with the PLO chairman. Torn between publicity and dignity, Rabin at first decided to leave the ceremony to Peres. The PLO did not respond, but the impression in Washington was that if Rabin was not coming Arafat too would stay away, and the organization would be represented by Abu Mazen. A further complication was that Arafat did not want the agreement to be signed until financial backing had been secured. The PLO chairman often referred to Mikhail Gorbachev's mistake in setting the Soviet Union on the road to change (and oblivion) without first obtaining Western financial commitments. According to a development plan for Gaza and the west bank prepared by Youssef Sayegh, a Palestinian economist, an investment of $13 billion was needed, including $2 billion in the first month. It did not prove possible to secure pledges for such huge sums in the time available.

Four days before the 13 September ceremony PLO headquarters announced that Arafat would attend in person. News of this decision reached Warren Christopher while he was entertaining a group of journalists at his home in Georgetown. After the reporters had left the secretary of state phoned Rabin, who replied: 'If he is coming, I have no other alternative. I'll come.'

Arafat travelled to Washington in King Hassan's aircraft, sitting alone reading the Koran, looking anxious. His calculation that he could get away with the agreement had so far proved correct, but how long would peace among Palestinians hold? Many Fatah commanders in the occupied territories had accepted that the struggle with Israel was over, but a faction called the 'Fatah Hawks' had rejected the agreement. This had resulted in clashes with Israeli forces in which some of the Hawks were killed. The mood was thus edgy, and the division within the PLO executive committee did not bode well. Some who had supported the agreement were now distancing themselves from it, and there was unease among Palestinian millionaires in the United States. Haseeb Sabbagh, chairman of Consolidated, had decided not to attend the White House ceremony. The former Washington delegates were divided too. Hanan Ashrawi had decided to be present, while Haider Abdel-Shafi chose to stay away.

One of the millionaires went to the Washington hotel where the PLO group was staying and found ten people in Arafat's bedroom and twice as many in the living room. Everyone was talking at once and the speech the chairman was to make on the lawn of the White House had not yet been written. The speechwriter later said it was the most difficult task of his life. He had only a few minutes in which to devise a concept and produce the necessary words. His concept was that Arafat should be cautious, because Rabin in Washington was like a fish swimming in home waters, while the PLO was out of its element.

Secondly, the speech should not be a lament for Palestinian suffering, because the occasion was inappropriate. Arafat should talk sense and use the opportunity to call for financial support. The result was a text which seemed to apologize for the past and beg for the future. Arafat was present as it was written and rehearsed, and made no changes.

The earlier worries forgotten, Arafat was in the best of spirits as he approached one of the greatest moments of his career. For years even American third secretaries had refused to talk to him, and now he was to be received by the president. The first suggestion made by the White House chief of protocol therefore came as a shock. The chief, who called at the delegation's hotel, wanted Arafat to wear civilian clothes, instead of his usual olive-green military fatigues. Knowing that no one would recognize him in a suit, Arafat adamantly refused.

Then there was the problem of his ever-present Smith and Wesson revolver. The protocol chief wanted Arafat to leave the gun at the hotel, but the chairman argued that the Palestinian revolution had never surrendered its arms. The chief insisted that it was against all regulations to enter the White House carrying a weapon. Arafat then suggested that as part of the ceremony he should hand the gun to President Clinton, as a symbol of peaceful intentions. The protocol chief found that idea too theatrical. Finally Arafat proposed leaving the ammunition at the hotel but carrying the gun. The protocol chief said that if Arafat did that, White House security men would be obliged to search him before he entered, which would be humiliating. Eventually the PLO chairman was obliged to accept that both gun and ammunition would remain at the hotel.

Rabin arrived at the White House before Arafat and stressed that he wanted the ceremony to be unostentatious, with no kissing or handshakes in front of cameras. He was prepared to shake hands with Arafat inside the White House, but not in public.

Arafat found Rabin's attitude offensive. His comment on Rabin's request was: 'He wants to insult me at a *zaffa* [a major event, especially a wedding ceremony] and make peace with me in an *atfa* [an empty lane].' Unknown to the PLO chairman, what was to happen when he, Rabin and Clinton stepped on to a podium on the south lawn had already been decided by Clinton's aides and rehearsed in the Oval Office. The moment calculated to make every television news bulletin around the world would come when Clinton stood between the two men and raised his arms in a gesture of reconciliation. Such theatricals without a handshake would have looked absurd. The White House had no intention of going along with the restrained ceremony Rabin wanted.

The two men shook hands inside the White House, as Rabin had suggested, but when they reached the podium the rest of the ceremony followed White House choreography. The following day most newspapers reported that Rabin had hesitated for many seconds before taking Arafat's outstretched hand. In fact the Israeli prime minister was simply taken by surprise, thinking that the handshakes were already over and that Arafat's gesture was out of order.

The contrast between Rabin's dark suit and dour manner and Arafat's tieless military uniform, black and white *kaffieyeh* and irrepressible grin could not have been greater. Rabin looked like a mourner at a funeral, Arafat an actor collecting his Oscar at a Hollywood ceremony. And yet when they made their speeches Rabin was inspirational and Arafat downbeat. There seemed to be no connection between body language and the spoken word.

Arafat said he had come to make 'the peace of the brave', and wanted to talk to Rabin 'as soldier to soldier', but the rest sounded like surrender. Rabin was eloquent and direct, and many in the Arab world wished Arafat had made a similar speech. Both were applauded by the 3000 guests, and the agreement was signed by Abu Mazen on behalf of the PLO and by Peres for Israel. Afterwards Arafat was in a capital mood as he greeted friends and former enemies, with encouragement from Clinton. Rabin escaped without being kissed, but not Larsen, who was recognized and saluted enthusiastically by Arafat.*

The *zaffa* was spoilt that night when Rabin and Arafat made further speeches. The Israeli prime minister sought to bring Arafat back to reality with harsh reminders of the limitations of the agreement and the difficult details which remained to be negotiated. Rabin's tone and manner, with heavy emphasis on Israeli security, suggested a deliberate effort to denude the occasion of glamour. Arafat, who had invited this rebuke by talking as if Israel had agreed to the creation of a Palestinian

* The Norwegian government subsequently rewarded Larsen for his efforts by giving him the title of ambassador.

state, then made matters worse. Speaking like a head of state, he referred to the cabinet he intended to appoint. Hanan Ashrawi was clearly embarrassed when Arafat mentioned his intention of giving her a high office. The Egyptians begged Rabin to be indulgent with Arafat's excesses on this occasion.

On the same day Yossi Sarid, an Israeli minister, said in a newspaper article that Israel had been created anew by the agreement. Until then Israel had had victory without legitimacy; now it had recognition and acceptance.

A week after the feast of Washington all was gloomy at PLO headquarters in Tunis. Still furious over Arafat's lack of consultation, Abu Mazen refused to take part in policy discussions, and the two men were not on speaking terms. Faisal Husseini had returned to Jerusalem and cut off all contact for ten days. Arafat's critics on the executive committee were reminding Arabs of the declaration of a Palestinian state in 1988. The effect of the Oslo agreement had been to cancel the state, by accepting something inferior. The Washington documents referred to Arafat as chairman of the PLO, not as president of Palestine. Arafat had made himself a hero for a day, at the price of his title and his state.

Another dispute broke out when Arafat asked the Palestinian press to attack Saudi Arabia for refusing to support the agreement. Exasperated colleagues pointed out that the PLO could ill afford to offend the Saudis. President Ali Abdullah Saleh of Yemen tried to smooth over the row, but was rebuffed by Prince Sultan, who told him: 'We will never shake hands with Arafat so long as this family rules Saudi Arabia.'

As if to prove that nothing had changed for the better, it was discovered that an important PLO administrator in Tunis was a spy working for Mossad. The man had placed bugging devices in the bedroom and office of Abdel-Hakam Bal'awi, the PLO's ambassador to Tunisia, who had taken over as chief of intelligence after the assassination of Abu Iyad in 1991. The bugs were detected by Tunisian intelligence and the man was arrested, but the discovery caused panic within the PLO. It was now obvious that the Israelis knew everything about the organization's internal splits and the gravity of its financial situation.

Hemmed in by worries of every kind, Arafat went to see King Hassan of Morocco and said that he felt like a man who had lowered a bucket halfway down a well but could not reach the water. 'Please help us get the bucket to the bottom and bring the water up,' he pleaded.

16

Flags of Fantasy

A month after the Washington ceremony PLO headquarters still showed no sign of overcoming its internal disagreements, nor of preparing to assume responsibilities in Gaza and Jericho. Rabin wondered whether Arafat realized how much remained to be negotiated before the handover could begin, and resented the PLO chairman's overblown rhetoric. 'The Palestinian state is within our grasp. Soon the Palestinian flag will fly on the walls, the minarets and the cathedrals of Jerusalem,' Arafat had said. This statement, first made in early September and repeated with variations during subsequent weeks, was aimed at reducing Arab objections to the deal, but inflamed right-wing opinion in Israel. Rabin and Peres faced angry demonstrations and demands for a referendum, and the coalition was deserted by the six deputies of the Shas religious party, reducing its majority in the Knesset to one. Army generals were pressing for answers on what they considered security matters, especially the issues of border control and the security of Israelis using roads in the occupied territories. Rabin was feeling the heat.

Responsibility for negotiating the hundreds of details still to be settled lay with Peres, but by early October, with no sign of activity, Rabin felt he could allow the drift to continue no longer. The prime minister asked President Mubarak to intercede with Arafat and persuade him to tone down his statements and press ahead with the talks. The request was accompanied by a threat that Rabin would be obliged to make harsh statements unless Arafat fell into line. Mubarak arranged for the two leaders to hold their first one-to-one talks in Cairo on 6 October.*

* In a speech at Fu Dan University, Shanghai, soon afterwards, Rabin said that the 6 October meeting was held at his initiative.

Before the meeting Arafat requested the US and Soviet governments through their ambassadors in Tunis to approach Rabin, asking him to take a lenient view of his difficulties. Both governments replied that the Oslo agreement had been reached without involvement by outside parties, and the negotiations should continue in the same way. It was natural, the two governments argued, that the process of turning a vague agreement into something workable should be fraught with disagreements. Washington and Moscow were not prepared to intervene in their roles as co-sponsors of the Washington talks unless they received a joint request from both parties.

Mubarak met the two leaders at the presidential palace in Cairo on 6 October and quickly withdrew, leaving them to resolve their differences alone. It was not a happy encounter. Two men with less in common than the taciturn blue-eyed general and the voluble, emotional freedom fighter would be hard to imagine. One came to discuss facts and timetables, the other to talk in broad political terms. Rabin wanted to firm up peace with an enemy, while Arafat sought to enlist Israel almost as a partner to overcome opposition within Arab ranks.

Arafat's eyes became sad as he explained the difficulties of rallying his disparate band of individualists in support of the agreement. Palestinians could only be persuaded to take the slow road to freedom if the ultimate goal was kept in sight. The PLO chairman knew how to barter future hope against present reality when talking to Arabs, but now he was facing a man with no instinct for intangibles. Rabin's attitude remained precise and pragmatic, betraying no sympathy for Arab political sensitivities. The Israeli prime minister was astonished that the leader of what he still regarded as a terrorist movement should ask for his understanding. To his ears, almost everything Arafat said was oratory, one long plea for help, bereft of specifics. Arafat further strained Rabin's patience by bringing up the PLO's financial problems, which were not Israel's concern. Rabin pointed out that the PLO would have no shortage of funds if it closed down its ninety-two foreign embassies. Two of Rabin's remarks made Arafat shiver: 'We cannot compromise on security,' and 'We will not give you control of our borders.'

As the meeting went on longer than expected, Yasser Abd-Rabbo became anxious to know the mood. In a note to Arafat he asked: 'Is it wheat or barley?' a Palestinian expression meaning good or not so good. Arafat sent back the reply: 'It is barley.' After an hour and a half of private talks the leaders emerged at 7 p.m. and held a session with the full delegations and the Egyptian president. Rabin said that he had not expected the private session to last more than half an hour. 'I have discovered that we have got two different readings of the Oslo agreement,' he declared to all present. 'We are facing conflicting interpretations of matters which I thought were clear. I wish I had met you [Arafat] before the signing, because there are matters which ought to have been made clear to you. There are some subjects on which I cannot compromise because they touch on the security of Israel.'

Arafat interrupted, saying: 'Mr Prime Minister, don't forget that you are the one who is putting your hand on my territory.'

Rabin shot an angry glance at Arafat, but controlled himself and said: 'Mr Chairman, there is no need for such talk. We are two negotiating parties facing one another.' Then he turned to other members of the delegations and said: 'I must confess that the gap between our positions is very wide. Our Egyptian friends wanted us to reach an agreement but I think that we have got some important issues to settle.'

Rabin and Arafat had agreed in their private session to set up four committees. The first was a liaison committee, involving Peres and Abu Mazen. The second was to deal with the interpretation and implementation of the Gaza–Jericho agreement, involving Nabil Sha'ath, the PLO chief negotiator, and Major General Amnon Shahak of the Israeli defence ministry. It was agreed that meetings of this second committee should be held in Taba on the Israeli–Egyptian border. The third committee was to discuss the transfer of authority, while the fourth would deal with economic questions.

Rabin returned to Israel feeling irritated with both Arafat and Peres. He was overheard saying to Lieutenant General Ehud Barack, the chief-of-staff: 'The man [Arafat] is a dreamer.' After a cabinet meeting Rabin told Peres that he should have made sure that Arafat understood the meaning of the Oslo agreement. The remark annoyed Peres.

The first practical results came in mid-October, when the Taba talks produced a timetable for releasing Palestinian political prisoners held in Israeli jails. No agreement was reached, however, on how many should be regarded as political prisoners. Israel put the number at 9500, while the PLO estimated that there were between 12,000 and 14,000.

One of the first to leave on 19 October was Mohamed Salim Zrii, who had spent no less than twenty-three years in prison. A further 700 were freed by 27 October, and over the following months many more went home.

Meanwhile the Clinton administration continued trying to soften the resistance Arafat was meeting. When Farouk Kaddoumi (Abu Lutf), the PLO member responsible for foreign relations, visited the US to attend the UN General Assembly he was invited to see Warren Christopher. To the surprise of the State Department, which regarded him as a hardliner, Abu Lutf assured Christopher that he would do all he could to bring the agreement to reality, so long as he did not have to deal with Israelis personally. Abu Lutf favoured progress on the Israeli–Syrian front, and thought this would reduce resistance to the Oslo agreement.* This pleased Dennis Ross, the State Department's special coordinator on the Middle East, who had long felt that accord between Israel and Syria should have priority.

Abu Lutf described the meeting with Christopher as 'positive', which was in itself a boost for Arafat. The remark was quoted in a report from the PLO representative in Washington, and Arafat added a handwritten note saying that it should be distributed to everybody. Even a single favourable word was now thought valuable in the struggle to wear down resistance to the agreement.

Arafat appointed Abu Lutf to lead the Palestinian delegation to the PLO–Israel economic committee, with Abu Ala as his deputy. Warren Christopher did not think this was a wise decision because Abu Lutf was a foreign affairs specialist, not an economist. Christopher was also disappointed by slow progress in early meetings of the committees. In a meeting with Arafat in Amman on 6 December, he expressed his reservations about Abu Lutf's appointment and urged the PLO chairman to speed up the talks, warning that slow progress was playing into the hands of the agreement's enemies.

A month earlier, on 9 November, Peres and King Hussein took a step towards an Israeli–Jordanian accord by holding a nine-hour meeting, at which an economic cooperation protocol was agreed upon. The meeting was supposed to be secret, not least because of anxieties that

* One of his reasons for opposing the Oslo agreement initially was the lack of consultation of Syria and Jordan.

any publicity might upset attempts to achieve an Israeli–Syrian agreement. Peres neither confirmed nor denied that the meeting had taken place, but added: 'We don't want to separate Jordan from Syria, but on the other hand a slow coach should not hold up a fast one.'

The Peres–King Hussein talks coincided with the first multi-party elections in Jordan for thirty-seven years, which were decisively won by groups loyal to King Hussein. Islamic fundamentalist candidates lost ground but remained the largest opposition group in the Jordanian parliament.

The Israel–PLO committees continued meeting but made slow headway, especially in the Taba talks between Nabil Sha'ath, the PLO chief negotiator, and Major General Amnon Shahak, his Israeli counterpart. The Israelis were insisting that Jericho should be defined as the municipal area, not the administrative district, and wanted to retain full control of the crossing points from Egypt and Jordan into the occupied territories.

At the same time Arafat was increasing his demands, insisting that Palestine should have some of the trappings of statehood from the beginning. It was vital that people crossing into the territories should be aware immediately that they were entering Palestine, whether the territory was under Palestinian control or not. Arafat wanted a Palestinian flag to fly from an old fortification on the Palestinian side of King Hussein Bridge, which the Israelis would not accept. The PLO felt that the first person to meet any visitor crossing the bridge should be a Palestinian officer, while Shahak insisted that an Israeli officer should take precedence.

A compromise suggested by the Palestinians was that people entering the territories should be met by a Palestinian officer but observed by an Israeli sitting in another room, watching arrivals through a screen of one-way glass enabling the Israeli officer to see without being seen. Those arriving would be admitted only if accepted by both the Palestinian and Israeli officers. Israel would not accept this suggestion, and the Palestinians feared that visitors to the territories would get the impression that nothing had changed. Another dispute centred on demands by Arafat that Palestine should have its own currency and issue its own passports. Israel objected that Jordan had always provided passports for Palestinians, whether living on the west bank or in Jordan. A further Israeli argument was that the PLO's proposal would create a separation between Palestinians living on the two banks of the river. Two million of the 3.8 million inhabitants of Jordan were Palestinians, and a further one million Palestinians were resident on the west bank.

A related problem was the vagueness of the Oslo agreement on the return of Palestinians from the diaspora. Like Jews before 1948, Palestinians were dispersed in many countries. According to United Nations estimates the total number of Palestinians who fled in 1948 and 1967, and their descendants, was 5,400,000. It was estimated that 210,000 were living in the United States, 15,000 in Canada, 350,000 in refugee camps in Lebanon, and 310,000 in Syria. Of the 2 million Palestinians in Jordan, 1,100,000 were recognized as refugees. Arafat said he planned to lead a return of 400,000 Palestinians within five years, but the Israeli government denied that there was any agreement to allow such an influx. The Israelis were willing to allow the return of 1000 people a year on a family reunification basis, and Yossi Beilin promised to raise this to 6000, which would permit the return of 30,000 people in five years.

By early December doubts were growing as to whether Israel intended to respect the timetable which called for withdrawal from Gaza and Jericho to begin on 13 December. The Israeli government insisted that there could be no departure until outstanding issues had been settled. Washington at first opposed any delay, but after a meeting between Warren Christopher and President Mubarak in Cairo on 8 December the US administration seemed more relaxed. During the same tour of the Middle East Christopher saw President Assad, who put his mind at rest about speculation that Syria might block the Oslo agreement.

Nearly three months had passed since the Washington signing ceremony, and the mood in the occupied territories was growing restive. Ordinary people saw PLO leaders on television apparently living in planes and luxury hotels, while the misery of their own daily lives continued. As disillusionment grew, violence crept back to the streets of Gaza. In a single week in early December, twenty-eight Palestinians and nine Israelis were shot, stabbed or killed in bomb blasts in the occupied territories. Some of the clashes were attacks by Israeli settlers on Arab communities, while others involved Hamas and Islamic Jihad commandos striking Israeli targets. Israeli undercover teams killed two suspected Hamas military leaders, Imad Aqal and Khaled Mustafa Zer, prompting demonstrations in which Israeli troops wounded thirty-three people and killed one.

Arafat held further talks with Peres in Grenada on 9 December and with Rabin in Cairo on 12 December. The atmosphere of the Rabin–Arafat talks was again tense, and afterwards Rabin refused to address a joint press conference and went straight to Cairo airport.

The two leaders had agreed to meet again in ten days, but the follow-up meeting never materialized. Rabin left direct dealings with the PLO chairman to Peres, but kept the foreign minister on a tight leash and insisted on reviewing everything the two men decided. Peres asked the Egyptian government to try to soften Rabin's attitude by inviting him to Cairo and explaining Arab views. The Egyptians tried to oblige, but had little success.

Soon after the Rabin–Arafat meeting, the atmosphere was further soured by claims in the Israeli and British press that Arafat was close to a nervous breakdown. The main character in this episode, apart from Arafat, was an Israeli officer of Lebanese origin, Colonel Jack Nerya. He was born and educated in Lebanon, and consequently spoke excellent Arabic. Nerya seemed torn between two cultures, unsure whether he was an Israeli Arab or an Arab Israeli. His knowledge of Arab ways was first put to use while serving in the Israeli army. Later, after reaching the rank of colonel, he came to Rabin's attention and was given a job in the prime minister's secretariat. Nerya came into contact with Stephen Cohen, which led to introductions to Palestinian representatives.

Because of his command of the language and his engaging personality, Nerya found that many doors were open to him. He rose to be director for Arab affairs in the prime minister's office, and was also attached to the Israeli delegation to the Abu Mazen–Shimon Peres liaison committee. As Palestinian delegates came to know Nerya, they realized that his special qualities made him the subject of jealousy and suspicion. Israeli foreign ministry officials were jealous because Rabin listened to Nerya's views more attentively than to theirs, while in the prime minister's office Nerya was seen as Rabin's favourite. Nerya was amused, and used these rivalries as a way of identifying with Arab negotiators. 'Those blue-eyed diplomats don't like us because we are Arabs,' he said. 'As long as my big turkey cock [meaning Rabin] likes me, what do I care about the others?' Remarks like that made Arab negotiators feel Nerya was more at home among them than with Israelis.

In early December Nerya was one of two special emissaries chosen to visit Arafat in Tunis, the other being Brigadier Gildat Amos, director of Rabin's office in the defence ministry. Before their arrival, Arafat heard from his representative in Israel, Dr Ahmed El-Tibi, that the purpose of the mission was to seek help in tracing the bodies of two Israeli soldiers who had been killed in southern Lebanon years earlier. All militias in Lebanon were aware that Israeli bodies could be traded for concessions in negotiations. It was common practice to bury the body of any Israeli killed in action in some secure place where it could later be disinterred. The two bodies had been the subject of much discussion in the Israeli press, and the Israeli government had even asked Washington to intercede with President Assad to use his influence in southern Lebanon to have them traced. Despite all efforts, no remains had been found.

Not wanting to fail at the first request from Rabin, Arafat had enquiries made before the mission arrived, and discovered that the one man who had known where the bodies were buried had himself since been killed. Realizing that he would be unable to help, Arafat thought of asking Israel to postpone the mission, but Dr Tibi counselled against such a move. 'Meet them anyway,' he suggested, 'because the fact that Nerya is coming may mean that Rabin wants to open a direct channel to you. He is not happy with your channel with Peres.'

The visit went ahead, and Arafat promised Nerya and Amos that he would send an envoy to conduct an investigation into the fate of the bodies.

Nerya and Amos asked Arafat for his views on the issues which were deadlocked in the committees. Arafat gave a long talk, but both men felt that he was lecturing rather than negotiating. The PLO chairman particularly stressed his demand that people arriving in Palestine should meet a Palestinian officer before seeing any Israeli officials. Jack Nerya interrupted to explain Israel's anxiety about security and the need to ensure that people who were considered a risk did not enter. This seemed to infuriate Arafat. 'If that's what you want, keep your agreement, I don't want it,' he shouted.

Nerya thought Arafat must be tired and suggested resuming the meeting the following day, but Arafat insisted that he was ready to continue until dawn. The PLO chairman said that Peres had seemed more sympathetic about the sensitivity of the border crossing issue: 'When Peres was in Oslo he understood our feelings and we thought that the agreement was clear.'

Nerya replied with a remark which made Arafat even angrier. 'Don't bring Peres into this, we are talking about Rabin,' he said. 'It is Rabin who is responsible for security problems, as minister of defence.'

According to Nerya, in a report he submitted to Rabin later, Arafat then began ranting and pleading and behaving strangely. A few days later an article appeared in *Y'di'ot Ahronot*, an Israeli mass-circulation newspaper, suggesting that Arafat was on the verge of a nervous breakdown. Nerya was not quoted directly, but the article spoke of the PLO chairman weeping and sweating profusely, and suggested that Arafat was feeling the strain of the huge gamble he had taken in accepting the Oslo agreement. A similar article appeared in a British Sunday newspaper.

Rabin was asked about the reports and was quoted as saying: 'I can't help it if Arafat is sweating. Let him sweat.'

Arafat replied two days later: 'He [Rabin] is going to be the one who sweats. I don't sweat. I am strong and fit and coming events will show who is sweating and who is weeping.'

Arafat felt that Jack Nerya must have been the source of the story, or alternatively that Nerya's report to Rabin had been deliberately leaked. The fact that Nerya had been seen by the PLO as the most understanding of Israeli negotiators made matters worse. Nerya was embarrassed that his report had reached *Y'di'ot Ahronot*, and suspected that the leak stemmed from intrigues within the prime minister's office. He did not think Rabin was responsible.

During the Tunis meeting but before the row, Arafat had suggested holding a special meeting in Paris of Israeli and Palestinian negotiators, outside the scope of the committee meetings. The aim was to prepare decisions which could be finalized at a meeting which Arafat and Peres had arranged to hold in Davos, Switzerland, in January. The Paris meeting went ahead, and was attended by Nerya despite the furore over the article. The Israeli team also included General Amnon Shahak and Joel Singer, the government lawyer, while the PLO was represented by Nabil Sha'ath and Said Kamal, PLO ambassador to Egypt.

Nabil Sha'ath went to the meeting convinced that friction between Rabin and Peres was the real cause of the deadlock, and that the Israeli military establishment was trying to derail the talks. Said Kamal, on the other hand, felt that the PLO should realize that there would be no withdrawal until Israel's security demands were satisfied. The original plan was to look at all eighteen main problems in the committee talks, but Sha'ath and Kamal realized that this was too ambitious. It would be best, they thought, to set aside matters on which the Israeli refusal had been most adamant and to concentrate on issues where there was more chance of success.

Before the meeting, which was to be held in a conference room at the Hôtel Crillon, Said Kamal decided to have a few words with Jack Nerya. They were sitting in a small salon just off the hotel lobby when Kamal noticed that most of the other chairs were occupied by unusually attractive women. 'It's very pleasant sitting here with all these beautiful ladies, but shouldn't we go somewhere where we can talk privately?' Kamal asked.

'Don't worry, the ladies are from Israeli security,' Nerya said. 'The beautiful ones, that is, not the ugly ones. They have to be beautiful to work in security.' Nerya explained that beautiful women were chosen because they were less likely to be identified as security agents. 'We would never leave the security of our delegation to French protection,' he added. 'It has cost Israel several million dollars to prepare men like Shahak for their mission, and we cannot afford to lose them.'

Nerya and Kamal joined the others in the conference room and Nabil Sha'ath outlined the PLO's position from a political viewpoint. When Sha'ath stopped speaking Shahak applauded. 'Nabil, you gave a very good lecture,' he said. 'But you know, I'm not Shimon Peres.'

Sha'ath replied: 'I am a politician and you are a military man, but I know that the Israeli military has a deep political culture.'

'Yes,' said Shahak. 'But I came here as a soldier to discuss security problems.'

After agreeing to postpone discussion of some of the more difficult problems, they tried to tackle the dispute over passports. The Palestinian delegation suggested returning to the practice used during the British mandate period, when passports carried Palestine as the main heading with 'Mandate Administration' underneath. Sha'ath suggested a similar arrangement but with an acknowledgement of the Israeli role. Shahak replied: 'Are you interested in travel or nationality? If it is nationality it is out of my jurisdiction.' If the Palestinians were interested in travel, he said, Israel was willing to allow them to have magnetic identity cards. 'But why do you want another passport?' he added. 'The Jordanians give you passports, and they would object if you had your own passports.'

'All right, what if we ask Jordan's permission?' Sha'ath asked. Shahak, however, continued to insist on the identity card offer, and it was clear that the Israelis would not budge.

Just when the meeting seemed to be heading for deadlock, Shahak disclosed that Israel was prepared to compromise on the size of Jericho, conceding something more than the twenty-seven square kilometres within the municipal boundaries, although he was not authorized to reach a deal himself because it was a political matter.

This was a step forward, helping to ease mutual suspicions. The PLO feared that Rabin or the Israeli army was trying to wreck the talks, while Israelis suspected that Arafat was deliberately introducing complications because he wanted to withdraw from the agreement. At the same time many in Israel were advocating that attention should be switched to the search for agreement with Syria. Sha'ath and Kamal sent a report to Arafat saying that some progress had been achieved.

Arafat's anger over the Nerya incident was reflected at a meeting of the liaison committee held in Norway soon afterwards. The instructions given to the PLO team amounted to an attempt to exploit differences between Rabin and Peres. The liaison committee delegations were normally headed by Abu Mazen and Shimon Peres, but because of continuing friction between Abu Mazen and Arafat, the PLO was represented instead by Yasser Abd-Rabbo, the chairman's political counsellor.

Abd-Rabbo told Peres that the PLO no longer knew who in the Israeli government to deal with: 'We have been meeting with you in these committee meetings thinking that you were authorized to act for Israel. But now Prime Minister Rabin has informed us that the responsibility is his, not yours. We are in a dilemma.'

'Who gave you this message from Rabin?' Peres asked.

'Jack Nerya,' Abd-Rabbo replied.

'I'll discuss that with Rabin,' Peres said. On his return to Israel Peres confronted Rabin with Abd-Rabbo's remarks. The prime minister called Nerya into his office and asked what he had said to Arafat. Nerya insisted that he had simply explained the division of responsibilities between the prime minister and the foreign minister. The division, which had begun under the previous government at the time of the Madrid conference in 1991, made the prime minister responsible for bilateral negotiations and the foreign minister for multilateral matters.*

Nerya denied having said anything of the sort alleged by Abd-Rabbo, but Rabin decided that an investigation should be carried out. In the meantime Nerya was banished from the prime minister's office and placed under General Shahak's authority. Arafat was thus allowed to take revenge on the supposed source of the *Y'di'ot Ahronot* article.

Despite everything Nerya was still much liked by members of the Palestinian delegation, who felt that he understood Arab views better than any other Israeli official. Some of the delegation went to Arafat and questioned whether the troublemaking message sent through Abd-Rabbo had really been necessary. Arafat replied that Nerya had to be punished for the remarks about sweating. Three months later, having served his time, Nerya returned to the negotiations. He later resigned.

* Peres appeared to be happy with this division of labour. During a meeting with Egyptian intellectuals at the Centre for Middle East Studies in Cairo, he said that the bilateral negotiations were dealing with problems of the past, while the multilaterals were looking to the future.

17

The Cairo Agreement

The fractious mood of the previous months gave way to an improved tone at the next round of the liaison committee, held in Cairo at the beginning of January 1994. Abu Mazen patched up his quarrel with Arafat and again headed the talks with Shimon Peres. The Palestinian delegation took up the offer Major General Shahak had made in Paris two weeks earlier of a compromise on the size of the autonomous area in Jericho. Provisional accord was reached, pending approval at higher levels, that the area from which Israel would withdraw would be about double the original offer of twenty-seven square kilometres. Some of Israel's security worries were eased by an understanding that settlers would be protected by Israeli forces inside the settlements, and responsibility for their security when in other parts of the west bank and Gaza would be shared by Israeli and Palestinian patrols. After two days of talks Peres said that the teams had reached 'a meeting of minds'. He reported back to Rabin with an optimistic account, and the impression was that a deal had been done.

When Abu Mazen briefed Arafat in Tunis, it became clear that a solution would not be that easy. Arafat was less than satisfied with the Jericho offer, and the Cairo meeting had not settled the questions of Palestinian border guards and flags. Rabin then accused Arafat of going back on the 'agreement', and suspended negotiations. The Egyptian government pointed out that talk of agreement was premature: what had been reached was an understanding. Rabin accepted this explanation and talks were resumed.

Arafat was again under pressure in January to accept the principle that important matters should be discussed within the collective leadership before rather than after major decisions. After a petition by 120 prominent Palestinians and a meeting with a delegation from the occupied territories, he appeared to understand the problem, but no changes emerged. Discontent with the leadership was underlined by an opinion poll in the occupied territories in mid-January showing that support for the Oslo agreement had dropped to 44 per cent, down from 68 per cent in September. As enthusiasm for the PLO waned, the religious ardour of Hamas found ever greater appeal among the disillusioned young men of Gaza. The personal austerity of its leaders contrasted with the expensive suits and jet-set lifestyle of the PLO negotiators. While Fatah hobnobbed with the gods of diplomacy, Hamas kept its feet on the ground.

The Egyptians and even the Israelis had long tried to make Arafat understand the full extent of the Hamas challenge. Dr Mustafa Khalil, the former Egyptian prime minister, had expressed amazement that the PLO was not trying to involve itself in the daily lives of the Palestinian people. Dani Rotchild, coordinator of civil administration, attempted to arrange a meeting with the PLO chairman to pass on his personal knowledge of what was happening. Arafat refused to see Rotchild and told the messenger who had brought the coordinator's request: 'Tell him not to waste our time trying to put wedges between us and them. Hamas is a part of our people and its roots go deep inside the Muslim Brotherhood, so don't think you can separate us.' This was not Arafat's real attitude, but what he felt should be said to Israelis. He understood the danger to the PLO but could not do much until the Oslo agreement was implemented and money began to flow from outside donors.

Arafat had tried to give the PLO a more religious image in Gaza by appointing Sheikh As'ad El-Saftawi as Fatah's representative in Gaza, but in November 1993, only two months after taking office, Saftawi was assassinated.

Yitzhak Rabin sent President Mubarak a tape-recording made in southern Lebanon of what appeared to be a conversation between a member of Hamas and the organization's spokesman, Dr Abdel-Aziz Rantisi. On the tape Rantisi was heard saying that as a young man studying medicine in Egypt, he had been in contact with the people who later assassinated President Sadat. The aim of Rabin's move was to increase Mubarak's concern about Hamas. Later it emerged that the man Rantisi had been talking to was an Israeli agent.

Washington continued to think that the key to peace was to bring about a Syrian–Israeli agreement. President Clinton held a three-hour meeting with Assad in Geneva on 16 January and claimed afterwards that they had taken 'an important step forward', though much remained to be done. Assad's public remarks did not confirm any change in the situation: 'We want a genuine peace which secures the interests of all sides and renders to all their rights. If the leaders of Israel have sufficient courage to respond to this kind of peace, the new era of normal, peaceful relations among all shall dawn,' he said at a press conference after the talks. Some in the West understood this to be a signal of flexibility, but in fact Assad had said nothing new. A 'genuine peace' meant total Israeli withdrawal from all occupied territories. The word 'normal' made Israeli ears prick up, but Assad did not define normality.

Peres said that the tone was too positive to justify disappointment, but the remarks were too general to give satisfaction. The 13,000 Israeli settlers in the Golan heights were becoming worried that an Israeli–Syrian deal might be close, and these fears grew when Yossi Beilin said that the construction of settlements in the heights had been a mistake. Amid demonstrations against a supposed 'Clinton–Assad' plan, General Mordechai Gur, Israel's deputy defence minister, told the Knesset on 17 January that any decision to withdraw would be subject to a referendum. By late January the Israeli–Syrian talks in Washington had resumed, and in a speech to the Council of Europe Rabin claimed: 'Syria is ready for a separate peace treaty [with Israel].' He added that he had received 'signals' of such readiness, but then seemed to go out of his way to annoy the Syrian president: 'For the moment President Assad has not done even 2 per cent of what Sadat did in his day to convince the Israelis.' Rabin reiterated his opposition to any global peace treaty between Israel and its Arab neighbours and his insistence on individual treaties with each country or group.

Few Arabs believed Rabin's remarks about Assad, because the Syrian president had always held out for a global settlement in the context of complete Israeli withdrawal. A theory which circulated at the time was that Rabin hoped the prospect of a Syrian–Israeli agreement would make Arafat move faster. Israel had tried that ploy on previous occasions, notably in 1992 during the Washington talks.

The death of Johan Jorgen Holst, the Norwegian foreign minister, brought Shimon Peres and Arafat together at the funeral in Oslo. The two men held three meetings on 21 and 22 January 1994, in addition to separate sessions with Warren Christopher, who had delivered the eulogy. An agreement in principle was reached that Israeli withdrawal from Gaza and Jericho should be achieved by 13 April, subject to settling the remaining problems. After a meeting with Egyptian foreign minister Amr Moussa in Jerusalem on 24 January, Peres said he now felt there was a basis for agreement.

Israeli and PLO delegations held talks in Cairo on 26 January, hoping to prepare a draft agreement for Arafat and Peres to sign at the end of the month. Both leaders had been invited to the World Economic Forum at Davos, and had arranged to hold a bilateral meeting at the same time. Little progress was made at the Cairo meeting, and a further three days of preparatory discussion between negotiators in Switzerland before the arrival of the leaders proved equally fruitless. The sticking points were still the size of the Jericho area, the issue of guards at the frontiers, and security measures for Israeli settlers.

Arafat and Peres came close to agreement on all remaining points at Davos, but when Peres left the room to consult Rabin by phone doubts began to emerge. Uzi Dayan, director of planning at the Israeli defence ministry, told the Palestinian delegates that Peres lacked authority to settle some of the points alone. Peres returned two hours later saying that the agreement would have to be postponed because certain points still needed to be cleared with the Israeli army. Some of the Palestinian delegates suspected that Dayan had intervened with Rabin.

Although nothing was signed, understandings were reached at Davos on numerous points. Arafat now seemed more resigned to acceptance of the revised Israeli offer of fifty-four square kilometres for the autonomous area in Jericho. The Israelis agreed that checks on Palestinians at the frontiers could be carried out by electronic scanning instead of physical searches. The Palestinians dropped their insistence on the withdrawal of Israeli troops from settlements in Gaza. Israeli patrols and mixed Israeli-Palestinian patrols would control three roads leading to the Gaza settlements. Special Palestinian passages would be set up to link King Hussein Bridge to Jericho, and Nebi Mussa to the Dead Sea. A Palestinian or Palestinian-Israeli hotel would be built beside the Dead Sea. Certain important religious sites would be placed under the control of their respective communities.

Peres claimed after the meeting that Arafat had clarified the PLO's position on the final status of Palestine, quoting the PLO chairman as saying: 'I know that you suspect that I want to achieve a separate Palestinian state . . . We have taken a decision to aim for a confederation with Jordan.' According to Peres, Arafat said that the decision was supported not only by Fatah but other PLO elements.

When the two men met again in Cairo a week later three main disputes remained to be settled. The Israelis were prepared to accept a Palestinian observer at each border crossing, while Arafat continued to insist on the principle that arriving visitors should be met by a Palestinian officer before seeing any Israelis. There was also a disagreement about the type of arms the Palestinian officer (or observer) should carry. The Israelis were unwilling to allow anything more than an electrical stick (a baton capable of delivering electric shocks), while the Palestinians wanted pistols. Within this second point there was also a disagreement about the calibre of the pistols. Finally, Arafat wanted the word 'withdrawal' to be in the agreement, while Rabin insisted that the removal of Israeli forces should be described as a 'redeployment'.

After the first day of talks on 7 February it was clear that Peres was being held back by Rabin. Nabil Sha'ath said: 'Peres was about to sign, then he phoned Rabin and came back looking sad. Every five minutes Peres received a call from Rabin or Ehud Barak.'

On the second day President Mubarak intervened repeatedly with both Arafat and Peres to urge flexibility, while further pressure came from the US administration. Finally on 9 February the text was ready for signing, together with a map of the fifty-four-square-kilometre autonomous area in Jericho and another map of the 360-square-kilometre Gaza area. The maps had been sent to Arafat before he arrived in Cairo three days earlier, but now he asked to see them again before signing. He also wanted confirmation that Peres was authorized to sign on behalf of Israel. The Egyptian government urged Arafat to avoid quibbles which could give an impression that he was looking for a pretext to withdraw from the agreement.

Peres was staying at the Meridian Heliopolis Hotel just across the road from Arafat's quarters in Andalus Palace (an ironic abode for the chairman, as Andalusia, which was under Arab rule from 711 to 1492, was the most famous part of the Islamic world ruled by caliphs to be lost before the Israeli conquest of Palestine).

Peres and Arafat and their aides assembled at Andalus Palace before moving to the presidential palace for the signing ceremony. Arafat had finished checking the text and the map of Gaza, but did not have a copy of the map of Jericho. As they were about to leave Arafat called Nabil Sha'ath and asked for the Jericho map. 'But I sent it to you in Tunis', said Sha'ath. He could have sent for a copy from the PLO's office in Cairo, but there was now little time before the ceremony. Arafat was not satisfied. In front of the assembled Israeli and Palestinian aides he said: 'You don't know them [the Israelis]. They would falsify anything, forge documents and swear to God they were genuine.' Sha'ath went to General Uzi Dayan and borrowed his copy of the Jericho map to show to Arafat.

The chairman inspected it and began asking questions about colour-coded areas showing zones under Palestinian, Israeli or joint control. Sha'ath realized that Arafat was trying to verify that the map was identical to the one he had been sent in Tunis. It was now time to go to the signing, and Amr Moussa, the PLO foreign minister, began urging Arafat to finish his inspection.

At that moment Yuri Savir came over and said that Peres was going to his hotel to make a phone call to Israel. Arafat shouted: 'It's Davos all over again. He won't come back. They [the Israelis] will postpone the signing again.' Amr Moussa assured Arafat that nothing of the sort would happen.

The Palestinian delegation felt that Arafat should be present at the ceremony, but should not sign himself. Arafat insisted that the Egyptians wanted him to sign personally, but Amr Moussa replied that it made no difference to Cairo. As a compromise it was agreed that the main signature would be that of Abu Ala, while Arafat would sign as a witness.

Peres returned, having phoned Rabin. Far from the 'second Davos' which Arafat feared, the Israeli foreign minister had secured a compromise on a point which was still troubling Arafat. Although he had reluctantly accepted Israel's final offer of fifty-four square kilometres, Arafat was not happy. Peres had arranged that Rabin would send him a letter promising to discuss the Jericho question when the two men next met.

There was then a dispute about the wording of the letter. Arafat wanted Rabin to promise to renegotiate the area, not just discuss it. Amr Moussa, anxious to smooth over these differences so that everyone could move to the signing ceremony, whispered that Peres had to convince Likud, meaning that Arafat should not push the foreign minister too hard. Peres overheard the remark and replied: 'I have to convince Labour, not Likud.'

Eventually Arafat accepted the argument and everyone went to the presidential palace, where television cameras had been set up in a ceremonial chamber to record an occasion which some considered historic. As the ceremony began Yuri Savir passed the text and maps to the two sides to sign in turn. Arafat looked around and asked: 'Where is Faisal?' Faisal Husseini was found and the PLO chairman insisted on him being present and visible to television cameras, in the hope of boosting support among Palestinians in the occupied territories. Before anything was signed Arafat again checked the text and the map of Gaza.

Then came the map of Jericho, but Arafat was still not convinced that this was the same as the one which had been sent to him. As Abu Ala picked up his pen Arafat whispered: 'Sign the Gaza one and the text, but just pretend to sign the Jericho map.' Both Arafat and Abu Ala then went through the motions of signing the Jericho map, for the benefit of the cameras, without actually doing so. In the confusion of the moment no one noticed. As the ceremony was ending and the parties were leaving, Savir spotted the omission and went to Peres. By that time Arafat had left the room and was striding towards the lobby. Peres snatched the Jericho map from Savir, confirmed that the signatures were indeed missing, and turned to President Mubarak. 'Mr President, stop the Chairman!'

Mubarak called after Arafat: 'Abu Ammar, come back.' Arafat returned and Mubarak asked why he had not signed.

'I wasn't paying attention,' Arafat replied.

'Do you think the man [Peres] is a street-corner *batata* seller?' Mubarak asked in Arabic. (*Batata* is a type of grilled sweet potato sold by street vendors.)

'Do you want to get me killed?' Peres asked. 'I'd be assassinated if I returned to Israel without your signature on that map.'

'Mr President, I haven't seen that map before,' Arafat said.

'Mr Chairman, that map was sent to you in Tunis,' Amr Moussa intervened. 'Anyway, Peres said that Rabin would send you a letter promising to discuss it again, and you accepted that.'*

'Oh yes, I'd forgotten that,' Arafat replied, and signed the map.

King Fahd wrote to Mubarak afterwards warning that the president was causing himself much public embarrassment by becoming involved in such squabbles.

The Cairo Agreement was an attempted compromise between Arafat's desire for the visible trappings of statehood and Israel's anxiety about security. This involved arrangements which were widely attacked in the Arab world as degrading. The agreement left overall control of security at border crossing points in Israel's hands, while the detailed arrangements amounted to a pretence of dual control. At each border crossing there was to be a single terminal containing a Palestinian section and an Israeli section, separated by a tinted glass window. People entering the terminal would go through an electronic gate, where they would be separated. Palestinian residents of the west bank and Gaza would go first to the Palestinian authority window to have their documents checked, then to the Israeli window. In front of the Palestinian side there would be a Palestinian flag and a Palestinian policeman, with equivalent arrangements on the Israeli side. Each side would have the right to refuse entry to anyone they considered a risk. Checks were to be carried out by electronic means whenever possible to avoid the indignity and time-wasting of physical searches. If the Israelis considered a physical check necessary, it would be carried out by a Palestinian official in the presence of an Israeli. Palestinian VIPs were to be exempt from the arrangements. Luggage was to be scrutinized by means of a conveyor-belt system similar to that used at airports.

The agreement gave the Palestinian authorities power to admit visitors for up to three months, provided Israel raised no objection. A three-month extension could be granted, subject to the Israeli authorities being informed. Any visitors staying more than six months would require Israeli approval.

The matters on which understanding had been reached at Davos, including Palestinian control of certain Muslim sites outside the auton-

* As expected, Rabin's letter undertook to 'discuss', rather than 'renegotiate', the autonomous area of Jericho.

omous areas, and special security arrangements for Israeli settlers in Gaza, were included in the Cairo Agreement.

The agreement aroused no enthusiasm in the Arab world and was vehemently attacked by the Israeli right. Rabin defended it by saying that no accord could give total security, but the new Palestinian authority would have an interest in maintaining order. 'I recognize the existence of a Palestinian entity . . . which is not a state but has a right to symbols such as a flag,' Rabin said in a television interview on 10 February.

After the Cairo Agreement negotiations continued in Taba on the powers of the Palestinian authority and on handover arrangements. On 23 February Sha'ath and Shahak reached agreement that Israeli troops would begin leaving Jericho and Gaza on 17 March and would complete their withdrawal by 12 April, a day before the target which Arafat and Peres had set in Oslo.

18

The Hebron Massacre

Deep in the subconscious mind of Israeli settlers there existed an inseparable bond between faith, patriotism, violence and territorial expansion. Nowhere was the power of these intangibles greater than at Kiriat Arba, a settlement of 7000 people on the northern edge of Hebron. Few would choose to live in such a place, surrounded by a hostile population, unless driven by an extreme commitment to 'Eretz Yisrael'.

It was no coincidence that Hebron was chosen by Rabbi Moshe Levinger when he led a small group of followers into the occupied territories in 1968 to found the first Jewish settlement. According to the Bible, the cave of Machpelah in Hebron was the burial place of Abraham and his family. The city was King David's capital for seven years. A Jewish settlement named Kfar Elsion was built near Hebron in the 1930s, but was occupied by the Jordanian army after the beginning of hostilities in 1948. The return of settlers to Hebron after the Israeli occupation of the west bank was seen as a religious duty.

In the minds of such people the Oslo agreement was a threat to everything they wanted to do. If the Palestinians regained control of even part of the occupied territories the rebuilding of biblical Israel would be impossible. The settlements, and therefore their homes, might be at risk once the final-status talks began. If the agreement was to be blocked, it had to be done before the Israeli withdrawal from Gaza and Jericho started on 17 March.

Any settler who wanted to wreck the agreement would have understood that a period ideally suited to political sabotage had begun on 11 February, two days after the Cairo Agreement. Ramadan, the ninth month of the Islamic year, was a time of fasts and abstinence and deep spiritual devotion. Observance of Ramadan was one of the five pillars, or basic duties, of the faith.* It was the month in which Prophet Mohamed received the first of the revelations from the angel Gabriel which became the Koran. Ramadan was thus the period of maximum sensitivity.

A settler wishing to provoke religious outrage would also have known that Hebron was the place to do it. Al-Khalili, the mosque built over the cave of Machpelah, was among the holiest sites in Islam. From the Muslim viewpoint the cave was the burial place of Ibrahim, the '*rassul*', or religious messenger, of monotheism. The fact that Muslims and Jews revered the same spot in different ways, and were forced to share the same main praying hall, made the Tomb of the Patriarchs the place of maximum sensitivity.

In the mind of Baruch Goldstein, a thirty-five-year-old American-born Israeli living at Kiriat Arba, these facts offered a sinister opportunity. Goldstein came from a middle-class family in Brooklyn, and had been religiously inclined since childhood. He grew up to be a follower of the fanatically racist leader Rabbi Meir Kahane, who started his career in America with verbal attacks against blacks, communists and Christian missionaries. In 1971 Kahane moved to Israel and began calling for the removal of Arabs from the west bank and Gaza. After qualifying as a doctor Goldstein followed his leader to Israel in 1983. When he married a fellow Kahane supporter, the ceremony was conducted by the rabbi himself. In 1990, when Kahane was assassinated by an Arab in New York, Goldstein vowed to revenge his death, and became a devotee of an ultra-extreme movement called Kahane Chai ('Kahane Lives').

In the early hours of 25 February, the fifteenth day of Ramadan, Goldstein wrote goodbye notes to a colleague at the medical clinic where he worked and to others, and put on his uniform as a reserve officer in the Israeli army. As he approached the mosque he was recognized by Mohamed Suleiman Abu Sarah, an unarmed guard. Goldstein had been to the tomb frequently to pray, and had provoked incidents with Muslim worshippers on several occasions. Goldstein knocked the guard down and entered the mosque, where some 700 Muslims were

* The other four pillars are the *shahadah*, the affirmation that 'Allah is Allah, and Mohamed is his prophet,' the five daily prayers (*salat*), alms-giving (*zakat*), and the once-in-a-lifetime pilgrimage to Mecca (the Hajj).

kneeling in pre-dawn prayers. Goldstein took aim and fired 111 bullets with a rapid-action assault rifle. Amidst the screams and panic which followed someone had the presence of mind to hurl a fire extinguisher, which knocked Goldstein off-balance. He was then beaten to death. In the rush to carry the wounded to hospital and the dead to their relatives there was no time to count the casualties accurately. Israeli officials found thirty-nine bodies when they arrived, but some had already been removed. The Palestinian count was fifty-two dead and seventy injured.

Even among a people inured to suffering the Hebron massacre was an immense shock. Any Palestinian could reel off the dates of half a dozen outrages committed by the Israeli army or its allies and stooges. The killing of 250 people at Deir Yassin, Palestine in May 1948 (before the declaration of the state of Israel), the Kibbya massacre in northern Jerusalem on 14 October 1953, the Sabra and Shatila massacres of 16–18 September 1982, and the slaughter of Palestinians in refugee camps at Tyre and Beirut in May 1985, were only a fraction of the aggression against non-combatants. The Israeli raid on the west bank town of Al-Samu on 13 November 1966, causing heavy civilian casualties, set a pattern of indiscriminate revenge. Israel had always replied to commando raids with retaliatory strikes, which was to be expected, but from Al-Samu onwards the targets were often heavily populated areas. The use of cluster bombs and napalm showed that the intention was to kill people without regard to any links with commandos. What made the Hebron massacre different was the deliberate intention to inflame religious feelings.

More than any other massacre except Shatila and Sabra, the Hebron outrage brought a torrent of international condemnation. Most countries apart from the United States appreciated that what had happened was a consequence of the settlement policy. The massacre was therefore on the conscience of the Israeli state, regardless of whether Goldstein had acted alone or with others.

The US administration found the act devastating, but the first priority was to save the Oslo agreement. President Clinton called Yasser Arafat to express his shock and revulsion, and said that the aggression was directed not so much against the worshippers in the mosque as against peace. Clinton, who had never phoned Arafat before, urged the PLO leader not to break off the remaining negotiations, and suggested that the talks should be transferred to Washington, where the negotiators would be insulated against fluctuations of Arab opinion. After the call Clinton told aides that he thought the PLO would return to the talks.

Warren Christopher, who phoned Arafat five times on the day of the massacre, argued that stopping the peace process would amount to rewarding the assassin. The American approach made a great impression on Arafat, who could scarcely believe the attention the US president and secretary of state were giving him. 'Clinton says I am the flag and the symbol of the Palestinian cause,' he told his entourage at one point during the calls. Abu Mazen reminded the PLO chairman that US leaders followed scripts written for them by State Department bureaucrats. The flattery was anything but spontaneous.

Arafat's initial feeling was that the massacre was part of a conspiracy against Rabin by the Israeli army to prevent any change in the status quo. This may have been correct, but it was not the right way to react. The challenge to Rabin, he thought, was like that posed by the French secret army in Algeria during Charles de Gaulle's negotiations to end the Algerian war.

The American influence was evident in a statement issued by Fatah a few hours after the attack: 'The negotiations with the Israelis are not suspended: on the contrary these acts demonstrate the urgency of peace.' It was immediately obvious that PLO headquarters was out of step with Arab capitals, which were issuing bitter attacks on Israel. Even Egypt, mediator of the Cairo agreement, denounced Israel in harsh language.

Arafat was digesting these views when reports arrived of massive disturbances throughout the occupied territories. In some of the most violent scenes for years nineteen Palestinians were killed and hundreds injured while confronting Israeli forces. The clashes and the massacre caused the highest Palestinian death toll on any single day since the 1967 war.

Palestinian fury was directed not only against the settlers, the army and the Israeli administration, but also against the PLO leadership. Faisal Husseini tried to enter Hebron to pay his respects and was driven back by a hail of stones. Pictures of Arafat were burned in the streets and demonstrators chanted accusations that the chairman had sold himself to the Israelis. Islamic leaders in Syria, Lebanon and the occupied territories called for retribution and denounced the PLO–Israel agreements, clearly linking the two issues.

The Israeli army cleared the bodies from the mosque while a huge crowd outside screamed abuse. Suddenly the crowd fell silent and then began chanting 'King Hussein!' A rumour had spread that the king was coming to pay his respects, and the people were delighted. The rumour proved false, but the masses had shown their feelings: the Jordanian monarch was welcome and the PLO was not.

Dr Ahmed El-Tibi, Arafat's representative in the occupied territories, commented on the Hebron scene in a report to Arafat. 'Where is the snag?' he asked. 'Is it in Oslo, or is it in our leadership? This massacre was the straw which broke the camel's back . . . [People feel that] it would not have happened if King Hussein had been in charge.' This view was supported, Tibi said, even by those who had been against Hamas and in favour of the negotiations with Israel.

Sheikh Suleiman El-Yadrasawi, the most important preacher of Al-Khalili mosque, commented: 'Our brothers are being massacred and our leaders are either asleep or negotiating with the Israelis.'

Bitter reactions were not confined to the occupied territories. In Egypt the Imam of El-Azhar called on Muslims to 'punish Israel for the massacre and the profanation of the Tomb of the Patriarchs'. Tens of thousands of people took to the streets to express their anger and grief. Students from Cairo University marched on the Israeli embassy a few hundred yards away across a Nile bridge, and Egyptian police were obliged to use tear gas and fire shots in the air to force them back. David Sultan, the Israeli ambassador, told Mubarak that police firmness had saved the embassy from being stormed. Some days later Arafat confessed to Mubarak that the Egyptian reaction to the massacre had alarmed him: 'It was as if a ghoul in the Egyptian soul had been awakened.'

Shimon Peres made repeated efforts to phone Arafat, but the chairman refused to accept his calls. Later Dr Tibi phoned to say that Rabin wanted to speak to Arafat, but wished to be sure that he would not be rebuffed. The PLO chairman decided to accept the prime minister's call. 'We can speak as soldier to soldier,' he told aides. Arafat went into a private room to talk to the prime minister, and said afterwards that Rabin had apologized. Rabin also sought permission to send a delegation to Tunis. The Israeli version of this phone call, given by a government source on 25 February, was that Rabin said he could not find words adequate to express his feelings of condemnation, and added that he felt ashamed of what had happened.

Rabin informed Mubarak that the Israeli cabinet would meet the following day to consider what measures to take. The prime minister read a statement to journalists on behalf of the government 'severely condemning' the massacre and expressing condolences to families of victims.

Rabin's apologies were not representative of all Jews. A spokesman for Kach, the organization founded by Kahane, described Goldstein as 'a sacred hero'. Some settlers openly rejoiced at the killings and said their only regret was that the death toll had not been greater. The massacre happened on the Jewish feast of Purim, a day of parades and dancing, and the festivities went ahead as planned.

When Egyptian foreign minister Amr Moussa heard that the Clinton administration had secured Arafat's agreement to continue the negotiations and transfer the talks to Washington, he phoned Arafat immediately. 'The Americans tell us that you have said yes to their request,' he said.

'I said "Yes, but." It seems they heard the yes, not the but,' Arafat replied.

If the chairman was beginning to feel uneasy about his initial decision, the next development made him more so. Evidence began to emerge that the massacre had not been the act of a single madman. Israeli soldiers had contributed by hurling smoke bombs which added to the confusion, delaying the evacuation of the mosque and enabling Goldstein to kill more people. The Israeli army version of this was that troops tried to intervene when they heard shots, but were blocked by worshippers pouring out of the mosque.

Moves to call a meeting of the UN Security Council to condemn the outrage began on the day of the massacre, but were blocked by Washington. Christopher told Arafat on 26 February that a Security Council resolution would complicate matters. As Washington had vetoed numerous UN resolutions condemning Israel in the past, this was no surprise.

Christopher was also unenthusiastic about the executive committee call for a UN peacekeeping presence, pointing out that UN forces in

Bosnia-Herzegovina had been largely unsuccessful in protecting Muslims there.

President Mitterrand, ever uncomfortable with US domination of the peace process, sent his adviser on Arab affairs, Ambassador Bruno Delaye, to discuss reconciliation efforts. Mitterrand's proposal was that the Socialist International should take over from Washington and that fresh peace efforts should commence with a breakfast for Arafat and Rabin at the Elysée Palace, hosted by the French president. Arafat sent Yasser Abd-Rabbo, a member of the executive committee, to Paris to explore the idea. At the same time Abu Lutf (Farouk Kaddoumi) was sent to Syria on the pretext of expressing condolences to President Assad, who had recently lost his son Basil in a car accident. The real aim of the trip was to ensure that the massacre did not add to the strains between the PLO and Syria.

By 27 February it was clear that the Israeli coalition was divided on how to react to the massacre. The MERETZ bloc demanded that Kahane's organization Kach and Kahane Chai should be banned, their members expelled from the Israeli army, and their weapons confiscated. Others argued that if Israel made concessions, greater demands would follow. This caution was reinforced by an incident in Jerusalem at Haram Es-Sharif, which Jews call the ruins of the Temple, where a group of Muslims pelted Jews praying at the Wailing Wall with stones. On Sunday morning a bomb exploded at a Christian Maronite church at Junieh, north of Beirut, killing nine people and injuring sixty others. Four other bombs in the church were found and defused. It was later alleged that the explosion at the church was planned by elements of the Maronite Lebanese forces. A Maronite leader known to be a friend and ally of Israel was arrested. The Lebanese authorities said he would be brought to trial in connection with the bombing.

After a five-hour Israeli cabinet meeting on 27 February only token measures against extremist movements were announced. The law was to be changed to make Kach and Kahane Chai illegal, and the arrest of five extremists was ordered, but three of them escaped before this could be implemented. Firearms licences were removed from eighteen people, and a commission of inquiry was set up. Arafat said these measures were 'insufficient and empty', while Hanan Ashrawi and Faisal Husseini insisted that apologies were not enough: all the settlers should be disarmed. Yasser Abd-Rabbo added that in all the negotiations Israel's security fears had been paramount, but the Hebron attack had demonstrated that Palestinians too needed security guarantees.

A few hours later the Arab League, meeting in Cairo, attributed responsibility for the Hebron attack to the Israeli government, and called on UN secretary general Boutros Ghali to provide protection for Palestinians. Syrian delegates attending the talks with Israel in Washington suddenly packed their bags and flew home. Soon afterwards the Lebanese and Jordanian delegations also suspended their participation.

Further demonstrations took place throughout the occupied territories on 28 February, and for the first time Israeli Arabs and Palestinians living in Jaffa, Galilee and the Negev joined the protests. Twenty-five people were killed during these demonstrations.

The following day, 1 March, the PLO executive committee reversed Arafat's decision not to suspend the negotiations. The committee insisted that condemnation and investigation of the massacre should precede any question of resuming talks. The PLO's conditions for resumption were security measures for Palestinians in Hebron, a United Nations resolution of condemnation, the presence of UN forces or observers in Hebron, and an increase in the Palestinian police force which was to take over Gaza and Jericho.

Arafat accepted the committee's views and offered an explanation for his initial acceptance of Washington's suggestions. He pointed out that the Americans had so far refused to become directly involved in the post-Oslo talks. In accepting the US request he had hoped to ensure their involvement.

As soon as news reached Washington of the executive committee's decision, Warren Christopher phoned Arafat. He said that Arafat had promised to continue the negotiations and transfer talks to Washington, and that he should keep his word. Arafat was tormented by conflicting pressures, not least because the Americans kept emphasizing his importance as the only leader capable of uniting the Palestinians.

Israelis were now braced for reprisals, but the first of these was not on their territory. On 1 March young members of the Lubavitch sect,*

* Hasidism is a Jewish pietistic movement. The Lubavitch sect, named after the Belorussian town which was its original headquarters, was run by a family dynasty of whom Rabbi Schnerson was the seventh in line of succession. The sect has been based in Brooklyn since 1941.

the most prominent American component of the ultra-orthodox Hasidism movement, became the targets of an attack. They had been to visit their ninety-two-year-old leader Rabbi Menchem Schnerson in a hospital in Manhattan. As they returned to the sect's headquarters in Brooklyn their minibus was raked with automatic weapons fire by a man shouting 'Death to the Jews.' One was killed instantly, another died later, and three were injured. A Palestinian was arrested the next day and charged with the killings.

In the days after the Hebron massacre Peres continued trying to reach Arafat, who persisted in refusing the calls. In total the Israeli foreign minister made nineteen attempts.

After receiving further reports from Dr Tibi entitled 'Public Opinion in the Palestinian Street', Arafat realized that anger in the occupied territories would not subside quickly. All the reports reflected continuing resentment against the PLO. Rabin still wanted to send a delegation to talk to him, but Arafat felt he could not be seen receiving Israelis in Tunis. He therefore flew to Cairo to meet Rabin's men on neutral territory.

Rabin's representatives were Jack Nerya and Gildat Amos, the same pair who had been involved in the disastrous meeting with Arafat in Tunis in December 1993.* The two Israelis briefed Arafat on the measures the Israeli government had taken against extremist parties. Arafat, who already knew these details, was irritated that they had no additional measures to offer, and hinted that he was half minded to call off the peace process and acknowledge that the hardliners had been proved correct. 'I will go to George Habash and tell him: "Hakim ['the Wise'], you were right all along,"' he threatened.

Rabin's request, conveyed through Nerya, was that the PLO should not reward the enemies of peace by stopping the talks. Arafat replied: 'And who are the enemies of peace? All the settlers, for a start.'

When Nerya said an investigation would be held, on the lines of the commission set up in 1982 under Chief Justice Kahan to probe the Sabra and Shatila massacres, Arafat replied: 'And what good did that do?' The thought of Sabra and Shatila brought tears to his eyes.†

* See p. 478.
† The findings of the investigation, announced on 26 June 1994, were that Goldstein acted alone, without complicity by his family, other settlers or soldiers. 'We cannot accuse anyone of negligence,' the commission said.

Nerya then promised further measures the following week. 'Why next week? Why not next month, or next year?' Arafat shot back.

The two Israelis said that Rabin wanted Arafat to know that withdrawal from Gaza and Jericho would go ahead by 12 April as arranged by Sha'ath and Shahak before the massacre. Rabin offered a compromise on the size of the Palestinian police force, which was still in dispute. The Palestinians wanted 12,000 men, while the Israelis had said that 6000 was sufficient. Rabin's new offer was 9000.

Arafat also expressed his anger over the lack of action by the UN Security Council, which had still not agreed on a resolution condemning the massacre, because of US objections to the wording. Nerya and Amos then returned to Israel to report to Rabin.

While in Cairo Arafat was again approached by Mitterrand's envoy Ambassador Delaye, who pressed the idea of a joint breakfast with Rabin at the Elysée Palace. Arafat said: 'I welcome the president's initiative but I cannot see Rabin now. The Americans asked me too, but my people would not accept a meeting at this time.' Delaye was surprised and annoyed.

After a pause for reflection the Egyptian government began to look for ways of restarting the talks under suitable conditions. Cairo's main aims were to complete the peace process, to ensure that Arafat extracted a political price from Israel for the resumption, and to keep the talks in Egypt.

A position paper prepared by Amr Moussa supported demands for greater security for Palestinians, but opposed any move to ask for an international military presence in the occupied territories, on the ground that the failure of UN operations in Somalia and Bosnia had shown this to be pointless. The PLO should, however, insist on the presence of UN observers. Moussa also advised Arafat to put the problem of the settlements on the political agenda immediately, without waiting for the final-status talks to begin, and to ask for disarmament of the settlers.

In the first week of March Dr Tibi informed Arafat that Israel was planning to send a high-level delegation to Tunis. It was assumed in Tunis that this meant Nerya and Amos, and permission was given for them to come. At this point Stephen Cohen approached the PLO urging that there should as a minimum be a meeting between Peres and Abu Mazen or Yasser Abd-Rabbo. Cohen's approach alerted the PLO to the fact that Peres was planning to head the delegation himself. The Israelis thought the PLO had agreed to receive Peres because of the reference to a 'high-level delegation'. A message was flashed to Tibi warning that if the foreign minister were aboard, the plane would not be allowed to land in Tunisia, which had no diplomatic relations with Israel. The authorities were prepared to close their eyes to the arrival of bureaucrats, but not politicians. Feelings were still running too high for any meeting between Arafat and Peres.

As the inquiry into responsibility for the massacre got under way, sloppy procedures practised by Israeli soldiers supposedly protecting the holy places were exposed. Although incidents between Jews and Muslims were not unusual at the Tomb of the Patriarchs, Israeli forces practised absurdly low manning levels. At any given time some of those supposedly on duty would be absent for one reason or another. On 10 March evidence emerged proving that the role of the guards was to protect settlers from Muslims, not to keep order in an impartial way. Meir Tayar, a police deputy commander in Hebron, said that security forces were under orders not to fire at settlers with live ammunition under any circumstances.

Later in the hearings two soldiers who had been on duty at the mosque on 25 February admitted that they fired their guns as worshippers were fleeing from the mosque. The soldiers denied having shot anyone. They said that Goldstein was carrying an M-16 rifle when he entered the mosque, which conflicted with evidence from army experts that all 111 bullets were fired from an Israeli Glilon assault rifle. Many Palestinians believed that two gunmen were involved, not one.

The inquiry also brought to light the extent of friction between Jews and Muslims at the Tomb of the Patriarchs. Although separate hours for prayers had been established, the Muslims felt progressively squeezed by Jewish encroachment. After the return to Hebron in 1968 Jewish groups rebuilt an ancient rabbinical school which had existed in the sacred area, and a preaching circle grew up, with 150 students and forty families living in three groups close to the temple. The Israeli residents carried Uzi sub-machineguns wherever they went in the city, flaunting their power over the population of 70,000. In time some began living in the school itself, thus establishing a full-time Jewish presence within a shared place of worship. Baruch Goldstein would frequently refuse to leave the main hall of the tomb when the time reserved for Jewish prayers ended, resulting in scuffles with Muslim worshippers. In October 1993 Muslim leaders complained to the government that Goldstein had poured 'flammable materials' on the mosque's carpet. In the twelve months before the massacre at least twenty-five 'incidents of friction' were recorded at the tomb.

Within two weeks of the massacre Goldstein's grave had become a place of pilgrimage for Zionists dedicated to 'Eretz Yisrael'. Far from showing remorse, the settlement of Kiriat Arba regarded Goldstein as a hero and an example to others. An ardent Zionist had his son baptized Goldstein and prayed at the Wailing Wall that the boy would grow up to follow Goldstein's footsteps.

In this atmosphere there was much scepticism among Muslims on 13 March when the legal changes banning Kach and Kahane Chai came into effect. The organizations joined a list of terrorist movements, making them subject to the same laws as Hezbollah (ironically the PLO was still on the terrorist list, although scheduled to be removed). Government spokesmen claimed that Kach and Kahane Chair had only a hundred members each, but the hatred and racism which they represented was clearly a wider phenomenon.

Throughout the second week of March the impasse in the UN Security Council continued to block diplomatic efforts to persuade the PLO to return to negotiations. Sensing that the Americans had locked themselves out through their support of Israel, the Russian foreign minister Andrei Kozyrev saw a long-awaited opportunity to play a role. Kozyrev toured the Middle East on 12 and 13 March, promoting the idea of a new Middle East peace conference. He met a frosty welcome in Israel, where his mission was openly regarded as interference. Arafat received him more warmly, and after talks in Tunis the PLO stated its willingness to return to talks once preconditions had been met, including a Security Council resolution of condemnation. This was not new, and Arafat was merely being polite. The truth that Russia had no role could not be disguised.

Arafat also held talks with US representatives, and it was agreed that the dispute over the wording of the Security Council resolution could be solved by voting on each sentence separately. This would allow the US to veto the parts it rejected and accept the rest. Dennis

Ross of the US State Department would then have further discussions with Arafat or Abu Mazen.

Another twist in the tortuous road back to the negotiating table came when the PLO indicated a wish to switch to Morocco instead of Egypt as an intermediary. The aim was to avoid further inflaming anti-Israeli feeling in Egypt, but the idea was not practical because Mubarak and Rabin had already worked out a strategy for bringing about a resumption of talks. After a two-hour phone conversation between Mubarak and Arafat, a solution was found. It was agreed that Faisal Husseini would meet Peres on the pretext of hearing what additional security measures Israel had to offer. This would amount to a *de facto* resumption of talks. The Security Council would then pass its resolution, and the Egyptian delegate in New York would announce that the resolution had paved the way for full resumption. After these steps an Israeli delegation at a higher level would be received in Tunis.

The agreed objectives were an international presence on the west bank, joint Israeli-PLO police patrols in Hebron, and the extension of the area in which the Palestinian police would operate. Instead of being confined to the autonomous areas, the police should be deployed throughout the west bank and Gaza from the start. It was realized that this last point had no chance of being accepted by the Israelis. Other demands certain to be rejected were that Israeli settlers should be disarmed and that the permanent presence of Israelis at the school in the Tomb of the Patriarchs compound should be ended.

In a flurry of moves on 16 and 17 March Rabin returned to Israel after talks with Clinton in Washington and the Pope at the Vatican, and immediately dispatched a delegation headed by Uri Savir to Tunis. Arafat reiterated the PLO's conditions for talks, and sent the team straight back to Israel.

On 18 March the Security Council passed Resolution 904 condemning the massacre and calling for the presence of international observers in the occupied territories on a temporary basis. Syria, Jordan and Lebanon then agreed to resume the Washington talks. The following day Israeli state radio announced that Rabin and Arafat had spoken on the telephone. The PLO was seeking a hundred Palestinian policemen in Hebron as well as Norwegian observers. Peres said that Israel was not against Palestinian police but wanted them to be under Israeli control.

Samir Ghoche, a member of the PLO executive, insisted on 19 March that talks between Arafat and Peres were out of the question until the method of implementing Resolution 904 had been decided. The following day an Israeli delegation including Savir, Shahak and Nerya went to Tunis to convey Israel's replies to the PLO's demands, while the US, Russia and Norway continued to play prominent roles.

Throughout the period since the massacre Israeli authorities had imposed a curfew on the district of Hebron to protect Israelis living in the precincts of the Tomb of the Patriarchs. Despite speculation in the Israeli press that the forty Israeli families would be centralized at a single location, or moved elsewhere, nothing was done and the curfew continued. Frustration in Hebron over this injustice resulted in clashes on 23 March in which five Palestinians were killed. Rabin told a Labour Party meeting the same day: 'One cannot hide the truth that we are keeping 120,000 Palestinians under curfew to protect about 400 Jewish settlers.'

Despite further serious incidents in the occupied territories on 28 March in which eight Palestinians were killed and fifty injured, the talks finally resumed in Cairo the following day. Palestinian leaders on the west bank and in Gaza sent a request to Tunis asking for a delay, but Arafat decided to go ahead. A fifteen-strong Israeli delegation led by Shahak and Nerya agreed with a PLO team that the international presence in Hebron should consist of ninety Norwegians, thirty-five Danes and thirty-five Italians, acting solely as observers.

By 5 April the roads out of Gaza and Jericho were choked with hundreds of Israeli army vehicles ready to start the withdrawal from the autonomous areas. At the same time advance groups of PLO organizers were permitted to enter across King Hussein Bridge and the Rafiah border crossing from Egypt.

Thirty-nine days had passed since the massacre, and all who understood the Muslim world knew that a crucial period was approaching. The long-promised revenge came the following day, hours after completion of the forty-day Muslim mourning period. The location was Afula, an Israeli town of 35,000 people, the majority of whom were Sephardim (and therefore more likely to vote Likud than Labour). A stolen car carrying a 175-kilogram bomb swung in front of a stationary bus and exploded as passengers were alighting, killing eight and wounding fifty-two. The car driver was Rashid Zakarna, a deeply religious nineteen-year-old Palestinian who lived near Afula. One of his cousins said Zakarna had been arrested in April 1993 and tortured while in custody. A spokesman for Hamas acknowledged responsibility for the attack and confirmed that it was in revenge for the Hebron massacre: 'The strategy of Hamas is to increase its action against military targets. We hold that Hamas has the right to act anywhere in Palestine.' It was the seventh attack by suicide bombers against Israelis in twelve months, but previous incidents had killed only the perpetrators.

Rabin replied: 'We will continue to negotiate as if there were no terrorism, and we will continue to fight terrorism as if we were not negotiating.'

The Afula attack placed Arafat in a delicate position. Soon after the Washington signing ceremony the previous September, an Israeli had been killed by an Islamic Jihad sniper. Rabin felt that the killing should be a test of Arafat's sincerity, and called on the PLO chairman to condemn the incident. The State Department contacted Nasser El-Kodra, PLO ambassador to the UN and Arafat's cousin, pressing the same demand. It was difficult for Arafat to condemn an act by Islamic Jihad, but a deal was made that he would do so on condition that the Israeli government condemned any future killings of Palestinians by Israeli settlers. The agreement resulted in the first condemnation by Arafat of an act of violence committed inside the territories. Some time later a Palestinian was killed by a settler, and the murder was condemned by Rabin. After the Hebron massacre, the Israeli government condemned the act both collectively and individually. Rabin went so far as to tell the Knesset: 'To Goldstein and his ilk we say: "You are not part of the congregation of Israel. Rational Judaism spits at you."' Even Binyamin Netanyahu, the Likud leader, said: 'It is a crime, a terrible crime, and I condemn it totally.' Arafat knew that the Afula bombing would be regarded by most Arabs as justified retribution, and that any condemnation on his part would be deeply unpopular. Hamas was now in the forefront of the struggle and had proved its ability to strike Israelis on their own territory, not just in the occupied territories. The Israeli and US governments called on Arafat to condemn the bombing, but he hesitated.

The Israeli government responded to the attack by closing entrances to Israel from the occupied territories, preventing the 100,000 Palestinian commuters with regular jobs in Israel from going to work. Opposition calls to suspend the talks were rejected.

In Paris Abu Ala and Avraham Shohat, the Israeli treasury minister, discussed creating a customs union between the Palestinian autonomous areas and Israel. Israel had already agreed to the creation of a central bank of Palestine to control local banks, but was not prepared to concede Arafat's demands for a Palestinian currency, arguing that the Jordanian dinar, the Israeli shekel and the Egyptian pound could be used.

Violence on both sides continued with an attack by Islamic Jihad in Ashdod, killing one Israeli and wounding four, and another incident in Hebron, in which Israeli forces shot and wounded eight Palestinians. On 13 April, Remembrance Day in Israel, a suicide bomber boarded a bus at Hedera and exploded a device, killing himself and five other people and injuring thirty. A Hamas spokesman said that this was only the second of five attacks planned in revenge for the Hebron massacre. On this occasion Arafat and Faisal Husseini condemned extremists on both sides.

Amid a seemingly endless spiral of aggression and revenge, the passing of the 12 April deadline for Israel to complete its withdrawal from Gaza and Jericho was no surprise. The withdrawal had been prepared, the lorries were waiting to move the troops out, but nothing had happened. The peace process was facing another period of uncertainty.

19

A Violent Peace

The darkest hour of the long night of confusion came in mid-April 1994. Opposition in Israel to the Oslo agreement had soared after the post-Hebron reprisals, leaving Rabin and Peres clinging to power by their political fingertips. Another attack against bus passengers, carried out by a seventeen-year old Palestinian Hamas supporter wielding an axe and shouting 'Allah Akbar,' brought tension to boiling point. Likud leader Binyamin Netanyahu said that Rabin would go down in history as the man who created an army of Palestinian terrorists.

The mood in the occupied territories was almost as hostile to the agreement as that in Israel, though for different reasons. Most Palestinians felt the PLO leadership had taken leave of its senses in resuming talks so soon after the Hebron massacre. Fury with Arafat resulted in a truce between Hamas militants and young members of Fatah, who had been involved in interfactional incidents. Leaflets distributed in Gaza in mid-April declared an intention by both groups to continue resisting Israel. In effect, militant Islam and militant nationalism were trying to set aside their differences with the intention of resuming the Intifada. At about the same time the Israeli military authorities announced that in the six years since the start of the Intifada 1045 Palestinians had been killed, 18,967 injured, and 140,000 had spent periods in prison. Israeli casualties during the same period were 219 dead and 7872 injured.

The sour atmosphere in the occupied territories was reflected in further bitter criticism of Arafat by his colleagues. Opponents of the Oslo agreement within the PLO had gained a fistful of new arguments since the Hebron massacre, and even supporters felt the peace process was in a muddle. There were now three different agreements, all called declarations of principles, each adding to or subtracting from the one before, and the leadership had lost track. After the Oslo agreement (August 1993), the Washington Declaration (September 1993) and the Cairo Declaration (February 1994), it now seemed that a fourth agreement would be needed to clear up loopholes in the previous three.

The critics had ample grounds for discontent. The size of the autonomous area of Jericho was still in doubt, and the letter Rabin had sent Arafat promising to discuss (not renegotiate) the provisional fifty-four-square-kilometre offer was considered too vague.* Palestinians had secured the right to cultivate the Mawady area in Gaza, but that had no value without an agreement on water allocation. The Israeli refusal to discuss east Jerusalem prior to the 1996 final-status talks was causing much anger. The whole leadership, and especially Farouk Kaddoumi, felt that Palestinians had been short-changed and that Israel was offering nothing but an opportunity to take over menial aspects of administration.

A beleaguered Arafat began to blame others for the untenable position in which the PLO found itself. Unable to criticize Egypt because of Cairo's vital importance as a mediator, he lashed out at Jordan, Syria and the Gulf states. He also tried to reduce his dependence on Cairo by finding another mediator between himself and the Israelis. In talks with King Hassan, who had a long history of secret negotiations with Israel, Arafat complained that the Israelis seemed not to understand that he had passed the point of no return. The king agreed that there was no way back; the Arabs had lost and should acknowledge this to themselves. King Hassan also counselled Arafat to continue negotiating and to bear in mind Israel's immense influence abroad: 'Those people [the Israelis] are very powerful. Consider what they have done for you. In twenty-four hours they changed your image from terrorist to peacemaker, enabling you to go to the White House, to dine at the State Department, to have lunch at the World Bank, to enter 10 Downing Street.'

As an illustration of Israel's hold over Washington, King Hassan disclosed what had happened when Baghdad asked him to intercede with the Americans. The Iraqi government wanted to know what it would take to bring about the lifting of the United Nations oil exports embargo. The advice which King Hassan obtained from US contacts,

* See pp. 488–9.

and passed on to Baghdad, contained three elements, one of which concerned the Arab–Israeli talks:* Iraq should not oppose or obstruct peace between Israel and its neighbours, whether Palestinian, Jordanian or Syrian. Baghdad would also do well, the king was told, to open a direct channel of communication with Israel, secret or otherwise. King Hassan clearly thought that Iraq should go along with these demands, confirming his reputation as the foremost pragmatist of the Arab world.†

Arafat decided he had no alternative but to continue trying to negotiate a more satisfactory agreement with Israel. Criticism within the PLO continued, related not just to the issues but also to the manner in which negotiations had been handled, and to Arafat's style of management. The earlier protests over lack of consultation had brought no changes, and the chairman's peripatetic lifestyle remained as hectic as ever, decisions being communicated to staff in terse phone calls from distant airports. With discontent growing Abu Mazen kept away from headquarters, and even Abu Ala was known to be unhappy.

Hani El-Hassan, one of Arafat's counsellors, felt that the chairman's carrot-and-stick method of management was no longer effective. The carrot had been the power Arafat derived from keeping total financial control in his own hands. The chairman still had control, but no money. The stick had been his personal authority, but with many in the PLO trying to dissociate themselves from the Oslo agreement, not much authority remained. Arafat had innovated a technique of punishment by neglect to keep colleagues on their toes, but that was ineffective at a time when many were happy to be neglected. The organization was full of rumblings about bad management, corruption and infiltration.

There were also broader criticisms of Arafat's approach to the problem. Critics felt that he was lending too much credence to the so-called

* The other two elements were that Iraq should cooperate unconditionally with international observers, and should recognize without discussion the revised borders which the Security Council had approved for Kuwait.

† The advice was not ignored. In April 1994, at a time when Morocco was a member of the fifteen-nation UN Security Council, Baghdad stepped up its diplomatic offensive to obtain the lifting of sanctions, and hinted at willingness to allow UN officials to complete their inspections of Iraqi military arsenals. Reports in the Israeli press in August 1994 claimed that contacts between Israeli and Iraqi officials had taken place in Europe.

'new world order', and was overawed by what he saw as American domination of the global game. The impact of the collapse of the Soviet Union on the PLO's bargaining position had been over-estimated, leading to unnecessary retreats. Worse, by giving the impression that the conflict was resolved, Arafat had enabled Israel to acquire a presence in countries which had previously refused contacts, including China, India, Malaysia and Indonesia.

Faced with a crisis of confidence, Arafat acted to quell the revolt. He told his critics that he had squeezed all that was humanly possible out of the Israelis in earlier talks, and promised to press for more in future negotiations. A new carrot was found, in the form of appointments to the twenty-four-member Palestinian administration which was to take over Gaza and Jericho. The process of selecting this team was spun out for months, though its usefulness to Arafat was limited by the reluctance of key people (including Hanan Ashrawi) to accept seats.

To show that rumours of corruption were not taken lightly, Arafat ordered several arrests. Among those held for questioning was his wife's uncle George Hawwa, a businessman who was picked up during a visit to Tunis. Mr Hawwa, who denied any wrongdoing, was imprisoned in a PLO detention house pending investigations into a deal with a construction company. In a highly charged atmosphere Arafat's wife, Suha Tawil, was too upset to speak to her husband. Instead she wrote him a terse formal note saying: 'Mr Chairman, will you please release my uncle?' Mr Hawwa was set free and was allowed to travel to Europe.

An important element in Arafat's strategy was the early development of a Palestinian sense of statehood. The reality remained distant, but psychological benefits could be derived as soon as the Oslo agreement went into effect. This hope lay behind the importance he attached to flags, passports, currency and border controls. Another symbol of statehood would be a Palestinian postal system. Arafat began showing colleagues designs for Palestinian stamps, portraying Saladin, Hajj Amin El-Husseini, and Abu Jihad. A fourth design carried his own likeness, which was considered by colleagues to be self-indulgence.*

* At the time of writing (1995), no decision had been taken on whether to use the design with Arafat's likeness.

Arafat also tried to restore optimism by suggesting that Gaza could become a free port, and that Palestine might develop into the Singapore of the Middle East. There was a limit to what the market for dreams would bear. In reality what Arafat was about to take over was more like a South African homeland, with too many people, not enough territory, hardly any water, practically no industry and only a veneer of autonomy. Worst of all, from Arafat's point of view, no money. The United States had so far delivered only $5 million, and that was earmarked for the Palestinian police.* At the same time Washington was giving Israel $148 million for the costs of redeploying forces away from Gaza.

Meanwhile the PLO–Israeli talks, which had resumed in Taba at the end of March, were working towards an agreement on detailed terms for implementing the three previous declarations. Arafat was eager that this new agreement should contain sufficient Israeli concessions to silence his critics. His hope was that the transfer of certain responsibilities could be brought forward, allowing Palestinians to take over as soon as the Israelis withdrew from Gaza and Jericho, instead of waiting until stage two of the Oslo agreement, which was to start after a council to administer the whole of the west bank and Gaza had been elected. Arafat instructed his negotiators to press for immediate Palestinian jurisdiction and for the establishment of a Palestinian water authority before rather than after elections. It was also vital, he thought, to set some kind of precedent concerning Jerusalem, possibly by securing control of taxation in the eastern part of the city.

The Israelis refused to make any concessions on Jerusalem. On the water authority, their argument was that Israel had to retain control because of the need to supply the settlements. As to taxation, Israeli negotiators sought to differentiate between general taxation and local taxes. The Palestinians were free to set what municipal taxes they wished, but 70 per cent of revenue raised through general taxation would go to Israel and only 30 per cent to the self-government authority. Arafat refused to accept so small a proportion. The Israelis were not prepared to bring forward or extend Palestinian jurisdiction.† Until

* Aid from Britain and France at that stage consisted of police equipment, not funds for government administration.

† The jurisdiction to be accorded to the Palestinian Council after elections was subject to limits. See pp. 453–4.

elections were held, that jurisdiction would be limited to settling disputes between Palestinians in the self-rule areas.

A way forward was eventually found during talks between Arafat and Peres in Bucharest on 21 and 22 April. The principles were that Israel should concede some of the symbols of statehood which Arafat wanted, and that the PLO would be more forthcoming on security. After this accord, PLO and Israeli negotiators quickly reached agreement on several details. Israel agreed to allow the Palestinian authority to issue passports to residents of the autonomous areas, to use its own postage stamps, and to have a separate international telephone dialling code. It was also agreed that a further 5000 Palestinians would be released from Israeli jails during the fortnight after signing the agreement.

The PLO's main concessions in return were that Israel should retain air rights over the autonomous areas, and that territorial waters off Gaza should be limited, though details of the limits remained in question. Arafat and Peres put off another matter whose symbolism seemed important to Arafat. This was a demand, carried over from the talks which led to the Cairo Agreement in February, that the Palestinians should station a policeman on King Hussein Bridge.

The long-running economic talks in Paris, which had begun in October 1993, came to an end on 29 April. Abu Ala and Avraham Shohat, the Israeli treasury minister, signed an eighty-page agreement at the Quai d'Orsay establishing a customs union between Israel and the autonomous areas. The agreement also dealt with the industrial and energy sectors and with control of banks, allowing the Palestinian authorities to set up a monetary authority but not to issue currency.

The accord reflected the reality that the Israeli economy was the only engine available to pull the Palestinian train. The Union Bank of Switzerland predicted in June 1994 that Israel would become the third most competitive country in the world, after South Korea and China, if it could secure peace agreements with all its Arab neighbours. The economic agreement was just as important to Israel as to the Palestinians. The Israeli Union of Industries and the Farmers Federation had been pressing Rabin to bring back cheap labour to Israel, and to gain access to wider markets in the Arab world.

The Paris talks also demonstrated that the Palestinian authority was bound to be dependent on outside financial support for some years. Quite apart from development costs, the Palestinians would be unable to cover their own routine expenditure. It was estimated that tax revenue would be between 300 and 350 million shekels (3 shekels = US $1) and that Israel would contribute 160 million shekels of the taxes deducted from wages of Palestinians working in Israel. This implied a total revenue of 460 to 510 million shekels. Assuming that the Palestinian authority had basic annual outgoings of 800 million shekels, there would be a budget gap of around 300 million shekels. Putting this another way, the Palestinian authority could cover only about 60 per cent of its outgoings through taxation.

It was agreed that the Palestinian authority could issue bonds and debentures on the Gaza stock exchange (another planned innovation), and Israelis would be free to buy these. However, without large-scale support, Palestine would soon become heavily indebted. By late April the World Bank had collected only a fraction of the $2.1 billion promised by forty donor countries. The bank insisted that only properly costed and financially transparent projects could be funded. A Palestinian Economic Council had been working for months to identify the most urgent infrastructure and service projects needing funding. Presided over by Abu Ala, this body had received 2600 proposals for projects totalling $3 billion. A first batch of projects was approved by the World Bank on 22 April for immediate financing, but what Arafat wanted was financial flexibility.

By the end of April the agreement on implementing the three declarations of principles was almost ready, and 4 May was set for the signing. Rabin, always uneasy when Peres was in the limelight, decided to sign on behalf of Israel. Arafat too wanted the Israeli prime minister to be the signatory, as it was clear that the Israeli army was calling the shots, and Rabin was their man. Cairo was chosen as the venue because Rabin wanted to placate President Mubarak, who had not been invited to the Washington signing in September 1993.

The two teams arrived in Cairo a day early to negotiate remaining points. While these talks were under way Israeli settlers staged noisy demonstrations in Jerusalem against expansion of the Jericho autonomous area, and 500 rabbis met to declare that the transfer of any part of Eretz Yisrael to non-Jewish hands was contrary to divine law.*

It had been agreed at the time of the Cairo talks in February that the next meeting between Arafat and Rabin would be the opportunity to rediscuss the size of Jericho. Rabin came to the 3 May talks with an offer to increase the area from fifty-four to sixty-two square kilometres, but Arafat was not satisfied. The demand for a Palestinian policeman on King Hussein Bridge was another sticking point. The talks continued late into the night, involving not only Mubarak, Arafat, Rabin and Peres but also Warren Christopher and Andrei Kozyrev, who had arrived in their roles as co-sponsors of the Madrid/Washington process. Eventually it was agreed that Rabin would provide Arafat with a letter assuring him that discussions on the unsolved issues would continue after the signing. Thinking that all was settled, the leaders went gratefully to bed at 2.30 a.m.

During the night the Israeli secretariat prepared files for the various delegations, while Egyptian organizers made the Cairo Conference Centre ready for the ceremony later that morning. The setting was designed by a team from Egyptian television, using a huge mural with a pharaonic theme as a backdrop. The unintended effect was to remind Israelis of the Exodus and Palestinians of Egypt's pride in its antiquity, which tended to detract from pan-Arab feelings. The unfortunate symbolism was completed by a picture of a woman kneeling before the pharaoh and serenading him with her lyre. The stage was set, but, as events proved, not all the actors were willing to follow their lines.

It was important to Mubarak that key figures in many fields should be present, to demonstrate that Egypt was united behind his policy of support for peace with Israel. Mubarak was therefore upset to learn that Arab League secretary general Esmat Abdel Meguid was not planning to attend, and had ordered all senior Arab League officials to stay away. At 7 a.m. Mubarak phoned Meguid and asked: 'Who are you trying to please – Libya or Syria?' Mubarak's office contacted the Grand Mufti (Sheikh Mohamed Sayed Tantawi) and Pope Shenouda III, the Coptic prelate, to make sure they would be present. All three men dutifully showed up at the ceremony. Only the Sheikh of Al-

* The objections were echoed by Likud after the signing. David Levy, former Likud foreign minister, said that the accord had started an uncontrollable process which would lead to a Palestinian state.

Azhar, Sheikh Gad-el-Haq Ali Gad-el-Haq, was spared this test, as he was in London for medical treatment. Intellectuals, actors and artists were invited, and Mubarak seemed assured of a spectacular success which would demonstrate that Egypt had been right all along to make peace with Israel, and that other Arabs had little choice but to follow.

The entire ceremony, which was televised around the world, was meant to last no more than twenty-five minutes. Mubarak, Rabin, Arafat, Christopher, Kozyrev, Peres and Abu Mazen were allotted a speaking time of three minutes each, and the signing was expected to take not more than three minutes. It was a timetable which did not allow for snags.

Apart from the backdrop, the stage was set with nothing more than a table and a chair. All the actors had to remain standing throughout the show, except when signing. The invited audience began to realize that something was wrong when Rabin, while sitting at the table, summoned Peres to his side. The foreign minister listened to the prime minister, took a message to Mubarak, then returned to Rabin. After a terse exchange Rabin strode over to Mubarak and began gesticulating. In a near-repeat of the Cairo ceremony in February, Arafat had signed the documents but not the six accompanying maps. For more than half an hour the 2500 guests could see but not hear a highly confused row taking place on stage, while the speeches went ahead as if everything was running smoothly. Warren Christopher and Kozyrev were heard praising the agreement while Peres was remonstrating with Arafat and Rabin looked furious.

Eventually the Egyptian foreign minister Amr Moussa, acting on instructions from Mubarak, asked Arafat to return to the signing table. There was applause from some in the mostly Arab audience when Arafat indicated his refusal. After further confusion the entire company left the stage and held a behind-the-scenes discussion. The problem turned out to be the written version of Rabin's promise to continue discussing the size of Jericho. Arafat had not seen Rabin's letter, though whether it had been missing from his file or he had simply overlooked it was unclear. The chairman was worried that if he signed the maps, Rabin would go back on the agreement.

Five minutes later the party returned to the stage and Arafat signed each map, adding the words 'pending agreement' beside his signature. This prompted Joel Singer, the Israeli delegation's lawyer, to ask:

'What does he mean, "pending agreement"? This is the agreement!' Rabin told Singer not to make a fuss and to let it pass. The crisis over, Rabin added his own signature to the maps and shook hands with all involved, including Arafat. Peres broke the tension with a joke: 'Nowadays you can see the process of giving birth on live television!'

Later some observers suggested that Arafat had deliberately milked the moment for drama to present himself as a tough negotiator. They were wrong. What had occurred was nothing more than a comedy of errors that left all concerned feeling frustrated, and none more than Mubarak, who was furious with Arafat for ruining his ceremony. The only real benefit of the affair for Arafat was that the media paid less attention to the fact that the ceremony was boycotted by Palestinian stars including Faisal Husseini, Hanan Ashrawi and Haidar Abdel-Shafi. Husseini had sent Arafat a fax saying: 'Mr Chairman, please do not sign this agreement.'

The theatricals also overshadowed a matter which caused some embarrassment. Although the PLO had had eight months to prepare, it was not ready to take responsibility for the autonomous areas. Part of the reason was Arafat's refusal to delegate and his reluctance to spend long periods in Tunis. The Israelis had understood that the first 1500 PLO policemen would enter Gaza the day after the agreement, but in fact only an advance party of twenty commanders arrived.

A depressed Arafat left Cairo to visit South Africa, where Nelson Mandela had just been elected president of the new multiracial state.* During his visit Arafat drew parallels between the PLO and the ANC, and implied that the Palestinian struggle could still be won. Addressing worshippers in a mosque in Johannesburg on 10 May, Arafat said that the *jihad* should continue, because Jerusalem belonged not just to the Palestinian people but to the whole Islamic world. He added that before signing the agreement in Cairo he had demanded a letter from the Israelis saying that the question of Jerusalem would be discussed earlier than the timetable laid down in the Oslo agreement. 'I insisted that it

* The Palestinians had always had to struggle to gain understanding of their cause in Africa, partly because newly independent African states in the 1960s tended to admire Israel's example. This problem was eased after Arab leaders managed to convince African counterparts of the similarity between apartheid in South Africa and Israel's treatment of the Palestinians. See p. 25.

should be explicitly established in this letter that we are responsible for all the sacred places, both Islamic and Christian.'

Arafat was unaware that his every word was being recorded on behalf of the Israeli government, which promptly sent copies of the tape to Mubarak and King Hassan, asking them to demand an explanation from the PLO chairman. The Israelis pointed out that Arafat's remarks on Jerusalem amounted to a breach of the agreement, and that unless he retracted Israel would no longer feel bound by its provisions. They also denied the existence of any secret letter or understanding that discussions on the status of Jerusalem would be brought forward. Arafat was forced to back down, though he claimed that he had used the word *jihad* in a figurative rather than a literal sense.

Back in Tunis after his ill-starred visit to South Africa, Arafat faced mounting demands to implement the agreement without further delay. The pressure came not from colleagues but from the Israeli army. Since the 4 May signing ceremony crowds had been gathering regularly at the Rafah border crossing in the hope of witnessing the arrival of Arafat's men from Egypt. The long delay had caused frustration, leading to violence, with youths stoning the Israeli soldiers guarding the crossing post. The troops replied first with gas grenades, then rubber bullets, causing dozens of injuries and a further cycle of anger. When the first batch of 280 PLO soldier-policemen arrived on 9 May it was already dark and the crowds had gone home disappointed. The Israeli troops could hardly wait to shake the dust of Gaza off their boots. 'Hold your nose, Arafat, soon all this will be yours,' an Israeli newspaper headlined an article about the impending handover. The Israelis tended to forget that poor sanitary conditions in Gaza were a product of poverty and overcrowding caused by Israel's policies.

Accelerating the arrival of PLO forces was not easy, because most of the soldiers who had been retrained as policemen were still at bases in Yemen. Arafat had to ask a friend sympathetic to the Palestinian cause to mediate with Saudi defence minister Prince Sultan to provide transport. Despite their past differences, the prince agreed to allocate six troop carriers to fly the men from Najran to El-Arish in Egypt. All the names had to be notified in advance to the Egyptian and Israeli authorities for permission to enter Gaza. When the planes landed the Egyptians found 102 soldiers whose names had not been on the list, and denied them entry. Arafat contacted Mubarak and asked him to intercede with the Israelis to allow the men to enter Gaza, but the Egyptian president refused. The men were flown back to Yemen the same night.

The long-awaited handover of power came on 13 May 1994, when General Biran, commander of the Israeli central sector, shook hands with Palestinian General Hajj Ismail at Jericho and wished his forces luck. Only 400 Palestinian policemen had arrived in Jericho at that point. Kach militants attempted to enter the town to disrupt the ceremony but were turned back by Israeli forces. The handover had been delayed for hours by the Israelis, in order to put pressure on the PLO to deliver a list of the twenty-four-member council of the autonomous areas. In the end they had to be satisfied with eighteen names, provided by Nabil Sha'ath. In Gaza Israeli forces were pelted with stones as they completed their second withdrawal in thirty-seven years.*

Three days after the handover the zealots of Kiriat Arba once again sought to wreck the peace. Students from a rabbinical school staged a provocative march from the settlement towards the centre of Hebron. After being pelted with stones the students opened fire, injuring seven Palestinians.† The anger caused by this incident led to wider clashes between Palestinians and Israeli troops in which a further twelve Palestinians were injured. The Norwegian, Danish and Italian observers in Hebron, who had begun their mission only five days earlier, were witnesses to these scenes but had no means or authority to intervene. The Israeli government censured the students for provoking the incident, but the students and settlers were unrepentant. The grave of Baruch Goldstein at Kiriat Araba had gained a new symbolism during the three months since the Hebron massacre. Pilgrims visiting the spot now spoke of Goldstein as a martyr who had fallen in the fight to restore the throne of David, king of all Israel from 1001 to 968 B.C.

The handover atmosphere was further marred when Islamic Jihad and Hamas claimed responsibility for a series of killings of Israelis, and when Israeli state radio broadcast the tape of Arafat's remarks in Johannesburg. Even Yossi Sarid, minister of the environment and probably the most doveish member of the Israeli government, was

* The previous withdrawal was in March 1957 and resulted from US and Soviet pressure following the Suez crisis.

† It was common practice for settlers to carry automatic rifles when outside their settlements.

disappointed with the first days of the new arrangements. The tension was further heightened by Shi'ite attacks on Israeli forces in southern Lebanon, and by a massive Israeli air strike against a Hezbollah training camp in central Lebanon on 2 June, in which forty-five people were killed and seventy-five injured. Victims of the attack, carried out by six fighter-bombers on the Ein Kawkab camp a few kilometres from the Syrian border, were mostly youths aged between twelve and eighteen. Speaking on Israeli radio, President Weizman praised the raid as 'a good operation'.* The French foreign minister condemned it. Two days later sixteen more Palestinians were killed in incidents in Hebron. The aftermath of the handover was thus an exceptionally violent 'peace'.

A bewildered King Hussein had been watching all these developments from the sidelines. His original intention was to keep a low profile, but with the situation deteriorating this proved impossible. 'Our brothers are dragging us towards ruin,' he told me. Apart from the terms of the 4 May agreement, which many Arabs considered acceptance of the unacceptable, the king had other reasons for concern. The Jordanian dinar, one of the two most widely used currencies on the west bank, was feeling the effects of instability in the occupied territories. With 400 million dinars in circulation on the west bank any sudden fall in value could expose the Jordanian economy to collapse. Moreover, Jordan had been drawn into a dispute with Israel over the reprisals carried out by Hamas following the Hebron massacre. Responsibility for the attacks was claimed by Hamas spokesmen resident in Jordan, giving an impression of Jordanian complicity. As early as 14 April Rabin had publicly accused Jordan of harbouring terrorists, which Amman denied. Israel was not satisfied with this denial, and Warren Christopher later sent a message warning that 'the Hamas declarations would lead to Jordan's inclusion on the list of countries supporting terrorism'.

Deciding that the time had come for Jordan to look after its own interests, King Hussein informed the British and American authorities that he was ready for an agreement with Israel. He held a last secret

* Ezer Weizman, nephew of former president Chaim Weizmann, had played a prominent role in talks leading to the Israeli–Egyptian peace treaty of 1979. See Part I, Chapters 14 and 15.

meeting with Peres in London at the beginning of June and then returned to Amman to announce that Jordanian–Israeli talks were about to resume. The Jordanian people were told that as coordination with other Arabs was not working, 'we will go ahead alone to defend our interests.' A few days later the Jordanian government was reshuffled, bringing in eighteen new faces representing all shades of opinion represented in parliament except the fundamentalists. This consolidated the king's domestic support as he prepared to test one of the few remaining barriers of the taboo: direct talks with Israelis on Jordanian territory.

While Jordan's moves were in preparation, the PLO repeatedly announced and postponed Arafat's arrival in the autonomous areas. The first date given was 5 June, then 15 June, and finally 25 June. There were several reasons for Arafat's hesitation. According to intelligence reports reaching the PLO, he would be assassinated as soon as he set foot on Palestinian soil. Certain groups, including Fatah (of which Arafat remained the leader), were accusing him of selling out to Israel. Arafat considered entering secretly but realized that this was not feasible. Secondly, most Palestinian dignitaries felt that if Arafat came to Gaza, he should come to stay, not just visit and depart. The chairman's view was that a permanent stay would place him at the mercy of the Israelis. Thirdly, Arafat wanted the effect of foreign donations to be felt before he arrived, so that he could enter Gaza on a groundswell of approval. By this time the World Bank had authorized the release of $360 million for approved development projects and $250 million towards the salaries of civil servants and for social security costs. Although this was a start, the bank's policy continued to deny Arafat any personal power of patronage. In an interview with an American television network Arafat said that if the international community did not honour its obligations, he would not go to Gaza.

Arafat also wanted to time his arrival to avoid being overshadowed by other world events. The original date, 5 June, was chosen for symbolic reasons, as the Israeli occupation had begun on the same day twenty-seven years earlier. Then it was realized that the Western focus would be on the fiftieth anniversary celebrations of the D-Day landings in Normandy, and Arafat would be eclipsed. Another date was unsuitable because it clashed with the World Cup football finals in the United States. Arafat also complained of feeling worn out and told colleagues he wanted a holiday. No one was sure whether to believe him.

Eventually there were no more excuses, and on 1 July, after giving aides only two days' notice, Arafat set out for Gaza. The Tunisians were not sorry to see the last of their most famous guest. President Zein el-Abdin ben Ali gave Arafat a big send-off and Mubarak accompanied him to El-Arish in an Egyptian aircraft. The Egyptian president persuaded the Israelis not to search Arafat's five-car convoy at the Rafah border crossing. Most of the Palestinian leadership, including Abu Mazen, who had negotiated and signed the Oslo agreement, refused to accompany the chairman. The Israeli authorities gave their own television station exclusive rights to cover Arafat's arrival, with the ironic result that Arabs had to watch pictures with the Israeli logo and the voice of a Hebrew announcer in the background.

After crossing the border with seventy guards, Arafat fell to his knees and kissed the sand of Gaza, then paused only for a moment to acknowledge the welcoming crowd before continuing his journey at high speed. Dignitaries who had waited under the scorching mid-afternoon sun to welcome him, including two sheikhs and Arafat's special representative in the occupied territories Dr Ahmed El-Tibi, could only scramble into cars and follow. Rumours were rife of assassination plots, and two Israeli cameramen were briefly detained on suspicion of possessing firearms, but later released.

A stage had been set up in Gaza's central square next to the former seat of Gaza's consultative council, which sat when the strip was under Egyptian rule. The crowd was packed so tightly that dozens fainted from heat-stroke, and at least ten people were hurt when a tree collapsed under the weight of children who had climbed into its branches for a better view.

Amid general applause, Arafat began his speech with a reading from the Koran, and then immediately reached out to supporters of Hamas by saying that the fight would not end until their leader Sheikh Ahmed Yassin, and other Palestinians, had been freed from Israeli jails.* Much of the speech, frequently interrupted by cheers, was an appeal for national unity. 'Big, big, big, big missions await us, to build this homeland and rebuild what the occupation has destroyed,' Arafat said.

* Israel had released a further 2500 prisoners on the day of the 4 May signing, as agreed.

The speech evidently hit the right note, because for two days the mood was euphoric and violence fell to a low level. Among those who came to pay homage to Arafat was a group of Arab Israelis, including Walid Zadek, deputy minister of agriculture. Late on his first night Arafat convened a sitting of the autonomy council, with only eighteen members. Six seats were left vacant as an invitation to Hamas and other groups to participate.

The enthusiasm was not shared by Haidar Abdel-Shafi, former leader of the Palestinian delegation to the Washington talks. 'No, my criticisms of the anti-democratic ways in which Arafat leads the PLO have not changed,' he told an Italian journalist, adding that the way the Gaza visit was arranged illustrated his views. 'He didn't consult anyone; he didn't even talk to his most faithful advisers. From one day to the next he let it be known that he wanted to undertake such an important step. To him it was obvious that everyone would have to obey.'* In fairness, Arafat's unpredictability was probably his best shield against assassination.

Violent protests against Arafat's arrival broke out in Jerusalem during the night of 2/3 July. Tens of thousands of demonstrators armed with stones and clubs attempted to enter the Arab quarter of the city, smashing shop windows and screaming 'Death to the Arabs, Death to Arafat. Jerusalem is only Jewish. Rabin is a traitor.' Israeli police beat the demonstrators back, but after dawn groups reorganized themselves to block traffic during the rush hour, spreading nails and oil at crossroads. Rabin was forced to delay a government sitting because ministers were late. 'The level of hate rising against Rabin seems to be approaching the intensity of that spread in 1982 against former defence minister Ariel Sharon,' commented Nachum Barnea, editorial writer of *Y'di'ot Aharonot*. By 4 July three different motions of no confidence in the government had been presented in the Knesset.

Arafat visited Jericho on 5 July, travelling in an Egyptian helicopter escorted by two Israeli military helicopters and taking a wide detour to avoid dangerous areas. The excitement of the Gaza visit did not follow him. A small crowd of perhaps 3000 people listened to a speech emphasizing the need for Palestinian unity. Arafat accused the Israelis of obstructing access by Palestinians, to which Rabin replied: 'We did

* *Il Corriere della Sera*, 4 July 1994.

not prevent anyone from going. Let him ask his people why they did not go.' The hidden hand of Jordan was evident in Arafat's lacklustre reception. Although King Hussein had cut his constitutional and political ties with the west bank in 1988, no one had any doubt about his real feelings. At the time of the 1988 announcement it was intended that Jordan would stop paying civil service salaries, and this led to panic and a run on the banks. The Jordanian government did not want to cause unnecessary suffering and decided to continue paying until alternative arrangements could be made. With donations from richer Arab countries, at least until the Gulf War,* Jordan was able to keep up many of its former obligations, including the salaries of local administrators in Jericho.

Arafat spent only a day in Jericho and then resumed his travels, this time collecting a peace prize from UNESCO in Paris, shared with Rabin and Peres. The three men also met in the French capital to discuss the Israeli promise, made during the run-up to the 4 May signing ceremony, to speed up talks on the second phase of the Oslo agreement. This implied a faster pace of transfer of a wide range of responsibilities for the whole of the west bank. It was agreed that three committees would be set up; one to deal with problems left over from the 4 May agreement, a second to discuss the transfer of more powers, and a third to look into refugee problems. A joint PLO–Israeli communiqué after the meeting said that Arafat planned to call a meeting of the Palestine National Council to approve 'the necessary modifications' to the Palestine National Charter. This arose from the letter Arafat had written to Rabin before the Washington signing in September 1993 recognizing the state of Israel and declaring that articles in the charter inconsistent with the agreement were no longer valid.

As Arafat had expected, the most urgent problem was money. He had been shocked by the wretched housing conditions in Gaza, the collapse of infrastructure and local services and the vast scale of unemployment. Something was needed to bring immediate hope. One of the first decisions of the autonomous council, immediately after a swearing-in ceremony in Jericho on 5 July, was that Palestinians released from Israeli jails should receive a monthly payment until they

* Jordan received less support after the Gulf War because the oil-producing states considered that King Hussein had been on Saddam Hussein's side.

found work. This marked only a beginning in facing vast social problems.

The World Bank was still not prepared to relax its rules on transparency and accountability to provide a quick cash injection. When Arafat expressed frustration, during his meeting with Peres and Rabin in Paris, Rabin urged him to use the fiscal system. 'If Arafat does not start exacting tax contributions, I don't know how his police and development programmes can be paid for,' he said afterwards. But as the Paris studies had already shown, tax revenue could produce only 60 per cent of the money needed for basic functions, without allowing for increased expenditure.

Arafat asked President Mubarak to arrange a meeting with King Fahd of Saudi Arabia, which was held on 10 July. The king was very frank: 'Abu Ammar, some people will tell you that it was the Americans who asked us to make our donations through the World Bank. Don't believe them. This was our own decision, and we advised everyone, including the Americans, to do the same thing. There must be accountability, and we must be sure that whatever is given is spent according to scientific plans. We fully understand that the Palestinian leadership needs some flexibility, that you need some funds at your disposal. This we are ready to do.' At the end of the meeting King Fahd handed a cheque for $5 million to Faisal Husseini, who had accompanied Arafat.

Meanwhile Nabil Sha'ath met World Bank representatives to ask for part of the $1.2 billion the bank was holding but not releasing. The representatives were even less sympathetic than King Fahd to arguments for a rapid release of funds, and Sha'ath was able to obtain only relatively small sums.

Arafat had realized from the earliest days of the Oslo agreement that cash was the key to success. According to a report by a team of PLO advisers led by the noted Palestinian economist Dr Yousef Sayegh, $11 billion would be needed in the first three years. Arafat held out for guarantees from the Americans that the funds would be made available, and tried to make this a condition for his signature on the agreement. He told a PLO executive committee meeting that he did not want to be remembered as the Gorbachev of Palestine: 'I am not ready to pay now and wait to be compensated tomorrow. That was Gorbachev's mistake; it will not be mine.' Arafat's demands received some response, but not as much as he would have liked. The total world pledges amounted, by July 1994, to about a quarter of what Sayegh thought necessary. Virtually all the money was tied by the accountability and transparency rules.

The long-expected breakthrough in Israeli–Jordanian relations came on 18 July, when King Hussein and Prime Minister Rabin held talks in a tent beside the Dead Sea, marking the start of a process expected to lead eventually to a peace treaty. Although most issues had been settled before or during the Washington talks, two important matters remained. There was a disagreement over 380 square kilometres of border territory, and a sharper dispute over the disproportionate share of water resources taken by Israel. A third issue raised by Jordan was the fate of Palestinian refugees displaced by Israel who had found refuge in Jordan. Shimon Peres said that Israel did not want to weaken the Hashemite kingdom: 'We don't want to prevent Jordan receiving water and we will steal neither its sovereignty nor its influence in the holy places in Jerusalem.'

A week later King Hussein and Rabin publicly declared the state of war between their countries to be over. In a highly publicized meeting at the White House with President Clinton, the Jordanian and Israeli leaders took a first step towards a peace treaty. An agreement was signed giving immediate benefits to both countries, including the opening of direct telephone links, connections between the two electricity generating systems, and arrangements for tourists to travel between Aqaba and Eilat. As this was supposedly only the second meeting between the two men, Clinton could not help noticing that they seemed well acquainted. 'Tell me, how long have you known each other?' he asked.

'Twenty-one years, Mr President,' Rabin replied.

The king's legendary prudence did not desert him. With a smile, he insisted that it was 'only' twenty years.

The three men agreed that the occasion was the culmination of the efforts begun by King Abdullah, who was assassinated in 1951 when his secret contacts with the Israelis came to be known.* Abdullah was killed at the entrance to al-Aksa mosque, at a time when Jordan controlled east Jerusalem and acted as protector of its holy places.

* See pp. 85–6.

Jordan's religious role was formally recognized by Israel in a statement issued by Rabin during the Washington meeting: 'Israel respects the present special role of the Hashemite kingdom of Jordan in Muslim holy shrines in Jerusalem. When negotiations on permanent status take place, Israel will give high priority to the Jordanian historic role in these shrines.'

The statement was a serious blow to Arafat, who considered control of the holy places to be a Palestinian prerogative. He also tended to link the religious issue with the Palestinian claim to sovereignty over the whole of Jerusalem. King Hussein, on the other hand, understood that there was no chance of persuading the Israelis to give up sovereignty of any part of the city, and that the real contest was over custody of the holy places. An Arab leader securing that role was assured of immense prestige throughout the Islamic world. The rivalry involved not just Hussein and Arafat, but also the Hashemite and Saudi monarchies. King Hussein's great-grandfather, Hussein Ibn Ali, Sharif of Mecca, had been the custodian of Mecca and Medina until his kingdom was attacked by Ibn Saud, ruler of the Nejd, after the First World War.* Saud and his successors thus became the custodians of two of the three holiest places in Islam. In the early 1990s Israel was offered huge investments in return for allowing the kings of Saudi Arabia to complete their collection with the Dome of the Rock in Jerusalem. A Saudi mission was sent to Israel to propose that, as a start, Saudi Arabia should carry out and pay for the restoration of the Dome of the Rock.† As Saudi Arabia had no diplomatic relations with Israel, members of the mission were issued with Egyptian passports and travelled from Cairo. The Israelis decided, however, to give King Hussein priority. The king announced that he was selling some property he owned in London for £8 million and would donate the money for the restoration work, which included regilding the dome. When the restoration was completed, the king held a celebration in Amman which the Saudis boycotted and the PLO did not attend.

Israel's recognition of Jordan's special role so annoyed Arafat that he called for a special meeting of the Arab League. At this meeting

* See p. 40.

† The Dome of the Rock and al-Aksa mosque lie within the Haram es-Sharif (The Noble Sacred Space), which Jews refer to as Temple Mount. The Jewish Temple, destroyed in 70 A.D., stood on the same site.

the Jordanians said they were interested only in the shrines, and had no intention of trespassing on the PLO's claim to sovereignty. They knew very well that in raising expectations among Palestinians that they might regain Jerusalem, Arafat had set a time bomb for himself.

The Jordanian–Israeli agreement was exceptionally popular with Israelis, receiving approval in the Knesset by ninety-one votes to three, with two abstentions. A joke in the Israeli press suggested that Israelis would welcome Hussein as their king too, just as Abdullah had hoped to be welcomed in the 1930s. As one of the steps towards peace agreed in Washington, it had been agreed that Jordanian and Israeli civilian aircraft could fly over each other's territory. The first Jordanian to test this new provision was the king himself, while piloting his plane from London to Amman on 3 August. By prior arrangement, Yitzhak Rabin waited in an open field near Tel Aviv with a telephone in his hand, and the two men exchanged greetings. 'Your Majesty, can you hear me?'

'I hear you, sir.'

'Welcome to the skies of Tel Aviv. I convey to you greetings from the people of Israel. I am really grateful to you, Your Majesty.'

'I am really very happy to start direct contacts between our two peoples. I congratulate you on the dawn of peace.'

'I hope we will see you on the ground in Israel very soon, Your Majesty.'

'I can see Jerusalem now.'

'You are welcome to visit it, Your Majesty.'

Five days later King Hussein's brother, Crown Prince Hassan, took part in a ceremony with Peres and Warren Christopher in which the frontier fence dividing Israel and Jordan was cut to create a border post linking Eilat with Aqaba.

The effect of these moves was to put Arafat on the defensive. After taking a step towards peace with Israel, Jordan was in a position to become economically stronger and politically more united, while the PLO seemed more isolated. A Palestinian newspaper was closed down by the Palestinian authorities after publishing an editorial praising the Israeli–Jordanian agreement.

When Arafat met Rabin at Erez, the border crossing between Gaza and Israel on 10 August, he made a long list of requests, including the release of Sheikh Yassin and financial aid. Rabin replied that if Arafat wanted help, he would have to cooperate in Israel's war against terrorism. The Israeli prime minister threatened to suspend PLO–Israeli negotiations if Arafat did not take action. Attacks on Israeli and Jewish targets both inside and outside Israel had continued at a high rate despite (or because of) Israel's agreements with the PLO and Jordan. More than ninety people were killed and 150 injured when a Jewish centre in Buenos Aires was blown up on 18 July, and a car bomb heavily damaged the Israeli embassy in London eight days later, injuring sixteen people. Incidents between Israeli forces and Hezbollah in southern Lebanon were continuing, with further casualties on both sides. After neutralizing Jordan, Rabin was in a position to squeeze Arafat financially and politically until he put a stop to attacks originating from Gaza.*

The Israeli prime minister knew that there was nothing Arafat could do about the situation on the Lebanese border. Israel was not prepared to give up its 'security zone' in southern Lebanon, and President Assad had no reason to use his influence in Lebanon to rein in Shi'ite militias. Warren Christopher visited President Assad five times between 30 April and 22 July trying to bring about an Israeli–Syrian agreement. The Syrian leader did not oppose King Hussein's decision to come to terms with Israel, but was determined that any Syrian–Israeli agreement should wait until Israel was ready to meet Syria's requirements.

Within days of the Arafat–Rabin meeting at Erez, Palestinian police detained forty-five Islamic activists and subsequently placed twelve of them under formal arrest. Those released after tough questioning included prominent Hamas political leaders, while those arrested were mainly suspected of membership of Ezzeldin al-Kassam, the armed wing of Hamas. Hundreds of Palestinians demonstrated in protest at the arrests, and Palestinian civil rights groups reported worrying signs that the new authorities were copying Israeli methods of coercion.†

* Rabin was concerned only about Gaza. Jericho was not a stronghold of militancy.

† In a report published on 15 June, Human Rights Watch, an organization based in New York, accused the Israeli authorities of the systematic use of torture during the interrogation of Palestinian detainees. The Israeli army denied the accusation. A few days earlier Israeli television broadcast a documentary on methods used by Shin Bet, the internal security service, to extract confessions. The documentary implied that most of the 80,000 Palestinians convicted by Israeli courts during the six years of the Intifada had confessed under torture. In September a Palestinian civil rights movement expressed fears that Palestinian police were applying the lessons they had learned from the Israelis.

The crackdown raised fears that the truce between Hamas and Fatah, stitched together with difficulty before the PLO chairman's arrival, might come apart.

The smack of firm government was not unwelcome to all Palestinians, and did not necessarily imply a general loss of confidence. Arafat might have his imperfections, but he remained the principal symbol of the cause. Palestinians were willing to give the Gaza–Jericho experiment a try, but they wanted to see their leaders putting in long office hours, not jetting around the world. The mentality of first-class tickets, born in Tunis, was now offensively inappropriate. As much as any other people the Palestinians needed their leaders to set an example. The building of a country, whether autonomous or independent, called for hard work, sacrifice and pride in achievement. If Arafat managed to bring that about, he would have passed a vital test of leadership. And if he managed to use Gaza and Jericho as a springboard for an independent Palestinian state, he would be remembered as a performer of miracles.

20

The Year of Disillusionment

When self-rule came to Gaza in 1994, most Palestinians thought they could make out a glimmer in the darkness of their future. A year later, after more twists in the tunnel of peace, most suspected that the light lay behind them, not ahead. Their declining morale had many causes, the greatest of which was dashed economic expectations. Far from improving, the Palestinian economy had plunged into decline.

Arafat had always realized that Palestinians would have to feel practical benefits in their daily lives if the elation of mid-1994 was not to give way to disillusionment. Even before signing the Oslo agreement the PLO chairman had insisted upon, and secured, promises of economic aid from international parties. With help from Shimon Peres – which later came to seem ironic – the developed world was persuaded to make pledges totalling $2000 million.* During the nine months before his return to Gaza in July 1994, Arafat sought the release of some of this money as seed capital for job-creating projects, but he soon found that donors imposed harsh accountability conditions.†

After his return the gap between promises and performance became wider. Just a trickle of money came through, sufficient to keep the lid on popular discontent, but not enough to breathe life into the economy. The donors justified their tardiness by accusing Arafat of incompetence, and by harping on the accountability question. This failed to take account of the difficulties of starting up a new administration without training or experience, problems of which the donors were aware before they made their commitments. Caught in a vicious circle, Arafat could not create a tight, modern administration because he had

* See p. 458.
† See p. 525.

no funds, and donors refused to help because the administration was considered sloppy or corrupt.

When the chairman tried to appease critics by distributing lucrative contracts for infrastructural development, he inadvertently fuelled the suspicions of sloppiness. A contract for a new telephone network was awarded twice to two rival consortiums, one American, the other French. Each had approached Arafat through its local middleman, and each received a promise and a signature.

Not all the criticism came from unsympathetic foreigners. Towards the end of 1994, at a time when the Palestinian Authority was complaining that donors had paid only 8 per cent of the $700 million promised for the year,* some of the PLO figures who had remained behind in Tunis were spreading rumours of mismanagement. Unsettled by such talk, a group of wealthy Palestinians who had set up a $50 million fund for investment in the self-rule area insisted on retaining control over the money through a management body. Arafat saw this as an unacceptable constraint on his authority, and refused. Despite negotiations no compromise was found and the fund did not materialize. Arafat complained to Haseeb Sabbagh, the multi-millionaire contractor:† 'It is a pity the Rothschild of the Palestinian cause has not emerged to shoulder his responsibilities.' Sabbagh replied: 'That is because the Ben-Gurion of Palestine has not emerged yet.' Other rich Arabs proved equally reluctant to help. The Saudis, preoccupied with their own problems, contributed only $30 million to an international fund for development of the self-rule area.

Within a few months of Arafat's return, the lack of funds had bred a whole cluster of related vicious circles. As economic disappointment set in, more and more Palestinians came to see Hamas, rather than the Palestinian authorities, as their hope for the future. The organization never lacked for young men willing to accept martyrdom, nor for chemists with bomb-making abilities. Attacks by Hamas suicide bombers became more frequent and much deadlier, bringing a shift of Israeli public opinion towards the right. Faced with a clamour of

* The donor countries, including Israel, reached an agreement with the Palestinian Authority in April 1995 to make up about half of the authority's budget deficit, the money to be used to pay the salaries of health workers, teachers and police.

† Haseeb Sabbagh was the chairman and owner of Consolidated, one of the most important contracting companies in the Arab world.

opposition, Rabin put intense pressure on Arafat to crack down on the fundamentalists, exposing the chairman to accusations of complicity with the Israelis. Rabin responded to every major Hamas attack by closing the border with Gaza, preventing Palestinians from going to their jobs in Israel. As unemployment soared Palestinian opinion shifted still further towards Hamas, and the peace process slipped ever lower in the popularity ratings. A few spins of these circles of despair were sufficient to wring all the optimism out of Gaza.

At the same time all Palestinians understood the risk of civil war, and most exercised a measure of self-restraint. Although Hamas struck Israeli targets frequently, the organization did not want to be held responsible by Palestinians for the failure of the Oslo accords, believing that an empty deal would ultimately collapse into its own vacuum. Secondly, Hamas could hardly resist the Palestinian Authority in the way it had fought the Israelis. For a time there was a tacit understanding that no Palestinian would point a gun at a fellow Palestinian.

As the weeks passed, Rabin broke one promise after another, refusing to meet agreed deadlines for the withdrawal (or, as the Israelis put it, 'redeployment') of troops from the main west bank urban areas. 'No date is sacred,' Rabin claimed, a remark which gained notoriety among Palestinians. The Israelis were also still far from meeting their promise to release 10,000 Palestinian prisoners. Arafat, whose credibility depended on implementation of the accords, found his position eroded, while Hamas gained wider acceptance of its argument that the deal had solved Israeli rather than Palestinian problems.

The Israelis justified their non-withdrawal by pointing to attacks by Hamas, and sought to force Arafat to cooperate with Israel in fighting the fundamentalists. Israeli officials gave him lists of suspects they wanted handed over to their jurisdiction, including people accused of acts committed outside the self-rule areas.

Events during the fourth month after Arafat's return brought Israeli pressure to unbearable levels. On a warm October afternoon a nineteen-year-old Israeli soldier was hitch-hiking along a road in central Israel when a car stopped to pick him up. The car's occupants were Hamas militants, who immediately took the soldier hostage. A few hours later Hamas carried out an attack in a popular restaurant district of Jerusalem only half a kilometre from the King David Hotel, where Warren Christopher was staying. Two Hamas commandos armed with assault rifles sprayed a pedestrian street with bullets, killing two people and wounding thirteen before being shot dead themselves by Israeli police. Responsibility for the attack was claimed by Izzeddin El-Qassam, the military wing of Hamas, in a statement which opened with a verse from the Koran saying that God rewards those who fight for him. The aim of the attack, it explained, was to avenge the deaths of twenty-one Palestinians killed by Israeli police in clashes at al-Aksa Mosque on Temple Mount on 8 October 1990.

A videotape sent to the Israeli media showed Nahshon Waxman, the kidnapped young corporal, with a masked gunman standing behind him. Looking terrified, Waxman said that he would be killed unless the government released Hamas founder Sheikh Ahmed Yassin and 200 other Palestinian and Lebanese prisoners from Israeli jails.

Amid scenes of mass indignation in Israel, with some 50,000 people praying at the Wailing Wall, the Israeli delegation taking part in talks with the PLO was called home from Cairo, and Shimon Peres said that Hamas had kidnapped not just a soldier but the entire peace of the Middle East. Rabin held Arafat personally responsible for Waxman's safety and insisted that the corporal was being detained in Gaza, despite Arafat's protestations to the contrary. The Egyptian government urged the PLO chairman to believe the Israelis, because Mossad and Shin Beit were well-informed. After Arafat had rounded up 400 suspects to appease the Israelis, it turned out that the soldier had been held all along in Israeli-occupied territory, at Bir-Nabala on the west bank. Ironically, the Israelis discovered this just as the Nobel Peace Prize committee was meeting in Norway to confirm its decision that Arafat, Rabin and Peres should share the prize for 1994.

On 14 October, a few hours after the Norwegian announcement, Israeli forces stormed the house in Bir-Nabala in a futile bid to rescue Waxman. The nineteen-year-old soldier was found dead after a fight in which three Hamas militants were killed and one captured. One member of the Israeli special forces died and twelve were injured.

Rabin accepted full responsibility for the bungled operation, which had been carried out while negotiations were under way, an hour before the deadline set by Hamas and twenty-five hours before a second deadline arranged by an Arab Israeli parliamentarian. A vindicated Arafat expressed his frustration in a revealing statement: 'I will not be treated like Lahoud,'* which was a way of saying: 'I am no Israeli puppet.'

When Rabin and Arafat met soon afterwards, the Israeli prime minister complained that Gaza was full of weapons. Arafat replied that most of them were coming from Israel, where right wingers within Mossad were trying to sabotage the peace agreement. To back up this assertion, the Palestinians gave the Israelis copies of a book by Victor Ostrovski, formerly a senior Mossad agent, who told extraordinary tales of his organization's covert operations. Extracts had been published in the Israeli newspaper *Y'di'ot Ahronot* at the end of September. The most bizarre episode was a failed attempt to assassinate President George Bush at the time of the 1991 Madrid conference, with the aim of aborting the peace process. A theory popular in some Palestinian quarters was that although Mossad had been created by Labour governments, its sympathies lay with Likud. As the main thrust of Mossad's activities had been the assassination of PLO members, many within the group saw Rabin's peace with Arafat as a betrayal.

Five days after Waxman's death, Hamas blew up an Israeli bus in Dizengoff Street, a busy thoroughfare of shops, restaurants and bars in the heart of Tel Aviv. As the red and white bus turned from the street into Dizengoff Square at 8.55 a.m., Salah Abdel Rahim Nazal Souwi, a twenty-seven-year-old Hamas militant, detonated a bomb containing ten kilograms of military-type TNT. Amid horrifying scenes of carnage police found pieces of twenty-two bodies, some of which had been hurled through first-floor windows above the shops.

The use of military explosives instead of home-made mixtures sent a shudder through the Israeli psyche, raising doubts about Shin Beit's effectiveness as a counter-terrorist service. Rabin closed the border with Gaza, but this was now a standard response after fundamentalist attacks, and the Israeli opposition demanded tougher action.

The talks in Cairo continued, but in a changed mood. Previously the Israelis had stalled on setting a date for the Palestinian elections; now they were openly refusing to implement the accords unless and until Arafat did more to curb Hamas and Islamic Jihad.

* Antoine Lahoud was the Lebanese commander of the Israeli-financed South Lebanese Army controlling the southern strip of Lebanon. Lahoud had replaced Saad Haddad (see p. 340), who died of cancer in 1984.

The dangers of Arafat's position were illustrated in early November, when Israel stepped up its campaign against the fundamentalists. One of the first victims was Hani Abed, a leader of Islamic Jihad, who was killed by a car bomb.* After the assassination Arafat went to the great mosque of Gaza, as an act of respect and mourning for Abed. His gesture was not appreciated by Abed's supporters. Amid shouts of 'collaborator', the chairman was jostled by young men who snatched his *kaffiyeh* and forced him to leave the mosque.

Islamic Jihad avenged Hani Abed's death ten days later. A twenty-one-year-old Palestinian wearing a bomb strapped around his waist rode a bicycle up to a group of Israeli soldiers near the Israeli settlement of Netzarim in the Gaza strip and detonated the device, killing himself and three soldies. Eleven other people were injured in the blast.

After the incident in the great mosque of Gaza, Shimon Peres realized the dangers of allowing Arafat's credibility to be destroyed, and persuaded Rabin to make a small conciliatory gesture. During a meeting with Arafat on 8 November 1994, Rabin agreed to implement certain elements of previous agreements, transferring responsibility for taxation, health, transport and social services throughout the west bank to the Palestinian Authority.

Every attack by fundamentalist groups brought further Israeli pressure on Arafat, and every concession the PLO chairman made to Israel increased the risk of fighting among Palestinians. Talk of civil war was no longer fanciful: even President Mubarak had warned that Gaza could become another Afghanistan, only worse. That risk seemed very real in the second half of November, when Palestinian police used live ammunition against fellow Palestinians to control rioting. The incidents began on 18 November, when 2000 worshippers emerged from the great mosque in Gaza after Friday prayers. When youths overturned two police cars and began hurling stones, the police fired directly into the crowd with automatic weapons, killing fourteen people and wounding about 150. This triggered an explosion of anger in which fundamentalists destroyed video shops and Gaza's two main cinemas.† The rioters screamed insults against Arafat with all the fury

* Hani Abed was killed on 2 November 1994. The attack was widely attributed to Shin Beit, an accusation that Israel did not deny.

† Video shops and cinemas were targeted because fundamentalists were opposed to films showing any part of a woman's body other than the face and hands.

which had previously been reserved for the Zionist state. Afterwards there were bitter accusations that the Palestinian police had been as bad as Israeli forces during the Intifada. A statement issued in Tunis by the Fatah central committee* described the killings as a 'monstrous massacre' and demanded the punishment of those responsible.

Tension between Palestinians was further marked by rival protest marches held in the days after the massacre. Thousands of PLO supporters chanting 'Arafat forever' turned out to show support for the chairman, who told the crowd: 'We will not allow anyone to destroy what we have built.' Hamas replied a few days later with a much bigger demonstration, attracting an estimated 40,000 supporters.

Meanwhile a further Israeli humiliation of Arafat was in the making. Benazir Bhutto, the Pakistani prime minister, wanted to visit Gaza, in the hope of boosting the Oslo accords. Her government made contact with the PLO through Egypt and tried to send an emissary to Gaza to make arrangements. When the envoy reached the Rafah crossing between Egypt and Gaza, he was denied entry, despite being accompanied by a Palestinian official. The border officials argued that Pakistan should have applied to Israel for a visa. Adding insult to injury, Rabin said: 'The lady [Bhutto] should learn some manners.' The Pakistanis were shocked, and the Palestinians were yet again reminded of how little autonomy they had acquired.

Another episode of Israeli obstructionism occurred when Arafat tried to rally the PLO executive committee. The chairman had been badly hurt by defections from the committee's ranks following the Oslo accords. Four members had resigned in protest in September 1993, including the poet Mahmoud Darwish.† Only six members agreed to go to Gaza and the majority stayed out, including Abu Mazen, the PLO's main negotiator during the Oslo talks, and Farouk Kaddoumi, who, as foreign minister of the Palestinian government in exile, understandably felt it was demeaning to ask the Israelis for permission to enter Gaza.

Arafat knew that if he could lure any of the defectors to Gaza his popularity would receive a much-needed boost. Darwish was perhaps

* The central committee included top figures such as Farouk Kaddoumi, the PLO foreign minister.

† See pp. 462–3.

the greatest prize because of his glamour as the poet of the Palestinian cause. After much persuasion Darwish accepted Arafat's invitation, but when he arrived in Cairo on the first leg of his journey to Gaza via Rafah he was told that the visit was off. The Israelis would not allow him to enter because some of his poems were considered to be anti-peace. Later Arafat and Darwish met in Paris, where the poet lived. Both avoided mentioning the incident, but Darwish had not softened his attitude towards the accords. 'Abu Ammar, it seems it will be Gaza first – and last!' he commented. After a moment of silence, Arafat murmured: 'Anything is possible.'

The winter of 1994 proved to be one of the darkest periods of Palestinian discontent. Repeated Israeli closures of the Israel–Gaza border had caused a 25 per cent drop in living standards,* and Israeli employers were dismissing Palestinian workers in droves, replacing them with labour hired from the Far East. Terje Larsen, originator of the 1993 'Oslo channel', said that he had never felt so pessimistic. When Arafat, Rabin and Peres collected their joint Nobel Prize on 10 December 1994, the gap between hope and reality could scarcely have been greater. Nothing remained of the hopes which had prompted the award. A joke circulating in Jerusalem said that Rabin and Peres had received the prize for making peace with each other, not for peace with the Palestinians, which remained to be achieved.

In eight months more than seventy Israelis had been killed in fundamentalist attacks, equivalent to two of the worst years of the Intifada combined. That toll rose to ninety-five the following month, when on 22 January 1995 two Islamic Jihad suicide bombers blew themselves up at a bus stop in front of Ashmoret prison near Netanya, on the coast north of Tel Aviv. The first explosion brought Israeli soldiers running to help the wounded, not realizing that they were entering a trap. The second commando then detonated his bomb, claiming more lives than the first.†

The Israeli government promptly closed the border again, this time

* Arafat said on 28 November 1994 that unemployment in Gaza and Jericho was about 58 per cent. Meanwhile Israel was enjoying a continuing boom: 'We have never had a better situation,' Peres said.

† The two explosions killed one civilian, eighteen Israeli conscripts, and the two fundamentalist commandos. Two of the injured, both Israeli soldiers, later died of their injuries.

dropping hints that the exclusion of Palestinians might become permanent. Rabin proposed that a barrier should be built along the entire demarcation line between Israel and the occupied territories, in addition to the fence already under construction between Israel and Gaza. President Ezer Weizman, who had been considered a dove since his role in the Egyptian–Israeli peace process eighteen years earlier, called for the suspension of talks with the PLO. After receiving phone calls from Arafat, King Hussein and President Clinton, Rabin decided not to take Weizman's advice, but granted still greater powers to Shin Beit and authorized a wave of arrests of Palestinian suspects.

The attack overshadowed a day of remembrance to mark the fiftieth anniversary of the liberation of Auschwitz by Soviet troops. The effects on Israeli opinion were measured in a poll conducted in late January by the Institute of Strategic Studies at Tel Aviv University, which found that the proportion of Israelis favourable to the process in general had slipped from 60 per cent in 1994 to 53 per cent, while support for the 'Gaza and Jericho first' formula had dipped from 43 per cent to 36. Only 29 per cent felt that the PLO could check terrorism, against 35 per cent previously. The majority now thought that Israel should reinforce its military capabilities rather than pursuing peace.

A reminder that fundamentalists (whether Muslim or Jewish) were not alone in opposing the Oslo accords came in early February, when tankers delivering petrol to Israeli settlements in the Gaza strip were ambushed. An Israeli guard was killed and another seriously injured. Responsibility was claimed both by Izzeddin El-Qassam and by 'Red Star', one of the groups within Nayef Hawatmeh's Popular Democratic Front for the Liberation of Palestine. Within twenty-four hours of the attack the Palestinian police had rounded up twenty leaders and militants of the Marxist group. This move heightened inter-Palestinian tension but failed to appease the Israelis. When Rabin and Arafat met at the Erez border post a few days later, on 9 February, the Israeli prime minister rejected the PLO chairman's demands for the border to be reopened and for the release of more Palestinian prisoners.

More humiliation for the Palestinians followed in the same month, when Ehud Olmert, mayor of Jerusalem, threatened to close down Orient House, the east Jerusalem building which had served as the unofficial seat of the PLO before the Oslo accords. Faisal Husseini, who had long worked from Orient House, maintaining a channel of communications between the PLO in Tunis and the Israeli authorities, found himself under fire from Olmert. His 'offence': holding a meeting at Orient House with a delegation of senior European Union ministers.* Olmert, supported by the Israeli government, considered this a violation of an Israeli law banning the PLO from conducting political meetings in the city.

With the peace process in deep disarray, a meeting was held in Washington in late March between Warren Christopher, Egyptian foreign minister Amr Moussa, Shimon Peres, PLO negotiator Nabil Sha'ath, and Jordanian foreign minister Abdel-Karim El-Kabariti. Another participant was Abu Medein, minister of justice in the Palestinian Authority, who said that the Authority could not be held responsible for violence inside Israel. When Peres claimed that Palestinians had danced in the streets of Gaza following suicide bomb attacks on Israeli targets, the Palestinian minister replied that Israelis had done the same thing after the Hebron massacre a year earlier.† Moreover, the gun used by Baruch Goldstein to slaughter Palestinian worshippers as they knelt in prayer had been returned to his widow by the Israeli authorities.

Once again there were moves by both sides to reduce the tension. Israel allowed some of the Palestinian workers to return to their jobs,‡ there was talk of building industrial parks along the Israel–Gaza border to create 10,000 new jobs, and a target date of 1 July was set for concluding negotiations on implementation of the stalled parts of the Oslo agreement.

Such moves were too limited and too late to offset the disillusionment in Gaza. Arafat expressed the feelings of the majority in an address to a conference of the Democratic Union in Gaza on 12 May 1995: 'We feel the Oslo agreement is impotent and deficient. We hoped it would be a beginning, but from our experience and dealings with the Israelis, especially over Jerusalem, we find that we were mistaken. We should be honest with ourselves and admit that Israel is the princi-

* The delegation was headed by Alain Juppé, then foreign minister and subsequently prime minister of France.

† See p. 497.

‡ After a Rabin–Arafat meeting at Erez on 16 February it was announced that 15,000 workers would be allowed to return. This was increased to 21,000 as a result of an Arafat–Peres meeting at Erez on 9 March.

pal enemy of the Palestinian people. It was the enemy in the past, it is the enemy in the present, and will continue to be the enemy in the future.'

Arafat's phrase 'especially over Jerusalem' was appropriate. Since the capture of the walled Old City in 1967, Israel had resisted all attempts to negotiate the status of Jerusalem, and had ignored the refusal of the rest of the world to accept its claim to the entire city as 'the eternal, undivided capital of the Jewish state'. The Oslo agreement gave an impression that Israel might, after all, be willing to discuss the matter, but that soon proved to be an illusion. Israel's tactic in accepting the principle of final-status talks had been to tranquillize the Arab world while it saturated east Jerusalem with Jewish housing projects and consolidated American support for Israel's claim to the entire city.

When President Clinton visited the Knesset in October 1994, Rabin used the opportunity to lobby for US support.* 'Jerusalem is the eternal capital of Israel and must remain under Israeli sovereignty,' he told the parliament, in Clinton's presence. Rabin was preaching to the converted, for the US president had already indicated that he was willing, eventually, to move the US embassy from Tel Aviv to Jerusalem. Clinton, however, wanted to wait for an opportune moment when the switch could be made with the minimum damage to US–Arab relations.

Clinton's 'later rather than sooner' approach was an easy target for the Republicans. Bob Dole, who was already pitching for the Republican nomination in the 1996 presidential race, quickly turned the issue to his advantage. In 1990 Dole had opposed a Senate resolution declaring Jerusalem to be the undivided capital of Israel, but in the spring of 1995 the senator reversed his stand and announced that he would introduce a bill to authorize the transfer of the US embassy. Newt Gingrich, the Republican Speaker, had already made a similar proposal in the lower house.

Meanwhile the Israelis were becoming more blatant about their plans to change the demographic balance of east Jerusalem. Ehud Olmert, mayor of Jerusalem and Likud member of parliament, had

* The main purpose of Clinton's visit to the Middle East was to attend the signing of the Israeli–Jordanian peace treaty (see p. 549).

been agitating for a policy of surrounding the Arab sector with Jewish suburbs, but until May 1995 the government prevaricated. However, with the Israeli general election only a year off, Rabin cast caution to the winds and authorized the confiscation of two tracts of Arab land, in north and south Jerusalem, totalling 53.5 hectares. The prime minister also stated openly at a press conference on 25 May that Israel's real aim in the 1967 war had been to capture Jerusalem. Labour was thus staking out Jerusalem as its battlefield for the election campaign, regardless of the Arab fury this was bound to provoke.

The first wave of opposition came simultaneously from the Palestinians and from Meretz, one of Labour's coalition partners. Yair Zaban, minister of immigration and a member of Meretz, described the decision as 'myopic' and contrary to Israel's interests. He also pointed out that land in east Jerusalem taken from Palestinians in previous confiscations had been used to construct 35,000 housing units for Jews, and none for Arabs.

Within days these initial reactions were overtaken by uproar throughout the Arab world and beyond. Control of Jerusalem remained, as it had always been, an issue to stir the passions of all three great monotheistic faiths. Fundamentalists of all colours, Christian and Jewish as much as Muslim, could imagine the struggle as a war of the gods, beyond the domain of mere mortals: Moses with the Torah, Jesus with the New Testament and Mohamed with the Koran struggling for supremacy in the holy city.

An Arab diplomatic offensive came close to achieving a UN Security Council vote to condemn the confiscation, forcing an embarrassed US government to use its veto to shield Israel. The Jordanian parliament met in extraordinary session, and sixty deputies demanded the suspension of relations with Israel. In Montreux, where further multilateral Arab–Israeli talks were taking place, Faisal Husseini called for the status of Jerusalem to be discussed immediately, without waiting for the final-status talks foreseen in the Oslo accords. Husseini, head of the Palestinian delegation, proposed the creation of a thirty-nation commission to study the issue.

If popular sentiment had been given free rein, Arab leaders could have found themselves forced into confrontation with Israel. The reaction was therefore anything but enthusiastic when the secretary-general of the Arab League proposed an emergency summit of all Islamic countries. President Mubarak, who was approached first, suggested that the secretary-general should see King Hassan of Morocco, head of the Jerusalem Committee.* The idea of including all Islamic countries scared the king, who felt that with tempers running high rash decisions might be taken. King Hassan proposed instead that a limited Arab summit be convened, at the same time setting impossible conditions, including a stipulation that countries could only be represented by their heads of state, and that foreign ministers would not be accepted.

The king sent his prime minister, Abdul Latif El-Filaly, to Cairo, Damascus and Jeddah to sound out the leaders. President Assad said he would not attend, and felt that if a summit were held it should be generalized to represent at least all Arabs, if not all Muslims, and that it should address not only the issue of Jerusalem but what had led to the present outrage. The Saudis could not see what a summit would achieve, and in any case King Fahd could not attend because he was going to the United States for an operation on his knee.

Ironically, Arab leaders were rescued from their dilemma by a handful of Arab deputies in the Knesset who put forward a motion of no confidence. The Rabin government at first thought it could defeat the motion, and then discovered that most Likud deputies planned to vote with the Arab left, even though they supported the confiscation decision.

Faced by a government crisis, Rabin backed off and put a temporary freeze on the confiscation. When Mubarak called other Arab leaders to inform them that the summit would not be necessary, there was a collective sigh of relief. The risk that a war of the gods might be transformed from metaphor into fact had been all too real.

The crisis had blown over, but an important point had emerged: people throughout the Arab world were unhappy with the Oslo accords, and their leaders were afraid that this unease could turn into something stronger. No one was more aware of the mood than Mubarak, and no Arab leader had more reason to feel personally let down by the Israelis. After making a great effort in 1993 and the first half of 1994 to bring Israel and the PLO together, the Egyptian government found that by 1995 its role was somewhat taken for granted. The lack of appreciation had first been noticed in September 1993 when, like a

* A long-standing institution established by an Arab–Islamic summit in 1969.

matchmaker who is not invited to a wedding, Mubarak was left off Bill Clinton's guest list for the White House nuptials between Arafat and Rabin. The Egyptian president took this in his stride, played a major role in the 1994 implementation negotiations, and demonstrated his continuing commitment by personally escorting Arafat to the Rafah crossing when the chairman entered Gaza in July 1994. After the start of Palestinian semi-autonomy, both sides continued to draw upon Egyptian mediation to resolve their many disputes.

Although the Egyptians were glad to help, the never-easy relationship with Israel was going through one of its more irritating periods. The Waxman affair had put Cairo in the awkward position of urging Arafat to accept Israeli information which turned out to be incorrect. Then came months of Israeli–PLO discussions, mainly conducted in Cairo, on the issues of Israeli 'redeployment' and Palestinian elections, matters which had supposedly been settled in principle in previous talks. The Egyptians urged the Israelis to go ahead with the agreements but met with vacillation.

The Israeli policy was to use delaying tactics to force Arafat to clamp down harder on Hamas. The chairman replied that so long as he was not elected he had no authority to do so. Until elections were held, the PLO would remain just another Palestinian organization, not very different from Hamas, with no mandate to represent the Palestinian will.

A further source of annoyance came in October 1994 when Israel left Egypt in the dark about its impending peace agreement with Jordan. Although Cairo knew from its own sources that a deal was imminent, Egyptian officials were miffed by Israel's silence. This strengthened an impression that whereas Egypt and Israel had once been partners for peace, Cairo's pivotal role was now being deliberately curtailed.

Soon afterwards Shimon Peres began hinting that Israel would like to take over Egypt's traditional role of political leadership in the Middle East. During a gathering of politicians and businessmen held in Casablanca in November, Peres told a closed session of some of the delegations: 'Egypt has led the Middle East for the last forty years. We can all see the results. Let Israel take the helm for the next forty years, and see what the results will be.'

The gathering had been called to discuss a proposal by Peres for a Middle East Market, similar to the European Economic Community before that body became the European Union.* Although it was dubbed an economic summit, the political leaders present were outnumbered by business tycoons motivated by a wish to free private enterprise from government restraints.

Egypt's feeling that it had been used and then rebuffed led to a growing sense of resentment. In an attempt to soothe ruffled feelings, Assad proposed that the leaders of the three big countries in the Arab east, Saudi Arabia, Syria and Egypt, should meet to coordinate. Egypt, glad of an opportunity to reassert its leading role, accepted with alacrity. The three leaders met in Alexandria at the end of December 1994 amid high expectations and reminders of the role the same group had played in the 1950s, when the three countries stood up to the Anglo–American inspired Baghdad Pact.† But as the leaders should have known, a summit called without thorough preparation usually raises false hopes. King Fahd came not knowing exactly what was on the agenda, and was too tired to attend the first meeting scheduled for 6 p.m. After waiting for him until 11.40 p.m., Mubarak and Assad went to the king's suite at Ras el-Tin Palace to hold the semblance of a meeting. A communiqué had already been drafted by the foreign ministers, and the next day the leaders signed. It proved to be a rehash of old positions, just a show of solidarity and an assertion that the Arab world retained an independent will.

The communiqué signatures were barely dry when Israel proposed a four-way summit between Israel, Egypt, Jordan and Arafat. This second meeting convened in Cairo six weeks after the first and was just as devoid of new ideas. But it served its purpose for the Israelis, which, as Rabin openly said, was to offset the impression that Arab resistance to Israel's growing role had begun to emerge at the Alexandria summit. Peres claimed that the four participants at the Cairo summit were the nucleus of a reorganization of the region, and announced that they had set up a permanent secretariat, although nothing more than a follow-up committee had in fact been agreed. Saudi Arabia and Syria were naturally upset, as indeed was Arab public

* The meeting resulted in a fourteen-point declaration in which the participants agreed to work towards a community based on the free circulation of goods, capital and people, beginning with the creation of a regional development bank.

† See Part I, Chapter 7.

opinion in general, especially when Israel began talking about joining the Arab League.

Meanwhile another issue was beginning to dominate the testy Egyptian–Israeli relationship. The Nuclear Non-Proliferation Treaty was due to expire in April, after completing the twenty-five-year term originally agreed, and the United States was lobbying hard for renewal. The issue was discussed at a special meeting of the non-aligned countries called to commemorate the fortieth anniversary of the famous Bandung conference, the Afro-Asian summit at which Nasser had emerged as a rising Third World star.* In 1968 Egypt had been one of eighteen countries which participated in drafting the NPT and submitting it to the United Nations. It signed the draft, but when Israel refused to sign the treaty in 1970, Egypt held back from ratifying it. In the period after 1970, when the NPT came into force, Israel became an important nuclear power. According to Mordechai Vanunu, the Israeli technician at the Dimona nuclear facility who was kidnapped, tried and imprisoned by the Israelis for divulging state secrets, Israel had 200 nuclear warheads in its arsenal by 1986.

Faced with US pressure to renew the treaty, Mubarak stated publicly that Israel's nuclear capability was a threat to Egypt's security, and called for a revision of the NPT. When the Egyptian president raised the issue with Peres, he was told: 'Your problem is not with us, it is with the Americans.' Mubarak sought to rally other Arab countries in objecting to an indefinite renewal of the treaty, and went to Washington to press his case.

The outcome did nothing to ease Cairo's fears that its views no longer carried much weight. The problem was not Mubarak's inability to prevent the unmodified treaty being renewed, which was hardly unexpected, but his lack of success in lining up other Arab countries behind him. Stung by this evidence of declining clout, Egypt resorted to verbal attacks against Israel and the United States. The Egyptian religious authorities promptly joined the fray, adding to an already tense atmosphere.

Both the PLO and Egypt thus had reason to feel that events since the Oslo accords had worked almost entirely to Israel's advantage. Their predicament was no surprise to President Assad, who had always

* See pp. 107–8.

understood that Israel's idea of 'peace' meant Arab surrender. If the Syrian president had been shocked by Sadat's decision to sue for peace after the Yom Kippur War,* he was devastated when the PLO succumbed. Palestine was not just a political issue but the cause for which Syrian blood had been spilt and Syrian territory lost. A further shock came in 1994 when Jordan settled, again without consulting him. The Jordanian–Israeli peace treaty exposed his country to danger, as Jordan had agreed to grant Israel a ninety-nine-year lease on land abutting on Syrian territory.

With Egypt, the PLO and Jordan out of the game, Syria remained the last redoubt of Arab resistance, still holding out for complete Israeli withdrawal from Syrian territory. Suited by character to a strategy of waiting, Assad had shown himself to be among the most astute of Arab leaders. Nevertheless, the loss of solidarity among Arabs had left him feeling exposed to American political pressure and Israeli threats, and deprived of any realistic military option. In addition he was approaching seventy, in poor health, and still recovering from the personal trauma of losing his eldest son in a car accident. Thus Assad too was ready for peace, if he could obtain acceptable terms.

As he told me in January 1995:† 'Peace is our strategic choice, but not at any price. Our conditions are complete withdrawal from the Golan and a balance of security guarantees.' At the time of our discussion, such terms were not available. Israel was holding out for security arrangements that Assad could not afford to concede, including a massive redisposition and restructuring of the Syrian army. All Syrian armour and artillery would have to be moved from Israel's borders to the Turkish and Iraqi frontiers, while the range of Syrian missiles would be cut to sixty kilometres.

Throughout the first year of Palestinian semi-autonomy Washington brought intense pressure to bear on Assad. Clinton went to see him in October 1994,‡ a move which tacitly acknowledged the absurdity of the State Department's continued blacklisting of Syria as a state

* See p. 220.

† Assad made the remarks quoted in this chapter during a six-hour meeting with the author on 5 January 1995.

‡ In a speech to the Knesset in that month, Clinton said that only peace with all its neighbours would give Israel real security. President Assad was serious about peace and had begun to speak in terms which Israelis could understand.

'sponsoring terrorism'. Warren Christopher or Dennis Ross, the State Department special coordinator for the Middle East, made monthly visits to Damascus. Ross, himself a Jew, was accompanied by four Jewish officials from the State Department and the National Security Council. The same Jewish contingent acted as hand-holders for Christopher on his trips. A bemused Assad told me: 'I have nothing against Jews, but it cannot be a coincidence that all the Americans who come to see me are Jewish. This cannot be an accurate representation of the ethnic distribution of the United States.'

The message the Americans pressed upon Assad was that he would be better off reaching an agreement with Rabin's government than waiting for the next Israeli administration. With Labour trailing in the opinion polls, Assad might have to contend with Likud's Binyamin Netanyahu after the 1996 elections.* During the year Netanyahu constantly baited Rabin for being soft on the Golan Heights issue.† The Americans went so far as to urge Assad to help bring about Rabin's re-election. 'The problem is that what can help Rabin with the Israeli electorate will not help me with the Syrian people,' Assad observed.

The Syrian leader had always been against concentrating on easy issues and putting off thorny ones, which was the formula for the Oslo accords. Peace, he said, was not a trick to be conjured up by sleight of hand. Real peace could be brought about only by facing reality.‡

As the first year of the Gaza–Jericho experiment drew to an end, Arafat, Mubarak and Assad all seemed to have lost some political ground. Arafat had been stripped of his freedom-fighter aura, Egypt's leadership of Middle East politics was under threat, and Assad's noble

* The situation was in fact more complicated. Israeli voters were due to choose their prime minister directly for the first time in 1996, instead of voting only for party lists. This raised the possibility that Rabin might be re-elected as prime minister while Labour and its allies lost their parliamentary majority, causing a paralysis of decision-making.

† In a speech to the Knesset in October 1994, made during President Clinton's visit, Netanyahu argued that the peace treaties Israel had reached with Egypt and Jordan were sufficient. If peace with the Palestinians and Syrians meant giving up the west bank and the Golan Heights, Israel could manage without.

‡ Direct talks between Israeli and Syrian delegations in Washington stopped in December 1994, with nothing left to say. Contacts continued between the Syrian and Israeli ambassadors in Washington, but there was no sign of the stalemate being broken until late May 1995, when formal talks resumed.

stand looked untenable in the longer term. Only one Arab leader could look back at the year with satisfaction. That leader was King Hussein of Jordan.

The king had been ready for peace with Israel since as far back as 1967, but had been restrained by the risk of a backlash from his Palestinian subjects. Once the PLO had made peace with Israel, the fact that a majority of the Jordanian population was Palestinian no longer presented a problem. Jordan and Israel ended their state of war in July 1994, only three weeks after Arafat had returned to Gaza, and at the same time Jordan secured formal Israeli recognition of its special role in the Muslim holy places in Jerusalem.* After that the only significant remaining issues were distribution of water resources and a relatively small disputed area of territory.

Solutions to these matters were found in mid-October, when Rabin spent a night in Amman talking to King Hussein. Ten days later Israel and Jordan conducted what was more a jamboree than a solemn peace ceremony. In a high-spirited atmosphere 10,000 coloured balloons were released and two children, one Israeli, the other Jordanian, distributed bunches of flowers to the guests. The treaty was signed by Rabin and Jordanian premier Abd El-Salam El-Majali, and by President Clinton, while others on the stage exchanged hats and greeted each other with cries of 'Shalom, Salaam, Peace.'† The speeches suggested the joy of a fresh start, and for a few hours the bitterness of the violent autumn was forgotten. Yehuda Waxman, father of Nahshon Waxman, was among the guests. 'I am not looking back,' he said. 'I ask all Israel to regard this as a day of celebration.'

When a grim-faced Rabin shook hands with Arafat at the White House in September 1993, no one could have doubted the enmity that had lain between them. The atmosphere at the Jordanian–Israeli ceremony, by contrast, was more like a party between old friends setting aside an awkward disagreement. And therein lay the heart of the matter: of all the Arab parties who had embarked on the journey of peace, King Hussein's load was the lightest.

To say this is not to suggest that the king took such a step lightly.

* See p. 527.

† During Clinton's visit a Hamas spokesman issued an open note to the president. It said: 'There is no difference between you and Rabin. How can you call this "peace", with so much injustice and humiliation?'

His commitment to his country and his people was beyond question, and his decision reflected what he perceived as Jordan's national interest. The king was convinced that cooperation with Israel was the only road to development, and was willing to dream of a kind of Middle Eastern Benelux comprised of Israel, Jordan and the west bank, with strong commercial links to the Gulf states. Israel encouraged him in this belief for its own reasons, one of which was a hope that economic development in Jordan might attract Israel's Palestinian inhabitants, thus consolidating the demographic balance of Israel.

As the dust settled on the first full year of Palestinian partial autonomy, it was realized that an anniversary had passed almost unnoticed. Few in Gaza or Jericho, let alone the occupied territories, had felt there was anything to celebrate on 4 May, the date of the Cairo agreement a year earlier which had set the Gaza–Jericho experiment in motion. The time for festivities, Palestinians felt, would come when and if the Israelis left them in peace.

Epilogue

Looking back over five decades of conflict, it is hard to avoid feeling that the true nature of the Arab–Israel conflict has never been grasped by the peacemakers. Every initiative so far has been based on finding a way for Arabs to surrender with a figleaf of dignity. Such an approach takes no account of the religious, historical and cultural dimensions of the dispute. Roots of Arab–Israeli discord reach into areas of the mind that lie beyond the antibiotics of surrender diplomacy. The bonds which tie the Palestinians to their country belong to the mysteries of faith, and of the subconscious. The land of the forefathers of the three great monotheistic religions will always be just as precious to Arab Muslims and Christians as it is to Jews.

Two different kinds of nationalism were violated in 1948 and 1967 – that of the Palestinians, and the separate ties of pan-Arab nationalism. Israel's conquests divided an Arab nation which considered itself one, whatever its religious diversity, and placed a barrier between its eastern and western land masses. The military might of Israel terrorized a great semi-circle of Arab peoples whose only strength lay in solidarity. The result was the Arab taboo, the most powerful blend of subconscious feelings and conscious ideas to have emerged in the Middle East in this century. Unable to defeat Israel in war, the Arabs sought a moral alliance with Asian, African and East European countries, as well as the Vatican, Spain and Greece. That alliance isolated Israel diplomatically and economically from much of the world, but not from its key sponsors. Israel's pact with the United States (and previously with Britain and France) allowed it to defy all moral pressure. With the principal superpower on its side, with the influence and economic power of worldwide Jewry, and with its own military strength, including the nuclear deterrent, Israel had little difficulty in remaining dominant.

The strategy followed by Israeli governments since 1948 has had three major themes, all of which are still in effect. The first is that Arabs should never be permitted any military gains. The second is the division of the Arab world, at first achieved by harnessing Hashemite ambitions and later by exploiting differences between rich and poor Arabs. The third element reflects the religious dimension. Since the 1980s the recreation of Eretz Yisrael has been pursued through the construction of settlements on Arab land. When the Rabin–Peres government came to power, many outside the Middle East supposed that the creeping annexation of the west bank had stopped. The reality was that territorial gains made since 1967 were consolidated through the Oslo agreement (which left control of settlements in Israel's hands), and the steady de-Arabization of east Jerusalem continued at an accelerated pace. The biblical imperative behind Israeli expansionism remained as powerful as ever. Ariel Sharon, champion of Jabotinsky's revisionist Zionism,* said on 27 March 1995 that the next Likud government would increase the number of Israeli settlers on the west bank from 140,000 to 500,000.

Israel's policies have so far produced four clear results. The removal of Egypt from the Arab political equation was a breakthrough, creating a wedge in the Arab world and making a united Arab counter-attack impossible. The second was the expulsion of the PLO from Lebanon, its banishment into exile 800 miles away, and the demonstration that Israel had the military capability to occupy an Arab capital. The third was the division of the Arab world into two camps, the conservatives and the radicals. The conservatives found themselves, whether intentionally or not, in an unwritten alliance with Israel. Finally, Israel persuaded some in the Arab world to accept its own definition of peace, as the Oslo agreement and the Israeli–Jordanian treaty demonstrated.

Israel had no master plan for these events. A consistent policy of exploiting the enemy's weakness and periodically wielding overwhelming power was sufficient to achieve every goal. The Arab world was left militarily and politically routed, its physical defences smashed and its psychological ramparts breached.

* See p. 26.

Israel is thus victorious, and yet its victory has been empty. The more Israel has defeated the Arabs, the more it has wrecked its own prospects of long-term security. The document signed by Anwar Sadat and Menachem Begin in 1979 was described as a peace treaty, and yet even sixteen years later relations could not be described as normal. Pope Shenouda III, the Coptic pontiff, continued in 1994 to forbid his flock from making pilgrimages to Jerusalem, saying: 'The Christians of Egypt will not be the traitors of the Arab world.' The Egyptian example should be a reminder that peace without justice cannot bring normalization.

The ephemeral nature of Israel's victory was always understood by a minority of Israeli intellectuals, but not by the decision-makers. Israeli politicians realized that security depended on acceptance, and yet could not bring themselves to make the necessary policy changes.

It was strange to see a nuclear power begging its impoverished neighbours to acknowledge its right to exist. A country which had thought there was no security without dominance had discovered that with dominance there was no security. That paradox gradually made some Israelis understand that a *fait accompli* could have no permanence without legitimacy, which could be conferred only by the vanquished. When Yitzhak Rabin took Yasser Arafat's hand in September 1993, he was acknowledging that fact.

There was, however, a flaw in the way the Israelis went about seeking legitimacy through the PLO. The organization was first obliged to adapt its appearance – to change its clothes and shave. The result was that Israel embraced a prettified PLO which no longer enjoyed the support of all Palestinians. Every sacrifice of principle left a moral vacuum, and the void was filled by competitors. Between 1992 and 1994 the PLO steadily lost ground to Hamas and Islamic Jihad, throwing into question its claim to be the Palestinian 'sole representative'.

The Oslo agreement received the acquiescence, reluctant or otherwise, of a majority of present-generation Palestinians. No one can guarantee that the same attitude will be taken by future generations. The Middle East cries out for peace, but peace with justice and dignity. An agreement reflecting 90 per cent of one party's demands and 10 per cent of the other's is not a settlement; it is a formula for future shock. Real peace calls for mutual understanding, respect and cooperation. If Israel wishes to be a partner in the Middle East a new way of thinking will be needed; one which takes account of the demographic balance of power, of long-term economic realities and of the true nature of security.

No one can say how long the unjust peace of Oslo will last, but the strength of Hamas and Islamic Jihad should be a signal. Islam is the only fortress of the old structure of the taboo still functioning. If Islam is being radicalized, it is because the Arab soul has been deprived of other defences, leaving faith as the last redoubt of a taboo broken but not appeased. And therein lies the portent of coming dangers.

INDEX

INDEX

Harold Wilson

Ben Pimlott

'One of the great political biographies of the century.'
A. N. Wilson, *Evening Standard*

'The rehabilitation of Wilson has begun – and Ben Pimlott, the best British political biographer now writing, has made a hugely impressive job of it . . . His narrative of the young Wilson, from sickly boy scout to academic pupil of the formidable William Beveridge, and then to chirpy junior minister is quite outstanding – clear, thoughtful and gripping. This early part of the book is central to its larger achievement, since Pimlott shocks the reader out of basic anti-Wilson prejudice by demanding a human sympathy for him. The little, blinking, stubborn boy, hiding his hurt with cocky self-confidence, lives on as a permanent presence within the powerful politician . . . Some biographies enter the political discourse at once, thanks to their innate qualities and lucky timing. There are so many echoes of the Wilson years in the politics of today that this happy fate must surely belong to Pimlott's book. Wilson's soured relationship with the press (and the terrible problems it caused for him) – the conflict within him between national leadership and good party management – even the growing debate about national decline – are all suggestive and worth lingering over. As, indeed, are almost all of these 734 well-researched and finely written pages.' Andrew Marr, *Independent*

'A masterly piece of political writing.'
Bernard Crick, *New Statesman*

'The narrative gallops along, sweeping the reader with it in a rush of excitement. A mass of complex detail is marshalled with the art that conceals art.' David Marquand, *Times Literary Supplement*

'Fascinating . . . Pimlott the X-ray has produced another work of formidable penetration.' Roy Jenkins, *Observer*

ISBN 0 00 637955 9

The Honourable Company

A History of the English East India Company

John Keay

'The first accessible narrative history of the English East India Company which has appeared for some time . . . Keay recounts his story with the sweep of a James Michener, but one anchored in the meticulous scholarship of historians . . . Commercial successes and failures, battles and politics from Table Bay to Tokyo Bay are treated with verve and clarity.'

Christopher Bayly, *The Observer*

Over two centuries, the East India Company grew from a loose association of Elizabethan tradesmen into 'the Grandest Society of Merchants in the Universe' – a huge commercial enterprise which controlled half the world's trade and also administered an embryonic empire. A tenth of the British exchequer's total revenue derived from customs receipts on the Company's UK imports; its armed forces exceeded those of most sovereign states. Without it there would have been no British India and no British Empire.

ISBN 0 00 638072 7

The Civilization of Europe in the Renaissance

John Hale

Winner of 1993 *Time-Life* Silver Pen Award

The Civilization of Europe in the Renaissance is the most ambitious achievement of Britain's leading Renaissance historian. John Hale has painted on a grand canvas an enthralling portrait of Europe and its civilization at a moment when 'Europe' first became an entity in the minds of its inhabitants. The book does not simply survey 'high' culture but with an astonishing range and subtlety of learning builds up a gigantic picture of the age, enlivened by a multiplicity of themes, people and ideas. It contains memorable descriptions of painting, sculpture, poetry, architecture and music; but Hale is not simply concerned with the arts: he examines the dramatic changes during the period in religion, politics, economics and global discoveries. At a time when we are thinking more and more about what 'Europe' and European culture mean, this is a book which shows us more than any other where we can find the roots of both of them, and how much the present and future can be illuminated by the past.

'A superb evocation of the Europe of "the long sixteenth century", wonderfully fresh and rich in its copious illustrative detail, full of innumerable incidental delights. [The book] takes its place as the summation of John Hale's career as a historian, and as the crowning achievement of a master-designer whose richly fabricated works have given so much pleasure.'
J. H. Elliott

'This study deserves to stand alongside Braudel's classic account of the Mediterranean in the time of Philip II. Hale is as generous as he is knowledgeable; his life's work has culminated in a meticulous masterpiece.'
Frederic Raphael, *Sunday Times*

'This is a magnificent book which fills a long-standing gap. It is the product of a lifetime's scholarship by someone with a quite irrepressible curiosity and prodigious breadth of reading . . . together with the enviable gift of writing clearly and beautifully.
A. V. Antonvics, *Times Educational Supplement*

ISBN 0 00 686175 X